REGULATION IN INDIA

The rise of the regulatory state has been a major feature of modern constitutional democracies. India, the world's largest democracy, is no exception to this trend. This book is the first major study of regulation in India. It considers how the development of regulation in India has altered the nature and functions of the state; how it is reshaping the relationship between business and the state; how it has called for the refashioning of established legal principles; and how it has raised new questions about the relationship between technical expertise and the rule of law. The chapters cover topics ranging from the foundations of the Indian regulatory state to the form of regulation across different sectors to regulation in practice. Together, the chapters reveal the challenges, promise, and limitations offered by contemporary regulatory practices, and they capture the close if sometimes fraught relationship that regulation must inevitably share with the political economy and constitutional schema within which it operates.

Volume 24 in the series Hart Studies in Comparative Public Law

Hart Studies in Comparative Public Law

Recent titles in this series:

The Nordic Constitutions
Edited by Helle Krunke and Björg Thorarensen

Human Rights in the UK and the Influence of Foreign Jurisprudence
Hélène Tyrrell

Australian Constitutional Values
Edited by Rosalind Dixon

The Scope and Intensity of Substantive Review
Traversing Taggart's Rainbow
Edited by Hanna Wilberg and Mark Elliott

Entick v Carrington
250 Years of the Rule of Law
Edited by Adam Tomkins and Paul Scott

Administrative Law and Judicial Deference
Matthew Lewans

Soft Law and Public Authorities
Remedies and Reform
Greg Weeks

Legitimate Expectations in the Common Law World
Edited by Matthew Groves and Greg Weeks

The Dynamics of Exclusionary Constitutionalism
Mazen Masri

Constitutional Courts, Gay Rights and Sexual Orientation Equality
Angioletta Sperti

Principled Reasoning in Human Rights Adjudication
Se-Shauna Wheatle

Human Rights and Judicial Review in Australia and Canada
Janina Boughey

The Foundations and Traditions of Constitutional Amendment
Edited by Richard Albert, Xenophon Contiades and Alkmene Fotiadou

The Federal Idea
Public Law Between Governance and Political Life
Edited by Amnon Lev

Regulation in India

Design, Capacity, Performance

Edited by
Devesh Kapur
and
Madhav Khosla

•HART•
BLOOMSBURY
NEW DELHI • LONDON • OXFORD • NEW YORK • SYDNEY

BLOOMSBURY INDIA
Bloomsbury Publishing India Pvt. Ltd
Second Floor, LSC Building No. 4, DDA Complex, Pocket C – 6 & 7,
Vasant Kunj New Delhi 110070

BLOOMSBURY, Hart publishing India and the Diana
logo are trademarks of Bloomsbury Publishing Plc

First published in India 2019
First published in Great Britain 2019

This edition published with permission from Bloomsbury Publishing Plc,
50 Bedford Square, London, WC1B3DP, UK

A catalogue record for this book is available from the British Library.
Library of Congress Cataloging-in-Publication data
Names: Kapur, Devesh, 1959- editor. | Khosla, Madhav, editor. |
Center for the Advanced Study of India (University of Pennsylvania), sponsoring body.
Title: Regulation in India : design, capacity, performance / edited by Devesh Kapur and Madhav Khosla.
Description: Oxford, UK ; Portland, Oregon : Hart Publishing, 2019. | Series: Hart Studies in Comparative Public Law. | "The chapters in this book were first presented at a workshop in New Delhi in March 2018, organised by the Center for the Advanced Study of India (CASI), University of Pennsylvania,
as part of its twenty-fifth-year celebrations." | Includes bibliographical references and index.
Identifiers: LCCN 2018052164 (print) | LCCN 2018055175 (ebook) | ISBN 9781509927739 (Epub) | ISBN 9781509927562 (hardback : alk. paper)
Subjects: LCSH: Trade regulation—India—Congresses. | Administrative law—India—Congresses.
Classification: LCC KNS982.A67 (ebook) | LCC KNS982.A67 R438 2019 (print) | DDC 342.54/06—dc23 LC record available at https://lccn.loc.gov/2018052164

ISBN: 978-93-88630-66-5

2 4 6 8 10 9 7 5 3 1

For sales in the Indian subcontinent only

Typeset by Compuscript Ltd, Shannon
Printed and bound in India by Rajkamal Electric Press

Bloomsbury Publishing Plc makes every effort to ensure that the papers used in the manufacture of our books are natural, recyclable products made from wood grown in well-managed forests. Our manufacturing processes conform to the environmental regulations of the country of origin.

To find out more about our authors and books visit www.bloomsbury.com and sign up for our newsletters

Acknowledgements

MANY OF THE chapters in this book were first presented at a workshop in New Delhi in March 2018, organised by the Center for the Advanced Study of India (CASI), University of Pennsylvania, as part of its twenty-fifth-year celebrations. We are deeply grateful to Dalip Pathak for making the event possible, and to Juliana Di Giustini and Georgette Rochlin at CASI, and Ruchika Ahuja, Shiv Dayal Gosain and Eswaran Sridharan at the University of Pennsylvania Institute for the Advanced Study of India, New Delhi, for their invaluable help. We are also grateful to the commentators at the workshop, who provided invaluable feedback on individual papers – Gautam Bhatia, Aparna Chandra, Shyam Divan, Navroz Dubash, Apar Gupta, Akshay Jaitly, KP Krishnan, Pradeep Ratnam, Harsha Vardhana Singh, TV Somanathan, Somasekhar Sundaresan, Arun K Thiruvengadam and Umakanth Varottil – and to Arvind Subramanian for his important observations at the event. We owe a special debt to Pratap Bhanu Mehta, Ananth Padmanabhan, Arun K Thiruvengadam and Raeesa Vakil for their help throughout this project, and to the team at Hart Publishing for their enthusiasm and forbearance.

Acknowledgements

[illegible]

Contents

Notes on Contributors

Farrah Ahmed is an associate professor at the Melbourne Law School, University of Melbourne.

Aditya Bhattacharjea is Professor of Economics at the Delhi School of Economics, University of Delhi.

Anirudh Burman is a Senior Research Analyst at Carnegie India, New Delhi.

Shibani Ghosh is a fellow at the Centre for Policy Research, New Delhi, and Advocate-on-Record, Supreme Court of India.

Akshay Jaitly is a partner at Trilegal, New Delhi.

Swati Jhaveri is an assistant professor at the Faculty of Law, National University of Singapore.

Amit Kapur is a senior partner at J Sagar Associates, New Delhi.

Devesh Kapur is the Starr Foundation Professor of South Asian Studies and Director of Asia Programs at the Paul H Nitze School of Advanced International Studies (SAIS), Johns Hopkins University.

Vikramaditya S Khanna is the William W Cook Professor of Law at the University of Michigan Law School.

Madhav Khosla is a junior fellow at the Harvard Society of Fellows.

KP Krishnan is Secretary at the Ministry of Skill Development and Entrepreneurship, Government of India.

Neel Maitra is an attorney in the Office of Chief Counsel, Division of Trading and Markets, US Securities and Exchange Commission.

Rahul Matthan is a partner at Trilegal, Bangalore.

Susan L Ostermann is an assistant professor at the Keough School of Global Affairs, University of Notre Dame.

Ananth Padmanabhan is a fellow at the Centre for Policy Research, New Delhi, and an SJD candidate at the University of Pennsylvania Law School.

Suyash Rai is a senior consultant at the National Institute of Public Finance and Policy, New Delhi.

Anirudh Rastogi is the founder of Ikigai Law, New Delhi.

K Vivek Reddy is an advocate at the High Court of Judicature at Hyderabad and Supreme Court of India.

Shubho Roy is a senior research associate at the National Institute of Public Finance and Policy, New Delhi.

Ajay Shah is a professor at the National Institute of Public Finance and Policy, New Delhi.

Justice BN Srikrishna (Retd) is a former judge of the Supreme Court of India.

Somasekhar Sundaresan is an advocate at the Bombay High Court and Supreme Court of India.

Raeesa Vakil is a JSD candidate at Yale Law School.

Umakanth Varottil is an associate professor at the Faculty of Law, National University of Singapore.

Table of Cases

References are to page number

Table of Legislation

Constitution of India

References are to page number

Table of Secondary Legislation

References are to page number

Table of Statutes

References are to page number

Table of Other Materials

References are to page number

Table of EU Material

References are to page number

Table of International Material

References are to page number

Table of National Material

References are to page number

Canada

England

Ireland

South Africa

USA

Part I

Introduction

Part I

Introduction

DEVESH KAPUR AND MADHAV KHOSLA

INTRODUCTION

1

The Reality of Indian Regulation

DEVESH KAPUR AND MADHAV KHOSLA*

INTRODUCTION

THE MODERN STATE has emerged as the most powerful territorially centralised form of organisation that shapes human affairs. Its focus has grown from minimalist 'night-watchman' goals to those that are far more wide-ranging. While the expanding goals of the state have been deeply contentious, with 'neoliberal' policies seeking to roll back the state in recent years, another dimension of contestation has been about means rather than ends – that is, how best to allocate economic resources, redistribute income and wealth, and affect the rate of economic growth. States have sought to achieve their goals via classic tax and expenditure policies, trade policies, expanding public sector employment and – especially in countries at earlier stages of economic development – building state-owned enterprises to promote economic development. The retreat of the state has been most pronounced in the direct production of goods and services (as distinct from their provision), where it has been replaced to a very large extent by the private sector.

While a principal goal of economic liberalisation has been the greater role of market forces and the private sector, it has also led to significant changes in state structures and market governance.[1] One of the ways in which state structures have undergone significant transformation is the astonishing growth of regulatory agencies. The rise of the 'regulatory state' is both part of a greater legalisation of the state and the judicialisation of the economy and society, as well as a part of greater formalisation of the relations between various actors in the capitalist economy. The redirection in the state's role from production to regulation has been mirrored in shifts in governments being organised around traditional branches – namely, the legislature, the executive and the judiciary – to governments that now encompass, in

* We are indebted to Ananth Padmanabhan, Milan Vaishnav and Raeesa Vakil for their help with an earlier draft.

[1] David Levi-Faur, 'The Global Diffusion of Regulatory Capitalism' (2005) 598 *Annals of the American Academy of Political and Social Science* 12.

addition, regulatory institutions with varying degrees of independence that incorporate elements of all three branches of government in their mandates.

We define regulation here as interventions by public agencies in the activities of a target population. The interventions that we have in mind are intentional and direct – involving binding standard-setting, monitoring and sanctioning – and which are exercised by public sector actors on the economic activities of private sector actors.[2] Regulatory agencies are thought to centre around four dimensions.[3] The first dimension relates to regulatory responsibilities: the extent of powers that agencies possess. The second dimension relates to managerial autonomy: to what extent do agencies have autonomy in their staffing, in their organisational structure, and in financial and budgetary matters? An important feature of the autonomy question is the separation between agencies and existing ministerial structures. The third dimension is concerned with political independence. What protection exists, such as perhaps the protection from being removed from office at will, that allows agencies to be immune from political forces? Finally, there is the question of accountability. What are the various forms of accountability that exist for agency behaviour? Are the forms of accountability vertical – that is, to the executive and/or legislature – or are they non-hierarchical forms of accountability that might exist, such as forms of accountability to stakeholders via participatory mechanisms?

While the rise of the regulatory state is a global phenomenon, its specific characteristics are rooted in distinct national contexts and the constellation of forces that led to the creation of specific regulators. As one might expect, the roots of the regulatory state lie in industrialised democracies. In the case of the US, regulatory institutions are deliberately 'politicised', with an underlying design philosophy that partisan political debate best ensures democratic accountability. Because they are faced with a powerful Congress intent on oversight, agencies are constantly exposed to the influences of majoritarian democracy. In contrast, the regulatory state movement in Europe has been driven by a very different force: the desire to 'depoliticise' contentious politically partisan issues and insulate technical matters from political pressures.

In the case of developmental states, such as in East Asia, the regulatory state rose in the context of democratisation and the crisis of the developmental state amidst financial globalisation. Pressures from the West and global forces called on the discretionary and collusive modes of doing business that were integral to the developmental state to be replaced by transparent and formally specified rules, which was effectuated by way of new regulatory agencies that would formulate and police those rules. Beyond developmental states, the rise of the regulatory state in the Global South, more broadly, has been shaped by three common contextual factors:[4] international

[2] Christel Koop and Martin Lodge, 'What is Regulation? An Interdisciplinary Concept Analysis' (2017) 11 *Regulation & Governance* 95.

[3] Jacint Jordana, Xavier Fernández-i-Marín and Andrea C Bianculli, 'Agency Proliferation and the Globalization of the Regulatory State: Introducing a Data Set on the Institutional Features of Regulatory Agencies' (2018) *Regulation & Governance* (forthcoming).

[4] Navroz K Dubash and Bronwen Morgan, 'The Rise of the Regulatory State of the South' in Navroz K Dubash and Bronwen Morgan (eds), *The Rise of the Regulatory State in the Global South* (Oxford University Press, 2013) 1.

pressures, especially from international financial institutions, to adopt the institutional innovation of regulatory agencies, particularly in infrastructure and financial sectors; a greater intensity of redistributive politics in settings where infrastructure services are deficient (and often non-existent); and limited state capacity. The first of these has resulted in weakly embedded regulatory agencies within the local political and institutional context; the second has inevitably drawn in other actors, especially courts and civil society; and the third encompasses a 'thin' and 'thick' dimension, the former covering organisational concerns of budget, personnel and training, and the latter the pressures on the state to manage multiple forms of engagement with diverse stakeholders in order to balance the competing concerns of growth, efficiency and redistribution.

The Indian experience is somewhat akin to that of other developmental states and the Global South. A *dirigist* state that was heavily interventionist found itself facing an economic crisis that led the state to withdraw from the direct control of large areas of economic life. The state subsequently moved in the direction of relying heavily on reformed, or newly created, regulatory agencies to manage economic life. These agencies were constructed to attempt to 'depoliticise' areas of economic life that had hitherto been heavily politicised. Since the liberalisation of the Indian economy in the early 1990s, the nation's governance structure has become increasingly regulatory in character. The admission of private actors into several domains meant that the prior model of administration, where the state had a monopoly and an executive ministry performed a managerial role, needed alteration. A notable feature of the new 'regulatory' structure was, and remains, the presence of regulatory agencies that operate with varying – and sometimes ambiguous and controversial – degrees of independence from the traditional political executive. Indeed, if economic liberalisation was meant to roll back the state, the rise of the regulatory state is a testament to the fact that, far from rolling back, the state has simply rolled over. It has, however, led to a more fragmented state apparatus. The emergence of the 'independent regulatory agency' has been a defining element in this institutional fragmentation, both in India and elsewhere.[5]

The principal reason cited for the rise of the regulatory state – the desire to de-politicise certain decision-making processes – and the concerns that have arisen with such regulation are familiar, both in India and elsewhere. Delegation to specialised agencies is a 'hand-tying' strategy that insulates 'technocratic' decisions from politically expedient ones. Agencies hold the potential to make determinations and exercise judgement based on expertise, as well as address issues on an ongoing basis. However, their structure and operation raise a range of questions relating to both democratic accountability and the rule of law.

Delegation has long occurred in constitutional democracies, and executive ministries have long engaged in regulation. But one consequence of the emergence of the

[5] See Karen Yeung, 'The Regulatory State' in Robert Baldwin, Martin Cave and Martin Lodge (eds), *The Oxford Handbook of Regulation* (Oxford University Press, 2012) 64. See also Daniel Halberstam, 'The Promise of Comparative Administrative Law: A Constitutional Perspective on Independent Agencies' in Susan Rose-Ackerman, Peter L Lindseth and Blake Emerson (eds), *Comparative Administrative Law*, 2nd edn (Edward Elgar, 2017) 139.

independent regulatory agency is that now, more than ever, a great deal of policy-making is performed outside of the legislature, inviting questions over the precise means through which such policy-making can be made accountable.[6] It is widely understood that regulatory states around the world must negotiate different kinds of tensions: the tension between the demands of the rule of law and formal constitutional principles; the demands of representation and accountability required by the democratic process; and the demands of economic efficiency.[7] In addition to these normative questions, there are a range of positive questions relating to the 'regulatory process' – these include agenda-setting; the negotiation of standards; and the implementation, monitoring and enforcement of actions through a welter of legal statutes, executive orders and judicial decisions, as well as the directives of regulatory agencies.

This volume is the first major study of regulation in India. Although several valuable studies of India's overall regulatory framework, as well as studies focused on specific sectors, have emerged in recent years, the scholarship on regulation in India is relatively sparse, especially given the growth in the scale and scope of the regulatory state in India.[8] A rare exception by economists examining the conduct of regulation in infrastructure and securities sectors in India asked whether regulators in the country were 'white knights that came to the rescue of sectors that were being mismanaged by public sector monopolies' or instead 'insidious de facto agents of government, perpetuating public sector control under a veneer of competitive forces'.[9] The authors concluded that performance varied across regulators, partly due to faulty design, but mainly because of 'lack of attention to the reform of the market structure and an inadequate understanding of the nature of interaction between the market structure and the effectiveness of the regulatory process'.[10]

The state of such a hypothesis today, well over a decade after it was made, is an important question and, in some ways, an open one. This volume considers an array of themes ranging from the legal and conceptual foundations of the Indian regulatory state, to its features across different domains, to aspects of its functioning and performance.[11] A significant portion of chapters concentrate on the legal

[6] See Susan Rose-Ackerman, 'Regulation and Public Law in Comparative Perspective' (2010) 60 *University of Toronto Law Journal* 519. See also Susan Rose-Ackerman, 'Citizens and Technocrats: An Essay on Trust, Public Participation, and Government Legitimacy' in Rose-Ackerman et al (n 5) 251.

[7] See Adrian Vermeule, 'The Administrative State: Law, Democracy, and Knowledge' in Mark Tushnet, Mark A Graber and Sanford Levinson (eds), *The Oxford Handbook of the US Constitution* (Oxford University Press, 2015) 259.

[8] For an overview of the Indian regulatory state, see TV Somanathan, 'The Administrative and Regulatory State' in Sujit Choudhury, Madhav Khosla and Pratap Bhanu Mehta (eds), *The Oxford Handbook of the Indian Constitution* (Oxford University Press, 2016) 386; Arun K Thiruvengadam, 'Flag-Bearers of a New Era? The Evolution of New Regulatory Institutions in India (1991–2016)' in Rose-Ackerman et al (n 5) 218.

[9] Saugata Bhattacharya and Urjit R Patel, 'New Regulatory Institutions in India: White Knights or Trojan Horses' in Devesh Kapur and Pratap Bhanu Mehta (eds), *Public Institutions in India: Performance and Design* (Oxford University Press, 2005) 455.

[10] Bhattacharya and Patel (n 9).

[11] It should be noted that this volume excludes those regulatory institutions that govern higher education and the professions, ranging from technical education (engineering and management) to medicine to architecture and so on.

architecture and framework at work. This focus is intended: the regulatory state is, after all, not merely structured and governed by law; the institutions and concepts that it involves are constructs of the law.[12] The rules that shape different sectors as well as the absence of rules in particular cases are constituted by the law, and underlining this fact is vital not merely in order to understand them but also to seriously pose the question of reform. Regulation in India is, perhaps even more than elsewhere, deeply embedded within the legal (and constitutional) framework operating in the country.

In this introductory chapter, we have chosen to resist exploring some of the general themes associated with regulation, from its capacity to respond to market failures and market limitations, to the ways to make it accountable. Instead, we have chosen to turn to certain features of Indian regulation that are distinctive. Our basic premise is that, for all the legal ambiguities and institutional weaknesses, studying the Indian regulatory state is unavoidable, and may even be the inevitable starting point for numerous other issues, from economic growth to inequality to democratic accountability. This premise is only strengthened by the fact that, despite the legal questions that critics pose, the reality remains that – as has been the case in many advanced democracies – Indian constitutionalism has 'accommodated' the rise of the regulatory state.[13]

I. DOCTRINAL INCOHERENCE AND UNCERTAINTY

In modern constitutional democracies, the executive, legislative and judicial branches of government are central actors in shaping the functioning of public institutions. However, in India, as in several other democracies, there has been a creeping expansion of judicial power.[14] The role of the judiciary with regard to the operation of regulators has been even greater given the absence of an overarching administrative law statute, such as the Administrative Procedure Act, 1946 in the US. As Raeesa Vakil's chapter shows, the Indian Supreme Court's approach began with a relatively thin conception of administrative law that was thickened over the years with the overlay of broad and somewhat ambiguously framed constitutional principles and rights jurisprudence.[15] Vakil captures how a field that is deeply embedded and nurtured

[12] This point about legal construction has recently been underlined in the context of law and economic relationships. See Katharina Pistor, 'A Legal Theory of Finance' (2013) 41 *Journal of Comparative Economics* 315; David Singh Grewal, 'The Laws of Capitalism' (2014) 128 *Harvard Law Review* 626.

[13] See Gillian E Metzger, 'Delegation, Accommodation, and the Permeability of Constitutional and Ordinary Law' in Tushnet et al (n 7) 409.

[14] See Ran Hirschl, 'The Judicialization of Mega-politics and the Rise of Political Courts' (2008) 11 *Annual Review of Political Science* 93.

[15] A fine example of this is the Supreme Court's approach towards the idea of natural justice. See Raeesa Vakil, 'Constitutionalizing Administrative Law in the Indian Supreme Court: Natural Justice and Fundamental Rights' (2018) 16 *International Journal of Constitutional Law* 475. On administrative review in India, see generally Prateek Jalan and Ritin Rai, 'Review of Administrative Action' in Sujit Choudhry, Madhav Khosla and Pratap Bhanu Mehta (eds), *The Oxford Handbook of the Indian Constitution* (Oxford University Press, 2016) 432.

with formal constitutional structures and practices has been translated to a new and complex arena – tribunals, regulators, agencies and authorities – with limited consensus among either scholars or the judiciary on even the most basic questions. Often, the dominant rights-based understanding of administrative law advanced by courts during the process of review deploys the language of fundamental rights violations, thereby limiting the growth and damaging the internal coherence of non-rights based – significant and distinct – grounds for review such as the doctrine of ultra vires or of legitimate expectations.[16]

A further feature noted by Vakil is that the much-needed renegotiation of the separation of powers doctrine has not occurred in India, with the Supreme Court continuing to be an overarching 'good governance' court while providing limited clarity on the permissibility and scope of delegation to the executive, on the specific demands from the legislative process, and on the norms involved in the establishment of regulatory agencies.[17] The idea of participatory rule-making, a major theme in the study of regulation globally, and one broadly seen as vital for democratic accountability and responsiveness, remains underbaked in the Indian context. Because the status of regulatory institutions in the three-branch separation is not adequately defined, such institutions often perform quasi-legislative functions without appropriate accountability and participatory mechanisms. The fact that Indian administrative law, crudely put, is 'missing in action' is further underlined by Farrah Ahmed and Swati Jhaveri's study of how the common law review of administrative action has been eclipsed by constitutional law, thereby resulting in doctrinal gaps and misalignments in addressing administrative failures and in providing guidance for administrators and citizens alike.

K Vivek Reddy takes the sub-optimal state of Indian administrative law one step further and provocatively questions its constitutionality. The constitutionality of the administrative state has, of course, been a matter of impassioned recent debate in the US.[18] Reddy notes, for example, that the separation of powers principle has only been applied to the regulatory state in narrow contexts such as judicial independence. In this context, the courts have certainly been vigilant in assessing the place that regulatory tribunals occupy within India's constitutional structure. A considerable degree of judicial doctrine has addressed the structure of regulatory tribunals (dispute settlement bodies to which regulatory decisions are appealed) in terms of their composition

[16] The nature of rights-based adjudication has also had a negative impact on the development of other areas of law. For a study in the context of private law, see Shyamkrishna Balganesh, 'The Constitutionalisation of Indian Private Law' in Sujit Choudhury, Madhav Khosla, and Pratap Bhanu Mehta (eds), *The Oxford Handbook of the Indian Constitution* (Oxford University Press, 2016) 680.

[17] This approach links, one should note, to the exercise of judicial review in India more generally. See Pratap Bhanu Mehta, 'India's Judiciary: The Promise of Uncertainty' in Pratap Bhanu Mehta and Devesh Kapur (eds), *Public Institutions in India: Performance and Design* (Oxford University Press, 2005) 158; Pratap Bhanu Mehta, 'The Indian Supreme Court and the Art of Democratic Positioning' in Mark Tushnet and Madhav Khosla (eds) *Unstable Constitutionalism: Law and Politics in South Asia* (Cambridge University Press 2015) 233.

[18] See Philip Hamburger, *Is Administrative Law Unlawful?* (University of Chicago Press, 2014); Adrian Vermeule, 'No' (2015) 93 *Texas Law Review* 1547; Philip Hamburger, 'Vermeule Unbound' (2016) 94 *Texas Law Review* 205.

and their staffing of judicial members, as well as their jurisdiction and how it relates to the jurisdiction of the Supreme Court and the High Courts under Articles 32 and 226 of the Constitution.[19] However, the constitutional legitimacy of other aspects of the regulatory state has not been sufficiently addressed.

Reddy points out, for instance, that the principle of collective responsibility – a core constitutional and political principle in parliamentary systems – has not been fully reconciled with the existence of regulatory agencies, which operate with varying and often unclear degrees of independence from the political executive. Courts often extend the same degree of deference to such agencies as they do to actions by traditional government ministries, an approach which has its justifications, but does not take into consideration the accountability vacuum present in the case of agencies. Traditional common law doctrines, such as the doctrine of ultra vires, have been less effective at regulating agency action than we might hope, for the mandates under which agencies operate are often defined in open-ended and even troublingly vague terms. Regulatory agencies in India thus operate under the blanket of ambivalent or antiquated doctrine, at times enjoying vast bundled powers of law-making, investigation, adjudication and enforcement, and resorting to new instruments such as close day-to-day supervision, inspection, detailed queries, advisory correspondence and guidance supervision.

There have, one should note, been some positive and important judicial interventions over time. The Supreme Court's recent decision in *Cellular Operators Association v Telecom Regulatory Authority of India* is one example.[20] This case involved both constitutional and legal challenges to a Telecom Regulatory Authority of India (TRAI) regulation that mandated one-rupee credits to subscriber accounts for each call drop occurring on telecom service provider (TSP) networks. In addition to raising standard administrative law challenges, including the claim that the regulation was ultra vires the parent statute, the TSPs alleged non-transparency on the part of the TRAI when weighing facts disclosed during stakeholder consultations.

The Supreme Court upheld the ultra vires challenge as well as declaring that the regulation violated Article 19(1)(g) of the Constitution. It could have allowed the TSPs' appeals on this basis without going any further, particularly because the TRAI Act, 1997 did not expressly delineate the 'transparency' requirement, despite mentioning it. But, instead, the Court chose to articulate new principles of regulatory review, relying in this regard on 'transparency' requirements fleshed out in a subsequent, unconnected enactment – the Airports Economic Regulatory Authority of India Act, 2008. While conceding that the TRAI carried out stakeholder consultations, the Court held that these fell short of the 'transparency' requirement because the post-consultation deliberations failed to reveal any discernible grounds

[19] Tribunals were enabled by an amendment to the Constitution in 1976 that inserted arts 323A and 323B into the text. See Arun K Thiruvengadam, 'Tribunals' in Choudhry et al (n 15) 412. Important decisions on tribunals include *L Chandra Kumar v Union of India* (1997) 3 SCC 261; *Union of India v R Gandhi* (2010) 11 SCC 1; *Madras Bar Association v Union of India* (2014) 10 SCC 1; *Madras Bar Association v Union of India* (2015) 8 SCC 583. For a recent decision on the question of appointments and composition, see *State of Gujarat v Utility Users' Welfare Association*, 2018 SCC OnLine SC 368.

[20] *Cellular Operators Association v Telecom Regulatory Authority of India* (2016) 7 SCC 703.

for disagreement with the TSPs' assertion that a sizeable percentage of call drops occurred due to consumer mistakes. Though refraining from holding this to be a general requirement across the board, the Court expressed the desire that Parliament would intervene to address the matter and enact legislation along similar lines to the Administrative Procedure Act in the US.

However, by and large, rather than carefully crafting a set of doctrinal principles that both enable and limit regulatory action in appropriate ways, the Supreme Court continues with its 'good governance' approach and sometimes resorts to blunt instruments such as bans, even if this approach does lend a degree of pragmatism to the process. This strategy of the Court is revealed by Susan Ostermann's chapter, which takes us through five different instances of judicial intervention – festival fireworks, correspondence courses in higher education, smoking in public spaces, the sale and registration of diesel vehicles, and highway alcohol sales. Judicially imposed bans in these cases emerge, she contends, when bottom-up 'fire alarm' mechanisms – whereby top-level leadership leverage citizen protests to expose egregious regulatory violations – fail to work due to weak state capacity on the enforcement front.[21] There is a fair degree of experimentation at play here as the Court attempts less harsh measures at first, converses with multiple stakeholders to gather information and graduates towards exemption-less bans only when other measures demand extensive monitoring and policing for them to work, or simply fall short of expected outcomes. Even in a case like the ban on highway alcohol sales, where the Court began with a ban without exemptions and did not explore other possibilities, Ostermann argues that an element of pragmatism is visible as the effort is to provide 'weak-link' actors with a simple enforcement tool rather than vest them with regulatory discretion. As these cases demonstrate, the judicial tendency is towards adjustments that can make bureaucratic functioning easier under extant circumstances rather than long-term capacity building that can enable more effective enforcement.

The claims offered by Vakil and by Ahmed and Jhaveri (that administrative law is under-utilised) and the one offered by Reddy (that administrative law is used but common law doctrines are less effective than we might suppose) may well be different sides of the same problem, which is that the judiciary appears to be making a conscious choice not to develop administrative law and instead relies on other methods, such as judicial overseeing, rights-based review and so forth. Together, these chapters indicate that the judiciary has been weakly invested in creating a new regulatory jurisprudence to meet the institutional changes in India's legal structure over the past three decades. Doctrinal changes and interventions have been piecemeal, and they are often situated oddly not only within the broader constitutional universe that structures the regulatory state, but also within one another. Why this is the case is a separate question. The answer is possibly rooted in what international relations

[21] Even in authoritarian China, the combination of strong coercive power but weak bureaucratic oversight has led to sub-optimal 'blunt force' regulation, especially in the case of environmental and financial regulation. See Denise van der Kamp, 'Blunt Force Regulation and Bureaucratic Control in Weak Institutional Environments' (draft on file with the authors).

scholars refer to as 'audience costs', a sort of populism that has afflicted the country's higher judiciary.[22] Judicial pronouncements rooted in the arcane minutiae of administrative law simply cannot match the publicity that constitutional jurisprudence attracts.

II. REGULATORY INCAPACITY AND STRUCTURAL WEAKNESSES

A second theme that looms large in several of the chapters in this volume is regulatory incapacity and a lack of systemic incentives to address this incapacity.[23] This incapacity is perhaps brought into sharpest focus when one considers situations where regulators are required to make scientific determinations, as seen in the context of air and water pollution as well as food safety. As Shibani Ghosh points out, India performs abysmally when it comes to drinking water quality, air quality, and general environmental and public health performance metrics. Focusing on the Water Act, 1974 and the Air Act, 1981, Ghosh argues that the effective implementation of both these enactments requires well-functioning boards supported by competent and adequate staff. The Indian Supreme Court has observed that the absence of technically competent leadership undermines the requirements of good governance.[24] The legislative and executive apathy towards regulatory incapacity is evident from a glance at the basic data. Ghosh notes that the Central Pollution Control Board has nearly 20 per cent of its sanctioned posts lying vacant as per its last annual report, and at least one State Pollution Control Board (the State of Karnataka) has 51 per cent of its posts unfilled. And the staff who are hired have a disproportionately high number of administrative members with no technical expertise, resulting in the paralysis of core functions.

The Indian state suffers from high levels of vacancies across all its organs, from the judiciary to the police and from the military to academic positions in universities. While the lack of competent personnel with adequate skills might be one explanation for senior-level appointments, it is belied by the fact that even local bureaucracies suffer from high numbers of vacancies. It is likely that politicians tend to underinvest in state capacity (staffing and training) because the electoral returns to these investments are diffuse and uncertain in contrast to the strong incentives to announce and inaugurate new and ambitious projects and programmes.[25] And there are, of course, questions relating to resource constrains. But there is another – and less generous – explanation, namely that understaffing is a deliberate strategy to enfeeble the regulators. However, while this might explain why the parent ministry might drag

[22] See James D Fearon, 'Domestic Political Audiences and the Escalation of International Disputes' (1994) 88 *American Political Science Review* 577.

[23] The problem of weak state capacity afflicts India's public institutions more generally and hence it is not surprising that this afflicts regulatory institutions as well. See Devesh Kapur, Pratap Bhanu Mehta and Milan Vaishnav (eds), *Rethinking Public Institutions in India* (Oxford University Press, 2017).

[24] See *Techi Tagi Tara v Rajendra Bhandari*, 2017 SCC OnLine SC 1165.

[25] Devesh Kapur and Aditya Dasgupta, 'The Political Economy of Bureaucratic Effectiveness: Evidence from Local Rural Development Officials in India' (draft on file with the authors).

its feet in selecting the members of the regulatory commissions, the hiring of staff is endogenous to the regulatory commission themselves.

Regulatory incapacity also chokes the process of standard-setting, which is critical to any domain where transgressions are measured and penalised based on scientific parameters. Over a range of industries, emission standards for severe pollutants are left underdetermined or, when determined, substantially higher than global standards, with little explanation for this variance. As Ghosh observes, source-based standards are problematic because they do not consider the capacity of the receptor – that is, the water body or local air – to absorb the effluents or emissions from multiple sources, even if the discharge from each individual source may be within legal limits. The absence of scientific capacity has doubtless contributed to a situation where the boards spend considerable efforts on licensing industries, much less on monitoring compliance with licence conditions, and perhaps least on developing and fixing standards. Is that a deliberate trade-off to encourage faster industrialisation at the cost of environmental protections, which was certainly the case in most countries at India's level of development? If so, it does not seem to have even served that goal.

In Vikramaditya Khanna's chapter on the regulation of food standards and safety, we are offered a disconcertingly similar narrative. Examining the Food Safety and Standards Authority of India (FSSAI), he divides its decision-making into two phases: pre-2015 and post-2015. The pre-2015 procedure involved product approvals for several commodities in respect of which standards were yet to be framed. Because the requisite capacity for scientific testing was not yet in place to consider these approval requests and scientific panels were over-stretched, the FSSAI started granting no objection certificates (NOCs) for products. These NOCs allowed products to be on the market for up to a year while awaiting panel decisions. It is only after 2015 – that is, after the Bombay High Court held this NOC procedure to be beyond the remit of the FSSAI's powers – that this regulatory authority started taking the standard-setting process more seriously.[26] But capacity deficiencies have stymied the process, resulting in a rather liberal importation of global standards and a reliance on industry players to help develop standards, train personnel and disseminate information on food safety more widely to the public. Khanna worries that the attempt at attenuating capacity gaps through reliance on external regulatory processes risks compromising fairness and neutrality in the decision-making process. A counter-argument – which we examine later – is that relying on an external 'anchor' could bolster the domestic regulator, not just by filling capacity gaps but also by staving off political pressures.

Moreover, the FSSAI has had a chequered track record of overriding scientific panels and taking important decisions without a clear scientific basis, partly due to its severe staffing limitations and excessive dependence on contractual staff. A Comptroller and Auditor General (CAG) report points out even a single qualified food analyst is not present in 15 of the 16 notified food laboratories, and quantifies a

[26] See *Vital Nutraceuticals Private Ltd v Union of India*, 2014 SCC OnLine Bom 165.

90 per cent shortfall of sanctioned food safety officers in 12 states.[27] Khanna reiterates the observations in this report that the FSSAI had no clear oversight procedures for evaluating lab performance, with many such labs running without the requisite testing facilities for pesticide residues, heavy metals and certain toxic substances. He argues that matters are only worsened by the enormous scale of regulatory activity expected from the FSSAI. Drawing parallels with China, he notes that regulators there have struggled to grapple with the local food diversity that makes standardisation difficult, and the massive production system, geographical size and number of market players that render monitoring and enforcement a gigantic task.[28] While self-regulation has its limitations, and it is unlikely that it can be a substitute for the scientific and technical capacity of regulatory bodies, given the challenges of regulating a large number of actors in large federal systems in terms of scale externalities and multi-level coordination challenges, there might be little alternative until state capacity is much more robust.

Neel Maitra examines the relationship between scale and regulatory efficacy in the context of a market that falls at the other end of the consolidation/concentration spectrum: the securities market. In his view, the Indian securities regulator – the Securities and Exchange Board of India (SEBI) – started with an easier task than some other regulators when it came to regulating stock exchanges. Limiting his study to members (and not all entities that issue securities), he unpacks a scenario where self-regulation works quite efficiently in India without the need for the regulator to make massive investments in internal capacity building. He argues that part of the reason for this are the early legislative choices, such as mandating that security trading can only take place over centrally recognised stock exchanges, and the placing of a premium on investor protection and transparency over competing market regulatory goals of efficient or liquid markets. But another important part is the regulator's own initiative in nudging the regulated market towards more standardisation and consolidation over time. SEBI has managed to achieve this through exercise of its delegated powers to recognise and de-recognise stock exchanges. Consequently, SEBI has been able to concentrate its regulatory capacity on a steadily decreasing number of recognised exchanges.

SEBI has also made full use of the legal embargo on trading elsewhere to orchestrate a virtuous cycle where entry barriers for new exchanges are kept high, and compliance and reporting norms for existing ones are stringent, leading exchanges to vigorously self-regulate and keep their members under check. Members too feel the heat of market non-participation in the event of de-listing or other sanctions imposed by exchanges, thus securing compliance with the self-regulatory regime. Drawing comparisons with the market structure in the US, he argues that the presence of alternative trading systems (ATSs) there alongside the securities exchanges undercuts the efficacy of self-regulation by exchanges. The cost of breach is never

[27] Comptroller and Auditor General of India, *Report on Performance Audit of Implementation of Food Safety and Standards Act, 2006* (Government of India, 2017).

[28] On the difficulties of food regulation in China, see John Yasuda, *On Feeding the Masses: An Anatomy of Regulatory Failure in China* (Cambridge University Press, 2017).

too expensive, as errant members can always move to trading in these ATSs. In India, SEBI has even minimised the possibility of regulatory arbitrage through member shift from one exchange to the other – the exchange market is effectively a duopoly now as two other exchanges are in exit stage – by pushing for identical or near-identical rules using its rule-making oversight. It has further tightened arbitrage, and promoted self-regulatory success, by making it difficult to switch from one business to another, such as from trading to investment advice. Maitra's major insight is therefore that SEBI has managed a striking degree of regulatory capacity by 'effectively delegating the regulation of market intermediaries to recognised stock exchanges, and has ensured that such regulation is effective by preserving the market power of these recognised exchanges'.

SEBI does, to be sure, have capacity-related concerns. As Umakanth Varottil highlights, SEBI fares better on the sanctioned strength versus occupied posts metric. But the growth in its sanctioned strength over a decade does not reflect the greater than sixfold growth in equity markets. Even from a qualitative perspective, he argues that the regulator's enforcement wing lacks the requisite skills and expertise to grapple with sophisticated market evolution, leading to a preference for blunt enforcement tools over more proportionate and nuanced responses.

In 2017, the US had 3,616 publicly listed companies, while 5,818 companies were listed on the Bombay Stock Exchange (BSE). As of March 2017, the US securities market watchdog, the Securities Exchange Commission (SEC), had 4,554 employees, while SEBI had 780. Thus, each listed company in the US was monitored by 1.26 SEC employees on average. In contrast, 780 SEBI employees were monitoring 5,818 listed companies in India, equating to each company being monitored by 0.13 employees – an order of magnitude difference. In key divisions, such as corporate finance, the SEC has more than 15 times as many employees as SEBI. This does not even control for personnel quality.[29] It should be emphasised that there are options to augment limited internal capacity, including outsourcing and crowd-sourcing data that is not sensitive, or instituting a strong whistleblower programme, with a reward correlated to the money collected from enforcements above a certain threshold.

Nonetheless, Maitra's comparisons between SEBI and the SEC in the US, and SEBI vis-a-vis other Indian regulators, presents a reasonably positive narrative on regulatory capacity and offers significant guidance on lessening the regulatory load while not compromising on the quality or efficacy of self-regulation. But there are two additional reasons why SEBI has been a more effective regulator. For one thing, its parent ministry – the Ministry of Finance – is itself widely acknowledged to have the most competent personnel across all departments. Additionally, India's need to attract foreign capital meant that the Ministry of Finance had a strong incentive to ensure that the regulator's effectiveness was not unduly compromised. However, these lessons cannot be easily extended to other situations, as Maitra himself acknowledges. Indeed, it is difficult to even stretch it to some of the other

[29] Krishnamurthy Subramanian, 'Building Regulatory Capacity in SEBI' *LiveMint* (3 September 2018), https://www.livemint.com/Opinion/JvxJZxGnegFSWS9jb6pIKP/Building-regulatory-capacity-in-Sebi.html.

functions discharged by SEBI. A good reason for this inability arises from another important and common concern with the Indian regulatory state: that of regulatory independence.

III. REGULATORY INDEPENDENCE AND DESIGN

Independence almost invariably has two dimensions to it: de jure and de facto. While regulatory design – such as ambiguity in the regulator's underlying statutes – can make it easier for the executive to override the regulator and compromise functional independence in a real sense, independence can be affected by another affliction of regulation and regulators, namely jurisdictional overlap and turf wars. An incessant need for a regulator to assert its jurisdictional legitimacy can easily undermine its public perception as an independent body. Both are detrimental for the regulator, albeit in different ways. Varottil's chapter provides interesting insights into the regulatory turf wars that presumably affect SEBI's ability to discharge its functions, as well as its public perception as an independent regulatory institution that can take firm decisions. SEBI has had to fight domain battles for years with the Ministry of Corporate Affairs (MCA), though it falls within the administrative oversight of the Ministry of Finance. The demarcation of powers, where SEBI administers those provisions of the Companies Act, 1956 relating to the issue and transfer of securities, has not been an exacting one. The *Sahara* case, where unlisted entities issued securities to thousands of investors by sidelining SEBI and filing paperwork with the Registrar of Companies (under the MCA), is a particularly egregious example of such a conflict.[30] The battle over who gets to set corporate governance norms in India also entails domain assertions from SEBI and MCA, with the latter winning in recent years.

Varottil also details turf wars between SEBI and other regulators such as the Reserve Bank of India (RBI) and the Insurance Regulatory and Development Authority, which lead to weakening public perception over workings of the overall financial regulatory structure. While his study is measured, seeing some episodes as having to do less with conflict and more with a lack of effective coordination, the real difficulty has been in creating institutional frameworks that resolve such coordination failures and strengthen the regulatory environment. For instance, the Financial Stability Development Council, established in 2010 to institutionalise and strengthen inter-regulatory coordination mechanisms, has not received much impetus. Subsequently, in 2013, the Financial Sector Legislative Reforms Commission recommended creating a unified regulator (to be called the Unified Financial Agency (UFA)) by merging the securities, insurance, pension, and forward markets regulators into the UFA.

Worldwide, countries have been grappling with financial sector regulation, given the frequency and virulence of financial crises. Disintermediation of the financial

[30] *Sahara India Real Estate Corporation Ltd v Securities and Exchange Board of India* (2012) 10 SCC 603.

sector has led to hybrid financial instruments that combine features of banking, insurance and capital markets. An overarching financial regulator appears attractive because regulated entities can (and do) take advantage of such fragmentation and engage in regulatory arbitrage, and, as Varottil argues, because fragmentation in regulating financial markets potentially causes uncertainties for market players. But super-regulators can also concentrate risk instead of spreading it across regulators. However, while both fragmented and consolidated regulatory authority have their merits and demerits, weak coordination is, in any case, a regulatory failure that impinges upon the overall independence of individual regulators as well as the regulatory system as a whole.

Another important design failure lies in the absence of proper consultative procedures that inspire faith in the regulator's accountability towards citizens and other stakeholders. In the case of SEBI, public consultations do exist, although questions remain as to how it deliberates upon the information gathered from such consultations. For instance, in 2018, SEBI's move to ban entities owned by people of Indian origin from operating as foreign portfolio investors backfired. While the intentions were sound – it was aimed at stamping out the practice of 'round-tripping', whereby India citizens had used relatives abroad to launder money and make investments in India while concealing their wealth from the authorities – it backfired when the magnitude of its effects became apparent. More troubling, as one observer noted, 'India is the only place I've seen where they announce rules without any discussion with the industry'.[31] With the regulation of other domains, such as in the air and water pollution scenario studied by Ghosh or the banking sector examined by Suyash Rai, there are no consultation requirements in place at all, resulting in decisions that are taken without stakeholder engagement even though they carry major consequences for the affected parties.

If the financial sector illustrates the challenges of horizontal coordination and turf wars among regulators, the power sector highlights the challenges of vertical coordination in India's federal system between the central and state governments. These federalism-related challenges are addressed in Akshay Jaitly's chapter on renewable energy. This sub-sector was targeted for differential and favourable regulatory treatment within the broader ambit of the Electricity Act, 2003. But, as Jaitly demonstrates, while these favourable policies have undoubtedly boosted the sector, interventions by state governments have significantly undermined the central government's vision. Jaitly also underlines the problem with misaligned objectives at the central level – that is, between the ministries of power, new and renewable energy, and finance that have different priorities – resulting in early benefits, such as accelerated depreciation and generation-based incentives being pulled back, re-introduced and again rolled back, thus sending conflicting messages to stakeholders as well as regulators. India's conflicting goals to procure cheap solar equipment on the one hand, while boosting a domestic manufacturing base through imposition of import duties

[31] At the time, it was estimated that of the $450 billion of foreign portfolio investment into India, $75 billion was funds managed by Indian origin investors. Simon Mundy, 'Indian Regulators Warned over Foreign Investor Plan' *Financial Times* (4 September 2018).

on the other, and simultaneously wanting to keep the lowest possible prices for power to help indebted and loss-making state-owned power distribution companies keep costs down is an impossible trinity.

States have sidestepped the feed-in tariff fixation system, which is meant to sufficiently incentivise renewable energy deployment by assuring attractive tariffs for power producers, in favour of competitive bidding that keeps tariffs low, in order to benefit their distribution companies and consumers. The implications of such low tariffs for the long-term sustainability of underlying projects and the overall growth of the sector seem reasonably clear. Moreover, falling tariffs have led to distribution companies unilaterally renegotiating or terminating their existing contractual arrangements with renewable energy generators. This, in turn, has resulted in a conflict between the Appellate Tribunal for Electricity (APTEL), which has held that a power purchase agreement can only be re-opened to provide thrust to renewable energy projects, and the State Electricity Regulatory Commissions (SERCs), that have largely weighed in favour of state-owned distribution companies. The issue points to the reality that problems in regulation might be rooted in underlying difficulties elsewhere, in this case the larger problem of contract enforcement in India.[32]

Similarly, renewable purchase obligations (RPOs) that were introduced to drive up demand for renewables have not been obeyed in letter or in spirit by the SERCs. The minimum targets set by SERCs for 'obligated entities' to fulfil, as part of their total energy purchase, have been typically lower than the recommended targets set by central government entities. SERCs have also ignored verdicts by APTEL and the Supreme Court, and either refrained from penalising or imposed paltry fines on state-owned distribution companies that fail to meet RPO targets. Jaitly concludes that these misalignments between state and central government actors, and within the central government itself, will likely get in the way of the sector's capability to attract the investments necessary for meeting India's nationally determined commitments under the Paris Climate Change Agreement.

The power sector exemplifies the challenges of regulatory independence in situations where the state, through its public enterprises, is a player in the sector under consideration. This leads to a scenario where a different set of norms are made applicable to the public entities, or one where even if the norms were the same, they are partially applied by the regulator due to pressures on its functioning. Banking is a classic instance of the former, while infrastructure and renewable energy exemplify the latter. Both jeopardise the 'level playing field' assertions behind India's transition from a licensed business regime to a regulatory state, with immensely detrimental consequences that are playing out even at present.

Suyash Rai's study of the banking regulatory system dives straight into the concern that occupies most observers of the banking system in India today. How

[32] According to the World Bank's 'Ease of Doing Business Indicators', the time taken to enforce a contract in India (in 2017) was 1,445 days, which was longer than it was 15 years ago (1,420 days), placing the country in 164th place in the global ranking on the Enforcing Contracts indicator. See http://www.doingbusiness.org/en/rankings.

did financial frauds and excesses in the public banking system go unnoticed for such a long time, only to suddenly appear with the flight and failure of high-net-worth individuals? Why did the RBI never intervene in a meaningful enough way and perform its task as a regulator? The answer, as Rai points out, is that even though public sector banks (PSBs) hold 68 per cent of the total deposits in the formal banking system, the RBI's regulatory powers are circumscribed, especially its ability to impose significant penalties on errant PSBs. When the Finance Minister disputed this, claiming that 'in the Indian system, we politicians are accountable, the regulators are not', the RBI Governor responded that 'the RBI's legal powers to supervise and regulate PSBs are also constrained. It cannot remove PSBs Directors or management who area appointed by the government of India, nor can it force a merger or trigger the liquidation of a PSB'.[33] It has, at best, some recommendatory powers against errant senior officials at these banks and participation through its nominees in their boards. Thus, the law provides for some minimal oversight by the RBI over the functioning of PSBs, with its primary task being confined to regulating private and cooperative banks.

The origins of this divided regulatory authority within the same sector go back to 1969, when then Prime Minister Indira Gandhi's government nationalised 14 private banks and concentrated the banking sector in the hands of PSBs. While policy priorities at the time of nationalisation or even a couple of decades later directed lending to the agriculture sector and other underserved sectors, the post-liberalisation exercise of this authority has largely benefited players in the infrastructure sector, with PSBs being compelled to grant loans to complex projects that they had little prior experience of dealing with. This was exacerbated by regulatory forbearance towards politically connected businesses. As Rai argues, excessive governmental control in the financial decision-making process, coupled with an alignment of political incentives that block any transition towards substantive regulatory oversight, have resulted in a moral hazard problem.

Until the passage of the Insolvency and Bankruptcy Code, 2016, the instruments of resolution and liquidation of poorly performing PSBs were vested with the Government of India and not the RBI, and there had not been a single exercise of this power. Instead, a vicious cycle had ensued in which poor performers were periodically recapitalised by governments willing to absorb their losses, leading the public to believe in the infallibility of the public banking system. Failures recur because PSBs have no real incentive to mend their practices, as they do not bear the massive adverse consequences of their actions. The public faith in PSBs, despite the abysmal track record of many of them, is rational given the record of bailouts, and spills over into the growth and competitiveness of the more regulated private banking system as they cannot boast of such assured bailouts. Faced with this reality where there is no run on the bank to justify regulatory intervention in the first place, the RBI has largely

[33] News Report, 'RBI's Regulatory Powers over PSBs are Weaker Than Those over Private Sector Banks: Urjit Patel', *Economic Times* (15 March 2018), https://economictimes.indiatimes.com/industry/banking/finance/banking/urjit-patel-opens-up-on-pnb-says-no-regulator-can-prevent-fraud/articleshow/63302101.cms.

refrained from intervening. It has sparingly exercised its power through members on PSB boards to adopt more prudent practices, as taking such an approach would place it in conflict with the government and its policy – or more likely its political – priorities. India's new insolvency and bankruptcy law appears to finally provide real powers to regulators to rein in the looting by big business. The RBI has leveraged the new law to force the hand of the PSBs to launch insolvency proceedings against major corporate defaulters, but its full impact remains to be seen.

The big beneficiary of PSB lending – the infrastructure sector – also faces issues of regulatory interference due to pernicious political pressures. As Amit Kapur outlines in his chapter, the pressures here fit broadly into two categories: preference for state-owned enterprises (SOEs) and undermining regulatory independence to suit the same, and the dilution of rule-based decision-making and disregard for contractual arrangements for political gains, such as providing free electricity and other 'welfare' measures. Kapur shows that the roots of the problem are somewhat like those in banking, where, until the early 1990s, the sector was heavily dominated by SOEs. Post-liberalisation, policy priorities shifted, pushing for vertically integrated SOEs (especially in the electricity sector) to be unbundled and corporatised into distinct functional entities, and for introducing competition into most segments of the value chain. But the actual realisation of these goals demands regulatory frameworks that guarantee and maintain a level playing field between new players and the dominant SOEs. Unfortunately, this has not happened to the requisite extent, despite the institutional presence of sector-specific regulators seemingly having the same kind of authority over both private players and SOEs.

Kapur points out that many of the sector-specific regulators are administratively located within and financially provided for by the concerned ministry, which also owns and controls the regulated SOEs. In addition, these regulators depend on the relevant ministry for staffing, often contractually engaging personnel from the regulated SOEs themselves. Completing the picture of dependence on the executive and non-separation from the regulated SOE is the fact that budgetary allocations are made from the ministry, with extensive reporting requirements placed on the regulator. In this scenario, it is evident to the regulated SOE as to where the real seat of authority lies: the ministry rather than the regulator. Therefore, when choosing between the regulator's verdict and conflicting policy directives from the ministry, SOEs ignore the former, diminishing market confidence in the regulator.

To demonstrate this point, Kapur uses the case study of open access, where independent power producers were legally entitled to access the publicly owned grid infrastructure and sell power generated at their end. The state transmission utility unilaterally chose to block such open access, and state governments acted in the 'public interest' to sequester the power thus generated to be sold to their utilities at a prescribed price. In effect, shortfalls due to deficiencies in the state distribution system were sought to be transferred to the private power generators by violating a legally guaranteed regulatory principle. Though the Central Electricity Regulatory Commission stepped in to secure the continuance of open access, its verdict was overturned by the Karnataka High Court, appeals against which decision have now been pending before the Supreme Court for the past seven years. Moreover, as Jaitly points out in his chapter, SERCs may have allied in principle with open access obligations, but have not fulfilled their mandate to reduce the cross-subsidy surcharge, which is a significant financial disincentive for consumers to opt for open access.

Similarly, Kapur argues that 'public interest' and welfare objectives have been used as a ruse to both overturn contractual commitments and limit pricing autonomy in infrastructure – where ex ante certainty is critical due to the long-gestation investments that investors need to make, and some assurance of viable returns over a long timeframe are needed to attract private competition in the first place. Regulators have not been proactive in taking prompt action against backtracking in relation to contractual commitments, including non-payment or delayed part-payment of tariffs, dues and carrying costs. Even legal provisions such as those in the Electricity Act, 2003, which aimed to give some pricing flexibility and to ensure that private players do not suffer the brunt of unsound subsidies granted due to political pressures, have been ignored by some state governments, with no respite from regulators to tackle these direct inroads into project viability. Like Jaitly, Kapur also concludes that the problems that the sector currently faces – namely, those relating to stressed assets and twin balance sheet woes – are unlikely to be easily cured without a better climate for investment, which in turn is hard to achieve given the current regulatory realities.

IV. NEW TECHNOLOGIES AND DATED REGULATORY FRAMEWORKS

One of the most demanding challenges facing regulatory design is how to deal with new technologies, especially disruptive technologies that upend the assumptions that informed prior regulatory design. It poses difficult questions not only on what or how to regulate, but crucially on who will regulate, provoking turf wars, as Rahul Matthan's chapter on telecommunications regulation illustrates. Technological change in this area has been so rapid that turf wars have been an endemic feature. The TRAI was created as an independent sector specific regulator in furtherance of India's international obligations as well as a Supreme Court directive. But the Department of Telecommunications (DoT) has enjoyed overriding powers over its decisions. As a result, over time, the TRAI was reduced to an expert recommendatory body on most cases other than those involving interconnection and tariff, where it can lay down rules that do not conflict with the operator licences issued by the DoT. On several occasions, and most notably with the controversial 2G spectrum allocation in 2008, TRAI decisions have been rejected or stalled by the DoT and have stymied the regulatory agenda.[34] In addition to departmental pressures, the TRAI's adjudicatory powers have been transferred wholesale to the Telecom Disputes Settlement and Appellate Tribunal (TDSAT) and it now faces further regulatory turf battles with the Competition Commission of India (CCI) over the issue of predatory pricing in the sector. In short, the TRAI is a specialised regulatory authority with reasonable

[34] The 2G spectrum allocation exploded as one of the most egregious corruption scandals in India, forcing the Supreme Court to step in and deliver several orders in relation to this issue. See *Centre for Public Interest Litigation v Union of India* (2012) 3 SCC 1; *Subramanian Swamy v Manmohan Singh* (2012) 3 SCC 64; *In Re Allocation of Natural Resources, Special Reference 1 of 2012* (2012) 10 SCC 1.

capacity but limited ultimate authority. However, despite this, the sector has grown explosively.

Matthan explains this puzzle by taking us through three objectives that have guided telecom regulations. These objectives – coverage and penetration, revenue maximisation, and national security – have been instrumental in shaping crucial policy decisions. The centrality of these objectives in creating and shaping a vibrant market where none existed emerges quite clearly from his discussion of decisions that have been taken by the DoT, with the first objective having been particularly influential. Early on, a cap was imposed on the number of operators in each circle to ensure that all of them did not gravitate to the more lucrative metropolitan areas. After ensuring the presence of operators in every circle, policy instruments subsequently aimed at maximising coverage within these circles. Positive measures to permit the sharing of passive telecom infrastructure also helped to lower entry barriers for new players. These steps deepened coverage and penetration with mobile subscribers increasing a hundredfold, from about 10 million in 2002 to 1.2 billion in 2018.

However, as Matthan notes, the current framework of departmentally driven regulation with clarity on the key regulatory objectives and little public consultation in the decision-making process, and a near-sidelining of the 'independent regulator' may have just about served its time. Today, the telecom sector's demands have changed as technological disruption is rife in this area. New technologies impact citizens differently without lending themselves to the triple-objective framing that has seen the sector grow from nothing to one that has among the lowest costs and second-largest subscriber base in the world. They also demand updating legal frameworks – the sector is, remarkably, still governed through an anachronistic enactment, the Indian Telegraph Act, 1885 – rather than governance through telecom service provider licences. Technological convergence – over voice and video, wireless and broadband – data protection and privacy, and emerging monopolies all even more require the TRAI's expertise and effective public consultation systems in not only recommending innovative frameworks but also putting them in place without further policy paralysis. The need for an independent regulator in the real sense of this term stands out ever more than in the past.

Rai's study of banking regulation offers the same observations regarding new technologies in the finance sector and the RBI's regulatory incapacity in playing catch up. He points out that technology can present the banking sector with five different kinds of scenarios – 'better bank', 'new bank', 'distributed bank', 'relegated bank' and 'dis-intermediated bank' – with policy and regulatory decisions influencing which scenario would dominate the sector's future in India. In such situations, the RBI will have to re-align its focus from the regulated entity's form to its actual functions, and develop mechanisms such as regulatory sandboxes to co-develop regulations for innovative business models. However, in order for this regulatory transition to be handled well, the organisation will have to be more open and consultative.

Inadequate attention to institutional design and independence is currently the situation when one considers the regulation of another technologically powered resource that is increasingly critical to national progress and economic growth: data. Ananth Padmanabhan and Anirudh Rastogi examine the rise of big data solutions and the startling inadequacy of India's legal and regulatory landscape to address this issue.

The Information Technology (IT) Act, 2000 – the applicable overarching legislation in operation in India – was enacted at a time when data storage was perceived to be vulnerable to attack, and the subsequent IT Rules, 2011, relating to sensitive personal data or information, added a few layers of protection in the light of increased data gathering. But Padmanabhan and Rastogi argue that the point of threat to individual and group rights has increasingly shifted from data gathering to data processing. The deep learning solutions of today are quite capable of profiling individuals and groups in extremely granular ways, and of re-identifying personal information and individuals even where the original dataset is bereft of personal details. No clear substantive safeguards against such practices, or robust regulatory mechanisms to mitigate these harms to individual and social rights, exist in India. The segregation of data security and these new kinds of challenges into separate policy silos is again unhelpful and out of sync with the reality of present-day threats.

Tracing the reason for these structural lapses to the relatively new recognition of informational privacy as a fundamental right in India – it was only in 2017 that a nine-judge bench of the Supreme Court of India unanimously held so – the authors build the case for stronger data governance principles and procedures going forward.[35] Drawing on recent government reports, they argue that protecting privacy is not only a matter of tightening consent notifications or differential treatment of sensitive personal data, but also about higher digital literacy and educating Indian users on the threats and consequences of data leaks and unlawful data processing. New notice requirements must be envisioned that serve this broader purpose, including the use of visual media, vernacular languages and simple writing. The authors argue that the end goal should be to nudge data controllers to introduce privacy-by-design and other data-respecting technologies, and strong internal procedures, rather than rely on an extensive state regulatory system. Their views seem to resonate with Khanna's on food regulation, where the scale of operations is too diverse and spread out – often happening behind 'closed doors' and in 'black boxes' – to make regulation meaningful or effective.

However, one area where Padmanabhan and Rastogi advocate higher regulatory independence and stronger frameworks is the use of big data solutions for public purposes. Using Aadhaar – India's biometric identity project – as a pivot for this discussion, they demonstrate how the Unique Identification Authority of India (UIDAI) serves as both the data custodian and regulator of this database, leading to a complete misalignment of incentives. As a regulator, it has no effective voice in deciding the public services for which the database would be used, while as custodian, it has no serious incentives to disclose the occurrence of a breach, despite the Aadhaar Act, 2016 vesting rights with the UIDAI, not the citizen, to be notified of data breaches and then decide how best to proceed. Similar flaws exist with the mass surveillance possibilities in this project and the oversight mechanisms for safeguarding against such possibilities. The authors anticipate these issues to worsen as big data solutions and algorithmic decision-making find increasing application in policy-making, the

[35] On the Indian Supreme Court's recognition of the right to privacy, see *KS Puttaswamy v Union of India* (2017) 10 SCC 1.

allocation of public resources, and the delivery of public goods and services. Without strong regulations and better-designed regulatory institutions that separate functions from the nodal ministries, discrimination harms against individuals and groups are likely to proliferate and remain unaddressed.

It is worth noting that one issue in this regard is relatively unaddressed. The proliferation of fake news and violence that undermine social trust and democracy, fuelled by the new social media technologies, are raising thorny issues of who – and how – this should be regulated.[36] The real puzzle here is how to regulate the systemic power of 'Big Tech' that is based on platform technologies. Big Tech straddles multiple markets (communications, media and, advertising) and, in terms of size, market impact and interconnectedness, it has become so embedded in everyday life that it is simply not easily substitutable. When antitrust regulation was introduced in the West, one important goal was to ensure that the economic power of large companies did not result in the corruption of the political process. For much of the twentieth century, antitrust policy was predicated on the welfare of the citizen. But, over time, emphasis began to be placed on business efficiency, which from the 1980s onwards came to be measured in consumer prices, a shift that clearly served the neoliberal politics of the time. However, such an understanding is increasingly questionable at a time when Big Tech offers products and services for 'free' in exchange for personal data. While there is increasing agreement that government intervention in Big Tech is needed, there is little consensus on who (that is, which institutions) should perform this regulation, about the trade-offs between innovation and regulation, privacy and free flows of data, and curbing manipulation and protecting free speech. Any solution to the problems of Big Tech will require innovation as well as regulation. This could include substantially larger fines (akin to the $2.7 billion fine on Google imposed by the European Union for manipulating its search engine results in order to favour its own shopping service) to insisting that individuals retain ownership rights of all the digital connections that they create.[37]

V. INTERNATIONAL REGULATION AS A DOMESTIC POLICY ANCHOR

As firms and markets globalise, regulation might be expected to follow suit. The integration of product and financial markets has internationalised these problems and has led to a shift from local and domestic to international standard-setting. Global agreements, institutionalised in intergovernmental organisations such as the International Monetary Fund, the Bank for International Settlements and the World Trade Organization, have further boosted the spread and power of international standards.[38] International regulatory standards then become instruments of

[36] For a recent intervention in the debate on social media and democratic values, see Cass R Sunstein, *#Republic: Divided Democracy in the Age of Social Media* (Princeton University Press, 2018).

[37] For the EU verdict, see EU Commission Decision, *Google Search (Shopping)*, Case AT.39740, 27 June 2017, http://ec.europa.eu/competition/antitrust/cases/dec_docs/39740/39740_14996_3.pdf.

[38] David Andrew Singer, *Regulating Capital: Setting Standards for the International Financial System* (Cornell University Press, 2007); Tim Buthe, 'The Globalization of Health and Safety Standards: Delegation of Regulatory Authority in the SPS Agreement of the 1994 Agreement Establishing the World Trade Organization' (2008) 71 *Law and Contemporary Problems* 219.

governance, acting either as norms or as government regulations, especially when incorporated into laws and regulations. There are several reasons why businesses and governments may adopt a particular standard. It might provide a superior solution to a technical problem; network externalities can create economic incentives for implementing a standard; information asymmetries in the market can create economic incentives for businesses to adopt standards; political-legal incentives or social pressure from third parties may induce government and firms to comply with standards that are seen as embodying 'best practice'; or compliance might be required by laws or regulations. Only the last is shaped by the power of business in lobbying governments.

Starting in the 1980s, divergent national standards became one of the most important non-tariff barriers to trade and, in the 1990s, a prominent barrier to the international integration of financial markets. Until the 1980s, there were only a few areas where standards had come into global use through intergovernmental organisations, such as the Codex Alimentarius Commission (a joint body of the UN Food and Agriculture Organization and the World Health Organization (WHO)), which had developed some food safety standards, and the International Telecommunications Union (ITU), which governed radio frequencies and standardised (some aspects of) related technologies. Today, the overwhelming majority of new standards for product and financial markets are developed in the expert committees of international (or sometimes regional) standard-setting bodies.

Most standards come from non-market private bodies, often international non-governmental organisations that have the backing of governments, but with the strong participation of market actors. Two prominent bodies of this type are the International Organization for Standardization (ISO) and the International Electrotechnical Commission (IEC), which jointly account for about 80 per cent of all international product standards. These two organisations have become prominent in part due to the Agreement on Technical Barriers to Trade, negotiated during the Uruguay Round of the General Agreement on Tariffs and Trade (GATT). It obliges all WTO member states to use international standards as the technical basis of domestic laws and regulations whenever international standards exist.[39]

Another area where global standard-making bodies heavily intrude into domestic regulatory processes is finance.[40] Thus, the Basel Committee on Banking Supervision – which develops global regulatory standards for banks and seeks to strengthen micro- and macro-prudential supervision – sets standards on capital adequacy of banks and liquidity coverage. With India represented on this forum by the RBI, these standards have found their way into Indian banking regulations. The International Organization of Securities Commissions (IOSCO) – a forum for the world's securities regulators that sets global standards for the securities sector – makes periodic assessments reports on Indian securities markets. India is represented through SEBI

[39] See Tim Buthe and Walter Mattli, 'International Standards and Standard Setting Bodies' in David Coen, Wyn Grant and Graham Wilson (eds), *The Oxford Handbook of Business and Government* (Oxford University Press, 2012) 440.

[40] Singer (n 38).

on its various policy committees and the standards that come out of these find their way into SEBI's regulatory practices.

Another salient private global regulator is the International Accounting Standards Board (IASB), which sets global accounting standards on corporate financial reporting. But accounting standards are not neutral. Accounting principles in Europe prioritised 'prudence' (emphasising judgement to avoid overstating capital or income), while the US system prioritised 'neutrality' (or the 'absence from bias') to facilitate trading in securities markets. Accounting standards affect how costly it is for a company to raise capital, the incentives to invest in research and development, and how it calculates risks (and thereby what risks it takes). For an emerging market like India, the adoption of global accounting standards by Indian firms affects their ability to raise capital in global markets or the possibility of Mumbai emerging as a global financial centre. While India has not adopted International Financial Reporting Standards in toto, it has developed Indian Accounting Standards (Ind AS) that are based on and substantially converged with International Financial Reporting Standards as issued by the IASB.[41]

An even more important role of international regulation is the de facto outsourcing of regulation. For instance, even as the airline industry in India expanded rapidly, the regulator – the Directorate General of Civil Aviation (DGCA) – was lackadaisical in discharging its responsibilities. But airline safety is an international issue since foreign airlines fly into India and Indian carriers fly into other countries. In 2012, a safety audit by the United Nations (UN) body, the International Civil Aviation Organization (ICAO), raised safety concerns about India's aviation system ranking India as the world's thirteenth-worst performer in safety. In 2014, the US Federal Aviation Administration downgraded India to Category 2 from Category 1, which effectively prevented Indian carriers from adding flights to the US or entering into any new code-share agreements for a year. This compelled the DGCA to align most of its rules (known as civil aviation requirements (CAR)) with the ICAO norms. The external regulators had highlighted the paucity of crucial personnel for flight operation inspectors and air traffic services, prompting the DGCA to hire the required flight operation inspectors in record time.[42] External regulation forced changes that the internal regulator was either unwilling or unable to do on its own accord.

A similar process has unfolded in the regulation of the food and pharmaceuticals industries. In the case of the former, Khanna's chapter demonstrates how India's food safety regulator (the FSSAI) set about standardising around 12,000 food items in

[41] Devesh Kapur, 'India and International Financial Institutions and Arrangements' in Waheguru Pal Singh Sidhu, Pratap Bhanu Mehta and Bruce D Jones (eds), *Shaping the Emerging World: India and the Multilateral Order* (Brookings Institution, 2013) 237.

[42] It did so by making the posts of flight operation inspectors attractive for experienced pilots and offering them a market-linked salary and 'managed to get the approval of the Finance Ministry within three days'. Tarun Shukla, 'ICAO Set to Audit India's Air Safety in November' *LiveMint* (10 January 2017), https://www.livemint.com/Politics/caywvFVaeGIwIJbgNQlfAJ/ICAO-set-to-audit-Indias-air-safety-in-November.html. See also Somesh Jha, 'DGCA Braces for ICAO Safety Audit' *The Hindu* (18 July 2017), https://www.thehindu.com/news/national/dgca-braces-for-icao-safety-audit/article19303296.ece.

harmonisation with globally recognised standards on food and food safety maintained by the Codex Aliementarius Commission (CAC). Similarly, the Global Food Safety Partnership (GFSP) – a public-private partnership established in 2012, which brings together governments, industry, multilateral organisations and other stakeholders promoting global cooperation for food safety capacity building in support of stronger food safety systems – has been working with the FSSAI in strengthening food safety standards and regulations.

Since the mid-2000s, the US has become a key market for Indian pharmaceutical firms, with about a third of its total sales coming from the US market. India's exports have almost doubled, from $8.7 billion in 2008–09 to $16.88 billion in 2016–17. Indian companies account for 40 per cent of the generic sales in that market.[43] India now has more than 600 US Food and Drug Administration (FDA)-approved facilities, the largest number of such manufacturing facilities outside that country, and Indian pharma firms received 301 US FDA generic drug approvals in 2017 (up from 177 in 2015).

Given the volume of generic drugs the US began importing, the US passed a Generic Drug User Fee Act (GDUFA) that made it compulsory for manufacturers of generic prescription drugs to pay a fee along with applications seeking permission to sell new drugs in the US and approval for generic products. The fee would pay for the US FDA to inspect the facilities of Indian drug exporters to the US for quality control. Since then, the Centre for Drug Evaluation and Research (CDER) division of the FDA has issued a large number of good manufacturing practices (GMP)-related warning letters and inspection reports (called '483' observations) to facilities in India (as well as China). The issues flagged included lack of scientifically sound laboratory controls, discrepancies in data maintenance records, ignoring high-end hygiene standards and problems with plant maintenance/factory environment. A landmark event in India's history with FDA compliance was the exposure by a former employee of an Indian firm (Ranbaxy Laboratories) laying bare how his former employer had failed to conduct proper safety and quality tests on drugs and had misled the US FDA about its procedures. When Ranbaxy was fined $500 million (and the employee earned $48 million through a whistleblower award from the US), the incident threatened to stymie one of the few success stories of Indian manufacturing.[44]

In 2015, nearly half of the FDA's warning letters were to Indian firms. Similarly, the European Medicines Agency carried out 1,333 inspections at 458 manufacturing sites around the world between 2011 and 2016, of which 49 per cent were in India.[45] Rising regulatory challenges and increasing competition led to the establishment of the Indian Pharmaceutical Alliance (IPA) – a group of leading Indian

[43] PB Jayakumar, 'The US Squeeze' *Business Today* (31 December 2017).

[44] Sohini Das, '10 Years of Pharmaceutical Sector: Controls, Regulations Stymie Growth' *Business Standard* (21 March 2018), available at: https://www.business-standard.com/article/companies/10-years-of-pharmaceutical-sector-controls-regulations-stymie-growth-118032001256_1.html.

[45] European Medicines Agency et al, 'Report on the International Active Pharmaceutical Ingredient Inspection Programme 2011–2016' (March 2018), available at: www.ema.europa.eu/docs/en_GB/document_library/Report/2018/04/WC500247387.pdf.

pharmaceutical firms, regulators, and other national and global stakeholder pharma companies – to form a quality forum in 2015. This forum developed guidelines for data reliability, investigations, process validation and good documentation practices, among other things. The guidelines appear to have worked to some degree. While quality issues are an ongoing challenge for the Indian pharmaceutical industry, in 2017 there were 192 FDA inspections, with India's share of warning letters falling to 29 per cent.

The international regulator – the US FDA – began working with its regulatory counterparts in India, including the Indian Export Inspection Council (EIC), the Drugs Controller General of India (DCGI), and the Joint Secretary of the Ministry of Health and Family Welfare. The All India Drug Control Officers Confederation (AIDCOC) organised workshops to train drug inspectors across the country and bridge the gaps that exist between industry and the regulators, while the Central Drugs Standard Control Organization (CDSCO) is trying to make the Indian regulators match international standards through such training sessions. With half of India's pharmaceutical exports going to highly regulated markets, the need to ensure quality assurance at the manufacturing level was manifest.[46]

The influence of external regulators has reached beyond federal agencies in India. The Gujarat government set up the Gujarat Food and Drug Control Administration (FDCA), which signed an agreement with the US FDA for training the drug control officials in capacity building, training, networking, knowledge sharing and compliance. With Gujarat accounting for 28 per cent of India's pharmaceutical exports and having the maximum number of 125 US FDA-approved pharmaceutical manufacturing units in the country, tying up with an external regulator provides another mechanism to augment weak domestic regulatory capacity.

CONCLUSION

The regulatory state in India has grown fast, but it has neither managed to fit neatly within the traditional constitutional framework, nor has its overall structural and design features enabled it to function in the most efficient and productive of ways. Even developed modern democracies, such as the US, struggle with adapting constitutional principles to new regulatory demands, and hence the difficulties of adaptation in India are hardly surprising. Furthermore, the character of the regulatory state in India has been shaped by the country's common law inheritance, the general lack of clarity on the place of administrative law within its written constitution, and the absence of a unifying legislative approach to the problem.

The structural and design themes underlined present a somewhat different set of problems, whether one considers staffing gaps, coordination failures or the lack of functional independence. Some elements of a fitting regulatory design in the context

[46] Sohini Das, 'Pharmaceutical Industry Improving Inspection Skills for Better Compliance' *Business Standard* (8 April 2018), http://www.business-standard.com/article/companies/pharmaceutical-industry-improving-inspection-skills-for-better-compliance-118040800024_1.html.

of India – from the role and composition of the board within an agency to the mechanisms for reporting and accountability – have been carefully underlined in the study by Shubho Roy et al. Some of the structural and design themes reveal failures in conception – say, a failure to properly frame the relationship between a regulator and an executive ministry, a lack of effort to align goals at different levels of government, contractions and tensions within statutes with regard to regulatory goals and means, and so on.[47] Others arise from problems which may be placed under the broad category of capacity.

In each of these instances, the regulatory state is a product of the political economy within which it operates.[48] The state's decision, for example, to leave the relationship between the formal executive and a specific regulatory agency open-ended is often taken for a reason to allow the state to exercise control when it desires and to claim independence when matters go awry. Incentives matter at a more internal level as well. As KP Krishnan and Anirudh Burman show, the internal motivation to improve regulatory processes within specific authorities is weak, as revealed by the improvised developments in administrative processes within regulatory agencies. The force exerted by the environment in which a regulatory state develops is powerfully captured by Aditya Bhattacharjea's chapter on India's regulatory approach to competition law enforcement. The presence of state-owned enterprises has, like in the case of banking regulation, shaped the regulatory apparatus that has developed to curb anti-competitive behaviour. Here, the ubiquity and power of SOEs has meant that the regulatory aims of competitive law were directly at odds with important organs of the state. In countries like India, as Bhattacharjea notes, the development of an antitrust regulator is also made harder by the existence of important welfare objectives. Such objectives invite attention as to whether a competitive environment is indeed ideal in all scenarios, and whether and when it should give way to other goals.

Some of the challenges enumerated above are inherent to the regulatory state itself. There is an intrinsic duality built into the regulatory state, one which is simultaneously a 'liberalising' and a 'controlling' project, where markets might be 'freer' but have 'more rules'.[49] The regulatory state reconfigures the role of the state from direct control to steering and balancing. The state establishes broad rules (like directives) in consultation with affected interests; these interests are then heavily involved in shaping the transposition of those rules into practical measures within specific sectors. Therefore, it should not be surprising that if delegation to independent regulatory agencies was meant to 'depoliticise' contentious issues, that can only go so far. Regulation is not a transitional arrangement between a statist economy and one where self-regulating markets reign supreme. The reason is that regulation is not just about

[47] See, for instance, Aditya Bhattacharjea and Oindrila De, 'Anti-cartel Enforcement in India' (2017) 5 *Journal of Antitrust Enforcement* 166 for a 'structural contradiction' in Indian competition law that hinders anti-cartel enforcement.

[48] See, for instance, Sudha Mahalingam and Deepak Sharma, 'Political Economy of Independent Regulation in India's Natural Gas Industry' (2017) 52 *Economic and Political Weekly* 44 for a discussion of how the political-economy context has shaped regulatory performance in India's natural gas sector. See also Dubash and Morgan (eds) (n 4).

[49] Steven K Vogel, *Freer Markets, More Rules: Regulatory Reform in Advanced Industrial Countries* (Cornell University Press, 1996).

efficiency – it is also about distribution, whether between producers and consumers or among different types of producers and consumers. And that always makes it intrinsically political. Thus, attempts to depoliticise regulation might be misplaced and perhaps could even worsen outcomes.[50]

Any regulatory structure – including not merely the institutions involved but also the overall practices and conventions that determine the exercise of power – is part of the overall governmental framework that exists. The legitimacy as well as the effectiveness of that framework thus shares an important relationship with the broader scheme within which it functions.[51] For instance, a perennial concern in the regulatory literature is the issue of 'capture' by the regulated entities. In India's case, concerns of capture are more about how the judiciary and the civil service have captured the regulators to create retirement jobs for themselves.[52] The weaknesses of other regulatory institutions not covered in this volume – the regulatory bodies that govern the professions and higher education in India in general – seep into the effectiveness of sector regulators. The information contained in financial statements presented to shareholders is based on discretionary accounting choices made by professional accountants, whose training and professional standards reflect the quality of self-regulation of organisations such as the Institute of Chartered Accountants of India. The wider failures of regulation in Indian higher education, whether it is desired or not, affects the quality of human capital staffing these regulatory institutions.[53]

Such debates are, of course, part of a more general inquiry into the possibilities and problems associated with liberalising the Indian economy. Even though liberalisation has occurred in important ways, there is much debate both about the overall goals of such liberalisation and the means that must be employed. A regulatory apparatus that is created within such debates will naturally have to negotiate the tensions that they involve, and so it is to be expected that many debates about regulation in India are debates about the Indian economy and – as the chapters in this volume make clear – about the nature of the Indian state. Many of the challenges in Indian regulation exist because of challenges relating to the Indian state, and perhaps that is revealed at a most basic and fundamental level when one considers questions of governance and of capacity. In the ultimate analysis, then, it is hard to resist the conclusion that the future of Indian regulation will turn on the extent to which the Indian state can address such questions at a systemic level.[54]

[50] For an argument in this vein in the case of India's electricity sector, see Navroz K Dubash, Sunila Kale and Ranjit Bharvirkar (eds), *Mapping Power: The Political Economy of Electricity in India's States* (Oxford University Press, 2018).

[51] This is commonly observed in studies of administrative power. See, for example, Peter Cane, *Controlling Administrative Power: An Historical Comparison* (Cambridge University Press, 2016).

[52] Some recent Indian literature has focused on post-retirement jobs for judges and the impact that this has on adjudication. See Madhav S Aney, Shubhankar Dam and Giovanni Ko, 'Jobs for Justice(s): Corruption in the Supreme Court of India' (2017), https://papers.ssrn.com/sol3/papers.cfm?abstract_id=3087464.

[53] For an analysis of regulatory challenges in Indian higher education, see Devesh Kapur and Pratap Bhanu Mehta (eds), *Navigating the Labyrinth: Perspectives on India's Higher Education* (Orient Blackswan, 2017).

[54] There is much ongoing debate on theory and practice of regulation in India, even as this book goes to press. This is revealed, for example, in a recent issue of the *Economic and Political Weekly* (53(38), 22 September 2018), which contains important contributions on themes ranging from data protection to telecom regulation and competition law.

Part II

Foundations

Part II

Foundations

Part II

Indian Administrative Law and the Challenges of the Regulatory State

RAEESA VAKIL

2

Indian Administrative Law and the Challenges of the Regulatory State

RAEESA VAKIL

> Over the course of the last two centuries, we have developed a new mode of governance – the administrative state – and it makes us feel miserable.[1]
>
> – Edward L Rubin

> 'The regulatory state' provides a sort of intellectual brazier around which we can all gather, to warm our hands and speak to each other, in a world of increasingly fragmented academic professionalism.[2]
>
> – Michael Moran

INTRODUCTION

Indian administrative law has been traditionally characterised by scholars of the field as apolitical and instrumental: apolitical in the sense that it is believed to consist of value-neutral rules that are applied to achieve administrative and constitutional goals; and instrumental in the sense that administrative law as a body is concerned primarily with procedure and not substance.[3] Even Baxi, who argues that Indian administrative law currently operates to the disadvantage of the 'constitutionally worst-off', ultimately concedes that administrative law is 'not really a subject or discipline of law'.[4] It strains belief, he goes on to say, in an introduction to Massey's volume on Indian administrative law, 'that one may ever specialize in the [Indian administrative law] as such. To understand the stuff of which [Indian administrative law] is made, one has to understand relevant domains of "substantive" law'.[5]

[1] Edward L Rubin, *Beyond Camelot: Rethinking Law and Politics for the Modern State* (Princeton University Press, 2005) 1.

[2] Michael Moran, 'Understanding the Regulatory State' (2002) 32 *British Journal of Political Science* 391, 412.

[3] IP Massey, *Administrative Law*, 8th edn (Eastern Book Company 2012) 2, 7; MP Jain and SN Jain, *Principles of Administrative Law*, vol 1, 8th edn (LexisNexis 2017) 13, 14.

[4] Upendra Baxi, 'The Myth and Reality of the Indian Administrative Law' in Massey (n 3) xvii–lvii.

[5] ibid xvii–xviii.

This thin Indian conception of administrative law admits the close relationship between constitutional and administrative disciplines, but privileges constitutional law. Constitutional law defines the goals of the state; administrative law provides the procedural framework by which to execute them. Nonetheless, constitutional litigation has expanded, relaxing rules of standing and extending the exercise of judicial review. This has entailed a general disregard for procedural consistency along with a pre-occupation with ends-based reasoning that characterises the Indian Supreme Court's approach to constitutional law and, particularly, to rights litigation.[6] These constitutional changes, in turn, have raised conceptual challenges to the idea of a thin, process-driven administrative law. Key scholars like Massey, Jain and Jain, and Baxi, all of whom take markedly different approaches to administrative law, are now all forced to concede that administrative law is no longer concerned only with processes, but also with outcomes, and yet are still not able to reconcile this thicker conception of administrative law with their original, limited definitions.[7]

The lack of fundamental conceptual clarity about the nature and scope of administrative law as a field ('the poor relation of public law; the hard-working, unglamorous cousin labouring in the shadow of constitutional law')[8] is possibly an explanation for why scholarship on the subject is particularly ill-equipped to cope with the rising demands of the regulatory state. The regulatory state is broadly defined in the Indian context as being composed of 'institutions operating at arm's length from the government, insulated from day-to-day political pressures and using technical expertise in challenging decisions'.[9]

The emergence of the regulatory state in global terms is undisputed; within India, it is linked to a large body of literature that is characterised by calls to scholarship to focus on themes, problems and issues specific to the Indian context. Thus, Somanathan writes that the Indian regulatory state is defined particularly by legal uncertainty, an overweening judiciary and excessive delegation of executive functions.[10] He notes specifically that Indian constitutional law struggles to cope with this phenomenon, stressing the need for scholarship to 'alternative metaphors' outside the traditional separation of powers in responding to changes wrought by the rise of regulation.[11] Rudolph and Rudolph focus on an acute gap in the constitutional literature, noting that an understanding of the transition of India's 'interventionist' state to its current regulatory avatar ought to take into account not only the Constitution itself, but

[6] For an elaboration on these themes, see section II.

[7] Baxi (n 4) xxxvi; Massey (n 3) 15; Jain and Jain (n 3) 16–18.

[8] Tom Ginsburg, 'Written Constitutions and the Administrative State: On the Constitutional Character of Administrative Law' in Susan Rose-Ackerman and Peter Lindseth (eds), *Comparative Administrative Law* (Edward Elgar, 2010) 117.

[9] TV Somanathan, 'The Administrative and Regulatory State' in Sujit Choudhury, Madhav Khosla and Pratap Bhanu Mehta (eds), *The Oxford Handbook of the Indian Constitution* (Oxford University Press, 2016) 386. See also Lalita Som and Faisal Naru, 'Regulatory Policy in India: Moving towards Regulatory Governance' (OECD Regulatory Working Paper No 8, 2017), http://dx.doi.org/10.1787/b335b35d-en.

[10] Somanathan (n 9) 401–10. On excessive delegation, see also Somasekhar Sundaresan, 'Subversion of Law in Law-Making' *Business Standard* (24 October 2016), www.business-standard.com/article/opinion/somasekhar-sundaresan-subversion-of-law-in-law-making-116102401342_1.html.

[11] Somanathan (n 9) 410.

also 'the commonly accepted rules, practices and institutions, and the symbolic constitution, consisting of collective representations, signifiers, and metaphors that help to define "India" and Indian-ness'.[12] More broadly, Morgan and Dubash call for a new approach to the regulatory state in the Global South, where regulatory environments are characterised by 'three shared contexts': the presence of external pressures from international financial institutions that propel internal reforms; the greater requirements of redistributive politics; and the problems linked to limited state capacity.[13]

The emergence of the regulatory state raises questions of legitimacy within the legal framework because citizens seek to establish democratic participation, accountability and controls over institutions by means other than the electoral process.[14] By immediate implication, this challenges long-held constitutional and administrative law doctrines concerning the rule of law and the separation of powers, as well as of the accountability and legitimacy of regulatory bodies. In addition to challenging long-held doctrines, regulation differs in fundamental ways from thin conceptions of administrative law. While regulation concerns itself with the ends and effects of legal regimes in achieving regulatory outcomes, legal approaches are concerned with the normative content of administrative law.[15] Yet, the distinction between these two approaches is increasingly blurred; administrative law scholars who adopt thicker 'understandings of the field might expand the scope of administrative law to concern themselves with outcomes, or ask, as Baxi does, "Who wins and loses, under the rule of law?"'[16] Additionally, as private actors increasingly constitute a part of the administrative law regime, it forces administrative law scholars to interrogate not only the normative content of the law, but also its prescriptive functions, and whether it should extend to private actors behaving in public capacities.[17]

Accordingly, scholarship in administrative law has to respond not only to questions of administrative structure and doctrine, but also to underlying questions about the aims of administrative law, and whether it is concerned with achieving regulatory and administrative outcomes, with norm compliance or with achieving public and constitutional values.[18] The response of Indian administrative law scholarship to these urgent calls has been remarkably weak, marked only by a few significant

[12] Lloyd I Rudolph and Susanne H Rudolph, 'Redoing the Constitutional Design: From an Interventionist to a Regulatory State' in Atul Kohli (ed), *The Success of India's Democracy* (Cambridge University Press, 2001) 128. See also Sujit Choudhry, 'How to Do Constitutional Law and Politics in South Asia' in Mark Tushnet and Madhav Khosla (eds), *Unstable Constitutionalism: Law and Politics in South Asia* (Cambridge University Press, 2015) 18–42.

[13] See Navroz K Dubash and Bronwen Morgan, 'The Rise of the Regulatory State of the South: The Infrastructure of Development' in Navroz K Dubash and Bronwen Morgan, *The Rise of the Regulatory State in the Global South* (Oxford University Press, 2013) 1–26, 4.

[14] Susan Rose-Ackerman and Peter Lindseth, 'Comparative Administrative Law: An Introduction' in Rose-Ackerman and Lindseth (n 8) 1–22, 7.

[15] Peter Cane, 'Administrative Law as Regulation' in Christine Parker, Colin Scott, Nicola Lacey and John Braithwaite (eds) *Regulating Law* (Oxford University Press, 2004) 207.

[16] Baxi (n 4) xxxv.

[17] See, eg, Shyamkrishna Balganesh, 'The Constitutionalisation of Indian Private Law' in Choudhury et al (n 9) 680; Cane (n 15) 210.

[18] See Cane (n 15) 213–16.

sector-specific contributions.[19] In general, it is a discipline in search of a theory, characterised by excellent scholarly interventions on specific questions without consideration of the field as a whole. The consequence is not only conceptual incoherence, but also active implications for how regulatory institutions are designed, function and are held accountable. In India, as elsewhere, 'the essentially administrative character of the modern state is irreversible'.[20] Administrative law therefore has to respond, adapt and transform. This is not a judicial and legislative endeavour alone, but also a scholarly one.

As such, this chapter sets out to achieve two aims. The first is a highly selective assessment of the current research on administrative law, focusing especially on the challenges raised by the rise of the regulatory state: legitimacy, participation and delegation. The second is to outline gaps and themes raised by these challenges in order to set out a partial agenda for future scholarship on administrative law. I have organised my analysis into four fields in which administrative law plays out: the Constitution, the Supreme Court, the executive and in citizenship. Although I do not identify the legislature as a separate field, a running theme through this chapter concerns the limitations of the role played by Parliament; consequently, it is discussed contextually and not by itself in order to avoid covering the same ground twice. Additionally, the focus is on central institutions, although a complete account of administrative law ought to take into consideration the impact of the regulatory state on federal relations as well. In each field that I consider, I return to specific challenges presented to administrative law by the regulatory state, while assessing existing literature on those topics. Through this analysis, I advance an overarching claim: administrative law scholars grappling with the regulatory state need to re-examine fundamental principles and concepts about the state, the Constitution and the role of administrative law.

I. THE CONSTITUTION AND ADMINISTRATIVE LAW

The Indian Constitution is famously long and detailed in scope; 'powerful in its vision and intricate in its formulation',[21] it contains provisions not only for the rights and obligations of citizens and governments, but also an unfolding account of the body of the Indian government. Provisions contained within the Indian Constitution cover broad allocations of power to the executive[22] and the judiciary,[23] detail specific provisions relating to the all-India civil services, and provide conditions for civil servants'

[19] See, eg, Arun K Thiruvengadam and Piyush Joshi, 'Judiciaries as Crucial Actors in Regulatory Systems of the Global South: The Indian Judiciary and Telecom Regulation (1991–2012)' in Navroz K Dubash and Bronwen Morgan (eds), *The Rise of the Regulatory State in the Global South* (Oxford University Press, 2013) 136–62; Navroz K Dubash, 'Independent Regulatory Agencies: A Theoretical Review with Reference to Electricity and Water in India' (2008) 43 (40) *Economic and Political Weekly* 43.

[20] Rubin (n 1) 19.

[21] Madhav Khosla, *The Indian Constitution: A Very Short Introduction* (Oxford University Press, 2012) xii.

[22] Constitution of India, pt V, ch I and pt VI, ch II.

[23] ibid pt V, ch IV, 'The Union Judiciary'.

employment and tenure.[24] Constitutional provisions provide for the creation of 'rules for the more convenient transaction of business' for the government,[25] for governing administrative relations between the centre and states,[26] and for allocating federal finances and managing government contracts.[27] Amendments have introduced specific frameworks for local governance in rural and urban areas[28] and for the creation of administrative tribunals to adjudicate disputes.[29] A host of regulatory and administrative institutions find their home within the constitutional architecture: the office of the Comptroller and Auditor General,[30] Public Service Commissions to determine issues of employment pertaining to civil servants[31] and an Election Commission to conduct elections.[32] Therefore, it is evident that the Indian administrative state is deeply embedded within the constitutional structure.

In debating the draft Constitution, a number of challenges were raised in the Constituent Assembly in relation to the inclusion of a detailed form of government within the constitutional framework. 'I agree that administrative details should have no place in the Constitution', conceded Dr Ambedkar, Chairman of the Drafting Committee, but went on, nonetheless, to rationalise their inclusion on several grounds. A unified civil service was provided for in elaborate detail in the text of the Constitution itself, which would enable the avoiding of inevitable conflicts within the federal structure of the Indian state; its inclusion, was not just advisable, but 'essential to maintaining the unity of the country'.[33] The form of administration, he noted, related closely to the goals of the Constitution; if the Constitution was to achieve its social goals, then an appropriately made administrative state was vital. Conversely, the form that the administrative state took could, in turn, easily subvert constitutional goals without actively amending constitutional provisions themselves. Although the administrative state could, in theory, be constituted by the legislature, Dr Ambedkar trusted neither the legislature nor the people to fulfil the constitutional imperatives that the Assembly was debating. 'Democracy in India is only a top-dressing on an Indian soil, which is essentially undemocratic',[34] he concluded. The Constitution was above all, a *moral* project; accordingly, constitutional morality had to be cultivated, and this cultivation was to take place, inter alia, through a carefully articulated administrative state that would serve the aims set out in the Indian Constitution.

In this sense, Indian administrative law is not unique: questions of administrative law in most modern democracies are inextricably constitutional.[35] Constitutions

[24] ibid pt XIV, ch I, 'Services'.
[25] ibid arts 53, 154.
[26] ibid pt XII, ch II.
[27] ibid pt XII.
[28] ibid pts IX and IX-A, introduced by the Constitution (Seventy-Third) and (Seventy-Fourth) Amendment Acts, 1992.
[29] ibid pt XIV-A, introduced by the Constitution (Forty-Second Amendment) Act, 1976.
[30] ibid art 148.
[31] ibid pt XIV, ch II.
[32] ibid art 324.
[33] BR Ambedkar, Constituent Assembly Debates Vol VII (4 November 1948), http://parliamentofindia.nic.in/ls/debates/vol7p1b.htm.
[34] ibid.
[35] See Ginsburg (n 8) 117–19.

shape the essential elements of delegation of power from legislatures to administrative and regulatory bodies, they lay down modes of redress (whether through rights and judicial review or institutional remedies) and they define principles that might not be embedded in the constitutional text, but are applied in its interpretation. Like constitutions, and perhaps even more so, the administrative state endures, but unlike constitutions, it does not lend itself as easily to convergence across states.[36] Yet, as the administrative and, later, the regulatory state expands to form new and independent institutions, a significant portion of administrative law operates outside the domain of constitutional law and of constitutional courts. The provision of services by agencies, the organisation of regulatory bodies and the manner in which regulation is conducted on a daily basis: all these are traditionally the domain of administrative law, but not necessarily of constitutional law.[37] Similarly, entire domains of constitutional law remain untouched by administrative law questions; consequently, the common law position traditionally saw 'constitutional law and administrative as occupying distinct provinces, but also a substantial area of common ground'.[38]

In detangling where constitutional law ends and administrative law begins, common law theorisation is divided broadly between two camps of 'red-light' and 'green-light' theorists.[39] 'Red-light' theorists have an understanding of administrative law in which the emphasis is heavily on controlling state action. Although it began with Dicey, this school went on to rely on constitutional theories about the separation of powers and checks and balances, arguing that the domain of administrative law was limited to controlling state power through the institution of courts[40] – in other words, the 'protection of individual rights against undue encroachment in the name of the public interest'.[41] The role of the state was envisioned as limited; consequently, the focus of administrative law was clearly demarcated from constitutional law and focused on procedure or, in other words, on the manner in which state power was exercised.[42]

Within Indian administrative law, Jain and Jain note that the function of administrative law is to 'ensure legal control of the administrative power and to provide protection to the individual against the abuse of power',[43] a clear, 'red-light' stance

[36] See Rubin (n 1); Ginsburg (n 8) 117.

[37] See generally Michael Taggart, 'The Province of Administrative Law Determined?' in Michael Taggart (ed), *The Province of Administrative Law* (Hart Publishing, 1997) 1, 1; Anthony M Bertelli, 'Law and Public Administration' in Ewan Ferlie, Laurence E Lynn Jr and Christopher Pollitt (eds), *The Oxford Handbook of Public Management* (Oxford University Press, 2009) 134.

[38] SA de Smith 'The Lawyers and the Constitution: An Inaugural Lecture' (1960), as cited in Michael Taggart, 'The Province of Administrative Law Determined?' in Taggart (ed (n 37) 1.

[39] The classification of 'red-light' and 'green-light' theorists originates with Carol Harlow and Richard Rawlings, *Law and Administration*, 3rd edn (Cambridge University Press, 2009) 23, but has since been widely adopted. See Peter Cane, 'Review of Executive Action' in Mark Tushnet and Peter Cane (eds), *The Oxford Handbook of Legal Studies* (Oxford University Press, 2005) 147–48.

[40] Harlow and Rawlings (n 39) 23; Cane (n 39)148.

[41] Cane (n 39) 147–48.

[42] See, eg, HWR Wade, *Administrative Law* (Clarendon Press, 1961) 3; HWR Wade and C Forsyth, *Administrative Law*, 9th edn (Oxford University Press, 2004) 4–5.

[43] Jain and Jain (n 2) 8. See also MP Jain, *The Evolving Indian Administrative Law* (NM Tripathi Pvt Ltd, 1983) 1–21.

that is almost immediately the subject of some theoretical muddying by the invocation of a 'human rights approach in administration' which advocates a less proceduralised administrative law.[44] This is echoed in other commentaries as well, which endorse well-established, red-light definitions of administrative law, then identify pressing green-light concerns, but fail to reconcile or address conflicts between the two approaches.[45] Therefore, it is unsurprising that Jain and Jain's attempt to detangle the aims of Indian administrative and constitutional law culminated in the mystifying claim that 'a student of Indian administrative law needs to have a good deal of knowledge of Indian constitutional law to better appreciate the nuances of Administrative Law as the Constitution being the fundamental law of the land conditions every law, much more Administrative Law'.[46] Massey similarly concludes his foray into differences between constitutional and administrative law with the unhelpful conclusion that 'whatever may be the arguments and counter-arguments, the fact remains that today administrative law is recognised as a separate, independent field'.[47]

'Green-light' theorists, on the other hand, project a broader understanding of administrative law that blurred these distinctions. Green-lighters interpret state power broadly and see administrative law as serving not just to constrain but also to facilitate the government in executing its functions.[48] This vision of administrative law admits an overlap in constitutional and administrative principles, but also expands the domain of administrative law away from courts, to nearly every matter that touches upon administration in expanding governments.[49] The resolution to conflicts, argue green-light theorists, is not in judicial review, but in administrative remedies outside courts. This, of course, partially removes administrative law from the domain of constitutional law.

Indian administrative law scholarship has had marginally more coherence, but less acceptance, when taking the green-light approach. Despite his aforementioned dismissal of the field as an independent area of study, two essays by Upendra Baxi written in 1982 and 2008, drawing heavily from his own work on the Indian Constitution, lay out this claim.[50] Baxi advocates a sociological and historical understanding of Indian administrative law. He traces its development from a coherent body of jurisprudence in the first few decades of independence to a vast, 'new Indian administrative law formation' that struggles to grapple not only with the demands of the expanding state, but also with the Supreme Court's rising pre-occupation with social justice.[51] Like other green-light theorists, Baxi highlights the rise of regulatory and administrative organs of the state, pointing to a 'contemporary Indian administrative law formation' that is characterised by 'de-constitutionalisation',

[44] Jain and Jain (n 2) 16–17.
[45] See, eg, Massey (n 3) 8, 10–11.
[46] Jain and Jain (n 2) 20.
[47] Massey (n 3) 16.
[48] Harlow and Rawlings (n 39) 31; Cane (n 39) 148.
[49] See, eg, WI Jennings, 'Courts and Administrative Law' (1936) 49 *Harvard Law Review* 426; J Griffith and H Street, *Principles of Administrative Law*, 5th edn (Pitman, 1973) 4.
[50] Baxi (n 4) xvii; Upendra Baxi, 'Developments in Indian Administrative Law' in AG Noorani (ed), *Public Law in India* (Vikas Publishing House, 1982).
[51] Baxi (n 4).

ie, increasingly functioning within the private and not the public sphere.[52] Despite noting these changes, Baxi is ultimately unwilling to concede a transformation, holding that Indian administrative law constitutes 'in a special sense, the common law of the Constitution, as for the most part it is uncodified'.[53] This understanding of the Indian administrative law assumes it to be a fundamental but subsidiary component of Indian constitutional law, 'reflecting it, but also shaping it'.[54]

Thus, it seems evident that neither red-light nor green-light theories, as they are currently formulated, are adequate to meet the challenges posed to administrative law by the rise of the regulatory state in India. Ultimately, the challenge faced by scholars is not to distinguish between constitutional and administrative law as a 'matter of organizational or pedagogical convenience';[55] nor can the issue be reconciled by proposing, as some do, that the distinction between administrative law and constitutional law is fundamentally irrelevant. These claims, whether they dismiss the relevance of drawing distinctions between the two fields[56] or argue for transcending them through the 'moral unity of public law',[57] usually assume a common method of reasoning, grounded in the same constitutional principles of freedom, dignity and equality, whether in constitutional law or administrative law.[58] Yet, a small and growing body of Indian scholarship suggests that such reconciliations between constitutional and administrative principles in jurisprudence is not as easy as suggested. It is only recently that the Supreme Court's misuse of administrative law principles of unreasonableness in the context of 'right to equality' cases has been identified by Khaitan as presenting particularly acute doctrinal challenges;[59] in addition, the variable use of 'principles of natural justice' in administrative and constitutional law has further resulted in a lack of clarity in terms of how and when these principles can be applied.[60]

The new regulatory state does not merely establish institutions; it transforms the theatre of administrative law, moving it from the sole domain of courts to tribunals, agencies and regulators.[61] As these theatres transform, so do the sources of administrative law – with the rise of tribunals, for instance, Indian administrative law increasingly grapples with new procedures that are formed and develop outside constitutional rights frameworks. Dubash points out a significant limitation of Baxi's claim regarding administrative law as the 'common law of the Constitution', since the recent 'explicit articulation of administrative procedures in legislation is a significant departure from past precedent in Indian administrative

[52] ibid xxx.
[53] ibid xvii, xviii.
[54] ibid.
[55] Cane (n 39) 148.
[56] See Harlow and Rawlings (n 39) 48.
[57] See TRS Allan, 'The Moral Unity of Public Law' (2017) 67(1) *University of Toronto Law Journal* 1, 2. See generally David Dyzenhaus (ed), *The Unity of Public Law* (Hart Publishing, 2004).
[58] ibid.
[59] Tarunabh Khaitan, 'Equality: Legislative Review under Article 14' in Choudhury et al (n 9) 699, 716.
[60] Raeesa Vakil, 'Constitutionalizing Administrative Law in the Indian Supreme Court: Natural Justice and Fundamental Rights' (2018) 16(2) *International Journal of Constitutional Law* 475.
[61] See section III.

law'.[62] Accordingly, in the regulatory state, administrative law will have to be understood as standing both within the shadow of the Constitution and also stretching far beyond it.

II. THE SUPREME COURT AND ADMINISTRATIVE LAW

The constitutionalisation of the administrative state by Ambedkar, as detailed above, was intended to secure the subversion of constitutional goals by articulating an administrative framework. Implicit in the resistance to handing over control to the legislature was an acceptance that the custodian of the constitution – and, in particular, the administrative state – was the Indian judiciary. Constitutional interpretation was to be the sole domain of the Indian Supreme Court; Article 145(3) of the Constitution required that all such questions would be heard by a bench of at least five judges; law pronounced by the Supreme Court was binding on all courts.[63] This was evidently to ensure that the interpretation of the Constitution would be consistent and authoritative, and the idea of vesting any other part of the state, such as the legislature or the executive, with the power of interpreting the Constitution was not seriously considered at any point during the drafting process.[64]

Indian administrative law, as Baxi suggests, is perhaps more deeply constitutionalised than its counterparts in common law countries; however, in order to understand the causes of this, we must first unpack the extent and nature of this constitutionalisation. It is not limited to constitutional architecture alone: the core of administrative law is the review of executive action, to hold the government and its agencies to account. Consequently, a major portion of administrative law tends to centre on the extent to which states permit judicial review of administrative action and the implications of this for democracy. The Indian Constitution sidesteps this debate by including constitutionally enforceable rights of citizens against the state,[65] along with unenforceable exhortations to the government on questions of public policy.[66] Rights, interpreted widely by the Supreme Court, supplement common law doctrines that allow review of administrative action: the state is vulnerable to legal challenge not only on standard common law grounds such as ultra vires actions, but also for violations of constitutional rights.[67]

Extensive jurisprudence from the Supreme Court and High Courts treats judicial review largely as a fait accompli: administrative law debates have traditionally centred not around whether we should have judicial review, but the extent to which it should be exercised.[68] Since judicial review of administrative action can co-extend

[62] Navroz Dubash, 'Regulation through the Back Door: Understanding the Implications of the Institutional Transplant' *Working Paper No. 42: Jerusalem Papers in Regulation & Governance* (2012) 16.

[63] Constitution of India, art 132.

[64] Raeesa Vakil, 'Jurisdiction' in Choudhury et al (n 9) 367, 377.

[65] Constitution of India, pt III, 'Fundamental Rights'.

[66] ibid pt IV, 'Directive Principles of State Policy'.

[67] See generally Jain and Jain (n 3) 147ff; D Basu, *Limited Government and Judicial Review* (LexisNexis, 2016).

[68] See, eg, Basu (n 67) 108–12; SP Sathe, 'Judicial Review in India: Limits and Policy' (1974) 35 *Ohio State Law Journal* 870.

with review of legislative action, administrative and constitutional law principles in India overlap and travel between the two fields.[69] Although the focus of judicial review even within administrative law has traditionally been on rights, such writing faces two significant limitations. First, doctrinal confusion arising from uniting rights review and administrative review has not been seriously analysed until recently, as I have indicated above. Second, scholars who focus on rights review tend to entirely elide the vast body of administrative law that deals with review on grounds outside fundamental rights, such as the doctrine of ultra vires or of legitimate expectations. A key study on judicial control of administrative action is devoted almost wholly to rights-based review, addressing only one paragraph to ultra vires as an 'alternative remedy'.[70] Similarly, Massey's treatment of ultra vires only enumerates some key grounds, refusing to delve into the development of the doctrine or address inconsistencies within it.[71]

Although theorisation on the causes and consequences is limited, administrative law scholarship in India does recognise the depth to which this doctrinal incoherence extends. Jalan and Rai, in their study of the review of administrative action in India, note that the Supreme Court has succeeded in articulating a framework for review, but then 'struggled to fit different levels of scrutiny within a common framework, leading to inconsistences in the application of tests'.[72] Jain and Jain note that the episodic development of administrative law points out that 'the emergence of a systematic, coherent body of principles is difficult through judicial process. Legislation may have to be undertaken to achieve such a result'.[73] Similar studies on the Supreme Court's use of the doctrine of proportionality and tests of reasonableness reveal deep conceptual disorder, reflected in erratic judicial pronouncements.[74]

Judicial interpretation of administrative law principles is also marked by a noted resistance to codification and systematisation within the judiciary. The Supreme Court refuses, first, to establish the bounds of judicial power, choosing instead to defer all such questions to 'facts and circumstances'. For instance, when examining the scope of its own discretionary power to hear appeals from administrative tribunals, the Court relies on justifications such as 'grave injustice' or 'shocking the conscience of the Court' instead of laying down conditions under which appeals may be accepted.[75] Second, when considering specific questions of administrative law, the Supreme Court often wavers between normative and ends-based applications

[69] Examples of this abound, but a key instance is the seminal case of *Maneka Gandhi v Union of India* (1978) 1 SCC 248, in which the Supreme Court heard a simultaneous challenge to the Indian Passports Act as well as to an order passed by an authority under that Act.

[70] BP Banerjee, *Judicial Control of Administrative Action*, 3rd edn (LexisNexis, 2016) 139.

[71] Massey (n 3) 135–48.

[72] Prateek Jalan and Ritin Rai, 'Review of Administrative Action' in Choudhury et al (n 9) 432, 447.

[73] Jain and Jain (n 3) 16.

[74] Chintan Chandrachud, 'Proportionality, Judicial Reasoning, and the Indian Supreme Court' (University of Cambridge Legal Studies Research Paper Series, 12/2016); Ashish Chugh, 'Is the Supreme Court Applying the Proportionality Principle?' (2004) 8 *Supreme Court Cases Journal* 33; Abhinav Chandrachud, 'Wednesbury Reformulated: The Indian Supreme Court and the Proportionality Principle' (2013) 13(1) *Oxford University Commonwealth Law Journal* 191.

[75] See Vakil (n 64) 371.

of principles. A significant instance of this is its wavering on the application of the principles of natural justice. The Court has sometimes required proof that 'actual prejudice' has been caused to the person claiming a violation before taking action,[76] even though at other times, it has characterised such an instrumental application of these principles as 'pernicious'.[77] Although this appears to be a debate about natural justice, it also reflects judicial uncertainty about the function of administrative law.

In addition to doctrinal incoherence within the field of administrative law, the Supreme Court's use of its powers of judicial review presents a challenge to administrative and regulatory governance. As is well documented, judicial interventions in administration and regulation are so frequent that some scholars have dubbed the Court a 'good governance court'.[78] The 'judicialisation' of governance in this manner is not unique to India; it is increasingly a global phenomenon, usually described as rising hand in hand with the growth of the regulatory state and its emphasis on procedures and constraints on regulatory actors.[79] Yet, Indian administrative law scholarship is curiously devoid of studies of how judicialisation has an impact on administrative law, and on administrative procedure, particularly.[80] More interestingly, scholarship on the judicialisation of administration does not yet address questions of how and why this process comes about, or how existing legal frameworks can accommodate it. As Ginsburg suggests: 'A complete account of judicialization in spheres of governance would include not only a discussion of its establishment but also of its endurance.'[81]

The Indian Supreme Court accordingly is under fire for rising doctrinal incoherence; this, coupled with polyvocality, a resistance to using five-judge authoritative benches, a disregard for precedent and an insistence on determining cases on the basis of 'facts and circumstances' instead of legal principles, has resulted in what Sathe calls 'systematic malfunctioning'.[82] While this raises a series of concerns, both political and constitutional, it also presents an acute challenge to the regulatory state. In one of the few studies of the Indian administrative and regulatory state,

[76] *Haryana Financial Corporation v Kailash Chandra Ahuja* (2008) 9 SCC 31, para 25 (the case concerned the question of whether a government employee was entitled to a copy of a departmental report on the basis of which he had been subjected to disciplinary action; the Court went on, applying established precedent, to hold that natural justice would entitle the petitioner to a copy of the report, but in the absence of proof of actual prejudice to the petitioner, the claim could not be allowed).

[77] *SL Kapoor v Jagmohan* (1980) 4 SCC 379. See also *Board of High School and Intermediate Education, UP v Chitra* (1970) 1 SCC 121.

[78] See Nicholas Robinson, 'Expanding Judiciaries: India and the Rise of the Good Governance Court' (2009) 8(1) *Washington University Global Studies Law Review* 1. See also SP Sathe, *Judicial Activism in India* (Oxford University Press, 2002) 123.

[79] See, eg, Tom Ginsburg, 'The Judicialization of Governance: Causes, Consequences and Limits' in Tom Ginsburg and Albert HY Chen (eds), *Administrative Law and Governance in Asia* (Routledge, 2009) 1–19; C Neal Tate and Torbjorn Vallinder, *The Global Expansion of Judicial Power* (New York University Press, 1995); Alec Stone Sweet, *Governing with Judges: Constitutional Politics in Europe* (Oxford University Press, 2000).

[80] Vakil (n 60).

[81] Ginsburg (n 79) 4.

[82] Sathe (n 78) 123. Sathe may be borrowing from John Hart Ely, who wrote of judicial review as a response to 'systemic malfunctioning', but applied the concept quite differently. See John Hart Ely, *Democracy and Distrust: A Theory of Judicial Review* (Harvard University Press, 1980) 105.

TV Somanathan points out that the Supreme Court has repeatedly intervened not only in reviewing administrative action, but also in reviewing legislation that directly affects the regulatory state.[83] The result has been 'a considerable degree of legal uncertainty' not just about the content of administrative law, but about the stability of administrative structures.[84]

As the Indian Supreme Court increasingly acts as the arbiter of policy-making choices, it is readily apparent that Indian administrative law is responding not only to legal claims, but also to political events and imperatives. Yet, Indian administrative law scholars tend to portray administrative law as an apolitical and process-oriented judicial product. Massey argues that Indian courts are engaged in 'making all concerted efforts to establish a rule-of-law society in India'.[85] Jain and Jain, while conceding that 'the judicial process has its own limitations',[86] argue nonetheless that administrative law as enforced by courts works 'to ensure that powers are exercised according to law, on proper legal principles, according to the rules of reason and justice; and not at the mere caprice and whim of administrators'.[87]

On the other hand, some administrative law scholars argue that despite criticisms of the Supreme Court, it remains the best recourse for administrative justice. While criticising the bureaucracy, Baxi says that 'I am not saying at all that the [Indian Supreme Court] has done better', but nonetheless argues that by providing access through public interest litigation, the Court has redeemed its errors and, consequently, that 'we must still count our thus offered constitutionally activist judicial blessings'.[88] In this vein, Thiruvengadam and Joshi present the claim that the Court's deep interventions in framing telecom policy in India are not only justified, but also constitute a 'constructive contribution', to the extent that they allow the Court to mediate conflicts in regulatory reform.[89] While acknowledging other criticisms of the Court, they put forward the claim that in this 'regulatory sphere, the Court acted in a relatively disinterested manner'.[90] Jacob, discussing the Court's approach to the doctrine of fairness, notes that '[t]he significant contribution of courts to make the system of administration tolerable, has been to devise a set of rules of fair administrative procedure',[91] referring to the undefined, uncategorisable 'rules of natural justice' that have since been the subject of much criticism.[92]

As a result, these accounts are of limited value when attempting to theorise administrative law in the regulatory state. Constitutional law theorists have pointed to several concerns in the manner in which the Supreme Court functions,

[83] Somanathan (n 9) 403. See also Rudolph and Rudolph (n 12) 162.
[84] Somanathan (n 9) 401.
[85] Massey (n 3) 28.
[86] Jain and Jain (n 3) 15.
[87] ibid 14–15.
[88] Baxi (n 4) liv.
[89] Thiruvengadam and Joshi (n 19) 136–62.
[90] ibid 141.
[91] Alice Jacob, 'Judicial Insistence on Fairness in Administrative Process' (1983) 25(2) *Journal of the Indian Law Institute* 195, 195.
[92] See Jain and Jain (n 3) 647.

comprehensively debunking the claim that it acts either apolitically or neutrally,[93] and particularly so when it comes to questions of procedural justice. Shankar's research in modelling judicial behaviour in civil liberties cases from 1950 to 2005 is one study that demonstrates this.[94] Additionally, Bhuwania's critique of the Supreme Court's relaxation of rules of standing in the public interest supports his claim that at the Supreme Court, 'the procedural is certainly political'.[95] While criticisms of this doctrinal incoherence are rife, analyses of its causes are less common. A recent, critical contribution to this is Chandrachud's comparative study of legislative overruling in England and India.[96] Chandrachud argues that for structural reasons, the Indian Supreme Court is constrained from expressing constitutional reasoning in judicial review of legislation and is instead required to employ an ends-based reasoning that contributes to doctrinal confusion.[97] The limitations of judicial power to fashion appropriate responses apart from judicial review is of critical importance when we consider the Court's engagement with questions of governance and policy.[98]

As Baxi points out, it is insufficient to rest a modern theory of administrative law on claims that the Supreme Court acts in a disinterested fashion; we must ask of administrative law as well as of the Court: 'Who wins, and who loses under the rule of law?'[99] More generally, once the role of the Court in shaping administrative action and choices of the government is established and acknowledged, administrative law scholars can engage with the idea that the legislature and executive, in making policy choices, are accounting strategically for the Supreme Court's role in future actions.[100] Somanthan, for instance, points out a series of Supreme Court judgments that overruled legislation constituting regulatory bodies, noting that this has forced the executive to take into account factors that might result in prospective overruling when designing new regulatory bodies.[101] This deepening judicialisation

[93] See, for instance, Pratap Bhanu Mehta, 'India's Judiciary: The Promise of Uncertainty' in Devesh Kapur and Pratap Bhanu Mehta (eds), *Public Institutions in India: Performance and Design* (Oxford University Press, 2005) 158; Pratap Bhanu Mehta, 'The Indian Supreme Court and the Art of Democratic Positioning' in Mark Tushnet and Madhav Khosla (eds) *Unstable Constitutionalism: Law and Politics in South Asia* (Cambridge University Press, 2015) 233. For more on the context of the manner in which Supreme Court judges are self-selected and appointed, see Abhinav Chandrachud, *The Informal Constitution: Unwritten Criteria in Selecting Judges for the Supreme Court of India* (Oxford University Press, 2014).

[94] Shylashri Shankar, *Scaling Justice: India's Supreme Court, Social Rights, and Civil Liberties* (Oxford University Press, 2012) (modelling decision-making by Indian judges in the context of civil liberties cases decided between 1950 and 2005).

[95] Anuj Bhuwania, *Courting the People: Public Interest Litigation in Post-emergency India* (Cambridge University Press, 2017) 134–42.

[96] Chintan Chandrachud, *Balanced Constitutionalism: Courts and Legislatures in India and the United Kingdom* (Oxford University Press, 2017).

[97] See ibid 1–29.

[98] Gautam Bhatia points this out in a review of Chandrachud's book. See Gautam Bhatia, 'Book Review: A Question of Design – Chintan Chandrachud's Balanced Constitutionalism' *Indian Constitutional Law and Philosophy* (23 June 2017), https://indconlawphil.wordpress.com/2017/06/23/book-review-a-question-of-design-chintan-chandrachuds-balanced-constitutionalism.

[99] Baxi (n 4) xxxv.

[100] Bertelli describes this function of judicial oversight as the 'thermostatic role of the courts', noting that: 'Of course, when making delegations, the sovereign *knows* of the courts' thermostatic role, relying on it when making its delegations'; Bertelli (n 37) 148.

[101] Somanathan (n 9) 396.

of regulatory bodies in turn affects not only in their systems of accountability and procedure, but also their structure and organisation, as well as influencing how the executive and the legislature shape the future of the Indian regulatory state.

The challenge for scholars in India will therefore be in terms of moving beyond acknowledgements of the Supreme Court's overwhelming role in shaping administrative law to demystifying the causes and consequences of this phenomenon. In doing so, we can look to scholarship outside India, but also specific to Asian contexts. Specifically with reference to the Global South, Dubash and Morgan suggest that the rise in judicialisation is a consequence of the regulatory state's emphasis on proceduralisation and redistributive politics.[102] Their approach accords the judiciary a central role in the regulatory state, not just as a bulwark against the misuse of regulatory and judicial power, but also as undertaking an active role in designing the shape of the regulatory state.[103] They trace the origins of this to active intervention by the World Bank in encouraging judicial reform in developing countries, partly to ensure the stability of legal relations in contract and property.[104] Ginsburg and Chen, on the other hand, evaluate administrative law in 11 countries in Northeast and Southeast Asia, and Ginsburg traces the rise of judicialisation not just to international influences, but also to economic and judicial factors, such as demands for strong enforcers in complex economic environments or the expansion of judicial power as a response to fragmented political power.[105]

We can also look within Indian scholarship outside of administrative law. The causes of the rise of judicial sovereignty over the regulatory state and the emergence of the 'good governance court'[106] have been analysed extensively by political and constitutional scholars. Some research links the expansion of judicial review to failures of representative institutions India to deliver on governance.[107] Another strand of thought traces extensive judicial review of administration to the tendency of a small, closely controlled professional judiciary to aggrandise its own power.[108] Bhuwania's anthropological research links the rise of the Supreme Court to the adoption of procedures that allowed citizens to approach the Court with 'public interest' litigation; the relaxation of rules of standing, for instance, 'delegitimized legal procedure', allowing courts to expand their power by departing from basic, constraining principles.[109] An argument I have advanced is that structural factors in the constitutional framework, such as provisions relating to the Supreme Court's jurisdiction, might have allowed the Court to interpret constraints on its powers liberally, thus expanding its jurisdiction.[110] Each of these approaches in turn can alter our understanding of

[102] Dubash and Morgan (n 13) 13.
[103] ibid.
[104] Dubash and Morgan (n 13).
[105] Ginsburg (n 79) 6–7.
[106] See Robinson (n 78).
[107] See Gerald E Beller, 'Benevolent Illusions in a Developing Society: The Assertion of Supreme Court Authority in Democratic India' (1980) 36 *Political Research Quarterly* 513.
[108] See Pratap Bhanu Mehta, 'India's Judiciary: The Promise of Uncertainty' in Kapur and Mehta (n 93) 158.
[109] Bhuwania (n 95) 26.
[110] Vakil (n 64) 367.

administrative law, as well as our prescriptions for its ailments, whether they take the form of proposed constitutional amendments, reforms to judicial appointments or a deep re-evaluation of the structure and procedures of administrative and regulatory bodies.

In acknowledging that the Supreme Court is not always motivated by apolitical concerns of fairness and justice, administrative law scholars are also forced to engage with the idea that judge-made administrative doctrines and procedures are vulnerable to similar critiques. Despite his support for judicialised remedies, Baxi's rueful but unaddressed acknowledgement is that 'the histories of [Indian administrative law] adjudication also show, even in the hands of India's most gifted and socially compassionate justices, the [Indian administrative law] developments as constituting an epic sorrow for the vast masses of the suffering Indian humanity'.[111] The regulatory state will, as I have suggested, raise challenges that are grounded in considerations of legitimacy, accountability and participation. The current jurisprudence of the Supreme Court is demonstrably inadequate to meet these challenges; accordingly, a new theory of administrative law cannot rely on traditional, apolitical conceptions and will have to root itself in an understanding of questions not only of *what* the Court does, but also of *why* judicial control over administrative law takes its current shape.

III. THE STATE AND ADMINISTRATIVE LAW

A key feature of the modern regulatory state is the delegation of functions to a number of governmental and administrative agencies.[112] Delegation is often criticised, but need not be inherently dangerous; while legislatures may be subjected to political and corporate interests that 'stack the deck' in favour of lobbies, delegation can also fight regulatory capture by the use of accountability mechanisms relying on constituencies outside these lobbies, such as citizen groups or expert and professional bodies.[113] Functionally, the rise of 'independent' agencies operating at arm's length from the government can serve to bridge concerns about political control, corruption and in relation to making policies in areas in which courts and governments may not have the necessary expertise.[114] At the same time, the rise of independent agencies in the regulatory state brings with it a number of constitutional, administrative and political concerns. These deal with aspects such as the legitimacy of independent agencies, their structure and appointments, questions regarding the level of public participation in their functioning, and concerns about their democratic accountability.[115]

[111] Baxi (n 4) xl.

[112] Susan Rose-Ackerman, 'The Regulatory State' in Michael Rosenfeld and Andras Sajo (eds), *The Oxford Handbook of Comparative Constitutional Law* (Oxford University Press, 2012) 672, 674–75.

[113] ibid 676.

[114] ibid.

[115] See Giandomenico Majone, 'The Regulatory State and its Legitimacy Problems' (1999) 22 *West European Politics* 1; Vrinda Bhandari, Renuka Sane and Bhargavi Zaveri, 'The Accountability Framework of UIDAI: Concerns and Solutions' *The Leap Blog* (10 August 2017), https://ajayshahblog.blogspot.in/2017/08/the-accountability-framework-of-uidai.html.

Delegation assumes significance, in part because the Indian central legislature is almost universally accepted as failing to fulfil its role of accountability, not just in relation to reasons of political composition and representation, but also because of structural lapses that prevent Parliament from holding the executive accountable.[116] Similar charges might be levelled at the deeply dysfunctional Indian administration, giving credence to the claim that 'the performance of India's public institutions has become a matter of serious concern, both for the quality of its democracy, and the well-being of its people'.[117] (Indeed, legislative and executive lapses and inaction are often taken as justifications for judicial intervention in questions of governance.)[118] The rise of independent regulatory agencies is usually viewed in this light as a response to failures by the state and lapses by the legislature, whether these failures take the form of a lack of capacity and expertise, corruption or the failure to secure capture by economic interests.[119]

India's regulators take three broad forms. First, there are regulators whose primary function is to frame policies and implement them, such as the Airports Authority of India or the Central Pollution Control Board. Second, there are tribunals, or primarily adjudicatory bodies that are not courts, but are sometimes described as 'quasi-judicial'[120] (for instance, the National Green Tribunal or the Securities Appellate Tribunal).[121] Third, there are regulatory bodies that combine adjudicatory and regulatory functions (consequently presenting challenges to the separation of powers), such as the Competition Commission of India or the Securities and Exchange Board of India. All three types of regulators operate under varying levels of government control and private participation; as a consequence, they not only blur the distinction between what is 'public' and 'private', but also the traditional distinctions between the executive, the judiciary and the legislature.

Administrative law scholars have focused primarily on the latter two categories, ie, tribunals and hybrid regulators. This is a field in which there is now a rich body of analytical literature. Critiques of the function of administrative and regulatory tribunals rest broadly on three prongs. The first prong points to the dubious constitutional origins of tribunals, beginning with the 44th Amendment, passed at a time of political emergency.[122] Tribunals were designed structurally as a response by the executive to judicial power; therefore, by design and intent, their aim is understood to

[116] See, eg, Arun Agrawal, 'The Indian Parliament' in Kapur and Mehta (n 93) 77; Babubhai Chinai, 'Parliament and Restraints over Executive Power' in LM Sanghvi (ed), *Parliament and Administration in India* (Metropolitan Books, 1970) 93–100; Devesh Kapur and Pratap Bhanu Mehta, 'The Indian Parliament as an Institution of Accountability' (2006) United Nations Research Institute for Social Development: Democracy, Governance and Human Rights Programme Paper No 23.

[117] Devesh Kapur and Pratap Bhanu Mehta, 'Introduction' in Kapur and Mehta (n 93) 1, 4.

[118] See Baxi (n 4); See also Robinson (n 78).

[119] For an overview, see Somanathan (n 9) 398. See also Navroz K Dubash, 'Independent Regulatory Agencies: A Theoretical Review with Reference to Water and Electricity in India' (2008) 43(40) *Economic and Political Weekly* 43.

[120] Arvind P Datar, 'The Tribunalization of Justice in India' (2006) *Acta Juridica* 288, 293–94.

[121] See generally, Arun K Thiruvengadam, 'Tribunals' in Choudhury et al (n 9) 412.

[122] Arvind P Datar, 'Tribunals: A Tragic Obsession' (2013), http://india-seminar.com/2013/642/642_arvind_p_datar.htm; Thiruvengadam (n 121) 416–20.

redistribute power from the courts to the executive and, accordingly, implicate separation of powers concerns.[123] Following this strand, the second prong of critique rests on repeated interventions by the Supreme Court to alter or strike down legislation constituting tribunals.[124] Tribunals have delegated functions that are essentially judicial; the argument raised before and accepted by the Supreme Court is that tribunals must accordingly be similarly designed with the safeguards to judicial independence that apply to courts.[125] Following this, a third and related line of critique of tribunals has rested on the structure of tribunals and regulatory bodies, and particularly on the practice of staffing of tribunals by retired judges and civil servants.[126] Datar, in particular, notes that any arguments justifying tribunals on the grounds of introducing expertise are eviscerated by these staffing practices:

> [T]ribunals are largely 'an excellent source of post-retirement opportunities' for persons with vested interests in their creation.[127]

Thus, existing administrative law critiques focus almost exclusively on the relationship between tribunals and courts, pitching the conflict as a battle between the executive and the judiciary for control over adjudicatory processes. 'There is an imminent threat', writes Datar, 'of the executive slowly, but surely and systematically stripping the High Courts of their powers and vesting them in tribunals controlled by the executive.'[128] Unlike most fields of administrative law, this conflict between the executive and judiciary has caught the interest of popular imagination.[129] Consequently, a recent battle between the executive to entirely restructure tribunals and take complete control of the appointment process away from courts has met with resistance not only from the Supreme Court, but also from public commentators.[130] Accordingly, commentators have rested their critique not only on structural flaws and judicial capture, but also on the failures of tribunals to fulfil their mandates of quick and effective dispute resolution.

In light of these developments, a few administrative law scholars have begun to note that the courts, the executive and the judiciary act strategically in determining the structure and functioning of regulatory bodies. It is well established that

[123] ibid.

[124] Datar (n 120) 293–94.

[125] ibid; Thiruvengadam (n 121) 425–29.

[126] See, eg, Prashant P Reddy, 'The Trouble with Tribunals' *OPEN* (18 May 2013), www.openthemagazine.com/article/india/the-trouble-with-tribunals (on the flaws in appointments to the National Green Tribunal).

[127] Datar (n 122).

[128] Datar (n 120) 294. *cf* SP Sathe, *The Tribunal System in India* (NM Tripathi, 1996) 221 (arguing that tribunals can, under certain circumstances, form a viable alternative to courts).

[129] Prianka Rao, 'Finance Bill 2017: Independence of Tribunals Could Be Affected' *Hindustan Times* (14 April 2017), https://www.hindustantimes.com/analysis/finance-bill-2017-independence-of-tribunals-could-be-affected/story-StaETXJ9sjqNHqRjbriCTI.html; Prashant P Reddy, 'Has the Executive Signed the Death Warrant for the Judicial Independence of 19 Tribunals?' *Scroll.in* (5 June 2017), https://scroll.in/article/839588/has-the-government-signed-the-death-warrant-for-the-judicial-independence-of-19-tribunals.

[130] 'SC Stays New Tribunal Rules' *The Hindu* (10 February 2017), www.thehindu.com/todays-paper/tp-national/sc-stays-new-tribunal-rules/article22709738.ece.

the regulatory state challenges traditional conceptions regarding the separation of powers,[131] a foundational concept in Indian administrative law. The rising 'rule of the unelected' (to use Vibert's phrase) coupled with Parliament's increasingly diminishing role are clear evidence that the separation of powers in the Indian regulatory state has changed significantly between constitutional design and constitutional politics. Recent studies reflect this redesign; for instance, the manner in which the Indian Competition Commission was framed, as well as the role of the Supreme Court in nudging the legislature to amend governing laws to secure the independence of the Commission has attracted scholarly consideration that focuses on the separation of powers, as well as legitimacy issues.[132]

Moving forward, such analyses of regulatory bodies and the laws they function within will also have to account for tribunals and other regulatory bodies as the site of contestation between the executive and the legislature. Increasingly, the executive uses a number of devices to secure legislative and governance measures that sidestep parliamentary involvement and oversight. Shubhankar Dam's study on the rise of presidential legislation through ordinances demonstrates that it is a process that effectively 'compromises parliament and voting in both process and substance'[133] by allowing the executive to effectively legislate outside the legislative process. Judicial review over ordinances has been traditionally more limited than review over legislative and executive action; consequently, it is unsurprising that the executive has increasingly used ordinances to constitute regulatory bodies and frame their functions.[134] Indeed, Dam's study demonstrates that the largest category of ordinances by far address administrative and regulatory matters.[135]

In addition to the use of ordinances, a developing parliamentary technique has been to use money bills instead of ordinary legislation in order to constitute and implement regulatory bodies. Money bills are specific forms of legislation with lower thresholds of oversight; as a result, they are easier to pass than legislative bills. Article 110 of the Indian Constitution purportedly limits their use to certain financial matters; however, they have been increasingly used to insulate and conduct significant administrative and regulatory changes. The introduction of India's controversial biometric identity system, including the creation of a regulatory authority to monitor the system, was achieved by the inclusion of substantive provisions in a bill authorising expenditure.[136] Similarly, a recent Finance Bill, a money bill that is intended to

[131] See generally Bruce Ackerman, 'The New Separation of Powers' (2000) 113(3) *Harvard Law Review* 633; Frank Vibert, *The Rise of the Unelected: Democracy and the New Separation of Powers* (Cambridge University Press, 2007).

[132] Aditya Bhattacharjea, 'Amending India's Competition Act' (2006) 41(41) *Economic and Political Weekly* 4314; Anusha Ramesh, 'Tribunalisation of India's Competition Regime' (2016) *NUJS Law Review* 259. See also Somanathan (n 9) 397.

[133] Shubhankar Dam, *Presidential Legislation: The Law and Practice of Ordinances* (Cambridge University Press, 2014) 3.

[134] Anirudh Burman, 'Ordinance Route' *Frontline* (9 August 2013), www.frontline.in/the-nation/ordinance-route/article4944717.ece

[135] Dam (n 133) 73.

[136] The Aadhaar (Targeted Delivery of Financial and Other Subsidies, Benefits and Services) Bill, 2016. See also Sruthi Radhakrishnan, 'Is the Aadhar Bill a Money Bill?' *The Hindu* (10 May 2016), www.thehindu.

give effect to the government's annual financial proposals, was the subject of great opposition and criticism when amendments introduced at the last minute attempted reforms to the appointment process in 19 administrative and regulatory tribunals.[137] The Supreme Court is currently seised of both these matters, although historically it has been reluctant to engage in the judicial review of money bills.[138] The issues of delegation that administrative law scholars grapple with are accordingly more complex when we account for instances in which the process of delegation, along with the act of it, is under question.

In the regulatory state, administrative law is concerned not only with how these regulators are shaped, but also by their role as sources of administrative law, particularly with reference to the procedures that they use. A common claim regarding the regulatory state is that it results in increased proceduralisation; the nature of this proceduralisation falls within the domain of administrative law, but is deeply under-analysed. Decision-making by regulatory bodies is defended on the grounds that it employs procedures that are informal and flexible, allowing the administration to modulate its approach not just to policies but also to individuals.[139] Jain has described the function of tribunal adjudication as responding to the need for 'an informal atmosphere untrammelled by too elaborate and technical rules of procedure or evidence. Effective implementation of new policies often demands speedy, cheap and decentralized determination of a large number of cases. These advantages are offered by administration adjudication'.[140]

The emphasis on flexibility and variation has meant that India, unlike the US or even the UK, has made little attempt at providing guidelines for the procedure followed by regulatory bodies. There has been no unifying legislation, such as the American Procedure Act; instead, it is common for statutes constituting regulatory bodies to merely state that they should employ 'the principles of natural justice' in decision making.[141] The principles of natural justice are famously undefined,

com/news/national/is-the-aadhaar-bill-a-money-bill/article14311812.ece; Amber Sinha, 'The Aadhar Act is Not a Money Bill' (24 April 2016) https://thewire.in/31297/the-aadhaar-act-is-not-a-money-bill; Gaurav Vivek Bhatnagar, 'The Rights and Wrongs of Aadhar as a Money Bill' *The Wire* (7 March 2016), https://thewire.in/24115/arun-jaitley-introduces-money-bill-on-aadhar-in-lok-sabha.

[137] Aman Sethi, 'Finance Bill: Govt Merges "Autonomous" Tribunals, Assumes Power to Appoint Chiefs' *Hindustan Times* (14 April 2017), https://www.hindustantimes.com/india-news/finance-bill-2017-govt-merges-top-tribunals-assumes-power-to-appoint-chiefs/story-ZWwZId9GgPW50u0KYxbTnN.html; Mayank Jain, 'Finance Bill 2017: How Tribunal Mergers Took Cover under Money Bill' *Bloomberg* (23 March 2017), https://www.bloombergquint.com/business/2017/03/23/finance-bill-2017-how-tribunal-mergers-took-cover-under-money-bill.

[138] Pratik Datta, Shefali Malhotra and Shivangi Tyagi, 'Judicial Review and Money Bills' (NIPFP Working Paper No 192, 7 March 2017), www.nipfp.org.in/media/medialibrary/2017/03/WP_2017_192.pdf.

[139] Cane (n 15) 233.

[140] MP Jain, *Principles of Administrative Law* vol 1, 6th edn (Wadhwa & Co, 2007) 643.

[141] A sample clause may be found in s 22B(1) of the Securities Contract (Regulation) Act, 1956, which reads: 'The Securities Appellate Tribunal shall not be bound by the procedure laid down by the Code of Civil Procedure, 1908 (5 of 1908), but shall be guided by the principles of natural justice.' Similar provisions may be found in a number of statutes. An indicative list is as follows: Administrative Tribunals Act, 1985, s 22; Railway Claims Tribunal Act, 1987, s 18(1); Legal Services Authorities Act, 1987, s 22D; Special Court (Trial of Offences Relating to Transactions in Securities) Act, 1992, s 9A; Securities and Exchange Board of India Act, 1992, s 15U; Recovery of Debts Due to Banks and Financial Institutions Act, 1993, s 22.

uncodified and the product of long and complex jurisprudence; the Supreme Court notes that they 'can be adapted and modified by statutes and statutory rules and also by the constitution of the Tribunal which has to decide a particular matter and the rules by which such Tribunal is governed'.[142] The result is certainly an amount of flexibility, but also one of tremendous uncertainty. Jain notes that there is now a 'a bewildering variety of procedures across the different adjudicatory bodies'.[143] This, in turn, renders the rulings of administrative tribunals vulnerable to repeated judicial review, in order to address the inevitable iniquitous outcomes of an erratic and variably applied procedure.

In their seminal work on law and administration, Harlow and Rawlings put forth the claim that: 'Behind every theory of administrative law there lies a theory of the state.'[144] The state is shaped by administrative law, but also defines it; red-light and green-light theories about the scope of administrative law are grounded in distinct ideas about the extent and scope of state power. Administrative law theorists in India, consequently, have to acknowledge not only that the rise of the regulatory agencies and mechanisms transforms the state, but also that it transforms their understanding of administrative law.

IV. THE CITIZEN AND ADMINISTRATIVE LAW

In examining the movement of administrative law principles in constitutional cases, Khaitan points to a significant consequence of the judicialised administrative state. The location of administrative law remedies primarily within the Supreme Court privileges certain routes of access to remedies.[145] He notes that when a constitutional court controls administrative relief: 'One implication of this move is that a challenge to unreasonable state action, even if it is only an administrative action, can only be made by following the procedure prescribed for a fundamental rights claim.'[146] This has tremendous implications for the access to justice, as it limits the availability of remedies to constitutional courts. Indeed, on a related note, Baxi notes that the rise of rights jurisprudence as a response to administrative concerns has its limits and that when deeply considered, 'administrative law in India emerges as an archive of production of human rightlessness for the Indian "masses" and a saga of solicitousness for the Indian middle "classes"'.[147] Even though perspectives on the rise of public interest litigation are gradually transforming from celebratory to sceptical, among some administrative law scholars, the use of public interest jurisprudence continues to be the key to achieving just and fair governance in the Indian state.[148]

142 *Union of India v Tulsiram Patel* (1985) 3 SCC 398, 477.
143 Jain (n 140) 647.
144 Harlow and Rawlings (n 39) 1.
145 Khaitan (n 59) 716.
146 ibid.
147 Baxi (n 4) xlii.
148 See Thiruvengadam and Joshi (n 19); Baxi (n 4).

However, within the regulatory state, decision-making is moving outside the realm of courts and into regulatory bodies. The limits of court-based tools and analyses accordingly become apparent. In previous sections I have discussed the tremendous shift to tribunals and the shrinking role of the legislature as implicating issues of legitimacy. However, tribunals also raise questions of participation in the regulatory state, from the involvement of citizens in the process of rule-making to the role of tribunals in individual dispute resolution. Significantly, participation also plays a role in holding regulators accountable for their acts. As Rose-Ackerman points out, '[p]ublic accountability goes beyond purely structural relations between government institutions'[149] and raises distinct concerns apart from political accountability.

The political accountability of regulatory institutions in states with parliamentary structures, like India, has traditionally been to the legislature, through parliamentary oversight and sometimes mediated through ministerial accountability.[150] Some limiting factors operate against this system of institutional controls. In India, ministerial accountability is minimal and ineffective,[151] and traditional legislative tools of accountability are increasingly assuming less importance as the executive sidesteps parliamentary procedures.[152] Therefore, it is generally agreed that the legislature as an organ of accountability is ineffective; in their detailed study, Kapur and Mehta note that traditional tools of parliamentary oversight, such as motions of no-confidence, and parliamentary committees have had limited and declining effectiveness.[153] In addition, while ministers can be held accountable for agencies directly under their control, the arm's-length operation of regulatory bodies is intended to insulate them from this kind of oversight. The cost of insulation from political control is a retrenchment from political accountability. An unsuccessful attempt at passing legislation to hold the heads of regulatory bodies directly accountable to Parliament is one proposed solution.[154] Although this issue has attracted attention from political commentators, it remains largely untouched by administrative law scholarship.[155] When combined

[149] Rose-Ackerman (n 112) 671, 679.

[150] See Somanathan (n 9) 396.

[151] MP Singh, 'Administrative Reforms in India' (2012) LVIII(4) *Indian Journal of Public Administration* 654; Ajay Shah, 'Ministry v. Regulator: How to Draw the Lines' *Business Standard* (17 October 2016), www.mayin.org/ajayshah/MEDIA/2016/department_vs_regulator.html.

[152] See section III.

[153] Kapur and Mehta (n 116).

[154] Ministry of Corporate Affairs, Government of India, 'Report of the Committee for Reforming the Regulatory Environment for Doing Business in India' (2013), www.mca.gov.in/Ministry/annual_reports/DamodaranCommitteeReport.pdf; Sujay Mehdudia, 'Heads of Regulatory Bodies Should Be Accountable to Parliament' *The Hindu* (23 September 2010), www.thehindu.com/todays-paper/tp-national/heads-of-regulatory-bodies-should-be-accountable-to-parliament/article5158456.ece; Surajeet Dasgupta and Indivjal Dhasmana, 'Damodaran Committee: Panel Slams Selection Process of Regulators' *Business Standard* (18 September 2013), www.business-standard.com/article/economy-policy/damodaran-committee-panel-slams-selection-process-of-regulators-113091601011_1.html.

[155] Srishti Pandey, 'After Autonomy, the Need to Fix Proper Accountability of Regulators' *Governance Now* (1 May 2014), www.governancenow.com/news/regular-story/after-autonomy-need-fix-proper-accountability-regulators; Harsimran Kalra and Sakshi Balani, 'Parliamentary Oversight of Regulator: Background Note for the Conference on Effective Legislatures' *PRS Legislative Research* (15 November 2012), www.prsindia.org/administrator/uploads/general/1370586800_Parliamentary%20Oversight%20of%20Regulators.pdf.

with the diminishing role that the legislature plays, it is evident that administrative law scholars will have to look for mechanisms of accountability outside traditional public institutions.

Some approaches to accountability in the regulatory state advocate the establishment of an additional branch of government, whose focus is oversight and control. Thus, Ackerman responds to the challenges of the modern state by advocating a 'constrained parliamentarianism' that rejects the traditional tripartite separation of powers.[156] His proposal calls on drafts of modern constitutions to form a distinct 'integrity' branch composed of a constitutional watchdog, 'armed with powers and incentives to engage in ongoing oversight'.[157] Ginsburg draws from the Chinese experience, discussing the existence of a 'control' branch of the government, whose sole function is to 'audit and fight corruption'.[158] In India, this is once again a field that has attracted extensive attention and literature; the Comptroller and Auditor General is a constitutional authority charged with auditing the finances of government bodies;[159] the Central Vigilance Commission and the Central Bureau of Investigation, constituted first by executive order and later ratified by statute, both oversee and inquire into corruption by government servants.[160] These institutions of internal accountability face their own challenges of independence and expertise, but, more generally, do not provide accessible and participatory forms of accountability to the government, and do not substantially exercise oversight in the regulatory state.

In response to the acute need for public accountability, proposals for a national ombudsman (a *Lokayukta*, or sometimes a *Lokpal*) have been in vogue since the 1960s, generating an equally rich body of commentary.[161] Jain and Jain, in an extensive evaluation of Lokayukta proposals, note that one factor behind them are inherent limitations in the judicial process, as courts have traditionally been reluctant to interfere with the exercise of administrative discretion.[162] This, coupled with the costs of litigation in courts, has resulted in a situation where 'the contest between the government and the individual is a very unequal one, and the dice is heavily loaded against the individual'.[163] Although some Indian states have had limited success in

[156] Ackerman, 'The New Separation of Powers' (n 131).

[157] ibid 633, 691.

[158] Ginsburg (n 8) 117, 124.

[159] Constitution of India, art 148.

[160] See Central Vigilance Commission Act, 2003; Delhi Special Police Establishment Act, 1946. See also Ronojoy Sen, 'Going beyond Accountability: The Changing Role of India's Auditor General' (2013) 72(4) *Journal of Asian Studies* 801.

[161] See, eg, MP Jain, *Lokpal: Ombudsman in India* (S Chand & Co, 1969); SP Sathe, 'Lokayukta (Ombudsman in India) A Socio-legal Study' (1989) 31(1) *Journal of the Indian Law Institute* 114; Anil Nauriya, 'Protecting the Cat from the Mouse: The Lokpal Bill 1985' (1986) 21(5) *Economic and Political Weekly* 1981; Chandra Pal, 'Recent Developments in Indian Ombudsmanship: The Lokpal Bill 1989' (1990) 32(2) *Journal of the Indian Law Institute* 189; Sriram Panchu, 'Lokpal: Where Do We Stand Now, and How We Got Here' (2011) 46(41) *Economic and Political Weekly* 19.

[162] Jain and Jain (n 3) vol 2, 2793.

[163] ibid 2795.

establishing an ombudsman watchdog,[164] attempts to establish a Lokpal at the centre have so far been unsuccessful.[165]

Proposals for a Lokpal have particular relevance to scholars of the regulatory state for three reasons. First, current Lokpal proposals engage strongly with the idea of extending oversight to non-governmental bodies; these include not only regulatory authorities, but other non-state actors that have an impact on regulation and administration (such as non-governmental organisations).[166] Second, although the institution of the Lokpal theoretically opens doors to citizen complaints in addition to being a watchdog, the proposed Lokpal imposes heavy costs if it finds those complaints to be 'frivolous or vexatious'.[167] Since the definitions are vague, this could operate as a disincentive to participation instead of enabling it. Third, and most significantly, the Lokpal itself raises questions that are posed by all regulatory bodies: of legitimacy, separation of powers, insulation from government control and oversight.[168]

Participation in the regulatory state is not limited to dispute resolution as a form of accountability. A significant mode of participation also occurs through direct involvement in the rule-making process, both at the legislature and in secondary rule-making by regulatory authorities. In 2014, the executive proposed a formalised mechanism for pre-legislative public consultations in all draft legislation – an innovation which addressed a tremendous gap in the legislative framework.[169] Although four years have passed since then, administrative law scholarship has not responded to this development at all; we have no assessments of how this policy is functioning, whether it is effective, or on the impact it has had on rule-making and legislation. Initial reports suggest that implementation might be erratic; a bill seeking to decriminalise the practice of beggary was preceded by public consultations, but only with representatives from state and union territories,[170] while a bill to criminalise instant, unilateral divorce among Muslims (triple *talaq*) was introduced with no consultation at all.[171]

[164] See, eg, A Narayana, S Krishnaswamy and V Kumar, 'Lokpal Bill: Lessons from the Karnataka Lokayukta's Performance' (2012) 1(7) *Economic and Political Weekly* 12.

[165] See K Deepalakshmi, 'The Long Wait for a Lokpal' *The Hindu* (27 April 2017), www.thehindu.com/news/national/all-you-need-to-know-about-the-lokpal-bill/article18254568.ece.

[166] See Sriram Panchu, 'Repairing the Lokpal Bill' (2012) 47(3) *Economic and Political Weekly* 10.

[167] Mandira Kala, 'A Citizen's Guide to Using Lokpal' *Governance Now* (2014), www.governancenow.com/news/regular-story/citizens-guide-using-lokpal.

[168] Amrita Johri, Anjali Bhardwaj and Shekhar Singh, 'The Lokpal Act of 2014: An Assessment' (2014) 49(5) *Economic and Political Weekly* 10; Ashok Kapur, 'The Lokpal Bill Could Create More Problems Than it Will Solve' *Hindustan Times* (24 April 2017), https://www.hindustantimes.com/opinion/the-lokpal-could-create-more-problems-than-it-will-solve/story-nPNGc9FFLBCKEWU7U4ZoyI.html.

[169] Law Department, Ministry of Law and Justice, Government of India, *Pre-legislative Consultative Policy* (5 February 2014), http://lawmin.nic.in/ld/plcp.pdf; Anirudha Nagar, 'Laws by the People, for the People' *The Hindu* (24 February 2014), www.thehindu.com/opinion/op-ed/laws-by-the-people-for-the-people/article5719578.ece.

[170] 'Government to Bring a Bill to Decriminalize Beggary' *Times of India* (19 October 2016), https://timesofindia.indiatimes.com/india/Government-to-bring-bill-to-decriminalise-beggary/articleshow/54940421.cms.

[171] Randeep Singh Surjewala, 'This is No Reform' *Indian Express* (3 January 2018), http://indianexpress.com/article/opinion/columns/this-is-no-reform-triple-talaq-bill-muslim-law-winter-session-5009174.

Consultations in rule-making procedures by regulatory bodies are also inconsistent. In the absence of common procedures on rule-making, most agencies follow individual and self-devised procedures. There is a wide variation in the level of public participation required and conducted by regulators. For instance, India's Telecom Regulatory Authority (TRAI) regularly conducts public consultations on proposed policies, fulfilling a statutory mandate to 'ensure transparency while exercising its powers and discharging its functions'.[172] The Supreme Court has reiterated this policy, loosely interpreting from the requirement of 'transparency' and accordingly setting aside a regulation when it found that the TRAI had failed to provide adequate reasoning in responses to stakeholder comments.[173] On the other hand, the Securities and Exchange Board (SEBI) occasionally conducts public consultations, but does not regularly respond; it is neither a statutory requirement for SEBI nor a judicially imposed constraint.[174] Therefore, it is unsurprising that an extensive analysis by Burman and Zaveri on regulatory responsiveness found that 'the degree of responsiveness of regulators seems directly proportional to the legal requirement for following participatory processes'.[175] A wide variation in consultation processes amongst regulators means that the level of participatory governance varies as well. Administrative law scholars who are examining the regulatory state in the context of both accountability and participation will thus have to engage with statutory and judicial frameworks governing dispute resolution as well as rule-making.

CONCLUSION

Administrative law scholarship in India has not seen the wide development and theoretical examination that it has received in countries such as the US or in England.[176] Although the regulatory state has expanded, the language of administrative law is still couched in terms of constitutional law and constitutional values, and has not yet transitioned to the more instrumental, ends-based syntax of regulatory studies. Part of this owes itself to the nature of Indian administrative law, which is deeply embedded within the constitutional frame and has accordingly developed hand in hand with constitutional jurisprudence. As section I has demonstrated, studies that are theoretical tend to focus on constitutional themes, often at the expense of developments in administrative law outside the Constitution.

A second, linked factor in scholarship in administrative law is the pervasive role that judicial review plays in the Indian state: unlike most academic schools, it is

[172] Telecom Regulatory Authority of India Act, 1997, s 11(4).

[173] *Cellular Operators Association of India and Others v Telecom Regulatory Authority of India and Others*, Civil Appeal No 5017 of 2016, Supreme Court of India (11 May 2016), para 66.

[174] Ajay Shah, 'The Agenda at SEBI' *Business Standard* (20 February 2017), www.mayin.org/ajayshah/MEDIA/2017/sebi_agenda.html.

[175] Anirudh Burman and Bhargavi Zaveri, 'Regulatory Responsiveness in India: A Normative and Empirical Framework for Assessment' (2016) Working Paper No 025-2016, Indira Gandhi Institute of Development Research, www.igidr.ac.in/pdf/publication/WP-2016-025.pdf.

[176] For an overview, see TRS Allan, 'Review of Executive Action' in Tushnet and Cane (n 39) 147, 149–50.

not the merits of judicial review, but the extent of it that has formed the bulk of academic inquiry. Judicial review is treated, by and large, as a fait accompli, and the linked questions of democratic legitimacy, the separation of powers, and participation accordingly receive little serious treatment. However, the rise of the regulatory state provides new reasons to re-examine these themes. Accordingly administrative law scholars may have to build from the ground up in order to have the tools to understand, analyse and respond to the regulatory state.

A third, structural reason factor that limits the growth of Indian administrative law is the episodic and unsystematic forms of its development. Administrative law in India has not been the subject of systematic, legislative reform; indeed, attempts at such reforms have been strongly resisted by courts, which favour the case-by-case application of common law principles. This approach is further extended by less qualified regulatory bodies, which use the same methodology to determine disputes, but often do not have quite the same level of expertise. The result is a diverse, vast field of jurisprudence that often defies attempts at the imposition of order or analysis. Despite this, laudable work in specific sectors is contributing to a body of scholarship which can form the basis of broader analysis.

I will point, finally, to two significant limitations in my analysis of challenges facing Indian administrative law today. I have not delved into the rich literature on the colonial roots of Indian administrative law, particularly when it comes to the inheritance of common law principles that continue to form the basis of modern administrative law. There are essentially three legacies of the post-colonial legal framework that continue to implicate regulation: the persistence of administrative structures and laws that were designed to secure colonial and not democratic control of the state;[177] the creation of plural domains in personal law that extend to commercial laws; and the displacement of informal pre-colonial regulatory systems with formalised judicial structures and codes.[178] With particular reference to the legacy of laws and legal principles, some research suggests that notions of justice as equity that thread through constitutional and administrative discourse in India today are traced back not just to the moment of India's Constitution, but also to colonial institutions and practices.[179] Moreover, the persistence of common law traditions is not confined to constitutional doctrine; these continue to represent themselves within the regulatory state.

A second, significant limitation is the rise of administrative law as a global and not a national phenomenon. Administrative law tends to be specific to national

[177] For instance, colonial structures that established the army, the police and the civil service continue in largely untouched forms. See Arvind Verma, 'The Police in India: Design, Performance and Adaptability' in Kapur and Mehta (n 93) 194; KP Krishnan and TV Somanathan, 'Civil Service: An Institutional Perspective' in Kapur and Mehta (n 93).

[178] See D Rohit, 'South Asian Legal Traditions' in James D Wright (ed), *International Encyclopaedia of the Social & Behavioural Sciences*, 2nd edn (Elsevier, 2015) 58–62.

[179] The clearest account of this approach is by Mithi Mukherjee, who differentiates between 'imperial justice' and 'colonial power', and examines how these have shaped constitutional institutions in India. See Mithi Mukherjee, *India in the Shadows of Empire: A Legal and Political History, 1774–1950* (Oxford University Press, 2010).

structures: 'But each system remains its own distinctive animal.'[180] It is therefore less likely to 'converge' on themes in a manner familiar to comparative constitutional law theorists.[181] In two ways, however, administrative law is increasingly moving outside the nation and into the world. Within the context of the Global South, the influence of external agencies and borrowings alters the regulatory state's framework. These external influences prompt institutional and policy transplants – a form of 'regulation through the backdoor' that shapes administrative structures, but also administrative procedures and laws.[182] In addition, as regulation attains a transnational character, so does administrative law; national administrative law regimes influence, and are in turn influenced by, global practice and development.[183] Global administrative law pushes not only for an increased understanding of convergences in administrative law, but also for the understanding of a distinct and global regime of administrative law. As India's participation in international institutions grows, global administrative law will continue to attain relevance, opening the door for leveraging national concerns.[184]

Administrative law in India is generally understood to be a field that endures rather than flourishes, but the regulatory state has demonstrably raised interest in the field. In order to respond adequately to the needs of the modern state, it is vital that administrative law scholars engage not only in scholarship that responds to periodic developments, but also in the endeavour of examining the underlying principles, assumptions and context within which the regulatory state is emerging. In rising to meet these new challenges, I hope that this chapter will help in setting an agenda for the growth of administrative law scholarship in India.

[180] Ginsburg (n 8) 117, 120.
[181] ibid.
[182] Dubash (n 62).
[183] Benedict Kingsbury, Nico Krisch and Richard B Stewart, 'The Rise of Emergence of Administrative Law' (2005) 68(15) *Law and Contemporary Problems* 15. See also the Global Administrative Law Project, https://www.iilj.org/gal.
[184] See BS Chimni, 'Co-option and Resistance: Two Faces of Global Administrative Law' (2006) IILJ Working Paper No 16, https://www.iilj.org/publications/cooption-and-resistance-two-faces-of-global-administrative-law.

3

Reclaiming Indian Administrative Law

FARRAH AHMED AND SWATI JHAVERI*

INTRODUCTION

THIS CHAPTER CLAIMS that constitutional law has largely eclipsed common law judicial review of administrative action in India; it argues that this development has diminished the efficacy of common law judicial review as a means of addressing administrative failures; and it offers proposals to address these concerns.

Section I offers a brief overview of common law grounds of review of administrative action. Sections II and III demonstrate how these grounds have been overshadowed through a study of two areas of Indian public law. Section II demonstrates that the jurisprudence around Article 14 of the Indian Constitution has overshadowed common law judicial review. Section III then demonstrates that constitutional jurisprudence on socio-economic rights has had much the same effect. Section IV argues that the dominance of constitutional law in these contexts has significant implications: unlawful administrative action is not met with the most suitable legal response; administrators are given inadequate guidance; doctrinal uncertainty abounds; and litigants have obstacles accessing justice.

The fifth and final section offers proposals for how to address these problems by reinvigorating common law judicial review or administrative law (the terms are used interchangeably in this chapter). Some proposals are aimed at increasing public awareness of administrative law – an issue which has received too little attention so far. Others are aimed at courts and involve change to legal doctrine. The proposals include constitutional avoidance, constitutional reference to administrative law and strengthening administrative law.

* This chapter benefited from insightful comments from participants at the 2018 Indian Administrative and Regulatory State Conference. Thanks are due to the Academic Research Service, Melbourne Law School for excellent research assistance. The chapter draws upon Farrah Ahmed and Swati Jhaveri, 'Arbitrariness and Judicial Review in India' in Swati Jhaveri and Michael Ramsden (eds), *Judicial Review of Administrative Action in the Common Law World: Legacies and Evolutions* (Cambridge University Press, forthcoming); and Farrah Ahmed and Tarunabh Khaitan, 'Constitutional Avoidance in Social Rights Adjudication' (2015) 35 *Oxford Journal of Legal Studies* 607.

I. COMMON LAW REVIEW OF ADMINISTRATIVE ACTION

Under the common law, judicial review of administrative action is available on a cluster of interrelated grounds. There is variation from jurisdiction to jurisdiction, and scholarship on how the grounds have evolved in common law Asia is still emerging.[1] A summary, necessarily rough-and-ready, of the key grounds follows:

Ultra vires: administrators should not exceed the powers granted to them by statute.

Relevant considerations: if a statute implicitly or explicitly requires administrators to consider or exclude particular considerations in making a decision, they should consider or exclude those considerations.

Proper purpose: administrators only use their powers for the purpose for which they are granted.

Hearing: administrators should hear from those affected by a decision before making a decision.

Reasonableness: administrators should not act unreasonably.

Bias: administrators should not make decisions based on biases. Administrators should not make decisions where they *appear* to be biased.

Legitimate expectations: administrators must honour the promises and follow the policies or practices they have made for themselves.[2]

Retaining discretion: administrators should not delegate their powers further and should not bind themselves to follow a policy inflexibly.

The grounds are described here in general terms; most of them admit of exceptions not discussed here. Upendra Baxi's assessments of early Indian administrative law reveal that judges invoked and reviewed administrative actions against practically all of these grounds.[3] Case law on some grounds was sparse, but their availability was not in doubt. It is against this background that the accounts below of how common law grounds of judicial review have been overshadowed by constitutional law must be understood.

[1] A particularly important project is being led by Swati Jhaveri: see Swati Jhaveri and Michael Ramsden (eds), *Judicial Review of Administrative Action in the Common Law World: Legacies and Evolutions* (Cambridge University Press, forthcoming).

[2] Farrah Ahmed and Adam Perry, 'The Coherence of the Doctrine of Legitimate Expectations' (2014) 73 *Cambridge Law Journal* 61. Chintan Chandrachud's work suggests that this ground has gained prominence in India only recently: Chintan Chandrachud, 'The (Fictitious) Doctrine of Substantive Legitimate Expectations in India' in Matthew Groves and Greg Weeks (eds), *Legitimate Expectations in the Common Law World* (Hart Publishing, 2017).

[3] Upendra Baxi, 'Developments in Indian Administrative Law' in AG Noorani (ed), *Public Law in India* (Vikas Publishing House, 1982); Upendra Baxi, 'Introduction to the Seventh Edition: The Myth and Reality of the Indian Administrative Law' in IP Massey, *Administrative Law*, 8th edn (Eastern Book Company, 2012).

II. THE ARBITRARINESS DOCTRINE

Article 14 of the Indian Constitution guarantees to everyone within India a 'Fundamental Right' to equality before law and equal protection of the law. In *EP Royappa v State of Tamil Nadu*,[4] this right to equality was interpreted to include protections from arbitrary state action. According to the Supreme Court, 'equality and arbitrariness are sworn enemies; one belongs to the rule of law in a republic while the other, to the whim and caprice of an absolute monarch'.[5] According to the Court, it followed that the constitutional protection of equality includes protection against arbitrary state action.[6]

While this reasoning has been criticised,[7] after *Royappa*, anyone wanting to challenge administrative action in India had an avenue to do so in addition to traditional common law grounds: constitutional judicial review by way of writ petition to the High Court or Supreme Court. A wide range of non-statutory bodies and decisions are subject to such review.[8]

The 'arbitrariness doctrine' has been strongly criticised for a number of reasons. A former Supreme Court justice, BN Srikrishna, expresses concerns with its legitimacy and legal basis:

> From *Royappa* it was a merry ride through *Maneka Gandhi, R.D. Shetty*, *Ajay Hasia*, and a host of other cases where the Supreme Court freely struck down actions of the other coordinate branches of the Government on the basis that it was not 'reasonable' or was 'arbitrary', a standard of judicial review, *neither contemplated by the framers of the Constitution nor by the plain text of Article 14*.[9] (Emphasis added)

There is also a fair degree of agreement that cases involving the arbitrariness doctrine provide little guidance on what qualifies as arbitrary state action. One of India's most distinguished senior counsel has characterised judicial pronouncements on the doctrine as 'in the main rhetorical praise of the concept of equality which by itself does not elucidate the legal content of Article 14'.[10] Scholars have expressed similar views on the emptiness or lack of clarity of the doctrine.[11]

The problems with the arbitrariness doctrine can be seen through a well-known case involving allegedly arbitrary executive action. In *Ajay Hasia v Khalid Mujib Sehravardi*,[12] the petitioners argued that the admissions process to a university course

[4] *EP Royappa v State of Tamil Nadu* AIR 1974 SC 555.

[5] ibid [85].

[6] ibid.

[7] Tarunabh Khaitan, 'Equality: Legislative Review under Article 14' in Sujit Choudhry, Madhav Khosla and Pratap Bhanu Mehta (eds), *The Oxford Handbook of the Indian Constitution* (Oxford University Press, 2016); Prateek Jalan and Ritin Rai, 'Review of Administrative Action' in Sujit Choudhry, Madhav Khosla and Pratap Bhanu Mehta (eds), *The Oxford Handbook of the Indian Constitution* (Oxford University Press, 2016).

[8] See, eg, *Ajay Hasia v Khalid Mujib Sehravardi* AIR 1981 SC 487; *Kumari Shrilekha Vidyarthi v State of UP* AIR 1991 SC 537.

[9] BN Srikrishna, 'Skinning a Cat' (2005) 8 *SCC* J-3, J-10.

[10] TR Andhyarujina, 'The Evolution of Due Process of Law by the Supreme Court' in BN Kirpal et al (eds), *Supreme But Not Infallible: Essays in Honour of the Supreme Court of India* (Oxford University Press, 2000) 206.

[11] Khaitan (n 7) 712; Jalan and Rai (n 7).

[12] *Ajay Hasia* (n 8).

was arbitrary because: (a) it assigned a very high weight to performance in an oral interview; and (b) the questions at the oral interview (which only lasted a few minutes) were not relevant to admission to the course.[13]

The Supreme Court referred to the admission practices for recruitment to government services and judicial comments on the appropriate weight to be attributed to interviews, and concluded:

> [H]aving regard to the drawbacks and deficiencies in the oral interview test and the conditions prevailing in the country, particularly when there is deterioration in moral values and corruption and nepotism are very much on the increase, allocation of a high percentage of marks for the oral interview as compared to the marks allocated for the written test, cannot be accepted by the Court as free from the vice of arbitrariness.[14]

Once the Court accepted that the test lasted 2–3 minutes and comprised irrelevant questions, it simply concluded that 'the oral interview test must be held to be vitiated and the selection made on the basis of such test must be held to be arbitrary'.[15]

This case illustrates how Article 14 has overshadowed administrative law grounds of review. In many Article 14 cases, these grounds are not mentioned at all, even though they are highly relevant. The matter is instead decided on the basis of Article 14, without any explicit connection being made between Article 14 jurisprudence and common law grounds of review (even though these grounds are recognised in India). *Ajay Hasia* is hardly an outlier in this respect.[16] In *Y Srinivasa Rao v J Veeraiah*,[17] the applicant challenged the decision of the petitioner to fill civil service vacancies through an advertisement that preferred candidates experienced in the relevant field of work and, where there were candidates with equal qualifications and experience, preference would be given to 'unemployed educated persons, ladies and handicapped persons'.[18] In a sparsely reasoned judgment, the Court concluded that this amounted to 'gross arbitrariness'.[19]

This approach to judicial review of administrative action has led traditional administrative law grounds of review to be heavily sidelined, so much so that many scholars conclude (incorrectly) that some common law grounds are no longer available, except under Article 14. For example, Prateek Jalan and Ritin Rai, writing in *The Oxford Handbook of the Indian Constitution*, assert that: 'Judicial review of the "reasonableness" of all government action – whether administrative or legislative – is rooted in Article 14 of the Constitution.'[20] Tarunabh Khaitan, in the same *Handbook*, takes the position that 'a challenge to unreasonable State action, even if it is only an administrative action, can only be made by following the procedure prescribed for a fundamental rights claim – that is, by filing a writ in a constitutional court'.[21]

[13] ibid [18].
[14] ibid [19].
[15] ibid [20].
[16] See, eg, *Zenit Mataplast P Ltd v State of Maharashtra* (2009) 10 SCC 388.
[17] *Y Srinivasa Rao v J Veeraiah* AIR 1993 SC 929.
[18] ibid [2].
[19] ibid [6].
[20] Jalan and Rai (n 7) 433.
[21] Khaitan (n 7) 716.

But judicial review on common law grounds – including unreasonableness – remains available in Indian courts. In *Ganayutham*,[22] the Supreme Court reviewed the *Wednesbury* test, and debates about proportionality in English courts, in great detail. Making no reference to Article 14, it laid out the position in India, implying that it was the same as in England and Wales:

> To judge the validity of any administrative order or statutory discretion, normally the Wednesbury test is to be applied to find out if the decision was illegal or suffered from procedural improprieties or was one which no sensible decision-maker could, on the material before him and within the framework of the law, have arrived at. The Court would consider whether relevant matters had not been taken into account or whether irrelevant matters had been taken into account or whether the action was not bona fide. The Court would also consider whether the decision was absurd or perverse. The Court would not however go into the correctness of the choice made by the administrator amongst the various alternatives open to him. Nor could the Court substitute its decision to that of the administrator. This is the Wednesbury test.[23]

Similarly, in *Chairman, All India Railway Recruitment Board v K Shyam Kumar*,[24] having discussed the place of both the *Wednesbury* and proportionality tests in English common law, the Court applied both these tests, making no reference at all to Article 14 (although the case was at least partly argued on Article 14 grounds).[25]

Courts have also reviewed administrative action against common law rules relating to natural justice without reference to Article 14. In *State of UP v Vijay Kumar Tripathi*, the Supreme Court said: 'The normal rule enunciated by this Court is that wherever it is necessary to ensure against the failure of justice, principles of natural justice must be read into a provision.'[26]

Despite the availability of review on common law grounds, it has been so overshadowed by Article 14 that it is overlooked even by careful commentators[27] (and, it seems, often by courts and counsel as well). A review of the arbitrariness doctrine thus offers a particularly clear picture of how Indian constitutional law has eclipsed Indian administrative law.

III. SOCIAL RIGHTS

The same pattern emerges from a study of social rights before the Indian Supreme Court.[28] A 2015 study by Farrah Ahmed and Tarunabh Khaitan found that in most cases, the Court overlooked the availability and significance of administrative law

[22] *Union of India v G Ganayutham* AIR 1997 SC 3387.

[23] ibid [28].

[24] *Chairman, All India Railway Recruitment Board v K Shyam Kumar* (2010) 6 SCC 614.

[25] ibid [21]–[40].

[26] *State of UP v Vijay Kumar Tripathi* AIR 1995 SC 1130 [7]. See also *AK Kraipak v Union of India* AIR 1970 SC 150, which is an important example of this point.

[27] See, eg, Jalan and Rai (n 7) 434; Khaitan (n 7) 716.

[28] Farrah Ahmed and Tarunabh Khaitan, 'Constitutional Avoidance in Social Rights Adjudication' (2015) 35 *Oxford Journal of Legal Studies* 607.

grounds of review in favour of constitutional law arguments.[29] (Madhav Khosla's work on the potential for tort claims in these social rights cases suggests that there is strong potential for constitutional avoidance in these cases, as discussed later in this chapter.) A more detailed analysis of three social rights cases is illustrative.

As a first example, the famous *Olga Tellis*[30] case proceeded on constitutional law grounds rather than administrative law grounds. This is despite the fact that administrative law review to protect legitimate expectations and procedural fairness was better suited to the issues that the Supreme Court grappled with. The government had a policy of carrying out a census of slum dwellers (except those living on pavements), allocating land for their resettlement and giving them identity cards. The Court held that such slum dwellers must be provided with alternative accommodation before they were resettled. The government had also (mistakenly) issued some people who were living on the pavements with identity cards.[31] The Court held that pavement dwellers who had been given identity cards must also be given alternative 'pitches' to the pavement.[32] It further held that:

> [S]lums which have been in existence for a long time, say for twenty years or more, and which have been improved and developed will not be removed unless the land on which they stand or the appurtenant land, is required for a public purpose, in which case, alternate sites or accommodation will be provided to them.[33]

Each of these orders could have been made under the doctrine of legitimate expectations. The Court was simply protecting the legitimate expectations created by the government's stated policy of providing alternative accommodation to those to whom it gave identity cards following the census, and the legitimate expectations created by the government's inaction in removing long-established slums. As a remedy, the Court required that notice be given to the pavement dwellers before they were evicted.[34] The Court also reviewed the reasonableness of administrative action and the fairness of the procedure followed by administrators.[35] Thus, the Court's remedies and concerns were administrative law ones, even though administrative law was not explicitly invoked.

The same could be said of the case of *Ahmedabad Municipal Corporation*.[36] In this case, the Supreme Court emphasised the importance of following a fair procedure before slum-dwellers were evicted, particularly in cases where they have been settled on land for a long time without any interference from the administrator.[37] Again, this finding is essentially based on an administrative law doctrine of legitimate

[29] ibid 614–17.

[30] *Olga Tellis v Bombay Municipal Corporation* AIR 1986 SC 180.

[31] ibid [16].

[32] ibid [57].

[33] ibid.

[34] ibid [46]. The Supreme Court's direction that slums would not be removed until after 31 October 1985 (the current monsoon season) could also be thought of as a requirement of notice: at [57].

[35] ibid [40], [42].

[36] *Ahmedabad Municipal Corporation v Nawab Khan Gulab Khan* AIR 1997 SC 152.

[37] ibid [9].

expectations.[38] The particular suitability of legitimate expectations doctrine is indicated by the Court's advice that the government remove encroachments as soon as they appear.[39] The relief granted to the 10 named petitioners amounted to a direction to the government to follow the schemes it had put in place and act in accordance with natural justice.[40]

The *Mohini Jain* case offers another helpful example in the context of the right to education.[41] The case involved a challenge to a fee that was charged for admission to a course of study. The fee appeared to be sanctioned by a notification issued by the state government of Karnataka under the Karnataka Educational Institutions (Prohibition of Capitation Fee) Act, 1984. However, the Supreme Court found that the notification, insofar as it appeared to sanction the fee in question to be charged, was ultra vires.[42] In fact, the fee in question was found to be precisely the type of fee that the Act intended to prohibit educational institutions from charging.[43]

Despite the grounds for the decision clearly being the canonical common law ground of ultra vires, the Supreme Court relied heavily on constitutional provisions, with potentially far-reaching consequences. It held:

> The 'right to education', therefore, is concomitant to the fundamental rights enshrined under Part III of the Constitution. The State is under a constitutional-mandate to provide educational institutions at all levels for the benefit of the citizens[44] … We hold that every citizen has a 'right to education' under the Constitution. The State is under an obligation to establish educational institutions to enable the citizens to enjoy the said right. The State may discharge its obligation through state-owned or state-recognised educational institutions.[45]

In the vast majority of social rights cases before the Supreme Court, even where administrative law is clearly applicable, the Court either ignores it altogether, in favour of constitutional law, or sidelines it (as in *Mohini Jain*) to emphasise the constitutional law arguments.

The next section teases out the worrying implications of this pattern, seen in both arbitrariness and social rights cases, and perhaps other areas yet to be studied.

IV. IMPLICATIONS OF THE ECLIPSE OF ADMINISTRATIVE LAW

The eclipse of administrative law leads to cases being decided on legal grounds which are not best suited to their adjudication, to administrators receiving insufficient guidance on their legal duties and to doctrinal uncertainty, conceptual confusion and inadequate access to justice.

[38] See also ibid [28].
[39] See ibid [20].
[40] ibid [30].
[41] *Mohini Jain v State of Karnataka* AIR 1992 SC 1858.
[42] ibid [29]–[31].
[43] ibid [28]–[29].
[44] ibid [14].
[45] ibid [17].

A. Suitability

To state what should be obvious, but is under-appreciated: when judges overlook administrative law in cases involving unlawful administrative action, they overlook the legal norms that are best suited to respond to that particular action. To take an example, the Supreme Court case of *Maharashtra Ekta Hawkers Union* was decided on the basis of Article 19(1)(g) of the Constitution.[46] This is despite the fact that the Court acknowledged that 'the problem [of the regulation of street vendors] has aggravated because of lackadaisical attitude of the administration at various levels'.[47] While there was a policy that purported to regulate street vendors – the national Policy on Urban Street Vendors 2009[48] – it was clearly not effective.[49]

Administrative law norms have developed to respond to precisely these kinds of problems. Judges over the years, and over several common law jurisdictions, have developed resources – norms, tests, analogies, rules of thumbs and remedies – that could aid judges in reasoning and crafting appropriate remedies. Ultimately, the Supreme Court directed that the 2009 policy should be implemented, giving direction to facilitate its implementation.[50] In doing so, the Court could have drawn on administrative law principles: both the principle of consistency and the doctrine of legitimate expectations direct administrators to apply policies that they have put in place. By ignoring administrative law, and focussing instead on Article 19(1)(g) of the Constitution, the Court lost access to enormously relevant intellectual resources which could have guided its decision-making.

Even where the Supreme Court recognises that the problem lies in the way in which the administration functions, it fails to consider administrative law. In *Court on its Own Motion*, the Court was concerned about 'the lack of public amenities, facilities, health care and particularly the high rate of mortality' of pilgrims to the holy cave of Amarnathji in Jammu and Kashmir.[51] The Court found that a large part of the problem lay with the administration: 'The management and arrangements for the yatris [pilgims] at the glacier and near the Holy Shrine are, to say the least, pathetic … the management suffers from basic infirmity, discrepancies, inefficiency and ill-planning.'[52] But it appealed to constitutional, not administrative law, in its reasoning and in fashioning remedies.

B. Lack of Guidance to Administrators

The *Ajay Hasia*[53] case discussed earlier demonstrates the lack of judicial guidance about what arbitrariness is and how it is to be avoided. While the Supreme Court was

[46] *Maharashtra Ekta Hawkers Union v Municipal Corporation, Greater Mumbai* (2014) 1 SCC 490.
[47] ibid [5].
[48] ibid [12].
[49] ibid [20]–[21].
[50] ibid.
[51] *Court on its Own Motion v Union of India* [2012] 13 SCR 1093 [2].
[52] ibid [9].
[53] *Ajay Hasia* (n 8).

concerned to offer guidance to the administrators in this particular case (suggesting that oral interviews should not be weighted at more than 15 per cent),[54] it offered no test or criteria for identifying arbitrary action. The explanation for why the respondents' actions were arbitrary was very closely tied to the facts.

This lack of guidance was acknowledged by the Supreme Court in *Kumari Shrilekha Vidyarthi v State of UP*:

> The meaning and true import of arbitrariness is *more easily visualized than precisely stated or defined*. The question, whether an impugned act is arbitrary or not, is ultimately to be answered on the facts and in the circumstances of a given case.[55] (Emphasis added)

The shortfall in judicial guidance can be seen in the social rights cases as well. In *Maharashtra Ekta Hawkers Union*, involving the non-application of policy, while directing that the policy should be implemented,[56] the Supreme Court did not say that administrators should *generally* follow the policies that they have set for themselves because of the principle of consistency[57] or legitimate expectations.[58] Similarly, in *Olga Tellis*, while the Court enforced legitimate expectations,[59] it did not say that administrators should *generally* take account of legitimate expectations that they have created.[60]

The sidelining of administrative law appears to be associated with a lack of judicial guidance to administrators about what they did wrong – what generalisable norm they contravened and what they can do to avoid unlawful action in the future.

C. Doctrinal Uncertainty

Further, administrative law does not escape the issues of doctrinal incoherence that face Indian law more generally. Raeesa Vakil's chapter in this volume documents the higher judiciary's failure to clearly establish the bounds of judicial power in reviewing administrative action or to identify the normative underpinning of administrative law doctrines.

Let us return for a moment to the case of *Mohini Jain*, where the Supreme Court declared a decision to charge a fee ultra vires and also made some (arguably unnecessary) findings on the constitutional basis of the right to education. The judicial pronouncements in *Mohini Jain*, besides being unnecessary to the order given in that case, caused confusion about the scope of the newly anointed constitutional right to education. The Supreme Court in *Unni Krishnan* was therefore called upon to resolve

[54] ibid [19].

[55] *Kumari Shrilekha Vidyarthi* (n 8). Somewhat ironically, this is a case where the Supreme Court does more than usual by way of guidance.

[56] *Maharashtra Ekta Hawkers Union* (n 46) [15].

[57] See generally Richard Clayton, 'Legitimate Expectations, Policy, and the Principle of Consistency' (2003) 62 *Cambridge Law Journal* 93.

[58] See generally MP Jain and SN Jain, *Principles of Administrative Law*, 6th edn (LexisNexis, 2013) 279.

[59] *Olga Tellis* (n 30) [46], [57]. See also *Ahmedabad Municipal Corporation* (n 36) [30].

[60] Jain and Jain (n 58) 279.

these doubts.[61] Sharma CJ and Barucha J, in *Unni Krishnan*, were implicitly critical of the breadth of judicial pronouncement on whether there was a fundamental right to primary education in *Mohini Jain*. They noted the obiter status of the remarks in *Mohini Jain*[62] and endorsed 'the well-established principle of not proceeding to decide any question which is not necessary to be decided in the case'.[63]

Indian high courts routinely review administrative actions based on constitutional provisions of questionable relevance to the facts at hand. The connection between a failure to give notice, honour promises or follow a set policy, and the right to life or livelihood is not an obvious one. It follows that the scope of these rights becomes highly uncertain.

D. Conceptual Confusion

Compounding these concerns about doctrinal uncertainty, these developments chip away at the conceptual basis of administrative law. It is true that the distinction, and the significance of the distinction, between constitutional law and administrative law is often questioned. Scholars across jurisdictions now talk of the blurring of lines between constitutional and administrative law. But in other work, Farrah Ahmed offers a theory of judicial review of administrative action which illuminates the distinction between the two bodies of law. Drawing on the widely endorsed idea that administrators are delegates, Ahmed demonstrates that common law grounds of review reflect the duties that administrators have by virtue of their status as delegates.[64] Refining John Gardner's distinction between constitutional and administrative law,[65] Ahmed concludes that constitutional law is the body of law whose core function is to regulate constitutional institutions *qua* constitutional institutions; administrative law is the body of law whose core function is to regulate administrative institutions *qua* administrative institutions where:

(a) constitutional institutions are state institutions whose powers are either inherent or in practice irrevocable by the delegating institutions; and
(b) administrative institutions are state institutions whose powers are in practice revocable by the delegating constitutional institutions.

Insofar as there is a conceptual distinction between these two bodies of law, the eclipse of the administrative law creates conceptual and, in turn, doctrinal confusion.

E. Access to Justice

When constitutional law eclipses administrative law, nudging applicants to use constitutional law to challenge administrative action, this has significant implications for

[61] *Unni Krishnan v State of Andhra Pradesh* AIR 1993 SC 2178.
[62] ibid [2]–[4].
[63] ibid [4].
[64] Farrah Ahmed, 'The Delegation Theory of Judicial Review' (Public Law Conference, Melbourne, 13 July 2018).
[65] John Gardner, *Law as a Leap of Faith: Essays on Law in General* (Oxford University Press, 2012) ch 4.

access to justice. Challenges based on breaches of fundamental rights proceed by way of writ petition to the High Courts or Supreme Courts. These constitutional courts are more expensive and difficult to access. Forcing more applicants to start their legal processes at that high level exacerbates India's massive problems with delays in litigation.

The sidelining of administrative law also contributes to a widespread dichotomic view of the Indian judiciary. The 'higher judiciary is often viewed as the panacea for the various endemic social and political problems that plague India'.[66] The lower judiciary, meanwhile, is 'purely pathological – inefficient, corrupt'.[67] This view naturally leads to very low levels of confidence in the lower judiciary amongst both the profession and the general public.[68] Lower courts are, on this view, 'hurdles to get over, or avoid altogether (for example, through the writ jurisdiction), rather than forums from which final resolution of disputes is expected'.[69]

No doubt there are genuine concerns about the quality of adjudication in the lower courts; the view is not pure caricature. There is also reason to suspect that these problems *caused* administrative law to be sidelined in favour of constitutional law to begin with. But the path we are on leads to an unmanageably top-heavy caseload. The need for (better functioning) lower courts to bear more of that load – including cases involving administrative wrongs – is clear.

V. REINVIGORATING ADMINISTRATIVE LAW

This section offers proposals for how to address these problems by reinvigorating administrative law. Some proposals are aimed at increasing public awareness of administrative law, an issue which has received too little attention so far. Others are aimed at courts and involve change to legal doctrine. The proposals involve constitutional avoidance, constitutional reference to administrative law and strengthening administrative law.

A. The Public

Sometimes an aspect of the law or legal process finds a place in the public imagination. Anuj Bhuwania makes a point about broad and deep public consciousness of public interest litigation (PIL) through illustrations of their place in Bollywood films and widely read newspapers.[70] While we know of no studies on the subject, there is reason to suspect that administrative law is at the other end of the spectrum of public consciousness. If higher court case law is any guide, the profession and judiciary pay it little mind; it seems even more unlikely to have made an impression on the public.

[66] Anuj Bhuwania, *Courting the People: Public Interest Litigation Post-emergency India* (Cambridge University Press, 2017) 3.

[67] ibid.

[68] Robert Moog, 'The Significance of Lower Courts in the Judicial Process' in E Veena Das (ed), *The Oxford India Companion to Sociology and Social Anthropology* (Oxford University Press, 2003) 1400.

[69] ibid.

[70] Bhuwania (n 66) 1, 5–6.

The status quo in India – the dominance of constitutional law – is such that this does not currently seem unnatural. Administrative law, it may seem, is like other 'technical and complex' areas of law. Administrative law cannot be understood by the layperson; it is of no interest to them; no good will come of their non-specialist involvement in the field in any case. What follows will challenge these assumptions.

The problem of poor administration is relevant to the lives of ordinary Indians. The overwhelming popularity of the anti-corruption movement associated with Anna Hazare suggests that ordinary Indians are aware of the importance of good administration. Administrative law, which regulates administrators at every level, including those whom ordinary people are highly likely to encounter, is therefore at least potentially of interest to the general public.

But even if the public has an interest in administrative law, do they have the capacity to understand it? Perhaps not the finer details. But much of administrative law involves holding administrators to the standards of behaviour that would be intuitive to most citizens.[71] Administrators must act fairly; they must not be biased; they must hear from those affected before making a decision; they must give reasons for their decisions; they must honour their promises; they must consistently follow the policies they set for themselves; and they must not do anything which they lack the legal power to do. The basic norms of administrative law can be easily communicated to someone without legal training. They should be easy to understand as they track so closely how a good administrator ought to act (morally speaking).

Even if the public *can* understand basic administrative law and are interested in doing so, why should they? First, it is important that the terms of the relationship between the administrators and those they govern is understood by all involved. If basic administrative law norms were widely understood, this would fundamentally alter everyday interactions between administrators and citizens. The former would moderate their behaviour and the latter would know when administrative behaviour crosses the line. Second, a basic understanding of administrative law would bolster forces for change, both large-scale change as well as individual action through complaint mechanisms.[72] Greater public awareness of administrative law, when combined with the strategies that the Right to Information Act, 2005 and PIL offer, could effect significant change.

B. Courts and Counsel

Reinvigorating administrative law also requires changes to doctrine, and to professional and judicial practice. At the most fundamental level, counsel and judges ought to be alert to administrative law issues in any given case. There are three broad strategies that would help to reinvigorate administrative law.

[71] See, eg, Farrah Ahmed and Adam Perry, 'Standing and Civic Virtue' (2018) 134 *Law Quarterly Review* 239.

[72] See, eg, initiatives like 'I Paid a Bribe': Janaagraha Centre for Citizenship & Democracy, 'I Paid a Bribe', ipaidabribe.com.

i. Constitutional Avoidance in Favour of Administrative Law

Where a matter can be decided on constitutional and non-constitutional grounds, constitutional avoidance refers to the practice of making the decision on non-constitutional grounds. Constitutional avoidance has been defended on the basis that it leads to stronger rights protection[73] because it allows the government greater flexibility,[74] and as a form of decisional minimalism, 'saying no more than necessary to justify an outcome, and leaving as much as possible undecided'.[75] However, there are dangers to constitutional avoidance. Indian administrative law has already been criticised as being overly deferential.[76] Constitutional avoidance may result in even more deferential review of administrative action (albeit that this chapter suggests strengthening administrative law to mitigate this concern). Many remedies are only available under constitutional law (though Ahmed has argued elsewhere for stronger remedies to be available for administrative law breaches).[77] The expressive aspects of the Indian Constitution are also such that citizens may feel hard done by if their constitutional claim is not decided, even if administrative law affords the same or better remedy. Clearly, though, while not always justifiable or feasible, constitutional avoidance in favour of administrative law would do much to reverse the eclipse of administrative law. If, and when, constitutional avoidance is not justified, constitutional law should develop to incorporate or explicitly reference administrative law norms, as the next section discusses.

ii. Referencing Administrative Law

Constitutional decision-making has occupied much of the field – the control of administrative action – that administrative law evolved to regulate. The term 'constitutional decision-making' and not 'constitutional law' is used advisedly here as many of the cases discussed so far demonstrate that decisions are often made appealing to constitutional provisions, but providing little substantive guidance on what is required of administrators.

Putting aside the option of constitutional avoidance, courts could offer clearer guidance to administrators by explicitly referring to administrative law as a source of constitutional norms. This strategy is illustrated by older Supreme Court cases that take an administrative law ground of review – particularly *Wednesbury* unreasonableness – as a guide to (constitutionally prohibited) arbitrariness. In *Kasturi Lal Lakshmi Reddy v State of Jammu and Kashmir*, Bhagwati J recognised that:

> The governmental action must not be arbitrary or capricious ... This rule was enunciated by the Court as a rule of administrative law and it was also validated by the Court as an emanation flowing directly from the doctrine of equality embodied in Article 14.[78]

[73] Ahmed and Khaitan (n 28).
[74] Jeff King, *Judging Social Rights* (Cambridge University Press, 2012) ch 9.
[75] Cass R Sunstein, 'Foreword: Leaving Things Undecided' (1996) 110 *Harvard Law Review* 4, 6.
[76] Baxi, 'Developments in Indian Administrative Law' (n 3); Baxi, 'Introduction' (n 3).
[77] Ahmed and Khaitan (n 28).
[78] *Kasturi Lal Lakshmi Reddy v State of Jammu and Kashmir* AIR 1980 SC 1992.

In *Tata Cellular v Union of India*, almost the entire judgment, decided on Article 14 grounds, is taken up by a detailed discussion of the doctrines of common law judicial review of administrative action.[79] The judgment takes for granted that arbitrariness is assessed by the *Wednesbury* test.[80] In *Om Kumar v Union of India*, the applicants were challenging disciplinary penalties imposed on them (as officers of the Delhi Development Authority) on the basis that they were not proportionate to the gravity of their misconduct.[81] The Supreme Court was very clear about the connection between the Article 14 arbitrariness doctrine and common law grounds of review. It emphasised that 'while judging whether the administrative action is "arbitrary" under Article 14 ... this Court has confined itself to a *Wednesbury* review always'.[82]

Reverting to this approach would represent an advance over the ad hoc decision-making with superficial reference to provisions in the Constitution seen in many cases adjudicated under Article 14.[83]

iii. Strengthening Administrative Law

Upendra Baxi has argued that contemporary Indian administrative law is too deferential to the executive.[84] Courts apply administrative law doctrines, he argues, in a way that does not rigorously hold administrators to account. If we take this worry seriously, we might wonder whether constitutional avoidance, or populating constitutional law with administrative law norms, is really well advised. Some may argue that in fact there is a reason for administrative law to give way even more to constitutional law. For Indian courts, they might suggest, are likely to be least deferential when holding the executive up to constitutional standards of behaviour. The Court's traditional view of itself as the guardian of the Constitution would add vigour and intensity to its scrutiny of administrative action when it is applying constitutional norms.

These are large claims, which are beyond the ambitions of this chapter. Let us assume that there is something to them. There is a need for great judicial creativity in shaping administrative law to address the challenges of poor administration in India, particularly where they affect constitutional rights.[85] I have argued elsewhere that, when fundamental rights are engaged, courts should apply a more demanding standard of administrative review and take a more generous approach to recognising the existence of legitimate expectations.[86] Indian courts may need to

[79] *Tata Cellular v Union of India* AIR 1996 SC 11, Subsequently applied in *New Horizons Ltd v Union of India* [1994] Supp 5 SCR 310.

[80] The judgment in *GB Mahajan v The Jalgaon Municipal Council* also proceeded on this assumption: *GB Mahajan v The Jalgaon Municipal Council* AIR 1991 SC 1153 [19].

[81] *Om Kumar v Union of India* [2000] Supp 4 SCR 693 [1].

[82] ibid [67].

[83] Khaitan (n 7).

[84] Baxi, 'Developments in Indian Administrative Law' (n 3); Baxi, 'Introduction' (n 3).

[85] See Ahmed and Khaitan (n 28).

[86] Courts should also be open to substantive protections for legitimate expectations. See Chandrachud (n 2) on how the Supreme Court's theoretical embrace of substantive protections is belied in practice.

expand the 'traditional' grounds of judicial review for administrative action; it may review for conformity with values of transparency, participation, consultation and accountability, for instance. Constitutional guarantees must be recognised as the legal-foundational background against which administrative law norms should be understood and developed.

CONCLUSION

Constitutional law jurisprudence in India – particularly the expansive interpretation of fundamental rights – has obscured the significance and distinctive nature of administrative law norms. In many cases, courts fail to recognise or respond to breaches of administrative law norms. This chapter has offered an account of the worrying implications of these developments and has made proposals – aimed at both the public and the courts – to reinvigorate administrative law.

Administrative law is not alone. The complaints raised here are echoed in assessments on Indian private law. Shyamkrishna Balaganesh, for instance, concludes that the Indian Supreme Court's 'fusion of constitutional law and tort law has successfully cabined the independent efficacy, normativity, and analytical basis of equivalent private law claims in Indian lower courts'.[87] These complaints, read with this chapter, paint a picture of non-constitutional areas of Indian law withering in the shadow of constitutional jurisprudence.

Nor is Indian law alone in facing these questions. Other jurisdictions which couple a common law heritage with an entrenched constitution – South Africa, for instance – wrestle with their relationship.[88] Thus, innovative ideas emerging from scholarship on comparative administrative law may usefully contribute to the future course of judicial review of administrative action in India.

[87] Shyamkrishna Balganesh, 'The Constitutionalisation of Indian Private Law' in Choudhry et al (n 7) 681.

[88] Cora Hoexter, 'South African Administrative Law at a Crossroads: The PAJA and the Principle of Legality' *Admin Law Blog* (28 April 2017), adminlawblog.org/2017/04/28; Kate O'Regan, 'The Constitution and Administrative Law: Insights from South Africa's Constitutional Journey' *Admin Law Blog* (12 April 2017), adminlawblog.org/2017/04/12.

4

Constitutional Regulation of the Fourth Branch

K VIVEK REDDY

INTRODUCTION

REGULATORY AGENCIES HAVE changed the landscape of governance in India. They have become a preferred administrative response to several challenging socio-economic issues. The government is increasingly becoming an aggregate of various regulatory agencies, leading many commentators to characterise such agencies as a 'fourth branch of government'. Regulatory agencies are based on the premise that experts would run agencies, which would promulgate regulations to meet the challenges of a modern, complex economy.

Although agencies have been present since Indian independence, they became pervasive after the nation transitioned to a market-oriented economy. In the initial phase, agencies were often transplants based on recommendations of international donor agencies. Over time, however, the agency model for regulation has become an accepted, even beloved, feature of modern government.[1] Their appeal is compelling: complex economics require a need for expertise and evidence-based regulation. Unlike departments within the government, where attention is often diffused and subject to several bureaucratic limitations, agencies that focus on one sector carry the promise of responding quickly to emerging situations and problems. Further, they can de-politicise regulation and help to see that it is informed by technical considerations.

The institutional benefits of agencies are well known, and the range of matters that they now cover is staggering. Yet, the precise division of power between an agency and the parliamentary executive has created a number of administrative and constitutional law challenges. In particular, agencies often involve bundling of the state's

[1] See Stephen J Choi and AC Pritchard, 'The SEC's Shift to Administrative Proceedings: An Empirical Assessment' (2017) 34(1) *Yale Journal on Regulation* 1.

regulatory power – the constitutional diffusion of power into the legislative, executive and the judicial arms are blended into one agency for the regulation of a particular sector. Unfortunately, the question of how we resolve some of these tensions has not received due attention in the Indian context. From an administrative law perspective, agencies raise accountability challenges. The current structure of administrative law is designed to deal with the abuse of power by departments of the government. Applying this model to agencies creates an accountability mismatch as they are not structured in the same way as a government department.

This chapter explores these issues and the bigger question of whether the Constitution permits a fourth branch of government.[2] In particular, what limitations are there in relation to the creation and design of agencies? The chapter proceeds through a study of two doctrines that are central to Indian constitutional law: the doctrine of separation of powers and the doctrine of collective responsibility. Both these doctrines have historically operated in competing spaces. While the doctrine of separation of powers contemplates a division of functions and checks and balances, the doctrine of collective responsibility reinforces the fusion of the executive and the legislature. While the former usually operates in a presidential form of government, the latter is an essential characteristic of a parliamentary form of government. In India, the former emanates from constitutional structure, while the latter has a strong textual foundation. Despite their conflicting orientation, both these doctrines have the common objective of holding the state to account for the exercise or non-exercise of power. This chapter first examines the constitutional foundation of both doctrines and the serious concerns over the design and practices of agencies if these doctrines are strictly applied. It then considers the accountability void created by applying the conventional administrative law doctrines to agencies. Specifically, it demonstrates the ineffectiveness of various existing mechanisms to make agencies accountable.

I. CONSTITUTIONAL FOUNDATIONS

A. The Separation of Powers

Once a constitution confers power on the state over its citizens, it also has to design mechanisms which will check any abuse of this power. Conventionally, constitution-makers have used two such mechanisms – bills of rights and the separation of powers. By dividing and diffusing sovereign power, the separation of powers enables each organ to check and balance other organs. The doctrine of separation of powers manifests itself in different ways – horizontal (division of power among the legislative, the executive and the judiciary) and vertical (division of power between the national and state governments). Even amongst each of these institutions, there can be further division of power, for example, in the form of bicameralism and veto rights.

[2] Some of these issues have been gestured at in the debate on tribunals in India. See Arun K Thiruvengadam, 'Tribunals' in Sujit Choudhry, Madhav Khosla and Pratap B Mehta (eds) *The Oxford Handbook of the Indian Constitution* (Oxford University Press, 2016) 412.

With regard to agencies, the doctrine of separation of powers is a major challenge, as it focuses on the design and structure of the government. The Supreme Court has declared this doctrine to be part of the basic structure of the Constitution. In *Clariant International v SEBI*, the Supreme Court warned that the wide jurisdiction conferred upon the Securities and Exchange Board of India (SEBI) would 'run counter to the doctrine of separation of powers'.[3] It highlighted that the vesting of legislative, executive and judicial powers in the same body in the future 'may raise several public law concerns as the principle of control of one body over the other was the central theme underlying the doctrine of separation of powers'.[4]

Since the separation of powers has not been expressly carved out in the constitutional text and operates as a background norm, the extent of applicability of this doctrine in the Indian Constitution deserves careful scrutiny. There are two broad approaches to this doctrine: the formalist and the functional.[5] The formalist approach to the doctrine of separation of powers pre-supposes that a constitution draws sharply defined and judicially enforceable lines amongst the three distinct branches of government.[6] Formalists assume that there is a free-standing separation of powers doctrine in a constitution and that the structure of the government should not fall foul of the formal lines of separation.[7] Justice Louis Brandeis illustrated this formalist approach when he observed that the purpose of the separation of powers was 'not to promote efficiency but to preclude the exercise of arbitrary power. The purpose was not to avoid friction, but, by means of the inevitable friction incident to the distribution of the governmental powers among three departments, to save the people from autocracy'.[8] The formalist approach extensively uses the language of 'encroachment', when one organ takes on the power of other organs. One branch aggrandising itself at the expense of others is a deeply disturbing feature for the formalist.

In contrast, functionalists reject the notion that 'the constitution contemplates a complete division of authority between the three branches' and instead stress that 'the separation of powers contemplates the integration of disbursed work into a workable government'.[9] The functionalist approach proceeds on the assumption that a constitution gives limited guidance about the exact nature of the allocation of governmental power among the branches. The functionalist approach focuses on maintaining balance in the division of power and ensuring adequate checks and balances as opposed to a strict division of power. The functionalist would ask the question whether a scheme or a structure of a governmental entity 'disrupts the proper

[3] *Clariant International v SEBI* (2004) 8 SCC 524 [75].

[4] ibid.

[5] See John F Manning, 'Separation of Powers as Ordinary Interpretation' (2011) 124 *Harvard Law Review* 1939.

[6] See Gary Lawson, 'The Territorial Government and the Limits of Formalism' (1990) 78 *California Law Review* 853, 859–60.

[7] Manning (n 5) 1944.

[8] *Myers v United States* 272 US 52, 293 (1926) (Brandeis J dissenting).

[9] See Manning (n 5) 1944, citing the US Supreme Court in *Nixon v Administrator of General Services* 433 US 425, 443 (1977) and *Mistretta v United States* 488 US 361, 386 (1989).

balance between the co-ordinate branches'.[10] Under the functionalist approach, the judicial role is confined to determining whether an enactment creating an entity 'so alters the balance of authority among the branches of government as to pose a genuine threat to the basic division of power'.[11] The functionalist would give substantial room for manoeuvre to the state on the design of the institutions as long as the design ensures adequate checks and balances. The focus is on preserving an overall balance of power and not on a strict line of separation. The functionalist would emphasise not only the separation of powers, but also the interlocking features whereby power is shared amongst the three organs. The emphasis is thus on the balance between the three organs and not the strict separation of power.[12]

The contrast between both approaches is crucial for determining how we approach regulatory agencies. Globally, the rise of the administrative state and the fourth branch of government is being challenged under the banner of the separation of powers. In the United States, which is the flag-bearer of this doctrine, courts and commentators have struggled to reconcile this doctrine with the powers that agencies deploy.[13] The fight against the expanding role of the administrative state is subsumed into the larger struggle between the progressives and conservatives regarding the role of the state. This is manifest in the judicial invalidation of the powers of agencies and restrictions on their ability to act outside the three branches of government.[14]

In India, the doctrine of separation of powers has been a judicial discovery. Even though there is no clear-cut demarcation of legislative, executive and judicial power in the Indian Constitution, there are provisions which do suggest a modest separation of powers. Article 50 requires the state to take steps to separate the judiciary from the executive. Article 246 confers legislative power on Parliament and the state legislatures, while Articles 53 and 154 confer the executive power on the President and the Governor. But there is also extensive functional overlap. The Constitution contains provisions where the legislature performs judicial functions (such as the impeachment of judges), the executive performs legislative functions (such as the issuing of ordinances by the President and Governor), the executive exercises judicial functions (such as the disqualification of a member of a House of Parliament) and so forth.

Despite these extensive functional overlaps, the Supreme Court has held that this doctrine of separation of powers forms part of the basic structure of the Indian Constitution. This was not always the case. In an early case, the Supreme Court, in an advisory opinion on delegated legislation, held that this doctrine had 'no place in the system of Government' envisaged by the Indian Constitution.[15] But this

[10] *Nixon v Administrator of General Services* 433 US 425, 443 (1977).

[11] *Borosher v Synar* 478 US 714, 776 (1986).

[12] Cynthia R Farina, 'Statutory Interpretation and the Balance of Power in the Administrative State' (1989) 89 *Columbia Law Review* 452, 496.

[13] See Gillian E Metzger, '1930s Redux: The Administrative State under Siege' (2017) 131 *Harvard Law Review* 1.

[14] This is revealed by a number of rulings from the US Supreme Court which suggest that central features of the modern administrative state may be unconstitutional. See ibid.

[15] *In Re Delhi Laws Act, 1912* AIR 1951 SC 332 [18].

position gradually changed. In *Ram Jawaya Kapoor*, the Court held that the doctrine is not recognised 'in its absolute rigidity', but there has been a sufficient differentiation of powers and 'consequently, it can very well be said that our constitution does not contemplate assumption, by organ or part of the state, of functions that essentially belong to the other'.[16] In 1964, the Supreme Court, in another advisory opinion, invoked the doctrine of separation of powers to assert judicial review over the actions of the house dealing with privileges.[17] In 1973, the doctrine was declared to be part of the basic structure of the Constitution of India.[18] Justice Shelat emphasised that the Constitution created a 'system of checks and balances by reason of which powers are so distributed that none of the three organs it sets up becomes so predominant as to disable the others from exercising and discharging powers and functions entrusted to them'.[19] Subsequently, the doctrine was held to invalidate the thirty-ninth constitutional amendment which contemplated parliamentary adjudication of disputes.[20] In 2007, a bench of nine judges of the Supreme Court held that 'the principles of equality and rule of law would be "redundant" if the legislative, executive and judicial powers are vested in one organ'.[21] The new position was firmly settled by 2012, when the Court declared that 'there is a distinct and rigid separation of powers under the Indian Constitution'.[22] Later, the doctrine was characterised as 'an essential constituent of rule of law'[23] and a violation of this doctrine to be a 'negation of equality under Article 14'.[24]

A close study of these rulings suggests that the Supreme Court emphasised a formal approach toward the separation of powers when judicial power was being threatened, but departed from this approach when the scope of legislative and executive powers was in question. When a scheme which allocated funds to Members of Parliament for development work was challenged on the ground that executive functions were being vested in the legislature, the Court adopted a functionalist approach when it held that the Constitution did not prohibit overlapping functions, but rather the exercise of functions by a branch in a way which 'results in wresting away of the regime of constitutional accountability'.[25] The Court found that there were adequate checks and balances in relation to the utilisation of the funds. It is evident that the separation of powers doctrine has been used to strengthen the independence of the judiciary rather than to demarcate and police boundaries between the three organs.

In a recent ruling, the Supreme Court considered the correct formulation of the doctrine. In *Kalpana Mehta*, the question arose as to whether a court in the exercise

[16] *Ram Jawaya Kapoor v State of Punjab* (1955) 2 SCR 225 [231].

[17] *In Re Powers, Privileges and Immunities of State Legislatures, Special Reference No 1 of 1964* [1965] 1 SCR 413 [38].

[18] *Kesavananda Bharati v State of Kerala* (1973) 4 SCC 225 [292] (Chief Justice Sikri observed that the separation of powers between the legislature, the executive and the judiciary is a feature of the basic structure of the Constitution).

[19] ibid [577].

[20] *Indira Gandhi v Raj Narain* 1975 Supp SCC 1 [691].

[21] *IR Coelho v State of Tamil Nadu* (2007) 2 SCC 1 [129].

[22] *State of UP v Sanjay Kumar* (2012) 8 SCC 537 [16].

[23] *State of Tamil Nadu v State of Kerala* (2014) 12 SCC 696 [126].

[24] ibid.

[25] *Bhim Singh v Union of India* (2010) 5 SCC 538 [78].

of its powers of judicial review can place reliance upon the report of the parliamentary standing committee.[26] The state contended that the doctrine of separation of powers would prevent the courts from subjecting the reports of the parliamentary standing committee to review. Justice DY Chandrachud, in his concurring opinion, explored the formalist and functional approach of doctrine of separation of powers, and concluded that:

> [W]hile the separation of powers, as a principle, constitutes the cornerstone of our democratic constitution, its application in the actual governance of the policy is nuanced. The nuances of the doctrine recognize that while the essential functions of the one organ of the state cannot be taken over by the other and that a sense of institutional comity must guide the work of the legislature, executive, and judiciary, the practical problems which arise in the unfolding of democracy can be resolved through robust constitutional cultures and mechanisms. The separation doctrine cannot be reduced to its descriptive content, bereft of its normative features. Evidently, it has both normative and descriptive features. In applying it to the Indian Constitution, the significant precept to be borne in mind is that no institution of governance lies above the Constitution. No entrustment of power is absolute.[27]

The ruling endorses the functionalist approach when it speaks of nuances, institutional comity and practical problems. These concepts are an anathema to the formalist approach with its insistence on rigid lines of separation. But it also encompasses the formalist approach when it asserts that the 'essential' functions cannot be encroached upon by other organs. The challenge is to identify the essential functions which cannot be taken over by other organs.

B. Collective Responsibility

Allied to the doctrine of separation of powers, the doctrine of collective responsibility directly implicates the design and structure of regulatory agencies. Unlike the doctrine of separation of powers, there is an explicit textual basis for this doctrine in the Indian Constitution – Article 75 mandates that Council of Ministers headed by the Prime Minister 'shall be collectively responsible to the House of People'. The Cabinet is thus answerable to the legislature for its actions and its policies. This principle had been held to be part of the basic structure of the Constitution of India.[28]

Agencies are, by their very nature, designed to be independent of the political executive. Their institutional merit lies in being outside the political control of the elected executive. The executive cannot be held accountable for the actions of agencies when it has no role in the policies or functioning of agencies. Unlike the elected

[26] *Kalpana Mehta v Union of India* (2018) 7 SCC 1.
[27] ibid [256].
[28] *Kesavananda Bharati* (n 18).

executive, there is an accountability deficit with regard to agencies since they are neither elected nor subject to ministerial responsibility of the legislature. Even when Parliament frames standards, the statutory limitations upon agencies are often vague. There is considerable scope for autonomy in terms of how legislative standards are applied by agencies.[29]

In the United Kingdom, which adopts a parliamentary form of government, William Wade noted that the design of agencies involves 'a sharp departure from the principle of ministerial responsibility'.[30] A committee of the House of Lords similarly recognised the accountability gap in the functioning of agencies.[31] In India, the concern over ministerial responsibility is perhaps even more serious, given its express constitutional basis.

Where do we locate regulatory agencies within the Indian Constitution? The Constitution does not provide a clear answer. It contains a limited vesting clause conferring powers on the legislature,[32] the executive[33] and the judiciary.[34] There is an express vesting clause of the executive power in the President and the Governor.[35] The prominent exceptions of bodies that exist outside the executive are the Election Commission and the Comptroller and Auditor General, but these institutions were deliberately meant to lie outside the three branches of the government and scrutinise the democratic process. Although there is a reference to the Reserve Bank of India (RBI) in the entries on the Union of India's legislative powers, the Constitution is silent on the powers that can be conferred.[36]

Article 53 vests the executive power of the Union of India in the President and cautions that this executive power 'shall be exercised by him either directly or through officers sub-ordinate to him in accordance with this constitution'. Thus, for agencies to fit within the executive department, they must satisfy two limitations. First, the agency has to be subordinate to the President, which effectively means the Council of Ministers. Is this constitutional subordination of the executive satisfied when an agency is created which has functions that are independent of the Union Cabinet? Second, all exercises of power by an agency are subject to constitutional limitations. In other words, agency design cannot permit exercise of powers that would undermine either Cabinet responsibility or the review of its actions by the judiciary.

[29] See SEBI Act, 1992, s 11(1) of which obliges SEBI 'to protect the interests of investors in securities and to promote the development of, and to regulate the securities market, by such measures as it thinks fit'. It is the prerogative of SEBI to devise standards and regulations as to how it will develop and regulate the securities market.

[30] HWR Wade and CF Forsyth, *Administrative Law*, 11th edn (Oxford University Press, 2014) 116.

[31] See Select Committee on the Constitution, *The Regulatory State: Ensuring its Accountability*, HL 2003–04, 68-I.

[32] See Constitution of India, arts 79, 245 and 246.

[33] See ibid art 53.

[34] See ibid art 32, 226, 124 and 214.

[35] See ibid art 53 and 154.

[36] See ibid, Entry 38, List I, Seventh Schedule.

II. AGENCIES AND THE CONSTITUTION

A. The Bundling of Powers

The major concern with regulatory agencies is the confluence of legislative, executive and judicial power in the same body.[37] In several agencies, the same body formulates rules, enforces them and adjudicates them. This confluence is exacerbated by the absence of internal division of power – the same personnel formulate the norms, oversee the enforcement of the norms and adjudicate any disputes arising from these norms. A glaring example of this is SEBI, which is governed by a Board comprising a chairman and members.[38] This Board exercises legislative power when it frames norms for market participants, executive power when it calls for information and enforces these norms against market players, and judicial power when it interprets and adjudicates any disputes arising from these regulations.[39] Although SEBI has created a separate cadre of 'Adjudicating Officers' who are appointed by the SEBI board for adjudicating any violation of the Securities and Exchange Board of India Act, 1992, the board has concurrent jurisdiction for enforcing any violation and often exercises it.[40]

Agencies also issue guidelines which interpret and resolve the ambiguity in their own regulations. When the power to write a law and to interpret it rests in the same agency, it raises several concerns relating to the separation of powers.[41] In an agency when this law-making and interpretive power rests in the same personnel, there is a tendency to push the law in a direction that is not discernible from the text of the regulations. When an agency issues interpretative guidelines, it is not required to go through the cumbersome process of rule-making. An agency with dual powers could announce new rules in the course of administrative adjudication. The larger question – if there is an ambiguity, to what extent should the courts defer to the agency interpretation of the parent statute and its own regulations – is yet to receive serious judicial attention in India.[42]

Executive adjudication raises graver concerns. In the traditional approach towards agencies, the executive's role was confined to the supervision of regulated entities. If a regulatory entity violated a role, the agency (by virtue of its expertise) would investigate the violation of the laws and regulations, and pursue enforcement action in a court of law. An agency could not, by itself, impose sanctions, and the

[37] In the American context, see Justice Gorsuch's opinion in *Gutierrez-Brizuela v Lynch* 834 F 3d 1142, 1149 (2016) (10th Cir).

[38] See Securities Exchange Board of India Act, 1992 (SEBI 1992), s 4.

[39] ibid ss 29, 30 and 11.

[40] ibid s 11c.

[41] See Justice Antonin Scalia's opinion in *Decker v Northwest Environmental Defense Center* 133 S Ct 1326 (2013).

[42] In the US, judicial deference to agency interpretation of its own parent statutes (*Chevron v Natural Resources Defense Council* 467 US 837, 865–66 (1984)) and judicial deference to agency regulations (*Auer v Robbins* 519 US 452, 461 (1997)) has raised a cottage industry on separation of powers concerns. See Cass Sunstein and Adrian Vermeule, 'The New Coke: On the Plural Aims of Administrative Law' [2015] *Supreme Court Review* 1.

adjudication before a court of law was a check on agency power. Only in rare exceptions would agencies adjudicate violations. Over the years, administrative adjudication has become the norm. These agencies decide cases that they themselves have investigated and decided to bring, under rules that they themselves have made.

Executive adjudication allows the agency to become a complainant/investigator/prosecutor/adjudicator. This may be illustrated through the SEBI Act, 1992. Under the SEBI Act, the SEBI board can issue a show-cause notice,[43] call for information,[44] conduct an investigation (by recording oral and written evidence),[45] prosecute the matter on the basis of the investigation[46] and finally adjudicate the matter.[47] The recent Finance Act, 2018 further enables the SEBI board to pass penalty orders for violating the provisions of the Act.[48] The SEBI board is thus a super-regulator. Not only would it exercise legislative powers, but it would also be able to authorise an enforcement action for a violation of the Act, oversee investigation and prosecution, and now exercise core judicial power by imposing penalties. And for good measure, it can approve a settlement for any violation of the Act. A violation of the SEBI Act becomes an in-house affair with no oversight from any external agency. In addition, a classic characteristic of a judicial function is that the adjudicator does not defend its action in a higher forum since it is not interested in the subject matter of the dispute. However, in agencies, the adjudicator also becomes the appellant, thereby compromising the independent element of adjudication.

Executive adjudication raises constitutional concerns. It is incompatible with the bedrock principle of natural justice of *nemo iudex in sua causa* – no man should be a judge of his own cause. This principle has long been a major justification for judicial review in a constitutional democracy.[49] This principle, which has its basis in administrative law, has now been elevated to a constitutional standard.[50] The absence of any checks violates even the functional approach to separation of powers. In the US, the Administrative Procedure Act requires that separate personnel perform the functions of investigation and prosecution on the one hand and adjudication on the other.[51]

Executive adjudication would also concern the functionalist, since it leads to a dilution of checks and balances. The US Supreme Court initially permitted executive adjudication on the principle that a combination of functions is necessary to secure expert administrative decision-making in a complex society and that the development of expertise would be hamstrung if agencies could not shape their

[43] SEBI 1992, s 11, 11(4), and 11B.

[44] ibid s 11(2)(ia), 11(2)(ib).

[45] ibid s 11c.

[46] ibid.

[47] ibid s 15I.

[48] Finance Act, 2018, s 179.

[49] See *Marbury v Madison* 5 US (1 Cranch) 137, 176 (1803): 'To what purpose are powers limited, and to what purpose is the limitation committed to writing, if these limits may, at any time, be passed by those intended to be restrained?'

[50] See *Union of India v Tulsiram Patel* (1985) 3 SCC 398 [72].

[51] 5 USC 554(d)(2) (2006). However, there is an exemption for top-level agency heads. See generally Adrian Vermeule, *The Constitution of Risk* (Cambridge University Press, 2014) 119, 120.

own regulatory agendas.[52] However, in a series of cases, the Supreme Court questioned the structure of agencies on the basis of the separation of powers doctrine.[53] Justice Neil Gorsuch, when serving on the US Court of Appeals for the Tenth Circuit, warned against permitting 'executive bureaucracies to swallow huge amounts of *core* judicial and legislative power'.[54] The Supreme Court invalidated provisions where an agency head could only be removed for cause as it impaired the ability of the President to oversee the control of the executive.[55] Chief Justice Roberts in a dissenting opinion observed that Congress cannot exercise judicial power on persons who do not have the safeguards enjoyed by judges.[56] In a recent ruling, the US Supreme Court held that any person who is facing an administrative enforcement proceeding within the Securities and Exchange Commission (SEC) is entitled to be heard by an adjudicating authority who is not just an employee of the SEC, but is an officer under the US Constitution (the appointment of an officer is subject to the Appointment Clause of the US Constitution, which is not the case in relation to an employee).[57]

In India, agency structure coupled with the enormous confluence of functions is yet to be tested on the basis of the separation of powers. To date, the Supreme Court has focused on the structure of tribunals and on ensuring its independence.[58] With respect to agencies, the Court has been more attuned to the nature of the personnel manning the agencies rather than the usurpation of the core functions or the checks and balances on the agency. For instance, in *State of Gujarat v Utility Users Welfare Association*,[59] the Court examined whether the functions of the Electricity Regulatory Commission were adjudicative in character and called for a member with judicial expertise. It did not ask the bigger question – whether there were sufficient checks and balances in the structure of the Commission. It came close to addressing this question in the case of the Competition Commission, where it suggested that the creation of two bodies within the Commission performing adjudicatory functions and the advisory/regulatory functions would satisfy the separation of power concerns and would be in line with global standards.[60]

B. Broad Mandates

Under conventional administrative law, the doctrine of ultra vires was a major safeguard to keep governmental action in check – the government as a delegatee cannot

[52] See *Withrow v Larkin* 421 US 35,47, 49–50 (1975). See generally Ilya Shapiro and Caitlyn W McCarthy, 'Are Federal Agencies the Sole Judges of Their Own Authority?' (2011) 34 *Regulation* 4, 5; Gary Lawson 'The Rise and Rise of the Administrative State' (1994) 107 *Harvard Law Review* 1231, 1248.

[53] See Metzger (n 13).

[54] *Gutierrez-Brizuela v Lynch* (n 37).

[55] *Free Enterprise Fund v Public Company Accounting Oversight Board* 561 US 477 (2010).

[56] *Wellness International v Sharif* 135 S Ct 1932 (2015).

[57] *Lucia v Securities and Exchange Commission*, US Supreme Court (21 June 2018).

[58] See Thiruvengadam (n 2).

[59] 2018 SCC OnLine SC 368 [114]; see also *Tamil Nadu Generation and Distribution Corporation Ltd v PPN Power Generating Company Private Ltd* (2004) 11 SCC 53.

[60] *Brahm Dutt v Union of India* (2005) 2 SCC 431.

go beyond the boundaries defined by the legislature. However, the application of this doctrine to regulatory agencies has been a challenge because their mandates are often defined in vague and open-ended terms. The classic instance of the wide ramifications of open-ended mandates is the Supreme Court ruling in the *Sahara* case.[61] SEBI was created in the early 1990s to regulate the securities market and in particular listed securities, and the regulation of unlisted securities fell under the domain of the Central Government.[62] However, Parliament defined SEBI's mandate 'to protect the interest of the investors in securities … by such measures as it thinks fit'.[63] This broad language was used by SEBI to regulate even unlisted securities. When this position was challenged, the Supreme Court relied on the expansive mandate in the SEBI Act to support SEBI's position.[64] Similarly, the language in the Telecom Regulatory Authority of India (TRAI) Act, 1997, enabling the TRAI to frame regulations 'consistent with purposes of the Act', was relied upon by the Supreme Court when it held that the legislative power of the TRAI to frame regulations is not even limited by the actual functions of the TRAI.[65]

The sole exception to this principle seems to be the Supreme Court ruling in *Petroleum and Natural Gas Regulatory Board (PNGRB) v Indraprastha Gas Ltd.*[66] The PNGRB framed regulations fixing the maximum retail price at which gas could be sold to the consumers. When this power was challenged, the PNGRB relied extensively on the broad language of the Petroleum and Natural Gas Regulatory Board Act, 2006, which created the PNGRB and conferred on it the powers to 'regulate the refining, processing, storage, transportation, distribution, marketing and sale of petroleum, petroleum products and natural gas … so as to protect the interest of consumers and entities'.[67] Despite this power, the Supreme Court held that the power to fix tariffs was not expressly conferred and, in the absence of such a conferral, the power could not be exercised. This approach is encouraging as it requires the legislature to expressly specify agency powers and prevent usurpation through an open-ended mandate.[68]

Open-ended mandates also lead to agencies exercising power in areas covered by other statutes enacted by the legislature. The TRAI invoked its power to regulate telecommunications to regulate even broadcasting content and pricing of the content, an area which was beyond its expertise and was covered by other statutes (including the Copyright Act, 1957). When the exercise of this power was challenged, a Division Bench of the Madras High Court struggled over this issue, given the lack of guidance in the TRAI Act, and the Court was left with the unenviable task of reconciling

[61] *Sahara India Real Estate Corporation Ltd v SEBI* (2013) 1 SCC 1.

[62] See Companies Act 1956, s 55.

[63] SEBI 1992, s 11B.

[64] *Sahara* (n 61) 304.5 and 305.

[65] See *BSNL v TRAI* (2014) 3 SCC 222 [100], holding that the power to frame regulations under s 36 of the TRAI Act is untrammelled by s 36(2) or ss 11, 12 and 13.

[66] *Petroleum and Natural Gas Regulatory Board (PNGRB) v Indraprastha Gas Ltd* (2015) 9 SCC 209.

[67] ibid [14].

[68] It is interesting to note that in this case, the Central Government did not support the Regulatory Authority's assumption of power.

an express right conferred by parliamentary statute with the exercise of regulatory power by a delegate.[69] A bench of the two judges of the Madras High Court differed on the issue of the powers of the TRAI to regulate broadcasting content. On appeal, the Supreme Court upheld the TRAI's power by relying on the expansive language of the TRAI Act to protect the interests of stakeholders and consumers.[70]

Finally, broad mandates to agencies often lead to conflicts with other agencies, thereby undermining the overall regulatory regime. Agency decisions end up being reflective of 'tunnel vision', ie, the agency's supreme confidence in the importance of its own mission.[71] This is illustrated in the jurisdictional battle between SEBI and the Insurance Regulatory and Development Authority (IRDA) over Unit Linked Insurance Plans (ULIPs), which are insurance products with an investment component. SEBI, exercising its broad mandate under the SEBI Act, banned 14 life insurance firms from issuing fresh ULIP schemes. The IRDA, in response, asked the insurance firms to ignore the SEBI order. The dispute was referred to the Finance Ministry, which advised the insurance firms to resolve the matter judicially. Eventually, an Ordinance was issued amending the SEBI Act to remove regulation of ULIPs from the SEBI's purview.[72]

C. The Exercise of Legislative Power

In several enactments, Parliament and the state legislatures delegate law-making power to the government. Administrative law mandates that when the government as a delegate exercises legislative power, it is in the same position as the legislature. Any law-making power exercised by the government within the scope of its delegated authority is entitled to the same deference and privilege attributable to a legislative act. The delegate is not required to comply with the principles of natural justice and is not under any compulsion to give reasons or give a hearing to the affected parties. If the rules framed by the government are challenged in a court of law, the rules are entitled to the same judicial deference as any law made by the legislature.[73] This traditional principle had an internal logic as the government was accountable to the legislature for its actions. The judiciary was thus required to defer to the government and restrain itself from undertaking any substantive review.

However, extending the same principle to agencies creates several accountability challenges. Several enactments creating agencies confer a vast legislative power. When the exercise of legislative power by agencies is challenged, courts often equate

[69] *Star India Private Ltd v Department of Industrial Policy & Promotion*, Madras High Court (2 March 2018).

[70] The TRAI regulations in question put a cap on pricing and discounts on packages offered by broadcasters to consumers. For the Supreme Court verdict, see *Star India v Department of Industrial Policy and Promotion*, Civil Appeal No 7326-7327 of 2018 (30 October 2018).

[71] Stephen Breyer, 'The Executive Branch, Administrative Action, and Comparative Expertise' (2011) 32 *Cardozo Law Review* 2189, 2190.

[72] Securities and Insurance Laws (Amendment and Validation) Act, 2010.

[73] See *Common Cause (A Registered Society) v Union of India* (2010) 11 SCC 528 [18], [19].

governmental law-making to agency law-making and extend the same deference given to governmental law-making to agency law-making. This extension creates several accountability mismatches. Unlike governments, agencies are not directly accountable to the legislature for their law-making. If an agency adopts a particular standard, the political executive avoids accountability for these decisions by disclaiming its role.

The accountability mismatch created by extending conventional administrative law principles to agencies is vividly illustrated by the ruling of the Supreme Court in *PTC India v Central Electricity Regulatory Commission (CERC)*.[74] The CERC was an agency created by the Electricity Act, 2003 to regulate the tariff for the generation and transmission of electricity. Like other agencies, the CERC was given the expansive power to 'make regulations consistent with this act and the rules generally to carry out the provisions of this act'.[75] In the exercise of its law-making power, the CERC issued regulations fixing a trading margin for interstate trading of electricity. The validity of these regulations was challenged before the Appellate Tribunal for Electricity created under the Electricity Act. The question arose as to whether an appellate tribunal can entertain a challenge on the validity of the law-making power. Conventional administrative law mandated that the invalidity of law-making power by the government can only be done in a public law remedy before the High Court or Supreme Court and not by invoking statutory remedies. The Supreme Court extended this principle to agencies by holding that any law-making power of an agency cannot be scrutinised by an appellate tribunal and can only be done by way of a judicial review challenge before the High Court or the Supreme Court.

The difficulty with this approach is that the law-making power of expert bodies like agencies is filled with technical standards which may not be ideally suited for effective scrutiny before a High Court. The exercise of ascertaining whether agency law-making is consistent with the statute in question and advances the purpose of the statute can be more effectively done by an expert tribunal than by a constitutional court, whose focus would be confined to whether the exercise of law-making power falls within the broad scope of delegation. Since agencies are not accountable to the legislature, the law-making power must be subject to intense scrutiny. If an agency becomes a victim of the regulatory capture, a broad and conventional public law remedy would be an inadequate remedy.

In the US, the Administrative Procedure Act, 1946 (APA) enables the courts to reject agency actions that are 'arbitrary, capricious, an abuse of discretion, or otherwise not in accordance with law'.[76] This standard has been used for 'resolutions of factual disputes implicating substantial agency expertise'.[77] From the APA requirement of every agency to give a 'concise general statement of their basis and purpose' for rules framed by it, the courts have evolved the 'hard look' review, which demands

[74] *PTC India v Central Electricity Regulatory Commission* (2010) 4 SCC 603.
[75] Electricity Act, 2003, s 178(1).
[76] 5 USC § 706(2)(A).
[77] See *Marsh v Oregon Natural Resources Council* 490 US 360, 376 (1989).

detailed explanation from agencies as to how the exercise of law-making power conforms to the mandate of the statute.[78]

In India, the only green shoot has been the Supreme Court ruling in *COAI v TRAI*.[79] This case dealt with 'call drops'. The TRAI, in the exercise of its legislative powers, framed call drop regulations penalising the telecom entity for every drop in phone calls, even in cases where the telecom entity was not at fault. The Supreme Court ruled that the TRAI call drop regulations defeated the purpose of the TRAI Act, which required the TRAI to ensure growth of the telecom industry.[80] Further, the regulation failed to meet the requisite standard of care and deliberation required, as it imposed penalties on the service provider without cause. The Court raised important concerns about the TRAI pre-determination of penalties.[81] It held that, prior to issuing regulations, the TRAI must hold due consultation with all stakeholders and allow stakeholders to make their submissions. All decisions must be fully documented and explained. This is a classic case of administrative common law being used to fill a statutory void. This decision is promising and may have important implications for the judicial review of agency action. The Court also urged Parliament to frame a law along the lines of the American APA.[82]

This is not the only arena where regulatory agencies have challenged conventional administrative law. Since the early case of *In Re Delhi Laws Act*, the Supreme Court has invalidated several pieces of legislation where a statute delegated the essential law-making function to the elected executive on the premise that the legislature must normally discharge its primary legislative function itself and not through others.[83] The Court has reasoned that the legislature cannot abdicate its essential legislative functions and, while entrusting power to an outside agency, such agency does not become a parallel legislature. There is a good reason for drawing some limitations to delegation. A delegate does not have the same democratic pedigree as the legislature and cannot be placed in the same position as the legislature. The application of this restraint on the delegating power of the legislature is a major challenge when it comes to conferring law-making power on unelected agencies. SEBI, IRDA and TRAI are mini-legislatures that have erected a complete legislative framework. Since delegation has become the backbone of the modern administrative states, there is now a formal abandonment of the limits of delegation.

III. ENFORCING ACCOUNTABILITY IN PRACTICE

What current mechanisms exist for the enforcement of agency accountability? Although the design and structure of India's regulatory agencies vary considerably,

[78] Sunstein and Vermeule (n 42).

[79] *Cellular Operators Association v Telecom Regulatory Authority* (2016) 7 SCC 703.

[80] ibid [41(d)] (rejecting the TRAI's submission that it was an active trustee and had framed the impugned regulations for the common good).

[81] *Cellular Operators Association* (n 79) [74].

[82] ibid [92].

[83] *In Re Delhi Laws Act, 1912* (n 15).

the measures that exist to ensure and enforce accountability are largely the same. Each statute creating a regulatory agency typically mandates that the regulations framed by the agency are placed before Parliament within a stipulated time period and that if Parliament modifies the regulations, they will have effect in the modified form; the government is empowered to issue directions to an agency on questions of policy after a prior hearing; agencies furnish reports to the Union on areas that they regulate; appellate tribunals can hear appeals by a party aggrieved by the actions of the agency; and so forth. Are these mechanisms effective in terms of satisfying the separation of powers concerns and ensuring that there are adequate checks and balances on the exercise of powers by regulatory agencies?

Every statute creating an agency invariably mandates that the rules and regulations framed by the agency shall be placed before the Parliament.[84] This ensures parliamentary scrutiny of the legislative power exercised by agencies. While the requirement to place the rules before the legislature has been complied with, the underlying objective of legislative scrutiny has rarely occurred. This is evident from the very few instances where Parliament has intervened to amend the regulations framed by an agency. Importantly, the laying requirement does not mitigate the above-mentioned constitutional concerns, such as excessive delegation, for the simple reason that Parliament does not vote on the regulations. This form of ex post intimation to Parliament, as opposed to formal ex ante approval by Parliament, does not result in effective oversight.

Although laws creating agencies provide and enable extensive legislative scrutiny, this is rarely seen in practice. In other jurisdictions, scrutiny of agencies is performed at a committee level. However, this has not occurred in India due to the absence of a dedicated parliamentary select committee reviewing the functions of each regulatory agency. Currently agencies are reviewed by department-related standing committees, which usually carry out a macro-review of agencies. To date, the only effective review of agencies was done by ad hoc committees of Parliament through Joint Parliamentary Committees, which reviewed telecom licensing and spectrum pricing in 2012 and scrutinised the working of SEBI and RBI in major stock market scams that occurred in 1991 and 2001. It was only pursuant to a 2002 Joint Parliamentary Committee Report that various steps were taken to strengthen the functioning of the regulators – the SEBI Act was amended to strengthen the regulator, interregulatory coordination which was recommended by the Committee was undertaken and quarterly meetings between the RBI and the Enforcement Directorate were instituted.[85] The Second Administrative Reforms Commission in 2009 recommended that legislative oversight of regulators should be performed by sector-specific committees and not a cross-sectoral committee reviewing the working of all regulators.[86]

[84] See Electricity Act, 2003, s 179; SEBI 1992, s 31.

[85] See Joint Parliamentary Committee, *Report on Stock Market Scam and Matters Relating Thereto* (Lok Sabha Secretariat, 2002).

[86] See Second Administrative Reforms Commission, *Organisational Structure of Government of India* (13th Report, Government of India, 2009).

Agencies are also not required to carry out regulatory impact assessment reports which could be reviewed by the public and scrutinised by the select committees of the legislature. This is hardly the situation in other jurisdictions. The Bank of England submits its reports on inflation and market stability to the Treasury Committee of the House of Commons, and its officers have to depose and provide evidence on the Bank's reports. Similarly in the US, the Federal Reserve Board is required to explain its monetary policy stance to the Banking Committee of both Houses twice a year.[87] There is also no structured practice in India through which regulatory bodies are required to minimise the regulatory burden and increase regulatory responsiveness.[88] Indeed, the 2006 Planning Commission consultation paper recognised the importance of a framework that involves a far greater role by Parliament and its committees.[89]

One mechanism for the legislature to effectively check agencies is via the power of the purse. The power to control the budget of the agency will enable the legislature and the executive to control the programmes and agenda of the agency. Historically, any penalties collected by the agency would be deposited in the Consolidated Fund of India. However, agencies have found a way round this in the form of fees and charges for services, which make them self-sufficient and less amenable to legislative control.[90]

Executive checks are another way of providing accountability. Statutes creating regulatory agencies have standard provisions that enable the government to issue directions to agencies.[91] In practice, however, there is little evidence of such power being exercised to control policies. If this power were to be robustly exercised, it could provide an answer to the collective responsibility concerns.

Judicial review has been similarly lacking in effectiveness. Unlike legislative or executive review mechanisms specified in the statute, the remedy of appellate judicial review is the only remedy available to an aggrieved party. As agencies are not subject to the same discipline of accountability as the elected executive, every statute creating the agency invariably constituted an appellate tribunal.[92] The appellate tribunal is usually expected to be an expert tribunal to review the actions of an expert body. It was a key component of the accountability enforcing apparatus. Ironically, however, the appeal process has been undermined by the judiciary itself. In *COAI v UOI*, the Supreme Court applied the conventional administrative law doctrine that the

[87] For a helpful comparative perspective, see PRS Legislative Research, 'Parliamentary Oversight of Regulators' (2012), available at: www.prsindia.org/administrator/uploads/general/1370586800_Parliamentary%20Oversight%20of%20Regulators.pdf.

[88] See Kaushiki Sanyal, 'Regulating the Regulators: Role of Parliament' (2016) 51 *Economic and Political Weekly* 16.

[89] Planning Commission, Government of India, 'Approach to Regulation: Issues and Options' (2006), available at: http://planningcommission.nic.in/reports/genrep/infra_reglawl.pdf.

[90] See Sanyal (n 88).

[91] See SEBI 1992, s 15K; Telecom Regulatory Authority of India Act, 1997, s 14; Electricity Act, 2003, s 110.

[92] Consider, for example, the Telecom Disputes Settlement Appellate Tribunal; the Securities Appellate Tribunal; the Competition Appellate Tribunal; the Food Safety Appellate Tribunal; and the Appellate Tribunal for Electricity.

fact-finding authority of courts is limited and that the judiciary must defer to the findings of the executive.[93] This was based on the traditional administrative law doctrine that the appellate body should not engage in de novo review. But this principle has evolved in the context of the elected executive and broadly at the time when the appellate authority did not comprise experts, which is not the case in modern appellate tribunals.

In *NSDL v SEBI*, the Supreme Court held that the tribunal's jurisdiction is confined only to the quasi-judicial actions involving the resolution of disputes and does not extend to either administrative or legislative actions.[94] This ruling was premised partly on the fact that the regulations framed are subject to legislative scrutiny since they are placed before Parliament.[95] Conventionally, the legislative power exercised by the government is not subject to any appeal and can only be challenged like any other form of legislation before the High Court or the Supreme Court. Yet, as noted above, this premise relies on practices that do not bear out in reality. Unlike the elected executive, which is accountable to the legislature for the exercise of legislative power, agencies are not susceptible to traditional methods of scrutiny and would therefore require more intensive scrutiny.[96] The irony is that the Supreme Court had itself recommended the creation of an expert appellate tribunal to review the exercise of power by an expert regulatory agency.[97] Furthermore, the distinction between the exercise of legislative power and the exercise of executive power in the case of agencies can be nebulous. Tariff fixation, for example, has always been considered to be legislative power and, under the Electricity Act, this power is subject to challenge before the appellate tribunal.[98] Since the appellate tribunal is the only effective forum to scrutinise the actions of agencies, the remedies available to an appellate tribunal should be effective in order to rectify any erroneous determination or wrongdoing by agencies. The England and Wales Court of Appeal was prepared to award substantial damages against erroneous determination made by the energy regulator which deprived the petitioner of financial benefit to which it was legally entitled.[99] This would create some kind of safeguard against the decisions of regulatory agencies.

The current structure of administrative law is designed to deal with agencies when they operate like a conventional government department and therefore insists that agencies issue notices and give reasons for their decision. The emphasis has been on ensuring slow and deliberative action. But with new challenges, agencies are becoming increasingly sophisticated and in their day-to-day practices operate unimpeded by the constraints of constitutional law and administrative law.[100] Financial

[93] *Cellular Operators Association v Union of India*, (2003) 3 SCC 186 [8].

[94] *NSDL v SEBI* (2017) 5 SCC 517.

[95] ibid [25].

[96] See *PTC India Ltd v Central Electricity Regulatory Commission* (2010) 4 SCC 603; *BSNL v TRAI* (2014) 3 SCC 222; *Clariant International v SEBI* (2004) 8 SCC 524 [71], [77].

[97] *West Bengal Electricity Regulatory Commission v CESE Ltd* (2002) 8 SCC 715.

[98] Electricity Act, 2003, s 111 and 121.

[99] See *The Gas and Electricity Markets Authority v Infinis plc & Infinis (Re-Gen) Ltd* [2013] EWCA Civ 70.

[100] See Note, 'Cashing out a Special Relationship? Trends toward Reconciliation between Financial Regulations and Administrative Law' (2017) 130 *Harvard Law Review* 1183.

regulatory agencies like the RBI are required to be decisive and agile, particularly when they are dealing with imperfect information in a crisis. These agencies are compelled to resort to new instruments of regulation like day-to-day supervision, inspection, intrusive queries, calls to regulated entities, advisory correspondence and guidance letters in order to enforce their norms. These are not norm-driven exercises, but rather outcome-driven exercises with a focus on taking quick decisions. Concerns over accountability are based more on achieving the desired result than on norm-based law enforcement. Administrative law, which is still mired in conventional notions of natural justice, requires re-engineering for dealing with new age instruments of regulation.[101]

The appointment of personnel to head agencies creates accountability deficits, since they are not elected and do not report to elected officials. The political executive avoids any accountability for the actions of the agency by asserting that it is maintaining an arm's-length distance from the agency, but at the same time it can nudge (or even direct) the agency in the direction of its choice by playing a role in the appointment of personnel. The power to appoint carries with it the power to influence policies. When political appointees are invariably appointed to head agencies, the agency policy often reflects political and not scientific considerations.[102] The abuse of the appointment power was widely documented in the field of energy regulation, where the agency heads virtually act on the fiat of the political executive ranging from tariff fixation to the removal of subsidies, and the political executive uses the cover of agency to avoid responsibility to the legislature for the agency's actions.[103]

A critical accountability concern with agencies is the issue of regulatory capture (or agency capture), where the regulator ends up advancing the interests of the regulated entities rather than acting in the public interest. This is a major challenge to administrative law, and other jurisdictions are struggling to evolve effective mechanisms to overcome this issue. Regulatory capture also manifests itself when an agency gets tied to an ideology or an approach. Regulatory capture is a complex theme and is beyond the remit of this chapter. In India, there have been complaints of agencies being beholden to a particular entity or being locked into a particular way of thinking.[104] However, it is important to point out that the consensus approach to root out regulatory capture is extensive oversight by other organs, strict judicial scrutiny and rigorous procedures requiring an agency to spell out its rationale for law-making.

[101] See Raeesa Vakil, 'Constitutionalizing Administrative Law in the Indian Supreme Court: Natural Justice and Fundamental Rights' (2018) 16 *International Journal of Constitutional Law* 475.

[102] Stephen Breyer, 'The Executive Branch, Administrative Action, and Comparative Expertise' (2011) 32 *Cardozo Law Review* 2189, 2190.

[103] Electricity Act, 2003, ss 62, 79 and 86; Navroz K Dubash, 'The New Regulatory Politics of Electricity in India: Independent, Embedded or Transcendent?', Paper presented at a workshop on 'The Politics of Necessity' Oxford, 9–10 September 2005, 16–17.

[104] A recent example relates to Reliance's foray into the telecom sector. See Kalpana Pathak, 'Reliance Jio May Expand Testing as Row with Telecom Lobby Reaches PMO', *Live Mint*, 12 August 2016, available at: https://www.livemint.com/Industry/8xP2wtJdiB6HU5SSUnlefI/Reliance-Jio-may-expand-testing-as-COAI-row-reaches-PMO.html.

As demonstrated above, weak legislative oversight and disguised executive control coupled with deferential judicial review provide a fertile breeding ground for regulatory capture in India.

Finally, the structure of regulatory agencies in India also raises larger constitutional accountability concerns. The rise of the regulatory state is marked by the shift in the modes of governance away from the direct provision of services by government to the arm's-length oversight by the government of other providers.[105] Agencies are a key instrument of this oversight model. But the Indian state under the Constitution also has redistributive obligations, which are expressed in the Directive Principles of State Policy. In a diffused regulatory state where sovereign power has been outsourced to multiple agencies, this obligation gets lost. Agencies are wedded to their parent statute and there is no institutional mechanism to ensure that the agencies comply with the broader constitutional responsibilities of the state. This became evident in the field of electricity regulation, where the limited scope of the electricity regulator 'rules out proactive attention to the social or environmental outcomes of reform'.[106]

CONCLUSION

Regulatory agencies occupy a peculiar place in India's constitutional framework. This chapter has highlighted some of the ways in which regulatory agencies stand apart from traditional executive ministries. Consider, for example, the fact that many statutes establishing agencies require that the chairperson and members of the agency can only be removed for cause.[107] How can the executive be accountable for the actions of the agency when it is not in a position to remove the members if their actions diverge from the government's policy? The chapter has also shown the ways in which India's regulatory structure is at odds with traditional public law doctrines. The legal framework in India has not adapted to the changed administrative structure that now governs the nation. India's Parliament has repeatedly given agencies like SEBI additional enforcement tools, and such agencies have managed to translate regulatory failures into broader authority in the form of additional enforcement tools.[108]

There are many ways to alleviate some of the concerns expressed in this chapter. The structure of agencies could be reformed to create an internal separation of powers whereby the same personnel do not perform the law-making, enforcement and adjudicative functions; agencies could be subjected to legislative oversight in the form of periodic reporting, and a dedicated standing committee could be instituted

[105] Colin Scott, 'Regulatory Governance and the Challenge of Constitutionalism' in Dawn Oliver (ed), *The Regulatory State: Constitutional Implications* (Oxford University Press, 2010) 17, 20.

[106] Navroz K Dubash and Sudhir Chellan Ranjan, 'Power Politics, Process of Power Sector Reforms in India' (2001) 36 *Economic and Political Weekly* 3367, 3380.

[107] SEBI 1992, s 6; Electricity Act, 2003, s 90.

[108] See Finance Act, 2018, ss 179, 180 and 182 (conferring additional powers on SEBI).

to scrutinise its functions on the basis of well-defined criteria; there could be the requirement of a rigorous procedure for law-making that requires agencies to hold an evidentiary hearing prior to enacting regulations and to demonstrate the evidence necessitating the proposed laws and its rationale for selecting one approach over the other; there could be much narrower mandates in statute drafting and far more careful judicial scrutiny over whether the agency has conformed to the parent statute; and so forth.

Regulatory agencies have been established, but the tools for making them accountable, and the specific nature and form of independence that they share from the executive are matters that require far greater attention. Constitutional and administrative law, which are focused on the conventional state, need to be re-engineered when it comes to regulatory agencies. Unless the accountability frameworks are strengthened, the objective of regulating the exercise of power risks being compromised.

Part III

Regulatory Domains

5

Securities Markets

UMAKANTH VAROTTIL*

INTRODUCTION

THE LEVEL OF investor protection conferred by law upon minority investors has a strong bearing on the quality and depth of the securities markets in a given economy. The tools employed to protect minority investors include disclosure and transparency rules, corporate governance norms and enforcement of shareholder rights. In several jurisdictions, as in India, the role of securities regulation is performed by a regulatory body that has been conferred the power to prescribe substantive rules of engagement and to enforce them through the power to impose sanctions on perpetrators of non-compliance. Such a regulatory mechanism provides flexibility and adaptability as it is implemented by the country's securities regulator, which is not only intended to be independent, but also possesses a great deal of domain expertise.[1] Given the emphasis on the regulator to craft subordinate legislation governing the securities markets, which it also administers and enforces, the system relies very little on the role of courts to use liability rules by way of private securities enforcement actions brought by investors.

Against this background, the emergence of India's regulator, the Securities and Exchange Board of India (SEBI), at the cusp of India's economic liberalisation is a watershed event as it introduced several groundbreaking reforms to the securities markets that arguably led to an era in which the Indian capital markets witnessed exponential growth, thereby attracting high-quality international investors. More importantly, SEBI's establishment as the earliest regulator of the modern era heralded

* I thank the participants at the Indian Administrative and Regulatory State Conference held in New Delhi in March 2018 and the 15th Asian Law Institute Conference held in Seoul, Korea in May 2018, including Jacques deLisle, Neeraj Grover, Devesh Kapur, Madhav Khosla, Aiman Mohd-Sulaiman, Susan Ostermann, Dan Puchniak, Vivek Reddy, Ajay Shah, TV Somanathan, Somasekhar Sundaresan and Wan Wai Yee, for helpful comments on a previous version of this chapter, and Sanjana Rao for excellent research assistance. Any errors or omissions remain mine alone.

[1] See NK Dubash and B Morgan, 'Understanding the Rise of the Regulatory State of the South' (2012) 6 *Regulation & Governance* 261, 262.

the advent of several other regulators.[2] As a result, it has played an influential role in the evolution of the regulatory state in India.

My goal in this chapter is to analyse the regulatory apparatus governing the capital markets in India and to explore the role and performance of SEBI. After examining the evolution of SEBI, the gradual expansion of its role and its positive impact on the capital markets, I provide a critical account of its structure and performance by discussing certain key issues and controversies surrounding its functioning. I seek to accomplish these goals against the backdrop of the broader framework relating to the rise of the administrative and regulatory state in India.

Interestingly, and unlike the case of several regulators in the utilities sector, SEBI's inception cannot be attributed substantially to external pressures such as conditions imposed by international funding agencies.[3] The need for the creation of a new securities regulator was borne out by internal demand. In that sense, SEBI had the power to chart its own destiny, subject to the circumscriptions set out by Parliament. As the earliest regulator in the post-liberalisation era, and one with a specific focus on the capital markets, SEBI's initial leadership was uniquely positioned to introduce reforms at a scale and speed hitherto unimagined. At the same time, it appears with the benefit of hindsight that SEBI began functioning with a relatively low base of powers to regulate the capital markets, which Parliament had to expand over a period of time through legislative amendments. Viewed from this perspective, the narrative is one of experimental regulation, whereby inadequacies in SEBI's powers experienced during various capital market debacles have compelled it episodically to seek additional authority from the legislature to embolden its functioning as a capital markets regulator.

SEBI's success as a credible regulator has been diluted by several constraints it has encountered in its functioning. Although it has a clear focus on the securities markets, SEBI has often become a victim of the 'siloisation' of the Indian financial sector architecture.[4] Not only has its relationship with government departments such as the Ministry of Corporate Affairs been strained on occasion, but it has often been forced to jostle for power with other regulators overseeing the banking and insurance sectors, which have created pockets of regulatory vacuum.

Like other independent regulators, SEBI operates as a mini-state,[5] exercising (quasi-)legislative (ie, subordinate legislation), executive and (quasi-)judicial functions. While its legislative powers (exercised through regulations, circulars and guidelines) have substantially enhanced the regulatory framework for the securities

[2] AK Thiruvengadam, 'Flag Bearers of a New Era? The Evolution of New Regulatory Institutions in India (1991–2006)' in S Rose-Ackerman, PL Lindseth and B Emerson (eds), *Comparative Administrative Law* (Edward Elgar, 2017) 227; D Raval, 'Improving the Legal Process in Enforcement at SEBI', *IGIDR Working Paper WP-2011-008* (2011) 3, available at www.igidr.ac.in/pdf/publication/WP-2011-008.pdf.

[3] See Thiruvengadam (n 2) 219.

[4] See L Som and F Naru, 'Regulatory Policy in India: Moving towards Regulatory Governance', *OECD Regulatory Policy Working Papers, No 8*, OECD, Paris (2017) 24, available at www.dx.doi.org/10.1787/b335b35d-en.

[5] TV Somanathan, 'The Administrative and Regulatory State' in S Choudhry, M Khosla and PB Mehta (eds), *The Oxford Handbook of the Indian Constitution* (Oxford University Press, 2016) 395; Government of India, *Report of the Financial Sector Legislative Reforms Commission* (vol 1) (2013) 6, 28 (hereinafter 'FSLRC Report').

markets, the independence and accountability of the regulator are determined by the process of regulation-making. While SEBI has been comparatively transparent in its regulatory process, it is arguably inadequate, thereby also raising concerns about the role of interest groups in influencing the shape of the regulation. Greater emphasis on regulatory impact assessment and a more robust and informative consultative mechanism will allay fears of regulatory capture.

Moving on to enforcement, SEBI's role in this realm has invited the most stinging critique. It has enjoyed limited achievement in bringing successful civil actions and criminal prosecution in high-profile insider trading and market manipulation instances (that strike at the heart of the integrity of the capital markets) and mixed success in defending challenges to its enforcement actions before the appellate tribunal. These have invoked the inevitable (and sometimes undue) comparisons with the US Securities and Exchange Commission (SEC), which has enjoyed comparatively greater success in such actions.[6] This necessitates a discussion about the relationship between regulation and the phenomenon of weak state capacity, wherein the implicit assumptions from Western literature about the expertise and capacity of regulators to design and enforce regulation may not be entirely appropriate in an economy like that of India.

Government-appointed committees, academics and other commentators have made proposals for radical reforms to address the issues pertaining to SEBI's regulatory set-up.[7] While some of those measures have been implemented, they have been marginal at best. It is not clear if there is sufficient political will and momentum to bring about reforms of the type required to induce greater technocracy, efficiency, transparency and autonomy that are essential for India's securities regulator to perform its role to the desired extent.

This chapter is organised as follows. Section I examines the evolution and expansion of SEBI's role in India's capital markets. Section II explores the relationship between SEBI and the Central Government as well as other independent regulators, and discusses the impact of regulatory turf wars that have erupted in the past. Section III examines SEBI's quasi-legislative function and how it maintains its independence and accountability. The role of interest groups in regulatory mechanisms is of particular relevance. Section IV considers SEBI's enforcement functions and identifies various shortcomings. Section V touches upon the weaknesses in state capacity in securities regulation and the various reform measures that have been suggested to improve its human resources.

I. EVOLUTION AND EXPANSION OF SEBI'S ROLE IN INDIA'S CAPITAL MARKETS

SEBI's emergence into the regulatory scene was in response to the need to create an independent regulator that is not impeded by the political environment. Under the

[6] See S Bose, 'Securities Market Regulations: Lessons from US and Indian Experience' (2005) *ICRA Bulletin* 83.

[7] See, eg, FSLRC Report (n 5); Planning Commission, Government of India, *A Hundred Small Steps: Report of the Committee on Financial Sector Reforms* (Sage Publications, 2009).

erstwhile position, the securities markets were regulated directly by the Government of India. Securities legislation consisted of the Securities Contracts (Regulation) Act, 1956 (SCRA), the Capital Issues (Control) Act, 1947 and the Companies Act, 1956. The primary securities legislation, the SCRA, was administered by the stock exchanges that were within the control of the Stock Exchange Division of the Department of Economic Affairs in the Ministry of Finance.[8] Primary markets in the form of issuance of securities to the public were overseen by the Controller of Capital Issues (CCI). The CCI had to approve each public offering of securities and its terms, including the price at which securities were to be offered.[9] Such a merit-based approach[10] involved extensive governmental oversight. Due to the resulting stringency in accessing the capital markets, public offerings of shares were not that prevalent.[11]

It is in these circumstances that SEBI was established in 1988, initially as an advisory body, to fulfil the twin objectives of promoting a healthy development of securities markets and ensuring adequate investor protection.[12] In 1992, SEBI was granted the status of a statutory authority under an ordinance, which then took the form of the Securities and Exchange Board of India Act, 1992 (SEBI Act). As a body corporate with separate legal personality, SEBI has been granted autonomy as a regulator.[13]

SEBI is helmed by a board of up to nine members comprising a chairperson, two members nominated from among officials of the Government of India, one from among officials of the Reserve Bank of India (RBI) and five others to be appointed by the Central Government.[14] SEBI also enjoys financial autonomy as it can meet its expenditure from fees and charges it levies without relying on the government.[15]

At the same time, concerns have been raised regarding the availability of certain powers of the Central Government that may impinge upon SEBI's autonomous functioning.[16] These include the power to remove the chairperson[17] and the

[8] G Sabarinathan, 'Securities and Exchange Board of India and the Indian Capital Markets: A Survey of the Regulatory Provisions', *IIM Bangalore Research Paper No 228* (2004) 10, available at www.ssrn.com/abstract=2152909.

[9] ibid 10–11.

[10] RJ Colombo, 'Merit Regulation via the Suitability Rules' (2014) 12 *Journal of International Business and Law* 1.

[11] U Varottil, 'The Protection of Minority Investors and the Compensation of Their Losses: A Case Study of India' in PH Conac and M Gelter (eds), *Global Securities Litigation and Enforcement* (Cambridge University Press, forthcoming) 8, available at www.ssrn.com/abstract=2421098.

[12] This is characteristic of regulatory bodies generally, by which they are required to perform two somewhat contradictory roles of promoting, on the one hand, the markets that they are tasked to regulate and, at the same time, to protect various constituencies from the risks emanating from such markets. It has been noted that 'this can result in the regulator thinking of the interests of the industry rather than the users of the industry'. L Som, 'Regulatory Policy in India: Moving towards Regulatory Governance' *The Leap Blog* (25 May 2017), www.ajayshahblog.blogspot.sg/2017/05/regulatory-policy-in-india-moving.html.

[13] SEBI Act, s 3(1); S Agrawal and RJ Baby, *Agrawal & Baby on SEBI Act* (Taxmann, 2011) 9–10.

[14] SEBI Act, s 4(1).

[15] ibid s 14.

[16] International Monetary Fund, 'India: Financial Sector Assessment Program: Detailed Assessments Report on IOSCO Objectives and Principles of Securities Regulation', *IMF Country Report No 13/266* (2013).

[17] SEBI Act, s 5.

non-ex officio members, as well as the power to supersede the board in exigent circumstances.[18] The Central Government is also entitled to issue directions to SEBI on matters of policy, which will bind SEBI's board in terms of the exercise of its powers.[19] Thus far, it appears that the availability of these powers with the Central Government have not, in practice, impeded SEBI's independent functioning.[20]

However, one issue continues to be a matter of consternation. Even though the SEBI Act recognises the regulator's financial autonomy, since 2011 the Government of India has sought to have SEBI's surplus funds (amounting to Rs 1,672 crores in 2017) deposited into a public account controlled by the government.[21] Successive chairmen of SEBI have resisted this move and thus far have retained control over these funds on the ground that 'keeping SEBI funds in Government account would seriously undermine the autonomy of the market regulator and would militate against the basic canons of governance of markets by statutory regulators as envisaged under the SEBI Act'.[22] Although SEBI is not the only regulator that has been the subject matter of the government's move to wrest control over its funds, such efforts hamper effective functioning of the independent regulators.

From a statutory perspective, SEBI's autonomy is subject to certain checks and balances.[23] The Securities Appellate Tribunal (SAT) exercises appellate authority over SEBI.[24] Moreover, SEBI's accountability to Parliament is evident in that its annual report as well as the regulations it issues must be placed before Parliament.[25]

SEBI's primary role is 'to protect the interests of investors in securities and to promote the development of, and to regulate the securities market, by such measures as it thinks fit'.[26] This general objective is supported by a range of specific powers that the SEBI Act confers upon the regulator for effectively discharging its functions. Several of these specific powers were inserted into the SEBI Act by way of amendments over the years due to gaps that were found to exist, especially when SEBI has been unable to unearth wrongdoing in the securities markets or to successfully enforce capital market regulation.[27] The range of powers includes suspending the trading of a security on a stock exchange, restraining persons from accessing the capital markets and prohibiting them from dealing in securities for a definite period of time, suspending the office bearers of a stock exchange or other self-regulatory organisation, and other types of orders including impounding the proceeds of the sale of shares effected in violation of securities laws, attaching property such as bank accounts and issuing restraint against alienation of property.[28]

[18] ibid s 17.

[19] ibid s 16.

[20] International Monetary Fund (n 16) 30.

[21] JP Upadhyay, 'Sebi Fights to Retain Rs. 1,672 Crore in Surplus Funds' *The Mint* (5 January 2018).

[22] '14 Regulatory Bodies, Including SEBI, IRDA, AICTE and UGC, Kept Public Money of Rs 6,064 Crore outside Govt Account: CAG' *MoneyLife* (27 December 2017).

[23] For a listing of these checks and balances, see Agrawal and Baby (n 13) 9–10.

[24] SEBI Act, s 15T.

[25] ibid ss 18, 31.

[26] ibid s 11(1).

[27] See, eg, Varottil (n 11) 13.

[28] ibid.

Unlike several regulatory statutes, the SEBI Act only sets out the broad objectives and principles regarding securities regulation, with the details left to be determined by the regulator.[29] This provides greater autonomy and flexibility to SEBI to determine the course of capital market regulation in India. It has promulgated a plethora of regulations on various areas of the securities markets, ranging from public offering of shares to corporate governance, takeovers, market misconduct and the like. SEBI has been prolific in regulating capital markets activity as some of these regulations have been overhauled on multiple occasions within a short span of time, indicating the dynamic nature of the securities markets. For example, SEBI's regulations on takeovers are currently in their third incarnation, with several amendments having been made in the meantime.

Undoubtedly, SEBI's role as a securities regulator has fostered the growth of India's securities markets. Its assumption of regulatory responsibilities in 1992 led to disclosure-based regulation of public offerings of securities by Indian companies.[30] SEBI's role has largely been to ensure accurate and timely disclosures to the markets, on the basis of which investors are free to invest in securities. Unlike fixed-price offerings, which were the only permissible method of securities issuances to the public under the erstwhile regime, SEBI introduced book-built offerings wherein issuers are free to invite bids from investors within certain indicative limits.[31] Depending upon the demand displayed for a company's securities, the pricing of the shares will be determined through a market-oriented mechanism. This triggered a slew of public offerings of Indian companies in the 1990s and 2000s that led to a dramatic upward swing in India's primary markets. SEBI's disclosure norms have developed substantially over the years and are now comparable to (or possibly even far exceed) those required in most developed markets.[32]

Apart from providing market-based pricing mechanisms for securities, SEBI's initiatives have also led to greater liquidity to securities holders. Measures initiated by SEBI include dematerialisation of securities that paved the way for electronic trading,[33] faster settlement and clearing,[34] and other innovations. The decision of policy-makers to enable the formation of the National Stock Exchange that began operations in 1994 brought about a fundamental transformation of the Indian securities markets.[35] Similar results are evident from the corporate governance perspective as well, in that India has catapulted into a stellar fourth position in the world when it comes to protecting minority investors in the Doing Business rankings published by the World Bank.[36]

[29] Raval (n 2) 9.

[30] JR Varma, 'Indian Financial Market Development and Regulation: What Worked and Why?' in M Kawai and ES Prasad (eds), *Asian Perspectives on Financial Sector Reforms and Regulation* (Asian Development Bank Institute, 2011) 253, 264.

[31] Varottil (n 11) 9.

[32] ibid. While SEBI's disclosure requirements have become extensive in nature, there is a fear of undue emphasis on quantity over quality, thereby making offer documents bulky and unreadable to the investors. See S Sundaresan, 'Now's the Time for SEBI to Embark on a Course Correction' *Huffington Post* (16 February 2016).

[33] Varma (n 30) 254–55; Sabarinathan (n 8) 44–45.

[34] Sabarinathan (n 8) 42–43.

[35] Som and Naru (n 4) 24.

[36] World Bank, 'Doing Business 2018: Reforming to Create Jobs' (31 October 2017) 167, available at www.doingbusiness.org/~/media/WBG/DoingBusiness/Documents/Annual-Reports/English/DB2018-Full-Report.pdfp.

In all, the emergence of SEBI as a regulator had a visible impact on India's securities markets. The reforms of the 1990s were indeed dramatic in nature[37] and in 'no other part of India's financial sector has such a radical reform agenda been executed, in such a short time'.[38] A lot has also been attributed to the challenge that was taken on by a fledgling regulator that was not only independent, but also had a clear and focused mandate.[39]

After reviewing the evolution and expansion of SEBI's role in Indian's securities markets, in the remainder of this chapter I address several inadequacies and controversies that have dogged SEBI's functioning over the years, and discuss several reforms proposed to address those from the purview of the administrative and regulatory state.

II. REGULATORY TURF WARS

Even though SEBI is an independent regulator whose sole focus is on the securities markets, experience has shown that, due to the fragmentation of the financial regulatory architecture in India, there could be a blurring of boundaries between SEBI's domain and that of the government or other regulators. Conflicts have arisen between SEBI and ministries within the Central Government, and also between SEBI and other regulators. It has been pointed out that these 'internecine steps were the result of an imperfect balancing of autonomy and accountability and a blurred picture on the type of principal-agent relationship'.[40] Such overlaps in jurisdiction cause a great deal of uncertainty to market participants and also raise questions regarding the regulatory state model given the inability of regulators to resolve jurisdictional conflicts. Here, it is worth considering a few instances of regulatory turf wars involving the securities markets.

I begin with a discussion of the relationship between SEBI and the Central Government.[41] Although SEBI is under the administrative oversight of the Ministry of Finance, it has had to exert itself to establish the extent of its powers over several aspects with the Ministry of Corporate Affairs (MCA). Prior to 2000, there was a clear demarcation of functions wherein SEBI drew its powers from the SCRA, while the MCA oversaw the implementation of the then prevailing Companies Act, 1956. This was found to be ineffective, especially in the context of companies offering shares to the public. Hence, in 2000 SEBI was given powers (for the first time) to administer the provisions of the Companies Act, 1956 to the extent that they related to the issue and transfer of securities and non-payment of dividends for listed companies or those companies intending to have their securities listed on a recognised stock exchange.[42]

[37] Varma (n 30) 260.

[38] Ajay Shah, 'Institutional Changes in India's Capital Markets' (1999) 34(3–4) *Economic and Political Weekly* 183, 188.

[39] Som and Naru (n 4) 24.

[40] FSLRC Report (n 5) 6.

[41] Since securities regulation falls within the purview of the Union List in the Seventh Schedule to the Constitution, SEBI has not had to lock horns with state governments.

[42] Companies (Amendment) Act, 2000.

While at first blush this may appear to be an elegant distribution of powers, it has not been devoid of conflicts, one of which came to the fore in the Supreme Court's decision in *Sahara India Real Estate Corporation Ltd v Securities and Exchange Board of India*.[43] In a nutshell, two unlisted companies of the Sahara group issued securities to thousands of investors in the garb of a private placement by filing requisite documents with the Registrar of Companies (which is overseen by the MCA) and sidelining SEBI altogether. The Supreme Court came down heavily on this activity and recognised the extensive powers available with SEBI under the SEBI Act, which it found to be a 'complete code' in itself.[44] By engaging in a harmonious reading of the SEBI Act and the Companies Act, 1956,[45] the Court reaffirmed SEBI's extensive powers to regulate public offerings of securities. SEBI emerged victorious as the Court clarified that companies will not be permitted to engage in regulatory arbitrage by seeking to invoke potential gaps in regulatory domains.

When it comes to corporate governance, the contest between SEBI and the MCA for regulating listed companies is subtler and more nuanced. In the 1990s and early 2000s, as part of its reform measures relating to the securities markets, SEBI was active in introducing and constantly enhancing corporate governance norms for Indian listed companies. This was based on the recommendations of several committees that SEBI had appointed to examine the issue.[46] SEBI was taking the lead in the field as its governance prescriptions (which applied to listed companies) were above and beyond those prescribed under the Companies Act, 1956. However, the occurrence of corporate scandals (including the infamous Satyam fraud exceeding US$1 billion) during the time that the Companies Act, 1956 was being overhauled tilted the scales, whereby the MCA wrested control by legislating extensively in the area of corporate governance in the Companies Act, 2013 that replaced the 1956 legislation. Arguably, the political implications of the Satyam scandal were significant enough to draw the attention of Parliament to intervene rather than to leave it to the domain of SEBI as an independent regulator. While in the early post-liberalisation era SEBI played a leadership role in corporate governance, the pendulum had swung with the enactment of the Companies Act, 2013, and SEBI in fact had to follow through by amending its regulations to synchronise them with the Act.[47]

[43] *Sahara India Real Estate Corporation Ltd v Securities and Exchange Board of India* (2012) 10 SCC 603.

[44] ibid para 57.

[45] ibid para 58.

[46] See, eg, Securities and Exchange Board of India, Report of the Kumar Mangalam Birla Committee on Corporate Governance (February 2000), available at www.ecgi.global/sites/default/files/codes/documents/corpgov.pdf; Securities and Exchange Board of India, Report of the SEBI Committee on Corporate Governance (February 2003), available at www.sebi.gov.in/reports/reports/mar-2003/the-report-of-shri-n-r-narayana-murthy-committee-on-corporate-governance-for-public-comments-_12986.html (hereinafter the 'Narayana Murthy Committee Report').

[47] A lateral consequence of the regulatory turf war is that the competition between the regulator and the government has also led to more stringent regulation in some areas, such as related party transactions. See S Godbole, 'Dispel Uncertainty over Related Party Transactions' *Financial Express* (25 December 2014).

The contest for regulatory leadership in the corporate governance arena has continued. In 2017, SEBI appointed a committee under the chairmanship of Mr Uday Kotak with a view to upping the ante on governance issues.[48] The committee issued a report with detailed recommendations,[49] but the striking aspect of the report is the objections of the MCA (which was also represented on the committee) to several of the committee's recommendations on the ground that they trespass upon the field occupied by the Companies Act and the rules issued by the MCA under that.[50] These developments in corporate governance have not only amplified the jurisdictional conflicts between SEBI and the MCA, but have also blurred the distinction between the regulation of listed and unlisted companies. In the end, an elegant solution would be to grant the remit to SEBI to regulate listed companies and their governance aspects, and leave it to the MCA to oversee unlisted companies. Such an approach would be consistent with SEBI's mandate under its parent legislation.

Domain overlaps have arisen between SEBI and other regulators as well. For instance, the regulation of foreign portfolio investments into the stock markets is carried out jointly between SEBI and the RBI. This could raise concerns, as one recent episode indicates. Usually, the RBI monitors the level of foreign investments allowed in an Indian listed company at the end of each day. However, on 17 February 2017, when the window was open for fresh foreign investments in HDFC Bank's stock, the RBI (based on data collected from intermediaries at frequent intervals) intervened to restrict trading in the stock on the ground that the statutory foreign investment limit was breached. SEBI viewed this RBI action as one that violated market sanctity without the concurrence of the securities regulator.[51] In another instance, SEBI issued a circular to all listed companies requiring them to make a public disclosure to the stock exchanges within one working day of defaulting on loans and other financial facilities.[52] However, this was contrary to RBI's stance of maintaining confidentiality relating to defaulters on loans in the broader interest of the economy through prohibition on disclosure of credit information. In an apparent turf war,[53] SEBI withdrew the circular prior to the date on which it was to become effective.[54]

[48] Securities and Exchange Board of India, Report of the Committee on Corporate Governance (October 2017), available at www.sebi.gov.in/reports/reports/oct-2017/report-of-the-committee-on-corporate-governance_36177.html (hereinafter the 'Kotak Committee Report').

[49] ibid.

[50] See M Doshi, 'SEBI's Corporate Governance Committee Proposes, Government Opposes' *BloombergQuint* (5 October 2017).

[51] See R Zachariah, 'SEBI, RBI Engage in Turf War over Stock Trading of HDFC Bank' *Economic Times* (6 March 2017).

[52] Securities and Exchange Board of India, 'Disclosures by Listed Entities of Defaults on Payment of Interest/ Repayment of Principal Amount of Loans from Banks/Financial Institutions, Debt Securities, etc.', Circular CIR/CFD/CMD/93/2017 (4 August 2017).

[53] See, eg, P Mittal, 'Supreme Court to Decide if RBI's Loan Defaulters List Can Be Disclosed or Not' *The Mint* (18 July 2017).

[54] Securities and Exchange Board of India, 'Deferment of Implementation of Circular', PR No 59/2017 (29 September 2017).

Finally, in one of the most high-profile instances, SEBI sparred with the Insurance Regulatory and Development Authority (IRDA) over the regulation of unit-linked insurance policies (ULIPs).[55] The controversy was finally set to rest by the Central Government, which, through an ordinance, handed the regulatory domain over the product to the IRDA.[56]

This is not to suggest a total lack of coordination between SEBI, the Central Government and other regulators. Indeed, both the Central Government and the RBI have their representatives on SEBI's board, who can facilitate coordination.[57] Further, there are various coordination committees among these agencies,[58] although they have drawn criticism on the ground of being 'toothless'.[59] In 2010, the government established the Financial Stability Development Council (FSDC) to institutionalise and strengthen the mechanisms for interregulatory coordination,[60] but that too does not appear to have received much impetus. Various committees appointed to review India's financial sector regulation have suggested unification measures to prevent fragmentation in the regulatory structure.[61] There is a strong push towards making SEBI the unified regulator for the markets, precisely with a view to avoiding the situations discussed above.[62] One important step taken in that direction is the merger of the Forward Markets Commission with SEBI, which now regulates both the securities markets and the commodities markets.[63]

From the purview of the regulatory state, the prevalent turf wars tend to impinge on the autonomy and independence of SEBI. Moreover, fragmentation in the regulation of financial markets could result in a great deal of uncertainty for market players.[64] In particular, the relationship between the Central Government and SEBI assumes tremendous importance: unless SEBI is given a free hand to regulate the securities markets, the benefits from an autonomous regulator for the Indian securities markets cannot be fully realised. The bigger risk is that regulated entities may take advantage of fragmentation in the financial sector regulation and indulge in regulatory arbitrage, which may militate against SEBI's regulatory goals.

In concluding this section, it may very well be that fragmentation has its own share of benefits such as specialisation on the part of the regulator and regulatory competition that might lead to optimal levels of regulation.[65] Moreover, an unhindered

[55] J Thakur, 'SEBI Bans ULIPs – But What about Other Similar "Insurance" Products?' *IndiaCorpLaw* (10 April 2010), available at https://indiacorplaw.in/2010/04/sebi-bans-ulips-but-what-about-other.html.

[56] M Halan, 'SEBI-IRDA Tiff: Who Wins, Who Loses' *The Mint* (23 June 2010).

[57] International Monetary Fund (n 16) 26.

[58] ibid.

[59] R Chakrabarti, 'Financial Development in India: Status and Challenges' in M Kawai and ES Prasad (eds), *Asian Perspectives on Financial Sector Reforms and Regulation* (Asian Development Bank Institute, 2011) 284, 300.

[60] International Monetary Fund (n 16) 26.

[61] See, eg, Planning Commission, Government of India (n 7) 121; FSLRC Report (n 5) 6.

[62] However, some argue that the political-economy barriers to a unified regulator are too high. J Bhagwati, MS Khan and RKR Bogathi, 'Financial Sector Legislative Reforms Commission and Financial Sector Regulation in India', *Indian Council for Research and International Economic Relations Working Paper 324* (2016) 2, available at https://ideas.repec.org/p/ess/wpaper/id10960.html.

[63] PTI, 'FMC Merges with SEBI' *The Hindu* (28 September 2015).

[64] M Lehmann, 'Legal Fragmentation, Extraterritoriality and Uncertainty in Global Financial Regulation' (2017) 37 *Oxford Journal of Legal Studies* 406.

[65] SR Pellerin et al, 'The Consolidation of Financial Market Regulation: Pros, Cons and Implications for the United States', *The Federal Reserve Bank of Richmond Working Paper No 09-08* (May 2009),

move towards regulatory consolidation could itself suffer from pitfalls,[66] which must be avoided altogether. It is therefore not surprising that the efforts towards consolidation are made in an incremental fashion rather than through a more radical approach.

III. BALANCING INDEPENDENCE AND ACCOUNTABILITY

One concern with the regulatory state is that independent regulators are bestowed significant powers to legislate without the requisite accountability, as regulations are drafted by unelected officials.[67] Moreover, since a regulator operates as a mini-state where the powers of the legislature, executive and the judiciary are vested in a single authority, the specific procedures by which the authority exercises its powers acquires prominence as a means to demonstrate accountability.[68] Appropriate stakeholder engagement will also induce a greater sense of legitimacy and broader support towards regulatory actions.[69] A robust consultative process will ensure that the regulator obtains adequate information from the market and stakeholders before devising regulation so as to enhance its success.[70]

Among the various regulators in India, SEBI has led the path in introducing transparency in regulation-making. Comparatively speaking, SEBI follows an elaborate consultative process before issuing regulations that affect the securities markets and also obtains feedback before finalising them. However, as I will discuss in this section, there continue to be several shortcomings in SEBI's approach, leaving considerable room for improvement.

The SEBI Act itself does not provide for any consultation mechanism before SEBI issues regulations.[71] However, SEBI commonly publishes a concept note or policy paper before formulating regulations.[72] In the case of significant reforms (such as corporate governance,[73] takeover regulation[74] and insider trading),[75] SEBI has also

available at www.richmondfed.org/~/media/richmondfedorg/publications/research/working_papers/2009/pdf/wp09-8.pdf.

[66] ibid.

[67] Som and Naru (n 4) 27; A Pattanaik and A Sharma, 'Regulatory Governance Problems in the Legislative Function at RBI and SEBI' *The Leap Blog* (23 September 2015), www.ajayshahblog.blogspot.sg/2015/09/regulatory-governance-problems-in.html.

[68] Somanathan (n 5) 395; FSLRC Report (n 5) xv.

[69] Somanathan (n 5) 398–99.

[70] Raval (n 2) 21.

[71] ibid 11.

[72] ibid.

[73] See n 46.

[74] Securities and Exchange Board of India, 'Justice P.N. Bhagwati Committee Report on Takeovers' (1997), available at www.takeovercode.com/committee_reports/pnbhagwatti.php; Securities and Exchange Board of India, 'Report of the Reconvened Committee on Substantial Acquisition of Shares and Takeovers under the Chairmanship of Justice P.N. Bhagwati' (2002), available at www.sebi.gov.in/reports/reports/may-2002/report-of-the-reconvened-committee-on-substantial-acquisition-of-shares-and-takeovers_13108.html; Securities and Exchange Board of India, 'Report of the Takeover Regulations Advisory Committee under the Chairmanship of Mr. C. Achuthan' (2010), available at www.sebi.gov.in/commreport/tracreport.pdf.

[75] Securities and Exchange Board of India, 'Report of the High Level Committee to Review the SEBI (Prohibition of Insider Trading) Regulations 1992 under the Chairmanship of N.K. Sodhi, Former Chief Justice' (2013), available at www.sebi.gov.in/sebi_data/attachdocs/1386758945803.pdf.

followed the practice of establishing committees comprising a diverse range of members to provide recommendations or even draft regulations. While SEBI also issues circulars and guidelines (in addition to regulations), it does not adopt an elaborate public consultation process for these.[76] Due to the absence of a legislative mandate, SEBI's approach towards a consultative process while issuing regulations lacks uniformity. This is exacerbated by the fact that SEBI's powers to make regulation are beyond the reach of the appellate jurisdiction of the SAT and the Supreme Court, as such jurisdiction is confined only to SEBI's quasi-judicial actions.[77]

Commentators have observed that the consultation process carried out by India's financial regulators does not compare with the high standards of transparency and organisation followed by some regulators such as the Airports Economic Regulatory Authority, which has displayed a stellar track record in this respect.[78] In the case of SEBI, one study of steps taken by SEBI during the period between June 2014 and July 2015 notes that 'SEBI sought public comments on 44.4% of its regulations and on 17.4% of its circulars'.[79] While the SEBI consultation documents outlined the objective of the proposed regulation, there was no cost-benefit analysis carried out, except on rare occasions.[80] It is a significant matter that very little time was offered for public consultation. SEBI allowed a median time of 23 days for regulations and 18 days for circulars, and there have been instances where the regulator allowed a period as short as 10–12 days.[81]

Concerns have also been raised regarding the quality and transparency of SEBI's consultation process. While SEBI has displayed its keenness to seek public comments, it is rather opaque regarding the process thereafter. SEBI does not publish the comments received or the action taken thereon.[82] This is unlike higher standards elsewhere, where the regulator publishes a response to the comments received so that stakeholders are aware of how their concerns have (or have not) been addressed.[83] Even though stakeholders commit their resources in responding to the request for public comments, they have no means to realise the manner in which their efforts have been considered.[84] Not only will such an approach cease to motivate stakeholders and thereby limit the scope of the consultation, but it will also fail to create the necessary ecosystem of regulation and standardisation of the process.

In the meantime, there has been a clamour for introducing regulatory impact assessments (RIAs) that create a structured process by which the regulator undertakes

[76] As a wider matter, SEBI has attracted concerns on the ground that it uses an unduly wide variety of instruments such as guidelines and circulars with varying degrees of formality to regulate the securities markets. See, eg, Raval (n 2) 12.

[77] *National Securities Depository Ltd v Securities and Exchange Board of India* (2017) 5 SCC 517.

[78] Pattanaik and Sharma (n 67); Som and Naru (n 4) 27.

[79] Pattanaik and Sharma (n 67).

[80] ibid. See also Indian Merchants' Chamber and FINSEC Law Advisors, 'Regulatory Impact Assessment: Is it Getting its Due?' (2013), available at www.imcnet.org/cms/public/content/publications/Regulatory%20Impact%20Assessment-%20Is%20It%20Getting%20Its%20Due.pdf, at 21.

[81] ibid.

[82] B Zaveri, 'Participatory Governance in Regulation Making: How to Make it Work?' *The Leap Blog* (17 January 2016), www.ajayshahblog.blogspot.sg/2016/01/participatory-governance-in-regulation.html.

[83] See, eg, Financial Conduct Authority (UK), 'Our Mission 2017: Feedback Statement' (April 2017), available at www.fca.org.uk/publication/feedback/fs17-01.pdf.

[84] Zaveri (n 82).

a cost-benefit analysis (both quantitative and qualitative) of a proposed regulation before it is enacted. The 12th five-year plan recommended that the Centre and States use RIA to analyse the need for new as well as existing regulations to be measured against specified criteria.[85] In its report, the Financial Sector Legislative Reforms Commission (FSLRC) also recommended the need for a robust consultation process for financial sector regulators, so that 'regulations will become more responsive to the needs of the financial system'.[86] The Indian Financial Code drafted by the FSLRC is accompanied by a 'Handbook on Adoption of Governance Enhancing and Non-legislative Elements of the Draft Indian Financial Code', which sets out the elaborate requirements for issuing regulations, including conducting a cost-benefit analysis of such regulation.[87]

Until any of the measures discussed above are implemented, SEBI's consultative process will continue to suffer from inconsistencies and inefficiencies. This raises significant questions about SEBI's accountability as an independent regulator. As mentioned earlier, the process is important to instil legitimacy, and hence needs better structure and organisation. In this regard, it would be useful for SEBI to take the cue from the decision in *Cellular Operators Association of India v Telecom Regulatory Authority of India*,[88] wherein the Supreme Court set out principles for transparency and openness in governance when regulatory bodies promulgate regulations and exhorted Parliament to enact a legislation along the lines of the Administrative Procedure Act in the US.[89]

Another dimension of the regulatory state and an extensive consultation process is that it creates opportunities for well-organised interest groups to have an excessive influence in determining the outcome of the regulatory process due to the enormous resources they are willing to invest.[90] On the other hand, diverse stakeholders who are large in number but may individually suffer minimal impact are less likely to participate in the consultation process due to collective action problems, as a result of which their voices may not be heard.[91]

In the securities regulation space, while it is hard to identify specific interest groups that may have lobbied for specific regulatory outcomes, it is possible to discern some broad trends. Professor Varma has argued that reforms in India 'have been pushed forward by academics, by the financial press, and by policymakers

[85] Planning Commission, Government of India, 'Twelfth Five Year Plan (2012–2017)', available at www.planningcommission.gov.in/plans/planrel/12thplan/pdf/12fyp_vol2.pdf, at 102.

[86] FSLRC Report (n 5) 30.

[87] Department of Economic Affairs, Ministry of Finance, Government of India, 'Handbook on Adoption of Governance Enhancing and Non-legislative Elements of the Draft Indian Financial Code' (26 December 2013), available at www.ccmrm.org/wp-content/uploads/2015/03/handbook_govEnhanc_fslrc-Dec-2013.pdf, at 39.

[88] (2016) 7 SCC 703.

[89] For a detailed analysis of the Supreme Court judgment and the broader aspects of consultation in regulation-making, see, V Reddy, ch 4 in this volume.

[90] Som and Naru (n 4) 19; RA Posner, 'Theories of Economic Regulation' (1974) 5(2) *Bell Journal of Economics and Management Science* 335; N Dubash and B Morgan, 'Understanding the Rise of the Regulatory State of the South', *Jerusalem Papers in Regulation & Governance Working Paper No 32* (2011) 9, available at http://citeseerx.ist.psu.edu/viewdoc/download?doi=10.1.1.454.5318&rep=rep1&type=pdf.

[91] Somanathan (n 5) 400.

(not necessarily in that order)'.[92] He then goes on to note that institutional investors (who may be the ultimate beneficiaries of stringent norms) have hardly played a role in driving securities regulation.[93] Even though the corporate sector has a great stake in securities regulation as more optimal regulation enhances their ability to raise capital on beneficial terms, it has not played any significant role in bringing about reforms to the securities markets.[94] Instead, it has 'usually been a bystander as reformers struggled against vested interests among market intermediaries'.[95]

To push this further, anecdotal evidence suggests that certain interest groups, principally controlling shareholders (known as 'promoters') of Indian companies, may have played an influential role in either stalling reforms that are adverse to their interests or may have helped shape regulatory reforms in a manner that enables entrenchment in the companies they control. This arguably militates against the interests of minority shareholders, including institutional investors who have not been sufficiently active in Indian corporate governance, at least until recently. I rely on a couple of illustrations to support this argument.

Beginning with takeovers, SEBI issued the first set of regulations in 1994.[96] This was replaced in 1997,[97] and that version underwent significant amendments in 2002.[98] Finally, these regulations too were replaced by a new version in 2011 that stands in force.[99] Except for the first set of regulations, all other reforms were based on the recommendations of committees.[100] While these efforts began with a desire to develop a market for corporate control in India by adopting global best practice, the ultimate regulatory outcome was far short of that, as SEBI made several compromises that resulted in a substantially modified version of the global benchmarks.[101] Interestingly, there has been no shortage of consultation. Each of these reforms was preceded by a great deal of transparency, which leaves some trail of the influence of interest groups. In fact, the interest group dynamics may have been the unintended consequence of a consultative process that is otherwise desirable. A lot tends to depend on the representation of the committees that proposed reforms. They not only had strong representation from the Indian industry, but also comprised leading Indian corporate lawyers. Indian industry received a dominant voice in the shaping of takeover regulation, as promoters of Indian companies were fearful of possible hostile takeovers of their companies by foreign acquirers. As I argue elsewhere,[102]

[92] Varma (n 30) 269.
[93] ibid 270.
[94] ibid.
[95] ibid.
[96] Securities and Exchange Board of India (Substantial Acquisition of Shares and Takeovers) Regulations, 1994.
[97] Securities and Exchange Board of India (Substantial Acquisition of Shares and Takeovers) Regulations, 1997.
[98] SEBI (Substantial Acquisition of Shares and Takeovers) (Amendment) Regulations, 2002.
[99] Securities and Exchange Board of India (Substantial Acquisition of Shares and Takeovers) Regulations, 2011
[100] See n 74.
[101] U Varottil, 'The Nature of the Market for Corporate Control in India' in U Varottil and WY Wan, *Comparative Takeover Regulation: Global and Asian Perspectives* (Cambridge University Press, 2017) 378.
[102] ibid.

the working of the interest group dynamics in emboldening incumbent shareholder interests in Indian companies has the effect of weighing against a meaningful market for corporate control.

Another example indicates the strength of informal pressure applied by domestic industry groups. In the initial years after SEBI introduced corporate governance norms in the form of clause 49 of the listing agreement that companies entered into with the stock exchanges, the general trend had been for companies to comply (at least in form) with the requirements of the norms. However, there were significant obstacles to the implementation of these norms and to their acceptability within the Indian corporate ecosystem. To begin with, there was considerable resistance to the stringent corporate governance norms even prior to their enactment in a detailed form. For instance, when SEBI strengthened its corporate governance norms in 2004 based on the recommendations of the Narayana Murthy committee report, they were not only met with a cold reception, but there were protestations and representations from industry, due to which the implementation of the revisions had to be postponed several times until they were finally mandated to take effect from 1 January 2006, and that too only in a diluted form.[103]

At the same time, the securities markets as well as the regulator have acquired greater sophistication and experience over the years. From a normative perspective, one can imagine a more nuanced balance of interests among various constituencies. For instance, institutional investors and other shareholder representatives (like proxy advisory firms) have begun to take a greater interest in influencing the tenor of securities regulation. Other sectors such as electricity regulation have demonstrated somewhat counterintuitive tendencies in that while large industrial consumers have been largely absent from the regulatory process, individuals and small groups have been more active.[104] Ultimately, it might well be that having a unified regulator for the markets will minimise the incidence of regulatory capture, as it has a wider range of regulated entities instead of specific ones.[105]

IV. ENFORCEMENT CONCERNS AND REGULATORY UNCERTAINTY

In the previous sections, I have examined SEBI's legislative functions[106] and its relationship with the government as well as other regulatory bodies.[107] Here, I discuss SEBI's quasi-judicial functions, which naturally involves an analysis of its relationship with the appellate bodies and the courts.

[103] Securities and Exchange Board of India, SEBI/CFD/DIL/CG/1/2005/29/3 dated 29 March 2005, available at www.sebi.gov.in/legal/circulars/mar-2005/corporate-governance-clause-49-of-the-listing-agreement_8348.html.

[104] NK Dubash and N Rao, 'Emergent Regulatory Governance in India: Comparative Case Studies of Electricity Regulation', *Working Paper* (2006) 23, available at www.regulation.upf.edu/bath-06/10_Dubash_Rao.pdf.

[105] Planning Commission, Government of India (n 7) 127.

[106] See section III above.

[107] See Section II above.

While the substantive laws relating to securities regulation have become progressively extensive and sophisticated in India, one principal concern has been SEBI's lack of effective enforcement of these laws.[108] Robust substantive laws lack the desired effect unless they are effectively enforced by the regulator. It is true that these legal constraints have been addressed by constant amendments to the SEBI Act that strengthen the regulator's hands, but they have not had the desired effect, arguably due to resource constraints that continue to plague it.[109] Moreover, there have been concerns about the manner in which SEBI has been exercising its powers and functions. For example, SEBI's track record is replete with instances where it has been taken to task by its appellate body (the SAT) and the courts for delays, inconsistencies and disregarding principles of natural justice, all of which have added to regulatory uncertainties in the securities markets. Here, I briefly explore some trends that demonstrate the point.

One study of SEBI's performance in its initial years, as compared with the SEC, shows:

> Between 1999 and 2004, the SEBI took action in 481 cases, as opposed to 2,789 cases for the SEC, even though the latter regulates a significantly more mature market. As a ratio of actions taken to the number of companies in their respective jurisdictions, SEBI's figure is an unimpressive 0.09, while that of the SEC is 0.52.[110]

Similarly, criminal enforcement, which can be a useful deterrent measure against market misconduct, has hardly been used. To my knowledge, SEBI has not managed to secure criminal convictions in any high-profile cases involving securities law violations, although it has enjoyed some success in the narrow area of unauthorised raising of funds by companies through collective investment schemes.[111] The reasons for this outcome range from the onerous nature of the evidentiary burden in criminal prosecutions (that SEBI has been unable to discharge) to the delays and inefficiencies in the criminal justice system in India.

SEBI has instead focused on exercising its general powers available under sections 11 and 11B of the SEBI Act[112] to issue wide-ranging orders, including to debar violators from participating in the securities markets for a period of time, often on an interim and *ex parte* basis as well. SEBI has also utilised the adjudicatory mechanism available under the SEBI Act to hand down penalties in the case of securities law violations. In that sense, its civil enforcement efforts have been relatively stronger than its criminal law prosecutions. This raises an important point: the incapacity of the regulator has resulted in the use of broader measures in the form

[108] Bose (n 6) 83.
[109] See section V below.
[110] Bose (n 6) 115.
[111] International Monetary Fund (n 16) 49.
[112] For example, the overbroad nature of SEBI's powers in s 11(1) of the SEBI Act to take 'such measures as it thinks fit' has been affirmed by the Supreme Court in *Sahara* (n 43) para 103. See also Reddy, ch 4 in this volume.

of 'blunt force' instruments rather than more precise and targeted measures against violators. In that sense, SEBI's enforcement efforts have been both under-inclusive and over-inclusive.

One method to ease the regulator of the burden of enforcement actions and to unclog an overburdened securities litigation system is to have a robust plea bargaining and settlement mechanism. Although SEBI established a consent and settlement mechanism in 2007, which it has progressively reformed,[113] it is arguably inadequate. Not only is the system riddled with uncertainties, it also excludes whole swathes of offences from qualifying for the settlement mechanism.[114]

The success of SEBI's enforcement efforts can also be measured by its ability to sustain its actions before the appellate authority and the courts. Here, SEBI's track record appears to be mixed. Anecdotal evidence suggests that while it has had some success before appellate bodies in defending its actions in fundraising violations[115] and against intermediaries,[116] its success against major corporates and market players in actions such as insider trading has been limited.[117] One study notes that in 'appeals before higher authorities, such as [the SAT] and the Finance Ministry, in 30–50 percent of cases, the decision has gone against SEBI'.[118]

A qualitative assessment of the outcome of appeals against SEBI actions also indicates the shortcomings in SEBI's enforcement measures. For example, SEBI's decisions on occasion have been found to be arbitrary while demanding turnover fee from brokers when none is due,[119] in shopping for clauses in different statutes in an arbitrary manner to impose sanctions on an issuer in a public offering[120] and in disposing of a consent application without giving an opportunity to the party against whom action was taken.[121] In certain instances, SEBI officials found to have acted in 'gross negligence'[122] have been rebuked for this 'irresponsible approach' and for functioning in a 'shoddy manner'.[123] Other concerns raised include violation of the

[113] This is currently administered through the SEBI (Settlement of Administrative and Civil Proceedings) Regulations, 2014.

[114] S Choudhary and S Ghosal, 'Why Sebi's Consent Mechanism Needs an Overhaul' *Business Standard* (11 September 2017).

[115] See n 43 and the accompanying text.

[116] Chakrabarti (n 59) 301.

[117] See, eg, *Rakesh Agrawal v Securities and Exchange Board of India* (2004) 49 SCL 351 (SAT); *Hindustan Lever v Securities and Exchange Board of India* (1998) 18 SCL 311 (AA).

[118] Chakrabarti (n 59) 301. It is a different matter, though, that not all decisions made by SEBI are challenged in appeal.

[119] *Time Capital Ltd v Securities and Exchange Board of India* [2006] 69 SCL 260 (SAT – MUM.)

[120] *DLF Ltd v Securities and Exchange Board of India*, SAT Order dated 13 March 2015 in Appeal No 331 of 2014.

[121] *Reliance Industries Ltd v Securities and Exchange Board of India*, SAT Order dated 30 June 2014 in Appeal No 1 of 2013.

[122] *Securities and Exchange Board of India v Vilas Vilunji*, SAT Order dated 28 June 2017 in Appeal No 68 of 2014.

[123] *Adventz Finance Pvt Ltd v Securities and Exchange Board of India*, SAT Order dated 15 June 2016 in Appeal No 206 of 2016. But see also *Adventz Finance Pvt Ltd v Securities and Exchange Board of India*, SAT Order dated 25 July 2016 in Appeal No 206 of 2016 (wherein the earlier order was modified).

principles of natural justice[124] and inordinate delays and indecisiveness. As for delays, the Supreme Court has come down hard on SEBI for 'dragging its feet' for seven years over a 'trivial issue' in the Satyam scam,[125] and has also expressed its apprehensions regarding SEBI's delays in clearing takeover offers that cause significant difficulties to acquirers engaging in such takeovers.[126]

Another major concern relates to the inconsistencies in SEBI's approach in cases that lead to uncertainties in the securities markets. Although found to be legal,[127] SEBI's model whereby it initiates parallel proceedings, one to pass sanctions (such as prohibitions from accessing the capital markets) and the other in the form of adjudication proceedings that seek to impose penalty on offenders, results in a multiplicity of actions that arguably amounts to harassment of alleged violators of securities laws.[128] Moreover, there are several instances where SEBI officials have adopted contradictory stances on legal issues without proper explanation, which has added to the uncertainty.[129] An internal research study conducted by SEBI analysed the orders of whole time members (who pass broader actions under sections 11 and 11B of the SEBI Act) and adjudicating officers (who decide upon penalty proceedings):

> [It] found that in cases of orders passed by Whole Time Members, in similar type of cases, while one member has passed orders for suspension in 8% of the cases, another one has done it in 0.5% of the cases and the third member has passed suspension orders in 25% of the cases. Similarly, debarment order has been passed in 50% cases by one member, in 75% of the cases by the second member and in 0.4% of the cases by the third member. The quantum of suspension order passed also varies vastly from member to member. In quantum of debarment orders, it varies from 50% to 1/3rd to 1/6th when the period of debarment of 2 years to 5 years is calculated.[130]

Although the numbers have to be considered in light of the fact that each case has its own set of facts and circumstances, a wide variation in the order that lacks clear explanation suggests arbitrariness and subjectivity.[131] There is a need for greater predictability in the orders passed by the whole time members and adjudicating officers.

[124] *Vinod Hingorani v Securities and Exchange Board of India*, Bombay High Court Order dated 10 March 2015 in Writ Petition No 639 of 2015.

[125] 'Supreme Court Slams SEBI for Delaying Rs 7,000 Crore Satyam Computer Scam' *Financial Express* (11 January 2017); 'Supreme Court Raps SEBI for Dragging its Feet in Satyam Auditor Case' *Business Standard* (11 January 2018).

[126] *Securities and Exchange Board of India v Akshya Infrastructure Pvt Ltd* AIR 2014 SC 1963.

[127] *Sunita Gupta v Securities and Exchange Board of India*, SAT Order dated 21 April 2017 in Appeal No 193 of 2016.

[128] Raval (n 2) 31–32.

[129] *Krishna Enterprises v Securities and Exchange Board of India*, SAT Order dated 20 April 2016 in Appeal No 131 of 2015; *Golden Tobacco Ltd v Securities and Exchange Board of India* [2014] 51 taxmann.com 51 (SAT – Mumbai).

[130] Letter dated 8 July 2011 from Mr UK Sinha, Chairman, SEBI to Mr R Gopalan, Department of Economic Affairs, Ministry of Finance, Government of India, available at www.issuu.com/moneylife/docs/sebi_litigation_fm, 4.

[131] ibid 5.

In all, while SEBI has brought about a significant enhancement of the securities markets in India, its enforcement track record requires greater attention. Not only has SEBI enjoyed mixed success in its enforcement efforts (especially when compared with its peers in developed economies such as the US), but its actions have also exposed several inconsistencies and inefficiencies. Given that the establishment of an independent regulator in the securities markets is aimed at ensuring efficiency in decision-making by experts in a timely manner, there are some concerns about the extent to which SEBI has achieved its objectives. A significant explanation for this state of affairs is the lack of adequate capacity in SEBI's regulatory establishment, a matter to which I now turn.

V. WEAK STATE CAPACITY

One of the key justifications for independent regulators is that they are in a position to build a cadre of competent personnel with specialised knowledge and domain expertise, coupled with human resources and policies and processes that are different from those of the government.[132] While this may hold true for the regulatory state in advanced economies, the same cannot be said for independent regulators functioning in India. Indian regulators such as SEBI fall short of the expertise and the resources required to oversee sophisticated market operations in the securities industry.[133]

As of 31 March 2017, SEBI had 788 employees on its rolls, out of which 692 were officers and 96 comprised secretaries and other staff members.[134] In contrast, the SEC houses around 4,600 employees.[135] Based on their respective annual reports, 'the SEC has almost one employee for each listed company',[136] while 'SEBI has one employee for six listed companies'.[137] Such a stark disparity operates in respect of key functions as well. For example, while the SEC's corporate finance department has 477 employees, SEBI's department handling the function employs only 31 individuals.[138] More crucially, while the SEC's enforcement division has 1,380 employees, SEBI's equivalent department has only 214.[139]

Moreover, the growth in SEBI's human resources has failed to keep pace with market developments. For instance, during the years between 2007 and 2017, the equity markets grew from a total turnover of Rs 18,463,603 crores[140] to Rs 115,696,292 crores,[141] ie, over six times. Market capitalisation too has risen

[132] FSLRC Report (n 5) 15.
[133] Som and Naru (n 4) 20; Dubash and Rao (n 104) 22.
[134] Securities and Exchange Board of India, *Annual Report 2016–17*, 195.
[135] US Securities and Exchange Commission, "Agency Financial Report: Fiscal Year 2017' (13 November 2017), available at www.sec.gov/files/sec-2017-agency-financial-report.pdf.
[136] Kotak Committee Report (n 48) 100.
[137] ibid.
[138] ibid.
[139] ibid.
[140] Securities and Exchange Board of India, *Annual Report 2006–07*, 47.
[141] Securities and Exchange Board of India (n 134) 59.

exponentially during the period. However, the number of officers (ie, non-secretarial staff) increased from 408 in March 2008[142] to 692 in April 2017,[143] that is, a little over 1.5 times.

This indicates a severe shortage of capacity within SEBI, which adversely affects its functioning, especially on the enforcement aspects, which require a great deal of effective resourcing. Suggestions have been made to increase the monitoring and enforcement functions of SEBI, including by outsourcing certain functions with appropriate safeguards.[144]

Even from a qualitative perspective, there are concerns about the skills and expertise of SEBI staff. As Professor Varma has noted:

> Enforcement … is not about a handful of people at the top; it is about a large army of competent (but not necessarily outstanding) foot soldiers. The constraints of a public sector compensation structure are far more stifling at this level … The regulator's low pay scale therefore makes it uncompetitive at this level as a long-term career.[145]

Although regulatory expertise has been in short supply, the method of transplanting civil servants and the regulatory structures of the civil service to authorities such as SEBI has not proved to be a useful strategy.[146] SEBI's ability to hire and retain the required talent is largely attributable to disparity in compensation packages between the regulator and the private sector.[147] Suggestions have been made that SEBI should emulate regulators in leading markets to create a revolving door policy that enables SEBI to laterally employ seasoned individuals with the requisite market experience.[148] Similarly, expertise needs to be built up by employing individuals with the required domain expertise in areas such as data science, accountancy, corporate law and academia.[149]

Unless SEBI undertakes ongoing efforts to build up its capacity on the enforcement front, the tremendous work it has done in the area of developing world-class substantive regulation will not bear fruit.

CONCLUSION

This chapter has sought to provide a critical account of SEBI's role as India's securities regulator over the last quarter of a century. SEBI's role has not only led to the

[142] Securities and Exchange Board of India (n 140) 130.

[143] Securities and Exchange Board of India (n 134) 195.

[144] Kotak Committee Report (n 48) 100.

[145] Varma (n 30) 279–80.

[146] FSLRC Report (n 5) 8.

[147] International Monetary Fund (n 16) 34.

[148] Kotak Committee Report (n 48) 101. At the same time, it is necessary to bear in mind the ill-effects of the revolving door policy. Necessary checks must be imposed to prevent behaviour involving bias and influence peddling. See B Protess and S Craig, 'S.E.C's Revolving Door Hurts its Effectiveness, Report Says' *New York Times* (11 February 2013); J Harrington, 'The Revolving Door at the SEC' *Huffington Post* (6 May 2015), available at www.huffingtonpost.com/john-harrington/the-revolving-door-at-the-sec_b_6785568.html.

[149] Kotak Committee Report (n 48) 100–01. See also Planning Commission, Government of India (n 7) 118.

growth and development of India's securities markets, but has also been a trailblazer in the regulatory sphere as one of India's earliest regulators in the post-liberalisation era. At the same time, as this chapter has sought to demonstrate, SEBI's role has been beset with legal and operational constraints that have prevented it from undertaking the desired role, particularly on the enforcement front. Its inability to fully and successfully enforce an extensive framework of well-developed legislative instruments has been a cause for concern. While a number of measures have been suggested by reformers over the years, the iterative process for enhancing SEBI's powers and resources has not kept pace with the needs of the securities markets. A more radical approach is necessary on this count.

6

Banking

SUYASH RAI

Banking is not only basically 19th-century technology, but it is disaster-prone technology.[1]

Merton Miller

INTRODUCTION

THE FINANCIAL SYSTEM plays an important role in mobilising savings, allocating capital in the economy, monitoring corporations, providing liquidity, helping individuals and firms manage risks, facilitating payments and other economic functions. There is significant evidence of the positive impact of financial development on the economy.[2] Financial systems of different countries differ in terms of their institutional structure, with some being largely market-based and others more bank-based.[3]

India's financial system is largely bank-based. As of 31 March 2016, about 45.5 per cent of borrowing of non-financial firms was from banks (see Figure 6.1). For private non-financial firms, the share of bank loans was 51.6 per cent, while bonds and foreign borrowing added up to less than a quarter of borrowing. As of 31 March 2016, the ratio of scheduled commercial banks' deposits to gross domestic product (GDP) was 67.8 per cent, up from 41.4 per cent at 31 March 1996. The total deposits with banks were Rs 103.6 trillion, while the total assets under management with mutual funds and the pension system were only Rs 13.5 trillion. Given the salience of banks in the economy, regulation of banking is a crucial function of the Indian state.

[1] Merton Miller, 'Financial Markets and Economic Growth' (2003) 11(3) *Journal of Applied Corporate Finance* 8, 15.

[2] See generally Raghuram G Rajan and Luigi Zingales, 'Financial Dependence and Growth' (1998) 88(3) *American Economic Review* 559, 586.

[3] Asli Demirgüç-Kunt and Ross Levine, 'Bank-Based and Market-Based Financial Systems: Cross-country Comparisons', World Bank, 1999, available at http://documents.worldbank.org/curated/en/259341468739463577/pdf/multi-page.pdf.

Figure 6.1 Sources of borrowing for non-financial firms (%) (data sourced from: Economic Outlook, Centre for Monitoring of Indian Economy, https://economicoutlook.cmie.com)

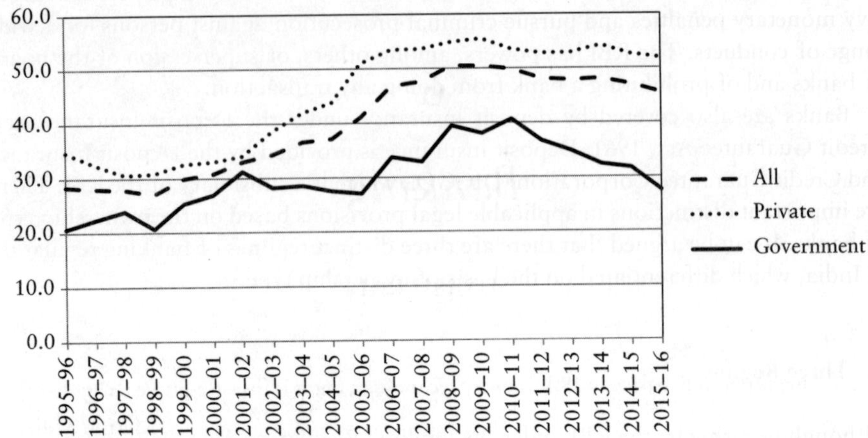

Mohan and Ray identify three distinct periods in the history of India's financial system: the 1950s and 1960s, with elements of instability associated with laissez-faire but under-developed banking; the 1970s and 1980s, which experienced the process of financial development across the country under government auspices, accompanied by a degree of financial repression; and the period since the 1990s, which has been characterised by gradual and calibrated financial deepening and liberalisation.[4] This chapter focuses on the latest of these periods.

I. BANKING REGULATION: THE PRESENT FRAMEWORK

The main law governing regulation of banking is the Banking Regulation Act, 1949 (hereinafter the BR Act). It defines *banking* as: 'the accepting, for the purpose of lending or investment, of deposits of money from the public, repayable on demand or otherwise, and withdrawal by cheque, draft, order or otherwise'. In addition to the business of banking, the BR Act allows banks to undertake certain related businesses (eg, borrowing money and lending money) and prohibits them from certain activities (eg, the buying or selling of movable property, except in connection with the realisation of security, and granting loans on the security of its own shares).

Beyond such permissions and prohibitions, the Act gives considerable powers to the Reserve Bank of India (RBI) to regulate the sector. The RBI can give any directions to banks (section 35A) based on a very broad set of reasons (in the public interest, in the interests of banking policy, to prevent the affairs of any bank from being conducted in a manner that is detrimental to the interests of the depositors or in

[4] Rakesh Mohan and Partha Ray, 'Indian Financial Sector: Structure, Trends and Turns', International Monetary Fund, 2017, available at https://www.imf.org/en/Publications/WP/Issues/2017/01/20/Indian-Financial-Sector-Structure-Trends-and-Turns-44554.

a manner that is prejudicial to the interests of the banking company, to secure the proper management of any banking company etc). The Act also empowers the RBI to levy monetary penalties and pursue criminal prosecution against persons for a wide range of conducts. The RBI has powers, among others, of supersession of the board of banks and of prohibiting a bank from doing any transaction.

Banks are also covered by deposit insurance under the Deposit Insurance and Credit Guarantee Act, 1961. Deposit insurance is provided by the Deposit Insurance and Credit Guarantee Corporation (DICGC), which is a subsidiary of the RBI. There are important distinctions in applicable legal provisions based on the ownership type of banks. It can be argued that there are three distinct regimes of banking regulation in India, which differentiated on the basis of ownership type.

A. Three Regimes

Although licensing by the RBI under the Banking Regulation Act, 1949 is mandatory for carrying out the business of banking in India, ownership type matters a great deal. There are three distinct types of banking institutions in India, which are as follows:

Public sector banks (PSBs): these are banks where a majority of shares are owned by governments in India. There are three types of PSBs. First, there are banks established by nationalisation laws. These include the State Bank of India (SBI)[5] and 19 nationalised banks. Second, there is one bank that is not governed by a nationalisation law, but has majority government ownership – IDBI Bank. Third, there are 56 regional rural banks (RRBs), where the Central Government owns 50 per cent of the shares, a state government owns 15 per cent and a 'sponsor bank' owns 35 per cent.

Private sector banks: these are banks where a majority of shares are owned by private individuals or organisations. At present, these include 37 Indian private sector banks and 43 foreign banks. Until recently, for anyone looking to establish a private sector banks, there were only two options: a universal bank or a local area bank.[6] Recently, small finance banks[7] and payments banks[8] have also been allowed. The Indian private sector banks include 21 universal banks, three local area banks, nine small finance banks and four payment banks.

Cooperative banks: these are cooperative banks registered under the cooperative laws of their respective states or under the Multi-State Cooperative Societies Act, 2002,

[5] From 1955 to 2007, the RBI held a majority stake in SBI. In 2007, the RBI's shares were transferred to the Government of India.

[6] Introduced in 1996, the local area banks are allowed to operate in a limited area of three contiguous districts.

[7] Small finance banks have a lower minimum capital requirement, but have to undertake more lending to certain priority sectors (agriculture, micro-enterprises etc) and have at least half of the portfolio in loans of less than Rs 2.5 million.

[8] Payments banks can accept limited amounts of deposits per customer (at present, Rs 100,000) and provide payment services, but cannot give credit.

which is a central law, and are licensed to undertake banking activities by the RBI.[9] The RBI regulates the banking functions of these societies, while the other functions are regulated by the state government or the Central Government, depending on the cooperative law under which the society is registered. There are 1,562 urban cooperative banks (including 51 multi-state urban cooperative banks), 33 state cooperative banks (StCBs) and 370 district central cooperative banks (DCCBs).[10] As at 31 March 2016, cooperative banks had just over seven per cent of the total deposits with banks. The share of public sector banks was about 68 per cent. Private domestic banks had about a 21 per cent share and foreign banks had a less than four per cent share. As at 31 March 2017, the deposit insurance system covered 2,125 banks, including private sector banks, PSBs, urban cooperative banks (UCBs), StCBs and DCCBs.

Although most of the powers of the RBI under the BR Act can be applied to all the banks, there are important differences. The BR Act prohibits the imposition of personal fines on board members of PSBs. The RBI can only recommend removal of chairmen, board members or senior officers but cannot take the decision. This limits the authority to hold board members accountable. The RBI cannot independently withdraw the licence of a PSB. The limited powers available to the RBI to initiate the process of resolution or liquidation of failing banks are not available in the case of PSBs. For instance, the RBI cannot force the merger of a PSB with another bank. Only the Central Government can use powers of amalgamation, liquidation etc under the respective nationalisation laws. Similar constraints exist for RRBs, which are governed by the Regional Rural Banks Act, 1976. On the other hand, there are some powers that the RBI has only over PSBs. RBI nominees are on the boards of all PSBs and they are also members of the management committees of boards, which take the major lending and write-off decisions.

The monitoring and enforcement responsibilities are fragmented. For UCBs, the banking function is supervised by the RBI, and the other functions are supervised by the respective state's Registrar of Cooperative Societies or, in the case of multi-state cooperative banks, by the Central Registrar of Cooperative Societies. For the supervision of StCBs, DCCBs and RRBs, powers have been delegated to the National Bank for Agriculture and Rural Development (NABARD) to conduct inspections. StCBs and DCCBs are also regulated and supervised by the states' respective Registrar of Cooperatives. For the cooperative banks, because of dual regulation, the RBI needs to work with the respective government to achieve the intended outcomes. The RBI has signed memoranda of understanding with various state governments. For the liquidation or winding-up of cooperative banks, the RBI can only ask the respective Registrar, who then has to initiate proceedings.

[9] The BR Act was amended in 1965 to extend its application to cooperative societies.

[10] Cooperative credit institutions also include primary agricultural credit societies (PACSs), state cooperative agriculture and rural development banks (SCARDBs), and primary cooperative agriculture and rural development banks (PCARDBs), but these are not under the purview of the Banking Regulation Act, 1949 and are not regulated by the RBI.

B. The Regulatory Framework

The RBI has used its powers to create a regulatory framework. The banking regulations can be broadly categorised into three types: prudential regulation for safety and soundness of banks; customer protection regulations focused on fairness in the conduct of banks; and distributive regulations relating to mandates given to banks to pursue social objectives.

Prudential regulation begins with licensing. For a long time, RBI followed a very restrictive licensing policy. After granting 10 licences in 1993–94, it did not give any universal banking licences for a decade. It then gave out only two more licences in 2003–04. After that, there was no licensing of universal banks for more than a decade, when, in 2014, in-principle approval was given for two more banks. In 2015, the licensing policy changed. The RBI gave a number of differentiated banking licences (in-principle approvals for 10 small finance bank licences and 11 payment banks).[11] In 2016, the RBI released guidelines for 'on-tap' licensing of universal commercial banks. Interestingly, the licensing guidelines prohibit large groups (assets of more than Rs 50 billion) whose income from non-banking sources is over 40 per cent of their total income from applying for a universal banking licence. The RBI imposes different licensing conditions, depending on the type of bank. It also now allows appeal against a decision to reject an application.

The RBI's prudential regulation, especially in matters of capital regulation, liquidity regulation and transparency for banks, has broadly followed the norms developed by the Basel Committee on Banking Supervision. The RBI issued regulations with an adaptation of the first Basel Accord in 1992. Subsequently, alterations to the Basel framework have to varying degrees been specified in regulations. In 2009, regulations for the implementation of Basel II norms were issued. In 2012, the RBI issued regulations based on the Basel III norms on capital regulation. The Basel III capital regulation was implemented from 1 April 2013 in India in phases and is expected to be fully implemented by 31 March 2019.

The Basel Committee on Banking Supervision conducts assessments of the implementation of 22 standards included in the Basel III Accord. In the assessment carried out in October 2017, the Committee found that: adoption was complete for seven standards; for two standards, rules had been published, but were yet to be implemented; for two standards, draft regulations had been published; and for the remaining 11 standards, no progress had been made.[12] This implementation status compares favourably with the implementation status in other countries. However, it is not sufficient to issue regulations with high standards. Supervision and monitoring by the regulator help to ensure that the regulations are truly followed. The supervision function is not directly observed by outsiders and is mostly revealed through outcome indicators relating to the performance of the regulated sector.

[11] Some of the approved applicants chose not to start the banks. Thus, nine small finance banks and four payment banks have been started.

[12] Basel Committee on Banking Supervision, 'Thirteenth Progress Report on Adoption of the Basel Regulatory Framework' (2017), available at https://www.bis.org/bcbs/publ/d418.htm.

Prudential regulations vary according to the institution type. The regulation of capital to risk-weighted assets ratio (CRAR) for StCBs and DCCBs was issued as recently as 2014.

On customer protection, the main focus has been on achieving safety and soundness of banks and providing redress for certain kinds of abuses. The former was to be achieved through prudential regulation and, in situations of bank failures, by deposit insurance and a forced merger of the failed bank with a healthy bank. Redress is provided through an Ombudsman scheme, which was introduced in 1995.[13] At present, there are 20 offices under the scheme. Appeals from the Ombudsman can go to a Deputy Governor of the RBI. In 2016–17, the scheme handled more than 100,000 complaints.[14] In 2017, the RBI expanded the scope of the Banking Ombudsman Scheme to include deficiencies arising out of sale of insurance/mutual fund/other third party investment products by banks and non-adherence to RBI instructions with regard to mobile banking/electronic banking as grounds for complaint.

Little attention has been paid to framing regulations against mis-selling and other forms of customer abuse, although this seems to be gradually changing. The RBI has begun looking at issuing regulations that outline the protections for customers. In 2014, the RBI issued a 'Charter of Customer Rights', which envisages five rights for customers: the right to fair treatment; the right to transparency, fair and honest dealing; the right to suitability; the right to privacy; and the right to redress of grievances and compensation. However, instead of formulating regulations to give these protections to customers, the RBI has only advised the banks to formulate their own board-approved policy incorporating these rights. These are small steps towards a regulatory framework for customer protection in banking.

Distributive regulations in banking have traditionally been concerned with ensuring the presence of banks in rural areas and the delivery of credit to rural areas and to certain priority sectors (agriculture, micro-enterprises etc). There is evidence to show that such interventions have helped reduce poverty[15] and improve per capita output.[16] These pursuits have continued, but their nature has been transformed. The focus is now less on ensuring that traditional bank branches are opened in rural areas and more on 'banking outlets' that may include agents. In 2006, the RBI allowed banks to appoint agents called 'business correspondents' to deliver services. This has enabled rapid expansion in the presence of banks in remote areas. Between 2010 and 2017, the total number of banking outlets in villages increased from 67,694 to 598,093.[17] While the number of bank branches in villages increased from 33,378 to 50,860, the number of business correspondent outlets grew 16 times, from 34,316 to 547,233. The presence of this channel has enabled the opening and servicing of low balance

[13] Bank customers also have the option of approaching the consumer courts.

[14] Reserve Bank of India, *Annual Report, 2016–17*.

[15] Robin Burgess, Rohini Pande and Grace Wong, 'Banking for the Poor: Evidence from India' (2005) 3(2–3) *Journal of the European Economic Association* 268, 278.

[16] Robin Burgess and Rohini Pande, 'Do Rural Banks Matter? Evidence from the Indian Social Banking Experiment' (2005) 95(3) *American Economic Review* 780, 795.

[17] Reserve Bank of India (n 14) Table IV.A.

accounts under schemes such as the *Pradhan Mantri Jan Dhan Yojana* (PMJDY). As at 31 March 2017, 533 million basic accounts, which do not require a minimum balance, had been opened.

Priority sector lending norms have also been partially reformed. The main reform is the introduction of priority sector lending certificates that enable banks to capitalise on their comparative advantages in lending to priority sectors. In 2016, the RBI issued guidelines that allowed banks to trade in these certificates. These certificates can be traded in sub-targets in lending to agriculture, small and marginal farmers, micro-enterprises and the overall priority sector lending target.

C. The Institutional Landscape

As discussed earlier, the latest phase in the history of India's financial system is characterised by gradual and calibrated financial deepening and liberalisation. Although the banking sector has not witnessed the kinds of far-reaching reforms that have been implemented in some other sectors such as equity markets, several significant shifts have occurred in banking regulation and in other policies related to banking regulation.

i. Macro-economic Reforms with Consequences for Banking Regulation

India witnessed considerable financial repression for a long time. A large proportion of bank assets were in the form of government securities. This mandate worked alongside the automatic monetisation of the fiscal deficit. Beginning in 1964, the statutory liquidity ratio (SLR) requirements were increased several times, and the cash reserve ratio (CRR) requirements were increased gradually during the 1970s and 1980s, but were raised sharply in the late 1980s as the fiscal deficit ballooned. The CRR requirement peaked in 1989–90, when it was raised to 15 per cent, a level maintained until 1993–94. The SLR requirement peaked at 38.5 per cent in 1990–91 and 1991–92. So, for two years, the combined ratio was 53.5 per cent.

This financial repression constrained lending. The share of credit in total assets of the bank hovered around 50 per cent from 1986–87 to 2004–05. The SLR and CRR yield low returns, but they are safe. As a result, safety and soundness of banks required relatively less emphasis on other instruments of regulation and supervision. Beginning in the late 1990s, these requirements have been reduced. The combined requirement is now 23.5 per cent (SLR: 19.5 per cent; CRR: 4 per cent). This was made possible by fiscal reforms, especially a reduction in deficits and the discontinuation of the practice of automatic monetisation. It is not clear whether financial repression is still happening due to these requirements, because banks often maintain higher than mandated ratios. However, this may be because of demand-side issues. In a time of a credit boom, it would become clear whether the present requirements are leading to financial repression. Moreover, since the requirements are general and not tied to bank-specific liquidity risks, in theory there may still be repression in some banks.

A recent reform impacting banking regulation is the creation of an empowered Monetary Policy Committee, with a clear inflation-targeting objective. There were potential conflicts between the monetary policy and banking regulation roles of the RBI. For instance, the expectation of high inflation calls for an increase in interest rates, which may, especially in times of downturns, push banks towards failure. By conferring monetary policy powers upon the Committee, this conflict has been reduced.

ii. Approach to Supervision

Until the late 1990s, the RBI had a supervisory approach that primarily relied on giving directions to specific banks, which amounted to micro-management.[18] The approach has now significantly shifted towards making general regulations for categories of banks and monitoring compliance against them. In 1991 and 1998, two committees under the chairmanship of M Narasimham recommended a number of reforms for the banking sector, including reforms of prudential regulation consistent with global standards, such as risk-based capital norms, standard accounting practices and so on. The RBI introduced regulations that were consistent with the Basel Accords, which emphasised more principles-based regulation, giving flexibility to banks to manage their risks within the given parameters.

Regulations can also facilitate monitoring by private stakeholders by mandating the release of structured information by auditors, rating agencies and accounting standards, and by creating incentives for private monitoring by allowing instruments such as subordinated debt to be included in capital. Barth et al have found that between 1999 and 2011, India registered the highest level of improvements in empowering private stakeholders for the monitoring of banks.[19]

iii. New Institutions

The RBI has issued more licences and has also allowed different categories of banks to be licensed. The introduction of business correspondents has changed the way in which banks reach remote areas and low-income areas in urban localities. This institutional innovation, coupled with the use of technology, has improved the economics of banking for low-income households and enterprises.

In 2000, the first credit bureau was established in India. Following the enactment of Credit Information Companies (Regulation) Act, 2005, multiple credit bureaus have been established. Similarly, following the enactment of the Payment and Settlement Systems Act, 2007, a number of payment service providers that work with banks have been licensed. Market infrastructure relating to interbank payments has also been overhauled. The Real-Time Gross Settlement (RTGS) system was introduced in 2004. The Clearing Corporation of India Ltd (CCIL), which is a central

[18] Savak Tarapore, 'Indian Banking: Preparing for the Next Round of Reform' in James Hanson and Sanjay Kathuria (eds), *India: A Financial Sector for the Twenty First Century* (Oxford University Press, 1999).

[19] James Barth, Gerard Caprio, Jr and Ross Levine, 'Bank Regulation and Supervision in 180 Countries from 1999 to 2011' (2013) 5(2) *Journal of Financial Economic Policy* 111, 219.

counterparty, was set up in April 2001 to provide clearing and settlement for transactions in government securities, foreign exchange and money markets in the country.

There have been institutional reforms relating to the recovery of bad loans by banks. The Recovery of Debts due to Banks and Financial Institutions Act, 1993 (hereinafter the RDBBFI Act) led to the establishment of Debt Recovery Tribunals (DRTs) and their appellate body – the Debt Recovery Appellate Tribunal (DRAT) – to help with the debt recovery for banks and other financial institutions. However, after the initial stages, the DRT system became clogged with a large number of pending cases.[20] In 2014, six new DRTs were added to the 33 existing DRTs. In 2016, the RDBBFI Act was amended to make certain changes that might help reduce the problems. These included: empowering the Central Government to provide uniform procedural rules for the proceedings in the DRTs and the DRAT, a higher retirement age of presiding officers of DRTs and the chairperson of the DRAT, the reappointment of presiding officers and chairpersons, an increase in the cost imposed on borrowers for delay in recovery timelines etc.

The enactment of the Securitisation and Reconstruction of Financial Assets and Enforcement of Security Interest Act, 2002 created a legal framework for recovery of loans by auctioning properties and also helped create an asset reconstruction industry. The recent enactment of the Insolvency and Bankruptcy Code, 2016 (IBC) is also beginning to help banks resolve their bad loans. The IBC also gives powers to DRTs to consider cases of bankruptcy from individuals and unlimited liability partnerships.

iv. Deposit Insurance Coverage

Before 1968, deposit insurance cover was up to Rs 1,500 per account, which covered less than a quarter of the total deposits. Beginning in 1968 and until 1993, deposit insurance coverage was increased periodically, so that at any given time, 60–75 per cent of deposits were insured and 95–99 per cent accounts were fully covered. This extensive coverage, coupled with public ownership of much of the banking sector, reduced the incentive to rely on regulatory and supervisory interventions for the safety and soundness of banks. Since 1993, the coverage amount has not been revised. As of 31 March 2017, only 29.5 per cent of deposits were covered, and 92.1 per cent of accounts were fully covered. This may have reduced the moral hazard arising out of high deposit insurance coverage and enhanced the incentive for regulatory as well as private monitoring of banks.

v. Customer Abuse Protection

Selling of third party products has become an important business for banks. At the same time, banks are becoming places where abuse of customers is taking place.[21]

[20] According to a question answered in Parliament, as of 30 June 2016, there were 109,518 pending cases in DRTs involving an amount totalling Rs 6.35 trillion (see http://164.100.47.190/loksabhaquestions/annex/12/AU2287.pdf).

[21] Renuka Sane and Monika Halan, 'Misled and Mis-sold: Financial Misbehaviour in Retail Banks?' (2017) 45(3) *Journal of Comparative Economics* 429, 444.

As discussed earlier, the RBI now seems to be recognising this problem and has taken steps to start building customer protection in the sector.

vi. Pricing Restrictions

Regulatory reforms have, over time, minimised the restrictions on interest rates both on the lending and deposit-taking sides. Much of this deregulation was carried out in the 1990s. Only a few rates remained regulated – interest on small loans up to Rs 200,000, rupee export credit and the savings deposit interest rate. The small loans and rupee export credit were deregulated in 2010, when the Base Rate system was introduced. In 2011, the savings account interest rate was also deregulated, subject to certain conditions.

vii. Application of the Anti-corruption Law

In 2016, the Supreme Court ruled that bankers, including those from private banks, are public servants under the Prevention of Corruption Act, 1988 (POCA). The decision was based on three laws: the POCA, the BR Act and the Indian Penal Code (IPC). The Court based its reasoning on section 46A of the BR Act: 'Every chairman who is appointed on a whole-time basis, managing director, director, auditor, liquidator, manager and any other employee of a banking company shall be deemed to be a public servant for the purposes of Chapter IX of the Indian Penal Code.' This Chapter of the IPC had certain corruption-related provisions that have been repealed and replaced by the POCA. The Court ruled that the legislative intent was to consider bankers as public servants for the purposes of anti-corruption provisions, which are now in the POCA. This decision has added a risk to the banking sector. Banking regulation seeks to build and sustain trust in banks, but by taking abrupt actions, such as conducting raids, the law enforcement agencies may create panic among depositors.

The question now is: what is next for banking regulation in India? Addressing this question requires an analysis of certain structural features of banking regulation, especially those relating to bank ownership, regulatory governance by the banking regulator, the legal process followed by the regulator, and gaps in the institutional architecture. In addition, given the ongoing developments in financial technologies, it is possible that in a few years' time, the banking sector may be forced to undergo important changes.

II. STRUCTURAL ISSUES

Banks are built on relationship-based intermediation and they preserve their businesses by maintaining a certain degree of opacity, because transparency may lead to the loss of business to the competition.[22] This inherent incentive towards opacity

[22] Raghuram G Rajan and Luigi Zingales, 'Financial Systems, Industrial Structure, and Growth' (2001) 17(4) *Oxford Review of Economic Policy* 467, 482.

makes banking regulation more difficult. For instance, large firms that can offer substantial business to banks can take advantage of the opacity of bank loans, which they would not be able to enjoy in market-based borrowing. Banking regulation is therefore a difficult kind of regulation, especially in a context of weak institutions. In this section, we take a strategic view of the sector and focus on the structural issues that seem to impede the effective regulation of banking in India.

A. Banking Regulation and Government Ownership: A Grand Bargain?

In 1969, 14 banks were nationalised by the Banking Companies (Acquisition and Transfer of Undertakings) Ordinance, which was confirmed by an Act of Parliament in 1970. In the two years prior to the nationalisation, many attempts were made by the RBI and the then Finance Minister Morarji Desai to avoid nationalisation by using alternative instruments of state power.[23] A number of governance reforms were introduced through an amendment to the banking laws that was notified in early 1969. These included: a majority of professional directors; representation on the board from agriculture and the rural economy, small industries and cooperatives; professional bankers instead of industrialists as chairpersons; a prohibition on lending to directors of the bank; RBI approval for the appointment and removal of auditors; and so on. The law also empowered the Central Government to acquire a bank if it failed to comply with the directions of the RBI or was being run badly. In the RBI's view, such governance reforms and greater social control over banks were better than nationalisation.[24] However, before these measures could be properly implemented, the government decided to nationalise the banks. In 1980, six more private banks were nationalised.[25]

There are theoretical arguments that support intervention in banking to ensure that it serves some specified idea of social good. Banerjee reviews and summarises evidence to show that in developing countries, the credit markets often do not serve borrowers in the agricultural sector or those running small enterprises, even though the positive externality of such loans may be high.[26] In practice, the welfare impact of government ownership of banks is not clear. For instance, Berger et al find that while government-owned banks in India are, predictably, more likely to lend to government-owned and rural firms, contrary to expectations, they are less likely to lend to smaller, informationally more opaque firms that government-owned banks are supposedly designed to serve.[27] There is also some evidence to suggest that even though government ownership may lead to development lending targets being met, this need not

[23] Reserve Bank of India, *The Concise History of Reserve Bank of India 1935–1981* (Reserve Bank of India, 2014).

[24] ibid.

[25] In 1993, the Punjab National Bank acquired the New Bank of India, leaving 19 nationalised banks.

[26] Abhijit V. Banerjee, 'Contracting Constraints, Credit Markets, and Economic Development' in Mathias Dewatripont, Lars Peter Hansen, and Stephen J. Turnovsky (eds), Advances in Economics and Econometrics: *Theory and Applications, Eighth World Congress, Volume III* (Cambridge University Press, 2003).

[27] AN Berger, LF Klapper, MS Martinez Peria and R Zaidi, 'Bank Ownership Type and Banking Relationships' (2008) 17(1) *Journal of Financial Intermediation* 37, 62.

have any significant impact on the real economy, thus putting into question the necessity of such intervention.[28] It is beyond the scope of this chapter to weigh up the merits and demerits of these arguments, or to assess their validity in India's context. However, the ways in which government ownership and intervention in banking affect regulation of banking are important to understand.

Nationalisation significantly altered the landscape of banking in India. Although their market share has fallen, PSBs continue to dominate banking. In 1989–90, about 91 per cent of bank deposits in scheduled commercial banks were with PSBs. In 2015–16, their share had come down to 74 per cent. Although the consistent downward trend in the share of PSBs was interrupted in the years following the global financial crisis (2008–09), it resumed in 2012–13.

Figure 6.2 Share in bank deposits mobilised by scheduled commercial banks (data sourced from: Basic Statistical Returns of Scheduled Commercial Banks, Reserve Bank of India, https://rbi.org.in/Scripts/AnnualPublications.aspx?head=Basic%20Statistical%20Returns)

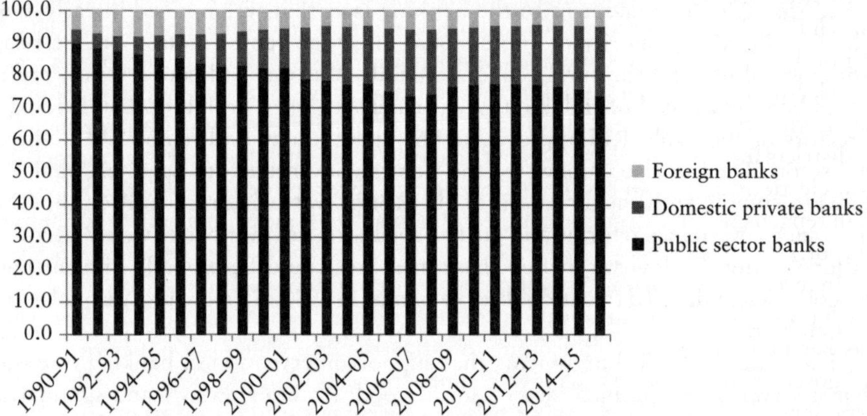

There are considerable differences in the financial performance of private and public sector banks, especially in times of crisis. At present, there is a crisis of bad loans in PSBs. As of 31 March 2018, the gross non-performing assets (GNPA) ratio of banks was 11.6 per cent. The ratio for public sector banks was 15.6 per cent, while that for private banks was just 4 per cent.[29] There are stark differences in terms of performance across a range of indicators.[30] Similar differences between PSBs and private banks were observed during the last crisis, which lasted from 1997 to 2002.[31] This begs the following question: why is this so, when both sets of banks operate in the same economy? There are certain structural differences between private banks and PSBs that could help explain these differences.

[28] Shawn Cole, 'Financial Development, Bank Ownership, and Growth: Or, Does Quantity Imply Quality?' (2009) 91(1) *Review of Economics and Statistics* 33.

[29] Reserve Bank of India, 'Financial Stability Report', June 2018.

[30] ibid.

[31] Rajeswari Sengupta and Harsh Vardhan, 'Non-performing Assets in Indian Banks: This time it is Different' (2017) 52 *Economic and Political Weekly* 85, 95.

i. Limits of Regulatory Powers

As discussed earlier, the legislative framework places certain constraints on the regulation of PSBs, which may limit the overall efficacy of regulations. For instance, the absence of the option to initiate the resolution or liquidation of a failing PSB limits the effectiveness of the suite of other supervisory powers. There are times when a bank cannot be improved by supervisory instructions and needs to be resolved or liquidated. But since the instruments of resolution and liquidation are in the hands of the government, this option does not exist with the regulator.

ii. Moral Hazard Due to Government Intervention and Support

The public ownership of banks is often associated with direct or indirect political intervention that may harm financial prudence in those banks. Sapienza finds that Italian public sector banks charge lower interest rates and that their interest rates are correlated with electoral results.[32] Khwaja and Mian note that Pakistani politicians enrich themselves and their firms by borrowing from government banks and defaulting on loans.[33] In India, Cole finds that lending by government-owned banks tracks the electoral cycle, with agricultural credit increasing by 5–10 percentage points in an election year.[34] There is significant cross-sectional targeting, with large increases in districts in which an election is particularly close. This targeting does not occur in non-election years or in private bank lending. This capture is costly: elections affect loan repayments and election year credit booms do not measurably affect agricultural output.

In recent years, the objective of political intervention seems to have been modified. It is no longer only about directing credit to agriculture or other such sectors. There has been a rapid increase in lending to infrastructure, which is a policy priority for the government. PSBs gave loans to complex projects with which they had little prior experience and took development risks they were not well placed to manage.[35] The government's priorities have also come to include getting accounts opened for the previously unbanked. Under the PMJDY, about 97 per cent zero-balance accounts have been opened by PSBs.

A related issue here is how government-financed loan waivers affect credit discipline and thereby placed stress on the financial health of banks. De and Tantri find that after a loan waiver in 2008, all groups of borrowers (those who received full debt relief, those who received partial debt relief and those who did not benefit), behaving strategically, defaulted and took longer to repay their loans than in the pre-waiver period, causing ex post inefficiency in the credit market.[36] The effects were found to

[32] Paola Sapienza, 'The Effects of Government Ownership on Bank Lending' (2004) 72(2) *Journal of Financial Economics* 357, 384.

[33] Asim Ijaz Khwaja and Atif Mian, 'Do Lenders Favor Politically Connected Firms? Rent Provision in an Emerging Financial Market' (2005) 120(4) *Quarterly Journal of Economics* 1371, 1411.

[34] Shawn Cole, 'Fixing Market Failures or Fixing Elections? Agricultural Credit in India' (2009) 1 *American Economic Journal: Applied Economics* 219.

[35] KC Chakrabarty, 'Infrastructure Financing by Banks in India: Myths and Realities', keynote address at the Annual Infrastructure Finance Conclave organised by SBI Capital Markets Limited, 2013, 9.

[36] Sankar De and Prasanna L Tantri, 'Borrowing Culture and Debt Relief: Evidence from a Policy Experiment' (2014) Asian Finance Association (AsianFA) Conference Paper.

be most negative for the formerly good borrowers who did not default before. The study also found that, anticipating adverse borrower behaviour, the lending institutions rationed credit, generating ex ante inefficiency and leading to lower access to credit for poor households.

It is not just that the government seems to intervene in the business of PSBs; it also absorbs the losses that may arise as a result of such business and other types of business of the PSBs. Government ownership of banks in India is seen as an implicit promise to support the bank if it faces a crisis. Although the laws do not promise this, the practice of repeated government-funded recapitalisation and the ambiguity in the laws have created the perception of a government guarantee.[37] The government has not allowed even the weakest PSBs to be resolved or liquidated.

This affects the perception of the safety of PSBs. Acharya and Kulkarni found that in the crisis of 2007–09, the vulnerable private sector banks experienced deposit withdrawals and shortening of deposit maturity relative to other private sector banks, but the vulnerable state-owned banks saw a relative growth in their deposit base (and even more so in terms of deposits) and increased their loan advances, at cheaper rates, and especially to public sector firms. These findings show that PSBs face weaker market discipline than private sector banks, perhaps because the former enjoy implicit government support. This may be distorting the incentives for those running the bank, and those depositing or lending money to them. If there is an implicit promise of a bailout, the incentive to exercise prudence is weakened. Evidence from other countries such as China also suggests that this effect is real.[38]

Recently, in a leading PSB, a scam was discovered that is reported to have led to losses worth about one-third of the bank's market capitalisation at that time.[39] That there was no run on the bank might suggest that the depositors expected the government to support the bank in a time of crisis. Similarly, some of the PSBs have very high GNPA ratios, but there are no signs of a run on such banks. For the governance and senior management of PSBs, the incentive to maintain safety and soundness is probably weaker because of this lack of market discipline. It seems that the confusion about incentives at PSBs percolates through the organisation and makes it difficult to enforce clear decision-making criteria and to hold persons and groups accountable. Perhaps through organisational culture, this also affects purely commercial lending decisions. Further, when systems are weak, those looking to conduct scams may feel emboldened to take advantage of the weaknesses.

The problem of moral hazard created by government intervention and support makes the regulation of PSBs more challenging. When government intervention imposes costs on banks or leads to imprudent lending practices, the RBI has to choose between two directions: either to not intervene or to use its powers (especially its membership on PSB boards) to force PSBs to follow more prudent practices.

[37] Although the nationalisation laws allow the government to merge or liquidate the PSBs, they prevent shares of the government from going below 50 per cent.

[38] Yizhe Dong et al. 'Ownership Structure and Risk-Taking: Comparative Evidence from Private and State-Controlled Banks in China' (2014) 36 *International Review of Financial Analysis* 120, 130.

[39] The scam involving the Punjab National Bank is reported to have cost more than Rs 140 billion.

The latter option essentially puts the regulator at odds with the government and its policy priorities, while the former may lead to a worsening of financial performance of the PSBs. It seems that the RBI has chosen some variant of the former path and this may be tied to the other side of government ownership – the implicit promise of support in times of financial distress.

iii. Weak Rationale for Regulation

Due to the moral hazard created by government ownership, the regulation of PSBs becomes more challenging, but at the same time, the rationale for regulation becomes weaker. Consider the basic rationale for banking regulation. First, as Freixas and Rochet observe, banking regulation is required due to the externalities of bank failures.[40] Bank failures impose losses on unsuspecting depositors, and banking crises have negative effects on the wider economy. Second, regulation is required to prevent runs on banks. Banks promise to return the deposits immediately without any deterioration of value, but use most of their funds to issue loans that are opaque, relatively illiquid. Banks have opaque balance sheets and the depositors are usually unable to assess their financial health. This introduces uncertainty in the system, and if one bank fails to make good on the promise of paying back the deposit, there is a risk of contagion. An important reason to regulate banks and to offer deposit insurance is that banks are prone to runs that are driven by contagion inspired by real or imagined failure.[41] Once a run begins, even a healthy bank may need to undertake a 'fire sale' of its assets, which may precipitate its failure. Allen and Carletti suggest that one of the market failures justifying the regulation of banking is a coordination problem – if people believe there is going to be a panic, then this can be self-fulfilling.[42]

The regulator seeks to sustain the safety and soundness of banks in order to assure depositors that their funds are safe with the banks. However, because of the implicit government guarantee and repeated experiences of bank recapitalisation, the perceived risk of PSBs failing is very low. India has had two significant banking crises in the last two decades – between 1997 and 2002, and the current crisis.[43] In both, the PSBs performed worse than the private banks, and some were on the verge of failure. However, there were no runs on PSBs. In addition to this near-impossibility of a run on PSBs, even the losses that are generated are mostly absorbed by the main owner – namely the government – through recapitalisation. Therefore, to the extent that regulatory capacity is a limited resource, there is an incentive to allocate less capacity to PSBs and more to other banks. As Laffont and Tirole demonstrate, transaction costs make it costly to create and enforce regulations.[44] Effective regulations

[40] Xavier Freixas and Jean-Charles Rochet, *Microeconomics of Banking* (MIT Press, 2008).

[41] Douglas W Diamond and Philip H Dybvig, 'Bank Runs, Deposit Insurance, and Liquidity (1983) 91(3) *Journal of Political Economy* 401, 419.

[42] Franklin Allen, and Elena Carletti 'What is the Rationale for Regulating Banks?' *Banking & Finance Monitor* (December 2007), http://finance.wharton.upenn.edu/~allenf/download/Vita/banking%20and%20finance%20monitor%20article.pdf.

[43] Sengupta and Vardhan (n 31).

[44] Jean-Jacques Laffont and Jean Tirole, *A Theory of Incentives in Procurement and Regulation* (MIT Press, 1993).

require intensive efforts, especially where moral hazard is significant. The RBI may not have sufficient incentive to expend regulatory and supervisory resources on these banks. It could be argued that the RBI may still regulate PSBs seriously in order to preserve its legitimacy in public opinion. This can be a real concern because the RBI is represented on the PSB boards. However, given that the RBI can cite limitations on its powers and government intervention in banks as challenges, the real effect on its legitimacy is difficult to determine.[45]

iv. Constraints on Information Supply

Even if the RBI tries to regulate PSBs effectively, certain constraints may impede these efforts. Regulators face informational constraints because they often do not observe endogenous variables such as decisions about efforts, the allocation of perks and indulgence in activities that privilege managers' career potential over efficiency. The regulated firms also have more information than the regulator about certain exogenous variables affecting their business.[46] For PSBs, the perception of government support limits the incentives for market participants to generate information about them.

This combination of limited regulatory instruments, policy-directed business decisions, the implicit promise of repeated bailouts, and the consequential changes in incentives of banks and their depositors and investors suggests an implicit 'grand bargain' between the regulator and the government. PSBs seem to serve as instruments of government policy, while also undertaking commercial banking, and, in times of financial distress, they are recapitalised by the government. On the other hand, the regulator does not seem to create impediments in this arrangement by using its powers to intervene in the business of banking in a manner that would slow down the pursuit of the government's policy priorities.

The consequences of public ownership go beyond the regulation of PSBs. They may also affect the risks faced by the private banks. As was seen during the 2008–09 crisis, there is a risk of PSBs crowding out private banks, especially in times of uncertainty. PSBs are largely kept safe by the implicit promise of a taxpayer-funded bailout. This promise has already cost more than Rs 2 trillion in the present crisis.[47] In times of uncertainty, depositors can flee from a private bank to a PSB looking for government-backed safety.

Privatising PSBs will help reduce the moral hazard. However, to ensure that this does not increase the overall fragility in banking, institutional reforms are required. These reforms would have to aim at transitioning to a system where trust in banking comes from sound regulation and one where when a bank fails, this trust is maintained by orderly bankruptcy resolution coupled with substantial deposit insurance protecting depositors without relying on a taxpayer-funded bailout. If such reforms

[45] In a speech delivered in March 2018, the RBI Governor Dr Urjit Patel offered an argument about the RBI's limited powers over the PSBs.

[46] Laffont and Tirole (n 44).

[47] Compiled from the budget documents of the Government of India.

are not done, simply privatising PSBs might increase fragility in the banking system and may even lead many people to move away from banks or force the government to again resort to bailouts.

B. Regulatory Governance and Due Process

A perspective that stands in contrast to the one discussed in the previous section is that even though the incentives to do so are weak, the RBI should still regulate PSBs properly and perform its statutory duties. In a study of banking regulation across the world, Barth et al have called this the 'public interest view', which assumes that regulators work to ameliorate market failures by directly overseeing, regulating and disciplining banks.[48] In contrast, the 'private interest view' holds that regulators do not maximise social welfare; they maximise their own welfare. From this viewpoint, powerful regulators may abuse their powers to serve their own interests, and simply empowering regulators might reduce bank efficiency.

Barth et al find that giving more discretionary powers to banking regulators in countries with weak institutional environments, where the rule of law, the information environment etc are under-developed, leads to lower levels of banking system development, greater corruption in lending and higher bank fragility. At the same time, regulations that encourage depositors and investors to monitor and discipline bank behaviour, such as the requirement to provide timely and transparent information, are positively related to bank efficiency. It is not reasonable to assume that the public interest will always be pursued. The design of regulatory agencies should balance the need for their independence with the necessity to hold them accountable for their performance. Further, checks and balances focused on transparency and accountability may take the shape of due process that the laws require the regulators to follow.

There are a number of institutional design issues in banking regulation. NABARD is supposed to supervise StCBs, DCCBs and RRBs, but it also undertakes the refinancing of loans for these banks. There is a conflict between its financing role and the supervisory role. The RBI's nominees serve on the Management Committees of PSBs, which take major lending and write-off decisions. This makes the RBI party to commercial decisions, and conflicts with its supervisory role. There are structural problems with the agency design of the RBI as a regulator that may affect its ability to perform its functions properly. These relate to the independence and accountability of the RBI.

For the central banking functions, Eichengreen and Dincer gave very low scores to the RBI in terms of both transparency and independence.[49] In fact, in relation to independence, they ranked the RBI the lowest in the world.[50] The absence of clear

[48] James Barth, Gerard Caprio and Ross Levine, *Rethinking Bank Regulation: Till Angels Govern* (Cambridge University Press, 2008).

[49] Barry Eichengreen and N Nergiz Dincer, 'Central Bank Transparency and Independence: Updates and New Measures' (2014) 10(1) *International Journal of Central Banking* 189, 259.

[50] The monetary policy reforms conducted after the chapter was published will help to improve the score on independence.

independence given in the law,[51] and the government's discretion on giving extensions to Governors and the Deputy Governor (as opposed to a full term) are some of the factors that impede the independence of the RBI even as a banking regulator. The pursuit of multiple, vaguely stated objectives creates opportunities to shun accountability. There are conflicts between banking regulation and some other functions of the RBI. The RBI's role as a debt manager for the government conflicts with its role as a banking regulator. Banks are the main purchasers of government debt and there is an incentive for financial repression. The RBI's role as a banking regulator can be seen to be in conflict with its role as a regulator of government bond markets because the development of bond markets may reduce reliance on banks.

Accountability is both external and internal. Within the organisation, the key form of accountability is primarily to the board. Accountability to the board is often exercised through the committee processes. Patnaik and Roy observe that the RBI does not have the kinds of committees that comparable central banks and banking regulators are known to have.[52] The Bank of England has committees on: audit and risk; nominations for promotions; remuneration, large-value transactions; and governing the affixing of official seal. These are in addition to committees mandated by law, such as the Monetary Policy Committee and the Financial Stability Committee. Apart from the statutory committees, the RBI's general regulations create just one Committee of the Central Board. The Committee enjoys wide and sweeping powers, but the quorum for the Committee of the Central Board is only two directors, one of whom shall be an independent director. This is a weak accountability arrangement.

After its Central Board meeting, the RBI only publishes a press release and does not publish the agenda or the minutes of the meetings. The RBI's press releases also do not give sufficient details about what transpired in the meetings. Typically, they contain records of attendance and a few lines summarising what was discussed. These problems are probably exacerbated by the larger context, in which Parliament seems to have become a less effective institution of accountability.[53]

In terms of regulatory capacity, the RBI seems to compare well to most other regulatory agencies in India. It has a strong cadre of employees, most of whom spend their entire careers in the RBI.[54] The RBI hires young people and trains them in the institutes it runs and on the job. RBI officials are usually considered to be knowledgeable and the general impression is that the RBI is not a corrupt organisation. However, good regulatory outcomes are not just the results of regulatory capacity and the personal integrity of staff, but also of due process followed in the exercise of regulatory powers. Due process in making and implementing regulations is an

[51] The government has the power to give directions to the RBI.

[52] Ila Patnaik and Shubho Roy, 'The RBI Board: Comparison against International Benchmarks' (2017), available at https://ajayshahblog.blogspot.in/2017/01/the-rbi-board-comparison-against.html.

[53] Devesh Kapur and Pratap Bhanu Mehta, 'The Indian Parliament as an Institution of Accountability' (2006) United Nations Research Institute for Social Development.

[54] The RBI has significantly reduced its staff strength during the last two decades. In 1997, it had 33,084 employees. In 2016, staff numbers had dropped to 15,461. This drop was mostly the result of reduction of the number of Class III and Class IV employees. The number of Class I employees has remained largely the same.

essential aspect of the rule of law. In the context of regulatory agencies, due process could mean a variety of features of the regulatory process: clarity of regulatory instruments; reasonable delegation of powers, with accountability of the board; a thorough consultation process while making regulations; a notice and hearing process before enforcement decisions; and so on.[55]

The BR Act is very sparse in terms of accountability, transparency and due process requirements. For instance, the power to give directions does not come with a process to be followed in order to ensure that the power is not misused. The power to inspect does not seem to distinguish between inspection and investigation. The objectives for which the powers are to be used are not precisely laid down in the law. The RBI uses instruments in a confusing manner. While 'Directions' usually mean regulations, 'Notifications' and 'Circulars' are used for regulations and supervisory instructions. The delegation of powers is not clear, as even important regulations are signed by mid-level staff in the RBI rather than the board. An important aspect of following due process in regulation is a participatory consultation process. The process should include at least: publication of draft regulations along with an analysis of the expected impact of the proposed regulation; allowing comments to be submitted for a reasonable period of time; publication of comments along with responses in general terms; and publication of the final regulations.

Before 2005, the RBI rarely published draft regulations. From 2005 onwards, a few draft notifications/guidelines have been published every year. In 2017, 380 notifications/guidelines were issued. From these, 59 were regulatory in nature, ie, they changed the obligations on market players. From the 59 regulations, eight were preceded by the publication of draft regulations, while for two other regulations, consultation papers or reports were published. The time given for submitting responses ranged from seven to 33 days, and the average was about 20 days. One could argue that the RBI might be optimising matters by publishing only select draft regulations. It seems that while all the regulations that were preceded by publications of drafts were substantive, not all substantive regulations were preceded by the publication of drafts. Regulations relating to liquidity standards, banking facilities for senior citizens and differently abled persons, the rationalisation of risk-weights and loan-to-value ratios for housing loans are examples of regulations that are substantive and could have benefited from a consultation process. So, the basis on which the RBI decides whether it should publish draft regulations is not clear.

Most of the regulations give only a brief statement of the rationale for the chosen regulatory intervention. None of the draft regulations are accompanied by an analysis of the expected regulatory impact. Methods of regulatory impact assessment can help in the choice of efficient regulatory approaches. For example, the regulation on banking facility for senior citizens and differently abled persons imposes a number of obligations on banks to help improve banking access for such persons. These include clearly identifiable dedicated counters or a counter which provides priority to senior citizens and people who are differently abled, the provision of doorstep banking etc. Such regulations can benefit from cost-effectiveness analysis.

[55] See Financial Sector Legislative Reforms Commission, 'Report of the Financial Sector Legislative Reforms Commission',2013, Ministry of Finance, Government of India.

Improving the processes for making and implementing regulations could help avoid decisions that may not be in the public interest. For instance, the decision to severely constrain the issuance of licences in a fast-growing economy for two decades could have been avoided if sound processes had been followed. In March 2013, the Financial Sector Legislative Reforms Commission (FSLRC) recommended a number of best practices of regulatory governance and legal process. In October 2013, in a meeting of the Financial Stability and Development Council (FSDC), a resolution was adopted stating that all the financial sector regulators would devise an action plan for the implementation of all the FSLRC principles relating to regulatory governance, transparency and improved operational efficiency that do not require legislative action. The resolution outlined the principles that the regulators need to follow. These principles have only been partially implemented by the RBI.

C. Institutional Architecture

Banking regulation in India is affected by certain lacunae in the financial regulatory architecture. There are four central financial sector regulators and numerous state-level regulators of financial services (eg, registrars of chit funds and registrars of cooperative societies). The RBI regulates the institutions it licenses and largely ignores the other institutions that may be performing banking-type activities. For instance, if an agency starts taking deposits without an RBI licence, the RBI usually does not pursue that institution in terms of taking enforcement action against it. This is partially because of ambiguity in the laws, which allow similar activities under different laws. If the RBI were to take an activity-based approach to regulation, it would concern itself with anyone carrying out an activity that looks like banking. To move towards an activity-based approach would require changes in the laws to give the RBI jurisdiction over all deposit-taking activities.

Bankruptcy resolution for banks is the other side of banking regulation. It begins when regulation fails. Some creative destruction of inefficient banks is good for economic efficiency. Bank failures require quick and orderly resolution to ensure that panic does not spread. For example, in the US, the Federal Deposit Insurance Corporation is supposed to ensure such resolution and has mostly been successful in doing so. When failure does not harm depositors, regulators are more likely to encourage competition in banking. India does not yet have a specialised mechanism for the resolution of failed banks. The absence of an effective resolution framework increases the cost of failure and has a direct effect on choices made by the banking regulator. The regulator has the incentive to be excessively conservative in the licensing and regulation of private banks. The weaknesses of some other parts of the institutional system affect the efficacy of banking regulation. Penalties need to be enforced through the court system. However, given the delays that mark that system, it is very difficult for a regulator to ensure quick enforcement. Also, some of the institutions created to expedite recovery of loans, such as the DRTs, are themselves becoming congested.

D. New Technologies and Business Models

The advent of new financial technologies (fintech) is changing the landscape of the financial sector. The Basel Committee for Bank Supervision has identified five scenarios for how banks may change due to the new financial technologies.[56] The 'better bank' scenario would mean the modernisation and digitisation of incumbent players, with banks retaining the customer relationship and core banking services, and leveraging technologies to change their business models. The 'new bank' scenario would see incumbent leaders of the sector replaced by challenger banks that are better able to use technology to improve efficiency and service quality. In the 'distributed bank' scenario, banking services would be fragmented among specialised fintech firms and incumbent banks, but the banks would continue to have a niche. In the 'relegated bank' scenario, the incumbent banks would become commoditised service providers, and customer relationships would be owned by new fintech intermediaries. In the 'disintermediated bank' scenario, banks might become irrelevant as the need for traditional banks for balance sheet intermediation or as trusted third parties is reduced, and as customers access services from individual fintech firms. In such a situation, banks would be replaced by platforms and technologies, which would ensure a direct matching of final consumers depending on their financial needs. Peer-to-peer lending platforms could take away a large part of banking business, while cryptocurrencies could enable payments without going through banks.

Some countries have begun changing their laws and regulations to benefit from these opportunities. In 2016, the UK Competition and Markets Authority issued an order requiring the nine largest banks in the country to allow licensed financial technology firms to access their data, including transaction data, subject to the consent of the depositor.[57] This has the potential to completely change the power that a depositor has vis-a-vis a bank. Banking regulations need to be modified in order to realise these opportunities. The RBI would need to focus on function over form, because the same functions of banking may come to be performed by very different institutional forms. Discovering the regulatory responses suitable for the emerging business models requires a different approach to making regulations. The RBI will have to be much more responsive. It would require mechanisms such as regulatory sandboxes to co-develop regulations for innovative business models. As discussed earlier, the RBI has not been a very open and consultative organisation. In order for India to benefit from the latest innovations, this regulatory approach will have to change.

CONCLUSION

There have been many important reforms of banking regulation. These reforms have led to increased competition, greater flexibility for banks to raise and price financial

[56] Basel Committee on Banking Supervision. 'Implications of Fintech Developments for Banks and Bank Supervisors' *Bank for International Settlements* (2018), https://www.bis.org/bcbs/publ/d431.htm.

[57] Rowland Manthorpe, 'To Change How You Use Money, Open Banking Must Break Banks' *Wired* (16 October 2017).

resources, more possibilities for delivering services through the use of technology and so on. However, certain structural problems persist. Regulation of PSBs is impeded by de jure constraints arising out of the legislative framework and de facto moral hazard and weak regulatory incentives due to public ownership. In recent years, the RBI has improved the transparency of its regulatory processes, but much more progress is required. Regulatory governance of the RBI has seen very few improvements. The challenge of banking regulation in today's India is not just to address these structural problems, but also to respond to new business models that seek to disrupt traditional banking business. This will require a pro-innovation stance, and mechanisms for allowing innovations and responding to them with suitable, proportionate regulations. It is time for a fundamental rethink of banking and banking regulation in India.

7

Infrastructure

AMIT KAPUR*

INTRODUCTION

REGULATION ORIGINATED OVER a century ago in the form of rate regulation of railroad and energy utilities in the US. The catalyst for this evolution was abuse of market power by monopolistic private enterprise and consumer grief due to apathetic public utilities. It sought to tackle problems posed by inefficient or inequitable market practices, and to mitigate their ill effects.[1] Economic regulation serves the important objective of replicating a competitive market with informed consumer choice in industries where such conditions do not exist. It thus seeks to minimise the adverse fallouts of market failures in settings where essential public services are supplied by non-substitutable monopolies or oligopolistic actors.

Economic regulation of infrastructure[2] addresses challenges relating to natural monopolies,[3] public goods,[4] externalities[5] and information asymmetry.[6] Intrinsically,

* The author gratefully acknowledges the invaluable contribution and assistance of his colleagues Subramaniam Nair and Abiha Zaidi in research and editing, with inputs from Radhika Seth.

[1] AC Pigou, *The Economics of Welfare* (Macmillan and Co, 1932).

[2] The Harmonized Master List of Infrastructure Sub-sectors notified by Ministry of Finance as on 14 November 2017 covers: (a) eight segments of Transport and Logistics; (b) six segments of Energy; (c) seven segments of Water and Sanitation; (d) three segments of Communication; and (e) 10 segments of Social and Commercial Infrastructure.

[3] This relates to a situation where it is less costly to society for production to be carried out by one firm rather than by several or many according to the economies of scale. This results in a lack of competition, with consequential adverse effects on pricing, entry barriers and quality of service.

[4] A commodity or essential service the benefit from which is shared by the public as a whole, where the supplier cannot exclude people who do not pay for it.

[5] Basically, these are economic side-effects of consequences for welfare of opportunity costs not fully accounted for in the price and the market system. External diseconomies of production (eg, pollution and congestion) and of consumption (eg, noise, smell and litter) diminish the welfare of the affected people. External economies of production (eg, research and development, and ancillary economic activity) and consumption have positive growth effects.

[6] AI Ogus, *Organization, Regulation, Legal Form and Economic Theory* (Hart Publishing, 1994).

regulation has a political economy aspect (distributive and allocative decisions), a technical aspect (optimal technical and economic solution – economies of scale and scope) and a legal aspect (protecting/enforcing rights of parties).[7]

The infrastructure regulatory mechanism must address these elements through incentives administered by a credible apparatus and by balancing the competing interests of actors such as the state, consumers, suppliers, investors/lenders and service providers. It must regulate investment decisions (how much to invest, in what, where, and return on investments), production decisions (quantity and quality), pricing decisions (whom to sell to and on what terms) and rules to compete for and in the market (including risk allocation). It must also balance the viability of investments with benefits of innovation, remaining flexible and responsive to emerging realities, all within the overarching regulatory principles.[8]

Before examining the specifics of India's regulatory apparatus in the infrastructure sector and the various tensions on account of competing interests, it would help to take note of some distinctive attributes of infrastructure that weigh significantly on its governance, regulation and operations:

(a) Infrastructure essentially retains characteristics of public goods, such as non-excludability[9] and non-rivalry.[10] Even where they do not, they bring about several positive externalities, ie, significant public benefits beyond the infrastructure provider's private returns. They are essential for a reasonable standard of living and are seen as an obligation of the state towards its citizens.[11] Infrastructure facilities are essential in supporting diverse economic activities and display high price sensitivity.

(b) Invariably, provision of infrastructure facilities is premised on concessions (a right/privilege to use some public good or facility) granted by the 'state' to the operator to establish, operate and supply essential services. The awarding of projects and their implementation often get questioned and evaluated in the context of allocation of public largesse.[12]

(c) Infrastructure creation requires significant upfront capital investments with long gestation periods and regulated returns. Further, its operation requires a steady working capital. Both kinds of capital must be repaid from the charges recovered from consumers. For such creation to be viable, the statutory and

[7] TV Somanathan, 'The Administrative and Regulatory State' in Sujit Choudhury, Madhav Khosla and Pratap Bhanu Mehta (eds), *The Oxford Handbook of the Indian Constitution* (Oxford University Press, 2016) 386.

[8] Darryl SL Jarvis, M Ramesh, Xun Wu and Eduardo Araral, Jr (eds), *Infrastructure Regulation: What Works, Why and How Do We Know it? Lessons from Asia and Beyond* (World Scientific, 2011).

[9] The practical difficulty in keeping consumers out of the common pool of resources, thereby resulting in free-riding problems.

[10] The enjoyment of the resource by one individual does not come at the cost of its consumption by another.

[11] Citizens' right of access to reliable facilities at affordable prices and universal supply obligations of the licensee/concessionaire.

[12] Standards of reasonable and fair conduct are expected from agencies and instrumentalities of the state when executing welfare projects that further the directive principles of state policy, including the optimal utilisation of scarce natural resources without creating monopolies.

policy framework contemplates that the same shall be operated on commercial principles[13] since:

(i) 75 per cent to 85 per cent of the capital is debt finance (from banks that lend citizens' savings) available for a tenure between eight and 15 years only against an asset life of 30–60 years,[14] which must be repaid with interest within the debt term. In fact, a continued challenge today is the mismatch between the debt-finance tenure and life of infrastructure facilities;

(ii) equity invested must earn a reasonable return.

(d) Since infrastructure facilities are by nature essential facilities with a lack of readily available substitutes, the option of denying supply for commercial reasons is invariably excluded or minimised by law.

(e) Given their significance, coupled with time and cost overruns, and potential inflationary impact, the construction and operation of infrastructure facilities must not be injuncted or obstructed/delayed.

(f) Ideally, the financing for such projects must be tied up against a predictable revenue stream embedded in long-term contracts spanning 10–30 years. Such contracts can never define, ex ante, all possible contingencies which could occur during the lifecycle of an infrastructure project,[15] and are acknowledged to be inherently incomplete. It is inherent in such long-term contracts that something unforeseen will come up during the lifecycle of an infrastructure facility.[16] As such, these long-term contracts must have a supportive framework which:

(i) allocates risk amongst the contracting parties at different phases of the design, construction and operation of the project;

(ii) puts in place a mechanism to tackle unforeseen developments that threaten to impair the sustainable operations of the facility.

In the light of these attributes, this chapter examines the nature of infrastructure regulation in India and, in particular, the tensions involved in creating well-functioning competitive markets built on private participation and contractual freedom, while navigating welfare goals, excessive state intervention and regulatory arbitrage favouring state-owned enterprises.

I. THE REGULATORY FRAMEWORK: EVOLUTION AND FEATURES

The importance of quality and affordable infrastructure for economic growth is well known. There are, however, limits to public financing. Moreover, public spending

[13] Unless subventions or subsidy is paid out of taxpayer monies, the project has to be viable based on tariff income (paid by consumers including interconsumer category cross-subsidy).

[14] This mismatch between the tenure of the loan and the life of an infrastructure asset results in the frontloading of the tariff burden on the public utility to discharge the interest and repay the principal.

[15] Inherently incomplete contracts due to the inability or costliness of accounting for all possible contingencies and contingencies which cannot be foreseen. The parties decide on which amongst the possible contingencies they want to include.

[16] Given the pace of technological innovation/disruption in terms of how markets function and business is organised, what may be a remote or unforeseeable reality today may emerge as obvious and reasonably foreseeable, like the global financial crisis and its implications on trade and finance, *force majeure* events and changes in the law/regulatory regime.

invariably has to prioritise welfare schemes and expenditure in the provision of education, health, skill-development etc, besides the popular distribution of freebies and free loan waivers. Infrastructure development comes a distant second for public expenditure. An analysis of public spending reveals that populist welfare schemes such as distributing jobs or direct wealth transfers can deliver political capital and a voter base much faster than provisions for infrastructure where such gains are realised in the long term.[17]

In this context, India's significant structural reforms over the past three decades, including new or amended laws and policies, have had a prominent role to play in its infrastructure growth. As part of the Indian transition from a controlled economy to a liberalised and delicensed one, vertically integrated state-owned enterprises have been unbundled and corporatised into distinct functional entities, introducing competition into most segments of the value chain. The dispensation regulating Indian infrastructure today has emerged as an interesting mosaic with industry-specific variations in both form[18] and substance.[19]

As compared to American and even European regulatory mechanisms, Indian infrastructure regulation is of recent origin,[20] emerging within the backdrop of the nation's constitutional imperatives to secure distributive justice, avoid resource monopolisation and maximise welfare.[21] India's socio-economic and political realities informed the constant effort to balance welfare objectives (access, affordability and environment) with financial viability. The first three decades post-independence witnessed increasing state control of key segments of the economy,[22] in pursuit of 'nation building' and 'welfare'. This culminated in the move towards nationalisation of key segments of the economy – banking, coal, oil and gas to name a few – starting with the late 1960s, and the acquisition and merger of erstwhile private entities in Central Government-controlled corporations like Oil and Natural Gas Corporation Ltd, Coal India Ltd, GAIL, NTPC Ltd, Power Grid Corporation of India Ltd etc. The original state can therefore be characterised by a dominance of state monopolies within a planned economy, with limited room for 'controlled' private participation. The mid-1980s marked a period of steady realisation among policy-makers that India needed to unshackle the state monopoly over the economy to attract private capital,

[17] Stuti Khemani, 'Political Economy of Infrastructure Spending in India' (2010) *The World Bank Group, Human Development and Public Services Team*, http://documents.worldbank.org/curated/en/997291468041960361/pdf/WPS5423.pdf.

[18] Some industries saw the emergence of statutorily established and empowered 'regulatory institutions' like the power sector. Others adopted the 'regulation by contract' model like highways and state ports. Most adopted a hybrid model, where some aspects were governed by the executive, while others were vested in regulators/contracts.

[19] Normally from amongst entry into and exit from the market, price, quality, access, safety etc.

[20] Widely acknowledged as a necessary outcome and accompaniment to the post-1991 liberalisation of the Indian economy.

[21] Article 39(b) and (c) of the Indian Constitution stipulates that the 'State' shall direct its policy towards securing that the ownership and control of the material resources of the community are so distributed as best to serve the common good, and that the operation of the economic system does not result in the concentration of wealth and means of production to the common detriment.

[22] This aspect was often referred to as the commanding heights of the economy being entrusted to the 'state' in industrial policies, guided by welfare and socialist imperatives, until the changes of 1991.

entrepreneurship, and research and development initiatives, as well as to benefit from a competitive market. Economic reforms in India commenced in 1985–86, culminating in the watershed reforms of July 1991.

As each infrastructure industry evolved its policy-regulatory compact to respond to various stages of market development and stated policy objectives, the government sought to be kept out of the regulatory oversight of infrastructure verticals. This was done both to prevent political economy distortions on account of the state presence and even dominance as a market player, and to place the specialised task of balancing affordability and viability in the hands of experts. The incumbent state-owned enterprises were required to grant non-discriminatory open access to the network infrastructure in order to establish a level playing field for private sector and Public–Private Partnerships (PPPs) to compete with them. Consequently, some or all of the elements – entry into, exit from and consolidation within the market, economic pricing such that prudent costs are recovered with a fair/reasonable return on investments, securing a reliable quality of supply, safety and competitiveness – were vested with the regulatory mechanism in each sector.

The budgetary constraints and limitations of public finance to fund all infrastructure needs is at the base of reforms which commenced post-1991, heralding the need for private participation in infrastructure such that public funds could focus on welfare programmes. This brought to the fore structural reforms with a focus on developing a framework for PPPs, where the transaction and monitoring costs were more than offset by the value-for-money proposition and welfare outcomes.[23] To effectuate the transition from previous state-owned/controlled regimes, legislative/policy frameworks governing infrastructure sectors (highways, telecom, power, ports, airports, petroleum, natural gas etc) were amended to provide for private participation, independent economic regulation governed by statutory principles (by regulators or by contract), and a level playing field for private and state-owned entities.

As a result, two alternate regulatory models evolved – one vesting regulatory functions in the hands of statutorily established expert regulatory bodies and the other embedding the regulation in long-term contracts monitored by a state instrumentality (invariably the concession-granting authority). Regulation in the telecom sector exemplifies the first type of structure, while highways and oil and gas exploration embody regulatory structures closer to the second type.

Similarly, from a functional perspective, we find two diverse approaches – the light-touch regulation of competitive segments of an industry versus more intensive regulation, either due to monopolistic activity or because of larger public interest concerns including health, environment, safety and national security. The former approach is found in the generation of electricity (which has been statutorily delicensed, with the role of regulators being limited to certain aspects)[24] and mobile

[23] NITI Aayog, 'Rebooting Public Private Partnership in India' (22 November 2017), www.niti.gov.in/content/rebooting-public-private-partnership-india. A Public-Private Partnership (PPP) is a long-term contract between the public sector, a public sector client and a private company or consortium of companies, a private entity, covering the design, construction, maintenance and financing of an infrastructure asset.

[24] *Tata Power Company Ltd v Reliance Energy Ltd* (2009) 16 SCC 659.

telephony (where the regulator chose to forbear once multiple licensees were operating in each area offering choices to the consumer on the basis of a reference tariff order).[25] The latter approach is more prominent in the functioning of the Petroleum and Natural Gas Regulatory Board, which regulates the refining, processing, storage, transportation, distribution and marketing of petroleum products, and the Airports Economic Regulatory Authority, which sets airport development fees, passenger service fees, and performance standards relating to the quality, continuity and reliability of airline service.

The telecom sector, over which the state had a monopoly, evolved into a vibrant competitive market. The sector remains regulated by the Telecom Regulatory Authority of India (TRAI), which is responsible for laying down the norms of open access, interconnection between different service providers and such other issues which require sharing of spectrum, a limited natural resource. Yet, in 2002, the TRAI adopted forbearance in telecom tariffs because consumers had enough information to choose freely amongst competing service providers and the benefit of a TRAI-notified reference tariff order that set the baseline norms for pricing.

Post-reform, the power sector has attracted significant private investment and efficiency improvement. Yet, the sector is still struggling with unresolved issues and risks. Faced with uncertainty in tariffs, private players are increasingly reluctant to invest. Additional factors such as the skew in risk allocation against the private sector, uncertainties regarding the availability of raw materials (in particular, the unreliable coal supply by Coal India Ltd) and unreliable contract enforcement due to excessive government intervention have made things more difficult.[26]

This sectoral contrast indicates how straddling the fine line between social welfare goals and market viability is a tough exercise. Regulatory frameworks and objectives differ across infrastructure sectors, resulting in divergence on the regulatory norms as well as coordination problems between sectoral regulators. Where the public and entrepreneurs see convergence and overlaps of opportunities to invest and optimise, there seems to be little convergence of ideas between regulators across sectors. Then there is the divergence of regulatory models – while there is an extensive network of regulators in the electricity sector, there is no independent regulator in the ports sector.[27] In the highway sector, the National Highway Authority of India is the operator and the regulator with no recourse to an independent body. The level of functional independence and autonomy also varies. The Forum of Indian Regulators established in 2000 as an informal mechanism to evolve a shared vision has not reported any significant positive outcomes.

An overlapping tier of regulatory oversight has added to the complexity with the enactment of the Competition Act, 2002 establishing a sector-agnostic competition regulator to keep a check on anti-competitive behaviour by dominant entities and natural monopolies, including allegations of cartelisation and abuse

[25] Telecommunication Tariff (23rd Amendment) Order 2002.

[26] Vijay Vir Singh and Siddharth Mitra, 'Regulatory Management and Reform in India', Background Paper for the OECD, www.oecd.org/gov/regulatory-policy/44925979.pdf.

[27] The proposed Major Port Authorities Bill, 2016 seeks to establish a Board of Major Port Authority (BMPA) for every major port: pib.nic.in/newsite/PrintRelease.aspx?relid=176352.

of dominant position.[28] The Competition Act contemplates a consultative mode of functioning amongst sectoral regulators and the Competition Commission.[29] This provision has rarely been used. Whenever consultative approaches were taken, outcomes were more holistic and workable than when the Competition Commission worked in isolation. When the issue of interoperability in DTH services arose, the Competition Commission dismissed an allegation of tying-in of the CAM Card in relation to set-top boxes. The Competition Commission took note of the recommendations of the Ministry of Broadcasting and of the TRAI, ie, that interoperability amongst the counter CAM Cards distributed by various broadcasters is not immediately possible due to incompatibility amongst different technologies in use, and that compatibility may be achieved over time.[30] In another instance, while examining allegations of predatory pricing raised against the National Stock Exchange (NSE) by its competitor Multi Commodity Exchange (MCX), the order completely missed out on an important fact that the regulator of the securities market (Stock Exchange Board of India (SEBI)) had denied a licence to MCX to operate in non-cash derivative segments, forcing MCX to rely on the cash derivative segment for its revenues, while the NSE operated in various other segments in the securities market.[31] Had the Competition Commission consulted SEBI, SEBI was bound to help define the relevant market in order to better analyse whether the zero-pricing policy by the NSE could be countered by competitive pressures from fresh market entry through new SEBI licences. Perhaps the provision for statutory consultation has not been used to its maximum potential by the Commission or other regulators because of its voluntary nature.

II. BASIC PRINCIPLES: REGULATION AND COMPETITION

The regulator is expected to perform a range of tasks to achieve stated objectives like balancing interests of consumers while attracting investments on commercial principles, maximising competition, limiting the free play of the market through universal service obligations and implementing welfare policies. The major challenge remains in striking the trade-off between welfare and economic objectives. While balancing between private and public interests, regulators must secure the successful implementation of the prevalent policy of the government.[32] Trade-offs amongst competing interests are intrinsic to the construct of any mechanism regulating public goods and natural monopolies – warranting policy decisions involving allocative and pricing choices.

[28] *Re: M/s Swastik Stevedores Private Ltd Jobra v M/s Dumper Owner's Association* [2015] CCI 42.

[29] Competition Act 2002, ss 21 and 21A.

[30] *Consumer Online Foundation v Tata Sky Ltd* 2011 SCC CCI 52.

[31] *MCX Stock Exchange v National Stock Exchange of India* 2011 SCC CCI 12.

[32] In *Energy Watchdog v CERC* (2017) 14 SCC 80, the electricity regulator was held to be bound by the competitive bidding guidelines, the tariff policy and other directives in exercise of its powers in the interpretation of *force majeure* and changes in the law provisions of the power purchase agreement. Further, the Supreme Court upheld the statutory power to 'regulate' unforeseen circumstances that are tantamount to restitutive remedy in order to restore economic viability in the project.

Often these regulatory choices are influenced by the type of infrastructure in question. Essential facilities pertaining to carriage such as railways and access to networks (power grid, gas pipeline, telecom interconnect or access to roads or ports) have predominantly remained with public players. Private entities are encouraged to participate in subsequent stages of the value chain through non-discriminatory open access. Legislation and/or suitable contractual arrangements addressing the initial phase of the project lifecycle is particularly important for those services or markets where more players must operate, and a competitive environment ought to be created by granting market access. To prevent abuse of market dominance by owners/operators of monopoly/bottleneck infrastructure facilities, a market-friendly regulatory mechanism – ex ante or ex post – must be enforced by the sectoral regulator or the competition regulator.

The choice between ex ante and ex post regulatory approaches is not an easy one. An ex ante regulatory approach, where regulation precedes actual market entry and operations, presupposes a deep knowledge of market elements and functioning. Ex post regulation, on the other hand, permits mistakes to be made, premised on the belief that the government can remedy these mistakes quickly and precisely after the fact. In the specific case of the infrastructure sector, an ex ante approach is usually preferred, despite its higher proclivities for regulatory capture, gaming, rent-seeking and abuse of regulatory processes by special interests, as well as the imposition of process and goal constraints that may impede innovation and experimentation. This preference is primarily justified because of the ability to set, in advance, consumer protection, efficient utilisation of resources and project viability as desired objectives/outcomes of the regulatory exercise, and thereby keep discretion under check. Moreover, long-term investments also demand prior regulatory certainty, a concern better addressed through ex ante regulations over ex post decision-making.

For any regulated industry, the regulated pricing of services must be cost-reflective and a zero-sum game in the hands of the supplier recovering prudent costs with a reasonable return without carrying forward any overall cash-gaps which would cast subsidy burden on tax-payers or impair the investment. The mechanism empowers regulators to secure affordable baseline supply for underprivileged citizens while allocating a share of their cost of supply to other customers who can afford to share it (cross subsidy). The subsidy decision is to be taken by the government such that some part of such cost may be borne by taxpayers. A significant challenge in the pricing of public goods is the welfare impulse keeping the tariff/pricing at uneconomic levels, contrary to stated statutory and regulatory principles. The need to secure sustainability/viability is widely recognised as fundamental in laws, policies and judgments in infrastructure industries. Regulatory functions must be exercised, keeping in view the careful balance between the welfare objectives and financial interests of the investors. All stakeholders must contribute their own share of services and finances so that end-users gain access to essential facilities for the reasonable charges they pay, while none of the market players are compelled to withdraw because of an impractical/excessive hike in fees and tariffs.

If the public good supply to a sector is partly financed by subsidy, it benefits a section of people using the good(s) (consumers) while imposing costs on a different set of people (taxpayers), although there may be some overlap. However, this can be permissibly resorted to within the budgetary constraints on public finance, to address multiple and competing welfare demands. Tariff-based financing with some checks and balances by regulators, including prudence checks to allow only efficient and legitimate expenses, targeted subsidies for the weaker sections, permissible cross-subsidies (whereby the more affluent share costs incurred for the under-privileged) to ensure availability and fairness of prices, is considered an acceptable model for the provisioning of public goods.

As mentioned above, regulation is considered necessary in sectors which have natural monopolies or bottleneck network industries and even more so where a universal service obligation exists.[33] Lack of access to the carriage segments in a sector would directly hamper competition and increase entry barriers. Once carriage is provided to users, any industry can benefit from adequate competition. A light-handed approach is considered more appropriate here, facilitating competition through the provisioning of market access. In this regard, there are differences between regulatory needs to promote competition 'in' the market, which demands only some degree of light-touch oversight and to promote competition 'for' the market, which necessitates a more active role in ensuring market access.

Most infrastructure regulation deals with supply-side concerns because it is assumed that the end goal of such regulation is consumer welfare as promoted through competition among supplier firms.[34] Consumer interest is safeguarded through remedies contained in the regulatory framework regarding reasonable tariffs, consumer choice amongst suppliers and remedies against abuse of a dominant position. In sectors where regulation is a necessity due to perceived market failure, regulators have tried to balance the contradictions amongst consumer interest and sustainable investments. The experiences of broadcasting, telecommunications, electricity and airlines post-1991 confirm that competitive conditions and consumer choice seem to better achieve this goal as compared to regulatory intervention, which has had patchy results. Having said that, the auction/bid procurement of investment has come into a series of contentious disputes due to a failure on the part of governmental agencies to meet conditions precedent regarding land acquisition and clearances, as well as reluctance of state-owned enterprises to abide by contractual obligations guaranteeing risk mitigation. Compounding this problem, we have witnessed several private sector bids which range from risky to opportunistic.

Accordingly, regulatory action should be limited to ensure that the essentials of a competitive market are established, providing a level playing field to market players. Some areas that need work to strengthen the existing mechanism that guarantees 'regulatory effectiveness' are: clarity on functions, powers, obligations and roles allocated amongst the government, regulators and utilities; harmonising regulatory principles; expeditious and predictable decision-making; effective monitoring of the quality of services; engagement of the 'voice' of various stakeholder groups; and regulatory accountability.[35]

[33] National Competition Policy 2011, www.mca.gov.in/Ministry/pdf/Revised_Draft_National_Competition_Policy_2011_17nov2011.pdf.

[34] Jarvis et al (n 8).

[35] Prayas undertook extensive evaluation of 12 electricity regulatory commissions and released a report in 2003 entitled 'A Good Beginning But Challenges Galore' in February 2003, highlighting issues

III. POLITICAL ECONOMY AND THE MARKET

Since 1991, with structural changes in the governance frameworks of infrastructure segments, the involvement of private investment has strengthened across the project cycle, ie, during the design, construction, operation and management. This is especially true post-2000. This change was dramatic in the backdrop of a four-decade-long mindset of keeping core industries and basic infrastructure reserved for the public sector for national development and welfare. Several challenges posed related to the need for viable pricing and budgetary constraints. Certain sectors like irrigation and water resources management, the construction of rural roads, capital dredging at major ports and infrastructure in economically or situationally disadvantaged regions remained more suited to public sector resources. Private sector investment has been strong in the remaining sectors, such as airports, power, telecom/IT and highways.

A. Private Participation: Goals and Reality

Opening up the telecom and power sectors in India shows direct benefits of significant private investments and capacity build-up in key infrastructure sectors. While the entry of private players has shown the increased efficiency and availability of cheaper and affordable services,[36] it has not come without a price and a set of unresolved issues. Investments by the private sector have not just been made in India, but also in China and other Organisation for Economic Co-operation and Development (OECD) countries with much power generation assets owned or operated by private entities. Public–private partnerships are helpful in offsetting higher financial costs, especially when they are operating in competitive markets.[37] A competitive bidding process is meant to result in the best price, encouraging bidders to share their efficiency gains (in terms of raw materials, finance, construction and operation) and eliminate gold-plating, ie, the unhealthy practice of changing the project scope midway through the process.[38] However, it has been noted that governments take a short-term project outlook, which can be detrimental in the long run,[39] while due to the stranded asset risk of long gestation period investments, private firms undertake detailed long-term studies.[40]

relating to the functioning of the Electricity Regulatory Commissions: (i) Independence & Autonomy; (ii) Empowerment; (iii) Accountability; (iv) Transparency & Public Participation; (v) Enhancing Quality of Professionals; and (vi) Sensitivity to Social Issues. see prayaspune.org/peg/resources/electricity-supply-monitoring-initiative-esmi/item/116.html.

[36] International Finance Corporation, 'Toward a Framework for Assessing Private v Public Investment in Infrastructure' (January 2017), https://www.ifc.org/wps/wcm/connect/e16e60fb-bc87-4f15-939d-c6636681aca4/EMCompass+note+29+Infrastructure+Framework+1-13+MB+NEW+rev+1.pdf?MOD=AJPERES.

[37] ibid.

[38] ibid.

[39] ibid.

[40] Report by the Comptroller and Auditor General, 'PFI: Construction Performance', *National Audit Office* (February 2003), https://www.nao.org.uk/wp-content/uploads/2003/02/0203371.pdf.

During 2002–07 (the Tenth Plan), out of the total investment in infrastructure of Rs 9,16,076 (five per cent of GDP),[41] the share of the public and private sectors was 78 per cent and 22 per cent respectively. During 2007–12 (the Eleventh Plan), private sector investment rose to around 38 per cent of the actual investment of Rs 19,00,063 crores (seven per cent of GDP) while the rest (ie, 62 per cent) was met by the public sector.[42] Riding on this growth phase, the Twelfth Plan (2012–17) envisaged a 48 per cent share of the private sector in projected investments in infrastructure.[43] However, actual private investments dropped to half of the target due to the 'twin balance sheet problem' of stranded corporate balance sheets and bludgeoning non-performing/stressed loans for banks.[44] Private investment is stated to be promoted by the government as a step in the right direction.[45] However, as the above numbers reveal, there is a clear divergence between goals and reality.

The Economic Survey of India (2016/2017) concluded that some of the key problems were higher costs (including time and cost overruns), lower revenues and greater financing costs (including the impact of adverse foreign exchange rate variations on debts), which squeezed corporate cash flow, leading to debt servicing problems.[46] Twin balance sheet problems tend to lower gross capital formation as stressed companies reduce new investments to conserve cash flow, while stressed banks are unable to lend more. In 2016–17, the private capital investment seemed to contract by more than seven per cent. In order to cushion the impact on the overall economy, public investment has been stepped up considerably, but this has still not been sufficient to prevent a fall in overall investment. The Economic Survey 2015–16 emphasised that addressing the stressed assets problem would require '4 R's: Reform, Recognition, Recapitalization, and Resolution'.[47] The recent Economic Survey has concluded that this twin balance sheet problem has, over eight years, deteriorated to a point where it is damaging economic growth and resulting in a failure of the market based mechanism.[48]

[41] High Level Committee on Financing Infrastructure, *Interim Report* (August 2012) 6.

[42] Planning Commission, *2nd Report of the High Level Committee on Financing Infrastructure* (June 2014) 1.

[43] Planning Commission, *XII Five Year Plan* (vol I) 88, planningcommission.gov.in/aboutus/committee/wrkgrp12/cit/vol1_IB.pdf.

[44] Prasantu Sahu, 'Infrastructure: Telecom, Power, Ports and Road Sector Hit by Tepid Private Investments' *Financial Express* (20 April 2017), www.financialexpress.com/industry/infrastructure-telecom-power-ports-and-road-sector-hit-by-tepid-private-investments/634800.

[45] A substantial rise in private investments from 20 per cent in the Tenth Plan to 30 per cent in the Eleventh Plan was planned for. In the Eleventh Plan, the public sector under-performed, achieving 86 per cent of the target investment, while the private sector over-performed at 113 per cent of the target. The Twelfth Plan has witnessed a significant reversal of the trend.

[46] Government of India, Ministry of Finance, 'Economic Survey 2015–16: Amidst Gloomy International Economic Landscape, India Stands as a Haven of Stability' *Press Information Bureau* (26 February 2016), pib.nic.in/newsite/PrintRelease.aspx?relid=136850.

[47] Ministry of Finance, Government of India, 'Economic Survey 2016–17' (2017), www.indiabudget.gov.in/es2016-17/echapter.pdf.

[48] Ministry of Finance, Government of India, 'Economic Survey 2017–18' (2018), mofapp.nic.in:8080/economicsurvey/pdf/068-081_Chapter_05_ENGLISH_Vol_01_2017-18.pdf.

For a long time, regulators have failed to provide interest or carrying costs on the deferred recovery of accrued dues (ironically called a 'Regulatory Asset'),[49] besides taking prompt action on defaults in the payments of tariffs. In infrastructure sectors, non-payment or delayed part-payment of dues and even of carrying costs – revenue streams that address the cash gap – could lead to the entire investment being rendered worthless. Similar issues arise due to denial or delay in tariff payments, which affects the repayment of even the principal amount. All of this has had a cascading effect on the loan-paying ability of investors, thereby affecting the banking/financial sector.

The spectre of increasing non-performing assets (NPAs) as defined by the Reserve Bank of India (RBI), which eroded investments, faces a renewed challenge by way of the RBI's revised framework for the resolution of stressed assets issued on 12 February 2018.[50] It is a directive to all Scheduled Commercial Banks in India requiring them to classify all loan accounts with incipient stress immediately on the non-payment of any part/instalment of debt, and to implement a resolution plan under the Insolvency and Bankruptcy Code, 2016.[51] It is estimated that a predominant share (70 per cent) of all NPAs and stressed/restructured loans of Rs 15,00,000 crores are in the infrastructure industry. It is believed that 75,000 MW of installed capacity of thermal power projects will attract these provisions due to uncontrollable events and regulatory lags, ie, the delays and refusal of state-owned distribution licensees to pay their dues on time, projected to be over Rs 500,000 crores, as well as delays of up to five to six years by regulatory commissions in determining and enforcing tariff adjustments due to changes in the law like the national coal distribution policy, taxes etc.[52] Should a reasonable resolution not be worked out at the earliest opportunity, the NPA crisis afflicting the Indian banking sector and stressed investments in power will be exacerbated, since 70 to 80 per cent of the capital expenditure for infrastructure is through debt financing.[53] Growing levels of stressed assets are

[49] 'Regulatory assets' refer to revenue which is recognised by the regulator as recoverable, but the recovery of which is deferred. Accounting for regulatory assets allows public utilities to defer the recognition of certain costs, bypassing the income statement in the short term by moving these costs to their balance sheet.

[50] Reserve Bank of India, 'Resolution of Stressed Assets – Revised Framework' (12 February 2018), www.rbi.org.in/scripts/FS_Notification.aspx?Id=11218&fn=2&Mode=0.

[51] Section 3(11) of the Insolvency and Bankruptcy Code 2016: 'debt' means a liability or obligation in respect of a claim which is due from any person and includes a financial debt and operational debt.

[52] Debjoy Sengupta, 'India's Thermal Power Generation to Reduce by Half in Next Five Years' *Economic Times* (4 March 2018), energy.economictimes.indiatimes.com/news/power/indias-thermal-power-generation-to-reduce-by-half-in-next-five-years/57466112; Veena Mani and Shreya Jai, 'Stressed Power Generations Firms Face Tough Insolvency Journey in Court' *Business Standard* (8 March 2018), https://www.business-standard.com/article/companies/stressed-power-generations-firms-face-tough-insolvency-journey-in-court-118030800009_1.html.

[53] The Resolution Circular of the RBI has been challenged by the Independent Power Producers Association of India before the High Court of Allahabad on the grounds that it fails to distinguish between various forms of stressed assets in different industrial sectors and, further, its failure to distinguish between genuine and wilful defaulters. The High Court of Allahabad by an order dated 31 May 2018 has temporarily stayed the implementation of the Resolution Order in respect of the members of the Independent Power Producers Association of India, to the extent that such members are not wilful defaulters.

affecting investor sentiments, with the bulk of them receiving their returns from the power, metal and construction sectors.[54]

B. Market Impairment

The post-reform experience in India from 1994–95 onwards testifies to the fact that regulatory decisions are not, and cannot be, completely insulated from the larger political economy in a democratic setting. Wherever the legal framework creates leeway for governmental intervention, the political economy has invariably driven distortions in regulatory decision-making, thereby eroding the potential benefits of private participation. India's experience is replete with internal conflicts within the regulatory apparatus that create and dismantle barriers to compete 'for' and 'in' the market through access to network infrastructure.

To give a recent example of access to such infrastructure and its importance as a regulatory matter, we need to look no further than the ongoing disruption in mobile telephony. In order to make the adoption of new technologies a reality, disruptors need to connect with the existing network infrastructure. Such interconnection is also extremely important from a consumer perspective. Consumers of telecommunication services cannot communicate with each other across the country unless necessary interconnection arrangements between telecom service providers (TSPs) are in place. This issue was the subject matter of a prolonged battle and an evolving reality of the interconnect regime. Recently the TRAI issued 'The Telecommunication Interconnection Regulations 2018', which mandates telecom operators to sign an interconnection agreement on a non-discriminatory basis within 30 days of receipt of a network connectivity request from a rival service provider. Similarly, the TRAI has directed well-established incumbents to provide sufficient Points of Interconnection (POI) to a new player in order to facilitate competition. Combined with allegations of predatory pricing by the new entrant, the legality of these directives is pending adjudication before the courts.

The above example illustrates the benefits to consumers of private participation, including the emergence of new players, and the criticality of access to network infrastructure to facilitate the same. Private players often face entry barriers compared to dominant and entrenched state-owned incumbents, due to a mix of preferential procurement bias, sunk costs and access to network/bottleneck infrastructure. The cost of access and competing in the market is critical to facilitate consumer choice 'in' the market, particularly because it can restrict competition. The predominance of state-owned entities in the carrier segment raises the risk of favourable terms for state-owned entities situated at the vertically downward level. For example, the transmission of electricity and coal is rife with instances of favourable terms and

[54] 'Gross NPA May Rise to Rs 9.5 Lakh Crore by March: Study' *Economic Times* (22 January 2018), https://m.economictimes.com/markets/stocks/news/gross-npa-may-rise-to-rs-9-5-lakh-crore-by-march-study/amp_articleshow/62603229.cms.

conditions for state-owned generators. This presents economic regulators with an important role, one they have handled with less-than-desirable neutrality in India.

In this regard, it is instructive to examine the experience of some independent power producers (IPPs) that entered into contracts with large consumers and traders to sell their output competitively. Around 10 years ago, the state transmission utility blocked the granting of open access to the grid, contrary to the regulatory framework. Some state governments acted in the 'public interest' to sequester the power thus generated to be sold to their utilities at a prescribed price. This mechanism in effect artificially transferred the inefficiencies of state distribution to the generators. The transmission utility was directed by the Central Electricity Regulatory Commission to grant open access, as its directions were found to fall outside the scope of section 11 of the Electricity Act. The aforementioned market access and freedom to generators was short-lived because the jurisdictional High Court intervened in the 'public interest' and disallowed open access. Appeals against this order have been pending in the Supreme Court for over seven years.[55] In an earlier case, the judiciary has followed the dictionary meaning of public interest to imply that it is something in which a class of the community has a pecuniary or some other interest which affects its *legal rights* or *liabilities*.[56] On the face of it, this concept cannot be used to justify blocking access to grid infrastructure in a manner that is legally impermissible under the Electricity Act.

In various cases, the states' regulators have created tariff barriers,[57] impairing the competitive advantage of any generator or licensee from outside a state in selling power to a consumer within the state in order to protect state-owned generation. This supply limitation on competition has come at the cost of consumer welfare in such states. The time taken (a minimum of two to three years) to dislodge or dilute these barriers by appeals is used to block competition within the state, with no deterrent costs or offsets.

C. Regulating State-Owned Enterprises: Bias and Arbitrage

Regulating state-owned entities brings various structural and behavioural challenges for regulators. Invariably each sectoral regulator is administratively located, and financially provided for, under the aegis of the concerned ministry, which also

[55] An order granting open access dated 22 January 2009 in Petition No 147 of 2008 was challenged before the High Court of Karnataka in Writ Petition Nos 2073/2009, 2733 of 2009 and 13338 of 2009. Initially, the order was stayed till these Writ Petitions were disposed of by the Karnataka High Court according to an order dated 26 March 2010 in Writ Petition Nos 590–91 of 2009. The Karnataka High Court Order dated 26 March 2010 was challenged before the Supreme Court in Civil Appeal No 3894-95 of 2011, which is currently pending.

[56] *Janata Dal v HS Choudhary* (1992) 4 SCC 305.

[57] This was done by imposing barriers to competitive access to the market in the form of an uneconomic cross-subsidy surcharge and an additional surcharge imposed under s 42 of the Electricity Act, 2003. The level of these charges was far beyond the level and scope of s 42 and the purpose for levying these charges, and in effect thrust inefficiencies and costs of State Discoms on to the generators or consumers seeking open access.

owns and controls the regulated state-owned entities. Most of the regulatory staff are recruited on a short-term contractual basis (three to five years) from the regulated public sector enterprises. Budgetary allocations for the regulators are made by the concerned ministry. These factors tend to make regulators, even if subconsciously, align with short-run welfare concerns as advanced by their political superiors over competitive concerns and interests that could work better in the long run.[58]

Further, the extent of reporting required from regulators to the concerned ministries also compromises their operational autonomy. Accordingly, the government has a greater incentive to monitor and control the regulator in order to protect its utilities or entities, as well as a greater opportunity to do so because of the regulator's place within the governmental hierarchy. For instance, in the telecom sector, the TRAI recommends the terms and conditions of a licence while the Government of India, which owns and controls one of the nation's biggest telecom players, Bharat Sanchar Nigam Ltd, exercises the power to grant such licences through the Department of Telecommunications.[59] Various policy decisions are taken by this department without consulting the TRAI. The Indian railways present an extreme situation where the government wears all three hats – policy-maker, regulator and operator.

Sanctions against state utilities have hardly deterred them from breaking regulatory directives or carrying out their operations in a commercially viable manner because state governments tend to make good the utilities' losses. As a result, regulated public sector entities do not appear to have much reason to abide by regulatory directives that conflict with the populist measures and policy decisions taken by the executive. Similarly, 'independent' regulators have limited authority and freedom to enforce regulations against state-owned entities to the same degree as against private players, leading to a form of regulatory arbitrage that helps state-owned entities. It is important to keep in mind that state utilities like NTPC Ltd and the Power Grid Corporation of India Ltd are mostly litigants pitted against private parties before regulators.

In view of the above problems, efforts must be made to reduce the governmental stake in the entities that play a pivotal role in infrastructure sectors. Further, the concessions or licences must explicitly define the relationship and role/risk allocations between the private entity and the state-owned entities, as well as those of the regulator. Private sector investments demand a conducive and independent regulatory environment that steers clear of bias towards public enterprises. This can be created either through a competitive market or through concessions given in a fair manner to

[58] *Bromley London Borough Council v Greater London Council* [1982] 1 All ER 129 recognised this aspect by observing that no public service undertaking can afford to say that it will ignore business principles, which are as essential to public service undertakings as to commercial ventures. The principle of reasonable return to commercial undertakings has also been recognised by the Indian Supreme Court in *Kerala State Electricity Board v SN Govinda Prabhu* (1986) 4 SCC 198. Indian courts have consistently observed that the regulator must base its decisions solely on plausible logic and a fair approach in the implementation of the applicable law. See *Chittoor Zilla Vyavasaya Adrula Sangham v AP State Electricity Board* (2001) 1 SCC 396; *Nand Kishore Garg v Government of NCT of Delhi* 2011 SCC Online Del 2366, 2011 ELR (DELHI) 0745; *Bromley London Borough Council v Greater London Council* (HL(E)) (1983) 1 QBD 484.

[59] 'Comparative Study of Regulatory Framework in Infrastructure Sector: Lessons for India', CUTS C-CIER, www.cuts-ccier.org/pdf/Comparative_Study_of_Regulatory_Framework_in_Infrastructure_Sector-Lessons_for_India.pdf.

the most competitive bidder, while ensuring that user charges are limited to a reasonable level and appropriate service standards are set by the regulations.[60] An added challenge remains the differentiated standards adopted by regulators in enforcing the legal and contractual obligations of public sector enterprises vis-a-vis a private sector entity – particularly when it comes to issues like specific performance of contracts, awarding interest/carrying cost/damages, strict adherence to agreed procedure in commercial issues etc. The 'welfare' bias of regulators, coupled with their excessive dependence on ministries that own regulated entities, appears to skew the apparent structural balance amongst contracting parties.

D. Freedom of Contract and the Pricing Function

Private sector investment in infrastructure brought to the fore critical aspects relating to fair pricing which ensures a reasonable return on investment (project viability). This aspect, in apparent tension with welfare outcomes/policy objectives, was not the subject of much attention, so long as infrastructure services were owned, operated and financed by the public sector. In a series of judgments from spanning the 1970s to the 1990s, the Supreme Court criticised the notion that public sector enterprises must not earn commercial profits, expressing concerns about growing deficit financing and rising debt in the public exchequer.[61] However, welfare objectives underlying the infrastructure continue to define and impact the entire lifecycle of infrastructure development and operation. This aspect has a two-way feedback impact on freedom to contract and regulatory adjustments to the same across the project lifecycle.

Parties to a contract wilfully and voluntarily bind themselves to perform reciprocal promises. Normally, in any lawful contract, citizens and corporations have the freedom to set their own terms as well as to choose the correct means for implementing such reciprocal promises, including the unforeseen change-based reset adjustment and dispute resolution mechanism. Contractual freedom gets redefined and somewhat constrained when contractual arrangements are entered into for any aspect of provision of infrastructure services/facility. The raison d'etre for such constraints is the shared public interest in the reliable provision of a reasonably priced facility/service, particularly since such facilities are seen as 'public goods' and involve the granting of certain 'largesse/concessions' by the state. Such constraints may be contained in the applicable legislation, delegated legislation, policy pronouncements or even contracts. This constitutes an area where the freedom of private law to contract interacts with public law's watchful protection of the public interest and welfare. It is in this context that the Supreme Court has delivered judgments balancing affordability, viability and risk-sharing.[62] These judgments have added a new dimension to the debates in law

[60] Planning Commission, *XI Five Year Plan* (vol I) 11, planningcommission.nic.in/plans/planrel/fiveyr/11th/11_v1/11th_vol1.pdf.

[61] See *ONGC v Association of Natural Gas Consuming Industries* 1990 (Supp) SCC 397; *DR Venkatachalam v Dy Transport Commissioner* (1977) 2 SCC 273; *Shashikant Laxman Kale v Union of India* (1990) 4 SCC 366; *Chittoor Zilla Vyavasayadarula Sangham v AP State Electricity Board* (2001) 1 SCC 396.

[62] *Energy Watchdog v Central Electricity Regulatory Commission* (2017) 14 SCC 80; *All India Power Engineer Federation v Sasan Power* (2017) 1 SCC 487; *Shivshakti Sugars v Shree Renuka Sugars* (2017) 7 SCC 729.

and regulation by mandating public interest-based restoration of an economic equilibrium where the statute so warrants.

Increasingly, the preferred mode of price discovery for infrastructure services is competitive bidding, which avoids the risk of abuse of dominance by a few well-entrenched players manifested through practices such as gold-plating or cartelised bids.[63] Where such bidding is not opted for, the tariff is determined by a regulator or in terms of a regulated contract (highway concessions, for example, have clauses where regulation is by contract) consistent with the statutory principles and procedure prescribed, which emphasise efficient cost-reflecting tariffs that ensure an affordable price for consumers, while securing reasonable cost recovery for the investor. For instance, the Airports Economic Regulatory Authority was established to create a level playing field amongst all major airports and to encourage investment in airport facilities. The Airport Economic Regulatory Authority of India Act, 2008 requires that, in determining tariffs, the viable operation of major airports, costs in improving efficiency and capital expenditure incurred should be factored in alongside the cross-subsidy from non-aeronautical revenue. Similarly, the 1995 amendment to the National Highways Act, 1956 empowers the Central Government to enter into agreements (concessions) with any person to develop and maintain national highways, wherein toll rates are to be determined on the basis of the interest on capital invested, the reasonable return and the volume of traffic.[64] Some discretion is left with the regulator to get affluent consumer categories to bear a part of the tariff for lifeline supply to the under-privileged by way of a cross-subsidy. Similarly, the government can choose as a matter of policy to partially bear the tariff burden of the under-privileged consumer category from public finance by way of subsidy (borne by the taxpayer/exchequer) which is required to be paid upfront.

A certain level of 'public interest' bias is virtually transposed when exercising pricing functions as most regulators are staffed by retired and serving bureaucrats/public servants. This is often manifested by regulators trying to keep the price uneconomically low, ignoring the viability aspect. Such orders have been challenged and the Supreme Court has clarified that the public interest does not mean the interest of public sector player(s) alone, but also demands a holistic view to achieve the statutory objectives of viable investments in the long run as well as assured supply.[65] There have been instances of policy directions to regulators issued by the government that directly contradicted the statutory framework, resulting in subsequent legal challenges. The regulator, being an independent and autonomous body, cannot blindly implement such directives in disregard of the letter and spirit of the applicable law.[66]

[63] Bids as the choice of the allocation mechanism have been held to be a policy decision of the procuring agency/government and not a mandatory mechanism by the Supreme Court in *Natural Resources Allocation, In Re, Special Reference No 1 of 2012* (2012) 10 SCC 1.

[64] National Highways Act 1956, s 8A.

[65] *APERC v RVK Energy Private Ltd* (2008) 17 SCC 769; *DERC v BSES* (2007) 3 SCC 33.

[66] *Chittoor Zilla Vyavasayadarula Sangham v AP State Electricity Board* (n 61); *Nand Kishore Garg v Government of NCT of Delhi* (n 61); *London Borough Council* (n 58); *Union of India v Madras Bar Association* (2010) 11 SCC 1.

In certain cases, the law has been extremely sensitive to the problems caused by limitations on pricing autonomy. The Electricity Act, 2003 was enacted, inter alia, to address the problems of creditworthiness crisis in the power sector due to uneconomic tariffs by distancing regulatory responsibility from the government and vesting it in an independent regulator. The tariff provisions required safeguarding the interests of consumers while ensuring the recovery of the cost of electricity in a reasonable manner. Anticipating the challenge of irrational tariffs dictated by political economy, section 65 of the Electricity Act required that a state government wanting to provide subsidised power (at a price below the economic tariff) must pay the amount of subsidy in advance to the licensee, who would otherwise suffer a cash flow shortfall due to the unpaid subsidy. This was meant to reduce the uncertainty of costs on investors and financial institutions involved in funding the project and to keep at some safe distance political motivations that distort economic tariff. While some governments followed this principle, most have directed state-owned utilities to refrain from filing for regular tariff revision.[67]

CONCLUSION

The sporadic critique and deliberations over the past decade, calling for the holistic overhaul of India's regulatory mosaic in the infrastructure sector, seem to have reached a tipping point.[68] Concerns exist across issues ranging from regulatory efficacy, independence, autonomy and accountability to impartiality. These challenges are exacerbated when public sector undertakings are part of the regulated entities which must compete with private sector and joint venture undertakings on a level playing field. Many sectors remain untouched by regulations that curb natural monopolies and display competition neutrality. Principles of competition neutrality therefore need strengthening, both at the policy and implementation levels.

The time is ripe for a comprehensive empirical evaluation of how regulatory mechanisms have fared with respect to their stated objectives. An area warranting serious introspection and reform is the character and space for regulation within the prevalent governance compact. The nature of regulatory agencies demands the ceding of some space by all three wings – the legislature, the executive and the

[67] Facing a crisis, the Union Ministry of Power was constrained to appear before the Appellate Tribunal for Electricity and seek a resolution which culminated in a full bench judgment on 11 January 2011 directing for regular tariff revisions (even *suo moto* if the utility in question does not file for it). See Op No 1 of 2011, Appellant Tribunal for Electricity (11 November 2011), aptel.gov.in/judgements/OP%20NO.1%20OF%202011.pdf.

[68] A study proposing a uniform baseline for the regulatory mechanism and principles of all infrastructure sectors was presented as a Report entitled 'Recommended Framework to Improve Regulatory Effectiveness in Indian Infrastructure Sectors' by the CII National Infrastructure Council (2006) to the Planning Commission of India. After a public consultation on the regulatory architecture in 2008, the Planning Commission issued for public consultation a draft Regulatory Reform Bill in 2009 and a revised version in 2013, which remained as drafts on the website of NITI Aayog. See www.jsalaw.com/wp-content/uploads/2015/09/regulatory-effectiveness.pdf.

judiciary – if these mechanisms must evolve as well-functioning bodies. A formal consultative process to evolve a national policy in this regard, with senior representatives from all three wings, is essential in minimising prolonged, disruptive disputes and changes. The challenge for Indian infrastructure regulation is to serve welfare through means that are economically viable in order to enable investment and supply.

8

Telecom

RAHUL MATTHAN*

INTRODUCTION

THE INDIAN TELECOM sector is a conundrum. It is beset with some of the most inexplicably draconian regulations anywhere in the world and is, as a result, a minefield to navigate. More often than not, telecom operators are flying blind, unable to assess the impact that adopting new technological enhancements will have on their business, unsure of when they will be confronted with yet another unexpected interpretation of the already hazy regulations. However, despite all of this uncertainty, the Indian telecom industry is one of the fastest growing in the world, adding new customers at a rate that other countries find it hard to match. And even with this rapid growth, customers in India still benefit from some of the lowest tariffs, and receive some of the most innovative products and services available anywhere.

How did this come to be? How is it possible that such growth and progress can emanate from a sector so ridden with uncertainty, unpredictable costs and variable regulatory focus? There is a considerable body of literature that has attempted to analyse these questions.[1] For the most part, this literature have attempted to analyse the evolution of case law, policies and regulations over the years, trying to tease out principles from the response of courts to transgressions by operators or from the manner in which the regulatory framework has been amended over time that will shed light on how the Indian telecom sector has reached its current place.[2]

This chapter engages with the issue slightly differently. By examining regulatory developments in the context of challenges faced by telecom operators (including some that have never been brought to the attention of the judiciary), the attempt has been made to illuminate the evolutionary trajectory of the sector through new dimensions.

* Special thanks to Arpitha Desai and Pushkal Dubey for their invaluable assistance.

[1] See Arun K Thiruvengadam and Piyush Joshi, *The Rise of the Regulatory State of the South* (Oxford University Press, 2013) 136–62.

[2] See C Agur, 'Re-imagining the Indian State: External Forces and the Transformation of Telecommunications Policy, 1947–Present' (2018) 20(1) *Global Media and Communication* 65.

Rather than laying out this analysis chronologically, this chapter presents this analysis from two distinct perspectives. We will first study the evolution of the sector by unpacking the administrative objectives that underpin the government's approach to regulation. Ever since the telecom sector was opened up for private sector participation, all policy changes have either been guided by or can be attributed to three broad objectives: coverage and penetration, revenue maximisation and national security. While the focus of telecom regulations has changed in response to evolutions in the technology as well as the maturation of the markets, these underlying objectives have remained the consistent basis for regulatory intervention throughout these developments.

At the same time, there are several characteristics, unique to the Indian telecom sector, that have had as much of an impact on its regulation as the objectives listed above. Like many countries around the world, telecom companies in India operate under a licence. However, the sector is still governed by an anachronistic law that was intended to regulate telegraphs at a time when the internet and all the other modern telecom technologies were not even contemplated. In addition, the sector is administered by two regulators – the Department of Telecommunications (DoT) and the Telecom Regulatory Authority of India (TRAI) – with different, often mutually inconsistent zones of authority, giving rise to an uncomfortable dynamic and considerable regulatory inefficiencies. Other overlapping influences contribute in their own way to the administrative complexity as regulators such as the Competition Commission of India and the Central Vigilance Commission have assumed jurisdiction over different aspects of the sector. Finally, since this sector operates at the cutting edge of technology, it has the additional burden of having to re-examine issues with greater frequency than is necessary in some other areas of regulation. It is here, at the intersection between the regulatory objectives based upon which the sector is administered and the particular characteristics that constrain its regulation, that explanations can be found for both the abstruse regulations that govern the telecom industry as well as the extraordinary success that the sector has enjoyed.

I. THE TELECOM ADMINISTRATIVE FRAMEWORK

How has the administrative framework of the telecom sector been organised? The bulk of the administration is carried out by the DoT, which operates both as the chief executive authority and as the entity responsible for day-to-day regulation. The Minister of State for Communications has charge of the DoT,[3] and the Telecom Commission is tasked with the role of formulating the policy and budget for telecom, getting it approved by the government and implementing telecom policy in the country.[4] The Telecom Commission is bound to adhere to the nation's National Telecom Policy and principles of administrative law.

The TRAI was originally envisaged as an independent regulator under the Telecom Regulatory Authority of India Act, 1997. As we shall subsequently see, over time

[3] Cabinet Secretariat, *Resolution: Constitution of Telecom Commission 1987* (No 15|1|2|87-Cab-I) s 3.
[4] 'Profile', *Department of Telecommunications* (21 December 2017), www.dot.gov.in/profile.

this role has been steadily reduced to that of an expert body limited to making recommendations on key policy issues in telecom. While it still has the mandate to make rules regarding interconnections and tariffs, these regulations cannot contradict the licence terms.[5] The adjudication of disputes arising out of licences and in relation to grievances against orders and directions of the TRAI are the domain of the Telecom Disputes Settlement and Appellate Tribunal (TDSAT).[6] TDSAT orders can only be appealed to the Supreme Court.[7]

Spectrum management is the domain of the Wireless Planning and Coordination Wing (WPC). The WPC is divided into three groups: Licensing and Regulation, the New Technology Group and the Standing Advisory Committee on Frequency Allocation (SACFA). SACFA is an interministerial body that is tasked with taking policy decisions about spectrum allocation and management. It comprises representatives from the Defence Ministry, the Airport Authority, the Home Ministry, the Wireless Department and the DoT.[8] The Telecommunication Engineering Centre (TEC) approves the hardware and other infrastructure equipment used in telecom operations.[9] The Telecom Enforcement Resource and Monitoring (TERM) Cell is the enforcement wing of the DoT.[10] It monitors the activity of telecom companies to ensure compliance with the regulatory framework. The Controller for Communication Accounts is responsible for internal administration and disbursement of the funds of the Department of Communications, and for disbursing subsidies from the Universal Service Obligation Fund.[11]

II. BROAD ADMINISTRATIVE OBJECTIVES

The evolution of the administration of the telecom sector in India has been guided by three broad objectives that have shaped the manner in which the executive has administered the sector. Most telecom regulations are best understood in the context of these three principles, and whenever the government decides how to address evolutions in technology, its decisions are almost always shaped by these three considerations.

Coverage and penetration – while the immediate need that was sought to be addressed with the opening up of the telecom sector was the creation of yet another sector into which the government could invite foreign investment, very soon thereafter, the focus shifted to ensuring coverage and penetration of telecom infrastructure throughout the country. To this day, these twin demands continue to drive the regulation of the sector.

[5] See *Mahanagar Telephon Nigam Ltd v Telecom Regulatory Authority of India* AIR 2000 (Del) 208.

[6] Telecom Regulatory Authority of India Act, 1997, s 14 (TRAI Act).

[7] ibid s 18.

[8] See Ministry of Communication and Information Technology, *Re: Constitution of SACFA 2007* (Memorandum K16011/01/2006).

[9] 'TEC Functions', *Telecommunications Engineering Center*, www.tec.gov.in/tec-functions.

[10] 'Telecom Enforcement Resource and Monitoring (TERM) Cells', *Department of Telecommunications*, http://dotosp.gov.in/homePage.do?methodName=getaboutTermCell.

[11] 'About CCA', *Department of Telecommunication* (11 February 2016), www.dot.gov.in/cca/about-cca.

Revenue maximisation – the government has always looked to maximise the revenue that it earns from the telecom sector. Early evidence of this philosophy was the transition from a fixed-price model to a revenue-sharing model. However, even thereafter, there have been many instances of regulatory intervention that have reinforced the importance of this objective. For instance, after the success of the 3G auction, realising that the real value in the sector resided in the spectrum (and not the licence), the government revamped the model of regulation to maximise revenue through the auction of the spectrum.

National security – telecom is a sensitive sector anywhere in the world, but given India's geopolitical reality, the focus on national security is considerably sharper. Given the concern that India's network infrastructure will be compromised by unfriendly neighbouring states, telecom operators in the country are subject to a unique set of national security restrictions that are often opaque and inexplicable to new operators.

In this section, we will examine each of these objectives in more detail. The examples selected to illustrate each of the stated objectives are representative. Consequently, it is likely that there are many other apposite examples of each of these objectives that have been left out.

A. Coverage and Penetration

In August 2017, there were 1.21 billion telephone subscribers in India. When compared with the numbers in 1991 – a mere five million[12] – this represents a significant growth in subscribers over a relatively short period of time. This growth is the direct result of a series of regulatory interventions that increased coverage and deepened network penetration in the country.

The National Telecommunications Policy of 1994 (hereinafter NTP 94) set out the government's objective to increase accessibility to telecom services.[13] At a time when tele-density was low, there was a need to ensure that as much of the population as possible got access to telecom connectivity. Accordingly, licences were granted to eight Cellular Mobile Telephone Service (CMTS) applicants with the additional condition that there would be just two operators in each of the four metropolitan cities. In December 1995, additional CMTS licences were issued in 18 state circles and Basic Telephone Service licences were issued in 27 cities and 18 state circles.[14] A cap was imposed on the number of operators in each circle in order to ensure that everyone did not gravitate towards the more lucrative metropolitan areas. This important administrative decision single-handedly contributed to the even spread of telecom coverage across the entire country.

[12] Telecom Regulatory Authority of India, *The Indian Telecom Services Performance Indicator Report April–June 2017*, 7.

[13] 'National Telecom Policy, 1994', *Centre for Internet and Society*, cis-india.org/telecom/resources/national-telecom-policy-1994.

[14] Ministry of Communication, Department of Telecommunication, *National Telecom Policy* (1994).

Once there were operators in every circle, the National Telecom Policy of 1999 (NTP 99) was redesigned to maximise coverage within the circles. Telecom companies were now obliged to cover the circle headquarters within a specified period and a majority of the rest of the circle shortly thereafter. Since all the licensees within a circle had to each individually meet this coverage obligation, this resulted in the rapid proliferation of cellular towers, resulting in a significant increase in mobile coverage across all the circles.

There is a limit as to how far the network can be expanded in parallel before inefficiencies, such as the clustering of towers, impedes network performance. Once the regulator realised that the inefficiencies had begun to creep in, further amendments were made to permit the sharing of passive telecom infrastructure. Telecom companies began to hive off passive telecom assets (towers, backhaul fibre and associated infrastructure) into separate infrastructure companies. These companies rented out space on a single tower to multiple operators, greatly improving the efficiency of their infrastructure utilisation. Telecom companies, which now no longer had to build or maintain this infrastructure themselves, were able to improve the quality of their operations. At the same time, the barriers to entry for new entrants were significantly reduced, given that the abundant availability of passive infrastructure considerably reduced their go-to market time and offered considerable savings in terms of capital and operating expenditure.

As a result of these timely administrative measures, India currently has the second-largest telecom network in the world, behind only China. However, while overall tele-density in the country is at a high 87.85 per cent, rural tele-density is 52.97 per cent, as opposed to urban tele-density of 164.13 per cent.[15] Despite the substantial increase in the reach of telecom services, around 30 per cent of the Indian population, mainly in far-flung rural and tribal areas, still do not have basic mobile services.[16] Geographically, 15 per cent of the country remains to be covered by the telecom service providers.[17]

Broadband coverage is still low across the whole country. As of June 2017, the total number of internet/broadband subscribers is a mere 431.21 million.[18] Despite the high indices on consumption, India is ranked 89 among 100 countries on average mobile internet connection speed at 4.9 megabits per second (Mbps), far behind other Asia-Pacific countries such as Sri Lanka (6.9 Mbps) and Thailand (8.6 Mbps).[19] When Reliance Jio, a new provider, recently launched its services in India, it offered low-cost LTE-enabled feature phones and WiFi hotspot devices, primarily targeting first-time internet users. Various other telecom companies have since launched mirror tariffs for bundled data packs to retain their customers, which has led to an overall decrease

[15] Ministry of Communication, Department of Telecommunication, *Annual Report 2016–17* (2017).

[16] 'Highlights of Telecom Subscription Data as on 30th April 2018', *Telecom Regulatory Authority of India* (26 June 2018) 5, http://trai.gov.in/sites/default/files/PRNo68Eng26062018.pdf.

[17] 'Highlights of Telecom Subscription Data' (n 16).

[18] Telecom Regulatory Authority of India (n 12).

[19] 'Q1 2017 State of the Internet: Connectivity Report', *Akamai* (31 May 2017), www.akamai.com/us/en/about/our-thinking/state-of-the-internet-report/global-state-of-the-internet-connectivity-reports.jsp.

in data prices. In the absence of the kind of significant regulatory intervention that resulted in the growth in coverage and penetration of telecom infrastructure in the late 1990s, it is likely that market measures such as this sort of data-led pricing is what will eventually lead to improved broadband coverage and penetration.

B. Maximising Revenue

The government has always sought to maximise revenue over all other considerations. The private sector has paid a hefty price for the privilege of being allowed to partake of what was, until liberalisation, the sole preserve of the government. This regulatory philosophy of revenue maximisation remains axiomatic of the sector and is exemplified in the manner in which licence fees have been charged and matters relating to spectrum have been addressed, and explains why the Indian government stringently regulates toll bypass and resale.

When the telecom sector was first opened up to private sector participation, it was on the basis of a fixed licence fee. Operators bid for a circle based on the fixed licence fee per subscriber that they would pay the DoT.[20] The licence fee projection was calculated as a lump sum increasing over the duration of the licence and was based on revenue projections per subscriber and estimates of growth in the number of subscribers over time.[21] However, the subscriber base grew at a much slower pace than anticipated and the government's interests of revenue maximisation could not be achieved as telecom companies generated far lower revenues than anticipated. By July 1999, private telecom companies owed almost $9 billion in licence fees to the DoT, nearly forcing them into bankruptcy. The government's approach to revenue maximisation was destroying the industry.

In NTP 99, the fixed-fee licence model was replaced with a revenue-sharing model.[22] Licensees were now required to pay the government 15 per cent of their Adjusted Gross Revenue (AGR) as a licence fee. Since the licence fee was now a percentage of actual income, it had a more direct bearing on their business than the earlier model, which was based on projections. However, since it was calculated on gross revenues, it had to be paid regardless of the profitability of their operations and included non-telecom streams of revenue (such as the sale of handsets).

When the private players were first allowed to participate in the sector, the government followed a first-come-first-served model – a minimum amount of spectrum was provided along with each telecom licence and once coverage obligations had been met, the telecom licensee would be granted additional spectrum at no further cost.[23]

[20] Vikram Raghavan, *Communication Laws in India: Legal Aspects of Telecom, Broadcasting and Cable Services* (LexisNexis, 2007) 77.

[21] ibid 83.

[22] Ministry of Communication, Department of Telecommunications, *New Telecom Policy* (1999) (NTP 99). See also Ministry of Communication, Department of Telecommunications, *Proposed Package for Migration of Existing Licenses of Cellular and Basic Telecom Services to New Telecom Policy – 1999 Regime* (No 842-153/99-VAS (Vol V) (Pt)).

[23] License Agreement, Unified Access Service License, 2009, pt III, cl 18.3.

As a result, until 2011, telecom spectrum was provided to telecom companies for free, based solely on the size of their subscriber base.

When countries around the world adopted the auction model for licensing 3G spectrum, the Indian government followed suit. The Indian 3G auction proved to be a huge success and a number of public interest litigations were immediately filed challenging the previous approach.[24] This was supported by a report of the Comptroller and Auditor General (CAG) that highlighted the loss to the exchequer that had resulted from the government's decision not to adopt the auction process sooner.[25] Finally, even the Supreme Court held that spectrum is a scarce natural resource that was best distributed through an auction process.

In 2012, the National Telecom Policy (NTP 12)[26] delinked spectrum from service type and technology.[27] The TRAI released a series of recommendations that have culminated in the notification of the Spectrum Liberalisation Guidelines and Spectrum Trading Guidelines in 2015.[28] As a result, auctioned spectrum today is simply earmarked for utilisation without specifying service or technology.[29] Due to the unusually large number of operators in the market, telecom companies still struggle from a relative paucity of available spectrum. In order to address this, the government amended the mergers and acquisition (M&A) guidelines in 2014. However, in yet another example of the government's focus on revenue maximisation, the new M&A guidelines introduced mark-to-market regulations that required acquirers to pay to the government the difference between the current price of the spectrum and the price at which the target company bought the spectrum.[30] One of the main reasons for consolidation was the opportunity to gain access to the spectrum of the target company at an affordable price. If the difference between the price at which the spectrum had originally been purchased and the current market price was to be paid to the government, consolidation no longer made commercial sense. Blinded by its imperative to maximise revenue, the government failed to achieve the necessary administrative objectives.

Data calls are a threat to licence revenue. When the internet is used to make calls, the revenue that the government might have earned from national and international calls falls dramatically. In 2004, Reliance Infocom carried international call traffic into India over its data network and then switched them onto the Public Switched

[24] *Centre for Public Interest Litigation v Union of India* [2012] 3 SCC 1 (Supreme Court).

[25] Comptroller and Auditor General of India, *Report of the Comptroller and Auditor General of India for the Year Ended March 2013, Union Government (Communications and IT Sector)* (20 of 2015).

[26] Ministry of Communications and Information Technology, *National Telecom Policy 2012* (2012) (NTP 12), III Objectives 3.3.

[27] ibid III 3.3 and 4.

[28] Ministry of Communications and Information Technology, *Guidelines for Liberalisation of Administratively Allotted Spectrum in 800 MHz and 1800 MHz Frequency* (J-14025/212/2015-CDMA); Ministry of Communications and Information Technology, *Guidelines for Trading of Access Spectrum by Access Service Providers* (L-14006/05/2015-NTG).

[29] Ministry of Communications and Information Technology (n 28).

[30] Ministry of Communications and Information Technology, *Guidelines for Transfer/Merger of Various Categories of Telecommunication Service Licenses/Authorisation under Unified License (UL) on Compromises, Arrangements and Amalgamation of the companies* (No 20-281/2010-AS-I (Vol VII)) (Merger Guidelines).

Telephone Network (PTSN). The only cost of these calls was the local call charge within the territory of India, allowing Reliance to price them at rates far lower than an International Subscriber Dialling (ISD) call would ordinarily have cost. The DoT disapproved of this approach, imposing a fine of Rs 150 crores on Reliance Infocom for the interconnection revenue that the National Long Distance (NLD) licensees had lost – a decision subsequently upheld by the TDSAT.[31]

Following a similar rationale, the government has, on numerous occasions, launched investigations into one-stop-shop managed data services businesses on the ground that the extending of these service offerings into India results in the resale of a telecom service without a licence. As a result of these investigations, various telecom companies that have no operations in India have been called upon to pay licence fees for the profit attributable to the Indian leg of their global telecom offerings.[32] To address the issue of resale, the Unified License (Virtual Network Operators) (UL(VNO)) licence was introduced, which separated network connectivity from the provision of service.[33] However, despite this, there are very few licensed UL(VNO) operators in India. The TRAI has recommended separating licences for network layer from the service layer under National Telecom Policy 2018.[34] If implemented, this could, in the long run, allow for greater flexibility in modelling licences for communication services in each industry.

C. National Security

The third and probably most aggressively monitored principle based upon which the sector is administered is national security. The Indian government has always regarded the telecom sector as sensitive, and telecom licences have always had provisions specifically aimed at ensuring national security. There has been a fear that unfriendly nation states would be able to capture elements or the whole of India's national telecom infrastructure that could paralyse defence infrastructure at a critical juncture. On the other hand, the government has always looked to be able to intercept messages and conversations over these private networks in order

[31] *Reliance Infocomm v Union of India* [2005] 2 Comp LJ 537 (TDSAT).

[32] See *Tata Communication v Union of India* [2012] Petition Nos 444 and 449 of 2011 (TDSAT); *Tata Communications Ltd v Union of India* [2014] Petition No 233 of 2013 (TDSAT); *AT&T Global Services India Private Ltd and Another v Union of India* (2017) WP (C) 3413/2017 & CM No 14921/2017 (Stay) (Delhi High Court).

[33] Telecom Regulatory Authority of India, *Recommendations on Introducing Virtual Network Operator in the Telecom Sector* (2015). Currently, a UL (VNO) requires a 7.5 crore entry fee and eight per cent of AGR as a licence fee along with Bank Guarantees. These costs can prove to be very high for service providers layering their services on dedicated connectivity. See Ministry of Communications and Information Technology, *Guidelines for Grant of Unified License (Virtual Network Operators)* (No 800-23/2011-VAS (Vol II)).

[34] Telecom Regulatory Authority of India, *Recommendations on Inputs for Formulation of National Telecom Policy 2018* (2018). In its current draft, the National Digital Communications Policy, 2018 recommends a separate licensing regime for each layer of the network – infrastructure, network, services and application. See Department of Telecommunications, *Draft National Digital Communications Policy 2018*.

to detect crimes being conducted using these communication networks. These twin concerns have wrapped themselves around the telecom regulatory framework, resulting in the inclusion of various restrictions aimed specifically at the security of the network.

When Vodafone sought approval for its investments in Hutchison-Essar, it had a 10 per cent stake in China Telecom. At around the same time, Videsh Sanchar Nigam Ltd was planning to use Huawei equipment in its network, because of the comparatively cheaper price at which this equipment was available. These two incidents, occurring as they did within roughly the same timeframe, drew attention to what was perceived to be the increasing influence of an unfriendly neighbouring state in the telecom infrastructure of the country. Concern began to be expressed about how easily foreign governments could exert control over telecom infrastructure, either through indirect foreign ownership or by inserting backdoors into the network infrastructure.

In response, the government introduced restrictions into the foreign direct investment regulations requiring telecom companies that had foreign investment to comply with various security conditions, including prohibitions on having foreigners in key positions in the company and on investments from 'unfriendly states'.[35] Over time, this initial restriction was diluted to allow such foreign nationals to be employed after security clearance. The government also introduced a security clearance procedure for imports, requiring telecom companies to apply for security clearance before placing the final procurement order for all equipment or software, either itself or through franchisees or agents.[36] Subsequently, various other regulations were issued with similar obligations on hardware and software testing and monitoring requirements.[37]

The regulations were worded so broadly that telecom companies had to subject all their software to a security threat check at the time of procurement and at specified instances thereafter. Telecom equipment suppliers chafed at the challenges that these regulations posed.[38] These obstacles resulted in a significant slowdown in their operations. Over time, the more onerous provisions were gradually done away with, but the government has recently reintroduced obligations requiring all telecom equipment to be approved by an accredited laboratory based on parameters yet to be notified.[39]

Telecom licences have always had legal intercept provisions requiring telecom service providers to allow government and law enforcement agencies to intercept

[35] Ministry of Commerce and Industry, *Enhancement of the Foreign Direct Investment Ceiling from 49 Percent to 74 Percent in the Telecom Sector* (2007), Press Note 3.

[36] Department of Telecommunications, *Amendment to License Agreement for Security-Related Concerns for Expansion of Telecom Services in Various Zones of the Country* (No 842-745/2005-VAS/Vol III).

[37] Ministry of Communications & Information Technology, *Amendment to the Unified Access Service License Agreement for Security-Related Concerns for Expansion of Telecom Services in Various Zones of the Country* (No 10-15/2011-AS.III (21)).

[38] John Ribeiro, 'Ericsson Objects to New Indian Telecom Rules', *CIO* (6 August 2010), www.cio.com/article/2416287/regulation/ericsson-objects-to-new-indian-telecom-rules.html.

[39] 'Telecommunications Engineering Centre', www.tec.gov.in.

conversations. These regulations originally required telecom companies to provide nine law enforcement agencies with a certain number of lines through which traffic could be intercepted and monitored.[40] This has now been replaced by an obligation to provide always-on connections to the Central Monitoring System (CMS).[41]

The ability of the government to intercept telephone conversations came up before the Supreme Court in *PUCL v Union of India*.[42] The Court held that the unregulated interception of telephonic conversations is violative of the right to life and liberty in Article 21 of the Constitution, and must be subject to substantive and procedural restrictions. Telephone conversations could only be intercepted for reasons of public safety and national security, and all such interceptions had to be governed by procedures that were just, fair and reasonable. The Court framed guidelines for legal interception which have now been incorporated under rule 419-A of the Telegraph Rules.[43]

During the terrorist attacks on the Taj and Oberoi hotels in Mumbai in 2008, the terrorists communicated with their handlers using Blackberry messenger. Since the Blackberry technology was designed with end-to-end encryption, law enforcement agencies were unable to intercept these messages. In the aftermath of the incident, the Indian government identified this as a security vulnerability that compromised national security and insisted that RIM (Research in Motion) should bring its servers into India so that the government could intercept all traffic in the future. For three years, RIM resisted the requests of the government until it finally capitulated, setting up its servers in Mumbai for the purposes of interception.[44] This was the first instance of data localisation a regulatory philosophy that has more recently been aggressively adopted by the government in the proposed data privacy law, the draft e-commerce policy and in relation to the regulation of financial transactions by the Reserve Bank of India.

But for the Indian government's strong focus on coverage and penetration, the telecom sector would not have grown as rapidly as it did to its current size. At the same time, the detrimental effect that both the focus on revenue maximisation and the inconstant and unpredictable implementation of security restrictions has had, and continues to have, on the sector is undeniable.

The sector has developed into one of the largest in the world, despite the fact that two out of the three central objectives behind the administration of the sector impose restrictions on the freedom to operate. The reason for this is the promise inherent in the Indian market. With an excess of a billion people wishing to take advantage of all that telecom connectivity has to offer, Indian telecom companies have always been willing to put up with some pain in exchange for the privilege of

[40] See License Agreement, Cellular Mobile Telephone Service (2011), pt VI 44.9.

[41] License Agreement, Unified License (2018), ch VIII 8.2, ch IX 8, ch X 5.2, ch XI 6.6, ch XII 7.5, 7.10. This change was made through amendments in the several access service licences in 2013. See Ministry of Communications and Information Technology, *Amendment to the Cellular Mobile Telephone Service (CMTS) License Agreement* (No 800-12/2013-AS.II.).

[42] *PUCL v Union of India* [1997] 1 SCC 301.

[43] Indian Telegraph Rules, 1951, r 419-A.

[44] Sanjay Singh, 'No Secrets on Blackberry: Government Gets its Way on Tapping Popular Messenger Service', *India Today* (7 April 2012), indiatoday.intoday.in/story/govt-to-tap-blackberry-messenger-security-privacy/1/183403.html.

tapping into a market of this size and scale. Key to their assessment of the value of the opportunity was the rate at which the industry de-regulated. By steadily opening up market access, the regulator created an aggressively competitive market in which commercial pressures have driven down prices to unprecedented levels. When coupled with the liberalisation of infrastructure sharing, the regulator was able to allow far more value to be unlocked from out of telecom assets in India than was ordinarily possible. That the regulator was capable of achieving such growth is particularly remarkable, given the special features of the Indian telecom market.

III. FEATURES OF TELECOM ADMINISTRATION

In order to fully appreciate the development of the Indian telecom sector, it is important to discuss some of the peculiar features that characterise the sector. These characteristics operate as constraints on telecom operators and subscribers to avail the full extent of the benefits that the sector could provide, while at the same time operating as restrictions on the ability of the regulator to appropriately administer the sector. There are five broad features that define and continue to influence the shape of current and future regulations:

Anachronistic law – the sector is governed by an old statute drafted in the pre-internet age. As a result, the sector is regulated on the basis of terms that were never intended to be interpreted in the manner in which they are currently being used. This philosophy of wresting meaning out of words and phrases has become a characteristic of telecom regulation and has led to much of the ambiguity that is currently a characteristic hallmark of its administration.

Regulation through licence – in the absence of a law, the sector is almost entirely regulated through the licence agreements that telecom companies enter into with the government. As a result, there is far greater informality in the regulation of the sector than would have been the case if regulation took place through laws or delegated legislation. Changes in policy are implemented through amendments to the licence agreements, eschewing the rules and regulations that are requirements under other statutes.

Two regulators – the telecom sector effectively has two regulators with distinct but often contradictory functions who are often portrayed as being in opposition to each other. This gives rise to a peculiar tension in the administration of the sector. While the TRAI was originally established as the regulator, its powers have been limited to tariff review and management of quality of service. While the TRAI does make policy recommendations, the DoT is not bound to comply with them.

Overlapping influence – the sector regulators operate amidst multiple, often overlapping, zones of influence that have an impact on the process of regulation. The telecom ministry exerts an unusual degree of influence. In addition, the telecom regulator is regularly subject to oversight from independent regulators such as the Central Vigilance Commission (CVC).

The influence of new technologies – telecom sector regulators have had to contend with the influence of new technologies that constantly challenge the manner in which the sector operates. Given the ambiguities in the manner in which regulations have been framed, telecom companies are constantly trying to exploit loopholes in the law by deploying new technologies that were never envisaged by the existing regulatory framework.

A. Anachronistic Law

The Indian telecom sector can trace its origins back to the British East India Company, which decided, in 1854, to establish a telegraph network for the Indian territories. Four successive telegraph laws had been enacted by the British since then to ensure their control over communications. This culminated in the Indian Telegraph Act of 1885, which is the law that currently governs all telecommunications in India.

Section 3 of the Telegraph Act defines the term 'telegraph' to include any appliance, instrument, material or apparatus used or capable of use for transmission or reception of signs, signals, writing images and sounds or intelligence of any nature by wire, visual or other electro-magnetic emissions, radio waves or Hertzian waves, galvanic, electric or magnetic means.[45] In *Balvinder Singh v Delhi Administration and Others*, the High Court of Delhi held that television and video both fall within the definition of 'telegraph' and a licence for public exhibition is necessary under the Cinematography Act, 1952, as well as under the Telegraph Act.[46] In *State v Mangal Rao*, it was held that a radio-set receiving communication is a 'telegraph' within this meaning.[47] Through a series of similar decisions, the courts in India have stretched the definition of 'telegraph' so wide as to encompass every new communication technology that has been developed.

This approach is unusual. Countries across the globe (such as Ireland and South Africa) with a similar colonial history have since adopted modern laws that better regulate these new technologies. Ireland, for example, repealed the Telegraph Act, 1863 and the Telegraph Act, 1869, replacing them with the Communication Regulation Act, 2002.[48] Similarly, South Africa enacted the Electronic Communication

[45] This definition has gradually been extended over time to include newer technologies within the ambit of the word 'telegraph', even though these technologies were developed long after the telegraph and the notification of the Telegraph Act, 1885. The legal basis for this emanates from an old Queen's Bench decision in *Attorney General v Edison Telephone Co of London* [1880] 6 QBD 244, where the government sued private telecom operators in court for challenging their monopoly over posts and telegraphs. The respondents in this case argued that the technology for telephone was developed long after the governing Telegraph Act in England and fell beyond the ambit of the word 'telegraph'. Therefore, the respondents could offer subscriptions to interconnect their subscribers. However, the Queen's Bench held that a telephone was similar to a telegraph as it was used to relay messages across a wire and it did not matter that the telephone used electricity, as it served the same purpose as a telegram. This was used as the basis for compelling telephone operators to obtain licences from the government and has served as the inspiration and legal basis for the Indian government to exert dominion over all forms of communication technologies.

[46] *Balvinder Singh v Delhi Administration and Others* [1984] AIR Del 379.

[47] *State v Mangal Rao* [1963] AIR SC 446.

[48] Communication Regulation Act, 2002.

Act, 2005[49] to repeal the Telecommunication Act, 1996[50] and the Broadcasting Act, 1999[51] that regulated telecommunications and broadcasting respectively. In India, however, telecommunication is still governed by a pre-independence legislation. The government made an attempt to repeal five colonial era laws of the land and replace them with the Convergence Bill, 2011, but as yet, the bill has not been tabled in the Parliament of India.[52] As a consequence, one of the most modern sectors of the economy finds itself governed by an archaic law whose terms are constantly being stretched to apply to technologies that had not even begun to be contemplated when it was drafted.

This approach of wresting meaning out of words and phrases so that they are made to apply to concepts that did not even exist when those clauses were first drafted has become a defining feature of the administration of the Indian telecommunication sector. From this has developed the habit of applying imprecise legislation replete with broadly defined provisions that regulated entities find hard to accurately interpret and which the regulator has to invoke against licensees and subscribers in ways that are hard to anticipate. This makes compliance with the Indian telecom regulation difficult and uncertain.

One of the best examples of this regulatory uncertainty is the other service providers (OSP) registration issued by the DoT to regulate entities providing 'application services'. The term 'application services' has been defined broadly to include tele-banking, tele-medicine, tele-education, tele-trading, e-commerce, call centres, network operation centres and other 'IT Enabled Services', which are provided by using telecom resources delivered by authorised telecom service providers. The inclusion of the phrase 'other IT Enabled Services' in the definition of 'application services' expands the definition to include every service that uses telecom resources. This could be interpreted to mean that virtually every modern business needs such a registration. While the regulator has been known to rely on this lack of clarity to send show cause notices to various businesses that have not obtained OSP registrations requiring them to provide reasons why they should not be prosecuted, hundreds of businesses have interpreted the regulations narrowly, assuming that they fall outside of the purview of these regulations. To its credit, the regulator largely leaves them alone.

B. Regulation Through Licences

The telecom sector is constructed as a state monopoly. Private sector participation is only permitted through licences granted by the state. It was not until 1991, when private companies were allowed to manufacture telecom switches for the first time,

[49] Electronic Communication Act, 2000.
[50] Telecommunication Act, 1996, s 2.
[51] Broadcasting Act, 1999, Preamble.
[52] Communication Convergence Bill, 2001.

that the telecom sector was opened up to limited private sector participation.[53] In 1994, as part of the liberalisation of the economy, the government allowed the private sector to apply for cellular mobile licences for metros and subsequently for the rest of the country.[54] Shortly thereafter, fixed-line telecom services and internet services were opened for private participation.[55]

The fact that the telecom sector has historically been regulated as a state monopoly continues to influence the regulatory approach towards its administration. The operating assumption is that everything which is not specifically permitted is prohibited. Since private sector participation in the sector is enabled through specific licences, only those activities that have been specifically permitted under the terms of the applicable license can be performed by the private sector. Given the government's penchant for using broad language while describing obligations and prohibitions, the exact obligations of the licensee often remains unclear.[56]

Among the many challenges with using licences to regulate the sector is the fact that the terms and conditions of the licence only bind regulated entities (the licensees) and, as a result, regulatory stipulations that ought to apply to the world at large are hard to enforce. In order to deal with this, the licence often includes language that requires licensees to contractually enforce these license obligations on their customers. This makes enforcement cumbersome. This issue came to the fore when the government tried to invoke the prohibitions contained in the Indian telecom licence against encryption against Blackberry. While the Internet Service Provider (ISP) licence contained stipulations that imposed restrictions on the levels of encryption that could be deployed, Blackberry was not a licensee and, as a result, these obligations could not be directly enforced against the company. In order to enforce compliance, the regulator had to issue notices to all telecom companies requiring them to terminate access to the Blackberry service through their telecom network. This is a cumbersome method of enforcement, but is unavoidable when regulation is carried out through licence. However, it has had the salutary consequence of ensuring that over-the-top operators have flourished, creating a rich economy of applications and services that have been built upon the telecom infrastructure.

Yet another challenge has to do with the rapid rate of change of telecom technologies. Licences were originally granted based on the nature of the service being provided. As a result, various technologies were used to provide services beyond the intended scope of the licence. In 2007, fixed services providers began to offer limited mobility services using cordless phones that could be carried around from place to place and which were, to that extent, not much different from cellular phones.

[53] SD McDowell and J Lee (2003) 'India's Experiments in Mobile Licensing' 27(5–6) *Telecommunications Policy* 371.

[54] ibid 377, 389–94.

[55] See 'Minister', *Department of Telecommunications* (4 January 2016), www.dot.gov.in/minister/minister.

[56] The fundamental requirement for a power to be delegated only under binding rules of conduct under a policy formulated by the legislature was first laid down in *Harishankar Bangla v MP State* [1954] AIR SC 465 and has successively been upheld by the Supreme Court. The licensing regime for telecom does not qualify this criterion, as the Telegraph Act grants unbridled power to license telecom services to the Central Government, and the various NTPs are more aspirational than binding in nature.

Cellular operators argued that fixed service providers should not be providing cellular services. The TDSAT agreed.[57] However, this TDSAT ruling never came into effect because shortly thereafter, the Unified Access Service (UAS) licence was issued, paving the way for a technology-agnostic implementation of access services.[58]

Despite the technology-agnostic nature of the licence, a similar issue arose during the 3G auctions.[59] Bidders for the 3G spectrum wanted to be sure that, in the event that they were not able to secure pan-India spectrum during the auction, they would, in those circles, be able to roam on the network of telecom companies that had obtained 3G spectrum. Since the licence already permitted both intercircle and intra-circle roaming without making a distinction between which bands of spectrum roaming was permitted on, it seemed that there would be no restriction on bidders implementing 3G roaming in those circles where they had not won spectrum. In order to be doubly sure, the bidders specifically asked this question during the bid consultations. They received non-committal answers.[60]

As anticipated, no one secured pan-India spectrum in the first 3G auction, and shortly after they launched their services in 2012, Bharti Airtel, Vodafone and Idea entered into agreements to provide each other with 3G roaming facilities in circles in which they had not won 3G spectrum. The DoT immediately declared that operators who had 2G spectrum in a given service area could not provide 3G services to their customers in those circles and imposed fines on all three operators.[61] The operators challenged this in court and eventually these arrangements were held to be valid. The government's approach of segregating cellular licences based on spectrum authorisation had worked to the detriment of telecom companies, subscribers and the objectives of the state.[62] It was only after the Unified License (UL) was rolled out that all voice and data services, regardless of band of spectrum, came to be jointly licensed under the heading 'Access Services'.[63]

Principles of administrative law require the executive to follow a specific process in the enactment of delegated legislation. Regulation through licences allows the government to bypass many of these requirements, including the obligation to lay new amendments before Parliament.[64] Infocomm Infotel was the only company

[57] *COAI v Union of India* [2003] 3 Comp LJ 337 (TDSAT).

[58] Telecom Regulatory Authority of India, *Recommendations on Issues Relating to Limited Mobility through Wireless-in-Local-Loop in the Access Network by Basic Service Providers* (2000), ch 1.

[59] Ministry of Communications and Information Technology, *Auction of 3G and BWA Spectrum: Notice Inviting Applications* (No P-11014/13/2008-PP).

[60] Ministry of Communications and Information Technology, *Auction of 3G and BWA Spectrum: Queries and Responses, Queries – 11, 12, 48, 230, 371.*

[61] *Vodafone and Others v Union of India* [2014] New Delhi Petitions 518–22 of 2011 and Petitions 308, 349, 353 of 2013 (TDSAT).

[62] ibid.

[63] Ministry of Communications, *Unified License*, 2.2(i).

[64] Before the split of the service provider and regulatory function of the Department of Telecom in 1999, it was a state public utility, fixed the tariffs under the Telegraph Rules and laid them before Parliament. The Madras High Court saw this as excessive delegation. However, this judgment became moot after private players licensed under s 4 entered the market for telecom services under NTP 94, as the terms imposed on them, including the fees charged under these licences, were never laid down before Parliament. As an aside, the levy of licence fees without any guidance on the rates would, in itself, constitute excessive delegation

that bid for and won 20 MHz of 4G spectrum for pan-India use in the Broadband Wireless Access (BWA) spectrum band – a band that had been earmarked for providing internet services. Shortly after the auction, the government amended the UL Guidelines to allow BWA licensees to migrate to the UL by paying the differential licence fee.[65] As a result, Infocomm Infotel, now Reliance Jio, was able to provide voice services over BWA spectrum, even though it had bid for a spectrum that had been exclusively earmarked for internet services.[66] This sort of a change in purpose is only possible when fundamental policy decisions are taken through a simple licence amendment without following any of the processes applicable to delegated legislation.

C. A Tale of Two Regulators

The need for an independent regulator arose early on in the evolution of the telecom sector. The Supreme Court had rebuked the government by pointing out that if the DoT was to be the regulator, policy-maker and monopoly service provider, it was evident that the government was not serious about private investment in the telecom sector.[67] In addition, India's international commitments under the Agreement on Trade-Related Aspects of Intellectual Property Rights required it to establish an independent regulator for the telecom sector in order to pave the way for the entry of private players into the telecom market. As a result, the TRAI was established through an ordinance and later under the TRAI Act in 1997.

Despite the creation of the TRAI, the DoT was unwilling to relinquish its jurisdiction over certain issues. For example, the TRAI and the DoT differed on whether it was necessary for the latter to consult the TRAI in the exercise of its licensing powers. In NTP 99, it was clarified that the TRAI had the power to issue directions to the government and to adjudicate disputes among service providers (among which were included the government-run incumbent telecom companies), but made it clear that the government's licensing and policy-making functions could not be delegated to the TRAI as they were derived from the government's sovereign authority. In time, the TRAI's adjudicatory powers were also handed over to a special tribunal created specifically in order to handle telecom disputes – the TDSAT. Today, the role of the TRAI is limited to making recommendations and issuing directions and regulations in strictly circumscribed areas. The regulatory authority of the TRAI continued to be challenged from time to time. In 2013, the Supreme Court reaffirmed the TRAI's regulatory authority and held that its directions could only be challenged in the High Court.[68]

as, according to the Supreme Court in *Municipal Corporation of Calcutta v Liberty Cinema* [1963] 2 SCR 477, it could amount to the levying of tax without any guidance. Nevertheless, the Supreme Court has continually validated the legality of licence fees on the ground that the licensee has accepted it. See *Union of India v Association of Unified Telecom Service Providers of India* [2011] 10 SCC 543.

[65] Ministry of Communications, *Guidelines for Grant of Unified License* (2014), 8.3 (ii).

[66] Ministry of Communications (n 65).

[67] *Delhi Science Forum v Union of India* AIR 1996 SC 1356.

[68] *Mahanagar Telephon Nigam Ltd v Telecom Regulatory Authority of Delhi* [2000] (52) DRJ (DB).

There have been several instances where TRAI recommendations have either been rejected or stalled by the DoT. In 2006, the TRAI's Recommendations on Next Generation Networks were not accepted by the DoT.[69] In 2008, the TRAI's Recommendations on issues related to internet telephony met a similar fate, being ultimately rejected.[70] In many instances, the delay in acting on the TRAI's recommendations has led to unnecessary stagnation in the regulatory agenda. After launching 3G services in the country, the government was supposed to roll out the Mobile Virtual Network Operators (MVNO) service with the objective of increasing competition and improving service conditions for customers. In 2008, the TRAI provided recommendations to the DoT on the licensing regime for MVNOs, but, due to a lack of consensus between the DoT and the TRAI on key issues, the Ministry of Communications did not act on it. The Telecom Commission finally cleared the proposal to allow MVNOs to launch operations in India in 2009, but it was not until May 2016 that the final guidelines for the grant of MVNO licences were released.

It is tempting to dismiss these as one-off instances of a legitimate exercise of regulatory discretion. Arguably, there are an equal if not greater number of instances where the TRAI recommendations have been accepted. However, it is worth reflecting on how these recommendations are issued in order to assess what the most optimal construct should be. The TRAI has a robust process by which it arrives at its policy recommendations. It prepares comprehensive consultation papers offering extensive policy recommendations and engaging with relevant stakeholders through a public consultation process before presenting a set of reasoned recommendations. The DoT, on the other hand, follows no such process and neither consults with the public nor provides any explanations when it rejects the TRAI recommendations. Since the TRAI recommendations are not binding on the DoT, despite of the high quality of its output, the government is not obliged to heed its recommendations.

This has resulted in an inadequate and counterproductive framework for expert choice. Though the TRAI clearly produces more considered recommendations, the current construct allows the DoT to ignore them, making the entire process of obtaining stakeholder inputs largely irrelevant. To an outsider who is unaware of this peculiar duality, the government seems like it is not following its own advice. Surely it would have been more efficient for the DoT to use the TRAI to formulate regulations that it would then implement as the regulator.

D. Zones of Influence

The relationship between various players in the telecom ecosystem – the DoT, its parent ministry, the courts and the legislature – is complex and worryingly opaque. However, even though the law empowers the government to issue licences and

[69] Telecom Regulatory Authority of India, *Consultation Paper on Issues Pertaining to Next Generation Networks (NGN)* (Consultation Paper No 2/2006).

[70] Telecom Regulatory Authority of India, *Recommendations on Issues Related to Internet Telephony* (2008).

notifications to private companies, these licences and notifications have to be issued in conformity with the policy directives of the parent ministry, the Ministry of Communications and Information Technology. Even though the decisions of the regulator are primarily subject to judicial review by the TDSAT, they can – and often are – challenged before the High Courts or the Supreme Court. Each of the government stakeholders are additionally subject to oversight by independent regulators, such as the CVC and, in all likelihood, the Competition Commission of India (CCI). It is therefore virtually impossible to accurately establish where their respective zones of influence extend.

The power to make regulations in consonance with the TRAI Act is a plenary power of the Authority.[71] However, in *MTNL v TRAI*, the Delhi High Court held this power to be subservient to the licence terms issued by the DoT under section 4 of the Telegraph Act,[72] as a result of which the TRAI can only make regulations within the framework provided by the Central Government.[73] Prior to the spectrum auction in 2007, the TRAI had recommended that there should be 'no cap' on the applications for the issue of licences. The DoT disregarded this recommendation and issued a press release stating that applications for issue of licences would only be accepted until 1 October 2007.[74] The Ministry of Communications and IT then arbitrarily decided, without reference to the Telecom Commission, as should have been the case, that the cut-off date for the issue of the Letter of Intent would be advanced to 25 September 2007, with allotment being decided on a first-come-first-served basis. As a result, not only did the government unilaterally influence critical policy decisions, but in doing so, it also made it all the more evident that the TRAI, which made the original 'no cap' recommendation, was a toothless regulator.

Similar overlaps exist in the zones of influence over adjudication. The TRAI was originally vested with broad powers, including powers of regulation and the responsibility to adjudicate disputes in the telecom sector. The government amended the TRAI Act in 2000 to establish the TDSAT, to which was transferred the TRAI's powers to adjudicate disputes between licensors, licensees, service providers and consumers.[75]

In the case of *Cellular Operators Association of India v Union of India*,[76] when the Cellular Operators Association of India (COAI) approached the TDSAT, challenging the decision of the TRAI approving the use of wireless in local loop (WiLL) technology by fixed line operators, the TDSAT held that the decision to allow WiLL technology was a policy decision and that the TDSAT could not interfere in matters of policy. The COAI then appealed to the Supreme Court, which held

[71] TRAI Act, 1997, s 36(1).

[72] *MTNL v TRAI* AIR 2000 Del 208.

[73] ibid.

[74] *Centre for Public Interest Litigation* (n 24) [26].

[75] 'It may be questioned whether the combination in one body of the regulator's rule-making function (quasi-legislative), its monitoring and enforcement functions (quasi-executive) and its dispute resolution function (quasi-judicial) is at odds with the principle of separation of powers-a principle which has been an important feature of the liberal democratic tradition of government at least since Montesquieu.' See Rory Macmillan, 'Reflections on Regulation and Dispute Resolution in the Indian Telecommunication Sector' (2005) 47 *Journal of the Indian Law Institute* 29.

[76] *Cellular Operators Association of India v Union of India* [2003] 3 SCC 186.

that, since the Tribunal was an expert body, the scheme of the TRAI Act required it to exercise its jurisdiction on matters such as this. In a subsequent case, *BSNL v TRAI*, the Court focused on the scope of the TDSAT's jurisdiction in respect to the TRAI's regulations.[77] Quoting its own decision in *L Chandra Kumar v Union of India*,[78] the Court held that while tribunals have the power to test the vires of subordinate legislation, this power does not extend to questions regarding the vires of the parent statute. In this case, the Court was of the view that the TDSAT did not have the power to examine the validity of regulations made under section 36 of the TRAI Act.[79]

While the objective of the TDSAT was initially to hear original and appellate cases, it now only has original jurisdiction, hearing mostly disputes between licensors and licensees in the first instance. However, telecom matters are routinely challenged before the High Courts, despite the existence of an expert judicial tribunal. In February 2012, the Supreme Court decided the controversy revolving around the UAS licences that were awarded in 2008 by cancelling all 122 licences on the ground that the procedure followed was arbitrary, illegal, and unconstitutional.[80] The judgment directed the TRAI to make fresh recommendations for the grant of licences and the allocation of spectrum through an auction process instead of the first-come-first-served policy that had been followed until 2008. The Court held that 'when it is clearly demonstrated that the policy framed by the State or its agency is contrary to public interest or violates constitutional principles, it is the duty of the Court to exercise its jurisdiction in the larger public interest and reject the stock plea of the State that the scope of judicial review should not be exceeded beyond recognized parameters'.[81]

The 2G scam, as it was called, also brought the sector under the scanner of the CVC. In the immediate aftermath of the 2G scam, officials of the DoT were so paralysed by the fear of being accused of corruption that for months, the Ministry was brought to a standstill, with officials refusing to take any action for fear of the repercussions. While this is an example of the chilling effect that investigations can have on the process of regulation, it is also evidence of the growing influence of the CVC in the telecom sector.

There is a likelihood that the influence of the competition regulator will continue to extend into the telecom space. From the perspective of the competition regulator, the sharing of infrastructure might well result in the cartelisation of infrastructure to the detriment of consumers. The telecom regulator, on the other hand, has mandated sharing in order to achieve greater efficiencies in the utilisation of assets. These contrary objectives are likely to result in regulatory conflict that will be hard to resolve. The TRAI recently issued a Consultation Paper on Anti-competitive

[77] *BSNL v TRAI* [2014] 3 SCC 222.

[78] *L Chandra Kumar v Union of India* [1995] 1 SCC 400.

[79] TRAI Act, 1997, s 36 (power to make regulations).

[80] *Centre for Public Interest Litigation* (n 24). See also *Tata Cellular and Others v Union of India* [1994] 6 SCC 65; *Delhi Science Forum v Union of India* AIR 1996 SC 1356.

[81] *Centre for Public Interest Litigation* (n 24).

Behaviour in Tariff Offers,[82] which has led to a tussle between TRAI and CCI over who should set the rules for predatory pricing in tariff.[83] We are likely to see more of these sorts of jurisdictional disputes between the regulators. The Supreme Court has held that it is ideal in such situations for the two regulators to work together towards a common solution.[84] However, the final word on this matter is yet to be delivered by the Court.[85]

E. The Influence of New Technology

As new technologies came on stream, they have had an impact on regulation, each new technology giving rise to a tension between the incumbents, who have invested in the existing technology, and new players, who would like to use these new advances to provide their services with greater efficiency. Given the rapidly advancing pace of technology in the sector, it would be impossible for any regulator to stay ahead of the game. We have seen many examples of regulation playing 'catch up'.

As discussed earlier, Reliance Infocom was fined Rs 150 crores in 2004 for carrying international calls into India over the data network and tampering with call line identification to obfuscate where the call originated from – a decision that was upheld by the TDSAT.[86] When the government permitted the use of WiLL technology, it intended for this to be a means to roll out the fixed line network without having to invest in physical last mile infrastructure. However, shortly thereafter, the TRAI received complaints that service providers were using their WiLL licences to effectively offer mobile services. The TDSAT held that Tata Teleservices' 'Walky' could not be used as a mobile wireless service, as that would be contrary to the licence granted to the company, and directed Tata Teleservices to pay an access deficit charge

[82] Telecom Regulatory Authority of India, *Consultation Paper on Regulatory Principles of Tariff Assessment* (Consultation Paper No 3/2017) 16–28.

[83] Tanya Thomas, 'Turf War Rages between CCI and TRAI over Telecom Tariffs', *Hindu Business Line* (27 July 2017), www.thehindubusinessline.com/info-tech/turf-war-rages-between-cci-and-trai-over-telecom-tariffs/article9791247.ece.

[84] *ONGC v Collector of Central Excise* [1992] Supp 2 SCC 432.

[85] The CCI has had to deal with a spate of telecommunication cases since the launch of Reliance Jio. While it is clear from the CCI's clubbing of the market for 2G, 3G and 4G services for ascertaining the relevant market for Jio's free services demonstrated in *Shanmugam v Reliance Jio and Others*, Case No 98 of 2017 (CCI) and *Bharti Airtel Ltd v Reliance Jio*, Case No 3 of 2017 (CCI) that its understanding of telecommunication services needs further refinement, a recent ruling of the Bombay High Court in *Bharti Airtel and Others v CCI* Writ Petition No 7173/2017 has quashed a CCI investigation into alleged cartelisation by some telecom operators on the grounds that the CCI has no jurisdiction over telecommunication matters. The CCI has appealed this order of the Bombay High Court in *CCI v Bharti Airtel and Others* in Petition for Special Leave to Appeal (C) No. 35574/2017. The CCI's jurisdiction over the telecommunication sector would ultimately be determined by the ruling of the Supreme Court in this matter.

[86] *Reliance Infocomm v Union of India* [2005] 2 Comp LJ 537 (TDSAT). See also R Mukherji, 'The Politics of Telecommunications Regulation: State-Industry Alliance Favoring Foreign Investment in India' (2008) 44(10) *Journal of Development Studies* 1405 for a more detailed analysis of the evolution and eventual demise of ADC in the Indian telecom regulatory framework.

(ADC) of Rs 300 crores to the state-owned BSNL.[87] On appeal, the Supreme Court upheld the TDSAT's order classifying the services provided by Tata Teleservices as limited mobile.[88]

When Reliance Jio acquired BWA spectrum, it had been earmarked for broadband and data services. It appears that the Telecommunication Engineering Centre had objected to this classification of the spectrum, since the capabilities of Long-Term Evolution (LTE) technology are much 'wider in scope than what is permitted in the ISP licence and since LTE is a technology which can be used for providing full-fledged mobile services along with high speed data services, it is possible for an ISP licensee to use LTE for both Internet services as well as full-fledged mobile services'.[89] Once they acquired the spectrum, Reliance looked to repurpose the spectrum to provide Voice over Long-Term Evolution (VoLTE) technology – a new evolution in technology that allowed 4G broadband spectrum to also be used for mobile voice.

In 2012, TRAI issued guidelines that replaced the licensing framework with a new UL regime, and ISPs were allowed to migrate into full service operators that offered voice services. In 2013, the conversion of ISP licences to the new UL was approved by the DoT. Reliance Jio paid an entry fee of Rs 15 crores and a migration charge of Rs 1,685 crores, and was granted a UL allowing it to provide voice services. The sector continues to deal with the relentless march of technology. Today these challenges include call drops (the unavoidable consequence of congested networks), net neutrality (an issue that is inevitable as more and more services increase their dependence on data) and entirely new technologies such as machine-to-machine (M2M) services. The TRAI has taken the lead by initiating consultations on all these areas and more. The challenge, as always, is to resist regulating where it is not entirely necessary and to make sure that when regulatory intervention is in fact called for, it is appropriate in the context of the objective that is sought to be achieved.

CONCLUSION

The characteristics listed above operate as constraints on the manner in which the telecom sector is currently regulated. The fact that India has still not rewritten the law since it was first enacted by the British, and that it still uses terminology designed to regulate the telegraph to administer the internet and modern cellular technology, has given rise to a culture of broad and ambiguous drafting used by regulator and regulated alike to their advantage. That everything not specifically permitted is prohibited means that telecom companies have to think long and hard before deploying new technologies, or take calculated risks that these new technologies fall within what is permitted under existing regulations.

[87] *Tata Teleservices Ltd v BSNL* Petition No 45 of 2005.

[88] *Tata Teleservices Ltd v BSNL* [2008] (10) SCC 556; *Reliance Infocomm Ltd v BSNL* [2008] (10) SCC 535.

[89] Comptroller and Auditor General of India (n 25) 44.

Indian telecom companies understand these peculiarities well, using them to their advantage while planning their business strategies. They know how to navigate the maze of conflicting influences and benefit from them to the greatest extent possible. As a result, they constantly push the boundaries of interpretation, innovating their services to operate within the realm of what is permissible. While the regulations offer a vast arsenal of regulatory ammunition to choose from, experience has shown that on balance, the Indian regulator is circumspect in deploying these weapons.

It is because of this appreciation of the regulatory reality that exists on both sides of the table, both with the regulator and the regulated, that telecom is the fastest-growing sector in the country. For the most part, this has been fuelled by the early regulatory decisions that ensured appropriate levels of coverage and penetration as the telecom network was rolled out across the country. Whether by accident or design, the fact that early versions of the telecom licences contained strict coverage obligations which were supplemented, at an appropriate time, with regulations that permitted the sharing of first passive and then active infrastructure was clearly responsible for the rapid growth of telecom subscribers in the country. Credit for the continued growth of the sector well up to the present day lies equally at the feet of a relatively benevolent regulator and operators who are deeply invested in the sector.

9

Renewable Energy

AKSHAY JAITLY*

INTRODUCTION

THE OVERARCHING LEGISLATION governing the Indian power sector is the Electricity Act, 2003, and regulators at the state and central levels deal with matters relating to both conventional and renewable energy. In this context, the evolution of the Indian renewable energy sector offers an interesting opportunity to study a sector accorded differential and favourable regulatory treatment within the broader ambit of the Electricity Act, which regulates the power sector more generally. It also enables us to look at the extent to which the objectives behind this differential treatment have translated into policy and regulatory decision-making. The mandate for preferential treatment of renewable energy has led to the development of this sector in an island of historically relatively light-touch regulation, in contrast to the more heavily regulated conventional energy sector.

This chapter analyses the evolution of the renewable energy sector from multiple lenses:

- first, the interplay of legislation, policy and regulations, and their impact on the sector;
- second, the balancing of competing interests and objectives at various levels – between different central government ministries, between the centre and the state, and between regulators at the state level and the appellate level; and
- third, the more recent closing window of lighter-touch regulation, with the roll-back of incentives and shift towards competitive bidding from feed-in tariffs.

This chapter aims to use these lenses while discussing four broad areas of regulatory oversight within the renewable energy sector – policy-making, tariff determination, renewable purchase obligation (RPO) and open access.

* Special thanks to Megha Kaladharan for her invaluable assistance.

I. EARLY OBJECTIVES

While the Electricity Act came into effect in 2003, discussions on the importance of renewable energy for India pre-date this enactment by several decades. The mandate to promote renewable energy can be traced back to the Indian Constitution, which imposes a fundamental duty on citizens to protect and improve the natural environment,[1] and directs the state to protect and improve the natural environment.[2] Recently, the Supreme Court,[3] in a matter relating to RPO compliance, recognised this constitutional mandate to promote renewable energy by referencing Article 21 of the Constitution, which guarantees the right to life, read with the other provisions of the Constitution mentioned above.

In the 1970s and 1980s, responding to the global energy crisis arising from petroleum shortages, Indian analysts, beginning to recognise the abundance of renewable energy sources in India, started advocating a gradual shift to renewable energy and called for a strategy directed at their development to reduce reliance on petroleum,[4] and were even discussing avenues for financing renewable energy initiatives.[5] One particularly far-sighted article from 1974 noted that:

> While it would take several years before there can be massive conversion of solar radiation and other renewable resources into mechanical and electrical forms, as fossil fuels are depleting, it would be useful to build up in India, an infrastructure which will be compatible with the new sources of energy and forms of utilization.[6]

In 1977, the Central Government constituted the Working Group on Energy Policy, one of the first committees focused solely on energy conservation.[7] In its report, the Working Group recognised the need to consider alternative sources of energy to generate electricity, given India's increasing energy demands. Even in 1979, when the discourse on renewable energy was at a nascent stage, the Working Group highlighted the need for 'adopting alternatives, less energy intensive technologies and also by substituting or supplementing conventional sources of energy by renewable sources'.[8] Subsequently, in the sixth Five Year Plan between 1980 and 1985, the Planning Commission highlighted the need to develop renewable sources 'with a sense of urgency'.[9]

While early scholarship and comment broadly espoused the need for renewable energy, a more focused effort to develop renewable energy came in the lead-up to the passing of the Electricity Act, 2003. In 2001, the Electricity Bill was introduced in the Lok Sabha. Parliamentary debates of the time refer to the Central Government's

[1] Constitution of India, art 51A(g).

[2] ibid art 48A.

[3] *Hindustan Zinc Ltd v Rajasthan Electricity Regulatory Commission*, judgment dated 13 May 2015 in Civil Appeal No 4417 of 2015 before the Supreme Court.

[4] DR Pendae, 'Dilemmas of Energy Strategies in India: Implications for Third World' (1984) 19(13) *Economic and Political Weekly* 564.

[5] Liaqat Ali, 'Financing New and Renewable Sources of Energy' (1981) 16(20) *Economic and Political Weekly* 913.

[6] BV Rangarao, 'Alternatives in Energy Development' (1974) 9(27) *Economic and Political Weekly* 1068.

[7] S Dhanalekshmy, 'The Energy Efficiency Policy Initiatives and Energy Security: Experiences from India' in WL Filho and V Voudouris (eds), *Global Energy Policy and Security* (Springer, 2013) 217.

[8] Planning Commission, 'Report of the Working Group on Energy Policy' (1979) [7.18(e)].

[9] Planning Commission, 'Sixth Five Year Plan' (1980).

failure to develop renewable energy, despite its potential and the presence of abundant renewable resources in India. However, the discussion on renewable energy was largely limited to the context of meeting the energy access needs of rural areas without grid connectivity.[10]

The Electricity Bill was eventually referred to the Standing Committee constituted by the Ministry of Power (MoP). The Standing Committee identified that the installed capacity of renewable energy sources was a mere three per cent of the total installed capacity at the time. It recognised the importance of meeting the country's growing energy demands in a sustainable manner through renewable energy and the need for states to meet at least a minimum quantum of their energy needs from renewable energy sources. Many of the recommendations of the Standing Committee encountered resistance from the states. For instance, the Standing Committee sought views from the states on whether mandating 10 per cent of energy generation from renewable energy sources was feasible. In an early sign of the divergence between the views of the centre and the states on the issue, which we will explore in more detail later, the states rejected this proposal, citing the high cost of renewable energy generation.

In its final form, the Electricity Act provided a reasonably clear path for India's renewable energy future by empowering state electricity regulatory commissions (SERCs) to specify the terms and conditions for the determination of renewable energy tariffs, guided by the objective of 'promotion of co-generation and generation of electricity from renewable sources of energy'.[11] This was in contrast to the competitive bidding regime established for conventional energy. The Electricity Act also required SERCs to set RPO targets for distribution companies (Discoms) to ensure a minimum quantum of power procurement from renewable energy sources by each state.[12]

At the time that the Electricity Act was passed, renewable energy sources were not well understood and was viewed largely as supplementary to conventional energy sources. Consequently, law-makers' approach to provide for preferential treatment of renewable energy was in many ways prescient, given that at the time the sector was new and untested, with the existence of nascent and at times unproven technology, uncertain markets, a paucity of data and technical challenges. On the other hand, while the objectives of the centre to promote renewable energy were clear, there was a clear gap between the centre's vision and the reticence of states to adopt renewable energy, and this has played out over the past decade and a half, including in the regulatory arena.

II. TURF WARS IN THE RENEWABLE ENERGY SECTOR: CONFLICTING OBJECTIVES AND POLICIES

The Electricity Act empowered SERCs to encourage the development of renewable energy by setting preferential tariffs and introduced a range of other incentives for

[10] Thirteenth Lok Sabha Debates, 'Further Discussion on the Electricity Bill, 2001' moved by Shri Anant Gangaram Geete (9 April 2003).

[11] Electricity Act 2003, s 61(h).

[12] ibid s 86(1)(e).

electricity generated from renewable energy sources. This enabling regulatory environment provided the backdrop within which significant investments have come into the sector and has contributed to its growth in the past decade.

As electricity is a concurrent subject under the Constitution, both the centre and the states can legislate on the matter. While the centre exercises jurisdiction over inter-state matters, states legislate over matters of and pass regulations on intra-state sale, purchase, distribution and supply of electricity. Theoretically, the delineation between the roles in the governance of the electricity sector of the centre and the states appears to be clear; however, in practice, the multiplicity of policies and institutional stakeholders and the different objectives of the Central Government and the state governments can translate into inconsistent decision-making at the central and state levels. While the centre can establish the broader policy, legislation and regulations to govern the sector, as in the case of the Electricity Act, states have considerable flexibility in the adoption and implementation of the centre's vision. This section highlights the competing objectives of key stakeholders and the resultant regulatory friction between them, including the centre and the states, in setting and pursuing RPO targets, and the shift towards competitive bidding for tariff discovery, and amongst regulators, ie, the Appellate Tribunal for Electricity (APTEL) and SERCs in the enforcement of RPO and open access. While the primary objective of the centre in this sector is the capacity addition of 227 GW of renewable energy by 2022 (recently revised from the earlier target of 175 GW), the focus of the states (and, to some extent, the centre) is to reduce the cost of electricity to consumers and protect the financial interests of Discoms. This concern gets accentuated in the run-up to the state or national elections. Even at the centre, the misalignment of objectives between different ministries, such as the MoP, the Ministry of New and Renewable Energy (MNRE) and the Ministry of Finance (MoF), can lead to uneven and at times contradictory policies, providing competing messages to stakeholders down the chain, including regulators.

A. The Evolution of Renewable Energy Legislation, Policy and Regulations

i. Policy and Regulatory Background

At the central level, the MNRE is the nodal ministry dealing with renewable energy. Its objective is to develop and deploy renewable energy to augment the energy needs of the country. Additionally, the Renewable Energy Corporation of India (the erstwhile Solar Energy Corporation of India (SECI)) is involved in all aspects of renewable energy, including owning solar power plants, generating and selling renewable power, and even manufacturing solar products and materials. The MoP formulates the broader electricity law framework through the National Electricity Policy and National Tariff Policy, along with amendments to the Electricity Act. Therefore, at the centre, the MNRE leads renewable energy development and deployment, but relies on the MoP and the MoF for large-scale policy changes and budgetary allocations to further its objectives. The centre has also launched schemes such as the Ujwal DISCOM Assurance Yojana (UDAY), which states can opt for by signing a memorandum of understanding (MoU) with the MoP. This scheme is aimed at improving the historically weak financial position of the Discoms, through which the centre offers financial restructuring assistance to Discoms,[13] subject to Discoms complying with the conditions set out in the MoU, as will be discussed in subsequent sections.

At the state level, there are nodal agencies and energy departments, which operate under the administrative control of state governments. These agencies channel central subsidies, implement pilot projects, coordinate among other local agencies and are also responsible for the implementation of the Energy Conservation Act, 2001. They also devise policies for the development of renewable energy within the state and oversee its implementation.

In addition to the various ministries and departments, state and central level regulators play a significant role. The Central Electricity Regulatory Commission (CERC) was set up in 1998 to oversee the development of electricity markets at the national level and design a regulatory framework for the states to follow. Subsequently, states set up SERCs, which regulate intra-state matters and oversee the implementation of various regulations. The CERC and SERCs formulate regulations that govern various aspects of the renewable energy sector, such as tariff determination, the implementation of RPO and open access. For instance, the CERC issued regulations in relation to RPO in 2010, further to which SERCs issued RPO regulations for their respective states. However, SERCs have the power to deviate from the regulations and directives of the CERC, as will be evidenced below.

After the Electricity Act came into force, provisions relating to renewable energy were incorporated in other national-level policy instruments such as the National Electricity Policy in 2005, followed by the National Tariff Policy in 2006. The National Electricity Policy stipulated a progressive shift from conventional sources to renewable energy and recognised the need to set preferential tariffs for electricity derived from renewable energy sources until it achieved grid parity. The latest version of National Tariff Policy in 2016 cites the promotion of renewable energy as a key policy objective. In 2008, the National Action Plan on Climate Change (NAPCC) identified eight core national missions running through 2017. One of the missions requires that a minimum renewable purchase standard be set, which is increased each year until a pre-defined cap is reached.[14]

Apart from the larger framework of the Electricity Act, policies targeting specific renewable energy sources such as wind, solar, biomass and small hydro[15]

[13] The UDAY scheme aims to reduce the interest burden, the cost of power and the technical and commercial losses of cash-strapped Discoms. Under this scheme, states would take over 75 per cent of the debt of Discoms over two years by issuing sovereign bonds to pay back the lenders. The scheme also provides that the remaining 25 per cent of the debt will be repaid through Discom-issued bonds.

[14] National Action Plan on Climate Change (2008), cl 4.2.2, www.moef.nic.in/downloads/home/Pg01-52.pdf.

[15] At present, India, unlike several other countries, excludes large hydropower projects from the ambit of renewable energy and only small hydropower projects (up to 25 MW) are considered as renewable energy projects, given the significant environmental impact of large hydropower projects. However, there have been recent reports of the Indian government considering the inclusion of large hydropower projects within the ambit of renewable energy. See S Singh, 'Government Mulling to Bring Large Hydropower Units under Renewable Energy Ambit' *Economic Times* (18 January 2016).

operate at both the central and state levels. Amongst the most significant drivers of the shift towards renewable energy was the Jawaharlal Nehru National Solar Mission (JNNSM), launched by the MNRE in 2010, with the ambitious goal of establishing India as a global leader in solar energy through solar capacity addition of 20 GW by 2022, a target which was revised in 2014 to 100 GW of solar power by 2022.[16]

A threshold problem with the Electricity Act is that while it provides the statutory framework and the legal impetus for the promotion of renewable energy, it does not chart out a clear path to achieve this objective. Also, it does not set out a system of sanctions or penalties for the failure of obligated stakeholders to meet their obligations. It is largely left to the states' discretion to pursue either an aggressive or a tepid path of enforcement of objectives and any associated standards to promote renewable energy within their state. Consequently, it is observed that regulators across states adopt different standards for adjudication when dealing with identical issues, leading to divergent outcomes and incentive systems amongst states and also between the state and the central policies.

ii. Incentivising Renewable Energy Generation: Competing Interests at the Centre

The early growth of the renewable energy sector in India was bolstered by various financial incentives extended by the centre to promote renewable energy. Amongst early incentives introduced to boost investment in the renewable energy sector, the accelerated depreciation scheme is notable. Accelerated depreciation allowed developers to write off a higher percentage of an asset during the initial years of ownership by increasing depreciation during the initial years of the asset's useful life, consequently reducing the developer's taxable income.

In 2009, the MNRE introduced the generation-based incentive scheme for wind power projects in which wind power projects not claiming accelerated depreciation were eligible for a generation-based incentive at the rate of Rs 0.50 per unit of power fed to the grid for a period of not less than four years and a maximum period of 10 years, subject to the ceiling of Rs 10 million per MW.

Accelerated depreciation and generation-based incentive benefits were withdrawn in 2012. For accelerated depreciation, there were concerns that since the tax benefit could be claimed simply by constructing and commissioning the project, investments were only being made to set up projects, but without regard to operational efficiency and effective maintenance. After the incentives were claimed, the developers often failed to maintain their wind farms and at times abandoned them entirely. After these incentives were withdrawn, wind generation dipped by 1500 MW in 2012–13 compared to the previous year.[17] Therefore, in order to revive the sector, generation-based incentives were reintroduced in 2013, followed by accelerated depreciation in 2014.

[16] Government of India Press Release, 'Revision of Cumulative Targets under National Solar Mission from 20,000 MW by 2021–22 to 100,000 MW' (Press Information Bureau, 17 June 2015).

[17] 'Wind Energy Dropped 1,500 MW Due to Withdrawal of Incentives' *Business Standard* (13 May 2013).

However, more recently, it appears that incentives for the renewable energy sector are being rolled back. The generation-based incentive scheme for wind projects came to an end in March 2017 and was not renewed, and the depreciation rate under the accelerated depreciation scheme for renewable energy projects was reduced from 80 per cent to 40 per cent with effect from April 2017. Coupled with this, an income tax holiday which had been applicable to all infrastructure and power projects since 2002, including renewable energy projects, ended in 2017.

This rollback of incentives is also indicative of an ongoing turf war between the MNRE and the MoF in shaping the renewable energy sector. In addition to the reduction or removal of incentives, it is relevant to look at certain other actions of the MoF, which include the impending imposition of a 25 per cent preliminary safeguard duty on solar cells imported from China and Malaysia,[18] the ongoing anti-dumping case[19] which appears to have the MoF's tacit support, a 7.85 per cent port duty on imported solar modules (which was previously exempted) and the imposition of the Goods and Services Tax with rates ranging between five and 18 per cent on various input costs for renewable energy projects. These measures are likely to affect the growth of the solar sector with an increase in project development costs, potentially resulting in higher tariffs. Recently, solar auctions in Karnataka and Maharashtra were postponed, since there has not been sufficient interest from bidders, given the lack of clarity on safeguard duties and port duty applicable to solar projects, coupled with the absence of a change in the law provisions in the bid document, which would allow bidders to seek a tariff revision if these duties subsequently become applicable.[20] The MNRE had apparently approached the MoF to scrap the duties on imported solar cells, arguing that the move affected the growth of the solar sector and would lead to tariff hikes. However, reports indicate that the MoF is unlikely to budge on this issue, citing that its decision was aligned with the Make in India policy, which aimed to promote domestic manufacturing across different sectors. The MNRE recently amended the solar bidding guidelines to allow duties to be passed through to become part of the tariff. This is a sensible step, but is one that will inevitably see bid tariffs rise as a consequence.

[18] The Directorate General of Trade Remedies (DGTR) has recommended the imposition of a safeguard duty on solar cells and modules imported from China and Malaysia for the coming two years in the following manner: 25 per cent duty in the first year, 20 per cent for the first half of the second year and 15 per cent for the remaining six months. In line with the recommendations of the DGTR, the Ministry of Finance is expected to notify the imposition of the safeguard duty. See Shreya Jai and Subhayan Chakraborty, 'Chinese and Malaysian Solar Panels Dace 25% Safeguard Duty in India' *Business Standard* (17 July 2018), https://www.business-standard.com/article/economy-policy/govt-imposes-25-safeguard-duty-on-chinese-malaysian-solar-cells-for-2-yrs-118071601050_1.html.

[19] Indian solar manufacturers have filed an anti-dumping petition with the Ministry of Trade and Commerce against Chinese solar modules and cells, hoping that an interim duty will be levied. This decision comes in the wake of India losing the World Trade Organization case which ruled that the provision for domestic content requirement discriminates against US solar cell manufacturers. In response, the MNRE has amended its guidelines under JNNSM to remove all provisions relating to domestic content requirement in the latest solar auctions.

[20] K Chandrasekharan, 'Fear of Safeguard and Anti-dumping Duty Hits Solar Auctions' *Economic Times* (5 March 2018), https://economictimes.indiatimes.com/industry/energy/power/fear-of-safeguard-and-anti-dumping-duty-hits-solar-auctions/articleshow/63161932.cms.

While the MoF's policy to roll back various incentives available to the renewable energy sector may reflect the growing maturity of the sector, its timing is likely to hinder the achievement of the enhanced renewable energy target of 227 GW by 2022. Further, the tariff increases likely to arise from the imposition of high duties on imported solar cells is at odds with the push towards the discovery of progressively low tariffs through competitive bidding.

Separately, the MoP is also engaged in a continuing attempt to balance competing interests in the power sector. There is a perceived need to make continued investments in coal, both to meet baseload power requirements and exploit domestic coal resources on one hand and to promote the large-scale deployment of renewable energy on the other. Against the backdrop of the rapid decline in renewable energy tariffs and the consequent increase in demand from offtakers, more and more thermal assets have come under financial stress, including state-owned thermal projects. Therefore, there is an inherent conflict of interest in the MoP making decisions concurrently in relation to the renewable and conventional power sector.

In the renewable energy sector, all issues are not resolved at the regulatory level, and the instances discussed above demonstrate the internal pulls and pushes at the centre. This also plays out as the tension between the stated goals of the centre to add renewable energy capacity on a large scale and many of the policies it has employed to achieve these goals. In this context, the Tinbergen Rule is instructive. It states that for each policy target or objective, there must be at least one policy tool. If there are fewer tools than targets, then some policy goals will not be achieved. The centre's approach does not appear to overcome the existing barriers to the deployment of renewable energy by offering specific solutions. For instance, the intention behind the imposition of duties on foreign solar modules is to promote domestic manufacturing; however, this sector would be better served by targeted policies or incentives, such as subsidies to domestic solar manufacturers, fiscal measures such as deemed export benefits leading to exemptions from terminal export duty, profit-linked deductions under section 80IA of the Income Tax Act and low-cost financing through the Indian Renewable Energy Development Agency.[21]

According to a recent study by the Centre for Financial Accountability, government-owned banks provided the majority of the financing for thermal projects in 2017, including nearly USD 4.5 billion to 12 thermal projects with a combined capacity of 17 GW. In contrast, government-owned banks formed only half of the top 10 lenders in renewable power projects.[22] It is therefore legitimate to ask whether the centre's commitment to the development of the renewable energy scale runs as deep as is officially stated. Matters are further complicated by competing policy decisions made by different ministries of the centre with jurisdiction over different aspects of the renewable energy sector. While it is inevitable that there will be some dissonance

[21] Akshay Jaitly, 'A Good Case for India to Lose?' *Business Standard* (11 May 2013), https://www.business-standard.com/article/opinion/a-good-case-for-india-to-lose-113051100630_1.html.

[22] Centre for Financial Accountability, *Coal v Renewables: Financial Analysis* (2018), 4, 10, www.cenfa.org/wp-content/uploads/2018/06/2017-COAL-vs-RENEWABLE-Report.pdf.

between policy decisions at the central and state levels, having a consistent policy stance at the central level, along with policy instruments targeting specific problem areas within the sector, is key to sustainable growth.

B. Tariff Determination

i. Feed-in Tariffs to Competitive Bidding: The Downward Tariff Spiral

As mentioned in section II.A above, the Electricity Act empowers SERCs to determine feed-in tariffs for renewable energy projects. A feed-in tariff is a commonly used policy tool to incentivise renewable energy deployment as it ensures an attractive tariff to renewable energy generators over long-term power purchase agreements (PPAs) executed with Discoms. In the Indian context, feed-in tariffs are determined on a cost-plus basis, where the tariff accounts for the capital cost of generation plus the operation and maintenance costs, and adds a specified return on equity, typically in the range of 16–18 per cent, for the project developer. More recently, however, the sector has seen a shift from feed-in tariffs towards the discovery of tariffs through competitive bidding.

In 2010, Phase I of JNNSM offered attractive feed-in tariffs and long-term PPAs to the developers who quoted the lowest capital grant to develop the solar projects. The feed-in tariff was complemented by support to Discoms by bundling solar power with conventionally produced electricity, reducing the average per-unit cost of solar power. To date, approximately 3 GW of solar projects have been commissioned under different phases of JNNSM.[23] Solar missions have been launched by several states since the launch of JNNSM, which has further driven the growth of the solar sector and the downward trajectory of solar tariffs. More recently, in 2017, the Central Government issued guidelines for the procurement of wind power through competitive bidding. Since the commencement of competitive bidding in the wind sector, wind tariffs have dropped by nearly 30 per cent in less than a year.[24]

Evidence of a clear policy shift towards competition in the renewable energy sector can also be observed.[25] It is also clear that the introduction of competitive bidding in the renewable energy sector has led to a significant reduction in tariffs, as evidenced by Figure 9.1 in the context of solar tariffs. However, it is useful to consider the implications of the low tariffs determined through competitive bidding on the long-term

[23] Migration program (PV – 48 MW and CSP – 2.5 MW), Phase I Batch 1 (PV – 140 MW and CSP – 200 MW), Phase I Batch 2 (PV – 330 MW), Phase II Batch 1 (PV – 680 MW), Phase II Batch 2 (PV – 1,400 MW) and other programmes; MERCOM Capital Group India, 'Q2 2017 India Solar Market Update' (2017).

[24] Saurabh, 'Wind Energy Tariffs in India Fall 30% in 10 Months' *Clean Technica* (2018), www.cleantechnica.com/2018/01/08/wind-energy-tariffs-india-fall-30-10-months.

[25] In an interesting analysis, which compares the frequency of occurrence of certain key words in the National Tariff Policy 2016 amendment against the 2011 version, the terms 'competition' and 'renewable' occur significantly more often in the 2016 amendment as compared to the previous version. See 'Analysis of Amendments in National Tariff Policy' (2016), blog by REConnect Energy, http://reconnectenergy.com/blog/2016/01/analysis-of-amendments-in-national-tariff-policy.

sustainability of the underlying projects and the growth of the sector as a whole. This in turn is important because it provides insights into the merits of competitive bidding as a regulatory tool, in the context of the objectives of renewable energy policy-making more generally.

Figure 9.1 Solar tariffs

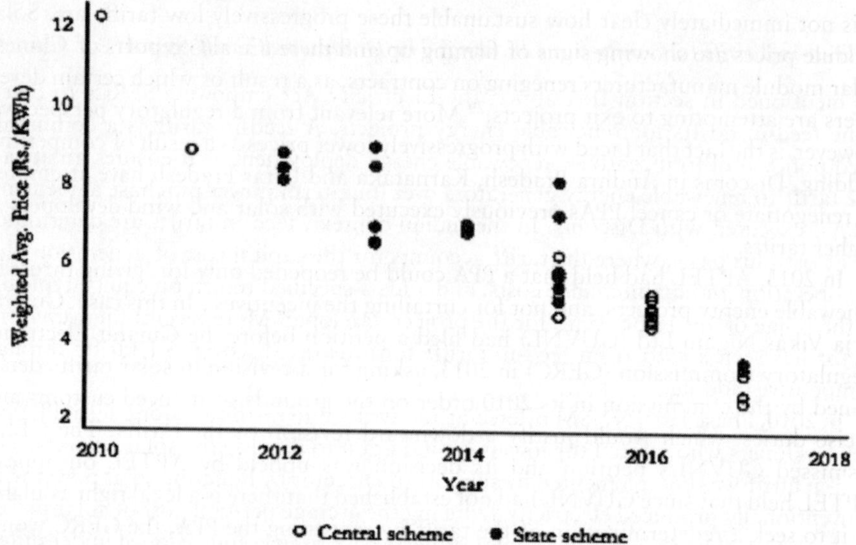

Source: Economic Survey 2017–18[26]

As can be seen in Figure 9.1 above, 2017 was a watershed year for the solar industry, which witnessed a significant drop in tariffs compared to the previous year, where tariffs for most tenders were around Rs 4.6 per kWh and dropped to under Rs 3 per kWh. The tariff spiral began with the Rewa project in early 2017, where the record lowest solar tariff at the time of Rs 2.97 per kWh (levelised tariff of Rs 3.29 per kWh) came about through competitive bidding. A few months after the Rewa bid, SECI's 750 MW utility scale auction in the Bhadla solar park saw tariffs fall to a new low of Rs 2.44 per kWh. The main contributor to falling solar tariffs was the sharp fall in module prices by nearly 30 per cent in one year. However, there were concerns that developers were not pricing risks and costs appropriately, largely relying on optimistic projections of a steady decline in solar module prices, coupled with increased competition amongst developers due to fewer new tenders and lack of pipeline visibility over the coming years.[27] Following the solar auctions, SECI carried out its first wind auction in 2016 for 1,000 MW, receiving the lowest bid of Rs 3.46 per kWh followed

[26] Ministry of Finance, Government of India, *Economic Survey 2017–18*, vol 2, 72, http://mofapp.nic.in:8080/economicsurvey/pdf/068-079_Chapter_05_Economic_Survey_2017-18.pdf.

[27] 'Indian Solar Tariffs Fall 25% in Three Months' *Bridge to India* (2017), www.bridgetoindia.com/indian-solar-tariffs-fall-25-three-months.

by an even lower bid of Rs 2.64 per kWh in SECI's 1 GW wind auction in 2017. The lowest tariff for both wind and solar is now below the average thermal power tariff.[28]

ii. Falling Tariffs: Contradictory Regulatory Responses

It is not immediately clear how sustainable these progressively low tariffs are. Solar module prices are showing signs of firming up and there are also reports of Chinese solar module manufacturers reneging on contracts, as a result of which certain developers are attempting to exit projects.[29] More relevant from a regulatory perspective, however, is the fact that faced with progressively lower prices as a result of competitive bidding, Discoms in Andhra Pradesh, Karnataka and Uttar Pradesh have attempted to renegotiate or cancel PPAs previously executed with solar and wind developers at higher tariffs.

In 2013, APTEL had held that a PPA could be reopened only for 'giving thrust to renewable energy projects, and not for curtailing the incentives'. In this case, Gujarat Urja Vikas Nigam Ltd (GUVNL) had filed a petition before the Gujarat Electricity Regulatory Commission (GERC) in 2013, asking for a revision in solar tariffs determined by the commission in its 2010 order on the grounds of reduced customs and excise duties, which would justify a downward revision of the tariffs. The GERC dismissed GUVNL's petition and its decision was upheld by APTEL on appeal. APTEL held that since GUVNL had not established that there is a legal right available to it to seek a redetermination of the tariff by reopening the PPA, the GERC would not be expected to revisit the generic tariff 'to dis-incentivise the project developers and consequently discourage future investment in the sector'.

However, despite this strong judicial precedent, which should have prevented any attempts by Discoms to renegotiate PPAs on arbitrary grounds, SERCs seem to be acting in the interests of Discoms in a spate of recent cases in which various Discoms and regulators in Karnataka, Andhra Pradesh, Uttar Pradesh, Jharkhand and Tamil Nadu have attempted to unilaterally terminate or renegotiate tariffs for existing PPAs. For instance, the Karnataka Electricity Regulatory Commission (KERC) passed an order in September 2017, setting a new feed-in tariff for wind power at Rs 3.74 per kWh, considerably lower than the tariff of Rs 4.50 per kWh set by it in October 2015, prompted by lower wind tariffs that came about through the SECI auctions. The KERC's decision has potentially jeopardised nearly 599 MW of wind capacity

[28] R Prabhu, 'Wind Becomes Competitive with Solar to a Record Low ₹2.64/kWh' *MERCOM India* (2017), www.mercomindia.com/wind-becomes-competitive-solar-tariff-drops-record-low-%E2%82%B92-64-kwh.

[29] Reports indicate that the Acme Group, which quoted the lowest solar tariff for the Bhadla Project, and the Inox Group, which quoted the lowest wind tariff for the 2017 SECI bid, are both looking to exit their projects. While there has been no subsequent move to exit the project and Inox has also recently won 200 MW in SECI's third wind power auction in February 2018 at a record low tariff of Rs 2.44 per kWh, it has also posted significant losses in its last three financial quarters, while it had been profitable only a year ago; see U Bhaskar, 'Acme, Inox to Explore Exit from Renewable Energy Projects Won at Record Low Tariffs' *Live Mint* (29 August 2017).

in the state for which PPAs were signed at the tariff of Rs 4.50 per kWh, but had not been ratified by the KERC. Similarly, in Uttar Pradesh, where the Discoms decided to unilaterally terminate PPAs, including for over 400 MW from Bajaj Energy's five power plants, the Uttar Pradesh Electricity Regulatory Commission (UPERC) recommended that instead of cancelling the PPAs, the tariff could be reduced. However, this decision of the UPERC directing tariff reduction is not supported by any law or regulations. The cancellation and renegotiation of PPAs took place despite prior warnings issued by the MNRE to various SERCs regarding the adverse impact of reneging on PPAs.

iii. Lessons for Competitive Bidding in the Renewable Energy Sector

The important issue of renewable energy tariffs highlights several regulatory and political economy issues within the sector, including in particular the regulatory autonomy of SERCs. It is self-evident that the credibility of a regulatory agency is predicated upon its autonomy and distancing of its decisions from considerations outside the regulatory and legal framework. However, given that SERC regulators are appointed by state governments, it is likely that such regulators are influenced by the political economy compulsions of the government and politicians appointing them. This is evidenced by instances of SERCs, such as the KERC and the UPERC, which have supported recent efforts by Discoms to renegotiate PPAs. Acting in contravention of APTEL's order on this issue in 2013 and failing to uphold the sanctity of previously executed PPAs, the SERCs have proceeded to set lower tariffs than pre-agreed ones.

The second issue is whether the approach towards shifting from a feed-in tariff regime to a competitive bidding model and, more particularly, the competitive bidding model adopted by the central and state governments is conducive to the long-term sustainability of the renewable energy sector. Well-established renewable energy markets, such as those in Germany and Japan, have only recently shifted to competitive bidding. Further, unlike markets in the developed world, where the emphasis is primarily on the replacement of conventional power capacity with energy from renewable sources, India is aiming at capacity addition through renewable energy to serve its growing population. While it seems likely that the competitive bidding model is here to stay, regulators and law-makers do not seem to have taken heed of the lessons learnt from competitive bidding in the conventional sector to avoid unrealistic bids, where the government revised the bid documents for coal-based power plants to introduce a floor price for fuel costs, allowing it to reject bids where fuel costs had been quoted below the floor price.[30] The absence of a floor price, inadequate

[30] The earlier version of the bid documents for coal-based power plants allowed bidders to opt for either escalating or non-escalating fuel costs. In their bids, bidders often chose the latter and accounted for a mix of domestic and Indonesian coal in their power plants, resulting in extremely aggressive tariffs. However, the bidders suffered major losses when prices of coal went up and their demand for a compensatory tariff were rejected by the APTEL. To avoid this situation in the future, the revised bid documents specified a floor price for fuel costs.

risk assessment by bidders and frequent policy changes lead to uncertainty and, at times, project abandonment. While it may be too early to assess the long-term impact of competitive bidding on the Indian renewable energy sector, it will be prudent to ensure that bids are designed with the objective of the long-term sustainability of the underlying projects and not just to arrive at the lowest tariff.

It does not take a great deal of imagination to see how these issues may work to reinforce each other, with regulators seeking to lower previously contracted tariffs on the basis of potentially unrealistic and possibly unsustainable tariffs determined through competitive bidding. Another aspect to consider is the mixed messaging sent to the states and project developers by the centre's inconsistency on various policy issues in the sector. There are similarities between the states' decision to renegotiate PPAs and the rollback of incentives and imposition of duties on renewable energy projects by the centre. Both actions were taken without forewarning investors in existing projects and negatively impact projected revenues. Further, both instances cause a change in the regulatory basis on which projects were bid out, with the same end result – in the case of renegotiation of PPAs, project developers are compelled to agree to lower tariffs, leading to losses, while the imposition of duties and the rollback of incentives lead to higher input costs for developers, resulting in a lower than projected realisation of revenues and profits.

C. The RPO and REC Mechanism

i. Setting RPOs: The Gap between the Centre and the States

The RPO mechanism was introduced by the Electricity Act and requires SERCs to set targets for 'obligated entities' – ie, Discoms, open access consumers and captive consumers – to procure a minimum percentage of their cumulative power requirement from renewable energy sources. The CERC (Terms and Conditions for Recognition and Issuance of Renewable Energy Certificate for Renewable Energy Generation) Regulations, 2010, which aimed to serve as a guiding document for SERCs, recommended a uniform RPO target of five per cent in every state with an annual increase of one per cent until 2020 in order to achieve the target of 15 per cent, in accordance with the NAPCC.[31] Subsequently, SERCs issued state-specific RPO regulations, where RPO targets were typically set lower than those recommended by the CERC and the NAPCC. As a corollary to RPO, the renewable energy certificate (REC) mechanism was introduced by the CERC to allow obligated entities in states with low renewable energy potential to purchase RECs[32] in order to bridge gaps in meeting their RPO targets. While there has been significant discussion on the RPO and REC mechanism and their contribution towards renewable energy deployment, in practice it has been a relative failure.

[31] Statement of Objects and Reasons on CERC (Terms and Conditions for Recognition and Issuance of Renewable Energy Certificate for Renewable Energy Generation) Regulations, 2010.

[32] Renewable energy generators who inject power to the grid are eligible to register for issuance and dealing in RECs, a tradable certificate of proof that 1 MWh of electricity has been injected (or deemed to have been injected).

The Comptroller and Auditor General's report in 2015 on the Indian renewable energy sector highlighted that while the NAPCC recommended targets were eight per cent and nine per cent for the years 2012–13 and 2013–14, the national achievement against this was only 4.28 per cent and 4.51 per cent, respectively. Further, only six states met their state level RPO targets, ie, Arunachal Pradesh, Meghalaya, Himachal Pradesh, Karnataka, Mizoram and Tamil Nadu, of which RPO targets were exceeded by only Himachal Pradesh, Karnataka, Mizoram and Tamil Nadu.[33] Discoms cite various reasons for their failure to meet the RPO, such as the relatively higher cost of renewable power procurement as compared to conventional power, coupled with their poor financial health and technical issues in integrating infirm power into the grid. However, despite such large-scale RPO non-compliance, the response of the SERCs in enforcing RPO and imposing penalties on Discoms has been tepid at best.[34]

ii. Enforcement of RPOs: Divergence between APTEL and SERCs

Despite the fact that there is no regulatory basis for this, SERCs routinely allow Discoms to carry forward their unmet RPO to the next financial year. In response to this, the Indian Wind Power Association approached APTEL to appeal the decision of the GERC to waive the shortfall of Gujarat Discoms in meeting their RPO target. APTEL held that the carry forward of RPO should be allowed by SERCs only if RECs are not available for purchase. APTEL also held that the SERC can revise the RPO targets only at the beginning of the relevant financial year if it deems such targets to be unrealistic, based on its experience from previous years.[35] In *Indian Wind Energy Association v APERC*,[36] APTEL reiterated its earlier decision and held that Discoms should prepare a plan for renewable energy purchase as part of their annual tariff petitions to the SERC. Subsequently, the Supreme Court in *Hindustan Zinc v Rajasthan Electricity Regulatory Commission (RERC)*[37] recognised the statutory authority of SERCs to impose penalties on Discoms under sections 142 and 147 of the Electricity Act as a necessary mode of ensuring RPO compliance.

While the decisions of the Supreme Court and APTEL are a step in the right direction, SERCs have not significantly changed their approach in enforcing RPO. For instance, in 2014, the Chhattisgarh State Electricity Regulatory Commission noted the failure of the Chhattisgarh Discoms to meet their RPO from 2011 to 2013, but did not impose any penalty for this non-compliance.[38] The Uttarakhand Electricity Regulatory Commission imposed a paltry penalty of Rs 20,000 on the Discom for RPO

[33] NITI Aayog, 'Report on India's Renewable Electricity Roadmap' (2015) 29.

[34] Presentation by USAID/INDIA, 'RPO Compliance Framework for Captive/OA Transactions at State Level' *Forum of Regulators* (2015), www.forumofregulators.gov.in/Data/Meetings/Minutes/51.pdf.

[35] *Indian Wind Energy Association v GERC and Others*, judgment dated 16 April 2015 in Appeal No 258 of 2013; Appeal No 21 of 2014 and IA-28 of 2014 before APTEL.

[36] Judgment dated April 20, 2015 in OP No 1 of 2013 and IA No 291 and IA No 420 of 2013, OP No 2 of 2013 and OP No 4 of 2013 before APTEL.

[37] Judgment dated 13 May 2015 in Civil Appeal No 4417 of 2015 before the Supreme Court.

[38] Order dated 15 October 2014 in *suo motu* Petition No 50 of 2013(M) before the Chhattisgarh State Electricity Regulatory Commission (CSERC).

non-compliance and stated that an additional penalty of Rs 2,000 per day would be imposed if the pending RPO was not met within a designated period.[39]

A token penalty was also imposed for RPO non-compliance – the Madhya Pradesh Electricity Regulatory Commission (MPERC) directed the Discom to pay Rs 25,000 for not meeting its solar RPO for over three years. However, the Discom's non-compliance continued and eventually the Green Energy Association filed another petition[40] before the MPERC to seek a cumulative imposition of solar RPO on the Discom for the financial year (FY) 2015–16. Surprisingly, despite the continuing non-compliance with its order, the MPERC decided to not impose any penalty on the Discom and allowed it to mitigate prior defaults through the excess purchase of solar energy in the coming years. This decision was clearly contrary to the principles established by APTEL in earlier orders. In 2017, the Maharashtra Electricity Regulatory Commission (MERC) allowed the Discoms and other obligated entities to fulfil their RPO for FY 2016–17 and FY 2017–18 cumulatively.[41] The MERC relied on its RPO regulations (amended in 2016), which gave it the discretion to allow variation of up to five per cent in fulfilment of RPO targets. This is a significant variation given that RPO targets set by the MERC for FY 2016–17 and FY 2017–18 were 11 per cent and 12.5 per cent respectively. The MERC also accepted the Discoms' argument that there was uncertainty in REC prices, since this matter was pending with the Supreme Court and it would be in the interests of consumers to await the outcome of the case as REC prices were likely to fall.

In another recent case, the KERC took a defensive stance when it was approached by the Green Energy Association to impose penalties on Discoms for their failure to meet the RPO. It was contended that the KERC should not have allowed a waiver of unmet solar RPO by Discoms, but the KERC responded that its decision was based on the non-availability of sufficient solar RECs in the market and, further, rejected the contention that any monetary penalties could be imposed on Discoms for non-compliance.[42]

Another roadblock in RPO implementation arises from the cascading effect of falling tariffs as a consequence of competitive bidding, causing several Discoms to stall their renewable energy procurement given the unpredictable tariffs. In this context, in early 2017, the KERC issued a directive barring Discoms from entering into any new wind PPAs until further review.

While the centre cannot directly intervene in cases of non-compliance with RPO by the states, it has attempted to follow a carrot-and-stick approach, where benefits from financial restructuring under the UDAY scheme available to Discoms were

[39] Order dated 22 January 2014 in *suo moto* proceedings initiated by the Uttarakhand Electricity Regulatory Commission (UERC).

[40] *Green Energy Association v MP Power Management Co. Ltd*, order dated 9 December 2015 in Petition No 34 of 2015 before the MPERC.

[41] *Petition of Reliance Infrastructure Ltd (Distribution) to Allow Cumulative Fulfilment of its Renewable Purchase Obligation Targets for FY 2016–17 and FY 2017–18*, order dated 14 July 2017 in Case No 35 of 2017 before the MERC.

[42] *Green Energy Association v BESCOM*, order dated 19 January 2017 in OP No 27/2015 before the KERC.

contingent on their compliance with RPO targets outstanding since FY 2012–13, in accordance with the timelines set by the MoP. However, the MoUs under UDAY signed between the MoP and Discoms do not refer to RPO compliance at all, with the exception of the Uttar Pradesh MoU. The Uttar Pradesh MoU provides that Uttar Pradesh Discoms are required to meet their RPO only three years after they break even, ie, by FY 2019–20. This is in contravention of the UPERC's RPO regulations and, further, there is no legal basis to link RPO compliance with the Discoms breaking even. While the centre has paid lip service to the importance of RPO compliance in achieving its ambitious target of 227 GW of renewable energy by 2022, it has faltered, much like the SERCs, in ensuring compliance in a situation where it has the power to do so.

The response of Discoms, SERCs and even the centre might lead one to the erroneous conclusion that RPO compliance by obligated entities is a matter of choice and not a statutory and regulatory mandate. On the other hand, it seems that SERCs, imbued with the concern for the poor financial health of the Discoms, choose not to impose penalties for RPO non-compliance which would further exacerbate the financial burden of Discoms. The failure of SERCs to penalise Discoms for RPO non-compliance and consistently allowing them either a waiver or carry forward of RPO is an instance where effective regulatory functioning has been curtailed by the regulators themselves, who have failed to give effect to regulations they have had a role in framing, with political economy considerations taking precedence.

D. Open Access

A key requirement for the successful large-scale deployment of renewable energy across the country is the availability and implementation of open access. Open access means the non-discriminatory provision for the use of transmission lines or distribution system or associated facilities by any consumer or power generator, with a connected load of 1 MW and above, to buy or sell power on the open market. The idea is that the customers should be able to choose among a large number of competing power companies instead of being compelled to buy electricity from the Discom. Open access is granted to entities subject to a payment of open access charges, comprising cross-subsidy surcharge, transmission charges, wheeling charges, additional surcharges (where allowed by the SERC), banking charges, scheduling and system operation charges and one-time charges like an application fee, in addition to levies such as transmission and wheeling loss. The Electricity Act requires SERCs to introduce open access in a phased manner and mandates that open access be allowed, subject to the payment of open access charges, to the Discom.[43] The Electricity Act also contemplates a progressive reduction of the cross-subsidy surcharge by the SERCs.[44]

[43] Electricity Act 2003, s 42(2).
[44] ibid s 39(2)(d) 2nd proviso.

i. State-Level Resistance to Implementing Open Access

Though open access has been allowed in principle, implementation has been far from encouraging, since the power generator requires a no-objection certificate (NOC) from the State Load Despatch Centre (SLDC). Under the Electricity Act, the SLDC is the statutory body responsible for the technical integrity and functioning of the grid. However, because of the close relationship between the SLDC and the Discoms as a result of both being government-controlled, open access approvals are often delayed or denied. Discoms rely on commercial and industrial consumers for a significant portion of their revenue. Therefore, given the precarious finances of Discoms, they are unwilling to grant open access to their bulk consumers.

In 2014 in Gujarat, a NOC for short-term open access was withdrawn by the SLDC, which cited constraints in the upstream network due to a rise in system demand. While the GERC[45] held such action of the SLDC to be arbitrary and directed the SLDC to grant open access, it also expressed its inability to provide compensation to the petitioner for the losses suffered by the consumers in the interim, since the regulations made no provision for this. In a similar case in Gujarat, APTEL in 2016 held that[46] open access should be provided subject to operational constraints and that in the case of denial of open access, the specific reason for such denial must be provided, in accordance with the SERC's regulations. In this case, APTEL observed that relevant facts on the system dynamics were not analysed or recorded by the SLDC, as was mandatory for denying the short-term open access permission under the state regulations.

In Maharashtra, various solar power developers were being denied permission for open access by the Discom ie, Maharashtra State Electricity Distribution Company Ltd (MSEDCL), which had cited deficiencies in the regulatory framework for giving such permission.[47] The MERC held that open access was a right of the consumers and that they could not be differentiated against on the basis of the source of energy. Further, it held that MSEDCL could not discriminate amongst different renewable energy sources and was obliged to provide open access to solar power developers. The MERC also directed MSEDCL to issue credit notes for the period in which the members of the petitioner were injecting power into MSEDCL's grid. In another case against MSEDCL, certain power-generating companies had approached the MERC seeking relief against MSEDCL's delay in providing open access permission to consumers within the state.[48] According to the Procedure of Distribution Open Access issued by MSEDCL in April 2010, MSEDCL was required to convey its acceptance or rejection of an open access application within seven days of the date of receipt of the application, and the open access permission was required to be granted

[45] *Sumeet Industries Ltd v SLDC*, order dated 16 January 2015 in Petition No 1407 of 2014 before the GERC.

[46] *SLDC, Vadodara v Steelcast Ltd and GERC*, order dated 7 April 2016 in Appeal No 70 of 2015 before APTEL.

[47] *Green Energy Association v MSEDCL and MEDA*, order dated 6 May 2014 in Petition No 44 of 2014 before the MERC.

[48] *Navlakha Translines v MSEDCL*, order dated 20 October 2011 in Petition No 41 of 2010 before the MERC; *Indo Rama Synthetics v MSEDCL*, order dated 8 December 2011 in Petition No 27 of 2011 before the MERC; *Indian Wind Power Association and Others v MSEDCL and MEDA*, order dated 27 April 2012 in Petition Nos 8, 18, 20 and 33 of 2012 before the MERC.

within 30 days from the date of the application. However, in certain cases, MSEDCL failed to grant open access permission for up to six months following the date of the application. MERC held that under the Electricity Act, it was a statutory obligation of the Discom to provide non-discriminatory use of its distribution system to all open access consumers. The MERC has, in cases relating to a delay or failure in providing timely open access, directed MSEDCL to provide non-discriminatory open access immediately to consumers. Further, the MERC has also held that in the event that energy was injected into the Discom's grid during the pendency of the open access application, MSEDCL must issue credit notes to the consumer.

Unlike RPO enforcement, SERCs have been largely proactive in holding Discoms accountable for granting open access approvals. This could partly result from the fact that unlike RPO, where SERCs have found ways to justify a waiver or carry forward of RPO by Discoms, there are no grounds to deny granting open access other than on very specific technical conditions. Another important distinction is that what while RPO requires a cash outflow from Discoms to purchase renewable energy or RECs, the impact of open access is in the nature of a potential loss in revenue. However, in both instances, SERCs have shown a reluctance to impose any monetary penalties on errant Discoms, reinforcing the view that their sympathy for the poor financial condition of the Discoms trumps their inclination to impose penalties authorised by law or regulation.

ii. The Position of States on Transmission Charges at Odds with Renewable Energy Targets

While SERCs have typically upheld the position that open access is a right of consumers and that Discoms cannot deny it, they have not fulfilled their mandate to reduce the cross-subsidy surcharge, which is a significant financial disincentive for consumers to opt for open access. Based on submissions by Discoms, state regulators revise open access charges every year. The cross-subsidy surcharge is usually the largest component of open access charges and can be unpredictable. For instance, in Gujarat, the cross-subsidy surcharge increased from Rs 0.39 per unit (for FY 2014–15) to Rs 0.59 per unit (for FY 2015–16) to Rs 1.45 per unit (for FY 2016–17), and was thereafter reduced to Rs 1.44 per unit (for FY 2017–18). Further, there is a wide variance in the cross-subsidy surcharge applicable in different states, as set out in Table 9.1 below.

Table 9.1 Cross-subsidy surcharge rates in Indian states

State	Cross-subsidy surcharge (Rs/kWh)
Gujarat	1.45
Punjab	0.89
Maharashtra	1.49
Rajasthan	0.13
Andhra Pradesh	2.07

Source: Forum of Regulators[49]

[49] Forum of Regulators, Minutes of the 55th Meeting, 22 July 2016, www.forumofregulators.gov.in/Data/Meetings/Minutes/55.pdf.

Very few states waive open access charges for renewable energy projects, and such waivers are typically limited to solar projects, for instance, in the case of Andhra Pradesh. However, given the trend to roll back incentives for renewable energy projects, such waivers may not continue. For instance, the KERC has rejected the possibility of extending exemption from wheeling, banking charges and cross-subsidy surcharge to solar projects beyond March 2018. Such waivers have also been rolled back without notice. In Ķarnataka, a cross-subsidy surcharge waiver for wind projects was abruptly discontinued in 2013. In *Bajaj Finserv Ltd v MERC*,[50] an appeal has been filed by various independent wind power producers against a 2016 MERC order where the MERC has: (i) done away with the separate categorisation for consumers procuring power through open access from renewable energy sources and has treated them as being on a par with other open access consumers by levying 100 per cent cross-subsidy surcharge, as opposed to 25 per cent, which was levied earlier; and (ii) imposed an additional surcharge of Rs 1.11 per unit on power procured on open access from renewable energy sources. This order has been challenged on various grounds, including violation of principles of natural justice, violation of Article 14 of the Constitution of India, the MERC's failure to act in accordance with the statutory mandate to promote generation of power from renewable sources, and the MERC's non-application of mind in determining and imposing an additional surcharge. The matter is currently pending before APTEL.

While there is significant interest in the procurement of renewable energy through open access, especially by large corporate entities with deep pockets, looking to meet their internal green energy targets, the resistance of Discoms in granting open access charges, coupled with prohibitive cross-subsidy surcharge rates approved by SERCs, militates against this interest. Recently, the MoP announced that no inter-state transmission charges and losses would be levied on solar and wind power projects commissioned up to 31 March 2022. While this provides some respite, especially to the solar sector, it leaves much to be desired at the state level since intra-state transmission charges continue to be excessive. Despite a broader policy directive under the Electricity Act to allow open access and reduce the cross-subsidy surcharge, states have been more inclined to protect their commercial interests and have been aided in this task by SERCs, with the question of regulatory autonomy continuing to hang in the balance.

CONCLUSION

Further to its obligations under the Paris Agreement, India's national climate goals include renewable energy generation of 227 GW by 2022. This target was recently increased in anticipation of achieving the original target of 175 GW prior to 2022. At present, India has nearly 70 GW of renewable installed capacity,[51] with another

[50] Appeal No 142 of 2017 before APTEL (decision pending).

[51] Central Electricity Authority, Monthly Report on Installed Capacity – May 2018, www.cea.nic.in/reports/monthly/installedcapacity/2018/installed_capacity-05.pdf.

40 GW in the tendering or construction stage. The additional 52 GW is estimated to require a further investment of USD 50 billion over the coming years; however, there does not seem to be a detailed and focused enough plan to attract such investment and resolve existing sectoral issues.

Attaining these goals depends upon various institutional stakeholders working in tandem and the acknowledgement and ironing out of inherent tensions between such stakeholders. As shown above, these tensions exist at various levels – in the Electricity Act itself at the very root, amongst different agencies at the centre, and between the centre and the states.

In the absence of the requirement to adhere to national standards in the sector, states have significant leeway in designing policies and regulations for the power sector as a whole. The varied views of the SERCs on the issues of RPO enforcement and the imposition of cross-subsidy surcharges are characteristic of the non-uniform approach towards renewable energy deployment in India. While, to some extent, such leeway is a necessary and inevitable outcome of a federal structure of government, an undesirable fallout is that political economy objectives often cloud regulatory decision-making. Even at the centre, where uniformity in policy-making could be expected, there are competing interests at play. As discussed, the imposition of safeguard duties on imported solar panels and the emphasis on the Make in India policy are at variance with achieving the ambitious 227 GW national renewable energy target. Therefore, there is an inherent friction and, at times, incompatibility amongst the policies pursued by the centre, and merely shifting the goalposts does not address the sectoral problems that arise from such incompatibility.

As discussed here, the actions of these stakeholders are not always consistent, and their competing interests and political economy considerations are often prioritised over both the sanctity of law and regulation on the one hand and potentially long-term sectoral sustainability on the other. While policy-making and administrative action will always be subject to pressures such as budgetary constraints, the financial health of Discoms and the need to keep electricity tariffs low for the consumer/voter, greater regulatory rigour and adherence to the rule of law will help to keep some of these tendencies in check.

10

The Environment

SHIBANI GHOSH*

INTRODUCTION

India is ranked 177th out of 180 countries on the 2018 Environment Performance Index;[1] 275 rivers in the country are polluted;[2] 6.3 crore people in rural areas do not have access to potable water;[3] 228 out of 280 cities in India do not comply with air quality standards for particulate emissions and 180 million people in these cities are exposed to levels that are twice the prescribed standards;[4] and 6,407 sq km of dense forests were lost in just the last two years.[5] Environmental health across indicators in India is rapidly declining and the Indian state's failure to regulate sources of, and causes for, environmental degradation has never been more apparent. The reasons for this failure are numerous and complex: conflicting interests in limited resources; inadequate regulatory capacity to design and enforce the law effectively; lack of interagency coordination; and environmental issues not being politically salient enough to trump competing policy interests and priorities. As the country grapples with an increasing array of environmental problems, which vary in terms of their magnitude and urgency, it is an important moment in time to reflect on the nature and quality of the environmental regulation that is in place.

Environmental regulation is a broad term that includes the law promulgated by the legislature and interpreted by the courts, as well as other forms of social control

* I am grateful to Mr Shyam Divan, Senior Advocate, the editors and other participants at the authors' conference held on 16 and 17 March 2018 in New Delhi for their insightful comments.

1 Yale Center for Environmental Law & Policy and Center for International Earth Science Information Network, Columbia University, *2018 Environmental Performance Index* (Yale University, 2018).

2 Central Pollution Control Board (CPCB), *River Stretches for Restoration of Water Quality* (CPCB, 2015).

3 Rosie Stewart, *Wild Water: The State of the World's Water 2017* (WaterAid, 2017).

4 Harshit Sharma, Lauri Myllyvirta, and Sunil Dahiya, *Airpocalypse II: Assessment of Air Pollution in Indian Cities* (Greenpeace India, 2018), https://www.greenpeace.org/archive-india/Global/india/2018/Airpocalypse_II_29Jan18.pdf.

5 Kumar Sambhav Shrivastava, 'Hold the Celebrations: Marginal Increase in India's Forest Cover is Masking Massive Deforestation' *Scroll.in* (15 February 2018), https://scroll.in/article/868606/hold-the-celebrations-marginal-increase-in-indias-forest-cover-is-masking-massive-deforestation.

which harness the state's authority along with that of the market, businesses and civil society to control the use (and abuse) of environmental resources and promote their conservation.[6] However, in the present discussion, I adopt a somewhat limited definition of environmental regulation: formal laws legislated by the Indian Parliament, the manner in which they are implemented, the actors responsible for their implementation, and their capacity to discharge their responsibilities.[7] I am consciously locating the Indian state (through its agencies) as a central actor, as it plays (and is likely to play in the foreseeable future) a dominant role in shaping and implementing environmental regulation in the country. This is not to underplay the very important role of other actors and processes in determining the level of protection accorded to the environment in the country – including businesses and their decisions to protect investments, shareholders and reputations; civil society campaigns; international scrutiny; and policy choices made for other, frequently incompatible, developmental imperatives.

While some forms of environmental regulation may be traced back to ancient Indian texts which prohibited injury to certain species of flora and fauna, the Indian Penal Code 1860 (IPC) is considered to be the beginning of modern environmental regulation in India.[8] The IPC introduced penalties for 'fouling water of public spring or reservoir' and for 'vitiat[ing] the atmosphere … so as to make it noxious to the health of persons'.[9] At around the same time, the colonial government introduced a law to manage forests to sustain supply of timber for railway sleepers.[10] Wildlife protection also began to receive legislative attention,[11] although the motivation may have also been to ensure adequate prey for royal hunts.[12] Several other legislations passed by the colonial government, such as the Easements Act, 1882, the Bengal Smoke-Nuisances Act, 1905 and the Bombay Smoke-Nuisances Act, 1912, also had some bearing on environmental issues.

The Constitution of India of 1950 did not contain specific provisions on the protection of the environment. Constituent Assembly debates on natural resources and agriculture took place in the context of federalism and which level of government should be given the administrative mandate.[13] The 42nd amendment to the Constitution in 1976 introduced Article 48A (a Directive Principle of State Policy to protect

[6] Neil Gunningham, 'Environment Law, Regulation and Governance: Shifting Architectures' (2009) 21(2) *Journal of Environmental Law* 179, 181.

[7] See Timothy F Malloy, 'The Social Construction of Regulation: Lessons from the War against Command and Control' (2010) 58(2) *Buffalo Law Review* 267, 268, where the author uses the concept of 'regulatory system' to 'include the formal structure and substance of the law, the manner in which it is implemented, and the capacities and activities of the implementing entities'.

[8] CM Jariwala, 'Changing Dimension of Indian Environmental Law' in P Leelakrishnan (ed), *Law and Environment* (Eastern Book Company, 1992) ch 1.

[9] Indian Penal Code 1860 (IPC), ss 277 and 278.

[10] Madhav Gadgil and Ramachandra Guha, *This Fissured Land: An Ecological History of India* (Oxford University Press, 1992) ch 4.

[11] For example, the Madras Wild Elephants Preservation Act, 1873, the Elephants Preservation Act, 1879 and the Wild Birds and Animals Protection Act, 1912.

[12] Mahesh Rangarajan, *India's Wildlife History* (Permanent Black, 2001) ch 4.

[13] K. Sivaramakrishnan, 'Environment, Law, and Democracy in India' (2011) 70(4) *Journal of Asian Studies* 905, 906.

and improve the environment and safeguard forests and wildlife) and Article 51A(g) (a fundamental duty of every citizen to protect and improve the natural environment). It also moved two entries – forests and protection of wild animals and birds – from the State List to the Concurrent List in the Seventh Schedule.

Since independence, regulations addressing different aspects of the environment – wildlife, forests, water, air and biodiversity – have developed in India at the national and sub-national levels. A mix of primary and secondary legislation and administrative actions, along with their judicial interpretation, establish the formal legal foundation of these regulations. A large network of institutional arrangements involving government departments, regulatory agencies and other statutory bodies, independent research institutions and laboratories and the judiciary, is responsible for implementing and facilitating the implementation of these regulations.

This chapter will focus on one set of environmental regulations – regulations preventing and controlling water and air pollution, and it will analyse, in particular, the design and implementation of two laws passed by the Parliament – the Water (Prevention and Control of Pollution) Act, 1974 (hereinafter the Water Act) and the Air (Prevention and Control of Pollution) Act, 1981 (hereinafter the Air Act).[14] The two Acts are similarly designed and are implemented by the same regulatory agencies, and regulated entities occasionally apply for a common regulatory approval under the two Acts. This chapter will describe the regulatory landscape with a view to understanding some of the important factors that contribute to the failure of pollution regulation in India.

The environmental rights jurisprudence developed by the Indian judiciary over the last four decades has been instrumental in addressing cases of aggravated environmental pollution.[15] But statutory mechanisms to regulate pollution, and not the rights-based judicial route, are the focus of the present discussion. The chapter also does not discuss issues relating to competing claims on water and the (unclear) regulatory regime governing the extraction and use of groundwater and surface water based on common law and state laws.

Section I analyses the framework of pollution regulation in India. It will examine the role of the main statutory environmental regulators, ie, the Pollution Control Boards, in implementing the Water Act and the Air Act, and the regulatory tools available to them to perform their statutory mandate. Section II analyses the tools for the enforcement of pollution regulation, both administrative and judicial.

[14] The Water (Prevention and Control of Pollution) Cess Act, 1977 is often discussed in the context of the pollution regulation in India, but is not dealt with here. It was repealed by s 18 of the Taxation Laws (Amendment Act) 2017. For four decades, water cess was an important source of funding for the Pollution Control Boards.

[15] See Lovleen Bhullar, 'The Judiciary and the Right to Environment in India: Past, Present and Future' in Shibani Ghosh (ed), *Indian Environmental Law: Key Concepts and Principles* (Orient Black Swan, forthcoming); Michael R Anderson, 'Individual Rights to Environmental Protection in India' in Alan Boyle and Michael R Anderson (eds), *Human Rights Approaches to Environmental Protection* (Clarendon Press, 1998) 199; Lavanya Rajamani, 'The Right to Environmental Protection in India: Many a Slip between the Cup and the Lip?' (2007) 16(3) *Review of European Community and International Environmental Law* 274.

Section III identifies some critical issues affecting the efficacy of the pollution regulation in India. This will be followed by a concluding section which proposes a way forward.

I. THE FRAMEWORK OF POLLUTION REGULATION IN INDIA: KEY ELEMENTS

Regulatory processes prescribed in the Water Act and the Air Act form the framework of water and air pollution regulation in India. This framework is complemented by processes and actions under other legislation such as the Environment (Protection) Act, 1986 (hereinafter the EP Act). This section will answer the following questions: (1) who are the principal regulatory actors and what are their functions; (2) who are the regulated entities; and (3) what are the tools for regulation employed?

A. Regulatory Actors and Their Functions

The key regulatory actors in the pollution regulation regime in India are the Central Pollution Control Board (CPCB) and the State Pollution Control Boards (SPCBs). When the Water Act was passed in 1974, it empowered the Central Government and the state governments to constitute the Central and State Water Pollution Prevention Boards to implement the provisions of the Act.[16] In 1981, the Air Act enlarged the mandate of these agencies to include powers and functions arising from it, and they were subsequently renamed as the Central Pollution Control Board and the State Pollution Control Boards. In the Union Territories, the CPCB exercises the SPCB's powers,[17] and over time these powers have been delegated to specially constituted Union Territory Pollution Control Committees.[18] Besides the Water Act and the Air Act, the Boards presently hold an extensive mandate under a large number of other environmental regulations.[19]

i. Composition

The CPCB and the SPCBs are similar in composition. They are multi-member Boards consisting of a maximum of 15 members, serving part time, along with a chairperson and a member secretary, with a maximum of five officials being nominated to represent the Central Government (in the CPCB) or the state government (in the SPCBs); a maximum of five persons nominated from amongst the members of State Boards

[16] Water Act, ss 3 and 4.

[17] ibid s 4(4); Air Act, s 6.

[18] For notifications on the delegation of powers, see www.moef.nic.in/division/water-pollution.

[19] For example, the Boards play an important role under the Noise Pollution (Regulation & Control) Rules, 2000, the Environmental Impact Assessment (EIA) Notification, 2006, the Solid Waste Management Rules, 2016 and the Hazardous and Other Wastes (Management and Transboundary Movement) Rules, 2016.

(for the CPCB) or the local authorities functioning within the states (for the SPCBs), a maximum of three non-officials to represent the various interests of agriculture, fishery, industry, trade or any other interest which in the opinion of the Central Government or the state government ought to be represented, and two persons to represent companies owned, controlled or managed by the Central Government or the state government.[20] Interestingly, there is no requirement for the representation of civil society groups, academics, researchers or community leaders. Members hold their post for a period of three years, after which they may be renominated.

ii. Qualifications

Under both Acts, the chairperson of the Boards must have 'special knowledge or practical experience in respect of matters relating to environmental protection'.[21] But under the Water Act, there is an alternate eligibility criterion for the chairperson which was not included under the Air Act, viz a person with knowledge and experience in administering institutions dealing with matters relating to environmental protection.[22] While the Chairperson of the CPCB is a full-time position, that of the SPCB may be a part-time one depending on the state government.[23] Member secretaries are required to possess 'qualification, knowledge and experience of scientific, engineering or management aspects of pollution control', and must be engaged on a full-time basis.[24] The two laws do not elaborate further on the qualifications of the chairperson and member secretary. They also do not lay down qualifications for other Board members; except under the Air Act, not less than two members of the Boards must have special knowledge or practical experience in matters relating to the improvement of quality of air.[25] The Central Government and the state government possess the rule-making powers to decide the terms and conditions of service of chairpersons, member secretaries and other members.[26]

iii. Functions

The functions of the Boards include advising the Central Government and the state government on matters concerning prevention, control or abatement of air and water pollution, planning and executing programmes for the prevention, control or abatement of pollution, and laying down standards for emissions, effluents and pollution control processes.[27] Although many of their functions are similar, the CPCB's role is

[20] Water Act, ss 3(2) and 4(2); Air Act, s 5(2). By the time the Air Act came into force, the CPCB had already been constituted. However, some states were yet to constitute the SPCBs. For such states, the Air Act laid down a similar composition of the Board, but with two important differences with regard to qualifications.

[21] Water Act, s 4(2)(a); Air Act, s 5(2)(a).

[22] Water Act, s 4(2)(a).

[23] ibid ss 3(2)(a) and 4(2)(a), proviso; Air Act, s 5(2)(a), proviso.

[24] Water Act, s 4(2)(f); Air Act, s 5(2)(f).

[25] Air Act, s 5(2), proviso.

[26] Water Act, s 63(2)(e); Air Act, s 54(2)(a), (aa) and (f).

[27] Water Act, ss 16 and 17; Air Act, ss 16 and 17.

more in the nature of a scientific and technical advisory body that collects, analyses and disseminates data on pollution control measures, while the SPCBs are invested with duties of regulatory oversight and enforcement.

The Boards meet periodically to take major decisions.[28] Daily functions are discharged by officers and employees appointed by the Central Government and the state governments to administrative, scientific, technical and legal posts.[29] SPCBs can also form smaller committees, such as the Consent Committee and the Standards Committee, to perform some of their tasks.[30] The Boards, along with their officers and employees, are under the direct supervision and control of their constituting governments, and are therefore accountable to them.[31] Additionally, SPCBs are also bound by directions given by the CPCB.[32]

iv. Funding

The Boards are body corporates[33] and are funded primarily by grants-in-aid from the Central Government and the state government, along with fees or charges received (such as for consent application fees under the Water Act and the Air Act). Until recently, the water cess collected under the Water Cess Act also formed part of the Boards' funding.[34]

B. The Scope of Regulation and Regulated Entities

The Water Act applies to entire states, unless the state government limits its application to notified areas.[35] The Air Act, on the other hand, applies only to identified 'air pollution control areas' notified by the state governments.[36] In reality, both laws apply across entire states, as state governments have not limited the application of the Water Act, and under the Air Act, the entire territory of states have been declared as air pollution control areas. State governments also have the power under the Air Act to apply different standards for fuel, appliances etc in different parts of the state to address specific causes of air pollution.[37]

[28] The law requires the Boards to meet at least once every three months, but the actual number of meetings varies across Boards. See Water Act, s 8; Air Act, s 10.

[29] Water Act, s 12(3); Air Act, s 14(3).

[30] Water Act, s 9; Air Act, s 11.

[31] It is interesting to note that unlike Independent Regulatory Authorities set up in post-liberalisation India (many of which are analysed in other chapters of this volume), the Pollution Control Boards function very much within the control and supervision of the Central/state government.

[32] Water Act, s 18(1)(b); Air Act, s 18(1)(b).

[33] Water Act, ss 3(3), 4(3), 34 and 35; Air Act, ss 5(3) and 32.

[34] The cess amount would be deposited by the state government with the Central Government, which would then disburse 80 per cent of the amount collected back to each state, while the remaining 20 per cent would be allocated to the CPCB.

[35] Water Act, s 19.

[36] Air Act, s 19(1).

[37] ibid s 19(3)–(5).

Definitions of key terms, such as pollution, air pollutant, emissions, sewage effluent, stream and trade effluent, under the two Acts are very broad[38] and potentially allow the Boards, and the governments, to comprehensively address water and air pollution. Further, certain provisions indicate the intention of the legislature to cast a wide net, as it were, for polluters. For instance, the Water Act prohibits all persons from knowingly causing or permitting any poisonous, noxious or polluting matter to enter any stream or on land.[39] Similarly, under the Air Act, the SPCBs can seek a restraining order from a court against any person, either operating an industrial plant or otherwise, who is likely to emit air pollutants in excess of the prescribed standards.[40]

However, the categories of regulated entities that have to obtain prior approvals, or 'consents', from the SPCB before establishment (ie, Consent to Establish (CTE)) and then before commencing operations (ie Consent to Operate (CTO)), are different under the two laws.[41] Under the Water Act, any person establishing an industry, operation or process, or any treatment and disposal system, or an extension thereto which is likely to discharge sewage or trade effluent, bringing into use any new or altered sewage outlets or making any new discharge of sewage has to first obtain these consents,[42] while under the Air Act, only industrial plants need to obtain these consents.[43] An industrial plant has been defined as a plant used for any industrial or trade purposes and emitting any air pollutant.[44]

Standards for vehicular emissions are proposed and decided by intergovernmental committees (with the participation of industry groups) headed by the Joint Secretary of the Ministry of Road Transport and Highways (MoRTH).[45] The Boards have a limited role to play with regard to vehicular emissions, other than laying down standards for emissions from vehicles.[46]

C. Tools for Regulation

There are primarily two regulatory tools employed by the Boards under the two Acts: (1) prescribing standards; and (2) the consent mechanism.

i. Prescribing Standards

The power to lay down standards is with the CPCB as well as the SPCBs under the two Acts. These include standards for quality of air,[47] for emissions of air pollutants from industrial plants and automobiles, or for emissions of air pollutants from

[38] See Water Act, s 2; Air Act, s 2.

[39] Water Act, s 24(1).

[40] Air Act, s 22A.

[41] See *Delhi Pollution Control Committee v Splendor Landbase Ltd* 2012 SCC OnLine Del 400, para 28.

[42] Water Act, s 25(1).

[43] Air Act, s 21(1).

[44] *Nitin Majumdar v State of Karnataka* 2007 SCC OnLine Kar 187, paras 8 and 9.

[45] See Gaurav Bansal and Anup Bandivadekar, *Overview of India's Vehicle Emissions Control Program: Past Successes and Future Prospects* (International Council on Clean Transportation, 2013) 35.

[46] Air Act, s 20.

[47] ibid s 16(2)(h). Exercising this power, the CPCB issued the National Ambient Air Quality Standards (NAAQS) in 2009. See Notification dated 18 November 2009, www.moef.nic.in/sites/default/files/notification/Recved%20national.pdf.

any source other than a ship or aircraft,[48] standards for a stream or well,[49] effluent standards for the sewage and trade effluents and for the quality of receiving waters resulting from the discharge,[50] and standards for treatment of sewage and trade effluents.[51] The Boards can prescribe new or revised standards, prohibit or regulate certain types of polluting activities, customise standards based on the tolerance of the receiving water body or airshed, and put in place plans and policies that can suitably respond to demands for environmental protection that are likely to arise in the future.

The Boards generally rely on emission and discharge standards prescribed by the Central Government for various industries, operations and processes in the Environment (Protection) Rules 1986 (hereinafter the EP Rules) issued under the EP Act.[52] For instance, the National Ambient Air Quality Standards 2009 (NAAQS) form Schedule VII of the EP Rules, and the EP Rules state that the combined effect of all industries, operations, processes, automobiles etc should not be permitted to exceed these standards.[53] However, the Boards may adopt more stringent standards than those prescribed in the EP Rules for a specific entity, depending upon the quality of the receptor (eg, a stream where the effluents will be discharged or the local airshed).[54]

ii. The Consent Mechanism

The consent mechanism requires regulated entities to obtain a CTE and a CTO from the Boards. These consent orders mandate that the regulated entity meets certain technical specifications in its operations and processes, and ensure that it does not discharge effluents or emissions in excess of the prescribed standards. Once an application is filed, the SPCB can undertake such inquiry as it may deem fit.[55] This could include a site inspection. However, there is no statutory requirement to conduct a public consultation with potentially affected persons as part of the consent granting process.

A CTO has to be renewed regularly. The periodicity of the renewal as well as the stringency with which a consent application is reviewed depends mainly on the categorisation of the industry as a Red, Orange or Green industry.[56] Recently, a fourth category of industries was created – the White category – which includes 36 'non-polluting' industries that do not need to apply for consents.[57] The SPCBs have the power to amend the conditions in a consent, cancel the consent before its expiry or refuse its renewal – after giving an opportunity to be heard to the regulated entity.[58]

[48] Air Act, s 17(1)(g).
[49] Water Act, s 16(2)(g).
[50] ibid s 17(1)(g).
[51] ibid s 17(1)(k).
[52] EP Rules, scheds I–VII. See also EP Rules, r 3(3A).
[53] EP Rules, r 3(3B).
[54] ibid r 3(2).
[55] Water Act, s 25(3); Air Act, s 21(3).
[56] CPCB, *Document on Revised Classification of Industrial Sectors under Red, Orange, Green and White Categories* (CPCB, 2016), http://envfor.nic.in/sites/default/files/Latest_118_Final_Directions.pdf.
[57] ibid.
[58] Water Act, s 25(4); Air Act, s 21(4).

Once consent is granted, SPCBs are expected to monitor compliance of the conditions set therein, along with other legal requirements, and regulated entities have to submit annual environmental statements to the SPCBs.[59] An integral part of the monitoring process are inspections carried out by the SPCBs, and the collection and testing of samples at recognised laboratories. For this purpose, SPCBs prepare inspection protocols indicating the periodicity of inspection (differentiated according to the category and size of the industry), the method of selection of industry to be inspected, the process for sample collection etc.[60]

Although the consent mechanism is similar under the two Acts, there are certain differences. Significantly, the Water Act contains a provision wherein if the SPCB does not decide on a consent application within four months of receiving it, the application is deemed to have been granted unconditionally.[61] Such a deeming provision does not exist in the Air Act.[62] Furthermore under the Water Act (and unlike the Air Act), if a regulated entity is operating without a consent, the SPCB has to first serve a notice on such an entity imposing such conditions as would have been imposed on it if it had filed an application.[63]

The Acts provide a statutory mechanism – Appellate Authorities – for aggrieved persons to appeal against the orders of the SPCBs.[64] State governments are required to appoint Appellate Authorities in each state, composed of one or three members.[65] The qualifications of persons who may be appointed is not specified in the Acts, although in a 1999 judgment, the Supreme Court issued certain directions in this regard.[66] However, a recent study shows that in some states, the Appellate Authorities are not functional, and their composition and functioning in many other states does not inspire much confidence.[67]

This section has provided an overview of the Boards, as well as the two mechanisms by which they regulate water and air pollution. What is of particular significance is that the two Acts give the Boards comprehensive powers to deal with increasing sources of pollution and types of pollutants, and to create new ways of remediating polluted environs. The next section discusses the mechanisms available to enforce the provisions of the Water Act and Air Act.

[59] EP Rules, r 14.

[60] See, for example, Inspection Policy of the Karnataka SPCB, http://kspcb.gov.in/OM_7158.pdf; and the procedure followed by the Maharashtra SPCB, www.mpcb.gov.in/consentmgt/pdf/Circular_SamplingprocedurethroughSoftare20062015%20%20.pdf.

[61] Water Act, s 25(7). See also *Som Distilleries and Breweries Ltd v State of Madhya Pradesh* MANU/MP/0509/1994.

[62] See *Proprietor, Sulaimaniya Bone Mill v Tamil Nadu Pollution Control Board* MANU/TN/0232/2011.

[63] Water Act, s 25(5).

[64] ibid s 28, Air Act, s 31. 'Aggrieved person' is not defined in the two Acts. However, the courts have held that it includes not only regulated entities, but also those likely to be affected by the functioning of such entities. See *District Collector, Nellai Kattabomman Dist, Tiruneveli and Another v The Rajapalayam Cement and Chemicals Ltd* 1997 Writ LR 157; *Gujarat Pollution Control Board v Parmar Devusinh Shersinh* 2000 SCC OnLine Guj 132.

[65] Water Act, s 28(2); Air Act, s 31(2).

[66] *AP Pollution Control Board v Prof MV Nayudu* (1999) 2 SCC 718.

[67] Shibani Ghosh, Sharachchandra Lele and Nakul Heble, 'Appellate Authorities under Pollution Control Laws: Powers, Problems and Potential' (2018) 14(1) *Law Environment and Development Journal* 47.

II. THE ENFORCEMENT OF POLLUTION REGULATION IN INDIA

The Water Act and the Air Act equip the Boards with various administrative instruments for the enforcement of pollution standards. Apart from these instruments, the Boards as well as affected – and concerned – persons can also approach appropriate judicial forums for the enforcement of pollution regulations and grievance redressal. This section provides an overview of these instruments and judicial forums.

A. Administrative Instruments

i. Directions by Boards to Regulated Entities

Initially the Water Act and the Air Acts only provided for criminal prosecution as the mechanism for enforcement. However, both Acts were amended in the late 1980s to give the Boards the power to issue directions, and persons to whom such directions are issued are bound to comply with them.[68] These include directions for closure, prohibition or regulation of any industry, operation or process, or stoppage or regulation of the supply of electricity, water or any other service.[69] Directions under these provisions are typically preceded by show cause notices from the SPCB to the regulated entities. Boards do not need the approval of an external agency (like the courts) to exercise this power. However, the successful implementation of these directions often requires interagency coordination between the SPCB, the electricity and water supply boards, and local administration. As this power to give directions is quite generally worded, Boards can invoke it in a variety of situations: if a person is violating the terms of a consent, is operating without a consent or is not complying with any other statutory requirement. However, the power cannot be invoked to grant compensation or impose a penalty.[70] Failure to comply with the directions could lead to criminal prosecution.[71]

ii. Directions by CPCB to SPCBs

The two Acts also empower the CPCB to give certain directions to the SPCBs in the performance of its functions.[72] These directions could, in turn, require the SPCBs to issue further directions to regulated entities within their states.[73] The CPCB has

[68] Water Act, s 33A; Air Act, s 31A.

[69] Water Act, s 33A, explanation; Air Act, s 31A, explanation. While discussing the ambit of closure directions, the High Court of Delhi in *Gopi Nath Pvt Ltd v Department of Environment Govt of NCT of Delhi* (1998) 72 DLT 536 held: 'Closing down all industrial activity is neither the purpose nor the object of the Act. Prevention of pollution is. If one particular component is the cause of pollution, the Board may well, subject to the provisions of the Act, direct its closure but it cannot seal the entire unit bringing thereby even unoffending activities to a standstill.'

[70] *Delhi Pollution Control Committee v Splendor Landbase Ltd* 2012 SCC OnLine Del 400.

[71] Water Act, s 41(2); Air Act, s 37(1).

[72] Water Act, s 18(1)(b); Air Act, s 18(1)(b).

[73] Water Act, s 33A; Air Act, s 31A.

exercised this power in many cases: for example, for the introduction of compulsory continuous emissions monitoring systems (CEMS) for 17 categories of highly polluting industries across the country;[74] imposing additional self-monitoring requirements on all red category industries in the National Capital Region (NCR) as a measure to improve air quality in the Region;[75] and bringing to the SPCB's attention specific statutory violations in its jurisdiction, directing it to take necessary action against the concerned regulated entities.[76]

As the CPCB's power to give directions is broadly worded and its functions include coordination of the SPCBs' activities, resolving disputes amongst them and implementing nationwide programmes for the prevention and control of pollution,[77] the CPCB is well placed to initiate and support programmes that are based on the sources, and receptors of pollution, rather than the geographical boundaries of states. For instance, the NCR has in recent years witnessed a sharp rise in air pollution. The affected areas form part of the same airshed, and the nature of sources is such that they can be tackled more effectively if a coordinated approach is taken by various states, with support from the centre. The Air Act suitably empowers the CPCB and the Central Government to resolve (most) jurisdictional conflicts which may arise.

iii. Directions by the CPCB to Regulated Entities

Like the Boards, the Central Government, in the performance of its functions under the EP Act, has the power to give directions to any person, and any such person is bound to comply with such a direction.[78] It has delegated the power to issue directions to any industry, municipal corporation or authority for violations of the effluent and emissions standards laid down in the EP Rules to the CPCB.[79] The CPCB exercises this delegated power to issue a variety of orders including closure orders and show cause notices against regulated entities, and to revoke closure orders.[80] However, it cannot take punitive action against defaulting units under the provision.[81]

iv. Other Instruments

SPCBs can reject applications for renewal of consents or withdraw valid consents if the regulated entity is found to be violating the conditions of the consent.[82]

[74] Letter to all SPCBs/PCCs dated 5 February 2014, http://cpcb.nic.in/displaypdf.php?id=Q1BBL0JfRGlyLnBkZg==.

[75] Letter to SPCBs/PCC of Delhi, UP, Rajasthan and Haryana dated 29 December 2017, http://cpcb.nic.in/openpdffile.php?id=UHVibGljYXRpb25GaWxlLzEzMjZfMTUxNzI5NzIxMV9tZWRpYXBob3RvMjE0NTQuMDE=.

[76] For directions issued by the CPCB under s 18(1)(b) of the Water Act and the Air Act, see http://cpcb.nic.in/cpcb-directions.php.

[77] Water Act, s 16(2); Air Act, s 16(2).

[78] EP Act, s 5.

[79] ibid s 23.

[80] For Directions issued by the CPCB under s 5 of the EP Act, see http://cpcb.nic.in/cpcb-directions-5ep.php.

[81] *M/s Champ Energy Ventures Pvt Ltd v MoEFCC and Others* 2015 SCC OnLine NGT 83.

[82] Water Act, s 27; Air Act, s 21(4), proviso.

Another mechanism that is increasingly being used by SPCBs to enforce compliance with statutory requirements is requiring regulated entities to deposit bank guarantees or performance security at the time of application for a CTE, or as a condition when allowing a regulated entity to continue functioning after a show cause notice is issued for some violation. This mechanism does not find a specific mention in the two Acts, but as a non-punitive condition has been found to be legal by the National Green Tribunal (NGT).[83] The guarantee amount is calculated by the SPCB based on the industry category and the investment/cost of the project. In the event of non-compliance with the conditions, the SPCBs encash full or part of the bank guarantee proportionate to the extent of the non-compliance.[84] Efforts have also been made to introduce an emissions trading scheme for particulate matter in certain industrial clusters in place of the conventional standards-based regulation under the Air Act.[85] However, the scheme has yet to come into force.

B. Judicial Forums

i. Criminal Courts

Violations of certain provisions in the two Acts constitute criminal offences, and the Acts prescribe imprisonment and fine as the punishment – the duration and amount varying depending on the offence.[86] Non-compliance with the conditions set out in the CTE or the CTO (eg, for polluting beyond permissible standards), knowingly introducing pollutants into the water, knowingly impeding the water flow which aggravates pollution, or failure to comply with directions issued by the Boards could lead to imprisonment of not less than one and a half years, which may extend up to six years, along with a fine. If the offence continues, an additional punishment may be imposed.

The court of competent jurisdiction under these Acts is the Metropolitan Magistrate or the Judicial Magistrate First Class. The prosecution may be initiated by the SPCB or by any person authorised by it, or by any other person, after serving necessary notice of his or her intention to approach the court to the Board.[87] The Boards can also approach the competent court for a restraining order against an entity which is likely to cause pollution in excess of the prescribed standards.[88]

[83] *State Pollution Control Board, Odisha v M/s Swastik Ispat Pvt Ltd and Others* 2014 SCC OnLine NGT 13; *Tarun Patel v Chairman, Gujarat Pollution Control Board* 2014 SCC OnLine NGT 1383.

[84] See the Maharashtra SPCB's Enforcement Policy dated 29 February 2016, available at http://mpcb.gov.in/consentmgt/pdf/Circular_Enforcement_Policy.pdf; Office order dated 22 February 2012 issued by the Rajasthan SPCB, available at https://www.pmar.in/asso/cir62.pdf.

[85] Esther Duflo et al, 'Towards an Emissions Trading Scheme for Air Pollutants in India: A Concept Note' (MoEF, 2010), available at https://gpcb.gov.in/Images/moef-discussion.PDF. See also Gujarat Pollution Control Board, 'Emissions Trading Scheme (Pilot Project)', available at https://gpcb.gov.in/emissions-trading-scheme.htm.

[86] Water Act, ss 41–48; Air Act, ss 37–41.

[87] Water Act, s 49; Air Act, s 43.

[88] Water Act, s 33; Air Act, s 22A.

ii. Under the NGT Act[89]

Civil action against pollution and violations of the Water Act and the Air Act can be sought by approaching the NGT. The Tribunal has original jurisdiction over all civil cases raising a substantial question relating to the environment, including the enforcement of any legal right relating to the environment.[90] Such question must arise from the implementation of six laws listed in the Schedule to the NGT Act, which includes the Water Act and the Air Act. The NGT has appellate jurisdiction over orders issued by Appellate Authorities under the Water Act and the Air Act, as well as directions issued by the Boards under the Water Act, but not over directions issued under the Air Act.[91]

The Tribunal can order relief and compensation to victims of pollution, and can order restitution of damaged property and for the restoration of the area's environment.[92] Compensation can be paid under heads mentioned in Schedule II to the NGT Act, which includes death, injury, loss of wages, medical expenses, expenses incurred by the government in providing relief, aid and rehabilitation to the affected persons etc.[93] The Act makes the person responsible for causing the damage to the environment (for example, the owner of a polluting factory) liable for paying the compensation as determined by the Tribunal.[94] In the case of an accident, the Tribunal has to apply the no-fault liability principle,[95] following the absolute liability principle laid down by the Supreme Court in the Oleum Gas leak case.[96] The Act also requires the Tribunal to apply the polluter pays, sustainable development and precautionary principles when deciding cases.[97]

The Tribunal is empowered to issue interim orders including injunctions or stays, and orders requiring persons to cease and desist from committing or causing any harm to the environment.[98] An order of the Tribunal can be appealed in the Supreme Court.[99]

The Tribunal has used its powers to issue a variety of orders to tackle different types of water and air pollution. It has issued closure orders to polluting industries,[100] directed polluting industries to install treatment facilities,[101] and ordered municipal corporations and industries responsible for polluting river water to pay environmental compensation and undertake remediation measures.[102]

[89] This section builds on Shibani Ghosh, 'Reforming the Liability Regime for Air Pollution in India' (2015) IV *Environmental Law and Practice Review* 125.

[90] NGT Act, s 14(1) read with s 2(1)(m).

[91] NGT Act, s 16.

[92] ibid s 15.

[93] ibid sched II.

[94] NGT Act, s.17.

[95] ibid s 17(3).

[96] *MC Mehta v Union of India* (1987) 1 SCC 395.

[97] NGT Act, s 20.

[98] ibid s 19(3).

[99] ibid s 22.

[100] See, for example, *MC Mehta v Union of India*, OA No. 200/2014, Order dated 26 April 2017.

[101] See, for example, *M/s Laxmi Suiting and Others v State of Rajasthan, through the Secretary and Others* MANU/GT/0042/2014.

[102] See, for example, *Vanashakti Public Trust and Another v Maharashtra Pollution Control Board and Others*, OA 37/2013(WZ), Judgment dated 2 July 2015; *Krishan Kant Singh v M/s Triveni Engg Industries*

In the context of rising air pollution in the NCR, the Tribunal has directed that diesel vehicles older than 10 years and petrol vehicles older than 15 years not be registered in the NCR,[103] and has issued detailed orders to reduce pollution caused from construction activities[104] and crop burning.[105] In November 2017, when Delhi experienced hazardous air quality, the Tribunal banned construction, industrial activities and the entry of trucks into the city.[106] To reduce air pollution in the Rohtang Pass region of Himachal Pradesh, the Tribunal has issued several orders, including restricting the number of vehicles going to the Pass per day and directing the payment of a fee for environmental compensation by each vehicle.[107]

iii. Proceedings before the Supreme Court

The Supreme Court of India has often been complimented for its green credentials and for its active role in protecting the environment. Some of its landmark environmental judgments have been delivered in cases concerning widespread water and air pollution. In such cases, the Court has relied on both a rights-based justification and on existing statutory provisions, often highlighting the executive's laxity in implementing the law.

The Supreme Court's orders and judgments addressing aggravated levels of pollution in the Ganga,[108] directing remediation of the environment in Bichhri village Rajasthan and sealing the polluting 'rogue industries',[109] and regulating the leather industry in Vellore while directing the payment of compensation to those affected by the industry's illegal actions[110] are some of its significant judgments on water pollution.

Similarly, on the issue of air pollution, the Supreme Court has played an important role – particularly in the NCR. In 2002, it directed the public transport fleet running in Delhi to move from diesel to compressed natural gas, which was then considered less harmful.[111] Over the years, it has directed concerned authorities to construct expressways around Delhi so that the traffic destined elsewhere can bypass the city, directed the introduction of an environmental compensation cess to be paid by heavy vehicles which pass through Delhi,[112] and imposed strict regulation on the use of

Ltd, OA 317/2014, Judgment dated 10 December 2015; *The Forward Foundation and Others v State of Karnataka and Others*, OA 222/2014, Judgment dated 7 May 2015.

[103] *Vardhaman Kaushik v Union of India*, OA No 21/2014, Order dated 7 April 2015.

[104] ibid, Order dated 4 December 2014.

[105] *Vikrant Kumar Tongad v Environment Pollution (Prevention & Control) Authority and Others*, OA 118/2013, Judgment dated 10 December 2015.

[106] *Vardhaman Kaushik* (n 103) Order dated 9 November 2017.

[107] *Court on its Own Motion v State of Himachal Pradesh*, OA No 237 (THC)/2015. See in particular Orders dated 6 February 2014 and 5 May 2015.

[108] *MC Mehta v Union of India* (1987) 4 SCC 463; *MC Mehta v Union of India* (1997) 2 SCC 411; and *MC Mehta v Union of India* (1988) 1 SCC 471.

[109] *Indian Council for Enviro-Legal Action v Union of India* (1996) 5 SCC 212.

[110] *Vellore Citizens' Welfare Forum v Union of India* (1996) 5 SCC 647.

[111] *MC Mehta v Union of India* (2002) 4 SCC 356.

[112] *MC Mehta v Union of India* (2016) 2 SCC 33.

pet coke and furnace oil.[113] In another case on air pollution in Delhi and surrounding areas, the Court issued a temporary ban on the bursting of firecrackers during Diwali.[114]

iv. Under General Criminal and Civil Law

Apart from the criminal proceedings under the Water Act and the Air Act, legal proceedings may also be initiated under general laws.[115] Actions causing water or air pollution could potentially be brought within the definitional ambit of 'public nuisance' in the Indian Penal Code.[116] Further, under the Code, polluting water ('fouling water') and air ('vitiates the atmosphere') are specific offences.[117] Action can also be taken by a magistrate under the Criminal Procedure Code to remove any cause of 'nuisance'.[118] This could include ordering the closure of any trade which is injurious to health or physical comfort, the removal of unlawful obstruction in a river or channel, or stopping the disposal of any substance that may conflagrate or explode.[119]

The enforcement of pollution regulation can also be pursued through an action against public nuisance under the Code of Civil Procedure 1908 or, as in any other civil suit, an order for declaration, injunction or any other appropriate remedy may be sought. Persons filing a suit against public nuisance need not prove that special damage has been caused to them.[120]

This section has reviewed the administrative instruments available to the Boards to enforce the provisions of the two Acts. It has also provided an overview of the judicial forums where cases relating to the enforcement of the Water Act and the Air Act can be adjudicated. From the array of options available to the Boards – both administrative and judicial – it would seem that the Boards have a reasonably heavy regulatory tool chest at their disposal and they could, depending on the severity of the violation or default, select one amongst many tools, viz issue a show cause notice, a closure order, a direction to desist certain polluting operations, or directions to install pollution abatement equipment, demand/forfeit a bank guarantee, withdraw

[113] *MC Mehta v Union of India* 2017 SCC OnLine SC 1378.

[114] *Arjun Gopal v Union of India* 2017 SCC OnLine SC 1203.

[115] The Supreme Court in *State of Madhya Pradesh v Kedia Leather & Liquor Ltd* (2003) 7 SCC 389 has clarified that the two procedures under the general law (Code of Criminal Procedure 1973) and under the special law (the Water Act) operate independently of each other, and the latter has not repealed the former.

[116] IPC, s 268.

[117] ibid ss 277 and 278.

[118] Code of Criminal Procedure 1973, s 133.

[119] The Supreme Court in *Kachrulal Bhagirath Agrawal v State of Maharashtra* (2005) 9 SCC 36 upheld an order under s 133 stopping the storing and transportation of dry chilies from a godown as it was held to be a public nuisance causing pollution and physical discomfort to persons residing nearby. The Court held: 'The guns of Section 133 go into action wherever there is public nuisance. The public power of the Magistrate under the Code is a public duty to the members of the public who are victims of the nuisance, and so he shall exercise it when the jurisdictional facts are present … The conduct of the trade must be injurious in presenti [sic] to the health or physical comfort of the community. There must, at any rate, be an imminent danger to the health or the physical comfort of the community in the locality in which the trade or occupation is conducted' (para 11).

[120] Code of Civil Procedure 1908, s 91.

consent, initiate criminal prosecution, seek an injunction, seek compensation etc. The only actions they cannot take are the imposition of a monetary penalty and reward compensation, but they can approach an appropriate judicial forum for such relief. In the next section I will explore some of the issues which impact the efficacy of pollution regulations in India and why the Boards, despite exercising wide jurisdiction and enjoying significant powers, are unable to utilise their regulatory tool chest to effectively regulate water and air pollution in the country.

III. CRITICAL ISSUES AFFECTING THE EFFICACY OF THE POLLUTION REGULATION

Despite an elaborate regulatory structure that has been in place for over four decades, a legal regime that could comprehensively address most causes of air and water pollution, regulators with a variety of enforcement tools at their disposal and a (usually) sympathetic judiciary, pollution regulation in India is failing. In this section, I discuss some of the critical issues that impact the efficacy of the pollution regulation regime.

A. The Institutional Capacity of Boards

The effective implementation of the Water Act and Air Act depends, in large part, on an effectively functioning Board supported by a competent and adequate staff. Over the years, several studies commissioned by the government, as well as some undertaken independently, reveal that the SPCBs do not have the capacity to perform the functions assigned to them under various environmental regulations. The lack of capacity in SPCBs is attributable to many factors: absence of technically competent leadership, inadequate sanctioned strength of personnel, high numbers of vacancies, absence of proper training for personnel, lack of pollution monitoring and abatement equipment etc.[121] I will look at a few of these factors in greater detail.

The Boards play a critical role in pollution regulation, and therefore their leadership and membership must mirror their statutory mandate. This issue of who is competent to head the Boards was raised before the Supreme Court.[122] The matter arose in an appeal against a judgment of the NGT, which directed all states to cancel the appointments of chairpersons and member secretaries of SPCBs that were not in accordance with the Water Act and the Air Act, and the Tribunal's interpretation

[121] Geetanjoy Sahu, *Environmental Regulatory Authorities in India: An Assessment of State Pollution Control Boards* (TISS, 2013); Centre for Science and Environment, *Turnaround: Reform Agenda for India's Environmental Regulators* (CSE, 2009); Departmental Parliamentary Standing Committee on Science & Technology and Environment & Forests, *192nd Report on the Functioning of Central Pollution Control Board* (2008); OECD, *Environmental Compliance and Enforcement in India: Rapid Assessment* (OECD, 2006); Planning Commission, Government of India, *Evaluation Study on the Functioning of State Pollution Control Boards* (Government of India, 2002).

[122] *Techi Tagi Tara v Rajendra Bhandari and Others* 2017 SCC OnLine SC 1165.

of the relevant provisions.[123] The Supreme Court set aside the Tribunal's judgment, holding that whether a person is qualified to be on the Board or not, and what should be the specific qualifications of candidates, was not within the Tribunal's jurisdiction to determine. However, the Supreme Court shared the Tribunal's deep anguish at the attitude of the state governments in appointing persons who were not adequately qualified to head expert bodies like the SPCBs. It observed:

> One of the principal attributes of good governance is the establishment of viable institutions comprising professionally competent persons and the strengthening of such institutions so that the duties and responsibilities conferred on them are performed with dedication and sincerity in public interest. This is applicable not only to administrative bodies but more so to statutory authorities – more so, because statutory authorities are the creation of a law made by a competent legislature, representing the will of the people.

The Supreme Court further noted that 'many of [the SPCBs] possess only a few or sometimes none of the above attributes of good governance and again a few or none of them are adequately empowered'. It directed all states to formulate rules and guidelines for recruitment to the Boards in light of the institutional requirements, legal provisions and recommendations of various committees over the years within six months. The state governments' inability – or reluctance – to properly constitute the Boards risks, at best, mediocre environmental decision making and, at worst, undesirable and irreversible environmental outcomes.

Given the nature and extent of their duties under the two Acts, along with other environmental regulations, the Boards require significant staff strength – technical and administrative – in order to be able to perform their mandate. However, even the sanctioned strength across Boards falls short of their basic requirements. According to a 2010 CPCB report, there was an additional staff requirement of 6,658 persons across SPCBs, of which 3,650 were required for scientific/technical and computerisation activities. At that time, the sanctioned strength of the SPCBs was 8,406, with only 6,005 positions filled.[124] After eight years, with sources of pollution and types of pollutants increasing, this assessment of additional staff requirement can only be revised upwards.

Even assuming the sanctioned strength has been reasonably determined – although it is unclear how this determination is made – the high rate of vacancies aggravates the situation. The CPCB's latest Annual Report 2015–16 states that of its 535 sanctioned posts, 101 were vacant. In fact, the post of the Chairperson of the CPCB was vacant for four and a half years before the current chairperson was appointed.[125] In performance audits conducted by the Comptroller and Auditor General of India (CAG), it

[123] *Rajendra Singh Bhandari v State of Uttarakhand and Others*, OA No 318/2013, Judgment dated 24 August 2016. See also Shibani Ghosh, 'National Green Tribunal Stops Chairpersons of 10 State Pollution Control Boards from Functioning', *Centre for Policy Research* (13 June 2017), www.cprindia.org/news/6236.

[124] See CPCB, 'Strengthening of Pollution Control Boards and Pollution Control Committees' (2010) (on file with the author).

[125] DNA, 'MoEF Appoints Full-Time CPCB Chairperson after Four years' DNA, 16 July 2016, www.dnaindia.com/india/report-moef-appoints-full-time-cpcb-chairperson-after-four-years-2234886.

was revealed that by the end of March 2017, in the Karnataka SPCB 51 per cent of posts and in the Rajasthan SPCB 34 per cent of posts were lying vacant.[126] Besides the vacancy problem, there is also the issue of many SPCBs employing a disproportionately high number of administrative staff with no technical expertise, who therefore cannot perform some of the core functions of the Boards.[127]

The composition and functioning of the Board itself is an area of concern. The composition of the Board is dominated by government officials, and the Member Secretary is generally an Indian Administrative Services or Indian Forest Services officer who comes through deputation, and her tenure is not fixed. On the one hand, the government is not required to appoint representatives from civil society groups or research institutions working on environmental conservation and pollution control to the Board, while on the other hand, they have representatives who are potential polluters, such as municipal corporations and industries.[128] Boards do not meet regularly, even though they are meant to meet once every three months.[129] There is no clear evidence that this structure – a multi-member Board, where all members other than the Member Secretary are serving only part-time, that enjoys significant decision-making powers but is under the direct supervision of the state governments, and that is supported by a permanent staff with limited expertise, training and autonomy – has been a successful model. In fact, the state of India's environment should urge us to rethink this structure.

B. Standard Setting and Pollution Control Measures

While designing pollution regulations, two determinations need to be made at the outset: first, ascertaining what should be the quality of water and air for a particular use or in a particular area – in other words, what it is that we are trying to achieve through the regulatory regime; and, second, what are the appropriate standards of discharge/emissions, fuel, technology, process etc that are required to attain this quality?[130] Both these determinations have to be arrived at after rigorous scientific assessment and after considering factors like human and animal health, biodiversity conservation, relevant environmental conditions etc. The entire regulatory regime is then structured in a way that supports these two determinations.

[126] Report of the Comptroller and Auditor General of India on Economic Sector for the year ended March 2017, Government of Karnataka, Report No 8 of the year 2017; Report of the Comptroller and Auditor General of India on Economic Sector for the year ended 31 March 2017, Government of Rajasthan, Report No 5 of the year 2017.

[127] Sahu (n 121). See, eg, CAG, Performance Audit on Environmental Degradation in the greater Guwahati Area with special emphasis on the role of the Pollution Control Board, Assam, Report No 3 of 2016, 7.

[128] Sharachchandra Lele and Nakul Heble, 'Changes in Pollution Board Undermine Accountability' *Deccan Herald* (16 June 2016).

[129] The Supreme Court noted in *Techi Tagi Tara* that the Uttarakhand SPCB met 15 times in 12 years. The CAG Report on Rajasthan SPCB states that between 2012 and 2017, the Board met eight times, instead of the stipulated 20 times.

[130] I would like to thank Sharachchandra Lele for this point.

In India, these determinations are either not made or are not made scientifically. The standard-setting function of the Boards (and the Environment Ministry) receives little attention. In 2017, the Supreme Court in an order noted that emissions standards for SOx and NOx had not been set for 35 industries.[131] Boards often do not maintain databases on even basic information about water bodies, number and type of pollution sources, pollutant load etc.[132] In the absence of this kind of information, Boards are not in a position to prepare location specific standards and introduce targeted pollution control measures.

The NAAQS prescribe, inter alia, permissible levels of particulate matter 2.5 (in μ/m^3) for industrial and residential areas annually as 40 and for a 24-hour period as 60. The World Health Organization (WHO) sets limits for the same parameter at 10 and 25,[133] while the United States Environment Protection Agency has pegged these limits at 12 and 35.[134] It is not clear how the CPCB has determined these standards, which are multiple times higher than the WHO standards.

The consent mechanism is currently designed to meet source-specific standards – standards which by themselves may not be scientifically designed – and do not consider the capacity of the receptor (ie, the water body or the local airshed).[135] Even if 10 factories discharge effluents which meet the standards prescribed in their respective consents, the water quality in the receiving stream may not meet the necessary standards for any type of consumption. In the context of air pollution, according to the EP Rules, the cumulative effect of emissions from all sources in an area should not exceed the relevant concentrations as stipulated in the NAAQS.[136] For that reason, Boards should grant consents to only those regulated entities in an airshed whose combined effect does not exceed the NAAQS. But unfortunately, the regulatory structure does not prioritise such holistic environmental outcomes and instead (unsuccessfully) focuses on regulating point sources.

Between their two core regulatory functions – prescribing standards and consent management – most Boards spend considerably more time on the latter and, given the limited technical staff strength, the former suffers. Even with regard to consent management, the Boards spend more time granting and renewing consents, and much less time and resources monitoring compliance with conditions. The 2017 CAG report for the Karnataka SPCB found that there was a shortfall of 44 per cent in inspections of regulated entities, based on the frequency of inspections required according to the SPCB's inspection protocol.[137]

[131] *MC Mehta v Union of India* (2017) 14 SCC 494.

[132] Report of the Comptroller and Auditor General of India, Performance Audit of Water Pollution in India, Report No 21 of 2011–12; Karnataka CAG Report (n 126) 41.

[133] World Health Organization, *WHO Air Quality Guidelines for Particulate Matter, Ozone, Nitrogen Dioxide and Sulfur Dioxide: Global Update 2005* (WHO, 2006) 9.

[134] United States Environment Protection Agency, *NAAQS Table*, https://www.epa.gov/criteria-air-pollutants/naaqs-table.

[135] See also Planning Commission of India, *Report of the Steering Committee on the Environment and Forests Sector for the Eleventh Five Year Plan (2007–2012)* (GoI, 2007) 47.

[136] EP Rules, r 3(3B).

[137] See also CAG Report on Rajasthan SPCB (n 126) 44.

Significantly, financial capacity is not necessarily a constraining factor. Annual reports and audit reports of several Boards show that the Boards do not spend the money allocated to them. More specifically, while funds under line items relating to personnel, which form a significant portion of the Boards' budget, are mostly spent, other line items like research projects and pollution control measures remain underspent.[138] For instance, it was reported that in the last two years, the Maharashtra SPCB has not spent 80 per cent of the funds allocated to it for air, water and noise pollution control measures.[139]

One of the main reasons for the failure of pollution regulations in India is that their goal is poorly defined. The goal is defined in terms of numbers of regulated entities rather than water bodies or airsheds with good quality usable water and breathable air. There is a myopic focus on consent management. Standard setting based on rigorous scientific assessment, and monitoring compliance with consent conditions, which ironically validates the consent granting process, are not a priority.

C. Issues with Enforcement

Despite an array of enforcement mechanisms to choose from, the implementation of pollution regulation in India is far from successful. A review of environmental cases before the higher judiciary reveals an abject failure of the regulatory agencies in exercising their own enforcement powers.[140]

Evidently the enforcement mechanisms are either inadequate or the Boards are reluctant to employ them often enough. According to the National Crime Records Bureau (NCRB), in 2016, nine cases were sent for trial under the Water Act and 26 under the Air Act. Further, while six cases under the Water Act were decided (three convictions and three acquittals), under the Air Act, only a single case was adjudicated, which resulted in an acquittal.[141] Even assuming under-reporting of cases and some methodological errors in data collection by the NCRB, these numbers indicate that criminal prosecution is not a chosen mechanism for Boards. This is also reflected in the data available from SPCBs. For instance, no cases were filed by the Gujarat SPCB in 2013–14[142] and the Odisha SPCB in 2015–16,[143] and in 2013 the Chhattisgarh Environment Conservation Board filed only nine cases.[144]

The reason is perhaps the resource-intensive nature of a criminal prosecution. A case goes through several appellate/revisional forums and each forum often takes a long time to conclude proceedings.[145] During the pendency of the case, unless an

[138] See for example, Performance Audit Assam SPCB (n 127) 6–7.

[139] Badri Chatterjee, 'Maharashtra Pollution Board High on Funds, Low on Staff, Equipment' *Hindustan Times* (27 June 2017).

[140] See, for example, *Ulhasnagar Municipal Corporation v Vanashakti Public Trust and Others* MANU/SCOR/42930/2017; *Indian Council for Enviro-Legal Action v Union of India* (1996) 5 SCC 281.

[141] National Crimes Records Bureau, *Crime in India 2016: Statistics* (NCRB, 2017) 480.

[142] Gujarat SPCB Annual Report 2014–2015.

[143] Odisha SPCB Annual Report 2015–2016.

[144] Chhattisgarh Environment Conservation Board, Administrative Report 2013–2014.

[145] See, for example, *Vikash Bansal v Delhi Pollution Control Committee*, Criminal Appeal No 112/17, Judgment dated 21 November 2017 (Tiz Hazari courts). See also *Uttar Pradesh Pollution Control Board v Mohan Meakins Ltd* (2000) 3 SCC 745.

injunction is specifically granted restraining the offending unit from continuing its operations, the unit may well continue to pollute. This long drawn-out legal battle is a strain on the SPCBs' limited resources, is certainly a disincentive for private citizens to initiate action and is hardly a cause for concern for the polluter, who is at minimal risk of conviction; therefore, it is not a very effective or timely way of enforcing environmental standards.[146]

The power to issue directions is broadly worded and can be invoked by the Board in a large variety of situations. But before it can issue such directions, the SPCB has to mandatorily issue a show cause notice to the establishment and give the owner time to respond. This is particularly important in cases of closure directions or directions to stop the water or power supply, which may have other unintended adverse consequences, such as on the labour force.[147] Although this mechanism is preferred over the initiation of criminal prosecution, the period of notice and reply often extends indefinitely, frequently involving several notices and not necessarily ending in any action by the Boards against the defaulting entity. During that time, the pollution may well continue, and the entity is not required to remedy the situation or compensate those who may have been affected due to its negligent action. The fear of criminal prosecution is clearly not an effective deterrent.

Certain Boards prefer the forfeiture of bank guarantees or performance security as an enforcement mechanism, and it is certainly appealing as it does not require a protracted legal proceeding and collateral damage is minimal. However, the mechanism is meant to be compensatory and not punitive, and this gives rise to the following concern: the amount of bank guarantee sought and forfeited has to sufficiently compensate for the environmental damage caused. Assessing the damage caused, the necessary remedial action and then initiating such action is a complicated exercise requiring expertise and resources, and an ex ante calculation of the monetary amount, without an option for future adjustment, may not be adequate. Unless the amount is sufficiently high to deter future violations or there is a real fear of strict punitive action in the case of repeated defaults, the bank guarantee mechanism may turn into a 'pollute and pay' system.

At the same time, it is important to consider the existing design and institutional capacity of SPCBs. Closure of an industrial plant or imprisonment for an environmental offence are perhaps the most stringent actions that can be prescribed, but the likelihood of either happening is very low because the Boards do not have the capacity to, for instance, make airtight prosecution cases which increase the probability of a criminal prosecution. Neither do they have the staff strength that can routinely monitor regulated entities and take timely action against the defaulters.

Increasing the SPCBs' enforcement powers will be to no avail if their capacity and competence to exercise these powers is not enhanced. If the law is amended allowing SPCBs to impose monetary fines on polluting units, the SPCBs must have adequate

[146] See also Shibani Ghosh, 'When the Court Convicted a Person for Polluting the Environment' *The Wire* (3 January 2018).

[147] See, for example, PTI, 'Labourers Went without Pay during Construction Ban: Delhi Govt' *Indian Express* (25 November 2017).

trained personnel to conduct proper inspections, assess environmental damage and necessary remedial actions, and then calculate the appropriate fine. Additional enforcement powers, such as those to impose monetary fines, will only increase the extent of their discretion, and mechanisms ensuring transparency and accountability will be essential in order to limit abuse.

D. Transparency, Public Participation and Accountability

Pollution regulations potentially impact – directly or indirectly – the lives of a majority of the Indian population. In such a scenario, transparency in the functioning of the regulatory actors, access to information about their actions, decisions, policies and processes, and the opportunity to participate in some of the decision making processes and hold erring regulators to account is critical.

As discussed above, operating without a consent or in violation of consent conditions is a criminal offence and could give rise to civil liability. The grant of a consent is also appealable before the NGT. Therefore, whether the consent has been granted and on what grounds are important facts which could have serious legal consequences. Information contained in consents is relevant while assessing the environmental impact of a regulated entity and, if necessary, to challenge its operation, and violations committed by it, in an appropriate forum.

The Boards clearly fall within the definition of 'public authority' under the Right to Information Act, 2005,[148] and are therefore under a statutory obligation to either *suo moto* disclose certain categories of information such as minutes of Board meetings, details of persons who have been granted consents by it and copies of the consent orders. The official websites of most SPCBs do not contain all this information, and although information when sought under the Right to Information Act is supposed to be supplied within 30–35 days, this is often not the case, and the appellate process is time-consuming.

The Water Act and the Air Act require the maintenance of a register by the SPCBs, recording the particulars of persons to whom the consent has been granted, the standards of emission laid down in the consent and other information, and making it available to the public for inspection.[149] However, performance audits conducted by the CAG of SPCBs over the years reveal that registers containing consent information are not maintained in accordance with the law.[150]

The application process and the conditions for the granting of consent require mandatory disclosure of certain categories of environmental impact information. Compliance with these consent conditions has to be disclosed in an annual

[148] RTI Act, s 2(h).

[149] Water Act, s 25(6); Air Act, s 51.

[150] For example, CAG Environment Audit Reports on Air Pollution, http://iced.cag.gov.in/wp-content/uploads/2013/02/ARs-on-Air-pollution.pdf; Audit Report (Civil and Commercial) for the year ended 31 March 2007 for Jharkhand; Report of the Comptroller and Auditor General of India on General and Social (non-PSUs) sectors for the year ended 31 March 2014, Government of Madhya Pradesh.

environmental statement to the concerned SPCB. The proportion of entities that submit annual environmental statements and what action SPCBs take based on the information submitted (or against non-submission) is unclear from publicly available information, and a summary review of the websites of some of the bigger SPCBs reveals that these annual statements are not accessible on their websites.

In terms of public participation in decision-making, the two Acts have very limited opportunities.[151] The consent-granting process, as well as the standard-setting process,[152] does not have a mandatory public consultation phase, unlike the environmental clearance process under the EIA Notification 2006. This is indeed deeply problematic as people have virtually no say in decisions, such as the siting of industrial plants or the renewal of consents of defaulting units in close proximity, which affect their lives and livelihoods.

Despite extensive powers and a broad mandate, Boards across India are underperforming. And while they undoubtedly suffer from a capacity crunch and there are internal (such as a lack of functional and financial autonomy) and external factors (such as overflowing dockets and protracted proceedings in courts) that influence their functioning, there are instances when the Boards and particular officials need to be held accountable for dereliction of duty, gross misconduct or even the abetment of crimes. In the *Bicchri* case, the Supreme Court suggested that:

> The heads of several units and agencies should be made personally accountable for any lapses and/or negligence on the part of their units and agencies. The idea of an environmental audit by specialist bodies created on a permanent basis with power to inspect, check and take necessary action not only against erring industries but also against erring officers may be considered.[153]

The High Court of Allahabad, faced with Uttar Pradesh SPCB officials colluding with brick kiln owners to illegally grant consents, emphasised the SPCB's role in protecting the environment and suggested that the Board's functioning should be screened by the Vigilance Department and other surveillance agencies.[154]

Currently there is no mechanism in the Water Act or the Air Act to hold errant officials responsible for their actions or inactions. No legal proceedings can lie against an official in respect of anything done in good faith or intended to be done in pursuance of the Acts or Rules framed under them.[155] While there is no statutory mechanism, the courts do have the power to hold them accountable – through judicially reviewing their decisions[156] and/or imposing costs on government agencies for their illegal

[151] CM Abraham and Armin Rosencranz, 'An Evaluation of Pollution Control Legislation in India' (1986) 11 *Columbia Journal of Environmental Law* 101.

[152] See also Shripad Dharmadhikary, 'Setting Environmental Standards Comparing Processes in Thermal Power Plants in India, US, and EU' (2017) LII(19) *Economic and Political Weekly* 93.

[153] *Indian Council for Enviro-Legal Action v Union of India* (n 109).

[154] *Shiv Shanker Yadav and Others v State of UP* MANU/UP/2769/2013.

[155] Water Act, s 59; Air Act, s 42.

[156] The Supreme Court of India in *Lafarge Umiam Mining Pvt Ltd v Union of India and Others* (2011) 7 SCC 338 summarised the grounds for review in environmental cases as follows: 'In the circumstances, barring exceptions, decisions relating to utilization of natural resources have to be tested on the anvil of the well-recognized principles of judicial review. Have all the relevant factors been taken into account? Have any extraneous factors influenced the decision? Is the decision strictly in accordance with the legislative

actions. The Supreme Court imposed costs of Rs 2 lakhs on the Environment Ministry for not finalising emission standards for two industries that had been proposed by the CPCB in 2014.[157]

The lackadaisical attitude of government officials in discharging their duties in not an uncommon occurrence in India, and therefore underperformance is not unique to the Boards. However, their neglect, inaction or condonation of illegal acts could lead to grave, and often irreversible, impacts on the environment and people's lives. Their accountability is necessary as the impunity they enjoy now contributes considerably to the failure of pollution regulation.

CONCLUSION

As a significant part of the Indian population suffers some form of pollution, and their quality of life is seriously threatened, India needs to urgently rethink its pollution regulation regime. The need for this reform has been expressed on several occasions by the public and the judiciary. In the recent past, several protests have taken place highlighting instances of widespread pollution and complete regulatory failure – for instance, against Vedanta's copper smelter plant in Thoothukudi, against Hindustan Unilever for mercury poisoning in Kodaikanal and against the spraying of endosulfan by the Plantation Corporation of Kerala. The judiciary in several cases has been dismayed by persistent regulatory inaction in tackling pollution. Even the government, as well as the committees constituted by it, has acknowledged the limitations faced in enforcing pollution norms.[158] Despite a clear demand for reform, comprehensive pollution regulation reform has not been undertaken.

Given how dysfunctional the regulatory system is, it is tempting to suggest a complete overhaul, repealing or amending the decades-old laws and setting up new institutions with structures and powers that respond to the nature and scale of the problem. Alternatively, it is also reasonable to consider the granting of additional powers to regulators so that they can perform their statutory tasks more effectively and achieve better environmental outcomes. But both of these sets of options are fairly radical. They require, at the very least, parliamentary action, and would also entail dismantling institutions with thousands of employees across several offices that have been functioning for decades, and which regulate a significant proportion of industries and other potentially polluting operations in the country.

policy underlying the law (if any) that governs the field? Is the decision consistent with the principles of sustainable development in the sense that has the decision-maker taken into account the said principle and, on the basis of relevant considerations, arrived at a balanced decision?'

[157] *MC Mehta v Union of India* 2017 SCC OnLine SC 1378. See also *Shiv Shanker Yadav v State of UP* MANU/UP/2769/2013; *Manoj Misra v Delhi Development Authority* 2016 SCC OnLine NGT 114.

[158] See, for example, MoEF, 'Discussion Paper: Workshop on Reforms in Environmental Governance: With Special Reference to Establishment of National Environment Assessment and Monitoring Authority (NEAMA)' (2010); Report High Level Committee to review various Acts administered Ministry of Environment, Forest and Climate Change (2014).

In any case, India has not experienced much success in designing effective and successful environmental regulators in the past. The Coastal Zone Management Authorities under the Coastal Regulation Zone (CRZ) Notifications of 1991 and 2011, as well as the Biodiversity Boards and Biodiversity Management Committees constituted under the Biological Diversity Act 2002, at the central, state and local levels are similarly struggling to meet their statutory mandate.[159] Bodies such as the Environment Pollution Control Authority (constituted to prevent and control environmental pollution in the NCR) and the Dahanu Taluka Environment Protection Authority (constituted to protect the ecologically fragile Dahanu Taluka) have had some success. But these are difficult to replicate as, first, their geographical and subject-matter mandate is much narrower than the other regulators, and, second, the judiciary's initial and/or continued engagement with issues that these bodies deal with is likely to have had a positive impact. However, one important commonality between these two bodies that has contributed to their effective functioning and could be an important learning is the active participation of technical experts.[160]

Therefore, proposals to set up new institutions and replace the poorly functioning Boards have to be carefully considered, lest we worsen the existing situation rather than ameliorate it. Meanwhile, it might be advisable considering some incremental changes that could lead to significant gains.

Filling up vacancies in Boards and appointing people with proper qualifications to the job is neither a politically sensitive issue nor a huge financial burden on the state exchequer. Nothing but bureaucratic and political disinterest, or even lethargy, explains delays in appointments. Similarly, enhancing the technical expertise and capacity of the Boards will go a long way towards improving the quality of standard setting, pollution control measures, the assessment of environmental impacts and remediation measures.

While the regulator's tool chest could accommodate more instruments, the problem is largely with the regulator and its capacity to select the appropriate tool and deploy it effectively. The so-called 'low-hanging fruits' of deliberate actions that strengthen the regulatory actors will fortify the regulatory structure from within and counter arguments to dismantle them.

[159] Manju Menon et al, *CZMAs and Coastal Environments: Two Decades of Regulating Land Use Change on India's Coastline* (CPR-Namati Environmental Justice Program, 2015); Kanchi Kohli and Shalini Bhutani, 'Biodiversity Management Committees: Lost in Numbers' (2014) XLIX(16) *Economic and Political Weekly* 18.

[160] Geetanjoy Sahu and Armin Rosencranz, 'Court-Appointed Monitoring Committees: The Case of the Dahanu Taluka Environment Protection Authority' (2009) 5(2) *Law Environment and Development Journal* 185.

11

Food

VIKRAMADITYA S KHANNA*

INTRODUCTION

FOOD REGULATION COVERS a vast area of activity of great importance to both health and safety. In light of this, it is not surprising that India has a series of enactments impacting the regulation of food. This chapter provides an overview of food regulation in India and discusses its implementation through key administrative and regulatory agencies. This in turn adds further information and insights on the operation of administrative and regulatory agencies in India.

This chapter begins in section I by cataloguing the various laws that specifically address food regulation in India, and enumerating the agencies and regulators involved in implementing and overseeing these laws. Although there are multiple regulators, this chapter focuses most of its attention on the Food Safety and Standards Authority of India (FSSAI). The FSSAI has been mired in controversy since its inception nearly a decade ago and is a particularly fascinating regulatory agency to study.[1]

Section II describes the FSSAI's structure and functioning, and how it is generally perceived in India. Overall, it appears that the FSSAI is thought to be one of the most poorly functioning regulators. However, in the last few years, there has been a marked increase in activity at the FSSAI – for both good and bad, it appears. The regulator has become more active in policing certain kinds of food safety issues (eg, Maggi Noodles), although not in a uniform or consistent manner (eg, policing milk adulteration).[2] Further, the regulator has demonstrated a greater

* My thanks to Devesh Kapur and Madhav Khosla for their helpful comments and discussion, and to Julie Gulledge and Ajitesh Kir for their excellent research assistance.

[1] See section III below discussing and critiquing the operation of the FSSAI. Food law is an area of active research in the US; see eg, Stephen Ansolabehere and Jacob Gersen, 'Eating Law', Draft 2018 (on file with the author); Emily M Broad Leib and Baylen J Linnekin, 'Food Law & Policy: An Essential Part of Today's Legal Academy' (2018), www.ssrn.com/abstract=3139958; Lisa Heinzerling, *Food Law: Cases and Materials* (CreateSpace Independent Publishing Platform, 2017); Michael T Roberts, *Food Law in the United States* (Cambridge University Press, 2015).

[2] See *M/s Nestle India Ltd v FSSAI and Others* (2015) 6 AIR Bom R 74 (judgment by the Bombay High Court, 13 August 2015) (involving Maggi Noodles); and *Swamy Achyutanand Tirth and Others v UOI and Others* (2016) 9 SCC 699 (discussing milk adulteration public interest litigation in India).

willingness to 'aim high' in terms of setting its goals by reference to the US Food and Drug Administration and to the internationally recognized *Codex Alimentarius* standards.[3] However, even this has generated debate both because these standards might be difficult to implement in India at the moment and because the FSSAI has explicitly stated that it would like to engage private sector entities (eg, multinational food corporations) in a collaborative model for food safety in order to achieve these standards.[4] The latter approach has generated significant commentary and concerns about potential conflicts of interest and undue influence.[5]

Section III examines some key critiques of the FSSAI by the judiciary and the Comptroller and Auditor General of India (CAG). Indeed, the beleaguered regulator has been subject to a searching inquiry by the CAG, which recently issued a scathing report on the FSSAI.[6] The CAG report suggests a very poorly functioning regulator with little internal control and minimal safety testing, amongst other concerns. Indeed, the CAG report highlights concerns that one sees with many regulators in India (albeit to different degrees) – insufficient expertise and regulatory capacity, poor interagency coordination, low salience and poor citizen knowledge of the issues, accountability concerns, and independence issues and conflicts of interest.[7] Moreover, recent reports about corruption within the FSSAI and associated entities promise to generate even more controversy.[8]

Section IV explores some potential reasons for the poor functioning of the FSSAI, whether recent reforms may provide some benefits, and what that might tell us about regulatory agencies in India. In particular, this section examines the impact on food regulation of weak state capacity and the scale of the food sector in India, and how these two factors interact to provide challenges to food regulation in India. This section also discusses some parallel issues of food regulation in China as a point of comparison. Further, it explores whether the greater reliance on industry expertise and increased use of global food standards as ways to benchmark regulatory performance might prove useful in the Indian food regulation environment.

[3] See 'FSSAI – Transforming the Food Safety and Nutrition Landscape in India 2016–2017', www.fssai.gov.in/home/FSSAI_Reports.html. For more discussion on the *Codex Alimentarius*, see www.fao.org/fao-who-codexalimentarius/en.

[4] See 'FSSAI' (n 3); Apurva Vishwanath, 'Maggi Case Still on, But FSSAI Ties up with Nestle to Improve Own Standards' *The Print* (14 September 2017), www.theprint.in/report/maggi-case-still-on-but-fssai-ties-up-with-nestle-to-improve-own-standards/10014.

[5] See Vishwanath (n 4); Arnab Dutta, 'Nestle and FSSAI Mend Fences Two Years after Maggi Ban' *Business Standard* (7 September 2017), www.business-standard.com/article/companies/nestle-and-fssai-mend-fences-two-years-after-maggi-ban-117090601353_1.html; Sumi Sukanya Dutta, 'Conflict of Interest Slur on India's Top Food Safety Regulator FSSAI' *New Indian Express* (20 January 2018), www.newindianexpress.com/nation/2018/jan/20/conflict-of-...1of23/30/18.

[6] See *Report of the Comptroller and Auditor General of India on Performance Audit of Implementation of Food Safety and Standards Act 2006*, Report No 37 of 2017, www.cag.gov.in/content/report-no37-2017-performance-audit-implementation-food-safety-and-standards-act-2006-union.

[7] See, eg, the chapters by Umakanth Varottil and Shibani Ghosh in this volume.

[8] See Press Trust of India, '11 Food & Pharma Organisations Demand a CBI Inquiry against FSSAI' *NDTV* (13 July 2017), www.food.ndtv.com/food-drinks/11-food-pharma-organisations-demand-a-cbi-inquiry-against-fssai-1225627 (describing the FSSAI as a 'den of corruption'); Aditi Tandon, '3 Ex-directors Allege Corruption in Apex Food Body, Write to Govt' *The Tribune* (7 June 2015), www.tribuneindia.com/news/nation/3-ex-directors-allege-corruption-in-apex-food-body-write-to-govt/90551.html.

I. AN OVERVIEW OF FOOD REGULATION IN INDIA

Food regulation can encompass a variety of activities ranging from setting food safety standards, developing nutritional guidelines, mandating disclosure of ingredients and nutritional content, devising certification standards (eg, what is considered 'organic'),[9] the testing of products, the imposition of sanctions (eg, penalties, 'recalls'), potentially allowing for private civil suits, and information dissemination to the general public about food safety, nutrition and perhaps general wellness. Given the plethora of things that might fall within the ambit of 'food regulation', it is not surprising that this area of law is not contained in one statute – rather, food is regulated through multiple statutes and regulatory bodies in India. Section I.A discusses the primary statute regulating food safety and standards – the Food Safety and Standards Act, 2006. Section I.B briefly discusses a few other areas of food regulation. Finally, section I.C notes the role of the courts in food regulation.

A. The Food Safety and Standards Act, 2006

The primary statute addressing food safety in India is the Food Safety and Standards Act, 2006 (hereinafter the 2006 Act), which consolidated a number of pre-existing laws and orders. These included the Prevention of Food Adulteration Act, 1954, the Fruit Products Order 1955, the Meat Food Products Order 1973, the Vegetable Oil Products (Control) Order 1947, the Edible Oils Packaging (Regulation) Order 1998, the Solvent Extracted Oil, De-oiled Meal and Edible Flour (Control) Order 1967, the Milk and Milk Products Order 1992, and orders under the Essential Commodities Act, 1955. These earlier laws and orders primarily attempted to police food adulteration and to regulate the process of producing, labelling and marketing certain food products.

The 2006 Act also created a new regulator – the FSSAI – to regulate the manufacture, storage, distribution, sale and import of food, to ensure the availability of safe and wholesome food for humans, and to lay down science-based standards for articles of food. The FSSAI comes under the Ministry of Health and Family Welfare, and has been granted powers to:

- frame regulations on food safety standards;
- provide scientific advice and technical support to the Government of India;
- contribute to the development of international technical food standards;
- delineate guidelines for the accreditation of laboratories for food testing;
- collect data on food consumption, contamination and food risks; and
- disseminate information on food safety and nutrition in India.[10]

[9] This is within the purview of the Agricultural and Processed Food Products Export Development Authority under the Union Ministry of Commerce and Industry.

[10] See FSSAI, 'About Us', www.fssai.gov.in/home/about-us/introduction.html; 'FSSAI' (n 3); Sounak Mitra, 'The Evolution of FSSAI' *LiveMint* (18 October 2017), www.livemint.com/Industry/NbljKgRzQhChgGZhtFPB0L/The-evolution-of-FSSAI.html.

There are 23 members of the FSSAI (one chair and 22 members) and it operates through seven offices in India (with headquarters in New Delhi).[11] The FSSAI not only puts forward standards on food safety, but also tests products, engages in consumer outreach and provides licences to food business operators to engage in the food business in India.[12]

In addition, the FSSAI is tasked with working with state-level food regulators to monitor and verify the requirements of the 2006 Act. It appoints state-level Food Safety Commissioners, who then appoint local Food Safety Officers, who have both investigatory and prosecutorial powers under the 2006 Act. Penalties under the 2006 Act range from regulatory to criminal and are supplemented by criminal provisions related to food adulteration under the Indian Penal Code 1860 (IPC).[13] Thus, although the FSSAI's mandate does not cover all kinds of food issues, it has a fairly broad jurisdiction.[14] I will discuss the structure and operations of the FSSAI in greater depth in section III below; however, before proceeding to that, I will discuss other legislation addressing food regulation in India and the role of the judiciary in order to round out the discussion.

B. Other Legislation Regulating Food in India

Food regulation in India spans beyond the 2006 Act and the FSSAI. For example: (i) the Ministry of Agriculture via the Department of Animal Husbandry, Dairying and Fisheries, and the Department of Agriculture and Cooperation have the responsibility for implementing the Livestock Importation Act, 1898 and the Plant Quarantine (Regulation of Import into India) Order 2013; (ii) the Ministry of Commerce and Industry via the Directorate General of Foreign Trade usually addresses food labelling concerns; and (iii) the Ministry of Consumer Affairs, Food and Public Distribution oversees the Legal Metrology Act, 2009 and its accompanying rules. Most of this regulation deals with a variety of issues beyond food safety, such as packaging, use of consistent weights and measures, livestock importation, plant importation and labelling.

[11] See FSSAI (n 10).

[12] See ibid.

[13] The Law Commission of India has recommended changes to the law to make the IPC and the 2006 Act more consistent. See *Law Commission of India Report No 264 – The Criminal Law (Amendment) Bill, 2017 (Provisions Dealing with Food Adulteration)*, January 2017, www.lawcommissionofindia.nic.in/reports/Report264.pdf (hereinafter LCI No 264).

[14] For example, the FSSAI does not directly regulate farmers or their use of pesticides, but rather checks for the maximum permissible residual levels in the final product. See E Kumar Sharma, 'How Effective is Pesticide Regulation in India?' *Business Today* (30 July 2013), www.businesstoday.in/current/policy/pesticide-regulation-in-india/story/197345.html. The key agencies regulating pesticides are the Central Insecticides Board and Registration Committee under the Ministry of Agriculture, and the Agricultural and Processed Food Products Export Development Authority under the Ministry of Commerce and Industry. Further, until very recently, the FSSAI had little role in regulating alcohol (eg, regulating its manufacture and sale was the responsibility of the states as per India's Constitution), but in April 2018, the FSSAI began regulating alcohol standards, labelling and related matters. See Item 8, List II of the 7th Schedule of the Constitution of India; Food Product and Safety Standards (Alcoholic Beverages Standards) Regulations 2018, www.fssai.gov.in/home/fss-legislation/fss-regulations.html.

An important area of regulation that is not yet subject to much oversight by the FSSAI is the regulation of genetically modified organisms (GMOs).[15] Regulation here covers two key areas – cultivation of GMO crops in India and then the use (or import) of GMOs in food products in India.

Cultivation of GMO crops is governed by the Rules for Manufacture, Use, Import, Export and Storage of Hazardous Micro Organisms/Genetically Engineered Organisms or Cells 1989 issued under the Environment Protection Act, 1986 (addressing research and application of GMOs in India). These rules create no less than four committees that have oversight (and hence vetoes) over the process.[16] This, and a fairly active anti-GMO lobby, has led to only one GMO being approved for cultivation in India thus far: Bt Cotton.[17] In addition, there are international conventions governing this area,[18] as well as domestic legislation – unrelated to food – that impacts the process. For example, individuals relied on India's Right to Information Act, 2005 (RTIA) to compel the government to provide information on the field tests for Bt Brinjal (eggplant). These tests suggested that strict standards were not maintained in testing Bt Brinjal, which then contributed to the commercial release of Bt Brinjal being delayed indefinitely.[19]

The use or import of GMOs in food products in India is overseen by at least three agencies. This can be seen in the 'Doritos Cool Ranch' saga, where some packages of these chips were allegedly found to have GMO corn in them (which is not permitted for importation into India), but the authorities simply held the items at the port of entry until the importer 'declared' that the products had no GMO corn in them.[20] After keeping some small samples, the authorities released the chips to the importer with no further inquiry, follow up or information about what happened thereafter.[21] This example underscores the standard concerns with poor interagency coordination and lack of accountability.[22]

One final topical and salient area of regulation is food distribution, which relates in part to storage practices and food distribution to the poor, and in part to whether and when foreign investment will be allowed in the food sector. The former issue is

[15] The FSSAI does have the power to issue regulations on GMOs (under s 22 of the 2006 Act), but has not yet done so and, given its manpower and other constraints, seems unlikely to do so in the near future.

[16] These four committees are: (i) the Genetic Engineering Approval Committee (GEAC), which is the apex body under the Ministry of Environment and Forests; (ii) the Institutional Biosafety Committee; (iii) the Review Committee on Genetic Manipulation; and (iv) the State Biotechnology Coordination Committee. See Sachin Verma, 'The Indian Bt Brinjal Controversy: Genetically Modified Food, Legal and Regulatory Framework' (Rajiv Gandhi School of Intellectual Property Law, IIT Kharagpur, 2010).

[17] The 'Bt' stands for Bacillus thuringiensis, a common soil bacteria used in producing Bt Cotton.

[18] See Convention on Biological Diversity, 1992 and the Cartagena Protocol on Biodiversity for GMOs, 2003. The precautionary principle is a part of Indian law (the Biological Diversity Act, 2002); see *Vellore Citizens Welfare Forum v Union of India* (1996) 5 SCC 647.

[19] See *Ms Divya Raghunandan v Department of Biotechnology*, Central Information Commission, Adjunct to Appeal No CIC/WB/A/2006/00548 dated 7 May 2007 and Appeal No CIC/WB/A/2009/000668 dated 16 June 2009 (noting that the government could not withhold these field tests under the RTIA on commercial confidence or trade secret grounds). See also Verma (n 16).

[20] See VS Viswambharan, '"Eat, Pray, Law": Implications of the Absence of a Coherent Regulatory Regime and the Problem of Genetically Modified Food in India' (2013) 2 *Nirma University Law Journal* 9.

[21] ibid.

[22] See, eg, the chapters by Varottil and Ghosh in this volume.

often addressed in policies to distribute food to the public (especially those in great need) through various public distribution schemes.[23] The foreign investment issue has garnered a great deal of attention because large foreign and domestic retailers are keen to enter India, which has a relatively low level of supermarket (or 'big box')-type penetration.[24] Indeed, Amazon's successful bid to enter the Indian food retail space has been closely followed by the media.[25] I do not discuss either of these areas because the FSSAI has little role to play in them, but I mention them here as examples of the breadth of food regulation in India.

C. The Role of the Judiciary

The Indian courts have played an integral role in food regulation through their decisions and the directions they, at times, give to the government. Below are two rather salient examples.

Maggi Noodles (manufactured by Nestlé) is one of India's favourite foods and in 2015 reports emerged that some Maggi Noodles appeared to have higher than acceptable levels of lead and monosodium glutamate in them.[26] In January 2015, a Food Inspector in Barabanki, UP sent a packet of Maggi Noodles to the State Food Laboratory in Gorakhpur, which found monosodium glutamate in the product.[27] Once the FSSAI and Nestlé became aware of this, Nestlé requested the sample to be sent to a Referral Laboratory in Kolkata (the type of laboratory which tests a product when there is a dispute about the accuracy of the State Food Laboratory's analysis).[28] The Kolkata Referral Laboratory found that the amount of lead in the packet was about five times the permitted content.[29] This result led to a series of further tests, where it was reported to the FSSAI that a number of samples had greater than permitted levels of lead.[30] The FSSAI met with Nestlé representatives on 6 June 2015 and a ban on Maggi Noodles was issued.[31]

Nestlé then brought a suit in the Bombay High Court seeking to overturn the ban. The Court decided in Nestlé's favour because: (i) the regulator did not give a proper

[23] For a helpful discussion of food distribution schemes in India, see Suman Chakrabarti, Avinash Kishore and Devesh Roy, 'Entitlement Fetching or Snatching?: Effects of Arbitrage on India's Public Distribution Scheme' (2016) International Food Policy Research Institute Discussion Paper No 01588, www.ifpri.org/publication/entitlement-fetching-or-snatching-effects-arbitrage-indias-public-distribution-system.

[24] See Subhayan Chakraborty and Karan Choudhary, 'Amazon Gets Nod for $500-Million FDI in Food Business' *Business Standard* (11 July 2017), www.business-standard.com/article/companies/amazon-gets-govt-nod-for-500-million-fdi-in-food-business-117071000994_1.html. See also Amy J Cohen, 'Supermarkets in India: Struggles over the Organization of Agricultural Markets and Food Supply Chains' (2013) 68 *University of Miami Law Review* 19.

[25] See Chakraborthy and Choudhary (n 24).

[26] See Sapna Agrawal and Sounak Mitra, 'Maggi Unsafe, Says Food Safety Regulator, Nestle Pulls Noodles from Stores' *Live Mint* (6 June 2015), www.livemint.com/Companies/VjP3K58x9WHHpCmj2lTJGJ/Maggi-safe-to-consume-says-Nestle-CEO.html.

[27] ibid.

[28] ibid.

[29] ibid.

[30] ibid.

[31] ibid.

opportunity to Nestlé to present its case and decided in an arbitrary manner; (ii) a number of the laboratories were not accredited; (iii) there was some concern that the laboratories did not follow testing procedures and protocols; (iv) the regulator banned nine variants of Maggi when only three were tested; (v) concerns about monosodium glutamate cannot justify a prohibition; and (vi) Nestlé already recalled the product the day before the ban.[32] The Court then quashed the ban and directed Nestlé to send samples of each batch of Maggi in its possession to accredited food laboratories and have them tested, and if they were within the acceptable limits, manufacturing of the noodles could commence.[33] By November 2015, Nestlé had met these conditions and started reselling Maggi Noodles.[34] Although Maggi sales picked up after the nearly five-month hiatus, they have not reached their pre-ban levels.[35] Moreover, the Court's decision has been appealed to the Supreme Court and a decision is awaited.

In another example, the Delhi High Court heard a public interest litigation in 2010 requesting the Court to issue directions to ban the sale of junk food in schools.[36] The Court agreed and directed the government and the FSSAI to take steps to establish such a ban.[37] The FSSAI produced guidelines in 2014 for banning the sale of certain kinds of junk food within 500 metres of a school (with which the Court seemed comfortable), but these were heavily objected to by the All India Food Processors' Association.[38] Before implementing these guidelines, the FSSAI formed an expert committee, which then proposed taxing junk food and banning advertisements for junk food during children's television shows.[39] This is the current proposal before the FSSAI, which, as of the time of writing, has not been implemented.

The panoply of laws described above and the fairly active role of the judiciary underscore not only the importance of food regulation in India, but also its breadth. In light of this, I will narrow the focus to the key regulator in this space – the FSSAI – and discuss its operation, performance and potential for improvement in the next few sections.

II. THE FOOD SAFETY AND STANDARDS AUTHORITY OF INDIA

The FSSAI is a relatively new regulatory body created in 2008 as part of the 2006 Act. Its mandate is quite broad and includes the setting of standards for food safety, the licensing of food business operators (FBOs) in India, enforcing the requirements of

[32] See *M/s Nestle India Ltd* (n 2).

[33] ibid.

[34] See Agrawal and Mitra (n 26).

[35] ibid.

[36] See Geeta Anand, 'One Man's Stand against Junk Food as Diabetes Climbs across India' *New York Times* (26 December 2017), www.nytimes.com/2017/12/26/health/india-diabetes-junk-food.html, accessed June 2018. For more details on the petition, see www.udayfoundationindia.org/petition-in-delhi-high-court-to-ban-junk-food-and-carbonated-drinks-in-schools.

[37] See Anand (n 36).

[38] ibid.

[39] ibid.

the law, and consumer education and outreach, amongst other things. It is an autonomous body headed by a chairman and a chief executive officer, and its budget is fairly secure given that it is empowered to keep the money it collects as fines and licence fees.[40]

The overall structure of the FSSAI is intriguing because it has a mandate to develop food safety standards and to monitor and test for them. Both require substantial technical expertise, but there is mounting evidence that the FSSAI does not possess these and that even where it is expected to delegate tasks to state regulators, those regulators are often under-staffed and poorly qualified.[41]

In describing the FSSAI and its operations, it is noteworthy that there were significant changes to its operations around 2015. Before 2015, the FSSAI issued many 'advisories' (not regulations) to govern its food safety processes. The Bombay High Court struck down this approach in 2015, thereby precipitating a new modus operandi.[42] Thus, I begin with the pre-2015 food safety processes, then move on to the post-2015 processes, and round out the discussion by examining some of the other matters that the FSSAI regulates (eg, licences for FBOs).

A. Pre-2015 FSSAI Processes

Before 2015, the FSSAI put food products basically into three categories: 'standardized', 'non-standardized', and 'traditional'.[43] Standardised products are those for which there is already a food safety standard in place and thus there is no need to seek product approval from the FSSAI (although a first-time manufacturer or importer would need a licence to be an FBO in India – more on that in section II.C).[44] In 2015, there were approximately 380 foods subject to standards.[45] Non-standardised products are ones that are not subject to existing food safety standards and they would require product approval by the FSSAI. In 2015, the FSSAI was working to standardise around 12,000 food items in harmonisation with the *Codex Alimentarius* – a set of highly respected and globally recognised standards, codes of practice and other recommendations on food and food safety maintained by the *Codex Alimentarius* Commission (CAC) (which has at least 186 member countries).[46] This underscores

[40] See FSSAI (n 10). The CAG notes that the FSSAI's current funds are about Rs 100 crore (Rs 1 billion or USD 15.384 million at an exchange rate of 1 USD = Rs 65). See *Report of the Comptroller and Auditor General of India* (n 6).

[41] See *Report of the Comptroller and Auditor General of India* (n 6).

[42] ibid.

[43] See Saurabh Arora, 'Food Regulations – What is the Current Scenario in India?' *Food Quality and Safety* (9 September 2015), www.foodqualityandsafety.com/article/food-regulations-what-is-the-current-scenario-in-india-2/; Mitra (n 10).

[44] See 'FSSAI' (n 3); Arora (n 43).

[45] ibid.

[46] ibid. The CAC was established by the Food and Agriculture Organization of the United Nations and was joined by the World Health Organization. For more details, see www.fao.org/fao-who-codexalimentarius/en.

the scale of the task facing the FSSAI. Finally, traditional foods in India do not require product approval. This seems to be because they have been consumed for centuries (presumably safely).[47]

A firm requiring product approval would apply and be subject to a 90-day outer limit for the FSSAI to respond.[48] If the product was referred to a Scientific Panel for further inquiry, then the time limit could be extended.[49] However, because of delays with decisions of the Scientific Panels, the FSSAI developed a system of 'No Objection Certificates' (NOCs) being given to products, allowing them to be on the market for one year while awaiting the Scientific Panels' decisions.[50]

When the NOC procedure was challenged in *Vital Nutraceuticals Private Ltd v Union of India*,[51] the Bombay High Court held that this procedure was not envisaged in the 2006 Act and was beyond the powers of the FSSAI.[52] Moreover, the FSSAI's procedure specifically violated the procedures in sections 92 and 93 of the 2006 Act (which require prior approval of the Ministry, prior publication by notification, and placing the notified regulations before Parliament) and sections 13 and 14 (which require that a decision on whether food is safe be made by a Scientific Panel rather than some other party).[53] The FSSAI appealed this to the Supreme Court and the appeal was dismissed in August 2015. Since then, the product approval process has been scrapped in favour of a system that relies on ongoing food safety standard development and enforcement.

B. Post-2015 FSSAI Processes

The FSSAI now operates on a new paradigm for regulation. The first thing to note is that the FSSAI is now interested not just in food sold in grocery stores and the like, but also in food in restaurants, at temples (eg, *prasadam*), at home, served by the Indian railways and so forth[54] – in other words, all the different venues in which food is provided to the Indian public.[55] Moreover, the FSSAI is adopting a more ongoing standard-setting process (which is common elsewhere too).[56] Of course, to do this, it needs a large number of experts to staff Scientific Review Panels and so forth. Given the regulatory capacity constraints, the FSSAI appears keen to 'borrow' standards

[47] See 'FSSAI' (n 3); Arora (n 43). I say 'presumably safely' because there may be some traditional food products that are not thought to be safe beyond certain amounts (eg, 'bhaang'). Of course, if the traditional food item has been changed from the original recipe, then it may require product approval. Exporting of food from India did not need product approval as it was not to be sold to Indian consumers. See Arora (n 43).

[48] See 'FSSAI' (n 3); Arora (n 43).

[49] ibid.

[50] ibid.

[51] *Vital Nutraceuticals Private Ltd v Union of India*, 2014 SCC OnLine Bom 165.

[52] ibid.

[53] ibid.

[54] See 'FSSAI' (n 3); Mitra (n 10).

[55] ibid.

[56] See 'FSSAI' (n 3).

from international bodies (eg, *Codex Aliementarius*)[57] and other countries (eg, the US Food and Drug Administration (FDA)) until it develops its own.

In addition, the FSSAI appears keen to modernise food safety testing in India with an earmarked Rs 482 crore (~USD 74 million at an exchange rate of USD 1 = Rs 65) for upgrading testing laboratories so that more of them are accredited under the National Accreditation Board for Testing and Calibration Laboratories (NABL), as well as setting up mobile labs in certain states.[58] The FSSAI also wants to encourage more third party auditing of food and food inspections more generally.[59]

Because of its regulatory capacity constraints, the FSSAI has started collaborating more with food providers to develop standards and to train its own officers, as well as engaging in greater dissemination of information to the public.[60] In relation to the former, it appears that the FSSAI considers that food businesses have an interest in food safety too (eg, sales for Domino's pizza would probably drop if customers thought the cheese was poisoned).[61] Further, the FSSAI is also inking deals with food businesses to help street vendors on food hygiene and safety.[62] For example, after the Maggi Noodles saga, the FSSAI announced in September 2017 that Nestlé would set up training locations in India for food safety that the FSSAI would also use and with which it would collaborate.[63] Although the potential conflicts of interest are palpable, it is also clear that producers such as Nestlé have substantial experience with food safety issues that may be of value in India.

More broadly, the FSSAI is keen to encourage food businesses to innovate and bring new food products to the market. Further, the FSSAI is interested in encouraging fortified food to become more easily available in the Indian market and promulgated a new regulation on this in late 2017.[64]

The overall impression conveyed is that the pre-2015 process was high in discretion, generated considerable delays with little clear connection to food safety, and was not governed by the required statutory processes. Following the *Vital Nutraceuticals* case and the arrival of a new Chief Executive Officer at the FSSAI in 2015, the

[57] ibid. The *Codex Alimentarius* refers to the *Codex Alimentarius* Commission, which is a joint intergovernmental body of the Food and Agriculture Organization of the United Nations and the World Health Organization.

[58] See 'FSSAI' (n 3); 'FSSAI Responds to the CAG Audit Report on Performance of FSSAI', *Food Safety Helpline* (23 December 2017), www.foodsafetyhelpline.com/2017/12/fssai-responds-to-the-cag-audit-report-on-performance.

[59] See 'FSSAI' (n 3) and draft regulations available on the FSSAI website – Draft Food Safety and Standards (Food Safety Auditing) Regulations, 2017, www.fssai.gov.in/home/fss-legislation/notifications/draft-notification.html and discussion thereof www.fssai.gov.in/home/safe-food-practices/THIRD-PARTY-AUDITS.html.

[60] See 'FSSAI' (n 3), 'FSSAI Responds' (n 58).

[61] ibid.

[62] See Vishwanath (n 4); Arab Dutta (n 5); Sumi Sukanya Dutta (n 5).

[63] ibid.

[64] See Food Safety and Standards (Fortification of Foods) Regulations 2017, File No 11/03/Reg/Fortification/2014 (pt I); Food Fortification, www.ffrc.fssai.gov.in/ffrc/home; 'India Revises Food Fortification Regulation' *Safeguards Food* (26 June 2017), www.sgs.com/en/news/2017/06/safeguards-09917-india-revises-food-fortification-regulation.

processes seemed to have been (or are being) substantially changed and brought more into line with global practices.

C. Licensing and Other Matters

All FBOs are required to have a licence or registration from the FSSAI in order to be in compliance with the 2006 Act and to sell food products in India. This requirement was operationalised in the Food Safety and Standards (Licensing and Registration of Food Businesses) Regulation 2011 (hereinafter the 2011 Regulations).[65] FBOs with an annual turnover of less than Rs 12 lakhs (ie, approximately USD 18,462 at an exchange rate of USD 1 = Rs 65) need a registration certificate, and those with an annual turnover exceeding this need a licence.[66] There are two kinds of licences – one issued by the Government of India (a 'central' licence) and one issued by any of the state governments (a 'state' licence).[67] Both licences are based on manufacturing capacity and turnover; however, if an FBO is operating in more than one state, then it needs both the state and central licences and if it is an importer (or exporter), then it needs a central licence.[68] An FBO can only obtain a licence to sell food products that have been approved in some sense (pre-2015), are subject to a food standard or are traditional. The licensing requirements have not been overturned by the courts and recently the FSSAI has issued draft regulations for e-commerce FBOs.[69]

Outside of licensing, there were additional rules regulating the importing of food into India that have caused considerable consternation and often resulted in the impounding of items at customs.[70] For example, under the 2011 Regulations, chocolates are to be prepared from milk and cannot contain vegetable fats or oil, and labels need to mention artificial flavours. If this does not happen, then chocolates are not permitted to enter India, which has led to Indian customs impounding chocolates, causing losses to large chocolatiers.[71]

III. CRITIQUES OF THE FSSAI

The FSSAI has, to put it mildly, come in for quite a lot of criticism from a variety of sources. In this section, I discuss the two broadest sets of critiques – one from the judiciary (section III.A) and the other from the CAG (section III.B).

[65] See www.fssai.gov.in/home/fss-legislation/fss-regulations.html.

[66] See 'FSSAI' (n 3); Arora (n 43).

[67] For a useful summary, see FSSAI, 'Frequently Asked Questions on Regulatory Compliance', www.fssai.gov.in/home/compliance/FAQs.html.

[68] See 'FSSAI' (n 3); Arora (n 43).

[69] See *Guidelines for Operations of Direct Selling Food Business Operators*, File No 13(12) 2016/DS Companies/Enf/FSSAI, 16 January 2017. For more discussion of this draft regulation, see www.ifoodlegal.blogspot.com/2017/10/the-food-recall-regulation-of-fssai_24.html.

[70] See *United Distributors Incorporation v Union of India*, 2014 SCC OnLine Del 4184 (appealed to the Division Bench of the Delhi High Court: (2015) 219 DLT 752 (DB)).

[71] ibid.

A. Judicial Oversight

In a telling 2016 decision, *Swamy Achyutanand Tirth v UOI*,[72] the Supreme Court decided a public interest litigation related to milk adulteration against the Government of India and various states. The Court noted that estimates suggest that about 68 per cent of the milk in India is adulterated, with some surveys suggesting adulteration being as high as 88–100 per cent in certain states.[73] Moreover, it appears that milk was being adulterated 'with hazardous substance[s] like urea, detergent, refined oil, caustic soda, etc. which adversely affects the consumers health'.[74] The Court issued a series of directions that essentially amount to instructions to the central and state regulators to take their duties more seriously under the 2006 Act, arrange for appropriate staffing and accreditation of food testing laboratories, develop and implement risk factors for food safety and engage in appropriate monitoring and sampling, devise mechanisms for checking corruption in this sphere, and take steps to inform concerned parties (eg, dairy operators, customers and children) about food safety and to educate them on ways to detect common adulterants via multiple modalities (eg, the internet).[75]

In another recent public interest litigation (*Centre for Public Interest Litigation v Union of India*),[76] the Supreme Court was approached for directions in relation to the sale, advertising, content and harmful effects of soft drinks on health (especially of children). After reviewing the 2006 Act and the accompanying rules, the Court noted that these laws covered the concerns of the petitioners, but that enforcement and implementation were weak.[77] It went on to say that any food product which is 'hazardous or injurious to public health is a potential danger to the fundamental right to life guaranteed under Article 21 of the Constitution of India'.[78] This imposes a clear duty on states to achieve the appropriate levels of protection.[79]

Overall, the Supreme Court's holdings have often taken the form of directing the FSSAI and state food safety regulators to develop processes or work more closely with other arms of the government, and to take steps to inform and educate the public on food safety and hygiene. These are not 'new' requirements, but rather directions to do what the FSSAI was required to do in the first place under the 2006 Act. Moreover, the Court has at times required the FSSAI to clear, or permit, products if there are ways in which the food provider can meet the requirements or cure any defect.[80] This type of oversight of day-to-day affairs suggests concerns with the operation of the FSSAI and various state food safety regulators.

[72] *Swamy Achyutanand Tirth v UOI* (2016) 9 SCC 699.

[73] ibid 703.

[74] ibid 704. Also, one can read more about this case in T Mohan, 'Supreme Court Suggests Life Imprisonment for Adulteration in Milk and Milk Products' *Live Law* (12 November 2014), www.livelaw.in/supreme-court-suggests-life-imprisonment-adulteration-milk-milk-products.

[75] *Swamy Achyutanand Tirth and Others v UOI and Others* (2016) 9 SCC 699, 705–07.

[76] *Centre for Public Interest Litigation v Union of India* (2013) 16 SCC 279.

[77] ibid 280.

[78] ibid 282.

[79] ibid.

[80] See *United Distributors* (n 70).

B. The Report of the CAG

The CAG issued a rather unfavourable report on the FSSAI in 2017.[81] The CAG's report was commissioned in order to ascertain whether the FSSAI was living up to its legislative mandates as provided in the 2006 Act. The CAG conducted a number of what might be called diagnostic tests and surveys to assess the performance of the FSSAI and state food safety bodies.[82] The results are not encouraging. They can be grouped into various categories, such as: (i) designing and implementing regulations; (ii) staffing levels and qualifications; (iii) overseeing food safety laboratories and enforcement; (iv) informing consumers about food safety; (v) FBO licensing; and (vi) interactions with customs offices. Although the FSSAI disputes some of these findings (as noted below), it is instructive to examine them as they essentially critique every aspect of the FSSAI's operations.

i. Designing and Implementing Regulations

One of the key concerns voiced by the CAG report and the court decisions is that the FSSAI has not framed regulations in many of the key areas of its responsibility (eg, accreditation, risk assessment and prohibiting unfair trade practices).[83] In some areas (eg, creating standards/product approvals), it has pursued paths (ie, the NOCs) that were later declared to be unlawful by the courts, with the result that some FBOs sold food products that did not meet existing food safety standards.[84]

Moreover, even where the FSSAI has taken some steps, the CAG found serious deficiencies. For example, scientific panels were often either not formed for investigating an issue (eg, regulations for proprietary foods) or no timeframes had been set for revising or processing standards. In addition, the FSSAI would often bypass scientific panels and not consider stakeholders' views before notifying regulations (a violation of section 18(2)(d) of the 2006 Act),[85] and often failed to develop mechanisms when required to do so.[86] It also wrongly operationalised the *Codex Aliementarius* standards for various commodities, and removed zinc from the list of contaminants and a host of other matters without Ministry approval and without clear scientific basis.[87] The FSSAI also did not initiate any mechanism to provide technical advice to Central and State Governments about crisis management, as it was required to do.[88] This all further contributed to the sense of general FSSAI unpredictability and mismanagement.

The FSSAI responded that it was a fairly new statutory body (although it is 10 years old now) and that it is evolving to fit its role under both manpower and resource

[81] See *Report of the Comptroller and Auditor General of India* (n 6).

[82] ibid 4–11.

[83] ibid para 2.2. For example, until November 2017 there were no regulations for organic food (ibid para 2.3).

[84] ibid para 2.8.

[85] ibid para 2.6.

[86] ibid para 2.13.

[87] ibid para 2.9.

[88] ibid para 2.13.

constraints.[89] The CAG did not find either of these responses to be persuasive. Moreover, the recent initiatives from the FSSAI (the online web-based inspection system and the single interface for food businesses)[90] seemed both fairly new (and hence the effects are still to be determined) and steps that were fairly obvious to consider even 10 years ago. Indeed, some of these measures have the feel of being developed in order to respond to critiques about the general ineffectiveness of the FSSAI.

ii. Staffing and Qualifications at the FSSAI

The CAG report frequently discusses staffing and qualifications problems at the FSSAI and associated entities. For example, the report criticises the FSSAI for excessive reliance on contractual employees (due to a shortage of regular employees).[91] At the end of 2016, there were 356 sanctioned posts at the FSSAI, of which 115 were filled with regular employees and 261 with contractual staff.[92] Going in the other direction, the CAG found that in the category of technical officers, the sanctioned strength of 17 was met with 93 individuals on a contractual basis.[93] In addition, it appears that the FSSAI was paying some contractual employees and consultants more than was permitted under regulations with no reasons provided for this.[94]

Concerns with the qualifications of staff and food analysts also drew the ire of the CAG. Section 45 of the 2006 Act read with paragraph 2.1.4(1)(i) and (ii) of the 2011 Rules provide the mandatory qualifications for food analysts (those who are to analyse food samples at laboratories).[95] In a check, the CAG found that 15 out of 16 notified food laboratories did not have a single qualified food analyst under the 2011 Rules.[96]

Further, the shortage of designated officers and food safety officers in the states badly affected the functioning of state food safety authorities.[97] It appears that in 12 states there was a 90 per cent shortfall in food safety officers as well as shortfalls in all states for such officers ranging from 33 per cent to 99 per cent.[98]

iii. Overseeing Food Safety Laboratories and Enforcement

The FSSAI's oversight efforts were considered to be failing. For example, the FSSAI has no procedure for laboratory oversight (eg, no procedure for surveillance audits,

[89] See 'FSSAI Responds' (n 58).

[90] These are FosCoRis (Food Safety and Compliance through Regular Inspections and Sampling), which is a web-based inspection system enabling the FSSAI to monitor digitally, and the Food Regulatory Portal, which will act as a single interface for food businesses to cater to both domestic operations and food imports. Along with this, the FSSAI has also put forward procedures for information sharing with other agencies (eg, customs), which should facilitate trade and investment. See *Report of the Comptroller and Auditor General of India* (n 6).

[91] ibid para 5.4.

[92] ibid.

[93] ibid para 5.4.1.

[94] ibid para 5.7 and 5.8.

[95] ibid para 4.6.

[96] ibid para 4.6.1.

[97] ibid para 5.9.

[98] ibid.

periodic spot checks, recognition of laboratories and monitoring of laboratories).[99] Indeed, out of 209 FSSAI recognised laboratories, only a small number were actually accredited by the NABL.[100] Moreover, the FSSAI appeared to notify some laboratories without approval from the Ministry, and laboratories often did not check all the required parameters for specific food items.[101] Indeed, the CAG's review noted that most laboratories do not have testing facilities for pesticide residues, heavy metals and certain toxic substances, amongst others.[102]

The FSSAI responded that it has been trying to ensure that laboratories have all the required equipment and are otherwise functional and it noted that the Government of India is investing substantially for laboratory enhancement.[103] There are also training programmes for staff (to meet NABL accreditation) and other 'handholding' steps. Although promising first steps, these do not appear to have generated a substantial increase in NABL-accredited laboratories.[104]

Finally, even when laboratories find that food products are adulterated or mislabelled, the penalties seem fairly lacklustre. Recently, information provided by the FSSAI indicates that conviction rates are low and that in the most recent year (2016–17), conviction rates in many states have actually declined (eg, in Maharasthra there were no convictions in 2016–17 from 313 criminal cases and only 24 convictions from 190 criminal cases in 2015–16).[105]

iv. Informing Citizens of Good Food Practices and Hygiene

It appears that few states had funds set aside for informing citizens about good practices or hygiene, and no regulations have been promulgated to utilise funds obtained by the FSSAI through its fees and so forth for informing the citizenry on appropriate food practices.[106] Even when the FSSAI has issued publications on food safety and hygiene, it has permitted two leading FBOs to place advertisements on the back of the publications, thereby creating the perception of FSSAI support or approval, which impinges on the FSSAI's ability to act (and being perceived to act) as an independent regulator.[107] The FSSAI argues that these activities were carried out by FBOs as part of their required corporate social responsibility initiatives (under section 135 of the

[99] ibid para 4.4.4.

[100] ibid para 4.2 and 4.3.

[101] ibid para 4.4 and 4.5.4.

[102] ibid para 4.7. The report also notes that some testing equipment does not work, that there is often a shortage of technical staff and food analysts, and other concerns.

[103] See 'FSSAI Responds' (n 58).

[104] ibid.

[105] See 'Answer from Shri Ashwini Kumar Choubey, The Minister of State in the Ministry of Health & Family Welfare' *Adulteration of Food Items*, Unstarred Question No 1318, to be answered on 22 December 2017 (Annexures II and III).

[106] See *Report of the Comptroller and Auditor General of India* (n 6) para 2.16. The fees collected by the FSSAI are estimated to be over INR 100 crore (ibid para 2.15.1).

[107] ibid para 2.17.

Companies Act, 2013) and that they should get credit for them.[108] Of course, the concern is that it appears that the FSSAI is approving of these efforts, not that the firms receive credit or recognition for them.

v. Food Business Operator Licensing

The FSSAI is responsible for licensing FBOs in India and yet it has no documented policy for risk-based inspections of domestically produced food.[109] Indeed, there were deficiencies in the required procedures for safe custody of samples (eg, freezing) where some samples were kept in cupboards and became spoiled.[110]

There are also substantial concerns with many irregularities surrounding the granting and renewal of FBO licences.[111] For example, the CAG found that roughly 53 per cent of issued state and central licences in their tested samples were issued with incomplete documentation.[112] To make matters worse, it appears that the FSSAI (without the approval of the Ministry) issued an advisory in 2013 transferring FBO-related enforcement to state food safety commissioners (which the CAG considers to be a violation of section 10(5) of the 2006 Act).[113] The FSSAI responded that this was done because states have greater manpower, to which the CAG responded that states are also manpower constrained and this is not permitted in the regulations.[114]

vi. Interactions with Customs

The FSSAI has considerable interactions with customs authorities with regard to food importation, yet it has a very thin presence at customs offices (eg, it had a presence at only 21 out of 635 entry points).[115] Further, the FSSAI would sometimes appoint customs officials as authorised officers, even if they did not have a degree in a prescribed discipline (which is in violation of the regulations).[116] Indeed, many of these were appointed in 2016 (a decade after the 2006 Act), which further suggests a 'last-minute dash' to appear better. The CAG also found that there were over 9,000 cases (between 2011 and 2016) where officers took food samples for analysis and did not issue any decision, leaving the consignments in a strange sort of limbo.[117] These types of concerns have led the Supreme Court in a recent decision to instruct the FSSAI and the customs authorities to 'work out the modalities of ensuring that the requirements of the FSS Act and the Regulations thereunder are complied with in respect of the import of food articles'.[118]

[108] ibid.
[109] ibid para 3.3.2.
[110] ibid para 3.3.3.
[111] ibid para 3.14.
[112] ibid para 3.5.
[113] ibid.
[114] ibid.
[115] ibid para 3.6.
[116] ibid para 3.6.1.
[117] ibid para 3.6.2.
[118] *Unlimited Nutrition Pvt Ltd v Commissioner of Customs and Others*, 2016 SCC OnLine Del 3192, para 39.

IV. WHY DOES FSSAI APPEAR SO DYSFUNCTIONAL?

Although the cacophony of problems with the FSSAI is quite remarkable, one is inclined to step back and ask what are the primary contributing factors for this type of subpar performance? In this section, I discuss two related, though distinct, factors that seem to contribute to the FSSAI's poor performance – weak state capacity and the scale and diversity of the food sector in India, which makes regulation even more of a challenge.

A. Regulatory or State Capacity

As with other regulators in India, it appears that the FSSAI suffers from insufficient regulatory capacity, weak interagency coordination, poor accountability, weak transparency, conflicts of interest and potentially poor information or salience with the public.[119] However, based on the CAG report and news stories about the public policing of food safety (eg, junk food and milk adulteration), one suspects that the primary factors are more regulatory capacity and accountability.

Indeed, one recurrent theme is that the FSSAI (and the state regulators) seem to suffer from a regulatory capacity problem – there do not appear to be enough qualified and experienced food officers at these regulators. Indeed, the courts, the CAG report and the FSSAI itself have highlighted these manpower concerns. Moreover, given that one of the core reasons for establishing a regulator is to rely on its expertise and independence,[120] it is hardly surprising that a lack of expertise would likely scuttle the ability of a regulator to function well.

This of course forces us to consider why it is that food regulation does not appear to be able to attract the necessary expertise. One reason may simply be that food corporations may offer more attractive packages for people with food expertise. However, this cannot be a complete explanation, because if the salaries and benefits in the private sector are large, that should induce more people to enter the field and if experience at the regulator is thought to be important, satisfying or useful, then some of these people will find it attractive to work for the regulator. Further, many regulators might face similar expertise constraints, but some have been able to attract talent. For example, individuals with finance and stock trading expertise might be able to make substantially more in the private sector than working with the Securities and Exchange Board of India (SEBI), yet SEBI has been able to attract expertise over the years, and while not to the degree required,[121] it is still more than the FSSAI has managed to achieve.

One way in which a regulator might address this concern (at least in the short term) is to collaborate more with industry (where the expertise might reside) either

[119] See, eg, the chapters by Varottil and Ghosh in this volume.

[120] See generally John F Manning and Matthew C Stephenson, *Legislation and Regulation: Cases and Materials*, 3rd edn (Foundation Press, 2017) ch 3.

[121] See, eg, the chapter by Varottil in this volume.

explicitly – via the FSSAI–Nestlé tie-up – or less directly where individuals from industry spend some time at the regulator and then move back to industry.[122] Further, collaboration may also lead to greater consensus in the design and implementation of regulation, and perhaps a lesser need for spending on extensive enforcement (relative to where regulation has little support in the regulated community). However, these approaches raise concerns about independence and accountability.

Enhanced transparency would have both salutary and potentially real effects, but there may be additional steps that can be, and perhaps are being, taken. The increasing desire to meet global standards might prove a useful benchmark. Reliance on the *Codex Alimentarius* and developments at other food regulators (eg, the US FDA) can be beneficial for India if utilised appropriately. It may not be the case that India can immediately implement these global standards, but awareness of them may be useful in monitoring the independence of the Indian regulator and the various collaborations into which it enters. If an FSSAI–industry collaboration produces standards that seem far removed from global standards, then that would raise proverbial 'eyebrows' and attract greater scrutiny. Of course, global standards may also be compromised in terms of independence from industry, but they do provide a useful benchmark as one develops expertise and capacity domestically.

However, I do not want to suggest that a blended reliance on industry and global food standards is a panacea for India. India's regulator will still have to develop its own standards to suit India's institutional and legal landscape, and will have to devote resources to more effective enforcement. Moreover, global food standards will not necessarily help to police the independence of enforcement activities in India (although a fairly active civil society might, as seen in the increasing number of right to information applications in the food sector and various news reports of increased public scrutiny in relation to food). Further, the interplay of interest groups in this area requires greater analysis before we can come to strong conclusions.

B. The Scale of Food Regulation in India

Regulating food in a country as large and diverse as India may present problems of scale that create their own challenges. A potentially useful comparison is food safety regulation in China (a country with a large and diverse population, but potentially stronger state capacity). In China, food regulation has been plagued by many problems even as the Central Government has made food safety a priority issue. John K. Yasuda recently argued that in addition to issues of state capacity and corruption, the scale of food production activities in China makes food safety a difficult area to regulate.[123]

[122] See ibid. Note that the 'revolving door' approach generates quite a lot of debate; see, eg, Ed deHann, Simi Kedia, Kevin Koh and Shivaram Rajgopal, 'The Revolving Door and the SEC's Enforcement Outcomes: Initial Evidence from Civil Litigation' (2015) 60 *Journal of Accounting & Economics* 65.

[123] See John Kojiro Yasuda, 'Why Food Safety Fails in China: The Politics of Scale' (2015) 223 *China Quarterly* 745.

Yasuda argues that China's 'massive production system, unwieldy bureaucracy and geographic size' present problems because handling this kind of scale in regulation – which tries to balance a need for standardisation of safety with local food diversity – gets more challenging as a result of the heterogeneity of the country and the number of players in its food market.[124] Of course, other countries and jurisdictions may face similar problems (eg, the EU), but Yasuda argues that China's food network (with millions of often small players) is larger and less developed than is the case in other places.[125]

Yasuda examines various strategies to address this scale problem in China (eg, coordination bodies, campaigns on food safety, and regulatory segmentation such as a tightly regulated export sector) and finds that they are unlikely to successfully address the scale problem.[126] Indeed, there may even be a push towards campaigns because of their high visibility in terms of appearing like they are taking food safety seriously.[127]

India presents similar sorts of scale issues – there are countless players in India's food sector who are often of limited size. This presents a challenge for regulation in part because there are so many different players compared to a situation where there are a few large players where regulation can be more easily designed and perhaps standardised.[128]

For example, consider how scale may impact the reliance on ex post or ex ante regulatory strategies. Many small diverse players make ex post strategies more difficult not only because designing appropriate standards is more of a challenge in the face of such diversity,[129] but also because ex post sanctions are less effective against judgment-proof entities (which are often small players).[130] This may push us towards more ex ante strategies and education campaigns, but this is also troubling because such measures and campaigns are harder to design nationally when there is a great variety in food practices.

When this is interacted with weaker state capacity or governance, we see even more layers complicating the regulatory landscape. For example, with slow courts and poor enforcement, one is inclined not to rely on ex post sanctions. However, with weak regulatory capacity and poor expertise, ex ante measures seem less plausible too.

Two other factors also impact food regulation in India. First, although food has considerable salience in India (occupying somewhat unique cultural, regional and religious lines), there are many potential causes of food-related illness or harm that may weaken the outrage that could propel regulatory or legislative action on food safety.

[124] ibid.

[125] ibid.

[126] ibid.

[127] ibid.

[128] ibid.

[129] ibid.

[130] There is much literature on this topic. For fairly recent discussions, see Brian Galle, 'In Praise of Ex Ante Regulation' (2015) 68 *Vanderbilt Law Review* 1715; A Mitchell Polinsky and Steven Shavell, 'Public Enforcement of Law' in Steven N Durlauf and Lawrence E Blume (eds), *The New Palgrave Dictionary of Economics*, 2nd edn (Palgrave Macmillan, 2008).

For example, if an otherwise healthy person suffers harm after eating something, one is not certain whether this was because of poor food safety, pesticides, water contamination, environmental pollution or poor hygiene. This may make outrage even more episodic and harder to use as the basis for consistent food regulation policy. This also means that food regulation shares some similarities with environmental regulation, where multiple causes of harm create their own challenges.

Second, India's version of federalism impacts its ability to engage in effective food regulation.[131] On one level, federalism allows for more variation in approaches, which might better address the issues raised by a large and diverse set of food practices (the scale issue). However, the complexity this adds is easier to operationalise in a jurisdiction with stronger regulatory capacity than is seen in India (and with better-functioning courts).

These considerations underscore the difficult trade-offs that merit greater exploration in the context of food regulation in India. Further, although the picture painted of the FSSAI and food regulation in India is rather bleak, there are some bright spots on the horizon. In a recent 132-page report, the FSSAI discusses a number of new initiatives, suggesting a new level of activity and verve at India's primary food regulator.[132] Of course, given concerns with regulatory capacity and scale politics, adopting a 'wait-and-see' approach might be judicious.

CONCLUSION

Food regulation is a topic that has been garnering greater attention both worldwide and within India recently. However, there is a general perception that India's food regulation and its primary regulator, the FSSAI, are woefully inadequate. Both the courts and the CAG take a largely negative view of the FSSAI's functioning, with repeated calls for the FSSAI to follow statutory requirements and procedures, and to ensure that experts in food safety are staffing the relevant parts of the food regulation processes in India. Problems of regulatory capacity and governance and scale politics in India's large and diverse food landscape all contribute to the reasons why food regulation is so problematic in India. This bears some similarities to issues raised in the experiences of other jurisdictions, including China.

In particular, it appears that food regulation in India is hobbled by the apparent dearth of qualified food experts to work with (or staff) regulatory functions. Given that one of the key reasons for creating a regulator is to provide independent expertise, it seems one of the primary reasons for the FSSAI's floundering has been a lack of such expertise. Attempts to address this by collaborating with food multinationals for safety standards and training, and reliance on global food standards as benchmarks might be beneficial, but could raise their own issues of ensuring independence

[131] See MP Singh (ed), *V.N. Shukla's Constitution of India*, 13th edn (Eastern Book Company, 2017) ch 1; Govinda M Rao and Nirvikar Singh, *The Political Economy of Federalism in India* (Oxford University Press, 2005) chs 1 and 3.

[132] See 'FSSAI' (n 3).

and transparency in India's regulatory and judicial environment. Further, the sheer scale, diversity and breadth of India's food landscape also raises issues for regulation, including balancing the need for standardisation with the need for local diversity. Moreover, when concerns with scale are overlaid on the regulatory capacity concerns in India, even more layers are added, complicating the analysis yet further. Nonetheless, it appears that the FSSAI is in a new era of leadership and has taken a more assertive role in ferreting out expertise (often from industry) to aid in food regulation and in examining ways in which food regulation might be taken forward in India. Although 'wait and see' might be the most judicious approach to take, it is clear that food regulation in India will be an area of great activity in the foreseeable future, and one with the potential to greatly impact the health and safety of people in India and those using Indian food products across the globe.

12

Big Data

ANANTH PADMANABHAN AND ANIRUDH RASTOGI*

INTRODUCTION

TECHNOLOGICAL INNOVATION, PARTICULARLY driven by large-scale gathering and processing of data,[1] is occurring at a frenetic pace. This has led to speculations on a 'fairly sizable chance' of attaining human-level machine intelligence within the next two to three decades, and a state of superintelligence 'fairly soon thereafter'.[2] But such hectic transformation comes with its set of costs and concerns. The unhindered erosion of human autonomy and its impact on individual and group rights, the centralisation of resources in the hands of a few technology companies with harmful consequences for open innovation, and the worrisome prospect of regulation playing catch-up with innovation resulting in sub-optimal outcomes are particularly serious problems.

Be it quicker information sharing, more efficient ways of doing business or newer means of social connectedness, the internet has facilitated these outcomes through its pervasive sectoral reach, evolutionary capabilities and openness to spawn further innovation.[3] In India, the Information Technology Act, 2000 (hereinafter the 'IT Act') and rules thereunder presently regulate digital storage and transfers, cyber-security, online behaviour and criminal conduct, intermediary liability and diligence standards, protection of sensitive personal data and online surveillance – key themes associated with the use of the internet. Yet, much has happened in the digital domain since the IT Act was passed or even after significant amendments to this legislation in 2008. This enactment was drafted during the read-write phase of the internet, popularly

* The authors are grateful to Pushan Dwivedi, Gaurav Rana and Tanya Sadana for their invaluable research assistance.

[1] Viktor Mayer-Schönberger and Kenneth Cukier, *Big Data: A Revolution That Will Transform How We Live, Work, and Think* (John Murray, 2013).

[2] Nick Bostrom, *Superintelligence: Paths, Dangers, Strategies* (Oxford University Press, 2014) 21.

[3] These three criteria determine any technology's status as a general-purpose technology. See John Naughton, 'The Evolution of the Internet: From Military Experiment to General Purpose Technology' (2016) 1 *Journal of Cyber Policy* 5, 6.

known as 'Web 2.0' and best identified through some of its core principles: cost-effective and scalable services; users as co-developers; device-agnostic and lightweight programming; and harnessing collective intelligence.[4] Many popular platforms, serving as intermediaries to host third-party content, were created during this phase.

The present phase – Web 3.0 or the 'semantic web'[5] – marks the transition to a machine-understandable web, with ubiquitous gadgets capable of mining human intelligence and deriving meaning.[6] The extensive tagging of content and linking of databases have brought structure and context to the emanating 'web of data'.[7] This transition started a little over a decade ago, broadly coinciding with when the last set of major amendments to the IT Act took effect. In Yochai Benkler's view, some of the major trends defining this transition have been: the emergence of the smartphone, app stores and a pervasive internet-of-things;[8] increasing mobile internet penetration;[9] cloud computing;[10] and big data and its uses in behavioural control.[11] While Benkler is rightly sceptical of the new kinds of control points over the internet that stem from these trends, they have also resulted in beneficial data insights and new kinds of innovation. They equally weaken several substantive safeguards in the IT Act to protect rights and freedoms of citizens, as well as stretch the limits of regulatory capacity envisaged therein.

This chapter maps, and responds to, important regulatory challenges in the new digital age. We have focused here on big data models, emerging concerns and possible regulatory responses for several reasons. The first of these is because data is arguably the most important asset for innovation and market dominance in the digital age. Therefore, guidance on regulating this asset is inevitable for the future of technology and innovation. The second is because data is a complex asset and ushers a host of new problems. Here, we identify a collective set of 'big data harms', with the most exigent of them being informational privacy and data security challenges. Web 3.0 depends on the limitless gathering and movement of data, be it personal, commercial or metadata, for rapid expansion. But alongside such expansion, it compels us to think more deeply about the implications of data leakage, and the erosion of both individual and group privacy. The third reason is because the challenges with regulating

[4] Tim O'Reilly, 'What is Web 2.0: Design Patterns and Business Models for the Next Generation of Software' (2007) 65 *Communications and Strategies* 17, 36–37.

[5] Tim Berners-Lee, *Weaving the Web: The Original Design and Ultimate Destiny of the World Wide Web* (HarperBusiness, 2000) 177.

[6] John Markoff, 'Entrepreneurs See a Web Guided by Common Sense' *New York Times* (12 November 2006), www.nytimes.com/2006/11/12/business/12web.html.

[7] The Resource Description Framework (RDF) is a metadata model that provides the structure to make statements about web resources in the form of 'subject-predicate-object' expressions called 'triples'. Additional ontology languages such as OWL have then been built on top of the RDF syntax model to strengthen the web's capabilities to express meaning and context. See Julien Mailland, 'The Semantic Web and Information Flow: A Legal Framework' (2010) 11 *North Carolina Journal of Law & Technology* 269, 284–85.

[8] Yochai Benkler, 'Degrees of Freedom, Dimensions of Power' 145 *Daedalus* 18, 21.

[9] ibid.

[10] ibid 22.

[11] ibid 23.

data also shed light on the challenges involved in regulating new technologies more broadly. Across various new technologies and their concomitant threats – drones and airspace intrusion, online aggregators and labour insecurity, cryptocurrencies and financial instability, gene editing and unethical practices – regulators increasingly run into difficulties gauging the modalities of optimal regulation. Sub-optimal responses either over-regulate, impeding innovation, or under-regulate, leading to spiralling threats. Even without a nuanced policy exploration into these technologies, our discussion on regulating data can provide a pathway for optimal regulations on this front.

This chapter first maps the separate evolutionary journeys of informational privacy and data security in the Indian context, and proceeds to demonstrate why big data models demand a more coherent regulatory vision towards these themes. It then examines the data governance principles required for this new world of Web 3.0 and big data solutions. It focuses primarily on the recent deliberations and recommendations of the Expert Committee on Data Protection headed by retired Justice Srikrishna to draft India's first personal data protection law. Both areas also discuss the recent decisions of the Indian Supreme Court on the right to privacy and the constitutional validity of the Aadhaar scheme respectively. The chapter subsequently examines the regulatory structure and design, independence and capacity requirements for the public and private use of big data, and where the current regulatory landscape in India falls short in these aspects. We would also like to highlight two major limitations here: first, that the chapter does not probe the issue of data nationalism and its various policy offshoots, including localisation, mirroring and cross-border data flows; and, second, that it does not explore in depth anti-competitive harms arising from various practices in the digital economy, most of which relate to the agglomeration of data in the hands of a few big entities.

I. INFORMATIONAL PRIVACY AND DATA SECURITY

A. The Indian Experience

Informational privacy and data protection, despite having captured the attention of scholars and policy-makers in the US and the EU for a long time, are relatively new to Indian jurisprudence. Up until the mid-1990s, India's tryst with privacy predominantly engaged with this right in its spatial sense, with the Supreme Court observing in early cases of investigative search and seizure,[12] and police surveillance[13] that the right to privacy was not a fundamental right in the Indian Constitution. *Gobind v State of Madhya Pradesh*,[14] an important decision where the Supreme Court partially recognised the constitutional moorings of the right to privacy, and

[12] *MP Sharma v Satish Chandra* AIR 1954 SC 300.
[13] *Kharak Singh v State of Uttar Pradesh* AIR 1963 SC 1295.
[14] *Gobind v State of Madhya Pradesh* (1975) 2 SCC 148.

Malak Singh v State of Punjab and Haryana,[15] which followed this decision, both dealt with the vires of police surveillance.[16]

Claims against disclosure of sensitive information,[17] unauthorised telephone tapping[18] and improper use of data furnished to a third party in confidence[19] set in motion[20] the gradual recognition of informational privacy as a category meriting constitutional protection in Indian law.[21] Though these decisions did not articulate the distinction between informational and other forms of privacy clearly enough, the recent verdict of the Supreme Court in *Justice KS Puttaswamy v Union of India* does so.[22] This verdict, arising within the context of a constitutional challenge to India's biometric identification project, the Aadhaar scheme, unanimously recognises the right to privacy, including informational privacy, as a fundamental right essential for human dignity. While doing so, the Court observes that privacy carries distinct connotations, including spatial control, decisional autonomy and informational control.[23]

However, a big gap continues to persist. The constitutionalisation of private law over the years has hindered the growth of tort law in India.[24] The tort of privacy, meant to provide relief against non-state actors, has suffered the same fate. As Gautam Bhatia points out,[25] the articulation of the right in constitutional terms, even in cases like *Rajagopal* or *Mr X*[26] that involve unauthorised disclosures by private actors, has resulted in a 'hopelessly incoherent' jurisprudence.[27] Far from resorting to

[15] *Malak Singh v State of Punjab and Haryana* (1981) 1 SCC 420.

[16] See Gautam Bhatia, 'State Surveillance and the Right to Privacy in India: A Constitutional Biography' (2014) 26 *National Law School of India Review* 127, 133–38.

[17] *R Rajagopal v State of Tamil Nadu* (1994) 6 SCC 632; *Mr X v Hospital Z* (1998) 8 SCC 296.

[18] *PUCL v Union of India* (1997) 1 SCC 301.

[19] *District Registrar, Hyderabad v Canara Bank* (2005) 1 SCC 496.

[20] As some scholars point out, the close coupling of computing and communications has led to a merger of data privacy and communications confidentiality, resulting in the broader category of 'information privacy'. See David Wright and Charles Raab, 'Privacy Principles, Risks and Harms' (2014) 28 *International Review of Law, Computers and Technology* 277, 281.

[21] Bhairav Acharya, 'The Four Parts of Privacy in India' (2015) 50(22) *Economic and Political Weekly* 32, 36.

[22] *Justice KS Puttaswamy v Union of India* (2017) 10 SCC 1.

[23] Justice Dhananjay Chandrachud's opinion is rich with references to academic scholarship on the multiple dimensions of privacy, including discussion of a typology of privacy developed in a recent law review article. This article identifies nine different types of privacy, namely bodily, spatial, communicational and proprietary privacy (which emphasise the freedom to be left alone), intellectual, decisional, associational and behavioural privacy (where emphasis is on the freedom of self-development), and informational privacy as an overarching category which secures both these freedoms. See Bert-Jaap Koops et al, 'A Typology of Privacy' (2017) 38 *University of Pennsylvania Journal of International Law* 483, 567–69.

[24] See Shyamkrishna Balganesh, 'The Constitutionalisation of Indian Private Law' in Sujit Choudhry, Madhav Khosla and Pratap Bhanu Mehta (eds), *The Oxford Handbook of the Indian Constitution* (Oxford University Press, 2016) 680.

[25] Bhatia (n 16) 138–40.

[26] ibid.

[27] Bhatia contends that one way to overcome this incoherence is to understand the judicial invocation of art 21 in these cases as being for the sole purpose of infusing the right to privacy with substantive content, without serving as a *ground for the decision*. See Bhatia (n 16) 154. This is, at best, a weak justification for a conceptually flawed approach. Presently, India cannot claim to have any clear principles guiding the granting of interim injunctions – which are particularly important in a legal system where cases go for trial several years after the date of filing – when privacy claims are asserted against non-state actors. See also Acharya (n 21) 37, who emphasises that the technical expertise to regulate data protection bears little relation to the constitutional, criminal and administrative law in relation to governing surveillance.

a common law approach that incrementally develops privacy norms and data protection practices through fact-sensitive adjudication, this has over time strengthened the call for a super-regulatory structure to fill the gap left by the absence of a robust set of private law remedies.[28]

Traditionally, informed consent lies at the heart of such regulatory approaches to the protection of personal data (in many jurisdictions).[29] In addition to enabling autonomy over personal data, consent facilitates 'privacy self-management'[30] by placing the responsibility of data protection on the person whose data is subject to collection and processing. Privacy policies serve as the operative document to both provide information and take consent. In India, statutory rules (the SPDI rules) similarly protect narrowly enumerated categories of sensitive personal information, including passwords, financial information, medical history, biometric information and sexual orientation, through a notice-and-consent model.[31]

Under the SPDI rules, body corporates and agents on their behalf that collect, receive, possess, store, deal with or handle sensitive personal information must provide for privacy policies – clear and accessible statements which outline data-handling practices, identify the type of personal data gathered, the purpose of collection and use, and the disclosure of such information – and ensure that such policies are available for viewing by information providers, thereby putting them to notice.[32] These rules, although they are an egregious case of poor drafting,[33] at least superficially incorporate several normative data protection principles contained in the Organisation for Economic Co-operation and Development (OECD) guidelines,[34] besides mandating express consent in writing from information providers before collecting sensitive personal information.[35] A glaring loophole is the absence

[28] Nimisha Srinivas and Arpita Biswas, 'Protecting Patient Information in India: Data Privacy Law and its Challenges' (2012) 5 *NUJS Law Review* 411, 420–21.

[29] Committee of Experts under the Chairmanship of Justice BN Srikrishna, 'White Paper on a Data Protection Framework for India' (Ministry of Electronics and Information Technology, 2017) 78, meity.gov.in/writereaddata/files/white_paper_on_data_protection_in_india_18122017_final_v2.1.pdf.

[30] Daniel Solove, 'Privacy Self-Management and the Consent Dilemma' (2013) 126 *Harvard Law Review* 1880, 1881.

[31] Information Technology (Reasonable Security Practices and Procedures and Sensitive Personal Data or Information) Rules 2011, r 3.

[32] ibid r 4.

[33] For a detailed critique, see Bhairav Acharya, 'Comments on the Information Technology (Reasonable Security Practices and Procedures and Sensitive Personal Data or Information) Rules, 2011' *The Center for Internet and Society* (31 March 2013), https://cis-india.org/internet-governance/blog/comments-on-the-it-reasonable-security-practices-and-procedures-and-sensitive-personal-data-or-information-rules-2011.

[34] Organisation for Economic Co-operation and Development, 'Guidelines on the Protection of Privacy and Transborder Flows of Personal Data, 1980' (2013), www.oecd.org/sti/ieconomy/oecd_privacy_framework.pdf.

[35] Under r 5 of the SPDI rules, these entities can collect only such information as necessary (*collection limitation*) for lawful purposes specified at the time of collection of such information, and only for such time until these purposes are achieved (*purpose limitation*). They must also take reasonable steps to provide information providers with knowledge regarding the fact that their information is being collected, the purpose behind this activity and the identities of information gatherers, custodians and intended recipients (*openness*), as well as permitting information providers to review their information and have it corrected when it is found to be inaccurate (*individual participation* and *data quality* principles), and must confine their use of such information to the purpose for which data has been collected (*use limitation*).

of a robust oversight and enforcement machinery, and clear principles for holding data controllers and processors liable. In any case, the rules exclude government entities from their ambit and only apply to 'sensitive personal data' rather than the larger category of personal data.[36] In the financial sector, the Credit Information Companies (Regulation) Act, 2005 and the regulations thereunder impose legal obligations on credit information companies to adhere to privacy principles at the stage of collection, use and disclosure of credit information, and to ensure that the credit information held by them is accurate, complete and secured against loss or unauthorised use, access or disclosure.[37] Privacy protection mandates in the telecom and health sectors are quite weak, relying predominantly on licence conditions for service providers in the former and codified professional ethics for physicians in the latter.[38]

The present regulatory mechanism in India, to the extent that it addresses data-related concerns, places much more emphasis on data security and technological protection following the gathering of data over informational privacy concerns that are largely assumed to arise when gathering the data in the first place and therefore to be addressed ex post through constitutional litigation or breach of confidence claims. The IT Act valued digital security as a focal theme during its evolutionary phase. The 2008 amendment defined 'cyber security',[39] imposed duties upon organisations dealing with sensitive personal data to implement reasonable security practices and procedures,[40] attempted to provide more weight to the Cyber Appellate Tribunal (CyAT),[41] authorised traffic data monitoring and collection to prevent the intrusion or spread of computer contaminant,[42] bolstered the punishment for attacks on protected systems forming part of India's 'critical information infrastructure',[43] proposed a national nodal agency responsible for protecting such infrastructure,[44] and envisaged the Indian Computer Emergency Response Team (ICERT) as the agency to coordinate cyber-incident response activities, issue timely guidelines and advisories, and undertake emergency measures for handling cyber-security incidents.[45] The ICERT has mandated chief information security officers handling government information assets in ministries and departments to establish an information security programme and issue security policies that aim to protect the personal data of citizens.[46] Similarly, independent regulators such as the Reserve Bank

Rule 6 requires prior permission from the information provider before disclosing sensitive personal data to any third party (*use limitation*), while r 8 mandates reasonable security practices and procedures as commensurate with the information assets being protected (*security safeguards*).

[36] Committee of Experts (n 29) 17.

[37] ibid 19.

[38] ibid 20–22.

[39] Information Technology Act, 2000, s 2(nb).

[40] ibid s 43A, read with the SPDI rules.

[41] Information Technology Act, 2000, ss 49–52.

[42] ibid s 69B.

[43] ibid s 66F.

[44] ibid ss 70, 70A.

[45] ibid s 70B.

[46] Nikhil Narendran, 'Policy Framework for Protection of Big Data in State Possession' in Baladevan Rangaraju and Vishnu Chandra (eds), *Blockchain for Property: A Roll out Road Map for India* (India Institute, 2017) 34, 37.

of India (RBI), the Securities and Exchange Board of India (SEBI) and the Insurance Regulatory and Development Authority have been proactive in issuing data security guidelines for industry players in their respective sectors and mandating independent data audits.[47]

The experience with some of these measures has been disappointing. CyAT functioned without a chairperson for more than five years,[48] finally resulting in its merger[49] with the Telecom Disputes Settlement and Appellate Tribunal. Though the National Critical Information Infrastructure Protection Centre (NCIIPC) was notified as the nodal agency for critical information infrastructure after a six-year hiatus, its functioning and response capabilities leave much to be desired. The story is similar with the ICERT.[50] Yet, as compared with informational privacy, where no oversight or enforcement mechanisms exist at present, data security has received some degree of special attention. However, big data models challenge existing conceptual assumptions and protective measures in both of these realms.

B. Big Data Challenges

Puttaswamy explains why emerging technologies threaten informational privacy and data security in ways that are different from before. Justice Dhananjay Chandrachud, writing for himself and three other judges who were part of the nine-judge bench, captures the tension between informational privacy and commercial interests in today's digital economy. As digital transactions grow exponentially, so do the electronic tracks left behind by consumers. The semantic web allows such crumbs to be *aggregated* by intelligent machines and algorithms to provide a comprehensive picture of an individual's preferences, personality traits and values, predict their next move and suggest specific choices.[51] Yet such practices run the risk of being reductive, incomplete and often divorced from the context in which the data was originally gathered.[52] Because of the efficiency involved in algorithmic perception, prediction and suggestion, and the recombinant nature of data, private actor incentives are aligned towards the unhindered amassing and processing of huge swathes of personal data, often for purposes not identified or even identifiable when the

[47] Ananth Padmanabhan and Deva Prasad, 'Designing Cybersecurity for the Financial Sector' *LiveMint* (22 May 2017), www.livemint.com/Opinion/LVq77kZ1YmRNSgn34kIdjO/Designing-cybersecurity-for-the-financial-sector.html.

[48] Anuj Srivas, 'The Tragic and Comedic Functioning of India's Cyber Appellate Tribunal' *The Wire* (12 December 2016), thewire.in/86414/tragic-comedic-functioning-indias-cyber-appellate-tribunal.

[49] Vijayashankar Na, 'Cyber Appellate Tribunal Goes into Limbo Again?' *Naavi* (20 June 2017), www.naavi.org/wp/cyber-appellate-tribunal-limbo-again.

[50] Kamlesh Bajaj, 'The Challenge of Cyber Security' (2016) 687 *Seminar* 36, 38–39.

[51] As Solove remarks about the Information Age, 'the data gathered about people is significantly more extensive, the process of combining it is much easier, and the computer technologies to analyse it are more sophisticated and powerful'. See Daniel Solove, 'A Taxonomy of Privacy' (2006) 154 *University of Pennsylvania Law Review* 477, 506.

[52] ibid 507–08.

original transaction or data exchange happened.[53] Often, these privacy invasions go undetected because of the non-rivalrous and invisible nature of data access, storage and transfers.[54]

Justice Sanjay Kishan Kaul, in his concurring opinion, similarly tracks the growth of technology and its implications for large-scale invasion of privacy by the state, including through surveillance and profiling. The several surveillance and predictive analytics projects active in India's present-day governance machinery[55] vindicate Justice Kaul's observation that 'surveillance is not new, but technology has permitted surveillance in ways that are unimaginable'.[56] Reading together these two opinions by five judges of the Court, we can perceive the recognition by a majority of the bench of what Daniel Solove characterises as 'architectural' problems or harms. They go beyond dignitary harms to 'the creation of the risk that a person might be harmed in the future' and are thus 'akin, in many ways to environmental harms or pollution'.[57]

Individuals, while not personally identifiable in these settings, may still be 'reachable' on account of being within a group targeted for prejudicial action based on data-driven inference and prediction.[58] Often, they are unaware of this 'membership' because the aggregated datasets are not pre-existing real-world groups, but invisible ones generated by algorithmic black boxes.[59] The excessive linking of multiple datasets also enables group profiling without any personally identifiable information being breached.[60] Of particular concern is the possibility of constructing 'demographically identifiable information', which then enables the classification, identification and/or tracking of a specific categorisation based on ethnicity, religion, gender, age, health condition, location or any other demographically defining factors.[61] Beyond the detrimental impact of big data analytics on individual privacy, these risks motivate the

[53] Jordi Soria-Comas and Josep Domingo-Ferrer, 'Big Data Privacy: Challenges to Privacy Principles and Models' (2016) 1 *Data Science and Engineering* 21, 22.

[54] *Justice KS Puttaswamy v Union of India* (2017) 10 SCC 1.

[55] Udbhav Tiwari, 'The Design and Technology behind India's Surveillance Programs', *The Center for Internet and Society* (20 January 2017), cis-india.org/internet-governance/blog/the-design-technology-behind-india2019s-surveillance-programmes.

[56] *Justice KS Puttaswamy v Union of India* (2017) 10 SCC 1, 618.

[57] Solove broadly separates architectural harms into two kinds: the high risk of identity theft or fraud due to voluminous personal information being available in public domain, often with the individual's consent, and imbalances in power through large-scale surveillance, resulting in a 'chilling effect' on public participation and criticism. See Solove (n 51) 487.

[58] Solon Barocas and Helen Nissenbaum, 'Big Data's End Run around Anonymity and Consent' in Julia Lane et al (eds), *Privacy, Big Data, and the Public Good* (Cambridge University Press, 2014) 44, 45.

[59] Ira S Rubinstein, 'Big Data: The End of Privacy or a New Beginning?' (2013) 3 *International Data Privacy Law* 74, 77–78; Davide Castelvecchi, 'Can We Open the Black Box of AI?' (2016) 538(7623) *Nature* 20.

[60] Mireille Hildebrandt, 'Defining Profiling: A New Type of Knowledge?' in Mireille Hildebrandt and Serge Gutwirth (eds), *Profiling the European Citizen: Cross-disciplinary Perspectives* (Springer, 2008) 17, 20.

[61] Nathaniel A Raymond, 'Beyond "Do No Harm" and Individual Consent: Reckoning with the Emerging Ethical Challenges of Civil Society's Use of Data' in Linnet Taylor, Luciano Floridi and Bart van der Sloot (eds), *Group Privacy: New Challenges of Data Technologies* (Springer, 2017) 67, 75.

re-imagination of privacy as a group right,[62] with distinct infractions upon this right due to technological innovation.[63]

Many of these privacy apprehensions arise during data processing, thereby shifting the focus from empowering individuals at the time of collection through data minimisation and informed consent to giving them a bigger say in how the data is used through higher transparency, access and accuracy.[64] Similarly, big data ecosystems are as much at risk from insider attacks, threats to any of the multi-level stacks for data processing, or vulnerabilities at endpoints where identification, authentication or other data use occurs, as externally driven direct attacks on the centralised servers where data is stored. The facile regulatory distinction in India between informational privacy and data security therefore needs rethinking. As big data leads to digital identities constructed through aggregation, data insecurity can result in identity theft and large-scale privacy erosion.[65] Even de-identification solutions, earlier relied upon to separate the privacy and insecurity problems,[66] have been rendered less effective. Moreover, big data models result in an *exclusion* problem, where individuals know precious little about, and have minimal say in, how their personal information is being used.[67] This in turn is closely related to insecurity as individuals are shut out from assessing the practices in place to secure their data.[68]

When intimate personal markers such as biometric information are used for identification, the problem worsens.[69] India's Aadhaar scheme, floated to make use of non-duplicable biometrics such as fingerprints and iris scans when verifying identity for welfare subsidies, is a case in point. The need for this scheme was primarily felt

[62] A recent work points out that group rights initially shaped spatial and decisional privacy zones, including religious choices and broader limits on state power contained in the Universal Declaration of Human Rights and the International Covenant on Civil and Political Rights, only to subsequently recede into the background as part of the increasing normative emphasis on rights of the individual. However, in the context of big data, groups regain importance due to an algorithmic ability to: (a) refine characteristics of an earlier grouping using new information; (b) create new groupings in collaboration with human analysts; and (c) create new groupings without human analysts even being aware of the same. Linnet Taylor, Luciano Floridi and Bart van der Sloot, 'Introduction: A New Perspective on Privacy' in Taylor et al (n 61) 1; Lana Kammourieh, 'Group Privacy in the Age of Big Data', in Taylor et al (n 61) 37, 41–42.

[63] As Taylor points out through actual case studies, resolving the problem of individual identifiability does not resolve rights infractions faced by groups. See Linnet Taylor, 'Safety in Numbers? Group Privacy and Big Data Analytics in the Developing World' in Taylor et al (n 61) 13, 32.

[64] Omer Tene and Jules Polonetsky, 'Big Data for All: Privacy and User Control in the Age of Analytics' (2013) 11 *Northwestern Journal of Technology and Intellectual Property* 239, 242.

[65] Solove (n 51) 515–16.

[66] These solutions were meant to ensure that even where data gets leaked, it will be in de-identified form, ie, by anonymising private details, removing personal identifiers or introducing noise into the data, so that personal information remains uncompromised. See Paul Ohm, 'Broken Promises of Privacy: Responding to the Surprising Failure of Anonymisation' (2010) 57 *UCLA Law Review* 1701, 1703.

[67] Tene and Polonetsky (n 64) 255.

[68] Solove (n 51) 521.

[69] Patrizio Campisi, 'Security and Privacy in Biometrics: Towards a Holistic Approach' in Patrizio Campisi (ed), *Security and Privacy in Biometrics* (Springer, 2013) 1. This introductory chapter highlights the privacy and security concerns with biometric systems, arguing for a joint optimisation of these problems rather than addressing them as two requirements hindering each other.

because of duplicate identities that beneficiaries of several state subsidies and other benefits kept, resulting in last-mile pilferages. At the same time, there were many who did not possess clearly verifiable identities despite entitlement to subsidies or benefits, often resulting in fake identities created by others to wrongly avail what was due to these intended beneficiaries. To address these problems, from 2010 onwards, the Government of India started rolling out a unique identification number that was tied to the demographic and biometric information of individuals. Several private operators were enlisted as part of the enrolment process, facilitating the capture of biometric information in centres across the country. Key to the understanding of this unique identities project is the fact that insistence upon getting the Aadhaar card was not a choice but a compulsion. Initially, the compulsion only operated in respect of targeted programmes such as food subsidies for economically disadvantaged sections of society. But over time, Aadhaar went through a 'mission creep' that saw its compulsory use being extended to several new schemes, both targeted and more general, as well as for tax filings, private banking services and telecom operator services. The hectic push by the state to seed Aadhaar numbers in multiple databases – pensions, health benefits, education etc – with the stated purpose of de-duplicating identities also facilitated effective tracking of various aspects of resident activity, resulting in fears of a grand digital surveillance apparatus.

Biometrics, often those that are already in the public domain, lack both the privacy[70] and alterability[71] of other kinds of passwords. Recent research also indicates that biometrics, particularly fingerprints, can be copied without much effort.[72] Without a proper assessment of the security and privacy fallout, the Government of India proceeded to create a big data ecosystem around the Aadhaar database. By linking Aadhaar numbers with several other government databases, important personal details such as demographic information started to reside unsafely in locations other than the central identities data repository (CIDR), which is the centralised database where the data is meant to be stored as soon as enrolment is complete.[73] These links have helped governmental entities obtain a '360-degree view' of the individual, a serious privacy concern.[74] By extending the database for private authentication, ie, the use of Aadhaar for identity verification when private actors dealt with individuals, the points of user interface with the biometric system rose exponentially, enhancing security[75] and leakage risks.[76] Use cases like Aadhaar and half-hearted

[70] Kevin Howell, '3 Reasons Biometrics are Not Secure' *Ipswitch* (28 August 2017), blog.ipswitch.com/3-reasons-biometrics-are-not-secure.

[71] Anil K Jain, *Introduction to Biometrics* (Springer, 2011) 283.

[72] Alienor, 'Biometric Authentication: Issues and Innovations' *Plixer* (23 March 2017), www.plixer.com/blog/cybersecurity/biometric-authentication-issues-innovations.

[73] Aman Sethi, 'Existence of Other Biometric Databases May Pose New Challenge to Aadhaar' *Hindustan Times* (21 January 2018), www.hindustantimes.com/india-news/existence-of-other-biometric-databases-may-pose-new-challenge-to-aadhaar/story-nv12eC1qypTVnSaLboc5cN.html.

[74] Vidyut Kale, 'Dear Centre & UIDAI, Please Stop Misdirecting Us On Aadhaar' *The Quint* (18 May 2018), www.thequint.com/voices/opinion/opinion-aadhaar-data-leak-supreme-court-hearing-privacy-uidai.

[75] Jain (n 71) 278–81.

[76] ibid 283–84.

responses to exposed vulnerabilities[77] further vindicate the need for a coordinated regulatory approach towards informational privacy and data security in big data solutions.

The close connectedness between privacy and security in cases of mass data aggregation is borne out from recent legal challenges to the Aadhaar ecosystem.[78] The constitutional validity of the Aadhaar (Targeted Delivery of Financial and Other Subsidies, Benefits, and Services) Act, 2016 (hereinafter the 'Aadhaar Act') has now been largely upheld by a five-judge bench of the Supreme Court.[79] A writ petition against multiple data leaks pertaining to the Aadhaar database is pending before the Delhi High Court.[80] Though the constitutional challenge was fundamentally built on the right to privacy and the security challenge before the High Court is constructed around non-compliance with security standards and practices under the Aadhaar Act and regulations, there are strong points of intersection between them. For instance, the security safeguards purportedly in place in respect of the CIDR heavily influenced the proportionality analysis that the Supreme Court carried out when concluding that the surveillance and privacy concerns with this Act and the Aadhaar project were mostly unfounded. Conversely, the apprehension of privacy being compromised through the mass leakage of sensitive biometric and demographic information has resulted in the challenge before the High Court. This challenge places the spotlight on the functioning of the Unique Identification Authority of India (UIDAI) that serves as the data custodian of the CIDR, its data security practices and redressal mechanisms available against data breaches.

Current structural safeguards against the privacy problem, such as informed consent, notice through elaborately drawn out privacy policies, and separating personally identifiable information (PII) for heightened protection work poorly in light of the harms outlined above. Consent-based frameworks work inadequately due to information asymmetries between the individual and the data controller.[81] In view of the rapidly evolving forms of personal data processing, users find it difficult to determine the purposes behind, or consequences of, such techniques.[82] With new

[77] Despite multiple leakages of the Aadhaar database from these other locations, government entities and data custodians have gone on record stating that all is well because the central identities data repository was never breached, thereby revealing an outdated understanding of system security. Srinivas Kodali, 'UIDAI's Defensive Stance on Aadhaar Security Breaches isn't Helping Anybody But the Government' *The Wire* (5 January 2018), thewire.in/politics/uidai-aadhaar-security-breach.

[78] Madhav Khosla and Ananth Padmanabhan, 'Only a New Law That Addresses Concerns Can Save Aadhaar' *The Print* (29 June 2018), https://theprint.in/opinion/only-a-new-law-that-addresses-concerns-can-save-aadhaar/76524. This is the last part in a four-part series highlighting various constitutional challenges to the Aadhaar Act.

[79] *Justice Puttaswamy v Union of India*, Judgment in WP (Civil) No 494 of 2012 and connected matters (26 September 2018), https://www.supremecourtofindia.nic.in/supremecourt/2012/35071/35071_2012_Judgement_26-Sep-2018.pdf.

[80] Apoorva Mandhani, 'Prof. Shamnad Basheer Moves Delhi HC against Aadhaar Data Leak; Demands Exemplary Damages' *LiveLaw* (18 May 2018), https://www.livelaw.in/prof-shamnad-basheer-moves-delhi-hc-against-aadhaar-data-leak-demands-exemplary-damages.

[81] Soria-Comas and Domingo-Ferrer (n 53) 22.

[82] 'Function creep', the practice of using data collected for one purpose for other non-consensual purposes, is a genuine risk. See Narendran (n 46) 41. As Solove points out, such 'secondary use' of data carries both dignitary and architectural risks. See Solove (n 51) 520.

modes of gathering and processing data such as the internet of things and remotely located cloud servers, privacy notices that are predominantly available on websites and mobile apps[83] are fast losing their relevance. The pervasiveness of digital technologies and applications has also resulted in consent fatigue due to the increasingly large number of requests for consent and the disproportionate time required to meaningfully assess such requests by the user on a routine basis.[84] Meaningful consent is further vitiated by a substantial number of companies adopting a 'take it or leave it' approach to privacy notices, with no room for negotiation.[85] Privacy notices also often suffer from verbosity and legalese.[86]

De-identification through removal of PII, though not mandated by the SPDI rules, has found industry approval in India[87] and has so far served as a legally acceptable strategy to facilitate privacy-sensitive data sharing in the EU, the US and the UK.[88] Unstructured streaming data presents new challenges for state-of-the-art anonymisation strategies developed to deal with static, structured and well-defined datasets.[89] Re-identification techniques have evolved in parallel, combining multiple PII-excluded databases to arrive at near-identical results as those emerging from the processing of a PII-inclusive database.[90] The newly created database can then be linked with other databases (even PII-excluded ones) to compromise their anonymity.[91] These techniques present a cautionary tale: against the ubiquity of 'data fingerprints' left by individuals and the excessive linking of multiple databases, PII protection can do much less than before.[92] Therefore, while the distinction between PII and other information, and anonymisation strategies built on such distinction, may still hold good to contain disclosures of sensitive information that can result in fully realised harm,[93] Indian law must explore solutions that go beyond de-identification of personal data.

In the context of Aadhaar, they call into question the very practice of seeding these numbers into multiple databases and making it easier to profile citizens, the constitutional vires of which has now been decided by a five-judge bench of the Supreme

[83] Committee of Experts (n 29) 92.

[84] Aleecia M McDonald and Lorrie Faith Cranor, 'The Cost of Reading Privacy Policies' (2008) 4 *I/S Journal of Law and Policy* 543, 565; Narendran (n 46) 40.

[85] Arthur Allen Leff, 'Contract as Thing' (1970) 19 *American University Law Review* 131.

[86] Narendran (n 46) 40.

[87] See Data Security Council of India, 'DSCI Submission to TRAI Consultation on Data Privacy in Telecom Sector' (2017) 8, www.dsci.in/sites/default/files/DSCI%20response_TRAI%20paper_Data%20 Protection.pdf.

[88] Committee of Experts (n 29) 415–18.

[89] Personal Data Protection Commission of Singapore, 'Guide to Basic Data Anonymisation Techniques' (2018) 4–5, www.pdpc.gov.sg/-/media/Files/PDPC/PDF-Files/Other-Guides/Guide-to-Anonymisation_ v1-(250118).pdf.

[90] For a particularly stark situation, where the de-identification was considered nearly foolproof and yet re-identified, see Jean Louis Raisaro et al, 'Addressing Beacon Re-identification Attacks: Quantification and Mitigation of Privacy Risks' (2017) 24 *Journal of the American Medical Informatics Association* 799, 800.

[91] Even were this not to happen, the entropy in the system is reduced, and each re-identification effort gets one step closer to revealing sensitive information about an individual. See Ohm (n 66) 1746, 1749–50.

[92] Ohm (n 66) 1723.

[93] ibid 1735.

Court.[94] The majority verdict by Justice AK Sikri took the view that a combination of three different measures – confining mandatory insistence upon Aadhaar authentication to schemes benefiting a 'particular deprived class', limited retention of authentication records and restricted gathering of metadata, and an embargo on any private authentication – will sufficiently protect against privacy invasions and surveillance fears.[95] But a more accurate line of inquiry, which Justice Chandrachud pursued in his dissent, was to critically examine Aadhaar's mission creep to new and originally unintended purposes. Based on this, he characterised insistence upon Aadhaar as a convenient ruse to cover every aspect of human life 'from delivery to deliverance', in the process building a profiling 'bridge across discreet data silos'.[96]

II. DATA GOVERNANCE PRINCIPLES

Acknowledging some of the above-outlined challenges, the Supreme Court in *Puttaswamy* advocated a dual-track approach to prevent the abuse of informational privacy: a robust fundamental right to privacy enforceable against state actors, which can only be restricted using proportionate means that advance a legitimate state aim, and a data protection law to regulate the conduct of the data economy. While the Court's observations on legitimate exceptions are better situated within the rightful status of informational privacy as a fundamental right against the state, a matter explored at greater length in the Aadhaar constitutional challenge and subsequent verdict, they do convey some of the inherent tensions that even a data protection law must grapple with. As the Chandrachud opinion elucidated, big data solutions are an unavoidable reality, deserving a qualified embrace due to the several benefits they potentially offer.[97] Rather than isolated responses to interlinked challenges within this big data ecosystem – privacy safeguards, information security, data-driven decision-making, responsible data sharing etc – a comprehensive data governance framework is required. Borrowing Lawrence Lessig's framework, technology regulation works through four instruments that often compliment, or interact with, each other: laws, norms, markets and physical architecture.[98] Whether in public or private big data

[94] *Justice Puttaswamy v Union of India* (n 79).

[95] ibid.

[96] ibid 907. See Madhav Khosla and Ananth Padmanabhan, 'On Privacy, Supreme Court's Aadhaar Verdict Doesn't Even Engage with the Concerns' *The Print* (27 September 2018), https://theprint.in/opinion/on-privacy-supreme-courts-aadhaar-verdict-doesnt-even-engage-with-the-concerns/125434.

[97] Ananth Padmanabhan, 'Privacy Verdict Presents Big Data as a Reality We Need to Work with, Not against' *The Print* (30 August 2017), theprint.in/opinion/privacy-verdict-presents-big-data-reality-need-work-not/8340. This is also recognised in the report of the Expert Committee constituted under the chairmanship of retired Justice BN Srikrishna to recommend a data protection law for India. See Committee of Experts under the Chairmanship of Justice BN Srikrishna, 'A Free and Fair Digital Economy: Protecting Privacy, Empowering Indians' (Ministry of Electronics and Information Technology, 2018) 5, http://meity.gov.in/writereaddata/files/Data_Protection_Committee_Report-comp.pdf.

[98] Lawrence Lessig, 'The Law of the Horse: What Cyberlaw Might Teach' (1999) 113 *Harvard Law Review* 501, 506–07.

uses, an optimal governance structure must necessarily make full use of these instruments to strike a workable balance without being excessive in terms of scope and application.[99]

The Expert Committee on Data Protection, constituted in 2017 under the aegis of the Ministry of Electronics and Information Technology and headed by Justice Srikrishna, is the second effort in recent times to develop a framework for India in this area since the Justice AP Shah Committee presented its report in 2012.[100] The Expert Committee identifies seven key principles as essential for any new data protection law in India: (1) technology agnostic and flexible enough to account for changing technologies and compliance standards; (2) holistically applicable to both the private sector and the public sector, with suitable modifications to further legitimate state aims; (3) informed consent as an expression of human autonomy; (4) data minimisation to ensure that data processing is kept to a minimum and only as necessary for the purposes for which data is sought, and other compatible purposes beneficial for the data subject; (5) data fiduciary/controller accountability for any processing of data, whether by itself or through entities with whom it may have shared the data for processing; (6) structured enforcement by a high-powered statutory authority and decentralised enforcement mechanisms; and (7) deterrent penalties for wrongful data processing.[101] Of these, a few need rethinking in the context of big data, along with some others on account of doubts relating to regulatory independence and capacity.[102]

Notice and consent requirements, though not particularly useful in expressing autonomy for reasons discussed above, still serve a valuable function – that of educating and informing users on the importance of informational privacy in a milieu where such consciousness is yet to sink in. But these requirements need restructuring in ways that are very different from the contractual language that has thus far been assumed to register autonomy and choice. The real test should be to evaluate whether, in the specific context in which users encounter any big data solution, the privacy policy is presented in a manner that best conveys the possible dangers of taking their data, the rights they pass on to the data controller, and the limitations on the controller. In short, education and information functions should best determine the appropriateness of privacy policies. Use of visual media, vernacular languages and simple writing must all play a role in this evaluation, with a strict mandate to companies that fail to meet the requisite standard to both erase all prior data collected by them and come out with new policies that serve these functions.

The draft Personal Data Protection Bill, 2018 suggested by the Expert Committee mandates many of these requirements, while stipulating a higher standard of explicit

[99] Tene and Polonetsky (n 64) 243.

[100] For a discussion on the various factors influencing this bill, see Amba Kak, 'The Emergence of the Personal Data Protection Bill, 2018' (2018) 53(38) *Economic and Political Weekly* 12.

[101] Committee of Experts (n 29) 204.

[102] The Expert Committee has now revisited and modified some of the terminology, with the final report and the draft Personal Data Protection Bill redesignating the 'data subject' as 'data principal', and the 'data controller' as 'data fiduciary'. See Committee of Experts (n 97) 7–8.

consent for processing 'sensitive personal data', a category already recognised in the SPDI rules, but given more coverage here.[103] This bill bars profiling, tracking or behavioural monitoring of children by 'guardian data fiduciaries' – defined to include those data fiduciaries processing large volumes of personal data of children – in what would qualify as the only absolute embargo on data profiling contained in it.[104] However, even with adult personal data, it creates a category of 'significant data fiduciaries' who will have to carry out a data protection impact assessment (DPIA) and submit it to the newly proposed Data Protection Authority (DPA) when undertaking any processing that involves new technologies or large-scale profiling.[105] Even for non-sensitive personal data, the enumerations under the notice requirement are quite elaborate, possibly veering towards the more cumbersome side when viewed from the perspective of data innovation.[106] In an unequivocal stance on data minimisation, it provides that data fiduciaries shall not make the provision of any goods or services, or the quality thereof, conditional upon consent from the data subject for processing any personal data that is unnecessary for this purpose.[107]

The draft Bill also creates important new rights and imposes elaborate responsibilities on data fiduciaries that are true to the underlying philosophy behind data protection that not everything can be left to the contract between data fiduciaries and principals. The right to confirmation and access entitles the data principal to obtain a confirmation from the data fiduciary as to whether the latter is processing or has processed personal data of the former, and a summary of such activities and data.[108] The data subject has the right to have his or her personal data corrected, completed or updated as the situation demands.[109] Concomitantly, the data fiduciary is responsible for taking reasonable steps to advance such data quality, with the necessity of these steps being determined on the basis of whether the personal data would likely be used to decide or disclose aspects of the principal's life.[110] The bill offers a watered-down 'right to be forgotten', which empowers the data principal to restrict or prevent the continuing disclosure of personal data by a fiduciary upon determination by an adjudicating officer that the disclosure has served its purpose or that the consent authorising such disclosure has since been withdrawn.[111] From the fiduciary's standpoint, the bill casts an obligation to retain personal data for 'only as long as may be reasonably necessary to satisfy the purpose for which it is processed' and to delete such data when the purpose is satisfied.[112] Despite these interventions,

[103] Personal Data Protection Bill, 2018, cll 3(35) and 18, available at http://meity.gov.in/writereaddata/files/Personal_Data_Protection_Bill,2018.pdf. See the note in this regard by Ms Rama Vedashree, a member of the Expert Committee, dissenting against the inclusion of financial data and passwords within the category of 'sensitive personal data'; Committee of Experts (n 97) post-Appendix material.

[104] Personal Data Protection Bill, 2018, cl 23.

[105] ibid cl 33.

[106] ibid cl 8.

[107] ibid cl 12(3).

[108] ibid cl 24.

[109] ibid cl 25.

[110] ibid cl 9.

[111] ibid cl 27.

[112] ibid cl 10.

a major shortcoming remains in the data protection landscape – that of protecting community data. The Expert Committee acknowledges this need, which is particularly amplified in the case of big data solutions that profile groups often as much as individuals using such community data and then make decisions that affect these groups and their privacy. However, the Expert Committee simply urges the Government of India to consider a separate law for this purpose, stating the need for class action remedies without further details.[113]

The draft Bill does not address situations where it becomes difficult to take express consent because of technological or interface limitations. A reasonably strong case can also be built, as was done by Rahul Matthan recently, that the notice-and-consent foundations of this bill can diminish the flexibility needed for new data technologies to scale and grow.[114] To remedy this concern, and the separate set of concerns arising from data asymmetry on account of consent fatigue, he recommends an Accountability Model with its focus on remediation rather than punishment and a system of data audits.[115] Without delving deeper into this issue, we believe that when interface limitations render it difficult to furnish information to individual users, as with the internet of things or drones, the state must mandate the publication of privacy policies in freely accessible online/offline locations depending on the use case. Data minimisation too would have to be operationalised in this manner because beneficial purposes are often not visible enough to both users and controllers at the time of gathering data. However, without more data, such purposes will not present themselves in due course. A workable balance is to enhance transparency without limiting the amount of data in the hands of fiduciaries/controllers.[116] Therefore, similar transparency requirements must follow whenever they expand the scope of processing to purposes unspecified when obtaining user consent before data gathering, with the option for users to opt out from these new purposes. Another response, already found within the draft bill, is to exclude the processing of anonymised data from statutory controls on processing.[117] To enhance choice for users, a strong right of data portability must be created so that users can easily switch from less responsible to more trustworthy data fiduciaries/controllers.[118]

In the case of sensitive personal data, the governance framework must continue to insist upon data minimisation, except where widely accepted de-identification techniques such as differential privacy methods are employed by the fiduciary/controller when storing and sharing the data. The preferential protection for sensitive personal data should also extend both when assessing the security standards employed to

[113] Committee of Experts (n 97) 45–46. For a detailed critique of the Bill, see Amba Kak, 'The Srikrishna Committee's Data Protection Bill Does Not Do Enough to Hold the Government Accountable for Use of Personal Data' *The Caravan* (28 July 2018), www.caravanmagazine.in/governance/government-policy/srikrishna-committee-data-protection-government-accountable.

[114] Matthan relies on various use cases possible in healthcare through big data analytics to strengthen this case. See Rahul Matthan, *Privacy 3.0: Unlocking Our Data-Driven Future* (HarperCollins, 2018) 167–71.

[115] ibid 185–87. Clause 35 of the draft Bill recommends data audits for significant data fiduciaries.

[116] The draft Bill broadly endorses this idea, enumerating transparency obligations for data fiduciaries in cl 30.

[117] Personal Data Protection Bill, 2018, cl 2(3); Committee of Experts (n 97) 29–30.

[118] Personal Data Protection Bill, 2018, cl 26; Committee of Experts (n 29) 135.

prevent data leakages and when awarding penalties to deter future leakages. Thus, to the extent that such data is handled, the Expert Committee's principles on data minimisation, controller accountability, enforcement structure and penalties must invite full applicability. Express consent too must be insisted upon, making the gathering of this data a matter of personal choice beyond societal education.[119] This will pre-empt technological design that captures sensitive data without accommodating an appropriate interface for users to expressly consent to the same.

Differential protection of sensitive data can also incentivise a gradual strategy shift within big data companies from either user self-management or grudging regulatory compliance to voluntary adoption of 'privacy by design'.[120] The latter is a new paradigm where 'system designers conduct privacy risk assessments and incorporate privacy as a fundamental design parameter'.[121] The Expert Committee has also recognised that privacy by design, coupled with demonstrable capacity within organisations to meet privacy objectives, is central to building meaningful data controller accountability.[122] A regulatory approach that places emphasis on educating users while doubling down on the protection of sensitive personal data and providing a strong right of data portability can lead to better norms around the use of data and the integration of privacy-enhancing technologies in the long run. These outcomes, in turn, can drive market-based solutions that lighten regulatory burden.

III. THE REGULATORY STRUCTURE

A. Design

In an important study of regulation, Ian Ayres and John Braithwaite draw on the premise that state interventionism should be responsive to the conduct of the regulated in order to develop various responsiveness models that are particularly useful when regulating new technologies.[123] Of particular relevance is a model that envisages

[119] Personal Data Protection Bill, 2018, cl 18.

[120] The strategy should be to 'change the legal entitlements in a way sufficient to change the incentives of those who architect the technologies of consent'. See Lawrence Lessig, 'The Law of the Horse: What Cyberlaw Might Teach' (1999) 113 *Harvard Law Review* 501, 519. Article 25 of the EU's General Data Protection Regulation is a recent example. Indeed, the gamut of architectural interventions to enhance privacy have now expanded beyond data minimisation and consent technologies to transparency-enhancing technologies and broader identity management solutions. For an overview of privacy-enhancing technologies, see Simone Fischer-Hbner and Stefan Berthold, 'Privacy-Enhancing Technologies' in John R Vacca (ed), *Computer and Information Security Handbook* (Elsevier, 2017) 759–75.

[121] George Duncan, 'Privacy by Design' (2007) 317 *Science* 1178; Ann Cavoukian, 'Privacy by Design: The 7 Foundational Principles' (Information and Privacy Commissioner of Ontario, 2011), www.ipc.on.ca/wp-content/uploads/Resources/pbd-implement-7found-principles.pdf. While this paradigm is not immune from criticism levelled on the grounds of both practical difficulties and market disincentives, there is an increasing public demand in privacy-aware societies for more responsible data handling practices. See Demetrius Klitou, *Privacy-Invading Technologies and Privacy by Design* (Springer, 2014) 279–82.

[122] Committee of Experts (n 29) 147; Personal Data Protection Bill, 2018, cl 29.

[123] See Ian Ayres and John Braithwaite, *Responsive Regulation: Transcending the Deregulation Debate* (Oxford University Press, 1992).

negotiations between the state and individual firms to jointly develop regulations customised to each firm.[124] Once the internal rules are approved, governmental inspectors are required to evaluate the independence of the organisation's internal compliance group and to audit their efficiency and stringency. Beyond monitoring, the state will legally enforce violations of these 'private' rules that are the outcome of a public ratification process.[125] A well-designed regulatory body is critical to this endeavour.

In a similar vein, the Expert Committee veers towards co-regulation[126] over excessive 'command and control' or weak 'self-regulation'. Suggested measures such as DPIAs by data fiduciaries prior to the rollout of potential privacy-intrusive projects, technologies and policies,[127] and data audits undertaken by regulated entities, either through external auditors or the regulator itself, to assess compliance with both legal obligations and respective industry codes of conduct[128] place emphasis on a joint effort by industry players and the regulator to bring in more privacy-friendly practices. Mindful of the entry and operational barriers that a regulatory system could create, the Committee considered the possibility of risk-based or size-based classification of data fiduciaries for the purposes of different compliances,[129] 'inherently risky' data processing practices for which strict liability would arise[130] and 'non-material harms' for which liability would only arise upon proof of failure on the part of the data controller to take the appropriate remedial measures.[131] Taking seriously the issue of transparency, the Committee places considerable regulatory focus on data breach notifications in the event of confidentiality, integrity or availability breaches.[132]

The Expert Committee has also given considerable thought to addressing major omissions in the IT Act and the SPDI rules – a strong enforcement mechanism, deterrent penalties and effective compensation for aggrieved individuals.[133] It has recommended an independent DPA to perform several important functions: monitoring, enforcement, investigation and adjudication; standard-setting, including codes of conduct, and standards for security, DPIA and notification of significant data fiduciaries; and awareness generation.[134] It has also recommended strong penalties,

[124] ibid 101.

[125] ibid 106–07.

[126] The Expert Committee understands this model as being the adoption of a general data protection statute with broad provisions, complemented with codes of practices or conduct formulated by the specific sectors and approved by the government or a newly created data protection authority. Committee of Experts (n 29) 145; Personal Data Protection Bill, 2018, cl 61.

[127] Committee of Experts (n 29) 168; Personal Data Protection Bill, 2018, cl 33.

[128] Committee of Experts (n 29) 169; Personal Data Protection Bill, 2018, cl 35.

[129] Committee of Experts (n 29) 171–72; Personal Data Protection Bill, 2018, cl 38; Committee of Experts (n 97) 161–62.

[130] Committee of Experts (n 29) 148.

[131] ibid 149. It bears noting that only some of these ideas have found expression in the draft Bill. For instance, there is no classification of harms into material and non-material ones when imposing penalties or awarding compensation, though some degree of granularity in punitive and compensatory remedies arises because of mitigating factors contained in cll 74(4) and 75(4) respectively in the draft Bill.

[132] ibid 161; Personal Data Protection Bill, 2018, cl 3(30), read with cl 32.

[133] Committee of Experts (n 29) 175, 185–86.

[134] Committee of Experts (n 29) 181–82, 188; Committee of Experts (n 97) 153–55.

quantified on the basis of per-day amounts for each day of continuing violation with an upper limit fixed at a percentage of the defaulting data controller's annual turnover and a right to compensation.[135] The adjudicating authority, when determining the quantum of the penalty, can take into account factors such as the nature and extent of violation of the data protection obligation, the nature of the personal information involved, the number of individuals affected, whether infringement was intentional or negligent, measures taken by data controller to mitigate the damage suffered and the previous track record of the data controller in this regard.[136] However, while imbibing global best practices in this regard, particularly those contained in the EU's newly in force General Data Protection Regulation (GDPR), the Committee has not sufficiently addressed the worrisome track record of Indian regulators on three fronts: independence, capacity and inter se coordination.

B. Regulatory Independence

In order to appreciate the concerns arising from inadequate regulatory independence, we need look no further than the UIDAI. This hybrid regulator and custodian of the Aadhaar database is a highly conflicted body. The Aadhaar Act vests power with the Central Government and the state governments to require that individuals undergo Aadhaar authentication to receive any 'subsidy, benefit or service for which the expenditure is incurred from, or the receipt therefrom forms part of, the Consolidated Fund of India'.[137] Besides the larger worry of this leading to a digital panopticon, the UIDAI has neither any say in the choice of public services for which the database would be put to use, nor the independence to freeze authentication when it fears that Aadhaar data is residing unsafely in government websites.[138] Being the data custodian, it has no serious incentives to disclose the occurrence of a breach, despite the Act vesting rights in the UIDAI, not the citizen, to be notified of data breaches and then decide how best to proceed. No grievance redressal mechanism or even data breach notifications are provided for individuals affected by such a breach, which worsens the problem and leads to more defensiveness than transparency on the UIDAI's part in the recent past. Similarly, it is conflicted when regulating the use of the Aadhaar database for private authentication. Being tasked with developing a revenue model around the biometric database through commercial arrangements with private requesting entities, while at the same time guaranteeing oversight over ways in which such entities use or abuse the database, is a structural design flaw that severely compromises the UIDAI's functional independence.

These concerns become more serious when factoring in the surveillance possibilities presented by Aadhaar's big data ecosystem. The IT Act vests authority with the

[135] Committee of Experts (n 29) 200; Committee of Experts (n 97) 164–65.

[136] Committee of Experts (n 29) 195; Committee of Experts (n 97) 164–65.

[137] Aadhaar (Targeted Delivery of Financial and Other Subsidies, Benefits, and Services) Act, 2016, s 7.

[138] Ananth Padmanabhan, 'The Three Sins of Aadhaar' *OPEN Magazine* (4 August 2017), www.openthemagazine.com/article/essay/the-three-sins-of-aadhaar.

centre and the states to monitor, intercept and decrypt information,[139] and enlists the assistance of intermediaries in this exercise,[140] for a wide range of purposes from state security, sovereignty and defence, to the investigation of any offence, and the maintenance of public order. They are also empowered to issue data retention mandates to intermediaries in order to enable quick accessibility to data.[141] There are no limitations on the extent to which data may be gathered, leaving the proportionality of privacy intrusions to the subjective satisfaction of the intercepting authority.[142] Surveillance procedures, including the present review mechanism, leave too much to bureaucratic good faith, failing to inspire confidence in the exercise of surveillance powers. They omit important principles for responsible, human rights-sensitive surveillance, including independent judicial evaluation, a fair and public hearing within reasonable time, user notification and systemic transparency.[143] This insufficiency, and possible illegality, of baseline norms governing surveillance in India extend beyond the IT Act to telephonic conversations and mass-surveillance programmes.[144] The Aadhaar Act broadly replicates this framework with the additional safeguard that a judicial order from a District Judge or senior in ranking must necessarily mandate the disclosure of any information,[145] except when such disclosure is required on the grounds of national security.[146] The UIDAI's powers are hardly those of a regulator, being much more in the nature of what technical intermediaries must do under the IT Act when faced with interception orders.[147] Yet, the UIDAI, not the aggrieved individual, is represented at the statutory hearing when the judicial authority considers disclosure requests, giving rise to serious worries about how the Aadhaar database will be put to use.

Some of these issues surrounding Aadhaar are discussed in the Expert Committee report accompanying the draft Bill.[148] The Committee has noted that in the light of the Government of India and various state governments making Aadhaar mandatory for several benefits and subsidies, it is imperative to make the UIDAI autonomous in its decision-making and to vest it with enforcement powers akin to those of a traditional regulator. On the enforcement front, the Committee has recommended

[139] Information Technology Act, 2000, s 69.

[140] ibid s 69(3), read with the Information Technology (Procedure and Safeguards for Interception, Monitoring and Decryption of Information) Rules, 2009.

[141] Information Technology Act, 2000, s 67C.

[142] Ananth Padmanabhan, 'Even after Privacy Verdict, India is Easy Game for Internet Monitoring' *The Print* (10 October 2017), theprint.in/opinion/internet-monitoring-in-india-a-post-privacy-analysis/12046.

[143] Maria Xynou, 'Policy Recommendations for Surveillance Law in India' *The Center for Internet and Society* (14 March 2015), cis-india.org/internet-governance/blog/policy-recommendations-for-surveillance-law-in-india-and-analysis-of-legal-provisions-on-surveillance-in-india-and-the-necessary-and-proportionate-principles.pdf.

[144] Vrinda Bhandari, 'India's Communication Surveillance through The Puttaswamy Lens' *The Leap Blog* (18 May 2018), https://blog.theleapjournal.org/2018/05/indias-communication-surveillance.html.

[145] Aadhaar (Targeted Delivery of Financial and Other Subsidies, Benefits, and Services) Act, 2016, s 33(1).

[146] ibid s 33(2).

[147] The UIDAI can be superseded and reconstituted by the Central Government for failure to comply with its directions, under s 48(1)(b) of the Aadhaar Act.

[148] Committee of Experts (n 97) 100–01.

additional powers to the UIDAI to impose civil penalties on errant or non-compliant entities, which will operate concurrently with the powers of the DPA to act against any entity in the Aadhaar ecosystem, including the UIDAI when it performs its role as a data fiduciary. On the independence front, the Committee has recommended bolstering the financial autonomy of the UIDAI by earmarking penalties imposed by this authority to a separate fund. However, we believe that these measures may not be sufficient in themselves to guarantee complete independence in terms of the functioning of the UIDAI. Any reasonable move towards securing the UIDAI's regulatory independence must necessarily involve separating the data custodian and data regulator functions rather than improving both, as the Committee seems to suggest.[149]

Many of these themes are addressed, though not in a uniformly satisfactory manner, in the Supreme Court's verdict on the constitutional validity of the Aadhaar Act.[150] The grievance redressal mechanism has been extended to cover private complaints. The disclosure of Aadhaar data on grounds of national security interest will now require some judicial scrutiny, and disclosure requests will have to emanate from an officer ranking higher than a joint secretary. As already discussed above, some brakes have been applied on excessive seeding and private authentication. Despite these positive outcomes, where the majority truly falls short is in taking a more principled view on the UIDAI and its current role. The plea on the vice of excessive delegation, which is very important in this regard as it focuses on the UIDAI's unfettered authority to both lay down policy and then implement it, has received little to no attention. The dissenting opinion takes this plea seriously, maps the range of powers vested with the UIDAI and concludes that this body does not meet the essential precondition of an independent monitoring agency required before embarking on technology projects such as Aadhaar that deal with sensitive personal data on a large scale.[151]

As big data solutions for public purpose gain momentum, it is therefore critical to have an independent institution to evaluate and monitor them. Differential regulatory treatment of public and private solutions is required. A technical body within the Department of Electronics and Information Technology may, subject to requisite capacity-building, serve the needs of evaluating algorithmic discrimination in the private sector. However, it cannot be considered independent enough to evaluate algorithmic bias in public decision-making across areas such as predictive policing, education and labour market reform, and resource allocation. Emerging research discusses the need for algorithmic impact assessments in these scenarios.[152]

[149] In this regard, the Expert Committee has made rather important recommendations to protect the privacy of individuals enrolled in Aadhaar, which seek to address the UIDAI's data custodian role. The Committee has recommended confining the use of Aadhaar for authentication – a process involving the sharing of biometrics from the individual's end and of demographic and other information from the UIDAI's end – to public entities performing a public function. See Committee of Experts (n 97) 100.

[150] *Justice Puttaswamy v Union of India* (n 79).

[151] Madhav Khosla and Ananth Padmanabhan, 'In Aadhaar, Supreme Court Did Not Probe if it is a Tool to Track Citizens' *The Print* (30 September 2018), https://theprint.in/opinion/in-aadhaar-supreme-court-did-not-probe-if-it-is-a-tool-to-track-citizens/127118.

[152] Dillon Reisman et al, 'Algorithmic Impact Assessments: A Practical Framework for Public Agency Accountability' *AI Now Institute* (April 2018), ainowinstitute.org/aiareport2018.pdf.

Without an independent regulator, these much-needed solutions to mitigate discrimination harms cannot be effectively deployed. Similarly, effective safeguards and transparency regarding public data breaches, linking of multiple government databases, and state surveillance demand an independent regulator that can push back against state overreach.

Concerns of independence are not unique to public big data solutions. This is evident from a cursory examination of the emerging problems that confront us and the trade-offs they involve. Algorithmic decision-making – a justifiable exercise towards greater efficiency – falls within the freedom of trade and business and must be delicately balanced against possible discrimination harms. Rampant dissemination of fake news – a direct outcome of more data and processing power with social media giants – remains, for all its ills, an exercise of free speech and expression.[153] Similarly, data-driven technology platforms have clear incentives to pursue network effects over profitability,[154] monopolistic control over data[155] and vertical integration through mergers.[156] Resulting data silos[157] can potentially lock down innovation, with huge repercussions in certain situations.[158] Here too, there is an apparent tension between the fundamental freedom to carry on business and the wider public interest. Only an independent regulator can inspire public confidence that ultimate resolutions of such tensions shall be fair and principled, soaring above both populism and industry capture. In addition to functional separation from the executive, an independent regulatory mechanism that meets this standard requires vigilant public scrutiny and feedback.

C. Capacity and Coordination

Regulatory capacity is also a significant hurdle when translating internationally accepted norms into real outcomes that benefit Indian citizens. A thoughtful analysis of the Expert Committee's provisional recommendations points out that India ranks much lower on this front than all other jurisdictions and data protection models from which the document takes inspiration.[159] The analysis argues that data protection addresses a wide array of highly discretionary and transaction-intensive activities, resulting in the need for higher regulatory capacity.[160] The big data economy also

[153] Apar Gupta, 'Dubious Concern' *Indian Express* (4 May 2018), indianexpress.com/article/opinion/columns/dubious-concern-5162551.

[154] Lina M Khan, 'Amazon's Antitrust Paradox' (2016) 126 *Yale Law Journal* 710, 785.

[155] ibid 783.

[156] ibid 792–93.

[157] Terrell McSweeny and Brian O'Dea, 'Data, Innovation, and Potential Competition in Digital Markets – Looking beyond Short-Term Price Effects in Merger Analysis' (2018) 2(2) *Antitrust Chronicle* 7, 8–9.

[158] Michael Mattioli, 'The Data-Pooling Problem' (2017) 32 *Berkeley Technology Law Journal* 179, 208–14 (demonstrating that competitive fears often motivate pharmaceutical companies to refuse data sharing for cancer research).

[159] Suyash Rai, 'A Pragmatic Approach to Data Protection' *The Leap Blog* (9 February 2018), https://blog.theleapjournal.org/2018/02/a-pragmatic-approach-to-data-protection.html.

[160] ibid.

gives rise to new challenges that demand the rapid upgrading of skills from the regulator's end. For instance, the opacity in unsupervised learning algorithms[161] cannot be sufficiently addressed through a mandate for human involvement in decision-making or a right to explanation as provided for in the GDPR[162] and yet, stricter remedies involving a technical evaluation of algorithms will considerably slow down regulatory functioning.[163] These considerations necessitate professional incentives to strengthen regulatory capacity, upgrade technical skills and infuse anticipatory governance[164] through interaction with scientific and technological communities, as well as periodic review of regulatory performance.[165]

They also prompt a necessary rethink on the optimal zoning between state-enforced data protection and self-regulation in the Indian context. Scholarly insights on smart regulation emphasise the need for regulatory pluralism and reliance on regulatory surrogates, including for-profit and not-for-profit actors, as part of the shift towards more flexible and imaginative forms of social control.[166] A central guiding principle here is the deployment of complementary instrument mixes over single instrument approaches. Real outcomes then depend on striking the right balance and keeping the instrument mix to as much as, and no more than, is required to achieve the desired result.[167] Smart regulation theorists advocate minimal interventionism as the first response, an escalating response model to increase dependability of outcomes through instrument sequencing, and encouraging businesses to go 'beyond compliance' within existing legal requirements.[168] Faced with capacity constraints, Indian regulatory response towards big data must inevitably incorporate these insights.[169]

[161] Frank Pasquale characterises this as 'a system whose workings are mysterious; we can observe its inputs and outputs, but we cannot tell how one becomes the other, or its use or consequences'. See Frank Pasquale, *The Black Box Society: The Secret Algorithms that Control Money and Information* (Harvard University Press, 2015) 3.

[162] Lilian Edwards and Michael Veale, 'Slave to the Algorithm? Why a 'Right to an Explanation' is Probably Not the Remedy You are Looking for' (2017) 18 *Duke Law and Technology Review* 51, 59–60.

[163] As Edwards and Veale point out in the context of the EU, 'neutral data arbiters' such as the State Data Protection Authorities are already struggling to regulate general privacy issues and will struggle even more with 'complex and opaque societal algorithmic harms'; ibid 77.

[164] Daniel Sarewitz, 'Anticipatory Governance of Emerging Technologies' in Gary E Marchant et al (eds), *The Growing Gap between Emerging Technologies and Legal-Ethical Oversight: The Pacing Problem* (Springer, 2011) 95, 100.

[165] The Australian government's Regulator Performance Framework helps here by prescribing key performance indicators (KPIs). These include an assessment of factors such as quality of communication and stakeholder engagement, compliance costs, regulatory approach towards small businesses and start-ups, steps to minimise unintended negative impact, risk assessment procedures, regulatory coordination to share information, and flexibility of the framework to adapt and change. See Department of Agriculture and Water Resources, 'Regulator Performance Framework: Deregulation Agenda' (Government of Australia, 2016), www.agriculture.gov.au/SiteCollectionDocuments/about/deregulation/regulatory-behaviour-performance/regulator-performance-framework-2016-17.pdf.

[166] Neil Gunningham and Darren Sinclair, 'Smart Regulation' in Peter Drahos (ed), *Regulatory Theory: Foundations and Applications* (ANU Press, 2017) 133.

[167] ibid 139–41.

[168] ibid 134–35.

[169] See Beni Chugh et al, 'Effective Enforcement of a Data Protection Regime' (Dvara Research Working Paper Series No WP-2018-01, 2018), https://www.dvara.com/blog/wp-content/uploads/2018/07/Effective-Enforcement-of-a-Data-Protection-Regime.pdf for a recent work that attempts to develop a risk-based granular set of enforcement toolkits.

With increasing reliance on the internet protocol for voice calls and the growth of digital media platforms, the Telecom Regulatory Authority of India has started examining various aspects of data governance, including regulation of over-the-top platforms, data protection and net neutrality. The Department of Telecommunications is now actively invested in policies and regulatory frameworks for the growth of digitally enabled new technologies, considering their importance for 'propelling' India forward.[170] The fake news problem has invited the attention of the Ministry of Information and Broadcasting[171] and the Election Commission of India,[172] while the RBI and SEBI grapple with problems relating to financial and transaction data and communications. In addition to the more obvious regulatory uncertainty that chequered decision-making can bring about, diverse stakeholders with decisive influence over regulatory or architectural choices present a deeper problem. Regulatory choices by each of the above-mentioned institutions, or others,[173] can fundamentally impact the big data economy.

The draft National Encryption Policy, circulated in 2015 for public discussion and shelved immediately thereafter, illustrates this problem. The Ministry of Electronics and Information Technology (MEITY) mandated data retention of plain text information (ie, in unencrypted format) through this policy. This choice towards further easing up of on-demand governmental access to private communications would have significantly reshaped the understanding of privacy over the internet.[174] Similarly, the RBI's recent data localisation directive – a poorly reasoned one-page order – disturbs the idea of a global, borderless internet that we have come to benefit from in India.[175] To resolve inter se coordination problems and ensure consistency of directional norms, the newly proposed DPA must have its say (final or otherwise) in all matters relating to data governance.[176] In addition, the authors recommend the following for India's big data ecosystem in order to pre-empt coordination failures and regulatory overreach.

First, information asymmetries between innovators and regulators regarding the risks involved with big data can potentially instigate ill-formed regulatory responses, hence the need for an interfacing agency between them, built on a public-private

[170] Ministry of Telecommunications, 'National Digital Communications Policy 2018 – Draft for Consultation' (New Delhi, Department of Telecommunications, 2018), www.dot.gov.in/sites/default/files/DNDCP2018.pdf.

[171] Karan Thapar, 'The "Fake News" Fiasco' *The Hindu* (6 April 2018), www.thehindu.com/opinion/op-ed/the-fake-news-fiasco/article23447264.ece.

[172] Devesh K Pandey, 'EC Seeks Help to Detect "Fake News"' *The Hindu* (9 April 2018), www.thehindu.com/news/national/ec-seeks-help-to-detect-fake-news/article23484897.ece.

[173] See Raghav Bahl, 'Walmart-Flipkart Deal: Young Entrepreneurs' Pride, Govt's Shame' *The Quint* (13 May 2018), www.thequint.com/voices/opinion/walmart-flipkart-deal-nda-government-indian-entrepreneurship.

[174] Govind Rammurthy, 'National Encryption Policy: Not Just Privacy, But also Feasibility and Security are at Risk' *Firstpost* (28 September 2015), www.firstpost.com/business/national-encryption-policy-not-just-privacy-but-also-feasibility-and-security-are-at-risk-2447308.html.

[175] Rajrishi Singhal, 'Like the Govt, RBI Policy Also Gets Unpredictable' *LiveMint* (29 April 2018), www.livemint.com/Opinion/uHT6wK5VUNDpb4Tw2OJMvK/Like-the-govt-RBI-policy-also-gets-unpredictable.html.

[176] The Personal Data Protection Bill, 2018, cl 67 provides for the DPA to consult other regulators or authorities when deciding upon matters involving concurrent jurisdiction, but says nothing about situations where such other regulators and authorities decide upon similar matters.

partnership. The National Investment Promotion and Facilitation Agency of India, set up as a non-profit venture under the Department of Industrial Policy and Promotion and serving as the first point of contact for investors, presents the template for a similar agency that could help data innovators interface with regulators better.

Second, time-bound regulations help build flexibility into the regulatory system by coming in with a 'sunset clause' that marks its expiry after a certain period. This compels the regulator to reassess the public policy rationale for the regulation in question, which is much needed in the context of technological innovation.[177] 'Experimental regulation' responds better to the dynamic nature of big data innovation by providing exceptions to existing regulation within a ring-fenced environment. They aid innovators to roll out new solutions in a limited, though real, consumer setting without extensive regulatory compliance.[178] They also help create a feedback loop for regulators and thereby inform risk-based responses that are customised to big data possibilities in specific sectors.[179]

Third, regulatory sandboxes can help operationalise such experimental regulation. These sandboxes are essentially test-beds, initiated by the sectoral regulator for live testing of innovations by private firms in a controlled environment.[180] They have gained traction in the data-driven financial technologies space where regulatory capacity is stretched, and the balancing of regulatory objectives is a complex exercise.[181] We believe that a similar sandbox approach is needed across verticals – healthcare, mobility, agriculture and other key sectors – to balance big data solutions with privacy, security and other concerns in a supervised environment without stalling innovation. This, in turn, is critical to both enhancing digital inclusion and influencing the deployment of responsible technology architectures early on.

CONCLUSION

Regulating new technologies comes with several challenges. Even a concrete mapping of the harms involved is often difficult, as seen here in the context of big data innovation. Gauging their seriousness and relative importance, as well as assessing the optimal zoning between state-enforced regulation vis-a-vis markets, technology and self-regulation, also involves considerable complexities. Questions of regulatory design, independence, capacity and inter se coordination again play out in ways very different from other sectors. Instead of strong command-and-control frameworks, it is better to build mechanisms that facilitate multi-disciplinary interaction among innovators, civil society and regulators, and to focus on regulatory responses that are

[177] Sofia Ranchordas, 'Innovation-Friendly Regulation: The Sunset of Regulation, the Sunrise of Innovation' (2015) 55 *Jurimetrics* 201.

[178] Anne Veerpalu and Nikolay Demchuk, 'Is it Time for a Sandbox for Start-ups in Estonia?' *NJORD Law Firm* (1 March 2017), www.njordlaw.com/time-sandbox-start-ups-estonia.

[179] ibid.

[180] Ivo Jenik and Kate Lauer, 'Regulatory Sandboxes and Financial Inclusion' (CGAP Working Paper, 2017), www.cgap.org/sites/default/files/Working-Paper-Regulatory-Sandboxes-Oct-2017.pdf.

[181] ibid 2.

graded and risk-based rather than a one size-fits-all approach. However, when core interests are involved – such as the privacy and security of sensitive personal data, the allocation of public resources and the protection of citizens against undesirable surveillance – the enforcement mechanism must be robust enough to make delinquent actors fall into line as well as to deter future misconduct. Above all, considerable flexibility needs to be built into the regulatory framework in order to implement responsive, rather than reactive, regulation.

Part IV

Regulation in Practice

13

The Enforcement of Indian Competition Law

Administrative or Regulatory?

ADITYA BHATTACHARJEA*

INTRODUCTION

THE PURPOSE OF competition law (or antitrust law, as it is known in the US) is to deter or modify certain kinds of business strategies that inhibit or prevent competition, which is regarded as a desirable feature of a market economy. Unlike the laws that are discussed in some other chapters in this volume, which regulate firms in particular sectors, the remit of competition law covers the entire economy, excepting those sectors that may be specifically excluded in the law itself or by government edict. Both sector regulation and antitrust seek to correct market failures, but of different kinds and with different interventions. I begin in section I with an outline of these differences, in the course of which I provide a brief exposition of the scope and basic principles of competition law and economics. However, the rest of the chapter shows that the reality is much messier. Section II asks whether advanced countries' competition law enforcement regimes can be classified as 'administrative' or 'regulatory'.[1] I also venture some comments on the system

* I would like to thank the editors of this volume for inviting me to contribute, for pointing me towards relevant source materials, and for their encouraging and helpful comments on earlier drafts. The usual disclaimer applies.

[1] There seems to be no consensus on the definition of these terms. Coming to this subject from a very different disciplinary perspective, my approach is synthesised from TV Somanathan, 'The Administrative and Regulatory State' in Sujit Choudhry, Madhav Khosla and Pratap Bhanu Mehta (eds), *The Oxford Handbook of the Indian Constitution* (Oxford University Press, 2016); and Navroz K Dubash and Bronwen Morgan, 'The Rise of the Regulatory State of the South' in Navroz Dubash and Bronwen Morgan (eds), *The Rise of the Regulatory State of the South: Infrastructure and Development in Emerging Economies* (Oxford University Press, 2013) 1. As I understand it, an administrative state is one that operates through ministries and departments of the executive, staffed by civil servants and functioning under direct political control, while a regulatory state operates through specialised agencies that are staffed

prevailing in the US and how the consensus on economic efficiency as the sole goal of antitrust is now being challenged. Section III goes further and shows that this consensus is of relatively recent origin and is not universally accepted in other jurisdictions. It examines how developing countries are different and what implications this has for their adoption of competition laws, which have proliferated in the last couple of decades. I trace the evolution of India's competition regime in section IV and discuss the pattern of appointments to the Competition Commission of India (CCI) in section V. In Section VI, I show that although the CCI has firmly asserted its jurisdiction over anti-competitive behaviour by state-owned enterprises and government departments, it has held back in some instances from condemning such activities when they concern complex and sensitive government policies.

I. SECTORAL REGULATION v COMPETITION LAW

The need for sector-specific regulation arises in two different contexts. The first is in sectors characterised by a 'natural monopoly', in which competition is infeasible because more than one firm would not be commercially viable in a particular territory. Examples are airports, major ports, pipelines for distribution of petroleum products, or wire networks for distribution of electricity or landline telecommunications. Second, regulation is required in sectors such as banking, insurance and securities markets, where excessive competition is undesirable. This is because free entry and vigorous price competition, which are regarded as desirable in other activities even though they result in elimination of inefficient firms, increase systemic risk in financial services: the failure of even one large firm may ravage the entire economy. Sector regulators of both types typically choose which firms are allowed to enter a particular activity or area, and lay down detailed rules and standards *before* they commence operations, regarding their pricing, quality of product or service, and access to their facilities or networks. In financial services, regulators must lay down capital adequacy and prudential investment norms to prevent excessive risk taking. Competition regulators, on the other hand, leave these operational decisions or outcomes to be determined by the competitive process, stepping in only when the process itself is endangered by certain types of behaviour by firms.

Competition laws usually cover three kinds of potentially anti-competitive behaviour: interfirm agreements that limit competition; abusive behaviour by a single large firm to retain or enhance its dominant position in a market; and interfirm mergers and acquisitions that result in fewer competitors.[2] The first two categories usually result in the initiation of an investigation or a case, on the basis of a complaint or information received by the competition authority, *after* the impugned conduct has

by technically qualified professionals, who enforce regulations whose primary if not sole objective is to promote economic efficiency, and who function at arm's length from the executive, insulated in particular from political pressures. We shall see that these categories sometimes blend into each other.

[2] For a slightly more elaborate non-technical exposition of the economics of antitrust, see the introductory section of Aditya Bhattacharjea, 'Of Omissions and Commissions: India's Competition Laws' (2010) 45(35) *Economic and Political Weekly* 31.

taken place, from a party that has been harmed. The third usually requires the merging parties themselves to notify their intentions to the authority; in most jurisdictions, this applies only to mergers in which the size of the transaction or the assets or turnover of the parties exceed specified thresholds. The authority then reviews the proposed merger from the competition perspective before it is allowed to proceed. (Firms that are subject to sector regulation also come under the jurisdiction of competition law in respect of these three types of conduct. In principle, these are distinct from the mandate of the regulators, but there may be overlaps and conflict in some instances.)

The most egregious form of anti-competitive agreement is a *cartel*, in which firms, instead of competing with each other, mutually agree to fix prices (or bids in an auction) or allocate territories or customers amongst themselves. In most countries, cartelisation is illegal 'per se' – only the fact of a collusive agreement or understanding has to be proved; its effects are irrelevant. This is because cartels almost invariably cause harm without any redeeming virtues. In many advanced countries, cartelisation is a criminal offence, with managers being liable for prison terms and personal fines, in addition to massive fines being imposed on the offending firms.

There are, however, other kinds of agreements that may restrict competition while generating some benefits for consumers. The same is the case with mergers, which may result in cost savings that can be passed on to consumers. Some kinds of allegedly 'abusive' behaviour may simply be symptoms of vigorous competition, which is the hallmark of a healthy market-based economic system. All such non-cartel cases require a detailed understanding of the extent of actual and potential competition in the relevant market (the definition of which is itself a non-trivial matter), whether the impugned conduct or merger is likely to result in significant harm to competition, and any offsetting benefits. All this requires a complex technical exercise that is best left to specialised agencies and tribunals.[3] Monetary penalties are usually imposed for infringements, along with a direction to terminate or modify the impugned agreement, practice or merger. The competition agency's decisions are usually subject to judicial review on the grounds of procedural fairness at a minimum, although superior courts in some countries have pronounced landmark judgments that have overruled these bodies as well as their own precedents, on the basis of a different set of economic arguments.

An overarching principle in most jurisdictions is that competition law is supposed to protect *competition*, not *competitors*. The competitive process produces both winners and losers: uncompetitive firms are forced to downsize or close, with consequent losses in terms of employees' jobs and investors' money. This provides a second reason for adjudication by independent regulatory bodies based on legal and economic principles – otherwise, the political process would invite intervention by the executive, based on which parties to the dispute command more influence with the government of the day.

[3] In the US, cases of this kind are also prosecuted in regular courts; even in cases in which the government would like to block a merger, the matter is decided in a federal court, as in the very recent case of *AT&T/Time Warner* (*US v AT&T et al, United States District Court for the District of Columbia* 17-2511, 2018).

In this respect too, competition law enforcement stands on a different footing from sectoral regulation. Regulators are often required to hold public hearings before taking crucial decisions so as to ensure a measure of legitimacy and also to take on board the views of different stakeholders. In contrast, antitrust/competition cases belonging to the first two categories distinguished above (interfirm agreements and single-firm dominance) are decided in judicial or quasi-judicial proceedings, where only the parties to the case are heard. Only in merger cases in which there is prima facie a likely adverse effect on competition are comments invited from other interested parties.[4] Another contrast is that agencies that regulate natural monopolies are supposed to prevent the monopolists from earning monopoly profits. But in modern competition law, large size, market domination, high profits or even a monopoly are not perceived as objectionable as such. What is condemned, in the oft-quoted words of a classic judgment of the US Supreme Court, is 'the wilful acquisition or maintenance of [monopoly] power as distinguished from growth or development as a consequence of a superior product, business acumen, or historic accident'.[5] Or, as the Competition Commission of India put it more pithily in a recent order: 'Dominance in itself is not bad, its abuse is.'[6]

These arguments provide further justification for leaving the enforcement of competition law to specialised agencies which are insulated from political interference that may cater to anti-big business sentiments on the one hand or crony capitalists on the other – in short, under the aegis of a regulatory rather than an administrative state. As compared to sectoral regulators, the possibility of 'regulatory capture' is less likely to arise. Competition agencies, because of their economy-wide mandate, are unlikely to develop a close nexus based on repeated interactions with a handful of firms in particular sectors. In addition, they do not require the industry-specific technical knowledge that allows for a 'revolving door' for a limited number of qualified personnel to move back and forth between the regulatory agency and the regulated entities. An independent and professionally staffed competition agency, then, seems to be the ideal vehicle for the enforcement of a competition law. However, even in mature jurisdictions, the reality is far from such an ideal, as I shall now show.

II. THE INSTITUTIONAL FRAMEWORK IN DEVELOPED COUNTRIES

The institutional structure of mature antitrust jurisdictions does not offer much guidance on whether an administrative or regulatory approach to competition law enforcement is preferable. The Canadian Competition Bureau is probably the best example of a competition agency operating within the regulatory framework.

[4] American courts sometimes allow amicus briefs on behalf of other interested parties for non-merger cases as well.

[5] *United States v Grinnell Corp*, 384 US 563 (1966) 571.

[6] Combined order dated 20 June 2018 in Case Nos 25–28 of 2017, *Meru Travel Solutions Pvt Ltd v ANI Technologies Pvt Ltd*, para 54 (available at www.cci.gov.in; there is no official reporting journal for CCI orders).

It is traditionally headed by a professional, is well-staffed and enforces what is probably the world's most economics-informed competition law. Other regimes are harder to classify. In the European Union (EU), the Directorate General for Competition is well-staffed by professionals and far removed from the national governments of the Member States. It frequently issues regulations and guidelines that incorporate economic thinking, but economic analysis often plays second fiddle to legal arguments, especially on appeal. It is headed by a career 'Eurocrat' and overseen by a Commissioner who gives political direction, influenced by the European Parliament. According to *The Economist*, the current Commissioner for Competition, Margrethe Vestager (a politician from the Danish Social Liberal Party), 'acknowledges that her job is political, but in a noble sense: the single market is an aspect of the EU that enjoys support even from Eurosceptics'.[7] As I shall point out below, the objective of maintaining the single market overrides standard competition analysis in the EU. In Britain, the competition agency is professionally staffed, but a Labour Party politician, Gordon Borrie, was head of the agency (then known as the Office of Fair Trading) from 1976 to 1992, and Andrew Tyrie, a Conservative Member of Parliament for two decades, has recently been appointed to head its current successor, the Competition and Markets Authority. All these agencies can independently investigate and decide cases, and impose substantial fines, but criminal cases for participation in a cartel can only be prosecuted in the regular courts. All decisions and penalties are appealable to higher judicial bodies.

Antitrust enforcement in the US is even more difficult to fit into an administrative/regulatory binary, or even along a spectrum. There are two federal antitrust agencies with substantially overlapping jurisdictions: the Federal Trade Commission (FTC) and the Antitrust Division of the Department of Justice (DoJ). They too are well-staffed by professionals, but cannot decide cases or even issue regulations; they can only bring cases before federal courts. So can the attorneys general of each of the 50 states. All these agencies often disagree with each other on particular antitrust matters; so do the federal district courts and the Circuit Courts of Appeal that decide the cases. The Supreme Court has the final word, often overturning the judgments of the lower courts and sometimes its own precedents, not just on procedural but also substantive matters. Antitrust issues are therefore decided by generalist judges, not by bureaucrats or independent agencies specialising in competition matters. The US Congress has effectively acquiesced to a complete reinterpretation of the antitrust laws by the courts, which at least in this domain exercise virtually legislative authority – but only while deciding cases that come before them.[8] (Merger review

[7] https://www.economist.com/europe/2015/05/02/the-enforcer. A noted European competition lawyer and scholar offers a much sharper assessment of Ms Vestager's priorities: 'A seasoned politician, Vestager knows that the payoffs of whacking a tech platform are immense in a continent rife with popular distrust against corporate bigness, U.S.-style capitalism and tech platforms' permission-less attitude toward innovation.' Nicolas Petit, 'EU Engaged in Antitrust Gerrymandering against Google', http://thehill.com/opinion/technology/399742-eu-engaged-in-antitrust-gerrymandering-against-google.

[8] See Thomas C. Arthur, 'Competition Law and Development: Lessons from the US Experience' in Daniel Sokol et al (eds), *Competition Law and Development* (Stanford University Press 2013) 71–76, which also cites several other scholars to this effect.

is an exception; most cases are settled between the federal agencies and the merging parties, with the courts deciding only in cases in which no settlement is reached.)

As for independence from political influence, which is a major issue in the administrative/regulatory debate, judges of the Supreme Court and federal courts, the Attorney General who heads the DoJ, the Assistant Attorney General who heads its Antitrust Division, and the FTC Commissioners are presidential nominees. Their appointments are subject to Senate approval, but the majority party can usually ensure the confirmation of nominees of a president from its own party, or block those of a president from the opposite party (however, the FTC's governing statute requires that not more than three of the five Commissioners can be from the same party). Most state attorneys general are directly elected on party platforms; the few remaining ones are elected by their state legislatures or are chosen by state governors. No doubt, the appointment of all these key decision-makers, although politically charged, is seldom based on their views on antitrust matters (except, of course, the FTC Commissioners and the head of the DoJ's Antitrust Division, who are chosen for their domain knowledge). But views on economic issues generally tend to be correlated with those on more politically salient issues along the ideological spectrum.

This highly fragmented system is saved from incoherence by the near-universal consensus in the last few decades amongst judges, lawyers and economists, regardless of their political affiliation, that economic efficiency should be the sole criterion for evaluating contested business behaviour, irrespective of the legislative intent behind the antitrust statutes.[9] It seems that the tensions between what Vermeule has called the three contending perspectives of 'law, democracy and knowledge' in the US administrative state (into which he subsumes government agencies) have been reconciled, at least in the antitrust domain.[10]

The focus on economic efficiency is the legacy of the Chicago Law School view of antitrust, which was in the ascendant during the 1970s and 1980s, and remains

[9] Disdain for legislative intent emerges clearly from the opinions of some prominent legal scholars and economists, quoted in Aditya Bhattacharjea, 'Who Needs Antitrust? Or, is Developing Country Antitrust Different' in Sokol et al (n 8) 55.

[10] Adrian Vermeule, 'The Administrative State: Law, Democracy, and Knowledge' in Mark Tushnet, Mark A Graber and Sanford Levinson (eds), *The Oxford Handbook of the US Constitution* (Oxford University Press, 2015). Still, political and ideological cleavages remain influential in some antitrust decisions. A comprehensive study of all cartel prosecutions in the US between 1969 and 2013 found that 'particular Presidencies matter for cartel prosecutions, and variation across Presidential administrations led to marked shifts in the total number of cartels prosecuted'; Vivek Ghosal and Daniel Sokol, 'Policy Innovations, Political Preferences, and Cartel Prosecutions' (2016) 48 *Review of Industrial Organization* 405, 405. This happened despite cartels being universally condemned as the most reprehensible form of anti-competitive conduct. Further evidence of political partisanship comes from two very recent high-profile cases. Media commentators opined that President Trump's hostility to Time Warner's television network CNN was behind the DoJ's attempt to block its acquisition by AT&T – the first vertical merger to be challenged in four decades. (A federal court refused to block the merger – see n 3 above.) In *Ohio v American Express Co* (585 US ____ (2018)), the DoJ and 17 state attorneys general had challenged a clause whereby American Express had prevented retailers from 'steering' consumers to use credit cards which charged lower merchant fees. Although the case involved technical issues of market definition in two-sided platform competition, the Supreme Court rejected the plaintiffs' arguments by a 5:4 split that exactly mirrored the conservative/liberal divide that is usually manifested in cases that involve, eg, civil liberties or social policy.

influential even after many of its formulations on specific kinds of business conduct have been challenged. It is applied in practice as a 'consumer welfare standard', according to which a business practice, agreement or merger escapes legal condemnation if it results in lower prices, better quality or greater variety for consumers, regardless of any adverse effects on inequality, employees, competitors or communities. Very recently, however, some American antitrust scholars have begun to question whether this standard is relevant or desirable, especially in dealing with giant technology-based firms like Apple, Amazon, Facebook and Google. Several such scholars are cited by Lina Khan in a widely noticed paper.[11] She draws extensively on the legislative history of the American antitrust statutes to argue eloquently for a return to its progressive origins, with its concern for the dispersal of economic and political power, and for preserving a competitive market structure and the competitive *process* rather than its outcome in terms of prices. This movement has not made much headway so far, with critics derisively referring to it as 'hipster antitrust'.[12]

III. IS ANTITRUST IN DEVELOPING COUNTRIES DIFFERENT?

While the privileging of economic efficiency characterises the dominant antitrust paradigm in the US, this is of relatively recent origin and is not universally accepted. The enactment of competition laws in advanced countries actually pre-dated the move from an administrative to a regulatory state by several decades and was motivated by very different objectives.[13] Beginning with the Wallace Act in Canada (1889) and the Sherman (1890) and Clayton (1914) Acts in the US, such laws were enacted for a variety of reasons, including the protection not only of consumers, but also of small enterprises (including competitors) from possibly more efficient larger firms, distrust of the concentration of economic and political power in the hands of big business, and the protection of investors and employees of 'failing firms'. For many decades, most European countries did not feel the need for competition laws, with some of them tolerating and even encouraging cartels. A unified set of broad competition law principles was encoded into the 1957 Treaty of Rome, the founding charter of the European Economic Community (EEC). The UK, which remained outside the EEC until 1973, had adopted its Restrictive Trade Practices Act in 1956. In Japan, both before and after the Second World War, cartels were encouraged as part of the state's industrialisation strategy, and vigorous price competition was discouraged. Similarly, the late-industrialising countries of East Asia had weak or no antitrust regimes. The promotion of 'national champion' firms, insulated from competition, was a major component of their development strategy. The economic efficiency paradigm

[11] Lina M Khan, 'Amazon's Antitrust Paradox' (2017) 126 *Yale Law Journal* 708.

[12] For contributions on both sides of the debate, see www.competitionpolicyinternational.com/antitrust-chronicle-hipster-antitrust.

[13] See Bhattacharjea (n 9) for a more detailed discussion of the history of competition laws in developed countries, and lessons for developing countries.

triumphed only in the 1970s in the US and more slowly and incompletely in other advanced countries over the next few decades. In the EU, the objectives of protecting the competitive process and ensuring the integration of the single European market continue to override efficiency arguments in respect of certain practices.

The discussion in the preceding paragraph might suggest that modern antitrust principles are not appropriate for today's emerging economies, which are presumably at a stage of development corresponding to the early years of the now-developed countries. I have expressed some sympathy for this view.[14] But these arguments are now moot, because in the past two decades, over 100 developing countries (including India) have transplanted or adapted competition laws of the more evolved kind that are now in vogue in the developed world, and have set up supposedly independent agencies to enforce them. How did this come about?

In advanced countries, the growth of the regulatory state in recent decades followed from the state's retreat as an owner of infrastructural and manufacturing assets, and a provider of goods and services. With these functions being increasingly left to private enterprise, some degree of regulatory oversight became necessary to ensure benefits to the public, while allowing entrepreneurs a satisfactory rate of return on capital as well as incentives to innovate. As for the present-day developing countries, the adoption of modern competition laws was usually a second-stage reform that followed policies of liberalisation, privatisation and globalisation. This process may seem to closely follow that of the advanced countries, but there were some major differences.[15] First, state intervention in developing economies had been far more extensive and intrusive, and the pull-back (especially in India) has been more gradual and partial. Consequently, state-owned enterprises (SOEs) continue to dominate many sectors of the economy. They now compete with private players for the same markets or supply them with essential infrastructure. Second, and contrarily, after signing up for membership of the World Trade Organization (WTO), developing countries committed themselves to dismantling barriers to competition from imports and foreign investment more rapidly than the developed countries had in the half-century following the Second World War.

These features impose another requirement on the regulatory apparatus, apart from technical expertise and independence from political pressure: in order to induce private investment, it has to ensure *competitive neutrality* between state and private (and between domestic and foreign) commercial entities. The new laws and enforcement institutions were often designed and put in place to provide comfort to trading partners and foreign investors who were chary of arbitrary, discriminatory or politically directed administrative decisions. The adoption of a non-discriminatory and

[14] See ibid.

[15] My analysis in the following paragraphs overlaps with, but goes beyond, Dubash and Morgan's catalogue of the three 'shared contexts' in which regulatory reform has been implemented in the countries of the South: external pressures to transplant particular kinds of regulatory institutions from the North; the greater intensity of redistributive politics; and limited state capacity. See Dubash and Morgan (n 1) 4. Their volume is confined to sectoral regulation; while acknowledging many similarities, I am dealing with competition law enforcement.

transparently enforced competition law was often mandated as a condition for entering into bilateral preferential trade agreements (PTAs), particularly with the EU, which also tried very hard (along with Japan) to secure a multilateral agreement that would impose the same requirement on all members of the WTO. These efforts were ultimately unsuccessful, but the advantages that were highlighted in this debate, as well as other pressures and inducements, may have convinced a large number of developing countries to adopt such laws.[16]

However, the political economy context in which competition laws have been adopted in developing countries differs considerably from that in developed countries, in ways that work against the forces outlined above. First, more extensive state ownership, combined with weak governance, meant that significant vested interests had built up around the SOEs – not just their employees and contractors, but also the associated political patronage and rent-seeking involved in appointing them. Second, the SOEs were also saddled with social obligations that private enterprises did not have to bear, making it impossible for them to compete on a level playing field. Third, other government policies and controls that interfered in the competitive process also survived, often geared towards ostensibly socially desirable goals. Finally, large sections of the population in developing countries lacked the education, skills and access to credit that are required to survive in a more competitive environment, and there are few or no social safety nets to protect those who are displaced by competition. In contrast, European competition regimes were set up after the establishment of universal literacy, significant and broad-based enrolment in higher education, substantial financial inclusion, and the safety nets of the modern welfare state, while the competition laws of Japan and Canada were ineffectively enforced until the 1980s, long after they had set up the required institutions.[17]

For competition purists in the antitrust community,[18] and more generally for 'neoliberals', all these are irritants that distract from the pursuit of economic efficiency. For them, the obvious way to cut the Gordian knot would be to privatise the remaining SOEs, replace the remaining controls with market-friendly mechanisms like direct transfers and subsidies, and let competition law do its job unfettered by such concerns. But in the real world, this would result in a democratic deficit that is not so easily sidetracked. All the features outlined in the preceding paragraph put a strain on purely technocratic decision-making by independent competition agencies of the South, even if their laws seem to conform to the templates of the North. I now provide a brief outline of the Indian competition regime, before showing how the pattern of appointments to the CCI and its emerging jurisprudence suggest some conflation of the administrative and regulatory approaches, thereby helping to reconcile some of these contradictions.

[16] For a review of this debate and a critique of the proponents' arguments, see Aditya Bhattacharjea, 'The Case for a Multilateral Agreement on Competition Policy: A Developing-Country Perspective' (2006) 9 *Journal of International Economic Law* 293. See especially section V of that article on the role of PTAs in encouraging developing countries to adopt competition laws. I discuss India's puzzling stance in the WTO debate in the next section.

[17] Bhattacharjea (n 9).

[18] See, eg, George L Priest, 'Competition Law in Developing Nations' and Allan Fels and Wendy Ng, 'Rethinking Competition Advocacy in Developing Countries', both in Sokol et al (n 8).

IV. THE MAKING OF INDIAN COMPETITION LAW

Long before the recent rush to enact competition laws, India already had one in place. The Monopolies and Restrictive Trade Practices (MRTP) Act was passed in 1969 and brought into force from 1970. Its ostensible purpose was to control the concentration of economic power, not only in individual product markets but also the aggregate size and growth of large business houses that controlled firms operating in multiple markets. However, the law allowed the government to bypass the MRTP Commission, or to ignore its recommendations, on precisely the categories of firm strategies that affect concentration: those that would today come under the rubrics of abuse of dominance and merger review. For anti-competitive agreements, the law only allowed the Commission to issue 'cease and desist' orders, without monetary penalties. It was feebly and inconsistently enforced by an underfunded Commission. After an amendment to the Act in 1984, the bulk of the Commission's workload was dominated by individual consumer complaints about defective products and deficient services. Competition-related cases were pushed to the margins. As part of the liberalising reform package of 1991, a further amendment deleted the entire chapter of the Act under which large and dominant firms had to obtain approval for mergers and acquisitions.[19]

In India, as in many other countries of the South, the reforms of the 1990s led to the creation of new regulatory laws and institutions. A new competition law was among them: the Competition Act of 2002. This covered all the three categories of competition regulation with a much more modern economics-based approach which targeted the effects of certain kinds of business conduct rather than the size of the firms. The CCI, unlike its predecessor, was empowered to impose substantial penalties for violations and to block or modify proposed mergers. The technical aspects of these substantive sections of the Act are not germane to this volume,[20] so I shall proceed immediately to the rather strange political circumstances under which it was passed and then remained in limbo for more than six years.

The issue of transplantation of foreign laws and institutions under external pressure is a central preoccupation of the literature on the regulatory state in the South. It is quite likely that there were similar pressures on India. However, it is difficult to trace these influences in the discussions of the time. In the case of the liberalising reforms of the 1990s, critics were quick to blame external agencies like the International Monetary Fund (IMF), the World Bank and the WTO. In the following decade, these reforms extended to the privatisation of some public utilities, entry by private players into sectors hitherto reserved for the public sector, and the creation of new sectoral regulators to oversee them at arm's length from the government. These were elements of the World Bank's well-known playbook. But there was no debate of this

[19] I have dealt with the background to the enactment of the MRTP Act, its many deficiencies and the Commission's unimpressive track record of enforcement in Aditya Bhattacharjea, 'India's New Competition Law: A Comparative Assessment' (2008) 4 *Journal of Competition Law and Economics* 609, 611–26. See also Bhattacharjea (n 2) 32–34.

[20] I have discussed these features in Bhattacharjea (n 19) 626–34 and some subsequent articles that analyse the economic reasoning adopted by the CCI in several cases.

kind in the case of competition law reform. While there may have been other considerations at work, what can be deduced from the documentary record is the possible impact of a contentious but now-forgotten debate that took place over the course of several years at the WTO.

The EU succeeded in getting a mandate for setting up a working group on trade and competition policy at the Singapore Ministerial meeting of the WTO in 1996. The proponents' ultimate objective was an agreement on competition policy as part of the WTO Single Undertaking, which would allow for enforcement through the organisation's dispute settlement mechanism. They pushed for an agreement that would require all members to enact competition laws prohibiting cartels and embodying the core principles of National Treatment (ie, non-discrimination between domestic and foreign enterprises), transparency and procedural fairness.

Dealing with this pressure did require considerable effort by the Indian government, but attracted little public attention. Committees were set up by different ministries to examine the issue. The most influential was the High Level Committee on Competition Policy and Law (Raghavan Committee). Its report, submitted in 2000, made a fairly good case for the need for a new competition law and outlined its scope. It made only a passing reference to the debate at the WTO, and its short chapter on the implications of the WTO regime for competition dealt almost exclusively with the possible incompatibility of various WTO agreements with existing government policies. However, the chapter commenced with a declaration that was entirely in tune with the EU proposal: 'It is axiomatic that the domestic Competition Law should not discriminate between Indian Companies and Foreign Companies.'[21] Contrarily, it recommended that the law should not apply to the procurement of goods for the public distribution system, and went even further to recommend that National Treatment should not apply to government procurement.[22]

In a number of places, the report mentioned fundamental differences between the committee members on how the law should treat particular business practices. Moreover, two of the Committee's nine members gave notes of dissent: one questioned the very need for a competition law, while the other opposed mandatory notification of mergers. Another two members gave 'Supplementary Notes' arguing that the law should be phased in gradually in order to allow for capacity building in the proposed Competition Commission as well as time for Indian industries (especially small enterprises) to adjust to competition. Similar concerns appeared in the business press. Impediments to mergers were opposed by several commentators. They argued that Indian industry, which had been fragmented during the control regime that preceded the reforms of the 1990s, needed more time to restructure and consolidate so that firms could grow large enough to compete globally and to face the challenge of multinational corporations that were increasingly entering the Indian market as restrictions on trade and foreign direct investment were relaxed.

[21] Report of the High Level Committee on Competition Policy & Law, http://www.ccr.org.in/uploads/2/1/9/6/21961628/report_of_high_level_committee_on_competition_policy_and_law.pdf, para 5.1.1 (no page numbers are given in this document).

[22] ibid para 5.3.7. India has not signed on to the WTO Agreement on Government Procurement, which mandates National Treatment, so this recommendation was WTO-compliant.

Nonetheless, the government moved fairly quickly. A Competition Bill was drafted, introduced into Parliament in August 2001 and referred to a Standing Committee. The Committee held 13 meetings over the course of a year, in which it heard the comments of a wide range of business representatives, professionals and financial institutions. After incorporating several changes, the Bill was passed by both Houses of Parliament in December 2002.[23] Interestingly, the debate was initiated by the Chairman of the Standing Committee, the (then) opposition leader Pranab Mukherjee, who strongly supported the Bill while asking for a few clarifications. He made only a passing reference to the ongoing debate at the WTO:

> Trade and competition is going to be a debatable subject in the series of negotiations, which are coming, related to the WTO. Therefore, it was considered necessary to have an appropriate legal framework to encourage competition and also to make a departure from the practices which we used to have.[24]

A Member of Parliament from the Communist Party of India (Marxist) saw the Bill as 'a tragic submission to the diktats of the international finance capital to allow multinational companies for plying our nation and it is a declaration to kill our national companies'.[25] A Congress member also asked: 'Is this [Bill] to placate the Western world, the WTO authorities, the World Bank, the IMF, the Americans, who are now able to direct not only our foreign policy, but also the economy?' He argued that enacting a new law would weaken India's bargaining position in forthcoming WTO negotiations on an agreement on competition policy. India should await the outcome of these negotiations, and meanwhile the MRTP Act could be suitably amended to remove unnecessary obstacles to firms. However, he supported the Bill with reservations.[26] Both these Members expressed apprehensions that National Treatment would result in unfair competition between giant multinational corporations that were entering the Indian market and small domestic producers. Other speakers expressed concerns about the fate of the employees of the MRTP Commission, which was to be replaced by the new Competition Commission. They also raised two issues that I shall address in the next section: the independence and composition of the new Commission. Several members presciently expressed their apprehensions that the Commission would become a 'parking lot', 'sanctuary' or 'dumping ground' for retired bureaucrats and judges.[27]

The Minister of Finance and Company Affairs, who piloted the Bill, gave assurances that these concerns would be suitably dealt with. He stated unambiguously that 'we do not intend to treat the Competition Commission as a kind of a parking lot where we have retired personnel finding their place' and that the Bill 'has not been brought because of any external factors'.[28] As for weakening India's position at the

[23] I have given only a selective summary of the debate in the Rajya Sabha (upper House of Parliament). The Lok Sabha (lower House) had passed the Bill a few days earlier after a similar debate.

[24] Rajya Sabha Official Debates, 197th Session, 20 December 2002, http://rsdebate.nic.in/handle/123456789/86732, 252.

[25] ibid 265.

[26] ibid 276–77.

[27] ibid 260, 264, 280.

[28] ibid 283.

WTO, he responded that 'the Ministry of Commerce which deals with the WTO negotiations has not communicated to us any such apprehension'.[29] He stated that different sections of the law would be brought into force in a phased manner: the CCI would play only an advisory role in the first year, then sections relating to anti-competitive practices and abuse of dominance would be activated in the second year, and merger review would commence only from the third year. He pointed out that the thresholds specified in the Bill for reviewable mergers were quite high and very few firms would be affected. No amendments were moved and the Bill was passed by a voice vote.

Ironically, meanwhile, India was spearheading the developing countries' opposition to the EU initiative at the WTO, even though the Competition Act was far more comprehensive than the basic anti-cartel legislation that the EU had been pushing for. The Act covered the full spectrum of horizontal and vertical agreements, abuse of dominance, and mergers. It implicitly adopted the principle of National Treatment by allowing no scope for discrimination on the basis of the nationality of firms, even though at the WTO, India had challenged the applicability of the principle to competition policy and had made a spirited argument for more lenient treatment of domestic firms.[30] In all these respects, the Act was a transplant of the kind of laws that were in place in mature jurisdictions. But there was no evidence of any one model being followed. In fact, the Act borrowed specific phrases from different foreign laws and regulations, often distorting their meaning.[31] Further, cartels were dealt with more gently than in most developed countries: They were deemed to be only presumptively anti-competitive rather than illegal per se, and even if they were ultimately found to be in violation of the statute, the responsible managers could only be fined, not imprisoned. Nonetheless, a few months after the Bill was passed, the visiting EU Trade Commissioner was quoted as saying that India's opposition to a WTO agreement on competition was 'only tactical because India's investment regime and competition law are already WTO-plus-plus'.[32] After meeting him, his Indian counterpart, the Commerce Minister (who, as Law Minister, had tabled the Competition Bill in Parliament and had spoken eloquently in its support in the final debate) was quoted as saying that 'developing countries were not geared to undertake the obligations of the World Trade Organization'.[33] A year later, the pushback by the developing countries succeeded in having the issue of trade and competition policy dropped from the WTO work programme.

[29] ibid 284.

[30] 'Communication from India to the Working Group on the Interaction between Trade and Competition Policy', Document WT/WGTCP/W/216, World Trade Organization, 26 September 2002, available at https://docs.wto.org.

[31] See Bhattacharjea (n 19) 627–32.

[32] 'India's Approach to Investment Tactical: EU', 14 March 2003, http://search.rediff.com/money/2003/mar/14wto1.htm.

[33] 'Leave Singapore Issues out: Competition, Investment Issues Need More Study, Jaitley Tells EU', *Business Standard*, 15 March 2003, www.business-standard.com/article/economy-policy/leave-singapore-issues-out-india-103031501073_1.html. Competition policy was one of the 'Singapore Issues', so called because they had been put onto the WTO programme at the 1996 Singapore Ministerial meeting.

I had a very minor role to play in these developments,[34] but it is still not clear to me what tactical calculations were involved in the government's apparently contradictory stance of enacting legislation in Delhi that went far beyond what it was strenuously opposing in Geneva. But, as it turned out, the actual implementation of the Competition Act was delayed far beyond the planned three-year transition period, thus validating in a way India's foot-dragging in Geneva and the disquiet of several members of the Raghavan Committee, media commentators and Members of Parliament. The reasons for this delay have a direct bearing on the issue of administrative versus regulatory institutional design and will be discussed in the next section.

V. THE COMPETITION COMMISSION OF INDIA

After it was passed by Parliament, the Competition Bill became an Act when it was signed by the President of India in January 2003. As originally enacted, section 8 of the Act provided for a CCI with a chairperson and between two and ten members, with the chairperson and one member to be appointed in the first year.[35] The section specified that:

> The Chairperson and every other Member shall be a person of ability, integrity and standing and who, has been, or is qualified to be, a judge of a High Court; or, has special knowledge of, and professional experience of not less than fifteen years in international trade, economics, business, commerce, law, finance, accountancy, management, industry, public affairs, administration or in any other matter which, in the opinion of the Central Government, may be useful to the Commission.

Section 9 prescribed that the 'Chairperson and other Members shall be selected in the manner as may be prescribed'. According to section 22: 'The jurisdiction, powers and authority of the Commission may be exercised by Benches thereof.' Each bench was to comprise not less than two members, including at least one 'judicial member' (defined as one who 'is, or has been, or is qualified to be, a Judge of a High Court').

To begin with, only some administrative clauses of the Act were brought into force, allowing for the appointment of the chairperson, members and staff of the CCI. The government notified the appointment of a chairman and one member, both senior civil servants who were close to retirement. The member took office in October 2003, but before the chairman-designate could take charge, the constitutional validity of some of the provisions specifying the procedures for appointing the chairperson and members was challenged in a writ petition that reached the Indian Supreme Court.

[34] Disclosure: I served on the Commerce Ministry's Expert Group on Trade and Competition Policy during 2002–03 while the WTO debate was at its peak. The Group met only twice during my tenure and was not asked for a report or for its views on the Competition Act. But some of its ideas apparently helped to formulate India's position during the discussions at the WTO. My own views on the issue of a multilateral competition agreement were published in Bhattacharjea (n 16).

[35] Here and below, all references to sections of the original Act are to the official version published in the *Gazette of India Extraordinary*, Part II – Section 1, No 12, 14 January 2003. For foreign readers, it should be pointed out that 'member' is an official designation which carries considerable weight in terms of remuneration and status. Members oversee the functioning of the CCI and also adjudicate on cases.

The petitioner contended that because the CCI would exercise judicial powers, the separation of powers between the judiciary and the executive required that the chairperson and judicial members should be senior judges chosen by the Chief Justice of India or a committee headed by him, and not by a committee set up by the executive. During the hearings, the Supreme Court expressed its displeasure over the exclusion of the judiciary, but its final judgment left open all questions raised by the petition because the government stated that it intended to propose suitable amendments to the Competition Act. The Court suggested that the government could:

> [C]onsider the creation of two separate bodies, one with expertise that is advisory and regulatory and the other adjudicatory. This followed up by an appellate body as contemplated by the proposed amendment, can go a long way, in meeting the challenge sought to be raised in this Writ Petition based on the doctrine of separation of powers recognized by the Constitution.[36]

Although the Supreme Court pronounced its judgment in January 2005, it was not until September 2007 that Parliament passed an amending act. It provided for a three-member Competition Appellate Tribunal (Compat), headed by a 'person who is, or has been, a Judge of the Supreme Court or the Chief Justice of a High Court', to hear appeals from CCI decisions. The strength of the CCI was reduced from 10 to seven. Its power to award compensation and impose imprisonment for failure to comply with its orders was taken away and given to Compat and a designated magistrate's court, respectively. Members of both the CCI and Compat would now be selected by committees headed by the Chief Justice of India or his nominee, with the Secretaries (top civil servants) of the Ministries of Law and Company Affairs as members. This reconfiguration of the institutional architecture was not challenged, even though it did not follow the design that the Supreme Court had suggested. The amending act also made extensive changes to the sections of the law dealing with mergers and anti-competitive practices.

The government took its time to activate the new selection mechanism and appointed the chairman and members of the full Commission only in early 2009. Significantly, this was just before a general election; it is possible that corporate lobbying had delayed the process. Sections of the Competition Act establishing the Compat and empowering the CCI to enforce the sections relating to anti-competitive agreements and abuse of dominance were brought into force by a set of government notifications on 15 May 2009, a day before the declaration of the election results. The MRTP Act was repealed later the same year. Sections of the Competition Act that dealt with merger review were bitterly opposed by Indian and foreign business lobbies, and were brought into force only in June 2011.

In the parliamentary debate summarised in the preceding section, several members had warned against populating the CCI with retired bureaucrats and judges. The Minister had given an assurance that the government did not intend to make it a 'parking lot' for retired people.[37] But things turned out rather differently. The 2007

[36] *Brahm Dutt v Union of India* (2005) 2 SCC 431.

[37] Rajya Sabha Official Debates (see text accompanying nn 27 and 28).

amendment had abolished the concept of judicial members and benches, and instead required the CCI to function as a collegium. Chairmanship of the Compat remained the only position statutorily reserved for a person with a judicial background. A former judge of the Supreme Court was duly appointed as Chairperson, but the other two members of Compat, as well as six out of the seven posts on the CCI, including that of the chairperson, were filled by retired or nearly retired bureaucrats. Ever since, regardless of the government in power, all chairpersons and almost all members of the CCI have been former civil servants; so were all members of Compat, whose chairpersons were invariably retired judges of the Supreme Court. Although not required by the governing statute, by convention a retired High Court judge has also been appointed as a member of the CCI; the original Act would have statutorily required one such judicial member on each bench. Thus, left with only two of the 10 positions available on the CCI and Compat combined, the judiciary was ultimately outflanked, despite the writ petition that had tried to give it a dominant role.

As Somanathan has pointed out, the retirement age specified in most statutes under which regulatory agencies have been set up is well beyond 60, the age at which civil servants retire, making these positions attractive post-retirement sinecures.[38] The Competition Act is no exception: the retirement age for the chairperson and members of the CCI, as well as for members of the Compat, is specified as 65 (sections 10(1) and 53F of the Competition Act), which would nicely coincide with the end of the statutory five-year term of office for a member who joins after retirement from the civil service. Their salaries are also fixed at levels much higher than those of the highest paid civil servants. Somanathan had also pointed to evidence suggesting an implicit truce in the turf war between the judiciary and the executive over what he calls 'equality of post-retirement opportunity': the retirement age has been set even higher for positions that are statutorily reserved on appellate tribunals for persons who have been judges of the High Court or Supreme Court, who retire at 62 and 65, respectively.[39] Consistent with this pattern, the retirement age for the Compat chairperson was fixed at 68.

These post-retirement possibilities have been severely crimped by recent developments. In May 2017, after an unexpected amendment to the Act, the Compat was abolished and all its functions as well as pending appeals were assigned to the National Company Law Appellate Tribunal. And in early 2018, the government announced that the CCI would be 'right-sized' by not replacing members as they retire, so that it would ultimately comprise a chairperson and three (rather than six) members. At the time of writing, its strength had fallen to the planned level. The posts of chairperson and two members have been advertised in anticipation of retirements that will take place over the next few months, and it remains to be seen what kinds of people

[38] Somanathan (n 1) 404. See also Devesh Kapur, 'Golden Parachutes, Leaden Results', *Business Standard*, 17 March 2013, https://www.business-standard.com/article/opinion/golden-parachutes-leaden-results-113031700334_1.html. For some insiders' views on the reasons why these positions are increasingly sought after by retired bureaucrats, see https://www.business-standard.com/article/economy-policy/civil-servants-rush-to-regulatory-bodies-as-post-retirement-jobs-dry-115110201338_1.html.

[39] Somanathan (n 1) 405.

are appointed. The rest of this section deals with the implications of the pattern of appointments that prevailed hitherto.

Two issues that were repeatedly raised in the parliamentary debate related to the technical competence and independence of retired bureaucrats and judges.[40] As regards the first, I do not subscribe to the view that bureaucrats are necessarily a bad choice on these two counts. The cohort of civil servants who have served and who are likely to be appointed in the next few years as members of these regulatory bodies joined the bureaucracy in the 1970s and 1980s, when it attracted the best and the brightest of Indian university graduates, before the liberalisation of the economy opened up much better career possibilities in the private sector. The diverse responsibilities these officials held in the course of their careers made them adaptable and quick learners. Although all the chairpersons and many of the members appointed so far have come from the generalist Indian Administrative Service (IAS), they have usually served in senior positions in SOEs and line ministries that required detailed knowledge of the functioning of economic sectors, industries and markets in the liberalised era. Many other members served in non-IAS branches of the civil service and have worked exclusively in such positions.

Given the paucity of such expertise outside the bureaucracy, there are few alternative talent pools. It might be possible to attract more candidates by waiving the requirement that members (if not already retired) must resign from their previous jobs. The corresponding positions in North American or European agencies are often filled by mid-career professionals on lien from academia, legal or consulting firms, to which they can return after their terms are over. The emerging antitrust bar has many lawyers who have been trained abroad and have worked in foreign law firms specialising in antitrust, but salaries that CCI members are paid, although generous by civil service standards, are no match for what these lawyers can earn by representing private parties. (The antitrust divisions of some prominent Indian law firms are in fact headed by former senior officials of the MRTP Commission and the CCI.) However, this expertise can contribute to the development of competition jurisprudence, even if it remains outside the Commission. Perhaps the arguments advanced by these lawyers, backed by some specialised consultants who have emerged on the scene, have contributed to the quality of the economic analysis on display in the CCI orders, which (with some exceptions that I have written about elsewhere) has usually been quite good. This is remarkable, especially given the lack of granular market data and the limited expertise of its members and its in-house staff, most of whom have been inducted on deputation from other government departments. The EU and the US have been providing technical assistance in capacity building, and the CCI has sent its staff on short-term visits to foreign antitrust agencies, but much of their learning and experience will be lost if they are later transferred to other government departments. Although it was set up with an official sanction for appointing over 100

[40] These concerns speak to the second and third of the 'shared contexts' in which Dubash and Morgan (n 1) frame the evolution of regulatory institutions in the South: the pressures of distributional politics and limited state capacity.

directly-recruited professionals in the fields of law, economics and accounting, the CCI remains severely understaffed as a result of the pervasive skill shortage in this domain.[41]

What about persons with a judicial background, whether retired or not? A detailed study found that in two-thirds of the cartel cases in which penalties had been imposed by the CCI between 2009 and 2016, the Compat had either quashed the finding of a violation, reduced the penalties or remanded the matter for rehearing. The major grounds given in the Compat orders were the CCI's arbitrariness in the calculation of the penalty, violation of the basic principles of natural justice, and inadequate evidence.[42] The Compat also reversed or reduced the fines in a high proportion of non-cartel orders in which the CCI found violations – this despite the CCI collegium including one member who had been a High Court judge. Of course, such reversals on points of law are fairly common in advanced countries. But these legal infirmities do not make a case for having a greater judicial presence on the CCI, especially with its size being whittled down to four members. Appeals to the Appellate Tribunal and then the Supreme Court are surely adequate to ensure due process. The CCI has begun to rectify some of its procedural lapses. In some cases, it has re-investigated the complaints and reheard the parties while ensuring due process, and then reimposed the penalties that were quashed by the Compat. But it has not followed the Compat's advice to formulate guidelines on penalties. In the EU, official guidelines lay down base penalties with increments and decrements for clearly specified aggravating and mitigating factors.

Another concern is whether filling the CCI with former judges and bureaucrats can compromise its independence.[43] The CCI has certainly imposed substantial penalties on prominent corporate defaulters in different sectors, including Google, the country's biggest real estate company, the powerful Board of Control for Cricket in India, almost all the private airlines and leading manufacturers (including multinationals with substantial Indian presence) of cars and cement.[44] It is true that no mergers have

[41] According to the latest available figures, as of 31 March 2017, only 54 out of the 122 sanctioned posts had been filled (calculated from Competition Commission of India, *Annual Report 2016–17*, Tables J3 and J4, 62–63). Disclosure: I have served a couple of times on selection committees for interviewing applicants for lower-level staff positions in the CCI. Most candidates, despite possessing postgraduate qualifications in economics and having already been filtered through a written test, have been quite ignorant of the economic principles and concepts that are relevant for antitrust analysis.

[42] Aditya Bhattacharjea and Oindrila De, 'Anti-cartel Enforcement in India' (2017) 5 *Journal of Antitrust Enforcement* 166, 180–90. We also point out that the Compat displayed a distinct lack of understanding of some basic principles of antitrust economics, resulting in unnecessarily high evidentiary standards.

[43] This is distinct from the concern expressed by Somanathan (n 1) and Kapur (n 38): the practice of appointing retired bureaucrats and judges to regulatory bodies is likely to compromise their independence in their *earlier* jobs by making them stay on the right side of the government in order to obtain these post-retirement positions.

[44] It must be pointed out, however, that in most cases the penalty imposed was much less than the statutory maximum specified in s 27(b) of the Act, ie, 10 per cent of the average turnover of the preceding three years. Moreover, as noted above, many penalties have been either quashed or reduced by the erstwhile Compat. Many others are still under appeal. In fact, much less than one per cent of the total penalties imposed by the CCI since its inception have actually been paid (calculated from Competition Commission of India (n 41) Table D1, 18).

been blocked. But in a few cases, the merging parties (including some of the world's leading multinational firms in biotechnology, cement and pharmaceuticals) have been told to license their intellectual property or to divest factories or product lines to independent competitors before their deals can go through.

My view is that it is harder to bribe or browbeat the majority in a collegium as compared to a single decision-maker. The statutory requirement that the CCI must give reasoned orders at every stage of the proceedings also helps to preserve its independence. These are publicly available and therefore subject to criticism as well as appeal. As a further safeguard, section 12 of the Competition Act prohibits any member from accepting employment with any enterprise which has been a party to a proceeding before the Commission for two years after 'ceasing to hold office'. There are, however, several implicit constraints on the Commission's independence from government influence. For one thing, post-CCI employment with the government, including employment in any statutory authority or corporation, is explicitly excluded from the two-year embargo – and the government and SOEs have been parties in several cases, as I shall show below. Moreover, the Commission's budget comes from the Ministry of Corporate Affairs (the fines it collects are paid into the Consolidated Fund of India). The government has the authority under section 55 of the Act to give binding policy directions to the CCI, and under section 56(1)(b) to supersede it if it does not comply with those directions. (There are similar clauses in the statutes that govern other regulators.) However, evidence of undue influence, whether by the government or private parties, is hardly likely to be available, and publishing it would in any case amount to contempt of a quasi-judicial body.

Two other concerns may arise regarding the composition of the CCI: has it inherited the agonisingly slow process of decision-making that plagues both the Indian bureaucracy and judiciary, and/or the opacity for which the former is notorious? On these, there is little cause for complaint, largely because of timelines and safeguards built into the Act. Apprehensions were expressed when the Act was being debated that merger proposals would be unnecessarily stalled, but these fears have been largely belied – in almost all the cases that have been notified to it, the CCI has managed to reach a prima facie decision within 30 days, excluding 'time-outs' for obtaining additional documentation. No timelines are specified for non-merger cases, but despite its severe staffing problem, the CCI has not taken significantly longer than the much better-resourced antitrust agencies in developed countries to dispose of fairly complicated cases. On transparency, apart from its reasoned orders, which are posted on its website, it has followed the statutory requirement of publicising and inviting comments on more complicated merger proposals. Although not statutorily required, it has done the same for proposed changes in its implementing regulations (which, being delegated legislation, are also subject to parliamentary approval). In many cases it seems to have acted on the suggestions received. Of course, it has not made public its internal deliberations or its responses to specific comments, but that would be expecting too much. Nevertheless, it could function more like a court and open its hearings up to the public.

VI. THE CCI AND GOVERNMENT RESTRAINTS ON COMPETITION

I would suggest that the composition of the CCI may have had a different kind of influence on its decisions. My co-authors and I have shown elsewhere that the agency has sometimes refrained from taking action against adverse effects on competition that are the result of government policies. Here, I provide only a brief summary of the relevant cases; that article may be consulted for details and citations.[45] I should emphasise that the views expressed below, although based on the cases discussed there, are entirely my own and should not be attributed to my co-authors, one of whom was a former member of the CCI who did not come from a civil service background.

Section 2(h) and (l) of the Competition Act defines 'enterprises' and 'persons' so as to cover SOEs and government departments performing commercial functions. The only explicit carve-out is for 'any activity of the government relatable to the sovereign functions of the government divisions or subsidiaries of the Central Government dealing with atomic energy, currency, defence and space' (section 2(h)). In a couple of early cases, the CCI's jurisdiction was challenged by the Steel Authority of India Limited (SAIL) as well as the Indian Railways (IR), both arguing that they were state-owned enterprises that were implementing government policies. The Ministry of Railways even argued that the carriage of goods on its network was a sovereign function of government. But the Delhi High Court upheld the CCI's assertion that:

> Welfare, commercial and economic activities ... are not covered within the meaning of 'sovereign functions', and the State while discharging such functions is as much amenable to the jurisdiction of competition regulator as any other private entity discharging such functions.[46]

Importantly, this holding covered activities of government ministries and departments, not just SOEs (or public sector undertakings – PSUs – to use the more familiar term). Following this, the CCI has imposed monetary penalties on Coal India Ltd (a public sector monopolist) and its subsidiaries, a state-owned housing development agency and four state-owned insurance companies.

However, in several other cases, the CCI finessed the issue of competitive neutrality between public and private enterprises. It has rejected many complaints alleging that the procurement rules and tender specifications of some PSUs and government departments were designed to exclude potential bidders. The public procurers had claimed that they had been forced to narrow the field of eligible bidders (or, in some cases, set up their own subsidiaries) because of the poor quality, unreliability and

[45] Aditya Bhattacharjea, Oindrila De and Geeta Gouri, 'Competition Law and Competition Policy in India: How the Competition Commission Has Dealt with Anticompetitive Restraints by Government Entities', *Review of Industrial Organization*, forthcoming, 2018, https://doi.org/10.1007/s11151-018-9641-0.

[46] Case No 64/2010, *Arshiya Rail Infrastructure Ltd (ARIL) and Another v Ministry of Railways (MoR) and Another*, Competition Commission of India interim order dated 3 May 2011, para 30, quoted and upheld in *Union of India v Competition Commission of India*, WP(C) 993/2012, Delhi High Court judgment dated 23 February 2012. However, in its final order dated 14 August 2012, the CCI held that the IR and its affiliate Container Corporation of India were not dominant in the relevant market and had not contravened the Act.

unethical practices of many private firms. Arguments along these lines would have gone down especially well with the CCI members who were formerly civil servants, as well as their professional staff on deputation from other government departments: most of them would have dealt with the complexity of public procurement in their previous assignments. They would also be acutely sensitive to the growing public sentiment against corruption and would appreciate the preference of PSU managers for dealing with other PSUs rather than laying themselves open to charges of collusion with private parties.[47] These are all legitimate concerns, and it is also true that even private firms prefer to deal with related parties in an environment in which contract enforcement is difficult. But with large public procurers, there is always the possible downside of foreclosing a lucrative market to more competitive private suppliers.

This issue was central in one of the cases in which the CCI asserted its jurisdiction over SAIL and the IR. JSPL (a private steel manufacturer) had challenged a contract whereby IR had committed to buy a particular specification of steel rails exclusively and indefinitely from SAIL, foreclosing competition from other suppliers. The CCI's own Director General, after an investigation, found this to be an anti-competitive agreement and an abuse of IR's dominant position. However, the Commission disagreed. Its order pointed out that the agreement ensured the 'safety of [SAIL's] investment' in a new and less profitable product line 'in national interest'; that JSPL could instead cater to the growing private market for these rails; and that taking quality and safety into account, JSPL had not met SAIL's 'comfort level' as a reliable and efficient supplier on a sustained basis. (Even though JSPL's rails had been certified by IR's own standards organisation, they were still being stress-tested on private sidings.) Although the Commission found it 'a bit disconcerting' that IR had provided no objective justification for not considering JSPL rails, it still held on these grounds that there had been no foreclosure.[48] Although this reasoning was somewhat persuasive, the CCI should not have endorsed a contract that permanently excluded competition.

The CCI's deference to government policies was more questionable in some other cases. In one such case, an individual challenged a policy that requires government employees and private individuals on government business to fly only on Air India – a chronically loss-making PSU that now faces vigorous competition from private airlines. This is clearly a hidden subsidy to keep it afloat. However, the CCI closed the case, holding that the government, as the consumer of air travel services, was free to choose its own suppliers. Admittedly, those who are forced to avail themselves of these services do not pay for them and are therefore not 'consumers'. But the CCI did not recognise the anti-competitive harm involved in foreclosing the market for government travel services.[49]

[47] Especially since 2013, when a Member of the CCI had to resign when he came under investigation for having favoured a private firm in his previous job as Secretary of the Coal Ministry. He was later convicted and imprisoned, although many believe that he was made a scapegoat.

[48] Case 11/2009, *Jindal Steel and Power Ltd v Steel Authority of India Ltd,* order dated 20 December 2011, 37–42.

[49] Case No 98/2015, *In Re: Mr Yeshwanth Shenoy v Air India and Others*, order dated 6 January 2016. In fact, the complainant had named five private airlines as other parties, alleging that despite knowing about

Another case involved a government policy that required the blending of bio-diesel with diesel fuel for environmental reasons. In 2006, three giant state-owned oil marketing companies (OMCs) were officially authorised to collectively fix the prices at which they procured bio-diesel from private suppliers. Separately, directives from the Ministry of Petroleum prevented the bio-diesel producers from selling their product on the open market, supposedly in order to prevent the adulteration of diesel. In the ensuing years of high oil prices, which the then government was unwilling to pass on to consumers, the OMCs kept their diesel prices low (incurring huge losses in the process) and calculated backwards to arrive at the price that they were willing to pay for bio-diesel. This price was often below the cost of production. The price of diesel sold by private OMCs was also regulated, limiting their ability to offer remunerative prices for bio-diesel. These practices were challenged by a bio-diesel manufacturer, who alleged that they were designed to block competition from private bio-diesel suppliers. The CCI's order set out these circumstances at length. It observed that 'even if an anticompetitive conduct flows from any policy of the Government, the Commission will still have jurisdiction to examine the impugned conduct' under the Competition Act. But it held that the behaviour of the OMCs could not be anti-competitive, 'taking into account the totality of the circumstance and the constraints under which PSU OMCs are functioning'.[50] An antitrust agency with a single-minded focus on anti-competitive behaviour would almost certainly have found the OMCs to be a price-fixing cartel. The bio-diesel producers were trapped in a vortex created by several official policies with different objectives: protecting the environment, preventing fuel adulteration, protecting consumers from high prices and preventing further increases in the OMC's losses, which were ultimately borne by the taxpayers. Not surprisingly, out of these incompatible policy objectives, it was environmental protection that lost out: no bio-diesel was actually supplied to the OMCs.

Corruption in public procurement, safety on the IR, the symbolism of a national 'flag carrier' airline, fuel pricing, PSU losses and the fiscal deficit – all these are sensitive political issues with ramifications that go far beyond economic efficiency. The CCI's forbearance showed its appreciation of their complexities. But it could at least have used the statutory authority it has been given under section 49 of the Act to undertake competition advocacy by suggesting measures to ameliorate the anti-competitive aspects of these policies. It has taken this route in some other cases. One arose from a statutory requirement that forces sugar mills to use only jute bags for packaging, allowing jute manufacturers to inflate their prices. Another was in relation to alleged cartelisation in the sugar industry itself. The CCI described a maze of regulations governing sugar prices, procurement, capacity, and duties on imports and exports. Although it found no evidence of cartelisation, the CCI made a case for policy reforms to promote competition while safeguarding social objectives.

these anti-competitive practices, 'they remained silent which may be attributed to a cartel amongst them or because of the fear of a regulatory backlash from [the government]' (at 4).

[50] MRTP Case No 1/28, *M/s Royal Energy Ltd v M/s Indian Oil Corporation Ltd and Others*, order dated 9 May 2012, para 7.10. (The CCI was given the authority to decide cases inherited from the MRTP Commission under the relevant sections of the Competition Act.)

All these cases reveal the CCI's limitations in protecting competition in a setting in which there are multiple government agencies intervening in the market in pursuit of multiple objectives. Anti-competitive Acts of State (eg, import restrictions, preferential government procurement policies, the granting of intellectual property rights, and agricultural support policies) are beyond the reach of antitrust law even in advanced jurisdictions. But state intervention has a much deeper and broader footprint in the Indian economy, even after nearly three decades of liberalisation. The competition regulators are accordingly more deferential, possibly because most of them have come out of the same system. They have sometimes made context-sensitive assessments of competition-restricting government policies that might have been condemned by a differently constituted Commission.

CONCLUSION

I began this chapter by explaining the scope of antitrust/competition law and why its enforcement should in principle be left to independent technocratic agencies with a narrowly focused agenda of promoting competition and economic efficiency. However, the rest of the chapter muddied these waters. It first showed that this principle has not been followed consistently, even in developed countries with adequate state capacity to enforce such laws. At different times, they have pursued a variety of 'political' goals and their competition agencies have usually been headed by political appointees. Only recently (and with some exceptions and qualifications) have they converged to an efficiency standard – although that is once again being questioned as giant firms come to dominate different sectors of their economies. Developing countries like India confront some of the constraints that these countries did in their earlier years, when they did not enact competition laws or enforced them only desultorily. But I also argued that developing countries have to implement competition legislation in a particular political economy context that results from the partial rollback of decades of promoting public sector enterprises and other government interventions that interfere in competitive markets.

I then described the evolution of Indian competition law, beginning with the largely ineffective MRTP Act which was in force from 1970 to 2009. I discussed the paradoxical manner in which the Indian government pushed through a new Competition Act in 2002 even while it was opposing a WTO agreement that would have required a much less ambitious law. A legal challenge to the composition of and selection procedures for the new Competition Commission of India stalled the enforcement of the new Act until 2009. Since then, almost all members of the CCI have been drawn from the ranks of retired or nearly retired civil servants, despite explicit assurances to the contrary given on the floor of Parliament when the Act was being debated. This pattern of appointments may have been inevitable, given the limited expertise available. On the whole, despite being severely understaffed, the CCI has done a fairly good job. Its orders are pronounced without inordinate delay and sometimes display an understanding of tricky economic reasoning. It has imposed penalties on major public-sector and private-sector firms, although its procedural mis-steps have resulted in many of these being quashed or scaled down by the Appellate Tribunal.

However, in some cases, the CCI did pull its punches in dealing with anti-competitive behaviour by SOEs when these flowed from government policies that would have been hard to modify without systemic repercussions.

In terms of the question posed in the title to this chapter, the CCI is unquestionably 'regulatory' in its independence and professionalism, but in cases involving government policies and PSUs, it has often shown an 'administrative' mindset in its holistic appreciation of the complexity of public policy-making. Perhaps one can conclude, then, that the enforcement of competition law is regulatory with (Indian) administrative characteristics.

14

Sanctions and Self-Regulation in the Securities Market

NEEL MAITRA*

INTRODUCTION

SELF-REGULATION IN SECURITIES markets may take a number of forms.[1] In one extreme case, regulation may be performed almost entirely by a public entity with exchanges responsible for the supervision of markets in very limited ways.[2] At the other extreme, the primary public regulatory authority may rely extensively on independent self-regulatory organisations (SROs) to perform a range of regulatory functions that go well beyond the operation of the market to members' business conduct and other matters.[3] Between these extremes exist hybrid possibilities which involve the delegation of varying levels of regulatory power to SROs. For instance, a public authority could act as the primary regulator while relying on exchanges to regulate market operations, as in Hong Kong or Singapore. Alternatively, a public authority could act as the primary regulator while delegating more extensive powers to exchanges to regulate both market operations and member conduct, as is the case in Australia or Japan.[4]

The precise position of the Securities Exchange Board of India (SEBI) on this self-regulatory continuum is debatable, but SEBI and Indian stock exchanges recognised by SEBI have extensive powers to discipline and enforce sanctions against exchange members. Moreover, the self-regulatory model in which SEBI and India's stock exchanges participate has been viewed as being successful in enforcing discipline against exchange members. The International Monetary Fund acknowledges this,

* The Securities and Exchange Commission disclaims responsibility for any private publication or statement of any SEC employee or Commissioner. This chapter expresses the author's views and does not necessarily reflect those of the Commission, the Commissioners or other members of the staff.

[1] The World Bank, 'India: Role of Self-Regulatory Organizations in Securities Market Regulation' (June 2007) 9 (hereinafter 'World Bank Report').

[2] The World Bank cites most EU countries as examples of such limited self-regulation; ibid 10.

[3] The World Bank cites the US as an example of such extensive self-regulation; ibid.

[4] ibid.

noting that SEBI has built up a reputation as a 'credible enforcement agency'[5] and that India's stock exchanges 'have established robust mechanisms for market surveillance, which are complemented by SEBI's own surveillance system'.[6] Notably, the IMF also states that: 'The enforcement actions taken by regulator [sic] are very high compared to other jurisdictions.'[7] The success of SEBI and the Indian exchanges in sanctioning members is notable because of the relatively low capacity of the Indian state and its public institutions to accomplish their administrative or regulatory goals.[8] It is also notable because, as this chapter discusses below, SROs in other jurisdictions have sometimes been less effective in enforcing discipline, even when they have significantly greater resources than SEBI and the exchanges.[9]

Two preliminary clarifications may be useful. First, this chapter offers no opinion on whether self-regulation in Indian securities markets, as a whole, is successful or whether Indian securities markets are efficient. The claim is more limited – it seeks to examine why SEBI and the recognised Indian exchanges are relatively effective in enforcing their regulatory regime against members. Second, the regulatory performance scrutinised here is the enforcement of discipline against members of stock exchanges, not of issuers of securities. This distinction is significant here because the regulation of members, ie, broker-dealers, is usually a core function of self-regulatory exchanges. As market operators, exchanges are almost always responsible, even if not solely responsible, for the creation and enforcement of the rules governing the markets they operate. The scope of exchanges' rule-making and enforcement activities varies considerably across jurisdictions, but most exchanges are rule-setters at least in respect of the admission of members, the admission of products to trading and the trading process itself.[10] Therefore, the enforcement of sanctions against members may serve as one important parameter for the comparison of the relative regulatory efficiency of SROs.

If self-regulation by India's securities markets is successful in terms of the effective enforcement of sanctions against members, what explains such success? This chapter suggests that such success may be largely attributable to a basic legislative choice that places a premium on investor protection and transparency over competing market regulatory goals of efficient or liquid markets. By statute, securities trading in India focuses almost entirely on stock exchanges recognised by SEBI, to the exclusion of other, non-exchange venues. The decision to regulate all trading through exchanges, and SEBI's rigorous recognition process for exchanges has had important, and beneficial, consequences for self-regulation because it has given exchanges the market power

[5] International Monetary Fund, 'India: Financial Sector Assessment Program – Detailed Assessments Report on IOSCO Objectives and Principles of Securities Regulation', IMF Country Report No 13/266 (August 2013) (hereinafter 'IMF FSAP'), 4.

[6] ibid.

[7] ibid 22.

[8] Devesh Kapur, Pratap Bhanu Mehta and Milan Vaishnav (eds), *Rethinking Public Institutions in India* (Oxford University Press, 2017).

[9] See section III below.

[10] International Organization of Securities Commissions, 'Regulatory Issues Arising from Exchange Evolution: A Report of the Technical Committee of the International Organization of Securities Commissions', Final Report (November 2006) 5.

necessary to regulate their members effectively. Equally, this regulatory choice poses some serious questions for India's securities markets. One such question relates to the impact on competition and the unavailability of alternative (ie, non-stock exchange) trading platforms in India, despite widespread acknowledgement that such trading platforms have at least some significant benefits for markets and certain types of investors.

This chapter begins with a brief overview of the regulatory structure governing India's securities markets and seeks to examine how the legislative choice to require all securities trading in India to be performed on-exchange enhances SEBI's disciplinary powers. This legislative decision to forego off-exchange trading entails certain consequences for innovation and efficiency in India's securities markets. However, this chapter argues that the trading of efficiency for effective sanctioning may arguably be justified by the nature of India's relatively nascent equities market. Yet, while SEBI and the recognised Indian securities exchanges may understandably wish to maintain the existing market structure to ensure the effective enforcement of regulations, it is unclear why institutional investors do not lobby more strongly for the availability of non-exchange trading venues, despite the apparent advantages of such trading venues. This chapter suggests that the purported advantages of off-exchange trading for institutional investors may be offset by other advantages available to market participants through the existing regulatory system. Finally, it points to some possible limits to SEBI's self-regulation model, and potential challenges to self-regulation that may arise with the continued growth of Indian markets.

I. SEBI's REGULATION OF STOCK EXCHANGES AND EXCHANGE SELF-REGULATION

As a historical matter, India's stock exchanges long pre-date government regulators. The Bombay Stock Exchange was established in 1875[11] and the Calcutta Stock Exchange was incorporated in 1908.[12] Several decades later, the role of the exchanges in regulating their members was recognised by the Securities Contracts (Regulation) Act of 1956 (SCRA), which, among other things, invited stock exchanges to apply to be recognised by India's Central Government.[13] The SCRA recognises the power of the exchanges to regulate a number of matters, including the contracts traded on the exchanges and the conduct of members.[14]

SEBI, a statutory authority, emerged as the Indian securities regulator in 1992. The legislation that established SEBI authorised it to promote and regulate SROs to carry out its functions.[15] This was implicit official recognition of the fact that SEBI came

[11] https://www.bseindia.com/downloads/Corporate_Profile.pdf.

[12] 'A Requiem for Calcutta Stock Exchange' *LiveMint* (23 May 2014), https://www.livemint.com/Companies/lbvFFIuG5PVuUo0w1iR1TP/A-requiem-for-Calcutta-StockExchange.html.

[13] SCRA, s 3(1).

[14] ibid s 9(1).

[15] SEBI Act 1992, s 11(2)(d). See also World Bank Report (n 1) 16.

into being, in part, because of the failures of exchange self-regulation. As SEBI noted in its annual report of 1992–93, its inspections:

> [R]evealed several inadequacies and deficiencies in the functioning of stock exchanges. It was noted that the stock exchanges were not functioning as effective self-regulatory organizations and regulating their own members effectively through enforcement of the bye-laws, rules and regulations of the Exchanges [sic]. The mechanism for enforcing discipline amongst the members was also found to be inadequate and the attention to redressal of investor grievances minimal.[16]

SEBI's scrutiny of stock exchanges arose from their centrality in India's legal regime. Several decades before SEBI came into existence, Section 19(1) of the SCRA required that all trades in securities in India be conducted *only* on stock exchanges recognised by the Central Government.[17] Following its establishment in 1992, SEBI, as an agency of the Central Government, was authorised to grant recognition to stock exchanges.[18] Accordingly, to this day, the only type of venue in India on which trading in securities can legally be undertaken is a stock exchange recognised by SEBI.

SEBI enjoys extensive regulatory powers over Indian stock exchanges. In its capacity as the Central Government's delegate, SEBI may, for instance, intervene in the management of stock exchanges,[19] suspend the conduct of business for significant periods,[20] call for and scrutinise returns and reports,[21] and initiate inquiries into the affairs of exchanges or individual members.[22] These regulatory powers are formidable, but they are effective in regulating securities trading primarily because of the existence of the SCRA, which requires securities trading to be done on recognised stock exchanges and vests in SEBI the sole power to recognise such stock exchanges. Self-regulation by Indian stock exchanges is therefore effective because members have no alternative but to trade through recognised stock exchanges. Members who have been sanctioned by a recognised stock exchange cannot avoid such sanction and 'simply and costlessly join a rival securities association'[23] or participate in the securities industry through an unrecognised stock exchange. By legislating out the possibility of alternative trading venues, the SCRA has ensured efficacy at two levels – it has ensured that SEBI's regulation of stock exchanges is effective and, at one remove, it has ensured the efficacy of self-regulation by recognised stock exchanges.

SEBI's power to grant recognition to and withdraw from stock exchanges has been a powerful tool against the fragmentation of the Indian securities markets.

[16] SEBI 1992–93 Annual Report at 12.

[17] Section 19(1) provides that no person shall, except with the permission of the Central Government, organise or assist in organising or be a member of any stock exchange (other than a recognised stock exchange) for the purpose of assisting in, entering into or performing any contracts in securities.

[18] SCRA, s 4.

[19] ibid s 12.

[20] ibid.

[21] ibid s 6(1) and 6(3)(a).

[22] ibid s 6(3).

[23] Jonathan Macey and Carole Novgorod, 'Enforcing Self-Regulatory Organization's Penalties and the Nature of Self-Regulation' (2012) 40 *Hofstra Law Review* 963, 967.

In fact, SEBI's power to recognise and de-recognise stock exchanges has resulted in the consolidation of securities exchanges in India. In 1992–93, in its first annual report, SEBI stated that it had inspected a total of 12 stock exchanges, including the Ahmedabad Stock Exchange, the Bombay Stock Exchange, the Calcutta Stock Exchange, the Hyderabad Stock Exchange, the Saurashtra Kutch Stock Exchange and the Vadodara Stock Exchange.[24] In its most recent annual report, in 2017–18, the number of stock exchanges was down to four exchanges with permanent recognition – the Ahmedabad Stock Exchange, the Calcutta Stock Exchange, the Bombay Stock Exchange and the National Stock Exchange. Of these, most trading was concentrated in the Bombay Stock Exchange and the National Stock Exchange.[25] Nor is the process of consolidation complete. SEBI noted that: 'Out of the four permanent exchanges, the Ahmedabad Stock Exchange and the Calcutta Stock Exchange are in the process of exit.'[26] Recognised securities exchanges in India therefore operate as a duopoly consisting of the Bombay Stock Exchange and the National Stock Exchange. Over its 25-year existence, SEBI has thus been able to concentrate its regulatory capacity on a steadily decreasing number of recognised exchanges.

II. SEBI's SELF-REGULATORY MODEL IN CONTEXT: MARKET STRUCTURE, MARKET POWER AND REGULATORY EFFICACY

In order to appreciate the scope of SEBI's regulatory power over recognised stock exchanges, and consequently, the power of stock exchanges to regulate the activities of their members, it may be useful to contrast India's securities regulatory with another model – that of the US. In the US, as in India, the principal securities regulator, the Securities Exchange Commission (SEC), regulates national securities exchanges, and the securities exchanges enforce their members' compliance with federal securities laws and exchange rules.[27] However, in the US, unlike in India, securities trading need not take place only on a registered securities exchange. A significant volume of trading[28] takes place on 'alternative trading systems' (ATSs) – automated trading systems that offered execution services comparable to those of exchanges.[29]

[24] SEBI 1992–93 Annual Report at 12.

[25] SEBI 2017–2018 Annual Report at 97. Just as the exit of certain stock exchanges has helped the efficient allocation of regulatory resources, the entry of the National Stock Exchange in 1992 may also have helped to improve the self-regulatory environment. In the wake of the exchange regulatory failures discussed in SEBI's first annual report, the National Stock Exchange expanded its membership beyond the relatively small group of brokers who had traditionally dominated the stock exchanges, while simultaneously maintaining stringent eligibility criteria for membership.

[26] ibid.

[27] Securities Exchange Act of 1934, 15 USC § 78f(a), (b)(1) (2006).

[28] In 2012, approximately 69 per cent of trading volume in national market system stocks was executed on exchanges, while 12 per cent was executed on ATSs and the remainder was executed on neither an exchange nor an ATS. See www.sec.gov/dera/staff-papers/white-papers/otc-trading-white-paper-03-2014.pdf. In 2005, the New York Stock Exchange alone executed 80 per cent of the trading volume in its listed stocks; by 2010, that figure had declined to 26 per cent. See Mary L Schapiro, Chairman, 'Strengthening Our Equity Market Structure', https://www.sec.gov/news/speech/2010/spch090710mls.htm.

[29] See generally Securities Exchange Act Release No 40760 (8 December 1998), 63 Fed Reg. 70844 (22 December 1998). The EU recognises a similar type of trading platform, the 'multilateral trading

Although they provide a platform for securities trading, ATSs do not perform the functions of SROs and are not regulated as securities exchanges. Instead, the SEC requires ATSs to register as broker-dealers.[30]

The substantial volume of trading taking place on ATSs indicates that they increasingly compete with securities exchanges. More importantly for the present analysis, the existence of a parallel universe of ATSs serves to undercut the efficacy of self-regulation by exchanges. Broker-dealers no longer need exclusively rely on exchanges for access to a pool of willing buyers and sellers. They 'can now provide 'marketplaces for securities themselves, establishing electronic trading networks outside of traditional stock exchanges.'[31] Accordingly, a US exchange's expulsion of a member need no longer result in its permanent exile from the securities markets.[32]

By statute, India's securities regime recognises no alternatives to recognised stock exchanges. Expulsion from a recognised stock exchange will therefore effectively mean near-permanent exile from Indian securities markets. The Rules of the Bombay Stock Exchange state that a person is ineligible to become a trading member of the Exchange if 'he has been at any time expelled or declared a defaulter by any other stock exchange'.[33] The Rules of the National Stock Exchange provide for a similar prohibition.[34] Members barred from trading on exchanges may, of course, resort to

facility' (MTF). The EU's Markets in Financial Instruments Directive II (MiFID II) defines an MTF as a 'a multilateral system, operated by an investment firm or a market operator, which brings together multiple third-party buying and selling interests in financial instruments – in the system and in accordance with non-discretionary rules – in a way that results in a contract in accordance with [MiFID II]'. Article 23(1) of the EU's Markets in Financial Instruments Regulation (MiFIR) appears, on its face, to create a structure similar to the SCRA's requirement that all trading occur only on recognised exchanges. Article 23(1) requires an investment firm to ensure that the trades it undertakes in shares admitted to trading on a regulated market or traded on a trading venue take place on: (i) a regulated market (MTF); (ii) a systematic internaliser (SI); or (iii) a third country trading venue assessed as equivalent in accordance with Article 25(4)(a) of MiFID II. Functionally, however, this amounts to the recognition of a much higher number of stock exchanges than India, in addition to MTFs and trading venues in other jurisdictions that the EU recognises as equivalent. Thus, despite the superficial similarity, art 23(1) of MiFIR does not result in the type of securities market concentration that has occurred in India.

[30] Rule 3b-16(b) 1 under the Securities Exchange Act of 1934 explicitly excludes certain systems that the SEC believed did not meet the exchange definition. Rule 3a1-1 under the Exchange Act exempts an ATS from the statutory definition of 'exchange', provided that it registers as a broker-dealer.

[31] Macey and Novgorod (n 23) 987. The same article notes that: 'The multiplicity of trading venues has crippled exchanges' abilities to exercise market power to discipline members as well as their ability to monitor individual member firms' (at 987–88).

[32] The Financial Industry Regulatory Authority (FINRA) has extensive procedures for reviewing the eligibility of prospective broker-dealers (see FINRA Rule 1013), which includes requiring information regarding regulatory and criminal actions against prospective broker-dealers. Article III, s 4 of FINRA's bye-laws and s 3(a)(39) of the Exchange Act have extensive provisions regarding circumstances which disqualify a person from becoming a broker-dealer. These eligibility requirements and disqualifications apply to entities that seek to operate an ATS, and which therefore have to register as broker-dealers. However, these requirements and disqualifications do not apply to entities that seek to trade on ATS, so that an entity that is barred from being a broker-dealer and trading on exchange can nevertheless proceed to trade on any ATS that permits it to do so. Recently, the SEC adopted regulations that impose extensive new transparency requirements on ATSs that effect transactions in National Market Stock (NMS). These new regulations do not appear to affect the powers of ATSs to admit entities to trading. See Securities Exchange Act Release No 83663, Regulation of NMS Stock Alternative Trading Systems (18 July 2018) (hereinafter 'ATS Final Release').

[33] See r 4(h) under ch III of the Rules of the Bombay Stock Exchange.

[34] See r 4(h) under ch III of the Rules of the National Stock Exchange, a near-identical provision to that of the Bombay Stock Exchange. It should also be noted here that under the SCRA, no recognised stock

trading over the counter, but this may severely reduce the amount of liquidity available to traders and generally results in more unfavourable terms of trade. Further, under the SCRA, some types of products, such as derivatives may only be available for trading on recognised exchanges – so that trading such products off exchange may be illegal.[35]

The SEC's dual exchange/ATS regime has consequences beyond those for effective sanctions. In early 2010, in its Concept Release on Equity Market Structure, the SEC described the structure of the US equities markets as 'dispersed and complex'.[36] It noted that its 'task has been to facilitate an appropriately balanced market structure that promotes competition among markets, while minimizing the potentially adverse effects of fragmentation on efficiency, price transparency, best execution of investor orders, and order interaction',[37] and that:

> When many trading centers compete for order flow in the same stock, however, such competition can lead to the fragmentation of order flow in that stock. Fragmentation can inhibit the interaction of investor orders and thereby impair certain efficiencies and the best execution of investors' orders. Competition among trading centers to provide specialized services for investors also can lead to practices that may detract from public price transparency.[38]

Unlike the SEC, SEBI does not deal with a 'dispersed and complex' market. As the IMF notes: 'In practice trading activity carried out in [recognised stock exchanges], excluding the two nationwide [recognised stock exchanges] is minimal or non-existent. Thus for practical purposes in this assessment the reference to [recognised stock exchanges] should be construed as referring to the [Bombay Stock Exchange] and the [National Stock Exchange].'[39]

Part of the reason for the concentration of trading on these two exchanges is through the operation of a virtuous cycle. As liquidity deepens on these exchanges, they attract more issuers and more members, who further contribute to increasing liquidity. In addition, SEBI's regulations further deepen the trend towards consolidation in the Indian securities markets. For example, in 2012, SEBI introduced new requirements for recognised stock exchanges, including net worth and trading volume requirements.[40] These have helped to increase entry barriers for exchanges and have effectively pushed a number of recognised stock exchanges to exit the market.[41]

exchange can amend its bye-laws without SEBI's prior approval. This effectively prevents a race to the bottom in which an exchange loosens its eligibility criteria to attract more business, even at the risk of admitting bad actors.

[35] SCRA, s 18.

[36] Securities Exchange Act Release No 34-61358, Concept Release on Equity Market Structure, 75 Fed Reg 3594 (21 January 2010) (hereinafter 'Concept Release'). More recently, the SEC noted that as of 31 March 2018, there were 21 registered national securities exchanges and 87 ATSs registered with the SEC. See ATS Final Release (n 32) 12.

[37] ibid 3597.

[38] ibid.

[39] IMF FSAP (n 5) 36.

[40] Securities Contracts (Regulations) (Stock Exchanges and Clearing Corporations) Regulations, 2012.

[41] '15 Regional Stock Exchanges to Shut Operations as SEBI Deadline Approaches' *LiveMint* (23 February 2014), www.livemint.com/Money/foV0xOfxkv4GSJjQ5z1PUL/15-regional-stock-exchanges-to-shut-operations-as-Sebi-deadl.html. See also SEBI 2016–17 Annual Report at 102 ('Exit of Stock Exchanges').

India's market structure thus appears to have followed the opposite trajectory to securities markets in the US – they are concentrated rather than dispersed. Market concentration comes with its own significant regulatory implications, notably for competition, but the impact of such concentration is obviously beneficial for the allocation of SEBI's resources, since there are now far fewer exchanges to supervise. Less obviously, however, such concentration has some benefits for self-regulation by the Indian exchanges.[42] As the number of recognised Indian exchanges decreases, and because each exchange denies membership to a member expelled by another exchange, members find it increasingly expensive to avoid sanctions imposed by exchanges. Given SEBI's oversight of exchange rule-making, recognised exchanges do not have to and likely cannot resort to regulatory concessions in order to attract members.

The Bombay Stock Exchange and the National Stock Exchange each have extensive power to regulate their members. Each exchange has disciplinary jurisdiction[43] over its members, and each requires its members to enter into arbitration for the resolution of claims against members.[44] Each exchange can exercise a range of disciplinary actions, including censure, fines, the suspension of rights and privileges, and expulsion.[45] Each exchange can exercise its disciplinary powers not just for breaches of the law, but also for conduct that does not rise to that level – conduct that is termed 'unbusinesslike' or 'unprofessional'.[46]

Each exchange's regulatory powers extend well beyond disciplinary jurisdiction. Both exchanges have, for example, rules governing default by members,[47] transactions and settlements,[48] and specific rules for specific market segments, such as the trading of futures and options.[49] Notably, in many cases, there appears to be relatively little difference between the rules and bye-laws of the Bombay Stock Exchange and those of the National Stock Exchange – indeed, many rules are identical or near-identical, possibly because SEBI oversees rule-making by the exchanges. This similarity in rules underlines the difficulty of regulatory arbitrage between the two exchanges, and the duopolistic structure of the market makes rule-breaking potentially expensive for market participants.

[42] The IMF appears to agree with this assessment. See IMF FSAP (n 5) 13.

[43] Chapter IV (Disciplinary Proceedings, Penalties, Suspension and Expulsion) of the Rules of the National Stock Exchange and the identical chapter in the Rules of the Bombay Stock Exchange.

[44] Chapter XI of the bye-laws of the National Stock Exchange and Chapter XIII of the bye-laws of the Bombay Stock Exchange.

[45] Chapter IV, r 2 of the Rules of the National Stock Exchange and the identical provision in the Rules of the Bombay Stock Exchange.

[46] Chapter IV, rr 4 and 5 of the Rules of the National Stock Exchange and the identical provision in the Rules of the Bombay Stock Exchange.

[47] Chapter XII of the bye-laws of the National Stock Exchange and Chapter XIV of the bye-laws of the Bombay Stock Exchange.

[48] Chapter IX of the bye-laws of the National Stock Exchange and Chapter X of the bye-laws of the Bombay Stock Exchange.

[49] Trading Regulations of the National Stock Exchange of the Futures and Options Segment, https://www.nseindia.com/global/content/regulations/NSEFOregulations.pdf; and Regulations of the Bombay Stock Exchange on the Futures and Options Segment, https://www.bseindia.com/members/downloads.aspx.

Sanctions imposed by a self-regulator can be less effective if market participants can switch from one trading venue to another at little cost. Self-regulatory sanctions can also be less effective if market participants can carry out a substantially similar business under the jurisdiction of another regulator.[50] A market participant who can easily switch from one business governed by one regulator to a similar business that is unregulated or governed by another regulator will be less amenable to disciplinary sanction. The rules of India's recognised stock exchanges have made it effectively impossible for market participants to evade regulation or disciplinary action by switching from one trading venue to another. But SEBI has also promoted self-regulation by making the other type of regulatory arbitrage – switching from one business to another – difficult. Thus, for example, SEBI's regulations for investment advisers provide that before registering an investment adviser, SEBI may consider 'whether any disciplinary action has been taken by SEBI or any other regulatory authority against any person directly or indirectly connected to the applicant'.[51] The term 'regulatory authority' is undefined in the investment adviser regulations, but will likely cover actions against members by a recognised stock exchange.[52]

The benefits for self-regulation brought about through the consolidation of India's securities markets illustrate, in an Indian context, a point made in the context of the US securities markets:

> [T]he success of industry self-regulation critically depends on the market power of the firms in the self-regulatory organization. If the firms have market power, then as long as the industry generates profits for members, self-regulation can work. But if either profitability or market power decline, self-regulation will fail.[53]

If this is true, then perhaps self-regulation succeeds in Indian stock exchanges because the securities market in India is effectively duopolistic. This duopoly may partly be attributable to the superior performance, products and efficiency of the stock exchanges in question, but it is also attributable to SEBI's own regulatory actions, particularly the tightening of regulatory standards for the operation of an exchange. It is also attributable to a legislative mandate that confines trading to recognised stock exchanges. The market power of Indian stock exchanges is thus at least partly shaped by regulatory choices, and the regulatory design that confers market power on these exchanges also enables the exchanges to self-regulate through effective sanctions. This regulatory arrangement is especially notable because it may constitute a relatively significant exception to failures by many other Indian administrative and regulatory institutions, as briefly discussed below. It is also notable because this regulatory arrangement minimises the burden on the regulator's capacity, and the capacity of the Indian state.

[50] Macey and Novgorod (n 23) 993–95 (discussing an increasing number of broker-dealers switching to being investment advisers).

[51] See reg 6(i) of the SEBI (Investment Advisers) Regulations, 2013.

[52] Similarly, SEBI has made liberal use of trading bans against a number of entities, and a list of entities banned by SEBI is maintained by the exchanges. See, eg, https://www.bseindia.com/investors/debent.aspx.

[53] Macey and Novgorod (n 23) 963.

III. EFFECTIVE SANCTIONS AND REGULATORY TRADE-OFFS

Recent work on India's public institutions contends that the Indian state is often undermanned and overbureaucratised, and 'that the Indian state is struggling to perform even the most basic functions of a sovereign state'.[54] The underlying institutional weaknesses of the state's public institutions 'stand in contrast to relatively dynamic private and civil society organizations'.[55] Kapur, Mehta and Vaishnav suggest that state capacity – the ability of the state to effectively design and implement public policies – varies greatly across India.[56] They note, in particular, that:

> Many regulatory bodies across India suffer from a common set of problems stemming from congenital birth defects reflected in their design: insufficient authority, circumscribed financial autonomy; weak human resources; multiple overlapping mandates; a lack of legitimacy; and unsurprisingly, political interference that is both the cause and consequence of their multiple weaknesses.[57]

This is a bleak diagnosis. Happily, however, SEBI seems to be in significantly better health than these ailing anonymous institutions. SEBI's relatively robust condition may be attributable to a number of causes that may be beyond the scope of this chapter – and, in any event, hardly anyone bothers analysing good news in great detail. Yet, SEBI's success in working with exchanges to produce effective self-regulation is attributable to a certain congenital strength, namely the SCRA's injunction to limit securities trading to recognised stock exchanges. It is probably unwise to extend the metaphor much further, but SEBI has certainly exercised itself diligently to reduce the number of recognised exchanges and create the degree of market power required to make self-regulation effective.

SEBI's regulatory choices have served to preserve, and even enhance, its regulatory capacity. It has preserved and maximised its own regulatory capacity by effectively delegating the regulation of market intermediaries to recognised stock exchanges, and has ensured that such regulation is effective by preserving the market power of these recognised exchanges. It has done this by promulgating and rigorously enforcing a variety of capital, governance and other rules for the operation of these exchanges. SEBI's regulatory approach was not a foregone conclusion. By definition, all securities regulators regulate their securities markets, but not all securities regulators hold all regulated markets to the same standards – sometimes, because they wish to encourage competition across markets. SEBI has eschewed competition across markets in favour of competition within markets, and this course of action has allowed SEBI to effectively leverage the power of the exchanges.

If the recognised Indian stock exchanges are successful in regulating their members, why is the regulatory and legislative structure that supports Indian exchanges not widely emulated by all regulators in major securities markets? Why do regulators

[54] Kapur, Mehta and Vaishnav (n 8) 5–6.
[55] ibid 7.
[56] ibid 6.
[57] ibid 11.

outside India worried by the prospect of market fragmentation and its consequences for self-regulation not seek legislation that is similar to the SCRA, or frame regulatory rules that severely restrict the number and nature of venues on which trading is permitted? One answer lies in the trade-offs that are required to be made within the set of competing regulatory objectives that confront each regulator.

As one commenter notes, regulatory trade-offs can be 'frustrating',[58] perhaps because they require the partial subordination of important principles that appear to be the kind of principles that we should never depart from or subordinate, such as fairness. Yet, regulatory trade-offs are common and trade-offs may even be inherent in certain questions relating to market structure. For example, in creating rules that affect the level of consolidation in a market, regulators must choose between competition among traders or intermediaries (which will occur in concentrated markets) or competition among market centres (which will occur in fragmented markets).[59]

In its Concept Release on Equity Market Structure, the SEC noted that:

> Congress found that it is in the public interest and appropriate for the protection of investors and the maintenance of fair and orderly markets to assure five objectives: (1) Economically efficient execution of securities transactions; (2) Fair competition among brokers and dealers, among exchange markets, and between exchange markets and markets other than exchange markets; (3) The availability to brokers, dealers, and investors of information with respect to quotations and transactions in securities; (4) The practicability of brokers executing investors' orders in the best market; and (5) An opportunity, consistent with efficiency and best execution, for investors' orders to be executed without the participation of a dealer.[60]

The SEC also recognised that 'these five objectives can, at times, be difficult to reconcile' and stated that its task had been to ensure an appropriately balanced market structure.[61] The SEC's recognition that regulatory objectives for a regulated market can be at odds with each other indicates that regulators may have to prioritise. The ordering of priorities may sometimes be pre-set – for example, where a hierarchy of objectives is ordered by legislation. In other cases, where the relative importance of a regulatory objective is not explicit, regulators may be forced to prioritise objectives based upon context. For instance, in large, well-developed, diverse and competitive market centres, competition may be relied upon to prevent or mitigate abuse of efficiencies.[62] By contrast, in smaller, less diverse marketplaces, stringent rules may be required to protect against abuse.[63]

The finding by Congress that competition between exchanges and non-exchange markets is a regulatory goal requires that the SEC consider this goal in regulating the

[58] Mattias Levin, 'Competition Fragmentation and Transparency, Providing the Regulatory for Fair, Efficient and Dynamic European Securities Markets, Assessing the ISD Review', CEPS Task Force Reports No 46 (1 April 2003) 64.

[59] ibid 64–65.

[60] Concept Release (n 36) 3597.

[61] ibid.

[62] Levin (n 58) 64.

[63] ibid.

securities market. This may explain why, despite the potential for market fragmentation and the resulting adverse consequences for self-regulation, the SEC continues to recognise ATSs as valid alternatives to registered securities exchanges. The SEC has also recognised that ATSs may 'advance the goals of the national market system'[64] in various ways. As the SEC noted, equity ATSs have become an integral part of the US national market system and are a significant source of liquidity for such equities.[65] The SEC also noted that the significant competition among exchanges and non-exchange markets might compel ATSs to innovate to attract more trading volume,[66] and that ATSs, like registered national securities exchanges, have used advances in technology to improve the speed, capacity and efficiency of their trading functionalities.[67] Certain types of ATSs, the so-called 'dark pools', were originally designed to offer some market participants, particularly institutional investors, the ability to minimise transaction costs when executing large-sized trades by completing their trades without prematurely revealing the full extent of their trading interest to the broader market.[68]

Institutional investors account for a significant portion of the US securities markets. One commenter observes: 'That the market for corporate securities traded on the New York Stock Exchange or the Nasdaq Global Market is no longer substantially retail in nature is now common knowledge.'[69] The Securities Industry and Financial Markets Association noted that in 2016, institutions accounted for 59.6 per cent of total US equities holdings.[70] Within this market structure, ATSs clearly fulfil a need for institutional investors. ATSs can offer liquidity, particularly in thinly traded stocks. Dark pool ATSs can enable institutional investors or other large traders to enter into transactions of significant size without moving or disrupting the markets. ATSs can often be nimbler and may allow for swifter, cheaper or bespoke trade execution for participants. They may also serve as laboratories for technological and logistical developments in trading, permitting players to experiment with high-frequency trading and other innovations.

Despite these considerable benefits, ATSs pose questions for regulators beyond their potential to cause market fragmentation. In 2015, the SEC expressed its concern regarding a lack of transparency around potential conflicts of interest that arise

[64] See Securities Exchange Act Release No 34-76474, *Regulation of NMS Stock Alternative Trading Systems*, 80 Fed Reg 80997 (28 December 2015), 80998 (hereinafter 'ATS Proposing Release').

[65] ibid 81000.

[66] ibid 81009.

[67] ibid. In July 2018, the SEC noted that '[NMS] ATSs have grown increasingly complex in terms of the services and functionalities that they offer subscribers, and they have used advances in technology to improve the speed, capacity, and efficiency of the trading functionalities that they offer to execute orders in NMS stocks'. See ATS Final Release (n 32) 14.

[68] ATS Proposing Release (n 64) 81009. The SEC noted, in this context, that the average size of the dark pool order was of significant size and could be as high as 500,000 shares per trade.

[69] Donald C Langevoort, 'The SEC, Retail Investors and the Institutionalization of the Securities Markets' (2009) 95 *Virginia Law Review* 1025, 1026.

[70] See Securities Industry and Financial Markets Association Fact Book 2017, www.lexissecuritiesmosaic.com/gateway/sec/public-statements/10_US-Fact-Book-2017-SIFMA.pdf, 82. This does not imply that retail investors' investments in US equities have declined in absolute terms. In fact, retail investors' investments in US equities markets have risen from $10,046.9 billion in 2007 to $15,621.5 billion in 2016; ibid 81.

from the activities of a broker-dealer operating an ATS and its affiliates, concerns which it has recently reiterated and sought to address.[71] Yet, the SEC concluded in 2015 that: 'Currently, the coexistence of national securities exchanges and [ATSs] seems to have beneficial effects on market efficiency.'[72] The SEC noted, among other things, that while not all trades that execute on ATSs are large block trades, those that are have been seen to be beneficial to market efficiency, and that if ATSs were not a viable trading venue for market participants, market participants might not execute large orders at all because of the price impact costs of executing on a securities exchange.[73]

The SEC's discussion of ATSs is a demonstration of how regulatory trade-offs may sometimes be necessary. Regulatory goals such as economically efficient execution and competition between and among trading venues may not always sit easily with transparency and fairness, ie, non-discrimination. In some cases, choosing a particular regulatory goal or set of goals may make regulation, or self-regulation, more difficult. Yet, regulators will prioritise their goals based on their particular contexts and the constituents they are required to serve, and some deference is due to these judgments, even when other similarly placed actors might come to different conclusions. Thus, while the existence of ATSs may make it more difficult for exchanges to regulate and sanction their members, a regulator may believe, under certain circumstances, that these difficulties are acceptable when viewed against gains in terms of goals such as efficiency, innovation and competition.

In its annual reports, SEBI often refers to three goals: (1) protection of the interests of investors in securities; (2) development of the securities market; and (3) regulation of the securities market.[74] These goals are very broadly, and perhaps ambiguously, worded, but operating in a context which is often very different from that of the US, SEBI may justifiably make different regulatory choices from the SEC. By many accounts, only a very small proportion of India's population invests in securities. One source estimated that in April 2016, 52 per cent of Americans owned stock – a record low, and down from 65 per cent in 2007.[75] By contrast, in a 2015 survey, SEBI estimated that only 33.7 million Indians (approximately 3.3 per cent of the population) owned equities.[76] SEBI defines a retail investor as an individual who applies or bids for securities of a value less than Rs 200,000[77] (approximately $2,800). An SEC rule defines a 'customer order', ie, a non-institutional order as an order for a quantity of stock with a value of less than $200,000.[78] Other differences, often very stark

[71] ATS Proposing Release (n 64) 81001. Amendments passed by the SEC in July 2018 to the regulations pertaining to certain types of ATS substantially expand transparency requirements for certain types of ATSs. See n 32 above.

[72] ibid 81117. In 2018, the SEC continued to state that: 'Currently, the coexistence of national securities exchanges and NMS Stock ATSs seems to have beneficial effects on market efficiency.'

[73] ibid 81001.

[74] See, eg, SEBI 2007–08 Annual Report at 1.

[75] See Justin McCarthy, 'Just over Half of Americans Own Stocks, Matching Record Low' (20 April 2016), http://news.gallup.com/poll/190883/half-americans-own-stocks-matching-record-low.aspx.

[76] 'SEBI Investor Survey 2015' (October 2016) 6, 112–14.

[77] See SEBI (Disclosure and Investor Protection Guidelines), ch I, 1.2.1 (xxiv(c)).

[78] See 17 CFR 242.600(b)(18).

ones, in relation to education, resources and access to redressal mechanisms may also distinguish the US investor from their Indian counterpart.

The differences between US and Indian markets and investors may indicate that differences in self-regulatory efficacy are a product of differing regulatory choices rather than differing regulatory performance. In the context of a nascent retail investor market characterised by relatively low household incomes, it may be possible to understand and even justify a regulatory posture which prioritises transparency, fair access and orderly growth over efficiency, innovation and speed. Retail investors are unlikely to be sufficiently sophisticated to use alternative trading platforms in significant numbers. Retail investors are also numerous, disorganised and dispersed, which makes them an ineffective pressure group to bring about regulatory change.[79] The availability of alternative trading platforms that are not regulated in the same manner as recognised stock exchanges would primarily benefit market participants with greater resources, typically institutional investors. These alternative venues may serve to deepen the chasm between retail and institutional investors by offering access on favourable terms to institutional or larger investors. The existence of a parallel set of trading venues subject to lower levels of regulatory oversight may also enable bad actors to continue to participate in the securities markets even after being expelled by securities exchanges. These concerns may explain why SEBI has shown relatively little interest in alternative trading platforms, despite their potential benefits for institutional investors.

IV. LIMITS AND NEW DIRECTIONS

This leaves us with a residual issue: the relative silence of India's institutional investors. If SEBI's apparent satisfaction with the existing regulatory regime is easy to understand, the relative silence of India's institutional investors on the absence of alternative trading platforms is intriguing. If the benefits of alternative trading platforms are apparent, then why do India's institutional investors not strongly lobby SEBI to permit their existence? It is difficult to give a definite answer to this question, but perhaps two speculative explanations could be advanced.

First, the types of large institutional investors who use non-exchange venues may already receive a sufficiently high level of service from brokers and recognised exchanges so that they feel no need to migrate to non-exchange venues. Institutional investors may be better able to leverage their market size and position to obtain better execution quality from their broker-dealers, whereas smaller customers may lack sufficient bargaining power to do so. If this is true, institutional customers may stand to gain little from a potentially expensive investment in alternative trading platforms. Second, major brokers and recognised stock exchanges may stand to lose significantly from a move to non-exchange trading, particularly where a former customer or member decides to operate its own trading platform to ensure better

[79] On the relative political weakness of anonymous and diffused groups to bring about political change, see Bruce Ackerman, 'Beyond *Carolene Products*' (1985) 98 *Harvard Law Review* 713, 729–30.

execution. These brokers and the stock exchanges are likely to be a major, organised and well-entrenched constituency against any change to the existing regulatory regime.

One powerful driver of changes to India's regulatory and self-regulatory structure may be investors' desire to access products that are not usually accessible through recognised stock exchanges. Alternative trading platforms that trade equities that are traded on recognised stock exchanges may offer advantages in terms of liquidity, anonymity and efficiency of execution, but they do not offer fundamentally different products. By contrast, platforms that trade products that are not listed on recognised stock exchanges may fulfil a need that no recognised stock exchange meets. For example, in 2014, there were reports that SEBI might consider the establishment of platforms for investors in private equity and emerging growth companies – entities whose securities are not available to investors on the recognised stock exchanges.[80] However, this initiative would be accompanied by its own set of regulatory trade-offs. Institutional investors, who might be particularly well suited to bear the risks associated with these types of investments, may already be well placed to invest in such companies through private contractual arrangements rather than through a new trading platform. A new trading platform for private equity and emerging growth companies might provide better access for retail investors, but such investors are poorly placed to bear the risks of these types of investments. It is also not clear whether SEBI would regulate such alternative platforms in a manner comparable to recognised stock exchanges, and regulatory choices made in this regard would have important consequences for self-regulation. An alternative trading platform for venture capital and private equity investments that is not subject to the same regulatory constraints as a recognised stock exchange might find it more difficult to regulate institutional members if expelled or suspended members can easily use private contractual mechanisms for investment.

More recently, there has been some speculation that SEBI might ease the listing norms for companies that are majority-owned by private equity or venture capital firms.[81] This may be a measure that SEBI is more comfortable with, since it is, in effect, no different from permitting the listing of relatively high-risk products on an existing recognised stock exchange. This measure would pose no serious challenge to the existing model of self-regulation by recognised stock exchanges, since all trading would continue to be done through the exchanges.

This type of measure could well be a relatively easy way for SEBI to continue to expand investor access to newer types of securities products. SEBI has promulgated extensive issuance, listing and disclosure requirements for various types of debt and equity securities.[82] In addition to these, prospective issuers seeking to list and trade

[80] Jayshree P Upadhyay, 'Sebi Mulls Platform for Pvt Equity, VC Securities' *Business Standard* (18 August 2014), www.business-standard.com/article/markets/sebi-mulls-platform-for-pvt-equity-vc-securities-114081801014_1.html.

[81] Anirudh Laskar, 'Sebi May Ease Listing Norms for Companies Majority-Owned by PE, VC Firms' *LiveMint* (14 June 2017), www.livemint.com/Money/rccsJQFxkyJ8amCw0GhzzJ/Sebi-may-ease-listing-norms-for-companies-majorityowned-by.html.

[82] See, eg, SEBI (Issue and Listing of Debt Securities by Municipalities) Regulations, 2015; SEBI (Listing Obligations and Disclosure Requirements) Regulations, 2015; SEBI (Issue and Listing of Non-convertible

their securities and exchanges must comply with additional requirements prescribed by the exchange on which the security is to be listed.[83] If SEBI and the exchanges could coordinate to relax or adapt these listing and disclosure requirements for new types of securities products, the Indian investor, whether retail or institutional, could have access to a more diverse market from which to build a portfolio.

If adopted, this approach to bringing new products onto existing exchanges will continue to embody SEBI's fundamental regulatory choice – an approach that favours competition within markets over competition among markets. Not only is this approach justifiable, as discussed earlier, in light of the need to protect India's small but growing market of retail investors, but it may even be the only approach that has political legitimacy under the SCRA. If SEBI were to recognise a second class of exchanges that operated very differently from the existing recognised stock exchanges, such recognition might amount to a hollowing out of the SCRA's requirement that securities trading be done on recognised exchanges. For example, SEBI's relatively recent ambivalence towards crowdfunding platforms may neatly illustrate how strongly SEBI considers itself to be bound the constraints of the SCRA. Through a letter issued in July 2017, SEBI directed angel investor networks and start-up funding platforms to warn investors through a disclaimer that crowdfunding platforms are neither stock exchanges nor authorised by the regulator to solicit investments. SEBI also required that the disclaimer state that the securities traded on crowdfunding platforms are not traded on any regulated exchange.[84]

SEBI's reaction to crowdfunding platforms also serves to indicate that the SCRA does not merely stipulate a formal rule to be adhered to – all exchanges are not created equal and recognition is not a mere technicality that SEBI can grant or withhold at its absolute discretion. Under the SCRA, recognised stock exchanges must, for example, have rules regarding their management,[85] the manner in which business is transacted,[86] and the admission, suspension, expulsion and re-admission

Redeemable Preference Shares) Regulations, 2013; SEBI (Public Offer and Listing of Securitised Debt Instruments) Regulations, 2008; and SEBI (Issue of Sweat Equity) Regulations, 2002.

[83] The website of the Bombay Stock Exchange states that it has a dedicated Listing Department to grant approval for listing of securities of companies in accordance with the provisions of the SCRA, the Companies Act, 1956, SEBI's Guidelines and Rules, and the bye-laws and regulations of the Bombay Stock Exchange. The website also notes that companies seeking to list their securities on the Bombay Stock Exchange are required to enter into and comply with the exchange's listing agreement. (https://www.bseindia.com/Static/about/listsec.aspx?expandable=2). Similar requirements apply at the National Stock Exchange, which has its own form of listing agreement (see https://www.nseindia.com/corporates/content/dpp_aggrement.htm).

[84] Anirudh Laskar, 'Sebi Wants Disclaimer for Crowdfunding' *LiveMint* (8 September 2017), https://www.livemint.com/Money/ic0BUI5NSsO1yeJSNAAP1I/Sebi-wants-crowdfunding-bodies-to-warn-investors.html. Also instructive in this regard is SEBI's experience with the Over-the-Counter Exchange of India (OTCEI), originally founded in 1990 as an exchange for small companies, and recognised by the Central Government as a stock exchange prior to the emergence of SEBI. By 2015, OTCEI, unable to meet SEBI's annual turnover requirements, successfully applied to SEBI to exist its role as a stock exchange. See Ashish Rukhaiyar, 'OTC Exchange of India Becomes 12th Bourse to Shut Shop' *LiveMint* (2 April 2015), https://www.livemint.com/Money/H4JJWaITip0HKAZEnzMcJP/OTC-Exchange-of-India-becomes-12th-bourse-to-shut-shop.html.

[85] SCRA, s 3(2)(a).

[86] ibid.

of members.[87] SEBI has also further circumscribed its own power to recognise stock exchanges by promulgating rules under the SCRA.[88] An approach which seeks to continue to confine securities trading to a small number of recognised exchanges achieves two regulatory objectives: it honours the legislative mandate laid out in the SCRA; and it does not strain SEBI's regulatory capacity by requiring it to supervise a large number of exchanges with differing types of products, participants and procedures.

Yet, this approach, for all its justifiability and political legitimacy, poses serious questions for SEBI's existing model. First, not all products are equally suitable to be offered to the investing public, particularly retail investors. Complex products such as certain types of derivatives may warrant restrictions on offering and resale.[89] Second, this approach risks placing a considerable burden on recognised exchanges, which would be required to monitor compliance with multiple sets of listing and trading criteria. To do so, exchanges may have to invest potentially substantial sums in infrastructure and the hiring, training and supervision of compliance and regulatory personnel. The costs of doing so may have to be passed on to members, and this may lead to the exit of members with fewer resources, particularly those who serve retail investors. Third, differences in products may also require a differentiation in the types of intermediaries who handle them. Broker-dealers who deal solely or largely in emerging growth companies may require to be regulated differently than brokers who deal largely in the securities of the top 100 companies by market capitalisation on the Bombay Stock Exchange.[90] For these reasons, among others, SEBI's exchange-centric model is subject to limits and cannot be extended infinitely, particularly as India's investor base changes.

Two broad types of related, but distinct, limits to SEBI's successful production of self-regulation are immediately discernible. The first type of limit is SRO capacity constraints. For example, the regulatory system may soon begin to show the preliminary signs of strain because of the number of entities that exchanges are required to regulate. The IMF noted that, as on December 2011:

> One of the challenges faced by the authorities is the sheer number of the intermediaries operating in the securities market such as brokers (19,557), sub-brokers (78,228), foreign institutional investors (1,767), merchant bankers (199), portfolio managers (246), custodians (19), depository participants (823).[91]

[87] ibid s 3(2)(c).

[88] Securities Contracts (Regulation) (Stock Exchanges and Clearing Corporations) Regulations, 2012. Among other things, these regulations prescribe a specific form in which recognition must be sought (see r 4, and Form A under r 3). Applicants seeking recognition as stock exchanges must comply with a range of requirements from infrastructure to governance. SEBI could certainly relax, amend or even partially waive these requirements, but it cannot do so in a manner that bypasses the SCRA or renders it nugatory.

[89] For example, this was recently recognised by the Alternative Investment Policy Advisory Committee (AIPAC), which was established by SEBI in its second report. The AIPAC notes that investment products like alternative investment funds require the participation of sophisticated investors. See AIPAC Second Report (1 November 2016) 63.

[90] For example, in the US, brokers who deal solely in municipal securities are regulated by the Municipal Securities Rulemaking Board and are subject to a different regulatory regime from other securities brokers, who are regulated by FINRA.

[91] IMF FSAP (n 5) 22.

The IMF goes on to note that the recognised stock exchanges have developed a risk-based approach to determine the intensity of inspections of its member brokers. Brokers have been divided into three categories based on a set of criteria that includes, among other things, trading volume, number of clients, funds settled and number of complaints.[92] As the number of intermediaries continues to increase, the burden on recognised stock exchanges will continue to mount. SEBI has already explored the possibility of increasing the types of securities products available to Indian investors. If SEBI decides to provide investors with access to these products by making them available through the existing recognised exchanges, the net effect will be to further increase the number of intermediaries that the exchanges are required to regulate. This, again, will burden the exchanges and test their ability to regulate their members effectively.

The second limit arises from India's evolving securities markets. As Indian retail investors seek to diversify their holdings, the pressure on SEBI and the exchanges to make more asset classes available will increase. If SEBI decides to make them available through existing exchanges, both it and the exchanges must consider the capacity constraints discussed above. SEBI may, however, consider other alternatives. First, it could simply ban or restrict access to an asset class, or work with other regulators to ban or restrict access to an asset. For example, SEBI may adopt some variant of this approach towards cryptocurrencies and other digital assets, in which many Indian investors have expressed an interest.[93] But if investor interest does not abate or if there is widespread circumvention of bans or restrictions, SEBI may be forced to consider allowing investors access through a platform other than the recognised exchanges. If such alternative platforms abound, self-regulation by the recognised exchanges may begin to lose its teeth.

The increased diversity of assets available to investors may also affect self-regulation in other ways. Exchanges are unlikely to be able to discipline their members in an effective manner if members can easily switch to other lines of business, including investment businesses in non-security products.[94] Further, as retail investors' deployable income increases and as such investors gain an appetite for risk, they may increasingly turn to foreign markets, which may begin to lessen the market power of the recognised Indian stock exchanges. These challenges are significant because they may call upon SEBI to rethink basic regulatory choices. A reassessment of the regulatory design underlying India's securities markets may require SEBI to confront questions not only regarding the evolution of these markets and the shifting needs and appetites of its investor, but also its own regulatory role, and, perhaps most importantly, of India's state capacity.

[92] ibid.

[93] 'SEBI to Crack down on Illicit Bitcoin Schemes, Says Can't Allow Gullible Investors to Be Taken for Ride' *Business Today* (19 December 2017), https://www.businesstoday.in/current/economy-politics/sebi-crack-down-illicit-bitcoin-scheme-investors/story/266203.html.

[94] Macy and Novgorod ((n 23) 1000) note, for example, that in the US: 'Several brokers expelled from the industry in the 1990s for infamous boiler room sales tactics have interestingly turned up in the jet brokerage industry.'

15

Regulatory Pragmatism
The Use of the Ban

SUSAN L OSTERMANN

INTRODUCTION

THOUGH THE INDIAN bureaucracy is often referred to as the 'steel frame of the state', the reality of the regulatory apparatus in India varies considerably from this clichéd image. To start with, the bureaucracy is understaffed. India has a fifth of the number of bureaucrats per person that the US has, for instance.[1] It should not be surprising then that the Indian state is often ill-equipped for enforcement or information-gathering operations that require large numbers of 'boots on the ground'. The Indian bureaucracy is also beset by principal-agent problems between the state and its bureaucrats.[2] These problems sometimes make it appear as if the state is trying to do one thing, while also working to accomplish the opposite. But if the Indian bureaucracy is both understaffed *and* inefficient, how does it sometimes achieve widespread compliance with unpopular state prerogatives? The answer may lie with the judiciary and its approach to regulation.

Unlike many similarly situated apex courts throughout the world, particularly if one looks at courts following the common law tradition, the Indian Supreme Court has taken a very active – rather than reactive – role. It has received scholarly attention for this in a number of areas,[3] but its track record on environmental issues is perhaps most famous and illustrative. Here the Court has interpreted the fundamental right to life and liberty enshrined in the Indian Constitution to include the right to a healthy environment. This has led to judgments, on cases typically taken up as

[1] P Swami. 'Figures Bust Myth India's Bureaucracy is "Bloated"' *The Hindu* (30 January 2012).

[2] SL Ostermann, 'Rule of Law against the Odds: Legal Knowledge, Poverty and Compliance along the India-Nepal Border', Doctoral dissertation, University of California, Berkeley, 2016.

[3] M Mate, 'Elite Institutionalism and Judicial Assertiveness in the Supreme Court of India' (2014) 28 *Temple International & Comparative Law Journal* 2; M Mate, 'The Rise of Judicial Governance in the Supreme Court of India' (2015) 33 *Boston University International Law Journal* 169.

public interest litigation and petitioned directly to the Supreme Court, which have required the bureaucracy to implement pollution controls, reduce noise pollution, cease issuing licences to manufacture certain harmful chemicals etc. The Supreme Court has even required that the government appoint a national environmental regulator. This is not the legal pragmatism described by Thomas Grey,[4] Daniel Farber,[5] Richard Posner,[6] Margaret Radin and Frank Michelman.[7] That pragmatism emphasised: (1) the importance of context; (2) the instrumental nature of law; (3) the unavoidable presence of alternate perspectives; and (4) the problematical nature of utilising any particular foundation for legal reasoning. The Supreme Court's actions go beyond the tidy role of passing judgment on particular cases in a pragmatic manner. Instead, I argue that the Indian Supreme Court is engaged in *regulatory* pragmatism.

This is evidenced by the fact that the Indian Supreme Court has taken on a dynamic role in handing down judgments that appear to match the strengths and weaknesses of the Indian bureaucracy charged with carrying out its orders; it also appears to have learned from its own past mistakes. Indeed, the Supreme Court, seemingly recognising India's weak state capacity – how poorly discretion is managed by its bureaucracy and how few resources it has to throw at large-scale enforcement operations – has handed down a series of bans. Bright-line rules of this variety come with costs, due to their over-inclusiveness, but they are relatively easy to apply,[8] in part because they limit bureaucratic discretion.[9] In a context in which corruption and rent-seeking behaviour may be facilitated by bureaucratic discretion,[10] such rules may be associated with increased compliance. They are also more effective when applied to a limited number of highly visible actors.[11] The fact that the Indian Supreme Court has largely limited its use of bans to those cases in which the Indian bureaucracy is well positioned to be effective or to circumvent an ineffective bureaucracy suggests an intentional and *pragmatic* strategy on the Court's part.

In this chapter, I review three Supreme Court bans and two cases involving bans that were subsequently adjusted: (1) the ban on the sale and registration of diesel cars in Delhi and their subsequent removal (*MC Mehta v Union of India*); (2) the highway liquor sales ban and subsequent restriction to non-urban areas (*State of Tamil Nadu v K Balu*); (3) the engineering correspondence course ban (*Orissa Lift Irrigation Corporation Ltd v Rabi Sankar Patro*); (4) the Delhi Diwali firework ban

[4] T Grey, 'Judicial Review and Legal Pragmatism' (2003) 38 *Wake Forest Law Review* 473.

[5] DA Farber, 'Legal Pragmatism and the Constitution' (1987) 72 *Minnesota Law Review* 1331.

[6] RA Posner, 'What Has Pragmatism to Offer the Law?' (1990) 63 *Southern California Law Review* 1653; RA Posner, *Law, Pragmatism, and Democracy* (Cambridge, MA, Harvard University Press, 2003).

[7] M Radin and F Michelman, 'Pragmatist and Poststructuralist Critical Legal Practice' (1991) 139 *University of Pennsylvania Law Review* 1019.

[8] CS Diver, 'The Optimal Precision of Administrative Rules' (1983) 93 *Yale Law Journal* 65.

[9] B Luppi and F Parisi, 'Toward an Asymmetric Coase Theorem' (2011) 31 *European Journal of Law and Economics* 111.

[10] S Gailmard, 'Expertise, Subversion, and Bureaucratic Discretion' (2002) 18 *Journal of Law, Economics, and Organization* 2; A Ogus, 'Corruption and Regulatory Structures' (2004) 26 *Law & Policy* 329.

[11] RA Kagan and JH Skolnick, 'Banning Smoking: Compliance without Enforcement', in RL Rabin and SD Sugarman (eds), *Smoking Policy* (New York, Oxford University Press, 1993); N Gunningham. RA Kagan and D Thornton, *Shades of Green* (Stanford, Stanford University Press, 2003).

(*Arjun Gopal v Union of India*); and (5) the ban on smoking in public places (*Murli S Deora v Union of India*). The fact patterns present in these cases, the Supreme Court's handling of them, and the language and logic that the Court used are revealing. They suggest that the Supreme Court responds to perceived weak state capacity with a pragmatic regulatory approach. In addition, when one examines the Supreme Court bans in chronological order, one can see that the Court is learning, over time, to be a more effective regulator.

I. BANS AS REGULATORY TOOL

Those following the Indian Supreme Court may have noted its use of an interesting remedy or tool: exemption-less bans on particular behaviours. This approach is quite different from that followed by many other apex courts throughout the world. Indeed, many courts tend to issue nuanced opinions, ones that betray an effort to interfere as little as possible in regulation, a task typically reserved for legislative bodies or for the bureaucracy. A review of the Delhi diesel vehicle bans of 2001 and 2015, the highway liquor sales ban of 2016, the engineering correspondence course ban of 2017 and the Delhi Diwali firework ban of 2017 suggests that the Court's emphasis on bans is an intentional response to perceived weak state capacity. The Court appears to be pragmatically attempting to make up for the failings of the Indian bureaucracy by restricting its scope for discretion and by making enforcement failures more readily visible to observers. However, in its efforts to increase bureaucratic effectiveness, typically by handing the bureaucracy simpler tasks, the Supreme Court has thus far stopped short of attempting to increase state capacity.

A. The Delhi Diesel Vehicle Ban

The Delhi diesel vehicle ban (*MC Mehta v Union of India*) arose over concerns about air quality in Delhi and the National Capital Region, and the government's failure to take appropriate steps to limit harm to public health. The question before the Court was whether Article 32 of the Constitution required a remedy in the case of an air pollution-based infringement based on the protections for health outlined in Articles 39(x), 47 and 48(a). In an earlier hearing, the Supreme Court had held that a remedy was required. The order at issue was an interim order that was later affirmed by the Court (in 2016 and again in 2018) prohibiting the new registration of vehicles with engine capacity greater than 2,000 cubic centimetres, prohibiting the transit of vehicles through Delhi that are not bound for Delhi, and requiring the payment of particular Environmental Compensation Charges (ECCs) by those vehicles bound for Delhi.

The origin of the case was a case under the same name that attempted to reduce pollution levels in Delhi by restricting vehicle traffic in the National Capital Region through a combination of traffic diversions and taxes on vehicles entering the area. The Supreme Court revisited the issue in 2015 when there were increased levels of public attention on pollution levels. While the initial case displayed some trust in the bureaucratic apparatus to conduct emissions testing and divert traffic, as well as a perhaps naïve belief that taxes and/or tolls might slow or halt the flow of polluting vehicles into the largest city in North India, the Supreme Court's 2015 attempt to regulate air pollution from the bench functioned much more like a precursor to its 2017 bans. In three fairly short opinions and orders issued in October, November and December 2015, the Supreme Court raised and then doubled the ECC on trucks entering Delhi, instructed that no vehicle not bound for Delhi could enter the National Capital Region on either of the two main highways, banned all vehicles manufactured prior to 2005 from entering Delhi due to their non-compliance with current emissions standards, and banned the registration of new diesel cars and SUVs with engine capacity larger than 2,000 cubic centimetres.

The iterative process of hearing and rehearing the Delhi diesel vehicle ban cases seems to have allowed the Supreme Court to refine its understanding of the nature of the problem and move closer to the heavy-handed ban approach it used in later cases. The Court first attempted to solve the perceived problem through a tax increase. By raising the ECC, the Court stated that it hoped to make it costlier for drivers to pass through Delhi, thus diverting some pollution around the city rather than into it. However, it soon became evident that this was not working:

> Mr. Harish N. Salve, learned senior counsel appearing as amicus, argued that imposition of ECC and the directions issued by this Court regarding diversion of commercial vehicles/ trucks to alternative routes has made some difference but the pollution levels continue to remain high despite such measures. He submitted by reference to the material placed on record that the level of pollution detected on or before 9th October, 2015 was in fact lower than the levels recorded on subsequent dates. Mr. Salve further submitted that although diversion of vehicles to alternative routes in terms of the order passed by this Court was given effect to belatedly on 6th November, 2015, yet the said direction has not been effectively enforced inasmuch as vehicles not bound for Delhi are being allowed to enter Delhi on payment of the prescribed ECC.[12]

Having more fully understood the nature of the problem and having seen specific evidence that its past measures were not working, the Supreme Court clarified that the ECC could only be paid by those vehicles *bound* for Delhi;[13] in other words, vehicles not having business in Delhi would not be allowed to enter the city: a ban.

However, the Supreme Court didn't stop there. With the consent of the Union of India and Delhi governments and on the advice of amicus curiae, it also raised the ECC dramatically, from Rs 700 for light-duty vehicles (two axle trucks) and Rs 1,300 for heavy-duty vehicles (three and four axle trucks), to Rs 1,400 and Rs 2,600, respectively, a 100 per cent increase.[14] It also exempted 'Passenger vehicles, ambulances and vehicles carrying essential commodities like food stuffs and oil tankers for Delhi' from the above charges.[15] Though this was certainly no ban – particularly with exceptions for trucks carrying food and oil in place – one must remember that these

[12] See *MC Mehta v Union of India* [2016] INSC 886.
[13] ibid.
[14] ibid.
[15] ibid.

are the charges collected from trucks that are *bound* for Delhi, trucks that must enter Delhi in order to carry out their business. It can be thought of as an additional thumb on the scale in a multi-pronged approach to pollution reduction.

With the last two aspects of its December 2015 order, the Supreme Court effectively issued two separate bans. The first was a ban on vehicles manufactured before 2005, the time when current higher emissions standards were put into place:

> We accordingly direct that while vehicles 'bound for Delhi' may enter on payment of ECC at the rates stipulated hereinabove, those registered in the year 2005 or earlier shall not qualify for such entry. State Governments and Union Territories concerned shall ensure that vehicles bearing registration numbers of the year 2005 or earlier do not enter Delhi.[16]

When it delivered this judgment, the Court was careful to assure the public, before making what was sure to be an unpopular bright-line rule, that this was not a hasty decision taken by the Supreme Court alone:

> There was a consensus among learned counsel for the parties even on this issue who submitted that Union of India or Government of NCT of Delhi have no real objection if a direction to that effect is issued.[17]

The Court then went on to issue a second ban: one on the registration of all new passenger vehicles with engine capacity greater than 2,000 cubic centimetres.[18] It did so after considering and deciding against a ban on light-duty vehicles (small trucks) for seemingly economic reasons:

> [W]e are of the view that the new commercial light duty diesel vehicles can for the present continue being registered in Delhi on account of the dependence of the public on such vehicles for supply of essentials. There is, however, no reason why registration of private cars and SUVs using diesel with an engine capacity of 2000 cc and above should not be banned up to 31st March, 2016.[19]

As the Court went on to explain, vehicles of this variety 'are generally used by more affluent sections of our society and because of the higher engine capacity are more prone to cause higher levels of pollution'.[20] In other words, the harm of such a ban would fall on those who could afford it most and who could least justify their actions. In later bans, the Supreme Court did not take such care to justify its regulatory approach, instead acting confidently and with limited reliance on the 'consensus' of other parties.

What is interesting about the Delhi diesel vehicle ban is that the Supreme Court did not specifically call out bureaucratic failures in this particular case, as it did in later cases, even while it appeared to be reacting to weak state capacity, taking charge of a regulatory process and learning which strategies are more or less effective. Indeed, in this first case, the Supreme Court sat with the relevant governments, individuals and

[16] ibid.
[17] ibid.
[18] ibid.
[19] ibid.
[20] ibid.

entities as seemingly willing partners. It also took a far-ranging approach, regulating vehicles, as discussed above, but also regulating dust and debris from building and road construction and pollution from the burning of solid waste. In taking a number of approaches to a multi-faceted problem, hearing the case repetitively and iteratively changing its orders, the Court appears to be experimenting and attempting to discern best practices. In some ways, this is regulatory pragmatism in its clearest form and the Court did settle on at least two fairly effective strategies: the blanket ban on cars manufactured before 2005; and the ban on the registration of new vehicles with 2,000 cubic centimetre engines. The sale and registration of such cars is readily discoverable, making monitoring fairly straightforward, even with limited state capacity.

This is particularly true when one considers the alternative, more commonly used approach: a ban on particular cars – not types of cars – that exceed emissions standards. Indeed, in Europe and the US, emissions testing is common, and permissible levels can vary by jurisdiction. Such a system allows for the repair or alteration of particular vehicles to meet emissions standards and enables consumers to freely choose the type of vehicle they want to drive, so long as it can pass an emissions test. Typically, emissions testing is required every year or every two years, and the renewal of vehicle registration is contingent upon a successful emissions test. An emissions testing system works well in cases where the bureaucracy can either administer these tests itself (implying a large investment of resources by the state) or, in the more likely case, effectively monitor independent and/or private testing locations. The opportunities for corruption in an emissions monitoring system are high, in that every test of a car presents an opportunity to break the law for those willing to tamper with the testing apparatus or the test-reporting software. In contrast, the system chosen by the Indian Supreme Court requires monitoring of particular classes of vehicles and presents far more limited opportunities to subvert the system. It also stops short of fostering stronger state capacity.

While we cannot know for sure, it appears as if it may have been this case or set of cases that convinced the Supreme Court that bans, when dealing with both public and bureaucracy, are more readily enforceable than more nuanced regulatory approaches.

B. The Highway Liquor Sales Ban

The Supreme Court's ban on the sale of alcohol on or adjacent to national and state highways (*The State of Tamil Nadu v K Balu*) is very much in line with the earlier Delhi diesel vehicle ban. The consolidated Supreme Court case related to highway liquor sales originated in a set of cases brought to court in states as distant and different as Tamil Nadu, Punjab and Haryana. The controversy at the heart of this case is whether the government can and should be doing more to reduce epidemic-level road deaths related to drunk driving. The question before the Supreme Court was whether liquor shops located near highways can have their licences confiscated in order to prevent highway deaths. The Court's judgment in 2016, which was slightly altered in 2017, held that there is no fundamental right to run a liquor shop under Article 19(1)(g) of the Constitution, and removing liquor shops from within 500 metres of national and state highways furthers constitutional protections for life, public health and public safety.

The issue here was quite simple: numerous vendors in each of these states – and, indeed, in every Indian state that allows the sale of alcohol – were selling alcohol from shops or stalls directly adjacent to highways. Those who brought the cases in the public interest argued that such ready access to alcohol was directly tied to epidemic rates of drunk driving and highway accidents; thus, they argued, its prohibition – while economically harmful to vendors already invested in selling alcohol near highways – was justified. The Supreme Court found these arguments to be persuasive and initially banned the sale of liquor within 500 metres of national highways in December 2016.[21] The Supreme Court then expanded the highway liquor sales ban to include state highways in March 2017, stating that there was no reason to discriminate between state and national highways, as drunk driving occurs in both places.[22] The ban, at least at the time, specifically included areas adjacent to state and national highways that fell in municipal areas.

In this case, more than in some others, the Supreme Court reveals the pragmatism behind its ruling quite clearly. To justify such sweeping policy-like action, the Court relied on the data, determinations and guidance issued by the Union of India regarding epidemic-level highway deaths:

> Intake of alcohol/drugs by drivers resulted in 16,298 road accidents and 6,755 fatalities in 2015 within the category of drivers' fault, intake of alcohol/drugs accounted for 4.2 per cent and 6.4 per cent respectively … In regard to the figures of death or injury due to drunken driving there is a tendency to under estimate or under-report in order not to impede the right of victims and/ or their legal heirs to receive compensation.[23]

In response to statistics like these, the National Road Safety Council, the apex body for road safety in India under the Motor Vehicles Act of 1988, 'unanimously agreed in a meeting which was held nearly thirteen years ago on 15 January 2004 that licences for liquor shops should not be given along the national highways'.[24] However, it took until 2007 for the Union Ministry of Road Transport and Highways (MoRTH) to issue an advisory to state governments to remove all liquor shops along national highways and refrain from issuing additional licences. Seemingly, very little was done in response to this advisory. Later, in 2011, MoRTH:

> [N]oted that India had reported the highest number of road accident fatalities in the world and data of 2009 indicated that a road accident occurred every four minutes. Drunken driving, it was stated, was a leading cause of road accidents with as many as 27,152 road accidents being caused under the influence of alcohol in that year.[25]

[21] The Supreme Court justified such sweeping regulatory action by first stating that 'the court must ensure that the parameters for the exercise of its jurisdiction are confined to the familiar terrain of enforcing the constitutional right to lead a life of dignity and self-worth' (see *The State of Tamil Nadu Rep by Sec and Others v K Balu and Another* [2016] INSC 895). The implication here seems to be that when lives are at stake, the Supreme Court is willing to act as regulator.

[22] See ibid.

[23] ibid para 4.

[24] ibid para 5.

[25] ibid para 6.

These statistics led MoRTH to again direct state-level attention to section 185 of the Motor Vehicles Act of 1988, which bans liquor sales from national highways.[26] Having encountered resistance from those negatively affected by these prohibitions and likely worried about how a decrease in excise tax collection might negatively affect their own finances, state governments failed to enforce these orders. With their inaction, state governments essentially admitted that either they could not or would not remove liquor shops from national highways. The answer is likely the latter, particularly because MoRTH had nearly no enforcement capacity of its own and could do little more than note state-level violations.

The Supreme Court, seemingly not ignorant of these problems and well situated to demand state-government compliance, specifically directed state-level Chief Secretaries and Directors General of Police, in consultation with State Revenue and Home Departments, to come up with a state-level enforcement plan within one month.[27] The Court was quite specific in its order: 'Responsibility shall be assigned inter alia to District Collectors and Superintendents of Police and other competent authorities. Compliance shall be strictly monitored by calling for fortnightly reports on action taken.'[28] By specifically calling out those responsible and issuing its orders and reporting responsibility to fairly local level actors, the Supreme Court suggested that it knows where the problems lie and will be watching. It also issued an exemptionless ban:

> For all these reasons, we have come to the conclusion that no licences for liquor shops should be allowed both on the national and state highways. Moreover, in order to ensure that this provision is not defeated by the adoption of subterfuge, it would be necessary to direct that no exception can be carved out for the grant of liquor licences in respect of those stretches of the national or state highways which pass through the limits of any municipality corporation, city, town or local authority. Necessary safeguards must be introduced to ensure that liquor vends are not visible or directly accessible from the highway within a stipulated distance of 500 metres form the outer edge of the highway, or from a service lane along the highway.[29]

In issuing a blanket ban with a harsh 500-metre rule rather than a more nuanced judgment, the Court handed a set of 'weak-link' actors a fairly simple regulatory and enforcement scenario.

The alternative and more commonly used approach to reducing drunk-driving behaviour is an individual-level enforcement system that is typically combined with harsh penalties. In much of the world and, in particular, in Europe and the US, individuals are free to consume some alcohol and drive, but they cannot drive if their blood alcohol content exceeds a particular threshold. Monitoring is done by police officers who suspect drunk driving either on the basis of observed behaviour or tip-offs from the public. If a driver is caught driving with more alcohol in their system than local regulations allow, they are typically arrested and will later face stiff financial penalties and the possibilities of losing driving privileges altogether.

[26] ibid.
[27] ibid para 24.
[28] ibid.
[29] ibid para 22.

Such a system relies on high levels of corruption-free monitoring and, implicitly, strong state capacity. Rather than focusing on policing the individual behaviour of drivers, which would require increased state capacity, the Indian Supreme Court's approach focuses on a small set of state-level actors who must ensure that liquor shops within a proscribed area are shut down. Doing so merely involves the non-renewal of licences to shops located near highways and potential enforcement against flagrant violators, tasks that can be completed even with limited state capacity. As in other cases discussed both above and below, any failure on the part of these state-level actors will be obvious and state government discretion has largely been removed. Failure in an individual-level policing regime would be far more difficult to discern.

Interestingly, this was not the final outcome in this series of cases. Following the Supreme Court's verdict, a number of state governments, recognising the sheer number of urban hotels located within the liquor ban area and the lost revenue they might incur from such a ban, moved to de-notify their own state highways within city or municipal limits. The argument put forth by a number of state governments was that their de-notification of state highways turned those highways that functioned like regular urban surface streets into exactly that. Such a move might have motivated the Supreme Court to issue yet another judgment, particularly since its initial judgments seemed directed at bypassing state government inaction, but the Court seems to have bought into state-government logic and has remained relatively quiet on the issue. If we believe that the Court is pragmatic about regulation, it may also have: (1) believed this to be a compromise in exchange for state efforts to enforce the ban outside of cities; or (2) recognised the difficulty of enforcing this particular ban in most urban contexts and believed this to be beyond the capabilities of those aspects of the bureaucracy responsible for this task. Subsequent cases suggest that it may have been the latter, as the Court is not insensitive to limits of its own rulings.

C. The Engineering Correspondence Course Ban

The Supreme Court's approach in the engineering correspondence course ban displays some of the same concerns and sensibilities in evidence in both the Delhi diesel vehicle ban and the highway liquor sales ban. In *Orissa Lift Irrigation Corporation Ltd v Rabi Sankar Patro*, the Supreme Court examined the case of a number of different 'Deemed to be Universities' that were offering distance learning courses beyond their areas of expertise – engineering in particular – without the approval of the relevant regulatory bodies, the University Grants Commission (UGC) and the All India Council of Technical Education (AICTE). The principal question in this case is whether degrees given by some institutions, even if not legally accredited, should be recognised by an employer for the purposes of hiring, promotion and pay changes. The question before the Supreme Court was one of jurisdiction: whether AICTE Regulations apply to 'Deemed to be Universities'. The Court held that these regulations do apply to institutions that are 'Deemed to be Universities' and thus such institutions were not justified in introducing new courses without the approval of the AICTE, nor was the UGC justified in granting ex post facto approvals to these institutions.

The issue that gave rise to this case was the experience of an individual who completed a distance learning course through a 'Deemed to be University' in order to gain a promotion at work; he was subsequently denied that promotion because the diploma he received was considered to be invalid by both his employer and the UGC. Subsequently, the UGC issued 'vide public notice No.F.27-1/2012 (CPP-II), dated 27.06.2013', which clarified that 'the UGC has not granted approval to any institution Deemed to be university to establish Study Centres'. In its opinion, the Court examined the relevant rules at length, as well as the correspondence between the UGC, the AICTE and the offending 'Deemed to be Universities'. Here the Court found the regulatory bodies to have communicated competently and adequately, but to have failed in effectiveness, as the offending institutions continued to offer their courses and then sought ex post facto approval for them. The Court, in its opinion, appears to be satisfied with UGC and AICTE rule-making, as well as with the substance of those rules, but not with other aspects of the conduct of these regulatory bodies. In other words, the Court was aware of the contours of state capacity in this particular arena.

However, the Court was not impressed with the way in which the relevant regulatory bodies chose to resolve the problem of illegally granted degrees by choosing to grant ex post approval. The Court first took issue with the fact that the UGC and the AICTE were unable to conduct their regulatory functions with respect to the past performance of 'Deemed to be Universities' that had illegally offered engineering courses and degrees. The problem here was that the quality of the degrees granted and, more specifically, the underlying practical education were completely unknown:

> Those study centres were not inspected at any stage, nor any facilities therein were assessed to see if they meet the standards prescribed for imparting courses in Engineering. Similarly, no authority had checked what kind of courses were being conducted nor was there any inspection at the time the examinations were said to have been conducted.[30]

At the same time, the Court recognised that students had spent time and money on these degrees and that to revoke them without remedy would be a kind of theft:

> Though we cannot wish away the fact that the concerned Deemed to be Universities flagrantly violated and entered into areas where they had no experience and started conducting courses through distance education system illegally, the overbearing interest of the concerned students persuades us not to resort to recall of all the degrees in Engineering granted in pursuance of said ex-post-facto approval.[31]

To solve these problems, the Court laid down two simple rules: (1) all students illegally granted degrees by 'Deemed to be Universities' would be given a chance to prove their skills through examination or request a refund of tuition paid;[32] and (2) going forward, no 'Deemed to be University' could offer a distance learning course

[30] See *Orissa Lift Irrigation Corporation Ltd v Rabi Sankar Patro and Others* [2017] 1 SCC 468, para 34.
[31] ibid para 46.
[32] ibid para 53.

without obtaining permission from the relevant authorities for each course offered and, specifically, at each location.[33] The same exam would apply to all students, thus allowing students who obtained their engineering degree in 'distance mode' to prove the quality of the underlying education.[34] At the same time, no further correspondence engineering degrees could be offered until strict standards had been met.[35]

The effect of these rules is to dramatically reduce regulatory discretion and, in particular, to grant ex post approval. This is something the Court seemed worried about:

> We direct the CBI to carry out thorough investigation into the conduct of the concerned officials who dealt with the matters and went about the granting permissions against the policy statement ... and into the conduct of institutions who abused their position to advance their commercial interest illegally.[36]

A more nuanced regulatory approach would have involved the Court allowing individual schools to demonstrate to the bureaucracy the merits of their past programmes. But such determinations, as the Court points out, would necessarily involve discretion, something both the bureaucracy and the 'Deemed to be Universities' had not proved themselves capable of in the past. There was also the issue of evidence. As the Court pointed out in paragraphs 28 and 46 of its opinion, the bureaucracy cannot conduct ex post inspections to determine the quality of the facilities and instruction, particularly when years have passed since instruction was given and degrees were granted.[37] In its judgment, the Court seemed to be convinced that weak state capacity is a fact that must be acknowledged and worked around.

The rules laid down by the Supreme Court in this case provide the bureaucracy with an improved regulatory scenario. They set a high bar for compliance and, in so doing, likely reduce the number of entities seeking approval. This necessarily reduces the workload for the bureaucracy. Implicit in this move is the idea that, with a reduced workload, even a bureaucracy with limited capacity will have little excuse for failure. And, once again, the Court stopped short of attempting to increase state capacity, focusing instead on 'tweaks' that should help a bureaucracy with limited capacity to nevertheless fulfil its mandate. The Court also deals with past degrees by offering an objective examination to students granted degrees illegally. In its circumvention of known problems, particularly in terms of ensuring quality of education/degree, and in its provision of justice for student victims of institutions granting degrees illegally, the Court's approach in the engineering correspondence course ban is further evidence of its pragmatism.

[33] 'We restrain all Deemed to be Universities to carry on any courses in distance education mode from the Academic Session 2018–2019 onwards unless and until it is permissible to conduct such courses in distance education mode and specific permissions are granted by the concerned statutory/regulatory authorities in respect of each of those courses and unless the off-campus Centres/Study Centres are individually inspected and found adequate by the concerned Statutory Authorities. The approvals have to be course specific' (ibid).

[34] ibid.

[35] ibid.

[36] ibid.

[37] ibid paras 28 and 46.

D. The Delhi Diwali Firework Ban

The same pragmatism in evidence in the engineering correspondence course ban was evident quite recently in the case of the 2017 Delhi Diwali firework ban (*Arjun Gopal v Union of India)*. This case arose over concerns that the use of fireworks in the National Capital Region was causing harm to peace, well-being and health, both physical and mental, during Diwali and the wedding season. It was originally filed on behalf of three infants from Delhi as public interest litigation, and the question was whether fireworks could be considered an invasion of the rights conferred on citizens by Part III of the Constitution of India. In an interim order issued in 2015, the Supreme Court held that fireworks, particularly in the quantities used during the festival and wedding season, are an invasion of protected freedoms, specifically those protected by Articles 48A and 51A of the Constitution. The Court then revisited the issue in 2016 and 2017, and provided a more thorough, but largely unchanged order.

After taking pains to clarify the connection between the chemicals in fireworks and air pollution in the National Capital Region, the Supreme Court opinion made it clear that it believed weak state capacity and bureaucratic ineffectiveness to be the main obstacles to air pollution reduction during Diwali:

> Have the steps already taken by the concerned authorities reduced air pollution during Diwali? It seems to us that the steps so far taken by the Government of NCT of Delhi are limited to issuing directions, which is merely paperwork … The response of the Government of NCT of Delhi is lethargic with the absence of any keenness to take proactive steps … Similarly, the Delhi Police has issued directions that are difficult to enforce such as restricting the time during which fireworks can be burst.[38]

The Court then went on to describe what it found most troubling about the case:

> What has really disturbed us is that the CPCB [Central Pollution Control Board] was directed on 11th November, 2016 to study and prepare a report within three months on the harmful effects of the materials used in the manufacture of fireworks. It is astonishing that the CPCB has not conducted the study and prepared a report as directed. Apart from the fact that the CPCB has not conducted any study, even otherwise, no standards have been laid down by the CPCB which could give any indication of the acceptable and permissible limit of constituent metals or chemicals used in fireworks and released in the air, beyond which their presence would be harmful or dangerous.[39]

Having carefully noted the inadequate actions taken by concerned authorities and particularly the absence of enforceable standards or rules, as well as a report substantiating the scientific basis for those rules, the Court then took it upon itself to regulate.

Interestingly, in laying out its own regulations, the Supreme Court seems to have found a complete ban to be unnecessary. It also noted that the 'Delhi Police ha[ve] issued directions that are difficult to enforce, such as restricting the time during which

[38] See *Arjun Gopal and Others v Union of India* [2017] 1 SCC 412, para 52.
[39] ibid para 57.

fireworks can be burst'.[40] The Court then went on to prohibit the further transport of fireworks into Delhi, allowing permanent licensees and a reduced number of temporary licensees to sell existing fireworks that do not contain antimony, lithium, mercury, arsenic, lead or strontium, and mandating that existing fireworks be labelled in accordance with rules 15 and 84 of the Explosives Rules.[41] The Court also banned the import of fireworks from China, as they typically contain strontium, a banned substance.[42] Given the high standards set by the Court, the number of licensed firework vendors who could possibly meet them was drastically reduced and the ruling amounted to a complete ban.

As with the Delhi diesel vehicle ban and the highway liquor sales ban, the Court proceeded with an approach that focused on applying a high set of standards to a limited number of largely repeat players. Alternatively, the Court could have prohibited the setting off of particular types of fireworks by the public at large. Such an approach would have required significant state capacity: a high regulatory/police presence on the streets during Diwali to patrol for illegal behaviour. Even with such capacity, it would be hard for the bureaucracy to enforce under such conditions. Once a firecracker has been used, it is difficult to tell who actually engaged in prohibited behaviour. It is also hard to tell, once the firecracker has exploded, whether it contained prohibited chemicals. Police could patrol the streets looking for those who possess fireworks, but this would be even more labour-intensive and invasive, in addition to giving rise to many more possibilities for corruption.

It is not surprising, then, that the Court's ruling left the bureaucracy with little room for discretion or excuse for inaction. Some chemicals were permitted, while a number of common chemicals used in the manufacture of fireworks were completely prohibited. Packages of fireworks for sale were required to be appropriately marked. There could be little mistake about who was at fault if highly visible violations continued. The Court even seemingly recognised that regulating vendors of fireworks is much easier than regulating the *use* of fireworks: 'one of the possible methods of reducing [pollution] during Diwali is by continuing the suspension of licences for the sale of fireworks and therefore implicitly, prohibiting the bursting of fireworks'. The Supreme Court's pragmatism in this case directly responds to the bureaucratic weaknesses it highlights in its own opinion. By laying down clear, readily enforceable rules and by reducing both the amount of fireworks in the capital region and the number of places in which they could be sold, the Court handed the bureaucracy a best-case enforcement scenario, one in which it stood a decent chance of succeeding. Still, it once again stopped short of an attempt to increase state capacity.

The above cases, while certainly varied, contain a number of similarities that are illuminating with respect to the Supreme Court's pragmatic approach to regulation. In particular, in the Delhi Diwali firework and correspondence course bans, as well as in the case of the initial Delhi diesel vehicle and highway liquor sales bans, over-inclusive rule application was undeniably in the public interest and the bans applied

[40] ibid para 54.
[41] ibid paras 59 and 60.
[42] ibid paras 33 and 34.

to a limited number of visible entities. While the sale of clandestine fireworks, much like that of illegal drugs, is a possibility in such a regulatory scenario, most individuals buy fireworks infrequently and thus the visibility of firework vendors is part of their marketing strategy. There are also a limited number of firework vendors. These two factors make them easy targets for enforcement. The same is true of those conducting correspondence courses, selling diesel vehicles and vending alcohol by the roadside. 'Deemed to be Universities', car dealerships and roadside liquor shops are all fairly visible entities, and those purveying goods through such forums largely *need* them to be visible. Their numbers are also limited. As a result, they too are excellent enforcement targets for the Indian bureaucracy.

In addition, bureaucratic accountability can be more readily secured in such scenarios; after all, it is relatively straightforward to determine whether bureaucrats are enforcing properly. If liquor shops are visible along the road, if diesel cars with engines larger than 2,000 cubic centimetres are available at dealerships, if correspondence course web space or study centres remain open and occupied, and if firework markets are plentiful and open for business, the bureaucracy is failing. The pragmatism of such bans is particularly clear when they are set in contrast to a less over-inclusive and more nuanced system. Take, for instance, a system in which only *polluting* diesel cars are banned. This type of system would certainly be fairer to individuals who want to buy vehicles with large engines that actually do comply with emissions standards. It would also be fairer to car manufacturers who have invested engineering resources into designing cars that are both powerful and efficient. But such a system was essentially already in place in Delhi and emissions standards are regularly flouted. Emissions certificates can be bought without emissions compliance and it is difficult for the authorities tasked with enforcing emissions standards against a large and rapidly expanding fleet of cars to determine true compliance from compliance secured through corruption. Given the regulatory realities in much of India, one can see why the Supreme Court might prefer bans in a number of similar regulatory contexts.

Using this same logic, we can also understand why the Court might have acquiesced to an exemption from the highway liquor sales ban in cities. Enforcing a ban on liquor sales along highways in cities necessarily involves investigating a large number of difficult to observe and trace transactions; it also involves bureaucratic discretion. The Indian bureaucracy cannot investigate all such transactions and, even if it did, it would end up preventing the consumption of alcohol by and associated revenue from many who had no intention of drinking and driving, the very behaviour the law was supposed to prevent. Thus, it would be all too easy for street-level bureaucrats to engage in rent-seeking behaviour as they enforce.

However, this explanation is complicated by insights from Olson.[43] The businesses that stood to lose the most from liquor sales in cities overcame collective action problems and lobbied governments to de-notify highways in cities. A small number of motivated actors can be a formidable adversary, as Olson notes, and the Supreme Court may have recognised this. Of course, the Court, which seems to use

[43] M Olson, *The Logic of Collective Action* (Cambridge, MA, Harvard University Press, 1965).

over-inclusive bans in support of the public interest, could have pressed on, but it would have struggled to justify its actions in a context in which the government is acting rather than failing to act. The broad lesson we can learn here is that while enforcement is certainly easier against a small group of visible entities and a pragmatic court can succeed in regulating from the bench in such scenarios, particularly when it has the public interest on its side, small group size also lends itself to collective action and a court's regulatory efforts can be more easily overwritten or altered by traditional regulators, namely the executive or the legislature. A pragmatic court would then likely do as the Indian Supreme Court did in the case of the highway liquor sales ban and 'step back from the fight'.

Given much of the above logic, save for the Olson caveat, one would think that a pragmatic Supreme Court would avoid using its regulatory powers in scenarios in which its rules would apply to a large and disparate number of difficult-to-view interactions. Interestingly, however, the Indian Supreme Court *has* used a ban in such a regulatory context: with respect to smoking in public places. In some ways this ban represents a misguided attempt to regulate individual-level behaviour. However, this case, which occurred early in the recent spate of bans, and the Court's subsequent restriction of ban use in similar regulatory scenarios, actually provides us with additional evidence of the Indian Supreme Court's pragmatism and willingness to learn from past mistakes.

II. THE LIMITS OF BANS: PUBLIC SMOKING

As alluded to above, there are limits to bureaucratic effectiveness when enforcing against large numbers of disparate violators, as well as to the Supreme Court's foresight. This was the case with the Supreme Court's early ban on smoking in public places. In *Murli S Deora v Union of India*, the Supreme Court quickly and summarily prohibited smoking in public places ranging from auditoriums to hospitals to offices. The principal question in this case is whether smoking should be allowed in public places given its known tendency to cause a variety of health ailments that can lead to premature death. The question before the Court was whether smoking in public places infringes upon citizens' right to life under Article 21. With support from the Attorney General of India, the Court held that smoking in public places, particularly in auditoriums, hospitals, health institutions, educational facilities, libraries, court buildings, public offices and public conveyances – places where people might have to go rather than choose to go – is a violation of the fundamental right to life.

As with its later cases discussed above, the Court pointed to existing legislation relating to tobacco, in this case the 1975 Cigarettes Act, and suggested that aspects of that Act acknowledged the harms of smoking in public places.[44] The Court then went on to state that the government had done little to implement the Act and instructed that it should do so post haste by ensuring that no smoking occurs in public places.[45] The government seemingly failed to submit briefs in the case and the Attorney

[44] See *Murli S Deora v Union of India and Others* [2001] 8 SCC 765.
[45] ibid.

General concurred that the prohibition of smoking would be advisable, so the Court acted unilaterally and faced no objections at all.[46]

At first blush, this seems like an ideal regulatory scenario and that government implementation would have been swift and at least somewhat effective, but this was not the case. The government was, in fact, debating similar legislation at the time, but it had not passed. There had also been several state efforts, including, as acknowledged by the Court in its *Murli* opinion, in Rajasthan and Delhi.[47] But with such disparate efforts, no regulatory body had been tasked with overseeing a public place smoking ban and the Supreme Court could do little but direct the Attorney General and Commissioners of Police to carry out its orders; it could not actually create capacity where none existed.

Given the prevalence of smoking in India, the Supreme Court's inability to create and staff a new regulatory body, and the overburdened police force, the Supreme Court's public place smoking ban was likely to be dead on arrival. This is particularly true because there would be few individuals motivated to bring forward subsequent cases to enforce the law or to report behaviour to police. Indeed, a ban on smoking in public places is unlike other, later blanket prohibitions on somewhat widespread practices, like sexual relations with child brides, in that individual instances of the prohibited behaviour are not likely to motivate individuals to bring cases of public smoking to the bureaucracy or to the courts, which would involve the investment of significant time and potentially other resources. In addition, the number of potential violators is too large and widespread, the activity too fleeting, to be a reasonable target for enforcement operations, particularly in light of weak state capacity. Thus, while this is an older example of the Supreme Court's use of bans as a regulatory tool, it is a poor example of the Court's *pragmatic* use of the tool.

However, this failure is illuminating with respect to the reasons why the Court has not yet moved, despite deteriorating air quality in Delhi, to ban crop burning in neighbouring states. Doing so would necessarily involve regulating a large number of disaggregated individuals and entities spread over significant territory (and in multiple states). If there were a readily available monitoring mechanism or if there were incentives for particular individuals to come forward to report crop burning, the Supreme Court might be able to pull it off. But the crop burning regulatory scenario is a challenging one and the Supreme Court, having learned from past failures, is actually displaying its pragmatism in not even attempting regulation. A failure might undermine its own reputation and perceived powers.

CONCLUSION

The Indian Supreme Court is enigmatic: while steeped in tradition, it never fails to surprise with its inventiveness. In this chapter, I have presented evidence suggesting

[46] ibid.
[47] ibid.

that one of the Supreme Court's innovations, the exemption-less ban, was not born out of the Court's arbitrariness or laziness, but out of its pragmatism.

Indeed, the Indian Supreme Court, already recognised for the active rather than reactive stance it has taken on a number of different issues, has iteratively developed and refined its use bans to respond to weak state capacity and the specific, perceived failings of various aspects of the bureaucracy. Here, I have examined an arc of recent cases ranging from the engineering correspondence course ban to the Delhi Diwali fireworks ban and have demonstrated, with respect to each case, the ways in which the Court's ruling: (1) eased the bureaucracy's enforcement burden by making violations more clear-cut or by reducing the number of regulated entities; and (2) made bureaucratic failure more obvious, thus putting the public in a position to hold the executive responsible for bureaucratic ineffectiveness. I have also demonstrated that while the Court's efforts serve to increase bureaucratic effectiveness, they stop short of actually increasing state capacity; instead, they increase the likelihood that the state can accomplish certain objectives at present capacity. Finally, I examine a challenging cases, the smoking in public places ban, in which the Supreme Court attempted to regulate a widespread, but disaggregated behaviour that many would assume difficult to regulate; here I explain the failure of the Smoking Ban and the implications for future bans in similar regulatory contexts.

While there is certainly room for the Supreme Court to expand its use of bans into new and different scenarios, the pragmatism that underlies the Court's use of this tool will likely restrict it to bans that are likely to be effective. This is particularly true in light of the fact that the Indian Supreme Court's bans have met with mixed or not-yet-measurable success. RK Puram's PM 2.5 readings from the Central Pollution Control Board in Delhi were 432.82 on 20 October 2017; they were 483.66 on 31 October 2016. While a 10 per cent reduction in toxic pollution is certainly a good thing and many observers noted that the use of fireworks in 2017 was far more muted than in previous years, the Supreme Court's efforts could not be called a resounding success. The Court's other efforts are more difficult to assess. We cannot yet measure the effectiveness of the Court's highway liquor sales ban, as it has only been a year since it went into effect and government statistics from the National Crime Records Bureau are not yet available. Meanwhile, objective measures of the number of diesel vehicles on Delhi's roads after the ban and the number of engineering correspondence courses still on offer are difficult to come by, even if these latter bans are widely perceived to have been successful. In light of this record, the true test of the Indian Supreme Court's pragmatism will come when it is presented with data that suggest that a ban has failed. If it rigidly adheres to past practice, we will have to reassess its character and approach.

Finally, it is worth thinking about state capacity itself, the role that the Supreme Court plays in the overall effectiveness of the Indian state, and the Court's capacity, as one part of that state, to achieve its own objectives. As Nafisa Akbar and I noted in 2015, the capacity of the Indian state varies tremendously from place to place and from agency to agency; it is also very tricky to measure.[48] The Indian Supreme Court

[48] N Akbar and SL Ostermann, 'Traditional, Modern, and Everything in between: Understanding, Defining, and Measuring State Capacity' (2015) 55 *Asian Survey* 845.

is widely viewed as one of the more capable aspects of the Indian state, but two aspects of its record stand out in this regard: its arbitrariness and its inability to actually do the things it demands of other parts of the state. Consider, with respect to the first, the Court's choice to ban diesel vehicles with engines larger than 2,000 cubic centimetres. The Court, so far as we know, had no specific reason for picking 2,000 cubic centimetres when it could have also chosen 1,900 or 2,100. It is the bureaucracy that *should* be making this choice, but the Court sometimes attempts to make up for the lack of capacity in other parts of the state with its own less-than-fully-informed standards. However, the Court's pragmatism is merely a plaster on a much larger wound and its behaviour is not likely to foster increased state capacity. After all, why should the executive develop the bureaucratic expertise necessary to determine how pollution should be tackled when the Supreme Court may just substitute its own judgment for that of the bureaucracy?

This is a problem because the Court has limited 'doing' power beyond hearing cases and issuing judgments. Take, for example, the Supreme Court's demand, in the *MC Mehta v Union of India* judgment, that the government build a circular highway around Delhi to reduce vehicular traffic and pollution in the city centre. This highway, well over a decade after the Court's demand, was finally completed in 2018. The reflections contained in a 1998 order in this case are illustrative of the conundrum facing the Court:

> To control vehicular pollution and protect environment is primarily the function of the executive. It is their obligation to devise suitable measures and provide machinery for rigid enforcement of such measures as are necessary to curb the menace of chaotic traffic conditions and vehicular pollution with a view to ensure the welfare of general public. The inaction on the part of the executive, however, impelled this Court to issue certain directions from time to time in this writ petition, but precious little appears to have been done despite those directions.[49]

As the Court noted, it is the executive/bureaucracy that is supposed to be setting standards, but it does not, so the Court steps in and issues orders. But, without the power to *do* the projects it proposes and without the ability to increase state capacity beyond the courts, the Court, with its pragmatic approach, is, at best, slowly pushing the rest of the Indian state to accomplish its objectives and, at worst, undermining the incentives for other actors in the state machinery to go about developing their own capacities.

[49] See *MC Mehta v Union of India and Others* [1998] INSC 581.

16

Statutory Regulatory Authorities

Evolution and Impact

KP KRISHNAN AND ANIRUDH BURMAN*

INTRODUCTION

A NUMBER OF statutory regulatory authorities have emerged in India since the 1990s. Statutes that have established regulators focus broadly on: (a) the design of the apex decision-making body (board or authority); (b) the substantive powers of the regulator, and; (c) accountability mechanisms such as audits, accounting and reporting. Such statutes are usually 'thin' on guidance to regulators on how to conduct their administrative functions. Consequently, statutory regulatory authorities are bound by the same principles of administrative law as other government agencies, as defined by the judiciary from time to time. However, independent regulators perform their functions in ways that are distinct from government departments.

First, statutory regulatory authorities concentrate legislative (regulation-making), executive (monitoring and supervision) and judicial (issuing orders) powers in contrast to the normal structure of government departments.[1] This structure potentially violates the principle of separation of powers and affects the design of statutory regulatory authorities. Second, the frequency and volume of regulation-making is significantly higher due to the responsibility of regulators to react to dynamic market requirements. Third, there is an independent and specialised appellate mechanism against the regulatory actions of most regulators.

The applicability of general administrative law to independent regulators is worth careful examination not just because of the distinct features stated above, but also due to the specific context in which regulators have been created in India. A critical

* The authors are grateful for the assistance provided by Ms Jai Vipra and Ms Trishee Goyal, researchers at the National Institute of Public Finance and Policy.

[1] See generally Financial Sector Legislative Reforms Commission, 'Report of the Financial Sector Legislative Reforms Commission', 2013, https://dea.gov.in/sites/default/files/fslrc_report_vol1_1.pdf.

but distinctive part of the context of the creation of independent regulators was to achieve nimbleness in regulating private markets. One part of this objective was to create specialised pools of human capital for regulating specific sectors. The other, importantly, was to enable regulation to be more dynamic, neutral between government-owned and private firms, and responsive to markets. Given these objectives, it is worth examining the applicability of general administrative law principles to regulators. It is also important to understand the degree to which courts have carved out administrative law principles applicable specifically to regulators, and the manner in which regulators themselves react to changes in administrative law.

In order to understand how administrative law is formed, we have to define what we understand by 'administrative law'. One definition of administrative law, the traditional definition, pertains to a series of external constraints placed on administrative bodies. These include due process requirements, natural justice requirements, and constraints imposed by statutes and courts. Decisions of courts are an important source of constraints and law-making since they create general rules of application based on specific cases. Another increasingly relevant way of understanding administrative law is to understand an agency's internal rules and regulations that enable/constrain the behaviour of its employees. The study of internal administrative rules has become a subject of the study of administrative law in recent years. For example, regulators use multiple instruments for substantive law-making functions – regulations, guidelines, circulars, even FAQs. In some cases, the use of such instruments is as per the requirements set out in the enabling statute (the Telecom Regulatory Authority of India Act, 1997 requires certain actions to be taken via orders and others via regulations). For the most part, however, it is unclear what dictates the choice of administrative instruments. India does not have a specific statute on administrative processes. It is therefore important to understand the sources of administrative law that determine the choice of administrative instruments and examine the necessity for a separate administrative law for independent regulators.

This chapter studies administrative law as applicable to independent regulators with the following objectives: to understand the role administrative law plays in issues such as regulatory efficiency and accountability; to study the impact of judicial decisions or external administrative law on the functioning of regulators; and to study the degree to which generally framed administrative law in India is relevant in the context of the specific features of regulatory agencies in India. This chapter looks at both external and internal administrative law as they apply to statutory regulatory authorities. By external, we mean largely common law principles of administrative law that are applied by courts. Therefore, by definition, such law is created or applied because of constitutional or statutory remedies for non-compliance with administrative law. The sources for many of these requirements are Articles 14 and 21 of the Constitution of India. As defined here, external administrative law includes the requirements of natural justice and due process, guarding against excessive delegation and abuse of discretion. Internal administrative law on the other hand includes:

> [P]rocesses, guidelines, and policy issuances that an administrative agency adopts to structure the actions of its own officials … internal management structures, which allow for

oversight of agency operations and enforcement of policies specified by agency heads, also constitute internal administrative law.[2]

Such law is usually created by the relevant agency for defining the methods of its own functioning, and stakeholders do not usually have access to remedies against non-compliance with such documents or instruments. At the same time, these documents, instruments and structures affect the decisions communicated to stakeholders in important ways, such as the levels of review or oversight possible against a decision taken by a junior employee. In some cases, no clear distinction between internal and external administrative law can be made. For example, the Office of Communications (Ofcom) law of the UK (dealing with the communications regulator) requires Ofcom to make 'effective arrangements' for consultations with consumers. It then proceeds to define the kinds of consumer groups with which Ofcom must have such consultations, the subjects on which consultations must be held and the institutional framework for holding such consultations.[3] This provides substantial guidance to Ofcom on how to structure its consultation process and, as such, the compliance of the process directly interferes in the internal organisation of the regulatory agency, while at the same time making such a process potentially reviewable by courts. We therefore study the structure, context and design of internal administrative law with a view to understanding its impact on the functioning of regulators.

I. STRUCTURE AND DESIGN OF REGULATORS

What are statutory regulatory authorities? TV Somanathan has recently drawn a distinction between regulators so called, and others that discharge regulatory functions as part of the larger administrative state.[4] Our point of departure is to consider regulators that have the following distinctive features: the regulatory agency is a creation of parliamentary law, and such law provides for operational independence except for accountability requirements clearly specified in the law; and the regulatory agency combines legislative, executive and quasi-judicial powers within the same agency.

These regulatory agencies can be said to have 'exited' the usual administrative framework of other government departments and can operate independently with respect to certain matters. For example, each regulator is free to create an internal organisational framework most suitable to its own objectives and constraints. Additionally, such regulators generally have independent funds that provide the statutory regulatory authorities with greater financial flexibility as opposed to government departments that rely on funds appropriated from the Consolidated Fund of India. On the basis of this classification, there exist the following 'statutory regulatory

[2] Gillian E Metzger and Kevin M Stack, 'Internal Administrative Law' (2016) 115 *Michigan Law Review* 1239, 1248.

[3] Communications Act, 2003, s 16.

[4] TV Somanathan, 'The Administrative and Regulatory State' in Sujit Choudhury, Madhav Khosla and Pratap Bhanu Mehta (eds), *The Oxford Handbook of the Indian Constitution* (Oxford University Press, 2016) 386.

authorities' in India: the Reserve Bank of India; the Securities and Exchange Board of India; the Pension Fund Regulation and Development Authority; the Insurance Regulation and Development Authority; the Telecom Regulatory Authority of India; the Petroleum and Natural Gas Regulatory Board; the Central Electricity Regulatory Commission; the Insolvency and Bankruptcy Board of India; the Competition

Table 16.1 Some independent statutory regulatory authorities

	Reserve Bank of India (RBI)	Securities and Exchange Board of India (SEBI)	Telecom Regulatory Authority of India (TRAI)	Competition Commission of India (CCI)
Governing legislation	Reserve Bank of India Act, 1934	Securities and Exchange Board of India Act, 1992	Telecom Regulatory Authority of India Act, 1997 (TRAI Act)	Competition Act, 2002
Interface with ministry (other than appointment and removal powers of central govt (CG))	CG has power to issue directions to the Bank in public interest (s 7)	Directions of CG on questions of policy bind SEBI (s 16 of the SEBI Act)	Directions of CG on questions of policy bind TRAI (s 25(2) of the TRAI Act)	Directions of CG on questions of policy bind CCI. (s 55 of the Competition Act)
Returns and filings	Weekly account of the Issue Department and of the Banking Department to the CG. RBI to also submit a copy of the annual accounts to the CG (s 53 of the RBI Act)	Annual Reports given to CG. Other reports as the CG may specify (s 18 of the SEBI Act). Rules and regulations framed to be laid before Parliament	Annual Report to be given to CG. CG to lay the report before Parliament (s 24 of the TRAI Act)	Returns and filings as specified. Annual reports to CG, which will then be laid before Parliament
Audit provisions	At least two auditors appointed by CG or audit by the Comptroller and Auditor General (CAG) (ss 51 and 52 of the RBI Act)	Audit by CAG (s 15 of the SEBI Act)	Audit by CAG (s 23 of the TRAI Act)	Audit by CAG (s 52 of the Competition Act)
Appellate authority	None – writ courts	Securities Appellate Tribunal	Telecom Disputes Settlement and Appellate Tribunal	Competition Appellate Tribunal

Commission; the Food Safety and Standards Authority of India; the Airport Economic Regulatory Authority; the Tariff Authority for Major Ports; and the Warehouse Regulation and Development Authority.

The real estate regulators under the states and the state electricity regulatory commissions under the Electricity Act, 2003 are statutory regulatory authorities established in states, but through a parliamentary law. Most such regulatory agencies have common administrative structures (see Table 16.1): the agency is headed by a collegial body called a board, commission or authority consisting of multiple members. This body is the 'legal entity' that is responsible for discharging the functions entrusted to the regulatory agency as per law. Parliamentary law generally lists the functions that the regulatory agency is expected to discharge, but is 'thin' on the manner in which such functions are to be discharged. The agency usually performs its functions by hiring personnel. Parliamentary law generally permits the board or commission to delegate its functions to subordinate officials. Certain laws impose limitations on what powers can be delegated, while others do not.[5] The parliamentary law usually provides powers to frame regulations, conduct audits, inspections and investigations, and to impose penalties by passing orders. Natural justice requirements that dictate minimum procedural requirements are usually provided only for quasi-judicial functions (passing orders). Table 16.2 provides a comparison of regulatory powers of certain statutory regulatory authorities.

Table 16.2 Regulatory functions

Legislative, executive, and quasi-judicial powers	**RBI**	**SEBI**	**CCI**	**TRAI**
Legislative functions – regulation-making	Section 58 gives the RBI the power to frame regulations on specified subjects. No procedural requirements are provided	Section 30 gives SEBI the power to frame regulations on specified subjects. No procedural requirements are provided. Regulations have to be placed before Parliament	Section 64 gives the CCI the power to frame regulations on specified subjects. No procedural requirements are provided. Regulations have to be placed before Parliament	Section 36 gives TRAI the power to frame regulations on specifiedsubjects. Section 11(4) requires the Authority to 'ensure transparency' in the discharge of its powers and functions. Regulations have to be placed before Parliament

(continued)

[5] For example, s 33 of the Telecom Regulatory Authority of India Act, 1997 prohibits the delegation of the power to settle disputes and frame regulations.

Table 16.2 *(Continued)*

Legislative, executive, and quasi-judicial powers	RBI	SEBI	CCI	TRAI
Executive functions – licensing, inspections, audits	Powers to grant licences are specified in the RBI Act, the Banking Regulation Act and other laws that RBI administers. RBI has general powers to inspect and audit banks, Non-Banking Financial Companies (NBFCs) and other regulated entities prior to registration, and also during the period of the entity's operations. It also has general powers to call for information from regulated entities (RBI Act and Banking Regulation Act)	Powers to grant licences are specified in the SEBI Act and the Securities Contracts (Regulation) Act. SEBI has general powers to inspect and audit exchanges, intermediaries such as brokers, mutual funds and other regulated entities. It also has general powers to call for information from regulated entities	CCI does not license entities, but investigates violations of competition law. It therefore conducts 'investigations' into allegations of agreements that result in 'dominant positions' and other 'combinations'. The Competition Act provides for factors to be taken into account while conducting an inquiry (for example, see ss 19, 20 and 21 of the Competition Act) and provides minimum due process requirements for investigations and inquiries	TRAI does not have licensing powers, but has the power to revoke licences. It has powers to investigate and audit regulated entities. This has to be done by passing orders. Due process requirements for passing orders are provided in the law
Quasi-judicial functions – investigations and penalties	RBI can impose monetary fines and also revoke the licence of a non-compliant entity. Rejection of licences, cancellation of registration etc have to be done through an order. Requirements of minimum due process are provided in the law. Sections 45J, 45K and 45L give RBI powers to issue directions. It is not clear if directions are legislative instruments or quasi-judicial ones	SEBI has the power to impose penalties for violations enumerated in the law. Rejection of licences, cancellation of registration etc have to be done through an order. Requirements of minimum due process are provided in the law	CCI passes orders based on the results of its inquiries. Requirements of minimum due process are provided in the law	TRAI has the power to revoke licenses and to impose penalties for violations of directions issued by it. Sections 11 and 12 give TRAI powers to issue directions. It is not clear if directions are legislative instruments or quasi-judicial ones

The exercise of powers in Table 16.2 is constrained by administrative law directly. Some procedural requirements are stated in the statutes that the statutory regulatory authorities administer, while others are part of the general administrative and constitutional law framework in India. The following sections analyse the exercise of the powers summarised in Table 16.2. We study the body of administrative law emanating from the review of actions of statutory regulatory authorities and critically analyse the impact of judicial decisions on independent regulators. In addition, we analyse the degree to which independent regulators are constrained by administrative law, and how this affects regulatory efficiency and accountability.

II. ADMINISTRATIVE LAW FOR STATUTORY REGULATORY AUTHORITIES

Administrative law is a subset of public law, and traditionally dictates and constrains mechanisms for the interaction and the resolution of disputes between state and citizen (due process, for example) on the one hand and different parts of the state on the other (for example, the Allocation of Business Rules, 1961).[6] The design of administrative law therefore both constrains and enables state functions as per constitutional limits. This proposition is equally applicable to statutory regulatory authorities. As agencies of the state, administrative law compels statutory regulatory authorities to regulate their jurisdictions within the constraints imposed by administrative law.

However, there are some key issues specific to statutory regulatory authorities that form the core of the development of administrative law. This flows from two key aspects of the way in which statutory regulatory authorities are designed: statutory regulatory authorities concentrate legislative, executive and quasi-judicial functions within the same agency, in violation of the principle of separation of powers, while statutory regulatory authorities enjoy a high degree of institutional independence compared to government departments. This includes the ability to design the internal organisation of the statutory regulatory authority (human capital, salaries, hierarchy etc) as well as administrative processes to be followed in discharging its functions (regulation-making processes, procedures for issuing show-cause notices, conducting inspections, issuing notices etc). This independence is guaranteed explicitly by law.

The key public administration concerns with statutory regulatory authorities – ensuring efficiency while balancing independence with accountability – are also key issues in administrative law: the exercise of delegated legislative powers, reasonableness and non-discrimination in administration, and natural justice and fairness

[6] MC Jain Kagzi, *The Indian Administrative Law*, 7th edn (Universal Law Publishing, 2014) 1–2.

in quasi-judicial functions. Table 16.3 provides a listing of the constraints administrative law poses to different administrative processes within a statutory regulatory authority:

Table 16.3 Administrative processes and the applicable administrative law

Administrative processes in statutory regulatory authorities	Administrative law applicable to administrative processes	Source(s) of law
Legislative process, ie, regulation-making	Substantive ultra vires; excessive delegation; statutory requirements	Article 14 of the Indian Constitution; judicial precedent; statute (for statutory law)
Executive (licensing, inspections, monitoring, audits etc)	Arbitrary or discriminatory treatment; violation of due process; statutory requirements	Same
Quasi-judicial (inquiries, investigations, orders, penalties)	Arbitrary or discriminatory treatment; violation of due process; violation of principles of natural justice; statutory requirements	Same

We therefore inquire into the sources of administrative law that affect statutory regulatory authorities in the following manner: the doctrines of administrative law applicable to the exercise of executive and quasi-judicial powers, including the development of these doctrines by courts and tribunals, and the doctrines of administrative law applicable to the exercise of legislative powers (delegated legislation), including the development of these doctrines by courts and tribunals. In Table 16.3, we state that statutory law is one of the sources of administrative law for statutory regulatory authorities.

An analysis of statutory law of four statutory regulatory authorities (the TRAI, the CCI, SEBI and the RBI) highlight the following: all the laws establishing the regulatory jurisdiction contain requirements guiding the use of quasi-judicial powers, namely with respect to passing orders, conducting inquiries and imposing penalties. These provisions incorporate basic requirements of due process and natural justice by usually stating that decisions or findings shall not be reached without giving the affected person(s) a hearing. In the case of the TRAI, there is an overarching requirement for the TRAI to be transparent in its functioning. In the case of the CCI, SEBI and the RBI, there is no legal provision that lays down or constrains the process of legislative activity, ie, regulation-making. Our analysis highlights that judicial review of the actions of these four statutory regulatory authorities has been focused predominantly on their quasi-judicial functions, with the exception of the TRAI (which has an explicit mandate to be transparent in all aspects of its functioning, including legislative and executive functions).[7] The quantum of challenges varies across statutory regulatory authorities.

[7] *Cellular Operators' Association of India v TRAI and Others*, MANU/SC/0551/2016. There have been subsequent challenges against TRAI regulation-making processes, but none has been upheld.

We find varying trends in the kinds of issues adjudicated before tribunals and courts, depending on the statutory regulatory authorities. A significant number of challenges to TRAI orders are based on the non-fulfilment of the conditions of transparency required in the TRAI Act, 1997. In *COAI v TRAI*, a number of telecom operators challenged the validity of the Telecom Consumers Protection (Ninth Amendment) Regulations, 2015. The challenge to the amendment regulations were based on the violation of Article 14 (arbitrariness), but also on the ground that the TRAI failed to meet the standards of transparency required under section 11(4) of the TRAI Act, 1997. The Supreme Court first held the impugned regulation to be arbitrary under Article 14 of the Constitution of India since it did not consider all the possible evidence while framing the regulations (non-application of mind).[8] In addition, the Court held that the TRAI had failed in its duty under section 11(4), since it found:

> [N]o discussion or reasoning dealing with the arguments put forward by the service providers, that call drops take place for a variety of reasons, some of which are beyond the control of the service provider and are because of the consumer himself.[9]

The Court therefore held the process followed by the TRAI to be deficient, even though the statutory regulatory authority had followed the process of putting out a consultation paper and allowing stakeholders to comment on it. Even though the TRAI had taken these steps, its process was considered deficient since it did not respond to the arguments put forward by stakeholders during the consultation process.

The Court also went on to add that although the petitioners had alleged a violation of the principles of natural justice, the action being challenged was of a legislative character, not an administrative one. The principles of natural justice do not constrain legislative action. The law as interpreted was subsequently used to challenge the TRAI's regulation-making process in the case of *Vodafone v TRAI*.[10] Vodafone challenged the refusal of the TRAI to disclose certain information it had requested as a breach of its duty to function transparently.[11] The Court noted that the TRAI had in fact conducted a consultation process and that its refusal to disclose the specific information requested could not be held to be derogatory to section 11(4) of the TRAI Act, 1997. It held that if the TRAI was held to the standard claimed by Vodafone, TRAI 'will have to conduct a full adjudicatory hearing prior to promulgating every rule – an untenability of procedure that would destroy the efficacy of delegated legislation'.[12] The Court further cautioned against holding the TRAI to higher standards of judicial review: 'The danger of judicial review interdicts in an ongoing law-making exercise by a regulator such as the TRAI is that absent facial or manifest omission of transparency, there are no discernible standards that can be enforced under Article 226, without in effect carrying out a premature "merits" review.'[13]

[8] ibid paras 30–46.
[9] ibid para 66.
[10] *Vodafone India Ltd and Others v TRAI*, MANU/DE/2883/2017.
[11] ibid paras 1–8.
[12] ibid para 30.
[13] ibid para 31.

Both points made by the Court are noteworthy: first, that unless there is an apparent and manifest dereliction of the requirement to be transparent, the Court will be cautious about holding the TRAI to a higher standard of review for fear of affecting its ability to effectively regulate its sector; and, second, in the absence of clear standards for the review of administrative process, judicial review can very easily become a review of substantive issues, allowing courts to intrude into the decision-making of statutory regulatory authorities.

In other cases – such as the Telecom Disputes Settlement and Appellate Tribunal cases *CITI v TRAI*[14] and *Zee Turner v TRAI*[15] – regulation-making processes have been successfully challenged on the ground that they did not meet the standards of transparency required under section 11(4) of the TRAI Act, 1997. Administrative law challenges to the CCI are of a different nature from those to the TRAI, owing to the difference in the regulatory process followed by the CCI. The CCI follows an adversarial process in making its decisions (see Table 16.2). Most of the challenges to decisions taken by the CCI therefore challenge quasi-judicial or administrative action rather than legislative action. A specific point of contention has been the process by which the CCI creates a prima facie opinion that leads to an investigation by the Director General of the CCI.

Recently, the Supreme Court framed a number of issues, four of which are relevant to our study.[16] They are: 'whether the directions passed by the Commission in exercise of its powers under Section 26(1) of the Act forming a prima facie opinion would be appealable in terms of Section 53A(1) of the Act?'; 'what is the ambit and scope of power vested with the Commission under Section 26(1) of the Act and whether the parties, including the informant or the affected party, are entitled to notice or hearing, as a matter of right, at the preliminary stage of formulating an opinion as to the existence of the prima facie case?'; 'whether it is obligatory for the Commission to record reasons for formation of a prima facie opinion in terms of Section 26(1) of the Act?; and 'what directions, if any, need to be issued by the Court to ensure proper compliance in regard to procedural requirements while keeping in mind the scheme of the Act and the legislative intent? Also, to ensure that the procedural intricacies do not hamper in achieving the object of the Act, i.e., free market and competition'.[17]

The Court held, first, that the grounds of appeal are limited to those provided in section 53(1) of the Competition Act: 'The orders, which have not been specifically made appealable, cannot be treated appealable by implication. For example, taking a prima facie view and issuing a direction to the Director General for investigation

[14] *Centre for Transforming India v TRAI*, MANU/TD/0022/2015.

[15] *Zee Turner Ltd v TRAI*, MANU/TD/0133/2010.

[16] For further cases regarding the due process requirements for the formation of a prima facie opinion, see *Aamir Khan Productions v Union of India*, 2010 (112) BomLR 3778; *Google v Competition Commission of India*, 2015 CompLR 391 (Delhi).

[17] *Competition Commission of India v Steel Authority of India*, Civil Appeal No 7779 of 2010 (Supreme Court of India) (8 February 2018), https://www.sci.nic.in/jonew/judis/36828.pdf, 16–17.

would not be an order appealable under section 53(1)(a).'[18] Second, it held that a party cannot claim a right to be heard at the stage where it is determined that a prima facie case exists to allow the Commission to direct its Director General to conduct an investigation. The nature of the function is an administrative or 'departmental' one and not an adjudicatory one.[19] Third, the Court held that the Commission is required to record 'some' reasons even while forming a prima facie view. It stated that while detailed reasons are not required, the decision must be explicit and recorded with reference to the furnished information.[20] Lastly, the Court held that procedural constraints must balance the need for expeditious disposal of matters before the CCI, while at the same time ensuring that the process is fair and reasonable for the concerned parties. It then proceeded to issue directions that effectively amended CCI regulations regarding the procedure for the formation of a prima facie opinion, the conduct of inquiries and the decision-making process of the CCI.[21] The Court's treatment of this specific issue explicitly highlights the tension between the constraints of administrative law and the need for efficacy in the regulatory process, and echoes the decision of the Court in *Vodafone v TRAI*.

The CCI has also faced challenges to its quasi-judicial functions. In *Board of Control for Cricket in India v Competition Commission of India*, the CCI launched an investigation into whether the Board of Control for Cricket in India (BCCI) was abusing its dominant position in the market to restrict other entities from organising professional league matches in competition with the Indian Premier League. The BCCI alleged that the Commission's definition of what was considered a 'relevant market' differed from that of the Director General, and that this was done without giving any notice or opportunity to be heard.[22] The tribunal held that since the CCI is discharging a quasi-judicial function, it is obliged to give an effective opportunity of hearing to the relevant person.[23] In one instance, the CCI has had its orders struck down because the orders were signed by members of the Commission in spite of them not having attended any hearings. Such orders were held to have violated requirements regarding the right to a fair hearing.[24]

SEBI's orders have been challenged for non-conformity with principles of natural justice as well as on the grounds of non-application of mind. Some challenges that have been dismissed by the Securities Appellate Tribunal (SAT) and other courts also highlight interesting points of law. An illustrative case is *Financial Technologies (India) Ltd v SEBI*.[25] Financial Technologies (India) Ltd (FTIL) was declared to be

[18] ibid 18.

[19] ibid 43–62.

[20] ibid 43–62.

[21] ibid 81–83.

[22] *Board of Control for Cricket in India v Competition Commission of India and Others* 2015 Comp LR 548 (COMPAT) (23 February 2015) para 9.

[23] ibid para 15.

[24] See, for example, *All India Organization of Chemists and Druggists v Competition Commission of India*, III(2015) CPJ4(TA) (27 April 2015).

[25] *Financial Technologies (India) Ltd v Securities and Exchange Board of India* [2014] 122 CLA 225 (SAT) (7 September 2014).

'not fit and proper' to transact in the commodities market by the Forward Markets Commission (FMC). Based on this order, SEBI declared it to be not fit and proper to transact in the securities market. However, the Court held that in its order, SEBI did not detail how for this case commodities and securities markets were similar, and that in the show-cause notice, SEBI did not provide enough details and reasoning, such that FTIL was not able to reply properly. SEBI relied on the conclusions drawn by the then the FMC rather than rely on the reasoning given by the FMC for its order.[26] However, the tribunal dismissed the appeal, holding that since the criteria of 'fit and proper person' applied by both the FMC and SEBI is similar, the conclusion arrived at by the FMC can be used by SEBI to exclude FTIL from the securities market as well.

In *Shankar Sharma v SEBI*, the Court, while accepting that the procedure followed by SEBI may have been erroneous, said that this was 'at best a matter of irregularity and erroneous exercise which in our view can be considered by the SEBI Board'.[27] In this case, the then SEBI Chairman issued an order restraining certain entities from trading in the securities market. The order was challenged, and the Court declared that the order and the affidavits filed by SEBI in court be treated as a show-cause notice, and that the Chairman pass a fresh reasoned order after granting a hearing to the concerned entities. In his revised order, the Chairman, after giving a hearing, reaffirmed his earlier order. He then proceeded to appoint an inquiry officer to investigate the charges on which the order was based.[28]

The five entities then appeared before the High Court in the present case. Dismissing the petition, it stated that the SEBI Board would be best placed to look into the fact that proper procedure was not followed while issuing a show-cause notice, and that in any case, SEBI's order would be appealable in the SAT.[29] On the one hand, the Court was right not to interfere with SEBI's investigative process, and its observation that the eventual order could be appealed before the SAT is correct. On the other hand, the facts of the case highlight wide deference to the statutory regulatory authorities by the courts. Since the Chairman's first order was not based on a formal investigative process, it is doubtful if the order could have been treated as a show-cause notice. The SEBI Chairman ought to have initiated an inquiry *before* the revised order was passed, not after it. Additionally, the inquiry officer's investigation would likely be clouded by the fact that his organisation's chairman had passed two orders finding the five entities guilty of having violated SEBI regulations. There were therefore very reasonable grounds to challenge the process that SEBI had adopted. However, the High Court left the issue of procedural irregularity to be resolved by SEBI itself.

In some cases, the tribunal has pulled SEBI up for not providing an opportunity of hearing to a regulated entity. For example, in *DLF v SEBI*, the tribunal held that SEBI had not followed proper procedure before invoking the Prohibition of Fraudulent and

[26] ibid para 10.
[27] *Shankar Sharma v Securities and Exchange Board of India*, MANU/MH/0233/2002, para 13.
[28] ibid para 2.
[29] ibid para 14.

Unfair Trade Practices Regulations against DLF and had not given them an opportunity of hearing (in addition to other grounds on which it struck down the order).[30] The tribunal held that:

> We note with concern that the above said due procedure established in the PFUTP Regulations has been blatantly violated by the Respondent. Formation of opinion/belief by the Board by an order in writing before invoking PFUTP Regulations on certain existing grounds is a pre-requisite. It is pertinent to note that no such 'order in writing' as to the satisfaction of the Appointing Authority regarding existence of certain grounds which could have led to the formation of belief that there was prima-facie violation of such regulations and the securities were being dealt with in a manner detrimental to the investors' interest is brought to our notice. Similarly, nothing was produced before us to show that the report, as required by law to level allegation [sic] of fraud against the Appellant, was considered by the Board and that a reasonable opportunity of being heard in consonance with the principles of natural justice was afforded to the Appellant before the impugned order could be passed.[31]

The tribunal went on to observe that SEBI's actions had in fact resulted in a loss to the securities market due to the adverse reaction to the order against SEBI by investors. Notably, SEBI was found to have violated its own regulations on the conduct of inquiries and investigations. The tribunal also addressed the issue of delay in writing the impugned order. It stated that the delay of close to nine months in writing the order was 'fatal' to the concept of a fair hearing and also violated Article 21 of the Constitution of India.[32]

One significant sub-set of challenges against SEBI's decisions has been the challenges to its interim orders on the ground that the concerned entities were not given a fair hearing before the interim order was passed. However, the SAT has rejected most of these claims.[33] Challenges in these cases have usually been based on the reasoning that the pre-decisional hearing was either not provided or not adequate, and that consequent to the final order, a provision of post-decisional hearing does not confirm to the basic requirements for a fair hearing. Yet, the SAT has consistently held that a post-decisional hearing is a well-known and acceptable aspect of providing the relevant parties a fair hearing. In all the cases, it has observed that SEBI has issued interim orders in matters of exigency, where doing so was in the interests of protecting investors in the securities market. It has also alluded to the fact that SEBI has expansive powers under section 11 of the SEBI Act. In doing so, it has located the legitimacy of post-decisional hearings within the powers accorded to SEBI under the SEBI Act.

[30] *DLF Ltd and Others v Securities and Exchange Board of India*, MANU/Sb/0006/2015, para 96.

[31] ibid para 96.

[32] ibid para 112.

[33] See, for example, *Beejay Investment and Financial Consultants v Securities and Exchange Board of India*, MANU/Sb/0047/2017 (27 March 2017); *Kailash Auto Finance v Securities and Exchange Board of India*, MANU/Sb/0261/2016 (27 October 2016); *Eco Friendly Food Processing Park v Securities and Exchange Board of India*, MANU/Sb/0263/2016 (27 October 2016); and *Citrus Check Inns v Securities and Exchange Board of India*, MANU/Sb/0109/2015 (24 August 2014).

A recent exception was the case of *Pancard Clubs Ltd v SEBI*.[34] SEBI passed an ex parte interim order against the appellant, directing it to shut down its business pending SEBI's determination of whether it was a collective investment scheme, and therefore subject to SEBI regulation.[35] It was argued that there was no reason for the urgency with which SEBI passed the order.[36] The tribunal noted that the appellant had approached SEBI, requesting it to clarify whether it fell within the definition of a collective investment scheme, to which SEBI had not replied for over a period of eight years. SEBI had also written to a Member of Parliament (pursuant to his query) that the entity was not covered within the definition of a collective investment scheme within its regulations.[37] The tribunal analysed the relevant provisions of the SEBI Act to state that the law did not provide 'boundary-less' discretion.[38] The tribunal struck down the order, stating that an authority has a duty to give a fair hearing to a person if it has the power to prejudicially affect him.

III. ANALYSIS AND FINDINGS

A. Administrative Law and Administrative Efficiency

Courts and tribunals across regulatory agencies have given deference to the functioning of the concerned statutory regulatory authority, except in cases of blatant disregard of process. A good example is the deference to SEBI's issuance of interim orders and conducting post-decisional hearings. Another way to consider the nature of constraints on the functioning of statutory regulatory authorities is to consider the impact of judicial decisions on the legislative, executive and judicial functions of statutory regulatory authorities separately.

We find very little review of legislative actions of statutory regulatory authorities, with the exception of the TRAI. The fact that regulation-making processes have been challenged on the grounds of violating statutory requirements of transparency indicates that a lack of such review in other cases is primarily due to the lack of statutory requirements for other statutory regulatory authorities. Similarly, judicial review of administrative action has been rare. In cases against the CCI, the Competition Appellate Tribunal (COMPAT) and other courts have differentiated between administrative (creating a prima facie opinion) and quasi-judicial functions (investigation and orders passed by the CCI). Judicial review is most frequent with respect to the quasi-judicial functions of statutory regulatory authorities. However, the courts and tribunals have construed administrative law requirements strictly, and with reference to the applicable statutory law and any regulations framed by the statutory regulatory authority with regard to such functions. However, as Table 16.2 shows, statutory requirements with regard to quasi-judicial actions are also the most elaborately detailed procedural

[34] *Pancard Clubs v Securities and Exchange Board of India*, MANU/Sb/0059/2014 (17 September 2014).
[35] ibid para 2.
[36] ibid para 9.
[37] ibid para 30.
[38] ibid para 32.

requirements in the statutes governing statutory regulatory authorities. Legislative intent is clear – judicial control on quasi-judicial functions is a necessary check on regulatory efficiency.

However, the nature of these checks affects different statutory regulatory authorities in different ways. For example, the CCI functions primarily by conducting investigations and passing orders. The impact of judicial review as a constraint in its functioning is therefore much higher than for a body like SEBI that performs a substantial degree of legislative and administrative functions, in addition to quasi-judicial ones. The TRAI does not perform a substantial degree of quasi-judicial functions. However, the statutory requirement for ensuring transparency in its functioning has been used to review its regulation-making processes. It is difficult to estimate whether these checks seriously affect regulatory performance. Courts and tribunals have consistently referred to the need for preserving the statutory regulatory authority's ability to regulate effectively and have construed administrative law requirements strictly. In some cases, such as that of *Shankar Sharma v SEBI*, the courts repeatedly allowed SEBI to proceed irrespective of serious procedural lapses. Additionally, we have just discussed the 'thinness' of administrative law (and consequent grounds for review) with respect to legislative and administrative functions.

B. Judicial Review

One way of understanding whether judicial review of statutory regulatory authorities has a substantive effect on their functioning is to analyse whether statutory regulatory authorities undertake corrective exercises if their actions are struck down by courts and tribunals. If judicial review points out lacunae or defects in the functioning of statutory regulatory authorities, one might expect authorities to correct such issues and create new *internal* administrative law.

In order to understand this process, we interviewed some past members of boards of statutory regulatory authorities.[39] The unanimous opinion was that statutory regulatory authorities have no systematic process to analyse the decisions of courts and tribunals in order to correct defects in procedures/processes. Individual officers sometimes take note of adverse findings in matters they have been involved in and try not to repeat mistakes. The degree to which this happens varies from one statutory regulatory authority to another. The members ascribed the reason for this to the systems of incentives and accountability applicable to statutory regulatory authorities. In the case of the CCI (where members of the Commission have signed orders without being present at hearings on more than one occasion), the interview revealed that CCI members do not have any incentives to lay down or follow processes, since an appointment as CCI chairperson is usually the last appointment in a person's

[39] We interviewed three past members of different regulatory bodies. The persons interviewed had been chairpersons/members of the Pension Fund Regulatory and Development Authority (PFRDA) (interviewed 22 January 2018), the CCI (interviewed 23 January 2018) and SEBI (interviewed on 25 January 2018), respectively. Interviews were based on pre-set questionnaires.

career. This problem of sinecures and lack of performance appraisals is an obstacle in ensuring proper procedural requirements in the case of the CCI.

A related issue is the degree of independence. One of the former members stated that heads of statutory regulatory authorities realise they have a great degree of independence in functioning once they move from government to a statutory regulatory authority. They therefore wish to avoid creating processes that could increase their accountability or impede their functioning. In fact, the problem of an unconstrained statutory regulatory authority was brought up by all the members we interviewed. When asked about why administrative processes in statutory regulatory authorities are strikingly similar to those of other government departments, one former member stated that since most members of statutory regulatory authorities as well as many of their officials (in the initial days at least) are from government departments, they copy existing government processes without any regard for whether this will be appropriate for the functioning of the market under their jurisdiction. Based on the discussions with former members and an analysis of the nature of cases reviewed by the courts, one may surmise that administrative law is not a substantial constraint to the functioning of statutory regulatory authorities from the point of view of ensuring fairness and deliberative regulation-making.

There are other reasons for this as well. The adoption of existing government processes by statutory regulatory authorities also points to the problem of state capacity. The human capital inside statutory regulatory authorities does not have the requisite capacity to innovate better and more accountable, deliberative forms of decision-making. Some of the violations of procedural requirements (signing orders without being present at hearings, initiating inquiries after passing the final order) also point to the absence of ex ante mechanisms to prevent abuse if the persons concerned are determined to subvert processes. To the extent that these issues are personality-dependent, it points to the failure of the appointments system for statutory regulatory authorities. This necessitates a proper focus on the appointment and recruitment processes of statutory regulatory authorities.

Issues of regulatory capacity, the problems of sinecure and issues of accountability and credibility can also be better understood by looking at the context in which statutory regulatory authorities have been established in India. These contextual factors have in turn also influenced administrative law provisions in existing laws and continue to influence the debate on improving accountability, transparency and state capacity. Though there has been a general trend towards the creation of statutory regulatory authorities in India since the 1990s, the motives for creating each regulator have been different. Different authorities were created at different points of time and with different motivations. In the electricity sector, for example, Navroz K Dubash argues that a dominant motive for the creation of the electricity regulator in Orissa was to send a 'signal of credibility to private investors and protect consumer interests'.[40] However, Dubash argues that electricity regulators were introduced *more* to signal credibility to investors than to protect consumers.

[40] Navroz Dubash, 'Independent Regulatory Agencies: A Theoretical Review with Reference to Electricity and Water in India' (2008) 43 *Economic and Political Weekly* 40.

SEBI was first established and then made a statutory regulatory authority in 1992 with the enactment of the SEBI Act, 1992.[41] As an authority, SEBI replaced the erstwhile Comptroller of Capital Issues, which was a part of the Ministry of Finance.[42] The driving motivation was to develop a thriving financial market and to create the required capacity to regulate the market effectively. In the case of telecoms, it was a desire to create a competitive industry, signalling that the government would regulate the sector in a neutral manner that led to the progressive reform of the telecom sector, and the establishment of the TRAI was a part of this reform.[43] It is useful to note that in at least some cases, one important motive in driving the creation of the authority has been to 'signal' credibility or a desire to create a competitive private market. The institutional quality and structure of the authorities is therefore likely to be affected by which value was predominant during the creation of the authority. In the case of the electricity regulators, for example, Dubash[44] implicitly argues that the *real* intention was to mimic a regulator rather than to structure the regulatory apparatus for technocratic decision-making.[45] On the other hand, the TRAI is one of the few Indian authorities that has an explicit requirement to be transparent in its actions.[46] This requirement precedes the Right to Information Act, 2005 and, as an outlier (the other being the Airports Economic Regulatory Authority), is indicative of the degree to which administrative structures are impacted due to separate contexts for the creation of authorities.

However, it is more difficult to determine the impact of the political economy on the nature of administrative *law* rather than administrative structure. If governments wished to signal credibility and dynamism, why did they not do so through creating better administrative mechanisms (a new administrative law) rather than creating statutory regulatory authorities? One answer is that a promise to reform administrative processes would have been far more difficult to implement. One consistent trend of the Indian reform story is the progressive creation of new institutions rather than the reform of existing ones. The other reason may have been that statutory regulatory authorities were fast becoming the dominant method by which many of these sectors were regulated globally, and therefore the decision to create regulators was significantly influenced by the desire to signal credibility to investors and financial institutions that India was serious about its reform path.[47]

[41] Securities and Exchange Board of India Act, 1992.

[42] Shaji Vikraman, 'From Early Battles to Position of Strength: Evolution of SEBI' *Indian Express* (2015), http://indianexpress.com/article/explained/from-early-battles-to-position-of-strength-evolution-of-sebi-2.

[43] Rahul Mukherji, 'Interests, Wireless Technology, and Institutional Change: From Government Monopoly to Regulated Competition in Indian Telecommunications' (2009) 68 *Journal of Asian Studies* 491.

[44] Dubash (n 40).

[45] See generally the literature on isomorphic mimicry, summarised in Philipp Krause, 'Of Institutions and Butterflies: Is Isomorphism in Developing Countries Necessarily a Bad Thing?' [2013] *Background Note, Overseas Development Institute* 1.

[46] TRAI Act, 1997, s 11(4).

[47] See generally Jacint Jordana, David Levi-Faur and Xavier Fernandez Marin, 'The Global Diffusion of Regulatory Agencies: Channels of Transfer and Stages of Diffusion' (2011) 44 *Comparative Political Studies* 1343; Navroz K. Dubash, *The Rise of the Regulatory State of the South: Infrastructure and Development in Emerging Economies* (Oxford University Press, 2013); Mukherji (n 43).

A third, less written-about issue is the question of capacity. In at least some sectors, the capacity required for regulating a diverse, private and competitive market requires technocratic specialisation. The administrative constraints impeding the creation of this specialisation in normal government departments are many (lack of fixity of tenure, manpower constraints and recruitment constraints, to name but a few). The creation of statutory regulatory authorities has enabled the Indian state to sidestep some of these issues and create pools of specialisation inside authorities to varying degrees. In this sense, statutory regulatory authorities succeeded in solving the critical issue of creating human capital required to regulate competitive markets. Because they have succeeded visibly where the traditional government departments have not, statutory regulatory authorities have in many cases used their legitimacy in their respective sectors to resist reforms in administrative law. A good example is the RBI's resistance to the establishment of an appellate body to judicially review its actions.[48]

CONCLUSION

The discussion in the previous sections highlights that judicial review of statutory regulatory authorities with respect to administrative law is heavily tilted towards a review of quasi-judicial functions unless specific requirements are placed in the law. This is a logical extension of the degrees to which administrative law constrains different regulatory functions. Judicial review of quasi-judicial decisions is most relevant in the case of the CCI, since the majority of its regulatory functions are discharged through quasi-judicial processes.

However, in the case of SEBI and the RBI, a large number of functions are discharged through legislative rule-making processes and receive comparatively little attention from the courts. In the few cases pertaining to regulation-making or executive decisions, we see wide deference accorded to statutory regulatory authorities. The degree of deference accorded by courts seems to be directly linked to the administrative law requirements related to these functions. Courts have interpreted agency actions narrowly in the case of the TRAI (where statutory requirements of transparency in regulation-making exist) compared to SEBI and the RBI (where none exist). This highlights the generally conservative and textual approach of the judiciary when seeking to impose limits on state action. Tellingly, in *COAI v TRAI*, while the Supreme Court discussed a number of transparency requirements and regulation-making processes present in other statutes, it did not bind the TRAI to any of these processes.

Statutory regulatory authorities have not created or have extremely 'thin' internal administrative law that guides or constrains agency actions. Such internal administrative law (process manuals etc) are unlikely to be developed due to problems with the incentives and accountability of the leadership of statutory regulatory authorities.

[48] Raghuram Rajan, 'Financial Sector Legislative Reforms Committee Report (FSLRC): What to Do and When?', https://rbi.org.in/scripts/BS_SpeechesView.aspx?Id=900.

The internal impetus to improve regulatory processes within authorities is weak, as evidenced by the ad hoc developments in administrative processes within regulatory agencies. There is no systematic review of procedural issues, and any corrective action is driven by individuals rather than institutional mechanisms. While statutory regulatory authorities are agents of Parliament, in many cases the legitimacy of an authority exceeds that of the political executive, allowing it to resist calls for reforms to its administrative process.

There is therefore a strong case for incorporating detailed requirements regarding transparency, consultations, due process and internal constraints in laws applicable to statutory regulatory authorities. The judicial approach to review of regulatory functions has been guided strongly by the statutory law and common law precedent applicable to the larger state. Consistent with its general approach of deferring to state action, the courts have granted deference to statutory regulatory authorities in the absence of specific constraints imposed by statutory law. Conversely, judicial review will not be an effective check on violations of good administrative law principles in the absence of specific statutory law. The Financial Sector Legislative Reforms Commission, which was set up in 2011 to review all financial sector legislation in India, recommended that a detailed body of administrative law processes and functions be included in statutory law for regulators.[49] A statutory framework based on similar principles must therefore be considered for improving administrative law-led accountability mechanisms for regulators.

[49] Financial Sector Legislative Reforms Commission, 'Report of the Financial Sector Legislative Reforms Commission' (2013), https://dea.gov.in/sites/default/files/fslrc_report_vol1_1.pdf.

17

Building State Capacity for Regulation

SHUBHO ROY, AJAY SHAH, JUSTICE (RETD) BN SRIKRISHNA
AND SOMASEKHAR SUNDARESAN

INTRODUCTION

When India embarked on market-oriented reforms in 1991, there was a desire to break with central planning, with detailed governmental control of entry barriers, product design and processes within firms. This is not synonymous with deregulation; there were market failures in many industries that required addressing. This led to the establishment of *regulators*. While the Reserve Bank of India has existed since 1934, there was a wave of establishment of new regulators after the Securities and Exchange Board of India (SEBI) was created in 1988.

Regulators were to have legislative powers and to write subordinate legislation which would embed intricate knowledge and change rapidly with the evolution of fast-paced private industries. They were intended to have executive power in licensing and investigations. They were designed to shield transactions (licensing, investigation) from political interference. They were expected to achieve greater state capacity when compared to departments of government improving upon processes such as human resource policies.

The early optimism about shifting from central control to specialised regulators has given way to concerns about the working of regulators. Regulators have also been plagued by poor state capacity. They have often veered into controlling as opposed to regulating, with creation of entry barriers and micro-management through regulations. Firms and groups of firms actively seek to co-opt regulators in their business objectives, which has given a return to the political economy of central planning. Entry barriers have sprung up with irrational and arbitrary decisions in licensing. The enforcement of regulations and substantive law-making are selective and weak. This has resulted in high costs for the economy. There is arbitrary power to initiate investigations and punish, and a climate of fear where private persons are afraid to criticise regulators. The India of 2018 is uncomfortably similar to the India of 1991. It is hence important to review the Indian experience, diagnose the sources of failure of existing regulators, and envision how high performance regulators can be obtained.

There are two blind alleys in this quest. It is possible to focus on one episode of a mistake by a regulator, and undertake analysis and advocacy to solve this problem. While a great deal of *knowledge* can be produced through case studies of failure, it is important to go upstream, to ask questions of incentives and information that lie at the source of repeated regulatory failure. The second non-solution is a focus on personalities. When institutions are weak, the character of the institution is determined by its staffing. There is, then, a clamour to recruit great men and to give them all power to do as they like (ie, extreme regulatory independence). It is important to look deeper and to build *institutions* that have impersonal capability. In order for any change to be more than skin-deep, it cannot be an idea in the minds of certain individuals; it has to be about the formal structures of governance, accountability and processes.

Conversely, individuals working in regulators sometimes take criticism personally. However, the failures of an organisation are primarily induced by the design of the organisation. The same individuals would deliver superior outcomes if placed in a better designed organisation. The focus must be on the incentives for the individuals who man the regulator. If regulators are merely given arbitrary power, public choice theory and the Indian experience show that this power will be used poorly. What is required are systems of accountability, and checks and balances, through which the individuals working inside regulators have incentives to do the right things. This requires seven elements:

Clarity of purpose: accountability for an organisation requires clarity on its goals. Every regulatory organisation must have a compact and clearly understood objective. Sprawling mandates, and particularly conflicting mandates, yield poor performance.

Role and composition of the board: the board must be dominated by non-executive members, through which the board can play the role of the principal vis-a-vis the management, which is the agent. The board must control the organisational design, including a hierarchy diagram of the organisation, internal process manuals and the budget process. The board must control the legislative function.

Legislative process: when Parliament places law-making power upon unelected officials in a regulator, this calls for commensurate checks and balances in the process of regulation-making. The regulation-making process must start from the board. The staff must document the problem that is sought to be solved along with the proposed intervention, and conduct a cost-benefit analysis. This packet must be put out for public comment. After this, the staff must address the public comments on the draft and make appropriate modifications to the draft regulation, and bring the draft back to the board for discussion. Finally, only the board should have the power to issue a regulation.

Executive process: sound processes are required in licensing and investigations, which protect citizens from arbitrary power. The non-award of a licence causes substantial harm to a person. It should not be done lightly or without clear demonstration that the applicant fails to meet the licensing condition. In civil or criminal proceedings, it is the duty of the plaintiff/prosecution to prove that the defendant carried out the actions which led to the liability/criminal act. Similarly, when rejecting a licence application, the regulator should marshal all evidence showing that the applicant is not eligible for the licence.

Judicial process: an administrative law department should contain administrative law officers who play no role in legislative or executive functions. This would yield an element of separation of powers. A hearing must take place before an administrative law officer, where the prosecution leads an argument and the defendant is given an opportunity to argue their case. This should lead to the drafting of a reasoned order as a structured document which shows the state of the law and the facts of the case, demonstrates that the law has been violated or explains why this conclusion cannot be reached, and uses proper reasoning to determine the penalty. Orders should be published. There should be the possibility of efficacious appeal at a court or tribunal against the order. These three stages of due process (internally at the administrative law officer and externally through publishing orders and at the appeal) put pressure upon the investigation and prosecution staff of the regulator to produce high-quality work and protect citizens from arbitrary power.

Reporting and accountability: regulators should be obliged to release statistical details about their functioning. Reporting should not concern the broader economic environment (eg, the fluctuations of the stock market index), but should focus upon the actual work of the regulator (eg, the win rate at the tribunal when orders are appealed). High-quality reporting of all aspects of the working of the regulator will create the pressure of accountability and will feed into the budget process where targets can be set and incremental resources allocated in a way that pursues those targets.

Role of the department: alongside the creation of well-structured regulators, there is a need to clarify the role of the relevant governmental department and create capacity in the functions that the department has to discharge.

These seven elements need to be coded into parliamentary law. This can be done at the level of one sector (eg, the draft Indian Financial Code, which envisages a single good governance framework for all financial regulators) or for all regulators in the Union government, as was done in the US by the Federal Administrative Procedures Act, 1946.

When compared with these seven elements of the design of a regulator which foster high performance, the present Indian landscape contains large gaps. The regulators of today are defined by skimpy laws, which give arbitrary power to the management and lack a principal-agent perspective upon the working of the regulator. The present legislative framework is grounded in the notion that regulators are good people and will work towards the welfare of the people. This creates poor incentives for good behaviour by regulatory officials. The Financial Sector Legislative Reforms Commission (FSLRC), which was chaired by one of the authors (Justice BN Srikrishna), drafted the Indian Financial Code from 2011 to 2015. This draft law embeds the key ideas of this chapter. Across the Indian landscape, many experiments are now taking place in building state capacity in regulators. This chapter provides a conceptual framework – and 140 sections in the draft Indian Financial Code provide the draft law – for this journey.

I. STATE CAPACITY AND REGULATION

Under central planning, the government intervened extensively in the economy through tools such as bans, price controls, public ownership, entry barriers and restrictions upon private persons. There were a large number of government schemes which intervened in the working of the economy in various ways. By 1991, it was clear that this amounted to an excessive involvement of the government in the economy. On many issues, there was a need to remove these restrictions upon the private sector. The liberal idea in Indian economic policy is to create private competitive industries as opposed to the old world of bans, price controls, entry barriers, public ownership, and onerous restrictions and schemes. There is a significant agenda of unfinished work of this nature. Indeed, the steady pace of introduction of new bans, schemes, price controls, government monopolies etc continues.

However, alongside this programme of establishing economic freedom, there are market failures which call for regulation. Across a large swathe of industries, there are concerns about health, safety and the environment, which require regulation of private industry. Concerns about consumer protection and market power motivate a parallel class of restrictions upon firms. In industries ranging from infrastructure to finance, there is often a role for regulation. Establishing a market economy is as much about removing the old ways of intervention as about establishing regulators.

In the India of old, coercion of private persons was done through a parliamentary law enforced by governmental departments. This approach had several difficulties: (1) with the fast-paced evolution of technology, products and processes, it was difficult for Parliament to keep up in terms of numerous amendments of the law; (2) laws required intricate industry knowledge, while Parliament worked at the level of high principles; (3) governmental departments had limited ability to police the compliance with law; (4) governmental departments had weak processes to absorb market feedback and low state capacity; (5) governmental departments were invested in a culture of central planning; (6) governmental departments were headed by ministers, which brought political considerations into individual transactions, as is the case in licensing, investigation and prosecution; (7) governmental departments have conflicts of interest through owning elements of the production process. Regulators would be at arm's length from the industry that they regulate.

A specialised organisation, the regulator, was envisaged to address these problems. The regulator would build dedicated teams with specialised knowledge and would improve upon processes that are utilised in governmental departments, thus developing greater capability. It would recruit experts and break with the established culture of central planning. It would have regulatory independence to the extent of shielding the processes of licensing, investigation and prosecution from political interference. These capabilities would enable the rapid evolution of subordinated legislation, the regulations, so as to keep up with the innovations and technological change of the private sector. They would also enable the sophisticated enforcement of these regulations. Governmental departments tended to own public sector companies and other elements of institutional infrastructure that directly participated in the market economy. Regulators would have the arm's-length arrangement: they would be referees and not players.

An integral part of the 1991 reforms was the programme of establishing regulators. The idea was to free up private persons to start firms and innovate in terms of what is done within firms, within a set of rules established by regulators that address market failures. While the first regulator, the Reserve Bank of India (RBI), had been established in 1934, a wave of new organisations came about, starting with SEBI in 1992. Other regulatory agencies were built in finance (the Pension Fund Regulatory and Development Authority (PFRDA) and the Insurance Regulatory and Development Authority (IRDA)), competition (the Competition Commission of India (CCI)), company law (the Insolvency and Bankruptcy Board of India (IBBI)), infrastructure (the Telecom Regulatory Authority of India (TRAI), the Central Electricity Commission (CEC) and the Airports Economic Regulatory Authority (AERA)), food (the Food Safety and Standards Authority of India (FSSAI)), real estate (the Real Estate Regulatory Authority) etc. Additional new regulators continue to be established.

The outcomes obtained in India through the establishment of regulators have been disappointing. Some regulators have been associated with important economic reforms (eg, SEBI and the TRAI). Other developments have been less desirable, such as the RBI's oversight of repeated banking crises. The main reason for the establishment of regulators was the desire to move away from central planning and towards dynamic competitive innovative industries. In most cases, regulators have created a new kind of central planning, where each detail of products and processes is codified into regulations, and the pace of innovation that is 'permissible' in the industry is determined by the pace of thinking at the regulator. As an example, India was the only country where the Uber cashless payment process was blocked by a regulator.[1] Similarly, we see newspaper headlines say that the RBI has introduced interest rate futures. The 'cost of doing business' in India is high and the conduct of regulators is an important part of this problem.

While regulators had an opportunity to use improved processes as compared to governmental departments, this opportunity has been utilised only to a limited extent. The weak processes in governmental departments have generally been carried forward into regulators. Regulators were intended to make a clean break with the culture of central planning, particularly with a new style of recruitment of practitioners and researchers. However, in practice, almost all recruitment by regulators has been from the pool of civil servants or based on recruitment practices of the government. This created a repeat of elements of the former socialist system. Regulators were envisioned to have regulatory independence in relation to individual transactions, but not in relation to questions of legislative functions and the governance of the regulator.

[1] Suyash Rai and Ajay Shah, 'RBI vs Uber, Continued' *The Leap Blog* (18 September 2014), https://ajayshahblog.blogspot.com/2014/09/rbi-vs-uber-continued.html.

Yet, all too often, regulators accepted political interference on individual transactions in return for reduced accountability and untrammelled regulation-making power. Regulators were also intended to avoid conflicts of interest – to be referees and not players. While this is generally true, there have been many deviations from this ideal. To give an example, the RBI is a participant in the markets that it regulates. At the RBI, old assets were not divested, and new assets have been steadily added.

New regulators have been a vital part of important economic reforms, such as SEBI's role in the equity market, the TRAI's role in the telecom reforms and the AERA's role in private airports. However, the overall picture of regulation in India is an unsatisfactory one. The India of 2018 is uncomfortably like the India of 1991, with entry barriers, central planning and the political economy of firms jockeying for competitive advantage by co-opting the regulator. The establishment of regulators in India raises traditional concerns about the administrative state. When power is wielded by unelected officials, this raises concerns. When the laws that define the checks and balances for regulators are weak, regulators amass arbitrary power. Under these conditions of the lack of the rule of law, private persons are fearful of regulators and fail to exert vocal or legal challenges against the actions of the regulator, even when appellate remedies are provided by law. This reduces the quality of checks and balances. When taken to an extreme, arbitrary power in the hands of regulators yields central planning, laziness, corruption and autocratic behaviour.

An important lens through which regulators should be examined is the separation of powers.[2] The separation of powers doctrine suggests that legislative, executive and judicial wings should be separated so as to reduce the concentration of power. Regulators worldwide obtain improved efficiency by fusing legislative and executive powers. While this yields greater efficiency at a practical level, it is important to see that this also induces the concentration of power, which makes it more difficult to achieve state capacity. In India, with pervasive gloom about the working of the judiciary, regulators such as the RBI and SEBI have also been assigned judicial functions, with the jurisdiction of courts being ousted by law. As a result of this, there is a violation of the separation of powers. Many regulators in India have legislative, executive and judicial functions. This exacerbates the concentration of power and makes it even harder to achieve state capacity.

The concept of a regulator continues to be an important one in the construction of the Indian state. But fresh thinking is now required on how foundational changes can be made in order to create high-performance regulatory organisations. The logic that motivated the establishment of regulators continues to resonate, but this do not immediately suggest a programme for action through which shortcomings can be addressed.

In the mainstream Indian debate, there is a lot of focus on and criticism of regulators and their actions. For the department, and for the larger policy community, there is a temptation to micro-manage the regulator and intervene in individual decisions made by the regulator rather than understand why the regulator is making these

[2] See MS Sahoo, 'Political Economy of Neo-governments' (2012) *Chartered Secretary* 1530.

wrong decisions. However, the existing structures of law that govern regulators have given regulators substantial powers. The cost to external parties of getting involved in a faulty outcome is fairly high. Hence, this approach for remedying bad regulatory outcomes can occasionally work, but it cannot be scaled up. The policy community should block the flow of bad regulatory outcomes at the root cause rather than fire-fighting the steady flow of failures.

The weak outcomes from regulators have placed pressure upon staffing. Many in India subscribe to a 'great man' theory of regulatory outcomes. There is an emphasis on the individuals who are hired for senior positions, particularly the chairperson. There has been a cycle of hope giving way to despair, where the media hails the appointment of a great man and then looks back at how little was done on his watch. The substantial power wielded by the chairperson has also created interest in obtaining the position for the wrong reasons.

However, building state capacity requires building capabilities in the institution and a reduction in the importance of individuals. We should go beyond individual regulatory actions and regulatory appointments, and look deeper. Why are regulators in India often performing poorly? Why are highly capable persons recruited for senior positions unable to deliver improved outcomes? This takes us to questions about organisational design and the nature of incentives. Here, we offer a set of features of organisational design which will induce improved performance. We offer arguments and examples which show the gains that can be obtained from these features. In this, we draw upon considerable international experience on these questions. To give an example, in the US, there was a wave of creation of regulatory institutions from the 1930s to the 1970s. There were concerns about arbitrary power being wielded by unelected officials, which led to the Federal Administrative Procedures Act, 1946 (APA). The APA establishes good governance procedures for all federal organisations, including all regulators. The APA has been highly influential worldwide in terms of the thinking about good governance procedures for regulators. The analysis of other advanced economies, such as Canada, Australia and the UK, also reveals a sophisticated doctrine of checks and balances through good governance procedures that induce high-performance regulators. The simple transplantation of law is of course not feasible across countries. We must think from first principles about the problems seen in the Indian environment, and design the checks and balances that will induce good incentives in the Indian context.

II. ELEMENTS OF A HIGH-PERFORMANCE REGULATOR

In our analysis, there are seven elements of a high-performance regulator: (1) clarity of purpose; (2) the role and composition of the board; (3) the legislative process; (4) the executive process; (5) the judicial process; (6) accountability through reporting; and (7) the role of the governmental department. These seven elements add up to a tangible set of actions in the law that governs the regulator and in the working of its parent department, through which state capacity can be obtained. We now turn to examining each of these in some detail.

A. Clarity of Purpose

Without clarity of purpose, there is no way for the legislature, or the broader public, to hold a regulatory agency to account for its functioning. When there is clarity of purpose, failures of the regulator create pressure upon the board members, in particular independent board members, who would translate the failures into modifications in the functioning of the organisation.

Table 17.1 Comparing objectives that regulators must pursue

Section 2 of the US Securities Act, 1933	Section 11(1) of the SEBI Act, 1992	Section 3(1) of the Payment and Settlement Systems Act, 2007
Whenever pursuant to this title the Commission is engaged in rulemaking and is required to consider or determine whether an action is necessary or appropriate in the public interest, the Commission shall also consider, in addition to the protection of investors, whether the action will promote efficiency, competition, and capital formation.	Subject to the provisions of this Act, it shall be the duty of the Board to protect the interests of investors in securities and to promote the development of, and to regulate the securities market, by such measures as it thinks fit.	The Reserve Bank shall be the designated authority for the regulation and supervision of payment systems under this Act.

The US Securities Act, 1933 captures the tension that the regulator has to maintain when regulating the securities market. The primary objective of the regulation is to *protect investors*, but the legislature also asks the regulator to balance this objective with the need to *promote efficiency, competition and capital formation*. This balances the regulator by requiring it to look at the bigger role of the securities market in a country, especially the raising of capital. There are clear objectives that the regulator has to meet. In comparison, the Securities and Exchanges Board of India Act, 1992 (hereinafter the SEBI Act) does not have this tension. The law oddly requires SEBI to protect the *interests of the investor* and *to promote the development, and to regulate the securities market*. Regulation is a means and not an end. The purpose of SEBI should not be to regulate the securities market.

Compared with US law, the objective of the regulator in India is less clear. The tension between protecting investors and making it easy to raise capital is not recognised in the law. The law also assigns a vague objective to SEBI as compared to that given to the US Securities and Exchange Commission (SEC): a 'market' is not an identifiable group, as it is difficult to measure if a market has developed. On the other hand, it is easier to measure the efficiency, competition and capital formation in the securities market. For example, one good measure of the efficiency of the securities market is the *bid-ask spread* of the most liquid securities. Similarly, capital formation ease can be measured by the *cost of raising capital* in a country. For example, the

US SEC compares the cost of raising capital in the US markets with those in other Organisation for Economic Co-operation and Development (OECD) countries as a measure of its efficiency.

The objective of the Payment and Settlement Systems Act, 2007 (PSSA) lacks clarity. In this Act, regulation is not the means; it is the end. There is no outcome that the regulator is required to deliver: all it is obliged to do is to use coercive power and regulate. If this power slows the development of the industry, harms the interests of consumers or prevents efficient payments, these outcomes do not offend the governing legislation in any manner. There is no possibility of any failures of the organisation creating pressures of accountability.

For the RBI, the problem of clarity of purpose is compounded by *conflicting* and *multiple* objectives. As the debt manager for the government, it is required to issue securities at the lowest price for the government. On the other hand, as the manager of inflation, it may be required to keep interest rates high, thereby increasing the cost of government borrowing. In addition to these conflicting targets, the RBI is expected to: (1) manage inflation; (2) regulate banks and their competitors – non-banking financial firms in the business of giving credit; (3) regulate debt securities; (4) regulate derivatives on currency and debt securities; (4) manage foreign exchange reserves; (5) control the flow of foreign capital; (6) manage debt for central and state governments; (7) regulate cooperative banks; (8) act as a development financial institution; (9) regulate payments; and (10) monitor and enforce social lending targets. It is hard for the principal (whether the RBI board, the Ministry of Finance or the Parliament) to judge the extent to which the agent is performing when the agent has such extensive and internally conflicting goals.

One element of the clarity of purpose is the distinction between player and referee. An organisation like the TRAI is purely a referee: it has no ownership or control over players of any kind. At the RBI, however, several infrastructure systems are directly or indirectly controlled by the RBI. These include the Subsidiary General Ledger, the Negotiated Dealing System (NDS), the National Payments Corporation of India (NPCI) and the Clearing Corporation of India Ltd (CCIL), among others. There are proposals to create more such elements, such as a public credit registry.[3] Achieving clarity of purpose requires divesting these assets and becoming a pure referee, as is the case with the TRAI.

B. The Role and Composition of the Board

Regulatory failures in India often elicit demands for the appointment of an exceptionally honest or competent person to lead the regulator. Alongside this, it is generally assumed that *regulatory independence* is required, which is used to lobby for reduced accountability. However, the feedback loop of elections leading to Parliament and the cabinet is a key source of accountability and performance. This is missing with

[3] See Prasanth Regy, 'RBI's Proposal for a Public Credit Registry' *The Leap Blog* (2 August 2017), https://ajayshahblog.blogspot.com/2017/08/rbis-proposal-for-public-credit-registry.html.

unelected officials. If unelected officials are hired to run an agency and are given job security and full freedom to do as they like, they are unaccountable.

At present, regulatory boards in India are often ineffectual and power is concentrated in the hands of the chairperson of the board who is also part of the management of the regulator (ie, an executive chairman). In addition, many boards have a substantial representation of interested parties who are not balanced by a healthy number of non-executive and non-government experts. As Table 17.2 shows, while some boards like that of the RBI have a predominance of independent non-executive members, other boards have flaws in composition.

Table 17.2 Comparing board composition of regulators

Regulator	Executive	Non-executive	Ex officio/government
RBI	5	8	2
SEBI	4	1	3
IBBI	3	0	4
IRDA	5	4	0

The institution of the board has matured to a greater extent in private companies through the Companies Act, 2013 and the global evolution of thinking on the role of the board. For example, listed companies in India are required to have at least one-third independent directors.[4] The RBI mandates that bank boards should have a non-executive chairman. This body of knowledge has important insights into the structuring of an effective board. Boards of commercial organisation have frequent feedback about the functioning in the form of profits and stock prices. The boards of government organisations do not get such feedback, which makes measuring the effectiveness of boards more difficult to achieve.

As a concrete example, we will imagine a regulatory board which is made up of the key managers of the organisation (one chairman and, say, two members), a nominee member (representing the relevant department) and a majority of independent members (say five). This adds up to a nine-member board. At a conceptual level, the purpose of the board is to be the hands-on principal that holds the agent (the management) to account. The five independent members, and the nominee member, should dominate board meetings and should challenge the work of the management (the three internal members).

The functioning of boards in Indian regulators today is opaque. Patnaik and Roy show that the functioning of the RBI board does not compare well with other central banks.[5] For example, while the minutes of a single meeting of the New York Federal Reserve Board are around 6,000 words, and those of the Bank of England Court of

[4] See Companies Act, 2013, s 149(4).

[5] Ila Patnaik and Shubho Roy, 'The RBI Board: Comparison against International Bench-Marks' *The Leap Blog* (24 January 2017), https://ajayshahblog.blogspot.in/2017/01/the-rbi-board-comparison-against.html.

Directors are around 2,100 words, the RBI only puts out a press release of 142 words. The Indian Parliament has set very low standards for the transparency and accountability of the RBI board. Details of the agenda, discussions, transcripts or votes are not released by the bank. Some other regulators in India work differently: SEBI publishes the board agenda and the decisions taken by the board on each agenda item on its website. However, the SEBI board functioning also has its weaknesses: the board routinely delegates to the executive chairman the full power to modify and finalise draft regulations that have been 'approved' by the board.

The difference in the transparency in meetings arises from the legal requirement placed on the regulator. As Table 17.3 shows, in India, this is left to the regulator. As an example, the US government in the Sunshine Act, 1976 lay down detailed requirements for any US agency/regulator board meetings. By default, meetings have to be held in the *open*: the public may watch and record the board meeting. Meetings can be closed only if they discuss items which are mentioned in the Act. Even in such closed meetings, detailed records about deliberations, transcripts of statements and voting records have to be kept by the regulator. Such records may become public after appropriate amount of time has passed.

Table 17.3 A comparison of requirements to publish meeting minutes

Section 552b(f)(1) of the US Administrative Procedure Act, 1946	**Section 22(1) of the Competition Act, 2002**
[T]he agency shall maintain either such a transcript or recording, or a set of minutes. Such minutes shall fully and clearly describe all matters discussed and shall provide a full and accurate summary of any action taken, and the reasons therefore, including a description of each of the views expressed on any item and the record of any roll call vote (reflecting the vote of each member on the question). All documents considered in connection with any action shall be identified in such minutes.	The Commission shall meet at such times and places, and shall observe such rules and procedure in regard to the transaction of business at its meetings as may be provided by regulations.

The regulations for the Competition Commission of India (CCI) were made by its board; unsurprisingly, there are no provisions governing minutes or voting. One additional function that should be placed with the board of a regulatory organisation is the legislative function. Every regulation-making project must start and end with the board. In India, many boards have ex officio members from other organisations. This has generally become a way for those organisations to obtain a veto power over board decisions. From the viewpoint of the management of a regulator, such passive members are convenient as they exercise their veto occasionally and otherwise do not hold the management accountable. However, on-management board members are the essence of regulatory accountability. This requires a lean board structure of the kind described above.

C. The Legislative Process

In a liberal democracy, the power to write law is ordinarily wielded by elected representatives of the people, who are accountable through elections. When the power to write law is given to unelected officials, this is an extraordinary arrangement. It requires a corresponding extraordinary set of checks and balances. This involves: (a) clarifying what falls under the legislative functions of the regulator; (b) the process that the regulator should undertake to make regulations; and (c) the method of parliamentary scrutiny.

Before any meaningful discussion about the quality of regulation making can be initiated, what constitutes regulations under law needs to be clarified. This is a murky area in India. As an example, financial sector regulators in India issue many *types* of instruments, all of which coerce private persons and thereby constitute 'law'. Box 17.1 enumerates the regulatory instruments issued in some regulators.

Box 17.1 A plethora of subordinate legislation instruments

Indian regulators issue a plethora of subordinate legislation instruments. There is usually no clarity as to why a specific type of legislative instrument is used for a particular purpose:

- **SEBI**

  Types: regulations, rules (made by government), circulars, general orders, guidelines, master circulars and press releases (since they are now used to stay the operation of circulars)

  Legislative scrutiny: rules and regulations only

- **PFRDA**

  Types: regulations, notifications, master circulars, circulars, orders and notices, public notices and exposure drafts

  Legislative scrutiny: rules and regulations only

- **IRDA**

  Types: regulations, guidelines, circulars, orders and notices

  Legislative scrutiny: rules and regulations only

- **RBI**

  Types: rules, regulations, notifications, press releases, directions, master directions, circulars and guidelines

  Legislative scrutiny: rules and regulations only

While section 31 of the SEBI Act, 1996 requires that every rule or regulation must be laid before Parliament, section 11B allows SEBI to make any directions on its own subjective satisfaction, without parliamentary review. Going beyond the scope of the parliamentary legislation, SEBI has created multiple types of legal instruments: rules, regulations, general orders, guidelines, master circulars, circulars and informal guidance. However, out of these, only regulations are laid before Parliament; the remainder face no legislative oversight. Since they are not considered to be judicial orders, there is also no possibility of judicial review of such legal instruments. Public choice theory predicts that the staff of SEBI will prefer the instruments which have no parliamentary oversight. SEBI does, in fact, favour issuing *circulars*.

While some regulatory instruments escape parliamentary scrutiny because the parliamentary legislation does not provide for them, in other legislation, the drafting of the law itself is flawed and enables the regulator to make subordinate legislation without any scrutiny. For example, section 35W(1) of the Reserve Bank of India Act, 1934 empowers the RBI to give directions to all entities dealing in securities. These directions are not required to be placed before Parliament. There is no definition of the nature of instruments which may be issued under any provision. This also allows the regulator to avoid the entire process mandated under the law for *effectively* making subsidiary legislation which affects all parties. The first step towards building state capacity in regulators is to require that there must be only one kind of legal instrument that regulators can issue: a 'regulation'.

Which process must the regulator follow to make regulations? Regulators are unelected officials who have been given an extraordinary law-making power by Parliament. Legal theorists and legislators have grappled with this problem in many countries and have come up with two main procedural checks drawn from the nature of regulators:

- *Address the democratic deficit*: since regulators are not elected and therefore do not reflect the *will of the people*, they must attempt to involve the public in their regulation-making process. This is done through processes called *public notice and comment*, where regulators provide draft regulations to the public.
- *Demonstrate expertise*: one reason for creating regulators is to bring in expertise which is not normally available in government. However, this expertise will not be *presumed*. The regulator must *demonstrate* that it has expertise in the subject of regulation by showing how the regulations will be beneficial for society. This is done by requiring the regulator to publish a documentation packet including a *cost-benefit analysis*.

These ideas are not present in the regulators in India today. Box 17.2 highlights some of the provisions governing the process of regulation-making by different regulators.

Box 17.2 Procedural requirements for making regulations

Currently, most regulators in India do not need to meet any procedural requirements before making regulations.

Section 30 of the SEBI Act, 1992 merely states: 'The Board may, by notification, make regulations consistent with this Act and the rules made there under to carry out the purposes of this Act.'

The Telecom Regulatory Authority of India Act, 1997 contains a general requirement which would apply to regulation-making in section 11(4): 'The Authority shall ensure transparency while exercising its powers and discharging its functions.'

The state-of-the-art legislation in India (in this respect) is the Airports Economic Regulatory Authority of India Act, 2008, where what constitutes transparent functioning of the board/authority has been defined in section 13(4) as:

(a) by holding due consultations with all stake-holders with the airport;
(b) by allowing all stake-holders to make their submissions to the authority; and
(c) by making all decisions of the authority fully documented and explained.

The way forward lies in requiring a regulator to comply with multiple steps which: (1) provide regulated persons with the reasoning behind the regulation; and (2) allow the public to *effectively* participate in the process of regulation-making. Box 17.3 contains extracts from laws in other jurisdictions which are analogous to section 30 of the SEBI Act. These requirements ensure that the regulator considers the costs and benefits of the regulation and allows effective participation. An analysis of requirements under various forms of legislation in other jurisdictions, the history of regulation in India, and best practices identified by organisations such as the OECD shows that there are some common requirements that all regulators should follow when making regulations, which are as follows:

(1) All regulations should commence from an instruction from the board of the regulator after a formal vote on the issue.
(2) After the formal board resolution, the employees of the regulator must make a documentation packet which answers the following questions with reason and evidence:
   (a) What is the problem we seek to solve?
   (b) Is it a market failure? Is it within the jurisdiction of this agency?
   (c) What is the proposed intervention?
   (d) Does the proposed intervention address the claimed market failure?
(3) This documentation packet must be accompanied by the following:
   (a) Cost-benefit analysis: do the benefits outweigh the cost? Was there an alternative intervention which would achieve the same outcome at a lower cost to society?
   (b) The draft regulation.
(4) The board of the regulator must approve these documents, agree that they meet the minimum quality standards and approve them to be published.

(5) This entire packet of documentation should be available for public comment for a reasonable period, say a month.
(6) All public comments should be categorised and then the management of the regulator must make a category-wise response to all the comments from the public.
(7) The first packet, comments from the public, categorised comments and the management response should be placed before the board for approval.
(8) The board of the regulator, in a formal meeting, by resolution should approve the final regulations for release.
(9) At some regular interval, say three years after a regulation is made, a formal review of the working of the regulation should be carried out. It should ask the following questions:
   (a) Was the problem solved?
   (b) Did the intervention solve the problem?
   (c) Was the original cost-benefit analysis correct or did it need to be reviewed based on the experience of implementing the regulation?
   (d) Are there any new interventions which could get the same outcome at a lower cost to society?

Box 17.3 The notice and comment procedure in the legislation

The UK Financial Services and Markets Act, 2000 lays down in some detail the processes that the UK Financial Conduct Authority (FCA) must carry out before enforcing regulations. Section 155(1)–(5) of the Act reads as follows:

(1) If the Authority proposes to make any rules, it must publish a draft of the proposed rules in the way appearing to it to be best calculated to bring them to the attention of the public.

(2) The draft must be accompanied by—

   (a) a cost benefit analysis;
   (b) an explanation of the purpose of the proposed rules;
   (c) an explanation of the Authority's reasons for believing that making the proposed rules is compatible with its general duties under Section 2; and
   (d) notice that representations about the proposals may be made to the Authority within a specified time.

(3) In the case of a proposal to make rules under a provision mentioned in subsection (9), the draft must also be accompanied by details of the expected expenditure by reference to which the proposal is made.

(4) Before making the proposed rules, the Authority must have regard to any representations made to it in accordance with subsection (2)(d).

(5) If the Authority makes the proposed rules, it must publish an account, in general terms, of—

(a) the representations made to it in accordance with subsection (2)(d); and

(b) its response to them.

In the US, the SEC is bound by the Administrative Procedure Act, 1946, which also mandates a system of notice and comment in Section 553.

…

(b) General notice of proposed rule-making shall be published in the Federal Register, unless persons subject thereto are named and either personally served or otherwise have actual notice thereof in accordance with law. The notice shall include—

(1) a statement of the time, place, and nature of public rule making proceedings;
(2) reference to the legal authority under which the rule is proposed; and
(3) either the terms or substance of the proposed rule or a description of the subjects and issues involved …

(c) After notice required by this section, the agency shall give interested persons an opportunity to participate in the rule making through submission of written data, views, or arguments with or without opportunity for oral presentation. After consideration of the relevant matter presented, the agency shall incorporate in the rules adopted a concise general statement of their basis and purpose …

In the US, cost-benefit analysis by regulators is mandated by a series of Presidential Orders.[6]

At present, this process is not required of any regulator in India. While some regulators may sporadically carry out public consultation, this is not meaningful. Burman and Zaveri show that regulators in India hardly follow through with public consultations.[7] There are long delays between consultation and final regulation, and there is no evidence that public consultation changes the thinking of regulators in any way. However, the authors do find that variation in the governing law of regulators (ie, laws which require some form of consultation) leads to relatively more involvement in regulation-making (they show that the TRAI, the telecom regulator, has more public engagement than SEBI, the securities regulator).

[6] The first major executive order was US Executive Order 12291 of 17 February 1981, 46 FR 13193. See generally Cass R Sunstein, *The Cost-Benefit Revolution* (MIT Press, 2018).

[7] Anirudh Burman and Bhargavi Zaveri, 'Regulatory Responsiveness in India: A Normative and Empirical Framework for Assessment' (2016), IGIDR Working Paper Series, https://EconPapers.repec.org/RePEc:ess:wpaper:id:11463.

The final legal process requirement is to subject the regulations formulated by the regulator to parliamentary scrutiny. Since Parliament is the sole repository of legislative power, laws usually require all subordinate legislation to be placed before it when it is in session. Parliament has some time (usually 30 days) to either modify or annul the regulations through a resolution. While regulators are required to place regulations before Parliament, this process suffers from two defects: first, as shown in Box 17.1, most regulatory instruments, which have the same effect as regulations, are never seen by Parliament; and, second, the current system places only the bare text of the regulation before the legislature. Neither the legislature nor the public is able to form an informed view about the appropriateness and quality of the subordinate legislation. For a counter-example, the Federal Register, which is the repository of all regulations made by the US regulators/government, contains the entire document packet of regulations, cost-benefit analysis, statement of purpose, public comments and response to public comments.

As a result of this poor *regulatory legislative process*, the regulator or its board: (1) does not have a systematic process to evaluate proposals to regulate that arise from the management of the regulator; or (2) does not receive any feedback from the regulated about the appropriateness of any proposed regulation. This is the root cause of the flow of poor, unenforceable regulations that are subject to frequent changes. Box 17.4 gives an example of an unexplained change in subordinate legislation.

Box 17.4 Regulatory uncertainty: an example

The basic tenet of securities regulation is to enable investors to make informed decisions about the issuer of a security. Banking regulation in India was not transparent on the issue of defaults. Information about defaults gets delayed as listed borrowers are not required to release information on defaults to banks. SEBI, the securities regulator, attempted to correct this situation with a *circular*, which required listed companies to disclose any delay in repayment of bank loans. The following is the series of events that followed.[8]

4 August 2017: SEBI issued a circular stating that there was a discrepancy about the level of information that listed companies have to release about default in payments. While a single-day single Rupee default in bonds is required to be disclosed, similar disclosures were not stipulated with respect to loans from banks and financial institutions. Therefore, from 1 October 2017, all listed companies would be required to report defaults to banks to the exchanges (public dissemination).

30 September 2017 (one day prior to the circular coming into effect): SEBI came out with a single-line *press release*, stating, in the passive tense, that

[8] Somasekhar Sundaresan, 'Without Contempt: Between What is Said and Left Unsaid' *Business Standard* (4 October 2017), https://www.business-standard.com/article/opinion/between-what-s-said-and-left-unsaid-117100401403_1.html.

the circular would be deferred until further notice. There was no information about the reasons for deferring the circular.

After the fraud at the Punjab National Bank at the end of February 2018, the demand for information about loan defaults was raised. However, by withdrawing its circular, SEBI undermined its own regulatory authority and reduced the clarity on upcoming regulations. Firms which had prepared to comply with the first circular wasted resources in setting up systems to report defaults. More importantly, investors expecting more clarity about issuers are now engaged in an indeterminate wait for disclosure requirements.

D. The Executive Process

The executive functions of a regulator are the third group of activities that are not regulation-making or quasi-judicial functions. This includes issuing licences or permissions to carry out regulated activity, inspecting regulated businesses, investigating alleged violations of the law etc. In the licensing, investigative and prosecutorial functions, governmental organisations run the risk of veering into arbitrary power, intimidation and corruption, which results in reduced capabilities.

High capability requires: (a) formal procedures with service-level assurances; and (b) the ability to demonstrate that the procedures are adhered to. While the importance of formal processes is well understood in private management settings, in public management, there is an additional requirement of adherence to two principles of the *rule of law*: (1) a substantial reduction in discretion; and (2) a duty to explain the reason behind any executive action. Private persons should feel there is high predictability before the event; this reduces regulatory risk. Once an action is taken, they should know the rationale. At present in India, there are many violations of these principles. For example, Roy and Shah show that the procedure for granting payment bank licences was inconsistent with the rule of law (see Box 17.5).[9]

Box 17.5 Payment bank licences

The process by which the RBI granted permission to open *payment banks* was similar to that of the coal block allocation through the committee system. This system was held to be unconstitutional by the Supreme Court in *Manohar Lal Sharma v The Principal Secretary*.[10] No identifiable criteria were identified for

[9] Shubho Roy and Ajay Shah, 'Payment Bank Entry Process Considered Inconsistent with the Rule of Law' *The Leap Blog* (1 September 2015), https://ajayshahblog.blogspot.in/2015/09/payment-bank-entry-process-considered.html.

[10] *Manohar Lal Sharma v The Principal Secretary* (2014) 9 SCC 516.

the selection of successful applicants. *After* the selection was complete the RBI released a press-release stating that the selection was done by an external committee which determined its own procedure and analysed the applications. While the press-release claimed that the applications had been granted based on some criteria, there was no explanation on how the committee evaluated each criterion. There was no explanation provided to the 30 applicants who were rejected. Instead the press-release stated:

The Reserve Bank believes that some of the entities who did not qualify in this round, could well be successful in future rounds.

It seems even the RBI was unsure about the reasons why these entities were rejected.

In addition to licensing, other executive processes need similar checks and balances. As Shubho Roy argues, regulators in India are particularly weak in *demonstrating* that there is a sound inspection process (see Box 17.6).[11]

Box 17.6 Missing inspection manuals

The recent Rs 11,400 crore bank fraud at Punjab National Bank, which was allegedly perpetrated by the billionaire Nirav Modi in collusion with a few bank employees, highlights the failure of inspection processes in banks. Section 35 of the Banking Regulation Act, 1949 empowers the RBI to carry out inspections. How the inspection will be carried out, what will be checked, how sampling will be done and other details of the inspection process are not provided in the legislation. It is expected that, based on this provision, the RBI would have developed rules, regulations and other documents setting out the detailed procedure for inspections.

In contrast, the Federal Deposit Insurance Corporation of the US (which plays a similar role in terms of bank inspections) releases detailed manuals on the process of inspections. The compliance manual is 1,275 pages long and has its own website. Anyone can read the manual and comment on the robustness of the procedures. All 128,755 words of the compliance manual are open to scrutiny. The Japanese financial regulator's inspection manual for deposit-taking institutions is 446 pages long. It provides detailed information about how inspections will be carried out, including a checklist for inspections.

[11] Shubho Roy, 'Rot in PSBs Part 3: Nirav Modi Scam Shows it's Time Parliament Reexamined Banking Laws, Brought in Transparency' *Firstpost* (22 February 2018), www.firstpost.com/india/rot-in-psbs-part-3-nirav-modi-scam-shows-its-time-parliament-reexamined-banking-laws-brought-in-transparency-4360917.html.

These principles are usefully applied to each of the three elements of the executive functions:

- *Licensing* should be given only on pre-determined criteria and evaluation processes. The denial of a licence imposes harm upon the applicant. Hence, if an application is rejected, it should be with a reasoned order (containing all the information the regulator relied upon) and after providing the regulated entity with a hearing. Denial of licence orders should be subject to judicial review.
- Inspections can easily turn into a tool for harassment and intimidation. The regulator must demonstrate that inspections are effective. The process manual used by inspectors should be visible to the inspected, who should be able to check for excesses. The findings of inspections should be recorded by the regulator and made available to the regulated. Inspection reports should be available for judicial scrutiny at a later stage.
- Investigations can easily turn into witch-hunts or continual harassment of regulated entities. Sometimes, open-ended fishing expeditions are begun, starting from one claim and ending up with a very different outcome. Investigation requires a clear direction from the regulator about the alleged violation, carried out in a time-bound manner and overseen by the judicial wing of the regulator. Before the investigator disrupts the functioning of any regulated entity or other person, they should be able to demonstrate (on record) reasonable grounds for doing so. If investigations do not find violations within a stipulated timeframe, appropriate closure statements should be provided to the entities under investigation.

When there are checks and balances on these issues, this simultaneously addresses the civil liberties objective and fosters the creation of state capacity. When there is unchecked executive discretion, this becomes an oppressive environment, which fails in relation to both objectives.

E. The Judicial Process

Regulators in India also have a judicial function: they assign punishments. This can be a dangerous function from the viewpoint of developing state capacity. If there is arbitrary power in awarding punishment, this leads to arrogance and corruption. If investigators and prosecutors know they can easily inflict punishment, they lose their incentive to do thorough work.

The moment we think of a state agency that assigns punishments, we envision the minimum rule of law machinery that must surround it. Once an investigation has been completed, a discussion should take place internally in the regulator with the prosecution team, which would judge the information that was obtained and decide whether there is a strong case. The prosecution team must be distinct from the investigative team. If there is a strong case, the first step should be that of issuing a show cause notice and giving the accused an opportunity to present their side of the story. After this, if the prosecution wishes to proceed, a hearing should take place in front of an adjudicating officer. The prosecution would show evidence and make the argument that there were violations of the law, while the accused would have an opportunity to defend themselves.

Sadly, this is not the starting position of quasi-judicial regulators in India. Indian quasi-judicial functions start with a *show cause notice.* A typical show cause notice requires the recipient to *show cause* why some penalty should not be imposed on the recipient. The starting position of the show cause notice is the *presumption* that the person has violated the law. The classical legal concept of *presumption of innocence* is turned on its head into a *presumption of guilt.* It is for the recipient to prove that they are innocent of the action for the regulator has already decided to impose a penalty. On many occasions, the information or evidence on which the regulator came to the conclusion is not provided to the defendant/accused. Even a basic right such as the right to have access to the evidence against a defendant is not established in the legislation. Parties have to resort to constitutional courts to gain access to documents, information and even the quasi-judicial decisions of a regulator.

One approach to make the quasi-judicial functions of a regulator fairer is to create an administrative law vertical. This is a separate department within the regulator (with Chinese walls) which solely works on adjudication and quasi-judicial functions. Like the judiciary in a country, staff in the vertical should not interact with the other departments of the regulator. This vertical should be headed by a member of the board who is referred to as the administrative law member. Employee performance assessments within this vertical would be insulated from unhappiness (or lack thereof) among investigators and prosecutors about the orders that were written by the adjudicating officers. Orders must be reasoned orders: they must state the position of law and the facts that were uncovered by the investigators, demonstrate that the law was violated and show the rationale for the punishment being assigned. A doctrine for calculating punishment is required in parliamentary law, which will then engender jurisprudence. Orders must be released in the public domain. This improves public scrutiny and hampers the arbitrary exercise of power. There must be an efficacious procedure for appeal against the order. As an example, orders written by SEBI, the IRDA and the PFRDA can be appealed at the Securities Appellate Tribunal (SAT).

These processes uphold the rule of law and ensure fair play. These are important values in their own right. But it is important to see that these good governance procedures are the pathway to state capacity. When prosecutors wield arbitrary power, the quality of work done by investigators and prosecutors will go down, and the arbitrary power will breed corruption. The checks and balances that have been described here impose pressure upon the investigation, prosecution and quasi-judicial parts of the regulator, resulting in higher levels of capability.

SEBI offers an interesting example of these links between fair play, the rule of law and state capacity. When SEBI was first created in 1991, there was no possibility of appeal against an SEBI order in a neutral judicial forum. An appeal was to be made to the Government of India. In 1995, the SAT was created, to which some of SEBI orders (adjudication orders imposing a monetary penalty) could be appealed. In 1999, every order of SEBI became appealable in the SAT. It was a new experience for SEBI to go from arbitrary power to the prospect of having numerous orders being scrutinised by the SAT. However, over the years, this drove SEBI towards higher levels of state capacity and higher-quality work in its investigative, prosecutorial and quasi-judicial functions. This has helped create significant state capacity within SEBI in relation to these dimensions.

F. Accountability through Reporting

Reports produced by regulators in India spend many pages discussing the overall environment. As an example, SEBI and the RBI make many reports discussing developments in the economy, even though the economy is not under the control or management of SEBI or the RBI. The focus of reporting should be upon the work of the organisation: to disclose the operational and financial Management Information System (MIS) of the organisation.

Transparency in executive procedures cannot be provided contemporaneously while the actions are underway. Post hoc disclosure creates checks and balances against wide powers. The operational MIS for SEBI should show detailed information about the working of the organisation – for example, how many days does it take for SEBI to process an Initial Public Offering (IPO)? How many investigations have been commenced? How many days were spent, on average, per investigation? What proportion of investigations resulted in a prosecution? What proportion of prosecutions led to an order with punishment? How many days did it take from the start of an investigation to the issuance of the order? What proportion of orders were appealed and what was SEBI's win rate at the SAT? These kinds of statistics reveal information about the performance of the organisation, which is under the control of the management. The management can be held accountable for the absolute values and the time-series variation in these measures.

Such reporting helps to identify the areas of concern and to guide the management and the board towards remedial actions. Such aggregate information also helps in justifying the resources employed by the regulator. Performance reporting by a regulator has to be supported by financial reporting of the executive functions. This reporting would clearly transmit to the public the level of resources that the regulator is investing in executive action. Parliament and the government would also be able to review the regulatory quality from aggregate statistics compared with the financial resources dedicated to executive functions. At present, this is not done in India. Table 17.4 compares the annual reports of the SEC and SEBI for the year 2011.

Table 17.4 Comparing SEC and SEBI annual reports (2011)

SEC	SEBI Report
201 pages for the entire report	172 pages for performance and accounts
10 pages on steps taken	85 pages on steps taken
4 strategic goals identified	No strategic goals
Each goal measured on 9–17 measures	No measurement of goals
Each measure has actual and target result	Report has no targets at all
Each section has deficiencies measured	No deficiencies identified
Corrective action plans for each deficiency	No future plans
Dedicated performance results	No performance results
Prosecution details with targets	Prosecution details but no targets

A reading of a number of annual reports of various regulators in India and regulators carrying out similar functions in other jurisdictions with high capacity throws up a thematic difference in the annual reports. Table 17.5 gives an analysis of the difference between the annual reports of Indian regulators vis-a-vis regulators and those from other jurisdictions.

Table 17.5 Summary of report-making

Feature	India	Other jurisdictions
Major part	Regulated markets	Functions of the regulator
Statistics	About regulated market	About regulator's functions
Targets	Broad targets	Broad and narrow targets
Metrics	None	Objective review, subjective review, independent review
Enforcement	Statistics	Expenditure, statistics, targets

Milestones and targets do not provide adequate information about the functioning of the regulator until the public and the legislature have been informed about the resources expended to achieve the target. This enables the board and the public to measure the efficiency of the regulator. Figure 17.1 provides an example of how the SEC reports targets in its annual report. For each outcome, the SEC:

- attributes the amount of money spent to achieve the outcome;
- provides a detailed definition of what constitutes *success* in terms of achieving the outcome;
- states the target that was set in the last annual report;
- compares it with the actual achievement in the present annual report; and sets out the target for the next year.

This in turn links the entire financial reporting of the regulator to its performance report. In addition to providing the normal balance sheet, a regulator is required to produce a financial statement which maps total expenditure onto each function that the regulator is required to carry out. This is not done in India. Indian regulatory annual reports rarely have information about the functioning of the regulator and do not map any functions onto expenditure. Without such financial and performance reporting, the board of the regulator is unable to make *strategic* decisions about spending and performance or to establish a link between the two. To summarise, sound reporting systems help create feedback loops that improve state capacity.

G. The Role of the Governmental Department

This chapter has discussed structural reforms of regulators that are conducive to state capacity. This logically leads to the following question: what is the role of the relevant governmental department? The 25 years of experience with regulators in India is a story of skirmishes between governmental departments and statutory regulators. How can we do better?

Each regulator is grounded in a law and has an administrative department of government. To give an example, Parliament enacted the TRAI Act, 1997. Parliament, represented by the Department of Telecommunications, is the principal and TRAI is the agent. The law, in this case the TRAI Act, is the contract that defines the relationship between the principal and the agent. A good contract should induce a good relationship. Both sides of a well-structured contract should work as a smooth machine. Most of the time, this has not been the result with Indian regulators. The leadership of departments has expressed myriad complaints about what regulators are doing and vice versa. There are some good periods, but they are usually the result of good interpersonal relations between the board of the regulator and the top management of the government department rather than because of proper systems being put in place. Low-intensity warfare is the norm, which periodically erupts into the public domain, with journalists taking sides. The media tends to assume that all regulators should have complete independence; however, placing absolute power in the hands of regulators is unlikely to deliver good outcomes.

We propose seven principles that should shape the relationship between the department and the regulator:

(1) Regulators *should* fuse legislative, executive and judicial functions. The regulator must have the authority to write law, which is termed a 'regulation', within parameters clearly laid down in the parliamentary law. Many departments are reluctant to give regulators this authority, and this is the incorrect approach.

(2) All members of the board of a regulator must be appointed by the department. The board should have a majority of independent directors. The chairperson of a regulator should gracefully accept the board recruitment decisions of the department, and the board should not be the appointing authority for membership of the board.

(3) The department must have one nominee member on the board. Membership of the board is a position of high responsibility, as the board's role is to push the management of the regulator towards performance. The board must continuously analyse the performance of the regulator, and reshape the organisational structure, process designs and resourcing. Failures of the regulator should result in feedback to the board, which should diagnose sources of failure and make the necessary changes. Regulatory staff should gracefully accept their accountability to the board, and the power of the board to continually reshape the organisation in order to improve performance. The nominee member should work to reach the necessary level of knowledge and hard work that is required to discharge the function.

(4) The staff of the regulator should not have the power to write law; this power must only vest with the board. This means that the department (in its capacity as a member of the board) must develop a point of view on all regulations. The appropriate forum for expressing these views is board meetings.

(5) External board members must not be involved in executive and judicial activities. This is the narrow space for regulatory independence. The department should have no say in any individual transaction, ie, licensing, investigation or orders. Phone calls should not be made by the department to the management asking for favours on transactions.
(6) When private persons are unhappy about an order written by a regulator (eg, rejecting an application for a licence), the appropriate port of call is an appellate tribunal and not the department.
(7) The department is the principal. It must constantly ask itself whether the contract (the law) is appropriate. It must regularly change the law in order to refine the principal-agent relationship and to modify the work allocation to the agent. Regulators should not have a say in the jurisdiction of the regulators or how the primary legislation governing them is drafted. The department must regularly modify the agency architecture in terms of what work is done by what agencies in the quest for performance.

The department should thus have four functions: (1) appointments; (2) regulation-making; (3) watching performance and continuously refining the organisational design of the agent; and (4) continuous refinement of the contract between the principal and the agent. It must create capacity for discharging these functions. This includes internal skills, connections with research institutions, a stream of conversations with practitioners, and process manuals.

In the Indian experience with regulation, there is a large degree of divergence from these principles. A low-level equilibrium that is often attained is one where the department asks for favours on transactions, ie, on executive and judicial functions, and in return cedes power on everything else. In the low-level equilibrium, the bureaucracy in the regulator zealously guards its turf, and the department stops thinking about regularly reshaping the regulatory architecture.

III. FROM THEORY TO PRACTICE

In the previous section, we have shown seven elements of the checks and balances through which the incentives of individuals inside regulatory organisations can be reshaped. How can these seven elements be operationalised? How does this programme for reform go from ideas to action?

A. The Principal and Agent

The difference between high-performing regulators in other jurisdictions and the behaviour of regulators in India can be traced back to the legislation governing the regulators. Parliament, represented by a governmental department, is the principal. In order to overcome the principal-agent problem, a contract has to be put into place that constrains the behaviour of the agent and establishes a structure of information and incentives. The law that defines the regulator is this contract. The seven elements described in this chapter must drive the drafting of the law that defines the regulator.

The seven elements described above need to be coded into the parliamentary law with considerable procedural detail. This is true in general in terms of thinking about contracts that seek to address principal-agent problems. In the India of old, a power purchase agreement used to be a skimpy document; it has now become a detailed document running to over 1,000 pages. In a similar fashion, we need to go from the overly concise SEBI Act, 1992, the Insurance Regulatory and Development Authority Act, 1999 or the TRAI Act, 1997 to a detailed treatment through which the agency conflict between Parliament/department and the regulator will be addressed. This can be done for one regulator at a time. To give an example, we can envision chapters in the Insolvency and Bankruptcy Code, 2016 (IBC) that place these provisions into the working of the new bankruptcy regulator, the IBBI. However, these ideas are general and need not be applied to one regulator at a time. As an example, the draft Indian Financial Code authored by the FSLRC has a single set of 140 sections of law, which set up these mechanisms for use with all financial agencies. Whenever a law has to be drafted in India that establishes a regulator, these 140 sections of law can be used. Similarly, in the US, the Sunshine Act, 1976 is a single law that governs the working of all federal agencies.

In India, in the past, the drafting of the law that establishes a regulator was often done by the regulator. As an example, the SEBI Act of 1992 and every amendment thereafter was first drafted by SEBI. The RBI Amendment Act of 2006 was drafted by the RBI. There is a conflict of interest rooted in public choice theory here. If the agent is given an opportunity to draft the contract between the principal and the agent, the agent is likely to favour more arbitrary power and less accountability. As such, it is important to ensure that regulators do not control the drafting of the laws that create regulators.

B. The Form of the Law

It is conventional wisdom in India that parliamentary law should never embed concrete detail and that well-drafted law is always principles-based law. It is useful to make a distinction between elements of the law that coerce private persons versus the elements of law that are designed to solve public administration problems. When the law is designed to prohibit persons from carrying out specific activities, it is indeed valuable to draft the law in a principles-based way. To give an example, the Indian Penal Code has defined theft in a timeless way. As the world changes and as new concepts of property and new concepts of crime arise, the definition of theft in the Indian Penal Code, 1860 will remain sound. Another approach to coercing private persons consists of writing down principles in the law and setting forth a regulator that translates these principles into regulations that change repeatedly.

However, when law is drafted to rein in the behaviour of governmental employees, the main focus is upon principal-agent problems and upon public choice problems. Here, giving officials the power to define their own procedures is inappropriate.

To give an example, the procedures that must be employed by a policeman before stepping into the home of a citizen have to be prescribed in an extremely detailed way in the primary law. If this is not done, public choice theory predicts that policemen will possess and abuse arbitrary power. As such, Parliament has drafted 40,000 words in the Criminal Procedure Code, all of which constrain employees of the state. This drafting has not been delegated to the police. While regulators do not have power to imprison a person, they have the power to, among other things, issue fines of an infinite amount or to ban a person from their business/profession, often resulting in the loss of their livelihood. However, existing laws are silent in relation to governing how these powers will be exercised. This in turn leads to arbitrary use of power by officers who may not even have legal training.

IV. RECENT DEVELOPMENTS

In the first flush of liberalisation in the 1990s, there was a broad notion that India needed to move away from central planning and that there was value in creating sectoral regulators that would address market failures. There was relatively little understanding of what regulation constituted, of the dangers associated with creating independent regulators, of the distinction between central planning and regulation, and of the hurdles in creating state capacity in regulation. A large number of regulators were created. In some areas, these regulators were part of important economic reforms (such as SEBI and the TRAI). However, the overall experience with regulators, both old and new, has been disappointing. The question of the age is about state capacity in regulators. How should high-performance regulators be constituted? A small set of recent developments shows the early beginning of this journey in India.

The laws that shape some regulators have improved provisions when compared to others. To give an example, the regulation-making process embedded in the law governing the AERA was unusually sound.[12] Similarly, the consultative processes followed by the TRAI have been superior to those of financial sector regulators like SEBI.[13] In the area of finance, in 2011, the Ministry of Finance created the *Financial Sector Legislative Reforms Commission*, chaired by Justice Srikrishna. This was an unusual project in that it set out to repeal all existing financial law and replace it with a single coherent law, the *Indian Financial Code*. As India lacks a general statute setting out administrative law governing regulators, the draft Indian Financial Code contains the 140 sections of good governance procedures that set the stage for a high-performance regulator. Most of the ideas in this chapter are expressed in version 1.1 of the draft Indian Financial Code, which was released in 2015. In 2014 and 2015, it was felt that enacting the Indian Financial Code would be a time-consuming

[12] Deepaloke Chatterjee and Shubho Roy, 'Legal Process in Rule-Making: A Success Story in an Unexpected Place' *The Leap Blog* (15 April 2011), https://ajayshahblog.blogspot.com/2011/04/legal-process-in-rule-making-success.html.

[13] Burman and Zaveri (n 7).

process, but good governance procedures could be brought about voluntarily by existing financial regulators even without a new law. The idea was the regulators would altruistically rise to higher standards of governance. This led to the drafting of a *Handbook on Adoption of Governance Enhancing and Non-legislative Elements of the Draft Indian Financial Code*.[14] This was associated with an MIS system for tracking the adoption by financial regulators of the elements of good governance embedded in the *Handbook*. These documents work out the thought process of this chapter in greater detail.

Public choice theory predicts that the management of a regulatory agency will favour arbitrary power over good governance procedures. This prediction was borne out: the present state of compliance by financial regulators with the requirements of the *Handbook* is close to zero.[15] This emphasises the idea that the principal (Parliament/governmental department) must place good governance procedures into the parliamentary law. When the IBC 2016 was enacted, it envisioned a new regulator, the IBBI. This was an opportunity to establish good governance procedure. However, the IBC 2016 uses the regulatory governance sections from the SEBI Act. This was a lost opportunity to improve the working of the IBBI. The Ministry of Company Affairs set up a Working Group to recommend the design of the IBBI, chaired by Ravi Narain. This report embedded many important improvements compared to conventional Indian regulators.[16] Some of these have found their way into the actual functioning of the IBBI.

From its outset in 2016, the IBBI was the first regulator in India where the judicial function is placed in a separate vertical wing where employees also do not perform legislative and executive functions. In 2018, the IBBI released a draft regulation that established good procedure for how the IBBI would make regulations. This would be the first formal regulation-making process, approaching FSLRC quality, among regulators in India. However, as these initiatives are not codified in the law, they can be dropped by future management teams at the IBBI. The Ministry of Skill Development and Entrepreneurship is in the early stages of creating a regulator of private industries that will provide skills and certification: the National Council of Vocational Training (NCVT). Early drafts of the legal instruments that will create the NCVT feature the full set of good governance provisions.

CONCLUSION

The world of Indian socialism was one where governmental departments indulged in bans, schemes, public sector enterprises (which were often monopolies), entry

[14] Department of Economic Affairs, Ministry of Finance, *Handbook on Adoption of Governance Enhancing and Non-legislative Elements of the Draft Indian Financial Code* (techspace rep, Department of Economic Affairs, Ministry of Finance, 2013), https://dea.gov.in/sites/default/files/Handbook_GovEnhanc_fslrc_2.pdf.

[15] ibid.

[16] See Working Group to Recommend the Design of the IBBI, *Building the Insolvency and Bankruptcy Board of India* (techspace rep, Ministry of Corporate Affairs, 2016), www.ibbi.gov.in/Wg-01%20Report.pdf.

barriers and price controls, and intervened in relation to products and processes. The objective of reforming the Indian economy was to create a scenario involving private competitive industries. However, there was a need to address market failures. It was felt that this would be done by specialised sectoral regulators, which would bring a new style of limited intervention into the working of private competitive markets. A few decades into this journey, the results are disappointing. At worst, the regulator has become like the erstwhile governmental department, operating bans, schemes, entry barriers, owning or controlling organisations that are players or even monopolies in the regulated industry, enforcing price controls and intervening in detail in relation to products and processes. These outcomes derive from a limited understanding of regulation in the 1990s, which led to errors in the drafting of law. There was inadequate understanding of what is a regulator and inadequate understanding of the principal-agent problems between Parliament/governmental department and the regulator. Too often, Indian laws have treated the text of the SEBI Act as a template for the construction of other regulators and this is a poor foundation to build on.

The way forward lies in focusing on the incentives of employees of the regulator. State capacity does not come from exhortations to better behaviour or by recruiting great men. The individuals who staff regulators respond to incentives. Institutional capabilities arise through modifications of these incentives. These incentives are determined by the text of the contract between principal and agent, ie, the parliamentary law that creates the regulator. The key insight lies in addressing these problems using the tools of public administration and legal thinking. A regulator will be put on the road to steadily improving state capacity when its foundational law has about 140 sections that set up good governance procedures for the clarity of purpose, the working of the board, the legislative process, the executive process, the judicial process and reporting. These features need to be codified in parliamentary law, with considerable procedural detail. If this detail is not specified, public choice theory predicts that individuals in the regulator will utilise the flexibility given to them in ways that diminish accountability.

This roadmap to state capacity is a finite and tangible action that can be undertaken by law-makers. However, it will not immediately create state capacity. It would create modified incentives and kick off feedback loops through which institutional capacity would be continually improved. The key feature of the path to state capacity is to initiate forces of accountability. Detailed reporting of the operational and financial MIS of the regulator would encourage the public and the board to ask questions about value for money, and improvements over time. These demands would become the feedback that continuously comes to the independent board members, who form the majority in the empowered board.

Efficacious challenging of orders at a tribunal would push the quality of investigation, prosecution and judicial functions within the competence of the regulator. Well-defined processes for the executive functions (licensing, investigation or prosecution) would remove arbitrary power from the hands of the regulator and would encourage regulated persons to challenge the regulator to a greater extent in the public discourse and in court. This would bring about increased capabilities in the regulator. An open and participatory process for the legislative function would help induce regulators to apply themselves more effectively when drafting regulations. The public and the board would put pressure on the staff of the regulator, which would improve the quality of the work in terms of writing regulations. A board dominated by external persons who held the management accountable and controlled the organisational design would yield greater deliberation and improvements within the organisation when compared with the present arrangement of an organisation controlled by its own management. India is a liberal constitutional democracy, and the exercise of legislative, executive and judicial powers must be undertaken within the rule of law. In this chapter, we see a happy synergy between constitutionalism and the objective of state capacity. The path to state capacity lies in upholding the rule of law: the dispersion of power, due process, and checks and balances create the incentives for persons in regulatory organisations to achieve knowledge and competence.

Index